Beginning Java Objects

From Concepts to Code, Second Edition

JACQUIE BARKER

Beginning Java Objects: From Concepts to Code, Second Edition

Copyright © 2005 by Jacquie Barker

ISBN (pbk): 1-59059-457-6

Printed and bound in the United States of America 9 8 7 6 5 4 3 2

Lead Editor: Steve Anglin
Technical Reviewer: James Huddleston
Editorial Board: Steve Anglin, Dan Appleman, Ewan Buckingham, Gary Cornell, Tony Davis, Jason Gilmore, Jonathan Hassell, Chris Mills, Dominic Shakeshaft, Jim Sumser
Assistant Publisher: Grace Wong
Project Manager: Beckie Stones
Copy Edit Manager: Nicole LeClerc
Copy Editors: Nicole LeClerc, Ami Knox
Production Manager: Kari Brooks-Copony
Production Editor: Katie Stence
Compositor and Artist: Kinetic Publishing Services, LLC
Proofreader: Sue Boshers
Indexer: Broccoli Information Management
Interior Designer: Van Winkle Design Group
Cover Designer: Kurt Krames
Manufacturing Manager: Tom Debolski

Distributed to the book trade in the United States by Springer-Verlag New York, Inc., 233 Spring Street, 6th Floor, New York, NY 10013, and outside the United States by Springer-Verlag GmbH & Co. KG, Tiergartenstr. 17, 69112 Heidelberg, Germany.

In the United States: phone 1-800-SPRINGER, fax 201-348-4505, e-mail orders@springer-ny.com, or visit http://www.springer-ny.com. Outside the United States: fax +49 6221 345229, e-mail orders@springer.de, or visit http://www.springer.de.

For information on translations, please contact Apress directly at 2560 Ninth Street, Suite 219, Berkeley, CA 94710. Phone 510-549-5930, fax 510-549-5939, e-mail info@apress.com, or visit http://www.apress.com.

The source code for this book is available to readers at http://www.apress.com in the Downloads section.

In loving memory of "the Weens"—sweet little Shylow and funny little Chloe—who graced our lives with unconditional love for almost 17 years.

Contents at a Glance

PART 1 ■ ■ ■ The ABCs of Objects

PART 2 ■ ■ ■ Object Modeling 101

PART 3 ■■■ Translating an Object Blueprint into Java Code

PART 4 ■■■ Appendixes

Contents

PART 1 ■■■ The ABCs of Objects

PART 2 ■ ■ ■ Object Modeling 101

■CHAPTER 8   The Object Modeling Process in a Nutshell 333

PART 3 ■■■ Translating an Object Blueprint into Java Code

PART 4 ■ ■ ■ Appendixes

About the Author

JACQUIE BARKER is a professional software engineer, author, and adjunct faculty member at both George Mason University in Fairfax, Virginia, and The George Washington University in Washington, D.C. With over 28 years of experience as a hands-on software developer and project manager, Jacquie has spent the past 12 years focusing on object technology, and becoming proficient as an object modeler and Sun Microsystems Certified Java programmer. She is the founder of ObjectStart LLC, an object technology mentorship and training firm, and she is also a senior member of the technical staff of Technology Associates, Inc. in Herndon, Virginia.

Jacquie earned a bachelor of science degree in computer engineering with highest honors from Case Western Reserve University in Cleveland, Ohio, where she was also inducted into the Tau Beta Pi National Engineering Honor Society. She later received a master of science degree in computer science, focusing on software systems engineering, from the University of California, Los Angeles, and has subsequently pursued postgraduate studies in information technology at George Mason University.

Jacquie's winning formula for teaching object fundamentals continues to receive praise from readers around the world, and *Beginning Java Objects: From Concepts to Code* has been adopted by many universities as a key textbook in their core IT curricula as a result. Her latest book, *Taming the Technology Tidal Wave: Practical Career Advice for IT Professionals*, is a light-hearted guide to maintaining leading-edge technical skills, and is similarly getting rave reviews.

On a personal note, Jacquie's passions include her husband, Steve; pet rats and miniature longhaired dachshunds (aka wiener dogs); teaching; writing; and programming in Java. When not engaged in computer-related pursuits, Jacquie and Steve enjoy taking motorcycle road trips through the Virginia countryside, tandem bicycling, enjoying quiet vacations at the lake, and spending quality time with family and friends.

Please visit Jacquie's web sites, http://objectstart.com and http://techtidalwave.com, for more information on her various publications and service offerings.

About the Technical Reviewer

JAMES HUDDLESTON is an independent consultant with over 30 years' experience in information technology. Revision author of Apress's *Beginning C# Databases: From Novice to Professional*, he's been a technical reviewer or editor for dozens of books on diverse computer topics. When not having fun writing programs for a living or translating Homer as a hobby, he delights in helping authors make good books better—and even more in playing with his three children, Jared, Quinn, and Tess.

Acknowledgments

My sincerest thanks go to

- James Huddleston, my technical reviewer, for his wise and thoughtful guidance in shaping this second edition of *Beginning Java Objects: From Concepts to Code*. James, you are a true Renaissance man and a delight to work with—not to mention **brilliant**!—and I look forward to many future collaborations with you.

- Beckie Stones, Nicole LeClerc, Katie Stence, and Steve Anglin, for their superb support in producing *Beginning Java Objects: From Concepts to Code, Second Edition*. I couldn't have done it without you! (Advance thanks to Paul Carlstroem and Stephanie Parker, as well, for lending their marketing wisdom in making my book a spectacular success.)

- Gary Cornell, author and publisher of Apress, for continuing to be a fan of and advocate for *Beginning Java Objects*.

- My friends Cathy McCabe and Brian and Cynthia Coleman, for informally reviewing my book and providing me with invaluable insights into how my message could be refined.

- Dr. Claudio Cioffi and my spring semester 2005 Computational Social Sciences 605 students at George Mason University, for helping me to hone my message for a broader audience.

- The many loved ones who patiently awaited my return from the "social abyss" known as writing a book:

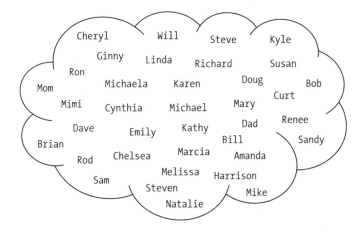

And most important, to the love of my life and my best friend, my husband Steve, for being such a supportive and understanding partner. I love sharing my life with you, "Klemmie"!

Preface

Welcome to the second edition of *Beginning Java Objects: From Concepts to Code*! Since the first edition of *Beginning Java Objects* was published back in November 2000, I've been delighted by the many emails and positive reviews that I've received from readers who found my book to be a perfect "jump-start" into Java and object-oriented programming.

My book is based on timeless principles that are language version independent, which means that it needn't be revised every time a new version of Java is released by Sun Microsystems. That being said, Java 2 Platform, Standard Edition (J2SE) 5.0 introduced some important new features that have significantly increased the power and versatility of Java as an object-oriented programming language. For this reason, I've deemed this to be the right time to "freshen" *Beginning Java Objects* in the form of a second edition.

I've also continued to teach the material of *Beginning Java Objects* since the first edition was published, and as a result of working with many students in both university and corporate settings, I've refined my message in important ways. Teaching, as learning, is a work in progress; one's message can never be 100% complete!

Noteworthy enhancements to *Beginning Java Objects* in this second edition include

- Emphasis on getting hands-on experience with Java much sooner (as of Chapter 2 versus Chapter 13 of the previous edition)

- A significantly improved discussion of model–data layer separation in Chapter 15, including a conceptual introduction to the JDBC API (used to communicate with ODBC-compliant databases)

- Greater focus on model–view separation, including a conceptual introduction to J2EE technology in Chapter 17

- Emphasis on the significant enhancements made to the Java language as of J2SE 5.0, highlighting their significance in OO terms

Recognizing that *Beginning Java Objects* has enjoyed widespread academic adoption as a textbook, I've made certain that the chapter outline of the second edition parallels that of the first edition, with only one exception: since the chapter formerly referred to as Chapter 16 had become so huge with this edition, I've split it into two chapters.

As always, I welcome reader feedback, and I hope to hear from you soon via either of my two websites, http://objectstart.com and http://techtidalwave.com.

Best regards,

Jacquie

Introduction

This is a book, first and foremost, about software objects: what they are, why they are so "magical" and yet so straightforward, and how you go about structuring a software application to use objects appropriately.

This is also a book about Java. It's not a hard-core, "everything there is to know about Java" book, but rather a gentle yet comprehensive introduction to the language, with special emphasis on how to transition from an object model to a fully functional Java application—something that few, if any, other books provide.

Goals for This Book

My goals in writing this book (and, hopefully, yours for buying it) are to

- *Make you comfortable with fundamental object-oriented (OO) terminology and concepts*

- *Give you hands-on, practical experience with object modeling*—that is, with developing a "blueprint" that you can use as the basis for subsequently building an object-oriented software system

- *Illustrate the basics of how such an object model is translated into a working software application—a Java application, to be specific*, although the techniques that you'll learn for object modeling apply equally well to any OO language

- *Help you to become proficient as a Java programmer along the way*

If you're already experienced with the Java language (but not with object fundamentals), it's critical to your successful use of the language that you learn about its object-oriented roots. On the other hand, if you're a newcomer to Java, then this book will get you properly jump-started. *Either way, this book is a must-read for anyone who wishes to become proficient with an OO programming language like Java.*

Just as important, this book is *not* meant to

- ***Turn you into an overnight pro in object modeling***. Like all advanced skills, becoming totally comfortable with object modeling takes two things: a good theoretical foundation and a lot of practice. I give you the foundation in this book, including an introduction to the Unified Modeling Language (UML), the industry standard for rendering an object-oriented "blueprint" of a software application. But the only way you'll really get to be proficient with object modeling is by participating in OO modeling and development projects over time.

  My book will give you the skills and, hopefully, the ***confidence*** to begin to apply object techniques in a professional setting, which is where your real learning will take place, particularly if you have an OO-experienced mentor to guide you through your first "industrial-strength" project.

- ***Teach you*** everything ***you'll ever need to know about Java***. Java is a very rich language, consisting of hundreds of core classes and literally thousands of operations that can be performed with and by these classes. If Java provides a dozen alternative ways to do something in particular, I explain the one or two ways that I feel best suit the problem at hand, to give you an appreciation for how things are done. Nonetheless, you'll definitely see enough of the Java language in this book to prepare you for a role as a professional Java programmer.

Armed with the knowledge you'll gain from this book, you'll be poised and ready to appreciate a more thorough treatment of Java such as that offered by one of the many other Java references that are presently on the market, or a deeper review of object modeling techniques from an in-depth UML reference.

Why Is Understanding Objects So Critical to Being a Successful OO Programmer?

Time and again, I meet software developers—at my place of employment, at clients' offices, at professional conferences, and on college campuses—who have attempted to master an object-oriented programming language like Java by taking a course in Java, reading a book about Java, or installing and using a Java integrated development environment (IDE) such as JBuilder or Sun One Studio. However, there is something fundamentally missing from virtually all of these approaches: a basic understanding of what objects are all about and, more important, ***knowledge of how to structure a software application from the ground up to make the most of objects***.

Imagine that you've been asked to build a house, and that you know the basics of home construction. In fact, you're a world-renowned homebuilder whose services are in high demand. You've built homes of every possible architectural style, using every known type of building material: brick, lumber, stone, metal, etc. So, when your client tells you that he wants you to use a brand-new type of construction material that he'll provide, you're happy to oblige.

On the day construction is to begin, a truck pulls up at the building site and unloads a large pile of odd-looking, star-shaped blue blocks with holes in the middle. You're totally baffled! You've built countless homes using more-familiar materials, but you don't have a *clue* about how to assemble a house using blue stars.

Scratching your head, you pull out a hammer and some nails and try to nail the blue stars together as if you were working with lumber, but the stars don't fit together very well. You then try to fill in the gaps with the same mortar that you would use to adhere bricks to one another, but the mortar doesn't stick to these blue stars very well. Because you're working under tight cost and schedule constraints for building this home for your client, however (and because you're too embarrassed to admit that you, as an *expert* homebuilder, don't know how to work with these modern materials), you press on. Eventually, you wind up with something that looks (on the surface, at least) like a house.

Your client comes to inspect the work, and he is terribly disappointed. One of the reasons he had selected blue stars as a construction material was that they are extremely energy efficient but, because you used nails and mortar to assemble the stars, they have lost a great deal of their inherent ability to insulate the home.

To compensate, your client asks you to replace all of the windows in the home with triple-pane thermal glass windows so that they will allow less heat to escape. ***You're panicking at this point***—swapping out the windows will require you to literally rip the walls apart, destroying the house.

When you tell your customer this, he goes ***ballistic***! Another reason he selected blue stars as a construction material was because of their modularity, and hence ease of accommodating design changes but, because of the ineffective way you assembled these stars, they've lost this flexibility as well.

This is, sad to say, the way many programmers wind up building an OO application when they don't have appropriate training in the fundamental properties of the building blocks of such an application—namely, software objects. Worse yet, the vast majority of would-be OO programmers are blissfully ignorant of the need to understand objects in order to program in an OO language. So, they take off programming with a language like Java and wind up with a far from ideal result: an application that lacks flexibility when an inevitable "midcourse correction" occurs in response to changing requirements after the application has been deployed.

Who Is This Book Written For?

Anyone who wants to get the most out of an object-oriented programming language like Java! It is for

- Anyone who has yet to tackle Java, but wants to get off on the right foot with the language

- Anyone who has ever purchased a book on Java—and who has read it faithfully—who understands the "bits and bytes" of the language, but doesn't quite know how to structure an application to best take advantage of Java's object-oriented features

- Anyone who has used a Java IDE but who really only knows how to drag and drop graphical user interface (GUI) components and to add a little bit of behind-the-scenes logic to buttons, menus, etc., without any real sense of how to properly structure the core of the application around objects

- Anyone who has built a Java application, but was disappointed with how difficult it was to maintain or modify it when new requirements were presented later in the application's life cycle

- Anyone who has previously learned something about object modeling, but is "fuzzy" on how to transition from an object model to real, live code (Java or otherwise)

The bottom line is that *anyone who really wants to master an OO language like Java must become an expert in objects* **first!**

In order to gain the most value from this book, you should have some programming experience under your belt; virtually any language will do. You should understand simple programming concepts such as

- Simple data types (integer, floating-point, etc.)

- Variables and their scope (including the notion of global data)

- Flow control (if ... then ... else statements, for/do/while loops, etc.)

- What arrays are, and how to use them

- The notion of a software function/subroutine/procedure: how to pass data in and get results back out

but you needn't have any prior exposure to Java. And, you needn't have ever been exposed to objects, either—in the software sense, at least! As you'll learn in Chapter 1, human beings naturally view the entire world from the perspective of objects.

Even if you've already developed a full-fledged Java application, it's certainly not too late to read this book if you still feel fuzzy when it comes to the object aspects of structuring an application; it ultimately makes someone a better Java programmer to know the "whys" of object orientation rather than merely the mechanics of the language. You'll most likely see some familiar landmarks (in the form of Java code examples) in this book, but you'll hopefully gain many new insights as you learn the rationale for why we do many of the things that we do when programming in Java (or any other OO programming language, for that matter).

Because this book has its roots in courses that I teach at the university level, it's ideally suited for use as a textbook for a semester-long university or advanced-placement high school course in either object modeling or Java programming. I've included some suggestions for how to use the book in that fashion in Appendix A.

What If You're Interested in Object Modeling, but Not Necessarily in Java Programming?

Will my book still be of value to you? *Definitely*! Even if you don't plan on making a career of programming (as is true of many of my object modeling students), I've found that being exposed to code examples written in an OO language like Java really helps to cement object concepts. So, you're encouraged to read Part 3, which steps through building a complete Java application, even if you never intend to set your hands to the keyboard for purposes of Java programming afterward.

How This Book Is Organized

The book is structured around three major topics, as follows.

Part 1: The ABCs of Objects

Before I dive into the how-to's of object modeling and the details of OO programming in Java, it's important that we all speak the same language with respect to objects. Part 1, consisting of Chapters 1 through 7, starts out slowly by defining basic concepts that underlie all software development approaches, OO or otherwise. But the chapters quickly ramp up to a discussion of advanced object concepts so that, by the end of Part 1, you should be "object-savvy."

Part 2: Object Modeling 101

In Part 2—Chapters 8 through 12 of the book—I focus on the underlying principles of how and, more important, *why* we do the things that we do when we develop an object model of an application—principles that are common to all object modeling techniques. It's important to be conversant in the UML, and so I teach you the basics of the UML and use it for all of the concrete modeling examples in my book. Using the modeling techniques presented in these chapters, we'll develop an object model "blueprint" for a Student Registration System (SRS), the requirements specification for which is presented at the end of this introduction.

Part 3: Translating an Object Blueprint into Java Code

In Part 3 of the book—in Chapters 13 through 17—I illustrate how to render the SRS object model that we develop in Part 2 into a fully functioning Java application, complete with a GUI and a way to persist data from one user logon to the next. All of the code examples presented in this section are available for download from the Apress web site (http://www.apress.com), and I strongly encourage you to download and experiment with this code.

The requirements specification for the SRS is written in the narrative style with which software system requirements are often expressed. You may feel confident that you could build an application today to solve this problem, but by the end of my book you should feel much more confident in your ability to build it as an **object-oriented** application. Three additional case studies—for a Prescription Tracking System, a Conference Room Reservation System, and an Airline Ticketing System, respectively—are presented in Appendix B; these serve as the basis for many of the exercises presented at the end of each chapter.

To round out the book, I've included a final chapter (Chapter 18) entitled "Next Steps," which provides suggestions for how you might wish to continue your object-oriented discovery process after finishing this book. In that chapter, I provide a list of recommended books that will take you to the next level of proficiency, depending on what your intention is for applying what you've learned in my book.

Conventions

To help you get the most from the text and keep track of what's happening, I've used a number of conventions throughout the book, for instance:

Notes are shown in this fashion, and reflect important background information.

Here are styles you'll find in the text:

- When I introduce important words, I **bold** them to highlight them.

- I show filenames, URLs, and code within the text like so: `objectstart.com`

- I **bold** lines of code within long code passages if I want to call your attention to those lines in particular, for example:

```
// Bolding is used to call attention to new or significant code:
Student s = new Student();
// whereas unbolded code is code that's less important in the
// present context, or has been seen before.
int x = 3;
```

- I use *italic* versus regular `code` font to represent pseudocode:

```
// This is real code:
for (int i = 0; i <= 10; i++) {
    // This is pseudocode!
    compute the grade for the ith Student
}
```

Which Version of Java Is This Book Based On?

As with any programming language, from time to time new versions of Java will be released by Sun Microsystems. The *good news* is that, because I focus only on core Java language syntax in my book—language features that have been stable since Java's inception—this book isn't version specific. The techniques and concepts that you'll learn by reading my book will serve you equally well when new versions of Java appear.

That being said, Sun Microsystems introduced some important new features with J2SE 5.0 (alternatively known internally to Sun as Java 1.5.0) that significantly increased the power and versatility of Java as an object-oriented programming language. I've adopted the J2SE 5.0 approach to coding in this second edition of *Beginning Java Objects*, which impacts the code examples of Chapter 6 and Chapters 13 through 16. For readers who are still working with an earlier version of the Java language, I've included notes in these chapters to guide you in adapting the code for earlier versions of Java, if desired.

SORTING OUT JAVA NOMENCLATURE

Since Java first made its public debut as a programming language in 1995, there have been some disconti-nuities in the way in which Java language versions have been referred to.

The first version of the Java language was referred to as 1.0; this was followed (logically) by version 1.1. When version 1.2 arrived on the scene, however, significant differences had been made to the language in terms of how GUI events were handled, such that Sun Microsystems anointed this version "Java 2" (but still alternatively referred to it as 1.2.*x*). Versions 1.3.*x* and 1.4.*x* of Java were subsequently referred to as "Java 2 Platform (Version) 1.*x.x*"; however, when Java 1.5.0 was released, it again incorporated significant enough differences to warrant a new name: J2SE 5.0. (I discuss some of the more significant J2SE 5.0 enhancements in Chapters 6 and 13, and again in Appendix G.)

Table 1 summarizes the naming history of the Java language through Java 2 Platform 1.5.0.

Table 1. *Java Naming History**

Actual Version Number	Preferred Name
1.0	Java Language 1.0
1.1.*x*	Java Language 1.1
1.2.*x*	Java 2 Platform
1.3.*x*	Java 2 Platform 1.3.*x*
1.4.*x*	Java 2 Platform 1.4.*x*
1.5.0 (now 5.0.*x*)	Java 2 Platform 1.5.*x* (now Java 2 Platform 5.0.*x*)

* Version numbers in this table apply only to J2SE and J2EE.

There have been similar discontinuities in the way in which the **Java Development Kit** (**JDK**) has been referred to. The JDK is the software "bundle" used by developers to build Java applications and consisting of

- The Java Virtual Machine (JVM)

- The Java compiler (`javac`)

- The Java Archive (`jar`) utility

- The Java documentation (`javadoc`) utility

etc. These discontinuities in naming are, in part, due to the fact that as of version 1.2 of the Java language, three Java "platforms" emerged:

- **Java 2 Platform, Micro Edition (J2ME)**: A pared-down version of Java ideally suited to programming consumer electronic devices such as mobile phones, pagers, personal digital assistants (PDAs), etc.

- **Java 2 Platform, Standard Edition (J2SE)**: The fundamental (and original) Java language and run time, used in building desktop applications such as we'll be building for the SRS in Part 3 of this book. J2SE also serves as the foundation for the *Enterprise Edition* of Java (J2EE).

- **Java 2 Platform, Enterprise Edition (J2EE)**: A set of component technologies used with J2SE to build multitier enterprise-level applications, as we discuss in Chapter 17.

Thus, the software bundle needed by Java developers has been alternatively referred to as follows:

- Java Development Kit (JDK)

- (Java) Software Development Kit (SDK)

- Java 2 Software Development Kit (Java 2 SDK)

- Java 2 Platform, Standard Edition (J2SE) Development Kit

etc. I'll refer to this software bundle as either the JDK or the SDK throughout the book.

Finally, there's the notion of the **Java Runtime Environment (JRE)**, that *subset* of the JDK consisting of the JVM, run-time class libraries, and Java application launcher that are needed to *execute* Java bytecode, but *omitting* developer tools such as the Java compiler (javac). For every release numbered 1.*x.x* of the JDK, there is a parallel release of the JRE.

A Final Thought Before You Get Started

A lot of the material in this book—particularly at the beginning of Part 1—may seem overly simplistic to experienced programmers. This is because much of object technology is founded on basic software engineering principles that have been in practice for many years and, in many cases, just repackaged slightly differently. There are indeed a few new tricks that make OO languages extremely powerful and that were virtually impossible to achieve with non-OO languages— **inheritance** and **polymorphism,** for example, which you'll learn more about in Chapters 5 and 7, respectively. (Such techniques can be simulated by hand in a non-OO language, just as programmers could program their own database management system (DBMS) from scratch instead of using a commercial product like Oracle, Sybase, or Microsoft SQL Server—but who'd *want* to?)

The biggest challenge for *experienced* programmers in becoming proficient with objects is reorienting the manner in which they think about the problem they will be automating.

- Software engineers/programmers who have developed applications using non-object-oriented methods often have to "unlearn" certain approaches used in the traditional methods of software analysis and design.

- Paradoxically, people just starting out as programmers (or as OO modelers) sometimes have an easier time when learning the OO approach to software development as their *only* approach.

Fortunately, the way we need to think about objects when developing software turns out to be the natural way that people think about the world in general. So, learning to "think" objects—and to program them in Java—is as easy as (Part) 1, (Part) 2, (Part) 3!

Please Tell Me What You Think

I, along with the Apress editorial and production staff, have worked hard to make this book as useful to you as possible, and we'd love to know what you think of it! We appreciate reader feedback, and take both constructive criticism and praise to heart in our future publishing efforts.

If you'd like to get in touch with anyone at Apress, please do so at info@apress.com or http://www.apress.com. You can contact me at jacquie@objectstart.com or via my web sites, http://objectstart.com and http://techtidalwave.com.

STUDENT REGISTRATION SYSTEM (SRS) CASE STUDY: SRS REQUIREMENTS SPECIFICATION

We have been asked to develop an automated Student Registration System (SRS). This system will enable students to register online for courses each semester, as well as track a student's progress toward completion of his or her degree.

When a student first enrolls at the university, the student uses the SRS to set forth a plan of study as to which courses he or she plans on taking to satisfy a particular degree program, and chooses a faculty advisor. The SRS will verify whether or not the proposed plan of study satisfies the requirements of the degree that the student is seeking. Once a plan of study has been established, then, during the registration period preceding each semester, the student is able to view the schedule of classes online, and choose whichever classes he or she wishes to attend, indicating the preferred section (day of week and time of day) if the class is offered by more than one professor. The SRS will verify whether or not the student has satisfied the necessary prerequisites for each requested course by referring to the student's online transcript of courses completed and grades received (the student may review his or her transcript online at any time).

Assuming that (a) the prerequisites for the requested course(s) are satisfied, (b) the course(s) meets one of the student's plan of study requirements, and (c) there is room available in each of the class(es), the student is enrolled in the class(es).

If (a) and (b) are satisfied, but (c) is not, the student is placed on a first-come, first-served waiting list. If a class/section that the student was previously waitlisted for becomes available (either because some other student has dropped the class or because the seating capacity for the class has been increased), the student is automatically enrolled in the waitlisted class, and an email message to that effect is sent to the student. It is the student's responsibility to drop the class if it is no longer desired; otherwise, he or she will be billed for the course.

Students may drop a class up to the end of the first week of the semester in which the class is being taught.

PART 1

■■■

The ABCs of Objects

CHAPTER 1

Abstraction and Modeling

As human beings, we're flooded with information every day of our lives. Even if we could temporarily turn off all of the sources of "e-information" that are constantly bombarding us— emails, voicemails, news broadcasts, and the like—our five senses alone collect **millions** of bits of information per day just from our surroundings. Yet, we manage to make sense out of all of this information, typically without getting overwhelmed. Our brains naturally simplify the details of all that we observe so that these details are manageable through a process known as **abstraction**.

In this chapter, you'll learn

- How abstraction serves to simplify our view of the world

- How we organize our knowledge hierarchically to minimize the amount of information that we have to mentally juggle at any given time

- The relevance of abstraction to software development

- The inherent challenges that we face as software developers when attempting to model a real-word situation in software

Simplification Through Abstraction

Take a moment to look around the room in which you're reading this book. At first, you may think that there really aren't that many things to observe: some furniture, light fixtures, perhaps some plants, artwork, even some other people or pets. Maybe there is a window to gaze out of that opens up the outside world to observation.

Now look again. For each thing that you see, there are myriad details to observe: its size, its color, its intended purpose, the components from which it's assembled (the legs on a table, the lightbulbs in a lamp), etc. In addition, each one of these components in turn has details associated with it: the type of material used to make the legs of the table (wood or metal), the wattage of the lightbulbs, etc. Now factor in your other senses: the sound of someone snoring (hopefully not while reading this book!), the smell of popcorn coming from the microwave oven down the hall, and so forth. Finally, think about all of the unseen details of these objects: who manufactured them, or what their chemical, molecular, or genetic composition is.

It's clear that the amount of information to be processed by our brains is truly overwhelming! For the vast majority of people, this doesn't pose a problem, however, because we're innately skilled at **abstraction**, a process that involves recognizing and focusing on the important characteristics of a situation or object, and filtering out or ignoring all of the unessential details.

One familiar example of an abstraction is a road map. As an abstraction, a road map represents those features of a given geographic area relevant to someone trying to navigate with the map, perhaps by car: major roads and places of interest, obstacles such as large bodies of water, etc. Of necessity, a road map can't include every building, tree, street sign, billboard, traffic light, fast-food restaurant, etc. that physically exists in the real world. If it did, then it would be so cluttered as to be virtually unusable; none of the important features would stand out. Compare a road map with a topographical map, a climatological map, and a population density map of the same region: each abstracts out different features of the real world—namely, those relevant to the intended user of the map in question.

As another example, consider a landscape. An artist may look at the landscape from the perspective of colors, textures, and shapes as a prospective subject for a painting. A homebuilder may look at the same landscape from the perspective of where the best building site may be on the property, assessing how many trees will need to be cleared to make way for a construction project. An ecologist may closely study the individual species of trees and other plant/animal life for their biodiversity, with an eye toward preserving and protecting them, whereas a child may simply be looking at all of the trees in search of the best site for a tree house! Some elements are common to all four observers' abstractions of the landscape—the types, sizes, and locations of trees, for example—while others aren't relevant to all of the abstractions.

Generalization Through Abstraction

If we eliminate enough detail from an abstraction, it becomes generic enough to apply to a wide range of specific situations or instances. Such generic abstractions can often be quite useful. For example, a diagram of a generic cell in the human body, such as the one in Figure 1-1, might include only a few features of the structures that are found in an actual cell.

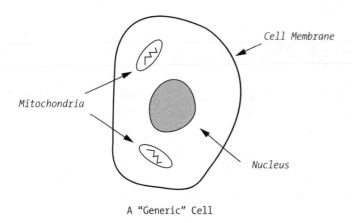

Figure 1-1. *A generic abstraction of a cell*

This overly simplified diagram doesn't look like a real nerve cell, or a real muscle cell, or a real blood cell; and yet, it can still be used in an educational setting to describe certain aspects of the structure and function of all of these cell types—namely, those features that the various cell types have in common.

The simpler an abstraction—that is, the fewer features it presents—the more general it is, and the more versatile it is in describing a variety of real-world situations. The more complex an abstraction, the more restrictive it is, and thus the fewer situations it is useful in describing.

Organizing Abstractions into Classification Hierarchies

Even though our brains are adept at abstracting concepts such as road maps and landscapes, that still leaves us with hundreds of thousands, if not millions, of separate abstractions to deal with over our lifetimes. To cope with this aspect of complexity, human beings systematically arrange information into categories according to established criteria; this process is known as **classification**.

For example, science categorizes all natural objects as belonging to either the animal, plant, or mineral kingdom. In order for a natural object to be classified as an animal, it must satisfy the following rules:

- It must be a living being.

- It must be capable of spontaneous movement.

- It must be capable of rapid motor response to stimulation.

The rules for what constitutes a plant, on the other hand, are different:

- It must be a living being (same as for an animal).

- It must lack an obvious nervous system.

- It must possess cellulose cell walls.

Given clear-cut rules such as these, placing an object into the appropriate category, or **class**, is rather straightforward. We can then "drill down," specifying additional rules that differentiate various types of animal, for example, until we've built up a hierarchy of increasingly more complex abstractions from top to bottom. A simple example of an **abstraction hierarchy** is shown in Figure 1-2.

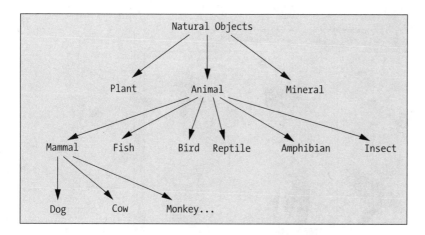

Figure 1-2. *A simple abstraction hierarchy of natural objects*

When thinking about an abstraction hierarchy such as the one shown in Figure 1-2, we mentally step up and down the hierarchy, automatically zeroing in on only the single layer or subset of the hierarchy (known as a **subtree**) that is important to us at a given point in time. For example, we may only be concerned with mammals and so can focus on the mammalian subtree, shown in Figure 1-3, temporarily ignoring the rest of the hierarchy.

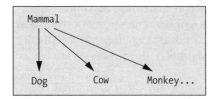

Figure 1-3. *Focusing on a small subset of the hierarchy is less overwhelming.*

By doing so, we automatically reduce the number of concepts that we mentally need to juggle at any one time to a manageable subset of the overall abstraction hierarchy; in our simplistic example, we're now dealing with only 4 concepts rather than the original 13. No matter how complex an abstraction hierarchy grows to be, it needn't overwhelm us if it's properly organized.

Coming up with precisely which rules are necessary to properly classify an object within an abstraction hierarchy isn't always easy. Take, for example, the rules we might define for what constitutes a bird: namely, something that

- Has feathers

- Has wings

- Lays eggs

- Is capable of flying

Given these rules, neither an ostrich nor a penguin could be classified as a bird, because neither can fly (see Figure 1-4).

Figure 1-4. *Deriving the correct classification rules can be difficult.*

If we attempt to make the rule set less restrictive by eliminating the "flight" rule, we're left with

- Has feathers

- Has wings

- Lays eggs

According to this rule set, we now may properly classify both the ostrich and the penguin as birds, as shown in Figure 1-5.

Figure 1-5. *Proper classification rules have been established.*

This rule set is still unnecessarily complicated, because as it turns out, the "lays eggs" rule is redundant: whether we keep it or eliminate it, it doesn't change our decision of what constitutes a bird versus a non-bird. Therefore, we simplify the rule set once again:

- Has feathers

- Has wings

Feeling particularly daring (!), we try to take our simplification process one step further by eliminating yet another rule, defining a bird as something that

- Has wings

As Figure 1-6 shows, we've gone too far this time: the abstraction of a bird is now so general that we'd include airplanes, insects, and all sorts of other non-birds in the mix!

Figure 1-6. *A rule set that is too relaxed is as much of a problem as an overly restrictive rule set.*

The process of rule definition for purposes of categorization involves "dialing in" just the right set of rules—not too general, not too restrictive, and containing no redundancies—to define the correct membership in a particular class.

Abstraction As the Basis for Software Development

When pinning down the requirements for an information systems development project, we typically start by gathering details about the real-world situation on which the system is to be based. These details are usually a combination of

- Those that are explicitly offered to us as we interview the intended users of the system

- Those that we otherwise observe

We must make a judgment call as to which of these details are relevant to the system's ultimate purpose. This is essential, as we can't automate them all! To include too much detail is to overly complicate the resultant system, making it that much more difficult to design, program, test, debug, document, maintain, and extend in the future.

As with all abstractions, all of our decisions of inclusion versus elimination when building a software system must be made within the context of the overall purpose and **domain**, or subject matter focus, of the future system. When representing a person in a software system, for example, is their eye color important? How about their genetic profile? Salary? Hobbies? The answer is, *any* of these features of a person may be relevant or irrelevant, depending on whether the system to be developed is a

- Payroll system

- Marketing demographics system

- Optometrist's patient database

- FBI's "most wanted" tracking system

Once we've determined the essential aspects of a situation—something that we'll explore in Part 2 of this book—we can prepare a **model** of that situation. **Modeling** is the process by which we develop a pattern for something to be made. A blueprint for a custom home, a schematic diagram of a printed circuit, and a cookie cutter are all examples of such patterns. As we'll cover in Parts 2 and 3, an **object model** of a software system is such a pattern. Modeling and abstraction go hand in hand, because a model is essentially a physical or graphical portrayal of an abstraction; before we can model something effectively, we must have determined the essential details of the subject to be modeled.

Reuse of Abstractions

When learning about something new, we automatically search our mental archive for other abstractions/models that we've previously built and mastered, to look for similarities that we can build upon. When learning to ride a two-wheeled bicycle for the first time, for example, you may have drawn upon lessons that you learned about riding a tricycle as a child (see Figure 1-7). Both have handlebars that are used to steer; both have pedals that are used to propel the bike forward. Although the abstractions didn't match perfectly—a two-wheeled bicycle introduced the new challenge of having to balance yourself—there was enough of a similarity to allow you to draw upon the steering and pedaling expertise you already had mastered, and to focus on learning the new skill of how to balance on two wheels.

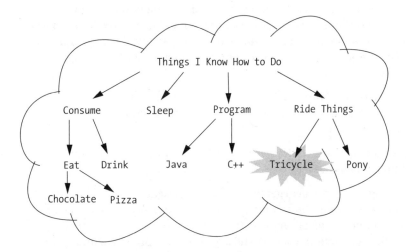

Figure 1-7. *The human brain is adept at learning by building upon already-established abstractions.*

This technique of comparing features to find an abstraction that is similar enough to be reused successfully is known as **pattern matching and reuse**. As we'll cover in Chapter 12, pattern reuse is an important technique for object-oriented software development, as well, because it spares us from having to reinvent the wheel with each new project. If we can reuse an abstraction or model from a previous project, we can focus on those aspects of the new project that differ from the old, gaining a tremendous amount of productivity in the process.

Inherent Challenges

Despite the fact that abstraction is such a natural process for human beings, developing an appropriate model for a software system is perhaps the most difficult aspect of software engineering, because

- There are an unlimited number of possibilities. Abstraction is to a certain extent in the eye of the beholder: several different observers working independently are almost guaranteed to arrive at different models. Whose is the best? *Passionate* arguments have ensued!

- To further complicate matters, there is virtually never only one "best" or "correct" model, only "better" or "worse" models relative to the problem to be solved. The same situation can be modeled in a variety of different, equally valid ways. When we get into actually doing some modeling in Part 2 of this book, we'll look at a number of valid alternative abstractions for our Student Registration System (SRS) case study that was presented at the end of the Introduction.

- Note, however, that there *is* such a thing as an *incorrect* model: namely, one that misrepresents the real-world situation (for example, modeling a person as having two different blood types).

- There is no acid test to determine if a model has adequately captured all of a user's requirements. The ultimate evidence of whether or not an abstraction was appropriate is in how successful the resultant software system turns out to be. We don't want to wait until the end of a project before finding out that we've gone astray. Because of this, it's critical that we learn ways of communicating our model concisely and unambiguously to the following people:

    - The intended future users of our application, so that they may provide a sanity check for our understanding of the problem to be solved before we embark upon software development

    - Our fellow software engineers, so that team members can share a common vision of what we're to build collaboratively

Despite all of these challenges, it's critical to get the up-front abstraction "right" before beginning to build a system. Fixing mistakes in the abstraction once a system is modeled, designed, coded, documented, and undergoing acceptance testing is much more costly (by orders of magnitude) than correcting the abstraction when it's still a gleam in the project team's eye. This isn't to imply that an abstraction should be rigid—quite the contrary! The art and science of object modeling, when properly applied, yields a model that is flexible enough to withstand a wide variety of functional changes. In addition, the special properties of objects further lend themselves to flexible software solutions, as you'll learn throughout the rest of the book. However, all things being equal, we'd like to harness this flexibility in expanding a system's capabilities over time, rather than in repairing mistakes.

What Does It Take to Be a Successful Object Modeler?

Coming up with an appropriate abstraction as the basis for a software system model requires

- ***Insight into the problem domain***: Ideally, we'll be able to draw upon our own real-world experiences, such as former or current experience as a student, which will come in handy when determining the requirements for the SRS.

- ***Creativity***: We must be able to think "outside the box," in case the future users that we're interviewing have been immersed in the problem area for so long that they fail to see innovations that might be made.

- ***Good listening skills***: These will come in handy as future users of the system describe how they do their jobs currently, or how they envision doing their jobs in the future, with the aid of the system that we're about to develop.

- ***Good observational skills***: Actions often speak louder than words. Just by observing users going about their daily business, we may pick up an essential detail that they have neglected to mention because they do it so routinely that it has become a habit.

But all this isn't enough. We also need

- An organized ***process*** for determining what the abstraction should be. If we follow a proven checklist of steps for producing a model, then we greatly reduce the probability that we'll omit some important feature or neglect a critical requirement.

- A way to ***communicate*** the resultant model concisely and unambiguously to our fellow software developers and to the intended users of our application. While it's certainly possible to describe an abstraction in narrative text, a picture is worth a thousand words, and so the language with which we communicate a model is often a **graphical notation**. Throughout this book, we'll focus on the Unified Modeling Language (UML; see Figure 1-8) notation as our model communication language (you'll learn the basics of UML in Chapters 10 and 11). Think of a graphical model as a blueprint of the software application to be built.

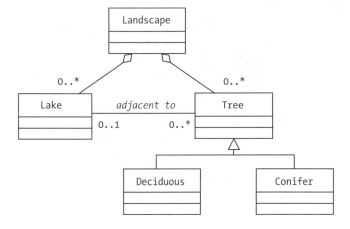

Figure 1-8. *Describing a landscape in UML notation*

- Ideally, we'll also have a ***software tool*** to help us automate the process of producing such a blueprint.

Part 2 of this book covers these three aspects of modeling—process, notation, and tool—in detail.

Summary

In this chapter, you've learned that

- Abstraction is a fundamental technique that people use to perceive the world.

- Developing an abstraction of the problem to be automated is a necessary first step of all software development.

- We naturally organize information into classification hierarchies based upon rules that we carefully structure, so that they are neither too general nor too restrictive.

- We often reuse abstractions when attempting to model a new concept.

- Producing an abstraction of a system to be built, known as a model, is in some senses second nature to us, and yet paradoxically is one of the hardest things that software developers have to do in the life cycle of an information systems project. It's also one of the most important.

IMPORTANT INFORMATION CONCERNING END-OF-CHAPTER EXERCISES

I've included exercises at the end of each chapter to assist you in your learning experience.

- Many of the exercises have been crafted as open-ended, thought-provoking questions suitable as homework assignments in an academic setting. Thus, there are no simple "one-size-fits-all" answers available for such exercises.

- Some exercises involve hands-on programming and are labeled as follows: [*Coding*] . . .

- You are encouraged to pose questions about the exercises, or about Java in general, via the Apress Forums online discussion group at `http://forums.apress.com`, where you get the benefit of insights from other readers, as well as from Apress authors/experts.

Exercises

1. Sketch a class hierarchy that relates all of the following classes in a reasonable manner:

   Apple

   Banana

   Beef

   Beverage

   Cheese

   Consumable

   Dairy Product

   Food

   Fruit

   Green Bean

   Meat

   Milk

   Pork

   Spinach

   Vegetable

   Justify your answer, noting in particular any challenges that you faced in doing so.

2. What aspects of a television set would be important to abstract from the perspective of

   - A consumer wishing to buy one?

   - An engineer responsible for designing one?

   - A retailer who sells them?

   - The manufacturer?

3. Select a problem area that you would like to model from an object-oriented perspective. Ideally, this will be a problem that you're actually going to be working on at your place of employment or that you otherwise have a keen interest in. Assume that you're going to write a program to automate some aspect of this problem area, and write a one-page overview of the requirements for this program, patterned after the SRS case study.

   Make certain that your first paragraph summarizes the intent of the system, as the first paragraph in the SRS case study does. Also, emphasize the *functional requirements*—that is, those that a non-technical end user might state as to how the system should behave—and avoid stating *technical requirements*—for example, "This system must run on a Windows NT platform, and must use the TCP/IP protocol to . . ."

4. Read the case study for a Prescription Tracking System (PTS) in Appendix B. In your opinion, how effective is this case study as an abstraction? Are there details that you think could have been omitted or missing details that you think would have been important to include? If you had an opportunity to interview the intended users of the PTS, what additional questions might you ask them to better refine this abstraction?

CHAPTER 2

■ ■ ■

Some Java Basics

The goals for this book are not only to teach you about objects and object modeling, but also to illustrate how objects translate into a working software application. So, before diving into the basics of objects in Chapter 3, we'll spend some time getting comfortable with Java fundamentals, as this is the programming language used to illustrate object concepts as they are introduced throughout the book.

Objects are "language neutral," and so what you'll learn conceptually about objects in Part 1 of this book, and about object modeling in Part 2, could apply equally well to Java, or C++, or C#, or an as-yet-to-be-invented object-oriented (OO) language. I've chosen Java specifically for the many advantages that this elegant OO programming language affords us as software developers, which we'll explore in this chapter.

In this chapter, you'll also learn about

- Primitive Java types, operators on those types, and expressions formed with those types

- The anatomy of a simple Java program

- The mechanics of compiling and running such programs

- Java's **block-structured** nature

- Various types of Java **expressions**

- Loops and other flow control structures

- Printing messages to the command window from which a program was launched, which is especially useful for testing code as it evolves

- Elements of Java programming style

If you're a proficient C, C++, or C# programmer, you'll find much of Java syntax to be very familiar, and you should be able to breeze through this chapter fairly quickly.

Why Java?

After learning what makes objects "tick" in Part 1 of the book and how to model an application to take advantage of objects in Part 2, you'll be ready for the grand finale: rendering an object model in code to produce a working Student Registration System (SRS) application in Part 3. As mentioned earlier, we *could* walk through building the SRS using any OO programming language. Why might we want to use Java? Read on, and you'll quickly see why!

Java Is Architecture Neutral

To execute a program written in a conventionally compiled language like C or C++, the source code must first be compiled into an executable form known as **binary code** or **machine code**. Binary code, in essence, is a pattern of 1s and 0s understandable by the underlying **hardware architecture** of the computer on which the program is intended to run.

Even if original C or C++ source code is written to be **platform independent**—that is, the program does not take advantage of any platform-specific language extensions such as a specific type of file access or graphical user interface (GUI) manipulation—the resultant executable version will nonetheless still be tied to a particular platform's architecture and can therefore be run on only that architecture. That is, a version of the program compiled for a Sun Solaris workstation will not run on a Windows PC, a version compiled for a Windows PC will not run on a Linux machine, and so forth. This concept is depicted in Figure 2-1.

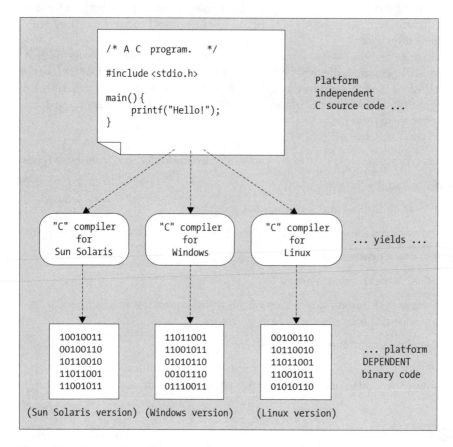

Figure 2-1. *Conventionally compiled languages yield platform-dependent executable programs.*

In contrast, Java source code is not compiled for a particular platform, but rather into a special intermediate format known as **bytecode**, which is said to be both platform independent and **architecture neutral**. That is, no matter whether a Java program is compiled under Sun Solaris, Windows, Linux, or any other operating system for which a Java compiler is available, the resultant bytecode turns out to be the same and hence can be run on any computer for which a (platform-*specific*) Java Virtual Machine (JVM) is available. This is illustrated in Figure 2-2.

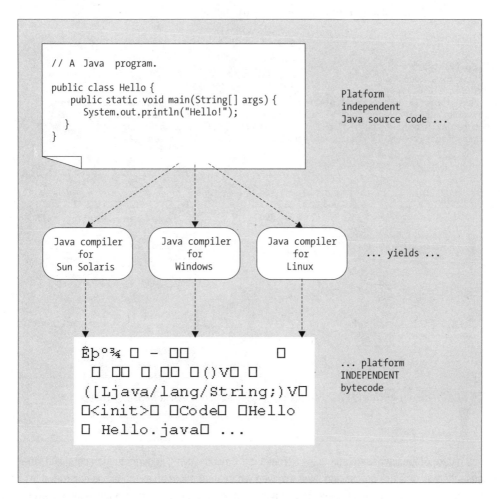

Figure 2-2. *The Java compiler yields platform-independent bytecode.*

The JVM is a special piece of software that knows how to **interpret** and execute Java bytecode. That is, instead of a Java program running directly under the control of the operating system the way traditionally compiled programs do, the JVM itself runs under direct control of the operating system, and our Java program in turn runs under control of the JVM, as illustrated in Figure 2-3. The JVM in essence serves as a translator, translating the universal Java bytecode "language" into the machine code "language" that a particular computer can understand, in the same way that a human interpreter facilitates a discussion between someone speaking German and someone speaking Japanese by translating their statements as they converse.

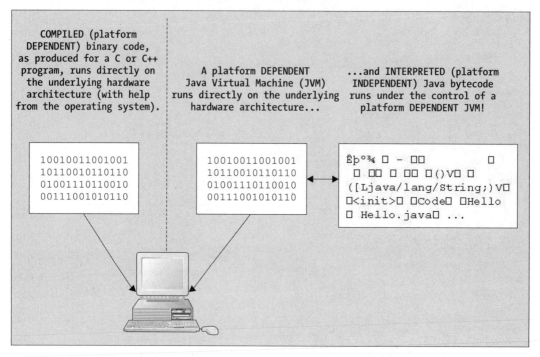

Figure 2-3. *A platform-dependent JVM is used to execute platform-independent bytecode.*

The interpreted nature of the Java language tends to make it a *tiny* bit slower, in general, than compiled languages because there is an extra processing layer involved when an application executes, as illustrated in Figure 2-3. For traditional information systems applications that involve a human user in the loop, however, the difference in speed is imperceptible; other factors, such as the speed of the network (in the case of distributed applications), the speed of a DBMS server (if a database is used), and especially human "think time" while responding to an application's user interface, can cause any JVM response time delays to pale by comparison.

As long as you have the appropriate JVM installed on a given target platform, you can transfer Java bytecode from one platform to another without recompiling the original Java source code, and it will still be able to run. That is, bytecode is transferable across platforms, as illustrated in Figure 2-4.

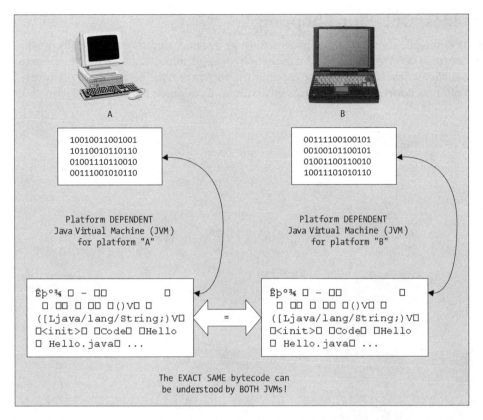

Figure 2-4. *The exact same bytecode is understood by JVMs on two different platforms.*

MIGRATING BYTECODE

There are two important caveats to keep in mind when migrating bytecode from one machine to another. The first involves migrating across different *versions* of the Java language, even if on the same platform. Java bytecode is, in theory, **forward compatible** with newer versions of the JVM, meaning that if a Java program is compiled with one version of the Java language—say, version 1.3.1—it will run correctly under a newer version of the JVM—say, version 1.4.2. However, there can be slight differences in the way an application runs under a newer version of the JVM, due to nothing more than perhaps that a minor bug in an earlier version of the Java language has been corrected.

Even when migrating to the *same* version of Java across *different* hardware architectures, however, minor incompatibilities can arise. Sun Microsystems is responsible for releasing new versions of Java for only a handful of platforms—in particular, newer "flavors" of Windows, Linux, and Sun Solaris (Unix). It's left up to other hardware vendors to provide compatible JVMs for their respective platforms (e.g., Apple Macintosh and SGI IRIX [Unix]). I've encountered situations where a particular vendor releases a version of Java that has the same version number as a Sun release of Java, but where the features of that vendor's version don't quite measure up to the similarly numbered version from Sun.

The bottom line is that it's best to recompile Java source code for a given target platform before transferring the resultant bytecode to that platform, if you have that luxury.

Java Provides "One-Stop Shopping"

With most conventional programming languages, the core language doesn't automatically provide everything that you'll need to build an industrial-strength application, with a GUI and access to a database management system. For these capabilities, you must typically integrate platform-specific (and often, *vendor*-specific) libraries into your application, as illustrated in Figure 2-5.

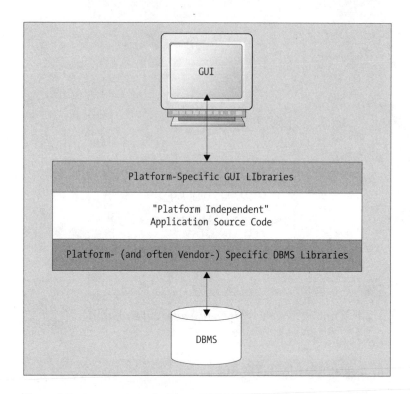

Figure 2-5. *Integrating platform-specific libraries into an otherwise platform-independent application*

The inclusion of such platform- and vendor-specific library calls hinders application migration from one platform to another, because not all library calls for a given platform *X* necessarily **have** an equivalent for a target platform *Y*—for example, not all Microsoft ActiveX controls (used to build GUIs for Windows computers) have an equivalent in the Motif library of GUI components (used to build GUIs for Unix machines), and vice versa.

Worse yet, the boundary between the platform-***independent*** and platform-/vendor-***dependent*** code is not really as clean as is depicted in Figure 2-5. Calls to these libraries are often scattered throughout an application, as illustrated in Figure 2-6, making the chore of migrating an application from one platform to another troublesome at best and prohibitively difficult in the worst cases.

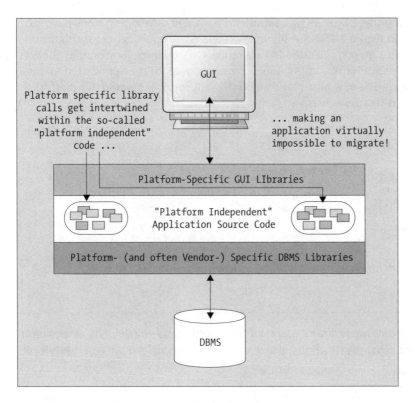

Figure 2-6. *The boundaries between platform-dependent and platform-independent code are unclear.*

If the boundary between platform-independent and platform-dependent components of an application is particularly messy, it's sometimes the lesser of two evils to rewrite the entire application from scratch rather than to attempt to migrate it.

There are some special third-party programs available called **emulators** that will simulate one operating system under another, thus enabling us (in theory) to execute a platform-dependent application on another incompatible platform without any modification. However, not all applications will necessarily run properly under an emulator, and those that do typically perform sluggishly.

In contrast, the Java language provides an extensive set of **application programming interfaces** (**APIs**) that provide a consistent, *platform-independent* means of accessing all underlying operating system functions, including GUI rendering and database management system (DBMS) access. We'll cover the following Java APIs later, in Part 3 of the book:

- `java.io`: Used for file system access (see Chapter 15)

- `java.sql`: The JDBC API, used for communicating with relational databases in a vendor-independent fashion (see Chapter 15)

- `java.awt`: The Abstract Windowing Toolkit, used for GUI development (see Chapter 16)

- `javax.swing`: Swing components, also used for GUI development (see Chapter 16)

And there are *many* more! If these built-in Java libraries are used in developing 100% pure Java applications as illustrated in Figure 2-7, the resultant Java code is truly portable across platforms and vendors. So, to migrate a *Java* application from Windows XP to Linux, for example, there's no need to rip out code (or your hair!): simply transfer the bytecode for the application to the new platform, and as long as the new host platform has the appropriate version of a platform-specific JVM installed, then you are good to go.

Figure 2-7. *A 100% pure Java application is platform-independent from GUI to DBMS.*

In Part 3 of the book, we'll discuss two *critically important* design techniques—**model-data access layer separation** and **model-view separation**—which will further ensure the vendor- and platform- flexibility of our applications.

Java Is Object-Oriented from the Ground Up

Before newer OO languages like Java arrived on the scene, one of the most widely used OO languages was C++, which is actually an object-oriented extension of the non-OO language C. As such, C++ provides a lot of "back doors" that make it very easy to write decidedly un-OO code. In fact, many proficient C programmers transitioned to C++ as a better C without properly learning how to design an OO application, and hence wound up using C++ for the most part as a procedural (non-OO) language.

If you're an experienced C++ programmer wishing to know more about the differences between C++ and Java, please refer to Appendix E.

In contrast, Java is object oriented to its very core. As you will learn in more detail in the chapters that follow, just about *everything* in Java is an object:

- All data, with the exception of a few primitive types, is rendered as objects.

- All of the GUI building blocks—windows, buttons, text input fields, scroll bars, lists, menus, and so on—are objects.

- All functions are associated with objects and are known as **methods**—there can be no "free-floating" functions as there are in C/C++.

- Even the main function used to launch an application (in Java it's called the **main method**) no longer stands alone, but is instead bundled within a **class**, the reasons for which we'll explore in depth in chapters to come.

Because of this, Java lends itself particularly well to writing applications that uphold the OO paradigm. Yet, as I pointed out in the introduction to this book, merely using such an OO language does not *guarantee* that the applications you produce will be *true* to this paradigm! You must be knowledgeable both in how to design an application from the ground up to make the best use of objects and in how to apply the language correctly, which are the primary intents of this book.

Practice Makes Perfect

The Java language designers at Sun Microsystems were able to draw upon the lessons learned from other OO programming languages that preceded it. They borrowed the best features of C++, Eiffel, Ada, and Smalltalk, and then added some capabilities and features not found in those languages. Conversely, features that had proven to be most troublesome in those earlier languages were eliminated.

Also, as of version 5.0 (aka1.5) of Java, several features of a *newer* language, Microsoft's C#, were retrofitted into Java.

This isn't to say that Java is a "perfect" language (no language is!), but simply that it has made some significant improvements over many of the languages that have preceded it.

Java Is an Open Standard

What significance does the fact that Java is an open standard hold for us as software developers? For one thing, all of the source code behind all of the built-in Java libraries is available for us to study and use as a basis for our own software design.

Also, the IT industry as a whole has been quick to embrace Java because no third-party vendors have been excluded, as is often the case with a proprietary/"closed" technology. Quite the contrary: Sun Microsystems has encouraged other vendors to adopt the Java standard and to incorporate Java capability in their products by allowing vendors to participate in the advancement of Java technology specifications through Sun's **Java Community Process**.

And, if the preceding reasons still aren't compelling enough to convince you of the merits of Java . . .

Java Is Free!

Sun Microsystems has ensured that Java enjoys widespread adoption, in part, by making the language and all of the basic tools necessary to develop Java applications *free*! Appendix C provides information on what you'll need to do to download the **Java 2 Software Development Kit** (**SDK**) from Sun's website (http://java.sun.com) to get started with Java development. (I provide instructions for how to compile and run Java programs a bit later in this chapter.)

The rest of this chapter introduces some elemental Java syntax, which we'll continue to build upon in subsequent chapters.

A Reminder Regarding Pseudocode vs. Real Java Code

I occasionally use little bits of pseudocode in the code examples throughout Parts 1 and 2 of this book to hide irrelevant logic details. To make it clear as to when I'm using pseudocode rather than real code, I use *italic* rather than regular SansMono condensed font.

This is real Java syntax:

```
for (int i = 0; i <= 10; i++) {
```

This is pseudocode:

```
    compute the grade for the ith Student
}
```

I'll remind you of this fact a few more times, so that you don't forget and accidentally try to type in and compile pseudocode somewhere along the way.

Anatomy of a Simple Java Program

Figure 2-8 shows one of the simplest of all Java applications.

```
File named SimpleProgram.java contains:
```

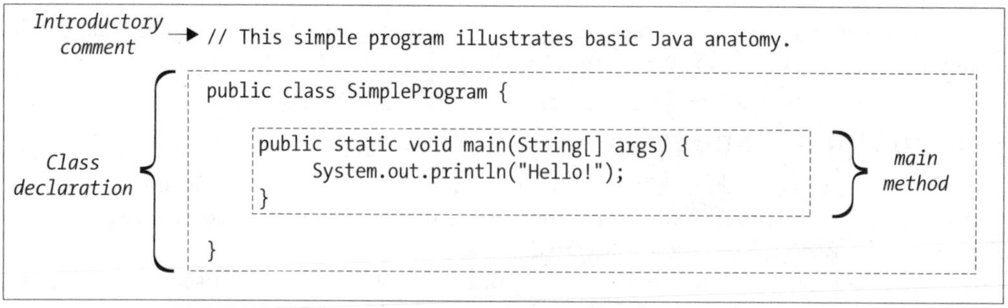

Figure 2-8. *Anatomy of a simple Java program*

Let's go over the key elements of our simple program.

Comments

The first thing we see in our simple Java program is an introductory comment:

```
// This simple program illustrates some basic Java syntax.
```

Java supports three different comment styles: traditional, end-of-line, and Java documentation comments.

Traditional Comments

Java **traditional comments** derive from the C language and begin with a forward slash followed by an asterisk (/*) and end with an asterisk followed by a forward slash (*/). Everything enclosed between these delimiters is treated as a comment and is therefore ignored by the Java compiler, no matter how many lines the comment spans.

```
/* This is a traditional (C-style) comment. */

/* This is a multiline traditional comment. This is a handy way to temporarily
   comment out entire sections of code without having to delete them.
   From the time that the compiler encounters the first "slash asterisk"
   above, it doesn't care what we type here; even legitimate lines of code,
   as shown below, are treated as comment lines and thus ignored by the
   compiler until the first "asterisk slash" combination is encountered.
x = y + z;
a = b / c;
j = s + c + f;
*/

/* We often use leading asterisks on the second through last line of a traditional
 * comment simply for cosmetic reasons, so that the comment is more visually
 * distinct; but, these extra asterisks are strictly cosmetic - only the
 * initial "slash asterisk" and the final "asterisk slash" are noted by the
 * compiler as having any significance.
 */
```

Note that we can't **nest** block comments—that is, the following will **not** compile:

```
/* This starts a comment ...
x = 3;
/* Whoops!  We are mistakenly trying to nest a SECOND comment
before terminating the FIRST!
This is going to cause us compilation problems, because the
compiler is going to IGNORE the start of this second/inner comment -- we're IN
a comment already, after all! -- and so as soon as we try to terminate
this SECOND/inner comment, the compiler will think that we've terminated the
FIRST/outer comment instead ... */
z = 2;
// The compiler will "complain" on the next line.
*/
```

When the compiler reaches what we intended to be the terminating */ of the "outer" comment in the last line of the preceding code example, the following two compilation errors will be reported:

```
illegal start of expression
  */
  ^
```

and

```
';' expected
    */
     ^
```

End-of-Line Comments

The second type of Java comment derives from C++ and is known as an **end-of-line comment**. We use a double slash (//) to note the beginning of a comment that automatically ends when the end of the line is reached, as shown here:

```
x = y + z;    // text of comment continues through to the end of the line ==>
a = b / c;

// Here's a BLOCK of sequential end-of-line comments.
// This serves as an alternative to using traditional comments
// (/* ... */) and is preferred by many Java programmers.

m = n * p;
```

Java Documentation Comments

The third and final type of Java comment, **Java documentation comments** (aka **Javadoc comments**), can be parsed from source code files by a special javadoc command-line utility program (which comes standard with the Java SDK) and used to automatically generate HTML documentation for an application.

We'll defer an in-depth look at Javadoc comments until Chapter 13.

The Class Declaration

Next comes a **class wrapper**—more properly termed a **class declaration**—of the form

```
public class ClassName {
    ...
}
```

For example:

```
public class SimpleProgram {
    ...
}
```

where braces { ... } enclose the **class body** that includes the main logic of the program along with other optional building blocks of a class.

In subsequent chapters, you'll learn all about the significance of classes in an OO programming language. For now, simply note that the symbols public and class are two of Java's **keywords**—that is, symbols reserved for specific uses within the Java language—whereas SimpleProgram is a name/symbol that I've invented.

The main Method

Within the SimpleProgram class declaration, we find the starting point for the program, called the **main method** in Java. The main method serves as the entry point for a Java program. When we execute a Java program by interpreting its bytecode with an instance of the JVM, the JVM calls the main method to jump-start our application.

With trivial applications such as the SimpleProgram example, all of the program's logic can be contained within this single main method. For more complex applications, on the other hand, the main method can't possibly contain all of the logic for the entire system. You'll learn how to construct an application that transcends the boundaries of the main method, involving multiple Java source code files, a bit later in the book.

The first line of the method, shown here

```
public static void main(String[] args) {
```

defines what is known as the main method's **method header**, and must appear exactly as shown (with one minor exception that I'll explain in Chapter 13 having to do with optionally receiving arguments from the command line).

Our main method's **method body**, enclosed in braces { ... }, consists of a single statement:

```
System.out.println("Hello!");
```

which prints the message

```
Hello!
```

---

to the (DOS/Solaris/Linux) command window from which our program is launched. We'll examine this statement's syntax further in a bit, but for now, note the use of a semicolon (;) at the end of the statement. As in C and C++, semicolons are placed at the end of all individual Java statements. Braces { ... }, in turn, delimit **blocks** of code, the significance of which I'll discuss in more detail a bit later in this chapter.

Other things that we'd typically do inside of the main method of a more elaborate program include declaring variables, creating objects, and calling other methods.

Now that we've looked at the anatomy of a simple Java program, let's discuss how such a program is compiled and executed.

Please refer to Appendix C for details on how to get the Java 2 Software Development Kit (SDK) properly installed on your computer before proceeding.

The "Mechanics" of Java

Once we have entered our program logic, as text, into a file, using either a simple text editor (such as Windows Notepad or vi) or a Java Integrated Development Environment (IDE) tool, we must first compile the source code into bytecode before we can execute it.

For folks just getting started with Java programming, I advocate using a simple text editor at first so that you aren't distracted by the bells and whistles of a specific IDE, and so that the IDE doesn't do so much work for you that you don't really learn what's going on at the most basic level. If you like working with IDEs, however, I recommend starting out with a very inexpensive tool called **TextPad**, available at `http://www.textpad.com`.

For folks who are proficient with vi (a Unix/Linux editor), note that there is a Windows/DOS-compatible version called **vim** that is available at no cost from `http://www.vim.org`—specifically, it can be downloaded from `http://www.vim.org/download.php`.

Once you've mastered the Java language, you can "graduate" to a more complex IDE if you wish.

The simplest way to compile and execute a Java program is via command-line commands, which are the same whether we're developing on a Sun Solaris, Linux, or Windows computer.

USING THE COMMAND PROMPT

In the case of Windows, open a **Command Prompt** window by selecting the Start ➤ Run menu, then type cmd in the dialog box that appears, as shown in the following image; then click OK.

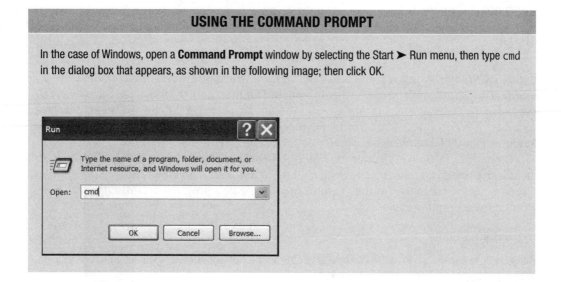

A sample Command Prompt window is shown in the following image.

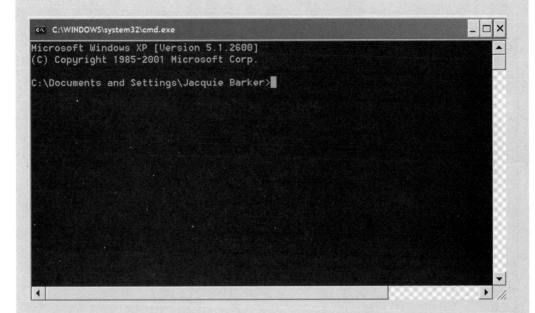

To expand the capacity of the Command Prompt window and/or to resize it, right-click the blue header bar of the window and choose Properties from the pop-up menu that appears, as shown in the following image.

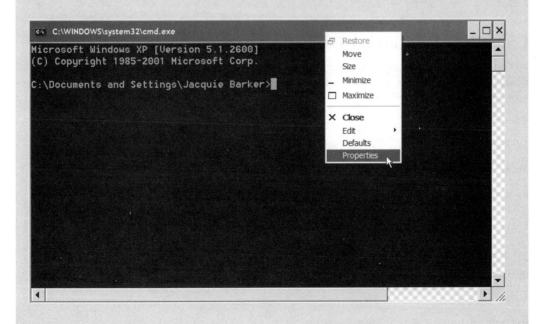

On the Layout panel of the dialog box that appears (as shown in the following image for a Windows XP computer), adjust the Screen Buffer Size and Window Size options as indicated.

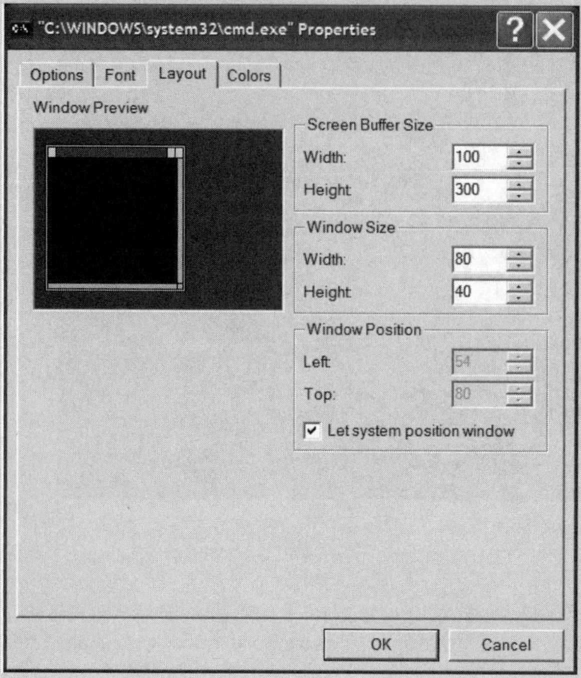

Compiling Java Source Code into Bytecode

To compile Java source code from the command line, we use the cd command, as necessary, to navigate into the working directory where our source code resides. We then type the following command:

```
javac sourcecode_filename
```

for example:

```
javac SimpleProgram.java
```

to compile it.

If there were more than one .java source code file in the same directory, we could either list the names of the files to be compiled, separated by spaces:

```
javac Foo.java Bar.java Another.java
```

or use the wildcard character (*), for example:

```
javac *.java
```

to compile multiple files at the same time.

If all goes well—namely, if no compiler errors arise—then a bytecode file by the name of `SimpleProgram.class` will appear in the same directory where the `SimpleProgram.java` source code file resides. If compiler errors do arise, on the other hand, we of course must correct our source code and attempt to recompile it.

Please refer to the section entitled "Common Compilation Errors" in Appendix C for a list of some of the common compilation errors and how to resolve them.

Executing Bytecode

Once a program has been successfully compiled, we execute the bytecode version via the command

```
java bytecode_filename       (note that we OMIT the .class suffix)
```

for example:

```
java SimpleProgram
```

Note that it's important to **omit** the `.class` suffix of the bytecode file name (which is called `SimpleProgram.class` in this case).

By default, the JVM will look in your default working directory along with the "home" directory where the Java language has been installed on your computer system for such bytecode files. If the JVM finds the specified bytecode file, it executes its main method, and your program is off and running!

If for some reason the bytecode you are trying to execute is in neither of these two default locations, you must inform the JVM of additional directories in which to search. You can do so by specifying a list of directories (separated by semicolons [;] under Windows, or by colons [:] under Solaris and Linux) after the `-cp` flag on the `java` command as follows:

```
java -cp list_of_directory_names_to_be_searched bytecode_filename
```

For example, on DOS/Windows:

```
java -cp C:\home\javastuff;D:\reference\workingdir;S:\foo\bar\files SimpleProgram
```

or on Solaris/Linux:

```
java -cp /barkerj/work:/java/examples/ex1 SimpleProgram
```

At a minimum, we typically want the JVM to search our **current working directory** for bytecode files. With version 1.4.x of Java and **later**, this happens automatically, as discussed earlier; for versions 1.3.x of Java and **earlier**, we must explicitly specify a single period (.), which is (DOS/Linux/Solaris) shorthand for "the current working directory", as a classpath entry; for example, for DOS/Windows:

```
java -cp  .  SimpleProgram
```

or

```
java -cp .;C:\home\javastuff;D:\reference\workingdir SimpleProgram
```

Please refer to the section entitled "Common Run-Time Errors" in Appendix C for a list of some common run-time errors and how to resolve them.

A Behind-the-Scenes Look at the JVM

Let's take a more in-depth look at what is actually happening behind the scenes when we type the command

```
java SimpleProgram
```

to run our program.

- The `java` command causes the JVM to be launched. Recall from an earlier discussion in this chapter that the JVM is a bytecode interpreter.

- The JVM in turn looks for the bytecode file that we've named in the command (`SimpleProgram.class` in this case), searching the directories enumerated by the `-cp` flag, if provided, or in the default working directory if `-cp` isn't used.

- Assuming that the JVM does indeed find the appropriate bytecode file, it loads the bytecode into its memory (conceptually, the bytecode serves as a "plug-in" for the JVM).

- Next, the JVM searches the bytecode that it has just loaded for the presence of the official `main` method header. If this method is found, the JVM executes it, and our program is off and running!

Now that we've looked at the mechanics of compiling and running Java programs, let's explore some of the basic syntax features of Java in more detail.

Primitive Types

Java is said to be a **strongly typed** programming language, in that when a variable is declared, its type must also be declared. Among other things, declaring a variable's type tells the compiler how much memory to allocate for the variable at run time, and also constrains the context(s) in which that variable may subsequently be used in our program.

The Java language defines eight **primitive types** (all eight of these type names are Java keywords), as follows.

Four types of *integer* numeric data:

- `byte`: 8-bit unsigned integer
- `short`: 16-bit signed integer
- `int`: 32-bit signed integer
- `long`: 64-bit signed integer

Two *floating-point* numeric types:

- `float`: 32-bit single-precision floating point
- `double`: 64-bit double-precision floating point

Plus two additional primitive types:

- char: A single character, stored using 16-bit Unicode encoding (versus 8-bit ASCII encoding), that enables Java to handle a wide range of international character sets.

- boolean: A variable that may only assume one of two values: true or false (both of these values are reserved words in Java). Boolean variables are often used as flags to signal whether or not some code should be conditionally performed, as in the following code snippet:

```
boolean error = false;  // Initialize the flag.
// ...

// Later in the program (pseudocode):
if (some error situation arises) {
    // Set the flag to true to signal that an error has occurred.
    error = true;
}
// ...

// Still later in the program:
// Test the flag's value.
if (error == true) {
    // Pseudocode.
    take corrective action ...
}
```

We'll talk specifically about the syntax of the if statement, one of several different kinds of Java flow-control statements, a bit later in this chapter.

An important reminder: If you wish to attempt to compile any of the Java code snippets that you come across throughout the book, remember that (a) pseudocode (*italicized*) won't compile, and (b) all code must, at a minimum, be enclosed within a main method, which in turn must be enclosed within a class declaration, as was illustrated in Figure 2-8.

Variables

Before a variable can be used in a Java program, the type and name of the variable must be *declared* to the Java compiler, for example:

```
int count;
```

Assigning a value to a variable is accomplished by using the Java **assignment operator**, =. An assignment statement consists of a (previously declared) variable name to the left of the =, and an expression that evaluates to the appropriate type to the right of the = (we'll cover various types of Java expressions later in the chapter). For example:

```
int count = 1;

total = total + 4.0;  // Here, we assume that total was declared to be a double
                      // variable earlier in the program.

price = cost + (a + b)/length;  // We once again assume that all variables were
                                // properly declared earlier in the program.
```

An initial value can be supplied when a variable is first declared:

```
int count = 3;
```

or a variable can be declared in one statement, then assigned a value in a separate statement later on in the program:

```
double total;
// intervening code ... details omitted
total = total + 4.0;
```

A value can be assigned to a boolean variable using the true or false literals:

```
boolean finished;
// ...
finished = true;
```

A literal value may be assigned to a variable of type char by enclosing the value (a single Unicode character) in **single** quotes:

```
char c = 'A';
```

The use of **double** quotes ("...") is reserved for assigning literal values to String variables, a distinct type discussed later in this chapter. The following would not compile in Java:

```
char c = "A"; // We must use single quotes when assigning values to char variables.
```

Variable Naming Conventions

When discussing Java variable names, there are two aspects to consider:

- First, is a particular name deemed **valid** by the Java compiler?

- Second, does a particular **valid** name adhere to the naming **convention** that has been adopted by the OO programming community across all languages?

Valid variable names in Java must start with either an alphabetic character, an underscore, or a dollar sign (whose use is discouraged, since it is used by the compiler when generating code), and may contain any of these characters plus numeric digits. No other characters are allowed in variable names.

The following are all valid variable names in Java:

```
int simple;              // starts with alphabetic character
int _under;              // starts with underscore
int more$money_is_2much; // may contain dollar signs, and/or underscores, and/or
                         // digits, and/or alphabetic characters
```

while these are invalid:

```
int 1bad;                // inappropriate starting character
int number#sign;         // contains invalid character
int foo-bar;             // ditto
int plus+sign;           // ditto
int x@y;                 // ditto
int dot.notation;        // ditto
```

That being said, the ***convention*** that is observed throughout the OO programming community is to form variable names using primarily alphabetic characters, avoiding the use of underscores, and furthermore to adhere to a style known as **camel casing**. With camel casing, the first letter of a variable name is in ***lowercase***, the ***first*** letter of each subsequent concatenated word in the variable name is in ***uppercase***, and the rest of the characters are in ***lowercase***. All of the following variable names are both valid and conventional:

```
int grade;
double averageGrade;
String myPetRat;
boolean weAreFinished;
```

Recall that, as mentioned earlier, Java keywords can't be used as variable names. The following won't compile, because `public` is a Java keyword:

```
int public;
```

In fact, the compiler would generate the following ***two*** error messages:

```
not a statement
int public;
^


';' expected
int public;
    ^
```

Variable Initialization

In Java, variables aren't necessarily assigned an initial value when they're declared, but all variables ***must*** be assigned a value before the variable's value is ***used*** in an assignment statement. For example, in the following code snippet, two `int`(eger) variables are declared; an initial value is explicitly assigned to variable `foo`, but not to variable `bar`. A subsequent attempt to add the two variables' values together results in a compiler error:

```
int foo;
int bar;
// We're explicitly initializing foo, but not bar.
foo = 3;
foo = foo + bar;    // This line won't compile.
```

The following compiler error would arise on the last line of code:

```
variable bar might not have been initialized
foo = foo + bar;
              ^
```

To correct this error, we would need to assign an explicit value to bar, as well as foo, before using them in the addition expression:

```
int foo;
int bar;
foo = 3;
// We're now initializing BOTH variables explicitly.
bar = 7;
foo = foo + bar;  // This line will now compile properly.
```

In Chapter 13 you'll learn that the rules of automatic initialization are somewhat different when dealing with the "inner workings" of objects.

The String Type

We'll look at one more important Java type in this chapter: the String type. A String represents a sequence of zero or more Unicode characters.

The symbol String starts with a capital "S," whereas the names of primitive types are expressed in all lowercase: int, float, boolean, etc. This capitalization difference is deliberate and mandatory—string (lowercase) won't work as a type:

```
string s = "foo";  // This won't compile.
```

Here is the error message:

```
cannot find symbol
symbol: string
```

(I'll explain the significance of the capitalization of String as a type in due time.)

There are several ways to create and initialize a String variable. The easiest and most commonly used way is to declare a variable of type String and to assign the variable a value using a **string literal**. A string literal is any text enclosed in ***double*** quotes, even if it consists of only a ***single character***.

```
String name = "Steve";       // Note the use of double quotes, regardless of the
String shortString = "A";    // length, when we're assigning a literal value
                             // to a String variable.
```

Two commonly used approaches for initializing a String variable with a temporary placeholder value are as follows:

- Assigning an empty string, represented by two consecutive double quote marks:

    ```
    String s = "";
    ```

- Assigning the value null, which is a Java keyword that is used to signal that a String has not yet been assigned a "real" value (as you'll learn later in the book, we'll use the null keyword in this same fashion for object references in general):

    ```
    String s = null;
    ```

The plus sign (+) operator is normally used for arithmetic addition, but when used in conjunction with Strings, it represents **string concatenation**. Any number of String values can be concatenated with the + operator, as the following code snippet illustrates:

```
String x = "foo";
String y = "bar";
String z = x + y + "!";  // z assumes the value "foobar!" (x and y's values are
                         // unaffected)
```

You'll learn about some of the many other operations that can be performed with or on Strings, along with insights into their OO nature, in Chapter 13.

Case Sensitivity

Java is a **case-sensitive** language. That is, the use of uppercase versus lowercase in Java is deliberate and mandatory, for example:

- Variable names that are spelled the same way but that differ in their use of case represent *different* variables:

    ```
    // These are two DIFFERENT variables as far as the Java compiler
    // is concerned.
    int x; // lowercase
    int X; // uppercase
    ```

- All keywords are rendered in lowercase: public, class, int, boolean, and so forth. ***Don't get "creative" about capitalizing these***, as the compiler will violently object—often with unintelligible compilation error messages, as in the following example, where the reserved word for is improperly capitalized:

    ```
    // The reserved word 'for' should be lowercase.
    For (int i = 0; i < 3; i++) {
    ```

    which in turn produces the following seemingly bizarre compiler error:

```
'.class' expected
For (int i = 0; i < 3; i++) {
     ^
```

- The name of the main method is lowercase.

- As mentioned earlier, the String type starts with an uppercase "S."

Java Expressions

Java is an **expression-oriented language**. A **simple expression** in Java is either

- A constant: 7, false

- A char(acter) literal enclosed in single quotes: 'A', '3'

- A String literal enclosed in double quotes: "foo", "Java"

- The name of any properly declared variables: myString, x

- Any *two* of the preceding types of expression that are combined with one of the Java **binary operators** (discussed in detail later in this chapter): x + 2

- Any *one* of the preceding types of expression that is modified by one of the Java **unary operators** (discussed in detail later in this chapter): i++

- Any of the preceding types of expression enclosed in parentheses: (x + 2)

plus a few more types of expression having to do with objects that you'll learn about later in the book.

Expressions of arbitrary complexity can be assembled from the various different simple expression types by nesting parentheses, for example: ((((4/x) + y) * 7) + z).

Arithmetic Operators

The Java language provides a number of basic arithmetic operators, as shown in Table 2-1.

Table 2-1. *Java Arithmetic Operators*

Operator	Description
+	Addition
-	Subtraction
*	Multiplication
/	Division
%	Remainder (the remainder when the operand to the left of the % operator is divided by the operand to the right; e.g., 10 % 3 = 1, because 3 goes into 10 three times, leaving a remainder of 1)

The + and - operators can also be used as unary operators to indicate positive or negative numbers: -3.7, +42.

In addition to the simple assignment operator, =, there are a number of specialized **compound assignment operators**, which combine variable assignment with an arithmetic operation, as shown in Table 2-2.

Table 2-2. *Java Compound Assignment Operators*

Operator	Description
+=	a += b is equivalent to a = a + b.
-=	a -= b is equivalent to a = a - b.
*=	a *= b is equivalent to a = a * b.
/=	a /= b is equivalent to a = a / b.
%=	a %= b is equivalent to a = a % b.

The final two arithmetic operators that we'll look at are the **unary increment** (++) and **decrement** (--) operators, which are used to increase or decrease the value of an int variable by 1 or of a floating-point (float, double) value by 1.0. They're known as unary operators because they're applied to a single variable, whereas binary operators combine the values of two expressions as discussed previously.

The unary increment and decrement operators can also be applied to char variables to step forward or backward one character position in the Unicode sorting sequence. For example, in the following code snippet, the value of variable c will be incremented from 'e' to 'f':

```
char c = 'e';
c++; // c will be incremented from 'e' to 'f'.
```

The increment and decrement operators can be used in either a **prefix** or **postfix** manner. If the operator is placed *before* the variable it's operating on (*prefix* mode), the increment or decrement of that variable is performed *before* the variable's *updated* value is used in any assignments made via that statement. For example, consider the following code snippet, which uses the prefix increment (++) operator. Assume that a and b have previously been declared as int variables in our program:

```
a = 1;
b = ++a;
```

After the preceding lines of code have executed, the value of variable a will be 2, as will the value of variable b. This is because, in the second line of code, the increment of variable a (from 1 to 2) occurs *before* the value of a is assigned to variable b. Thus, the single line of code

```
b = ++a;
```

is logically equivalent to the following *two* lines of code:

```
a = a + 1;  // Increment a's value first ...
b = a;      // ... THEN use its value.
```

On the other hand, if the increment/decrement operator is placed *after* the variable it's operating on (*postfix* mode), the increment or decrement occurs *after* the variable's *original* value is used in any assignments made via that statement. Let's look at the same code snippet with the increment operator written in a *postfix* manner:

```
a = 1;
b = a++;
```

After the preceding lines of code have executed, the value of variable b will be 1, whereas the value of variable a will be 2. This is because, in the second line of code, the increment of variable a (from 1 to 2) occurs *after* the value of a is assigned to variable b. Thus, the single line of code

```
b = a++;
```

is logically equivalent to the following *two* lines of code:

```
b = a;       // Use a's value first ...
a = a + 1;   // ... THEN increment its value.
```

Here's a slightly more complex example; please read the accompanying comment to make sure that you can see how x will end up being assigned the value 10:

```
int y = 2;
int z = 4;
int x = y++ * ++z;   // x will be assigned the value 10, because z will be
                     // incremented from 4 to 5 BEFORE its value is used in the
                     // multiplication expression, whereas y will remain at 2 until
                     // AFTER its value is used in the multiplication expression.
```

As you'll see in a bit, the increment and decrement operators are commonly used in conjunction with loops.

Relational and Logical Operators

A **logical expression** compares two (simple or complex) expressions *exp1* and *exp2* in a specified way, resolving to a boolean value of true or false.

To create logical expressions, Java provides the **relational operators** shown in Table 2-3.

Table 2-3. *Java Relational Operators*

Operator	Description
exp1 == *exp2*	true if *exp1* equals *exp2* (note use of a *double* equal sign for testing equality).
exp1 > *exp2*	true if *exp1* is greater than *exp2*.
exp1 >= *exp2*	true if *exp1* is greater or equal to *exp2*.
exp1 < *exp2*	true if *exp1* is less than *exp2*.
exp1 <= *exp2*	true if *exp1* is less than or equal to *exp2*.
exp1 != *exp2*	true if *exp1* is not equal to *exp2* (! is read as "not").
!*exp*	true if *exp* is false, and false if *exp* is true.

In addition to the relational operators, Java provides **logical operators** that can be used to combine/modify logical expressions. The most commonly used logical operators are listed in Table 2-4.

Table 2-4. *Java Logical Operators*

Operator	Description
exp1 && *exp2*	Logical "and"; compound expression is true only if **both** *exp1* **and** *exp2* are true
exp1 || *exp2*	Logical "or"; compound expression is true if **either** *exp1* **or** *exp2* is true
!exp	Logical "not"; toggles the value of a logical expression from true to false and vice versa

Here's an example that uses the logical "and" operator to program the compound logical expression "if x is greater than 2.0 and y is not equal to 4.0":

```
if ((x > 2.0) && (y != 4.0)) { ... }
```

Logical expressions are most commonly seen used with flow-control structures, discussed later in this chapter.

Evaluating Expressions and Operator Precedence

As mentioned earlier in the chapter, expressions of arbitrary complexity can be built up by layering nested parentheses—for example, $(((8 * (y + z)) + y) * x)$. The compiler generally evaluates such expressions from the innermost to outermost parentheses, left to right. Assuming that x, y, and z are declared and initialized as shown here

```
int x = 1;
int y = 2;
int z = 3;
```

then the expression on the right-hand side of the following assignment statement

```
int answer = ((8 * (y + z)) + y) * x;
```

would be evaluated piece by piece as follows:

$$((8 * \underline{(y + z)}) + y) * x$$
$$(\underline{(8 * 5)} + y) * x$$
$$\underline{(40 + y)} * x$$
$$\underline{42 * x}$$
$$42$$

In the absence of parentheses, certain operators take precedence over others in terms of when they will be applied in evaluating an expression. For example, multiplication or division is performed before addition or subtraction. Operator precedence can be explicitly altered through the use of parentheses; operations performed inside parentheses take precedence over operations outside of parentheses. Consider the following code snippet:

```
int j = 2 + 3 * 4;      // j will be assigned the value 14
int k = (2 + 3) * 4;    // k will be assigned the value 20
```

In the first line of code, which uses no parentheses, the multiplication operation takes precedence over the addition operation, and so the overall expression evaluates to the value $2 + 12 = 14$; it's as if we've explicitly written 2 + (3 * 4) without having to do so.

In the second line of code, parentheses are explicitly placed around the operation 2 + 3 so that the addition operation will be performed first, and the resultant sum will then be multiplied by 4 for an overall expression value of 5 * 4 = 20.

Returning to an earlier example

```
if ((x > 2.0) && (y != 4.0)) { ... }
```

note that the > and != operators take precedence over the && operator, such that we could eliminate the nested parentheses as follows:

```
if (x > 2.0 && y != 4.0) { ... }
```

However, the extra parentheses certainly don't hurt, and in fact it can be argued that they make the expression's intention clearer.

The Type of an Expression

The **type of an expression** is the Java type of the value to which the expression ultimately evaluates. For example, given the code snippet

```
double x = 3.0;
double y = 2.0;
if ((x > 2.0) && (y != 4.0)) { ... }
```

the expression (x > 2.0) && (y != 4.0) evaluates to true, and hence the expression (x > 2.0) && (y != 4.0) is said to be a boolean type expression. And, in the following code snippet

```
int x = 1;
int y = 2;
int z = 3;
int answer = ((8 * (y + z)) + y) * x;
```

the expression ((8 * (y + z)) + y) * x evaluates to 42, and hence the expression ((8 * (y + z)) + y) * x is said to be an int(eger) type expression.

Automatic Type Conversions and Explicit Casting

Java supports **automatic type conversion**. This means that if we try to assign a value to a variable

```
// Pseudocode.
x = expression;
```

and the expression on the ***right-hand side*** of the assignment statement evaluates to a ***different*** type than the type with which the variable on the ***left-hand side*** of the assignment statement was declared, Java will automatically convert the value of the right-hand expression to match the type of x, but ***only if precision won't be lost in doing so***. This is best understood by looking at an example:

```
int x;
double y;
y = 2.7;
x = y;  // We're trying to assign a double value to an int variable.
```

In the preceding code snippet, we're attempting to assign the double value of y, 2.7, to x, which is declared to be an int. If this assignment were to take place, the fractional part of y would be truncated, and x would wind up with an integer value of 2. This represents a loss in precision, also known as a **narrowing conversion**.

A C or C++ compiler will permit this assignment, silently truncating the value. Rather than assuming that this is what we intend to do, however, the Java compiler will generate an error on the last line of code as follows:

```
possible loss of precision
found: double
required: int
```

In order to signal to the Java compiler that we're willing to accept the loss of precision, we must perform an **explicit cast**—that is, we must precede the expression whose value is to be converted with the target type, enclosed in parentheses:

```
// Pseudocode.
x = (type) expression;
```

In other words, we'd have to rewrite the last line of the preceding example as follows in order for the Java compiler to permit the assignment of a more precise floating-point value to a less precise integer variable:

```
int x;
double y;
y = 2.7;
x = (int) y;   // This will compile now, because we have explicitly
               // informed the compiler that we WANT a
               // narrowing conversion to occur.
```

Of course, if we were to *reverse* the direction of the assignment, assigning the int value of variable x to the double variable y, the Java compiler would have no problem with the assignment:

```
int x;
double y;
x = 2;
y = x;     // Assign a less precise int value to a double variable that is capable of
           // handling more precision - this is fine as is.
```

In this particular case, we're assigning a value of *less* precision—2—to a variable capable of *more* precision; y will wind up with the value of 2.0. This is known as a **widening conversion**. Such conversions are performed automatically in Java, and need not be explicitly cast.

Note that there's an idiosyncrasy with regard to assigning constant values to variables of type float in Java; the following statement won't compile:

```
  float y = 3.5;   // This won't compile!
```

because a numeric constant value with a fractional component like 3.5 is automatically treated by Java as a more precise double value, and so the compiler will view this as a narrowing conversion and will refuse to carry out the assignment. To *force* such an assignment, we must either explicitly cast the floating-point constant into a float:

```
float y = (float) 3.5;    // This will compile, thanks to the cast.
```

or, alternatively, we can force the constant on the right-hand side of the assignment statement to be viewed by the Java compiler as a float by using the suffix F, as shown here:

```
float y = 3.5F;    // OK, because we're indicating that the constant is to be
                   // treated as a float, not as a double.
```

Yet another option is to simply declare double rather than float variables whenever we wish to represent floating-point numeric values in a program.

We'll typically use doubles instead of floats whenever we need to declare floating-point variables in our SRS application in Part 3 of the book, just to avoid these hassles of type conversion.

Expressions of type char can be converted to any other numeric type, as illustrated in this next example:

```
char c = 'a';

// Assigning a char value to a numeric variable transfers its
// ASCII numeric equivalent value.
int x = c;
float y = c;
double z = c;

System.out.println(x);
System.out.println(y);
System.out.println(z);
```

Here's the output:

```
97
97.0
97.0
```

The only Java type that can't be cast, either implicitly or explicitly, into another type is the boolean type.

You'll see other applications of casting, involving objects, later in the book.

Loops and Other Flow-Control Structures

Very rarely will a program execute sequentially, line by line, from start to finish. Instead, the path of execution through a program's logic will often be **conditional**.

- It may be necessary to have the program execute a certain block of code if some condition is met, or a **different** block of code if the condition **isn't** met.

- A program may have to repeatedly execute a particular block of code a fixed number of times, or until a particular result is attained.

The Java language provides a number of different types of loops and other flow-control structures to take care of these situations.

if Statements

The if statement is a basic conditional branch statement that executes one or more lines of code if a condition, represented as a logical expression, is satisfied. Alternatively, one or more lines of code can be executed if the condition is *not* satisfied by placing that code after the keyword else. The use of an else clause with an if statement is optional.

The basic syntax of the if statement is as follows:

```
// Pseudocode.
if (logical-expression) {
    execute whatever code is contained within these braces
    if logical-expression evaluates to true
}
```

Or, adding an optional else clause:

```
// Pseudocode.
if (logical-expression) {
    execute whatever code is contained within these braces
    if logical-expression evaluates to true
}
else {
    execute whatever code is contained within these braces if
    logical-expression evaluates to false
}
```

If only one executable statement follows either the if or (optional) else keyword, the braces can be omitted, as shown here:

```
// Pseudocode.
if (logical-expression) single statement to execute if logical-expression is true;
else single statement to execute if logical-expression is false;
```

For example:

```
if (x > 3) y = x;
else z = x;
```

But it's generally considered good practice to always use braces as follows:

```
if (x > 3) {
    y = x;
}
else {
    z = x;
}
```

A single boolean variable, as a simple form of Boolean expression, can serve as the logical expression/condition of an if statement. For example, it's perfectly acceptable to write the following:

```
// Use boolean variable "finished" as a flag that will get set to true when
// some particular operation is completed.
boolean finished;

// Initialize it to false.
finished = false;

// The details of intervening code, in which the flag may or may not get set to
// true, have been omitted ...

// Test the flag.
if (finished) { // equivalent to:  if (finished == true) {
    System.out.println("We are finished!  :o)");
}
```

The ! ("not") operator can be used to negate a logical expression, so that the block of code associated with an if statement is executed when the expression evaluates to false instead:

```
if (!finished) { // equivalent to:  if (finished == false)
    System.out.println("We are NOT finished ... :op");
}
```

When testing for equality of two expressions, remember that we must use *two* consecutive equal signs, not just one:

```
if (x == 3) { // Note use of double equal signs (==) to test for equality.
  y = x;
}
```

A common mistake made by beginning Java programmers—particularly those who've previously programmed in C or C++—is to try to use a *single* equal sign to test for equality, as in this example:

```
// Note incorrect use of single equal sign below.
if (x = 3) {
    y = x;
}
```

In Java, an if test must be based on a valid *logical* expression; x = 3 isn't a logical expression, but rather an *assignment* expression. In fact, the preceding if statement won't even compile in Java, whereas it *would* compile in the C and C++ programming languages, because in those languages, if tests are based on evaluating expressions to either the *integer* value 0 (interpreted to mean false) or nonzero (interpreted to mean true).

It's possible to nest if-else constructs to test more than one condition. If nested, an inner if (plus optional else) statement is placed within the else part of an outer if. The basic syntax for a two-level nested if-else construct is shown here:

```
if (logical-expression-1) {
    execute this code
}
else {
    if (logical-expression-2) {
        execute this alternate code
    }
    else {
        execute this code if neither of the above expressions evaluate to true
    }
}
```

There's no limit to how many nested if-else constructs can be used, although if nested too deeply, the code may become difficult for a human reader to understand and hence maintain.

The nested if statement shown in the preceding example may alternatively be written without using nesting as follows:

```
if (logical-expression-1) {
    execute this code
}
else if (logical-expression-2) {
    execute this alternate code
}
else {
    execute this code if neither of the above expressions evaluate to true
}
```

Note that the two forms are logically equivalent.

switch Statements

A switch statement is similar to an if-else construct in that it allows the conditional execution of one or more lines of code. However, instead of evaluating a logical expression as an if-else construct does, a switch statement compares the value of an int or char expression against values defined by one or more case labels. If a match is found, the code following the matching case label is executed. An optional default label can be included to define code that is to be executed if the int or char expression matches *none* of the case labels.

The general syntax of a switch statement is as follows:

```
switch (int-or-char-expression) {
    case value1:
        one or more lines of code to execute if value of expression matches value1
        break;
    case value2:
        one or more lines of code to execute if value of expression matches value2
        break;
    // more case labels, as needed ...
```

```
     case valueN:
         one or more lines of code to execute if value of expression matches valueN
         break;
     default:
         default code to execute if none of the cases match
}
```

For example:

```
// x is assumed to have been previously declared as an int.
switch (x) {
     case 1:  // executed if x equals 1
       System.out.println("One ...");
       break;
     case 2:  // executed if x equals 2
       System.out.println("Two ...");
       break;
     default:  // executed if x has a value other than 1 or 2
       System.out.println("Neither one nor two ...");
}
```

Note the following:

- The expression in parentheses following the switch keyword must be an expression that evaluates to a char or int value.

- The values following the case labels must be constant values (a "hardwired" integer constant or character literal).

- Colons (:), not semicolons (;), terminate the case and default labels.

- The statements following a given case label don't have to be enclosed in braces. They constitute a **statement list** rather than a code block.

Unlike an if statement, a switch statement isn't automatically terminated when a match is found and the code following the matching case label is executed. To exit a switch statement, a break statement must be used. If a break statement isn't included following a given case label, execution will "fall through" to the next case or default label. This behavior can be used to our advantage: when the same logic is to be executed for more than one case label, two or more case labels can be stacked up back to back, as shown here:

```
// x is assumed to have been previously declared as an int
switch (x) {
     case 1:
         code to be executed if x equals 1
     case 2:
         code to be executed if x equals 1 OR 2
     case 3:
         code to be executed if x equals 1, 2, OR 3
         break;
     case 4:
         code to be executed if x equals 4
}
```

for Statements

A for statement is a programming construct that is used to execute one or more statements a certain number of times. The general syntax of the for statement is as follows:

```
for (initializer; condition; iterator) {
    code to execute while condition evaluates to true
}
```

A for statement defines three elements that are separated by semicolons and placed in parentheses after the for keyword: the **initializer**, the **condition**, and the **iterator**. The *initializer* is used to provide an initial value for a **loop control variable**. The variable can be declared as part of the initializer, or it can be declared earlier in the code, ahead of the for statement, for example:

```
// The loop control variable 'i' is declared within the for statement:
for (int i = 0; condition; iterator) {
    code to execute while condition evaluates to true
}
// Note that i is no longer recognized by the compiler when the 'for' loop exits,
// because it was effectively declared within the 'for' loop - we'll talk about the
// scope of a variable later in this chapter.
```

versus

```
// The loop control variable 'i' is declared prior to the start of the 'for' loop:
int i;

for (i = 0; condition; iterator) {
    code to execute while condition evaluates to true
}
```

The *condition* is a logical expression that typically involves the loop control variable:

```
for (int i = 0; i < 5; iterator) {
    code to execute as long as the value of i remains less than 5
}
```

The *iterator* typically increments or decrements the loop control variable:

```
for (int i = 0; i < 5; i++) {
    code to execute as long as the value of i remains less than 5
}
```

Again, note the use of a semicolon (;) after the initializer and condition, but **not** after the iterator.

Here's a breakdown of how a for loop operates:

1. When program execution reaches a for statement, the initializer is executed first (and only once).

2. The condition is then evaluated. If the condition evaluates to true, the block of code following the parentheses is executed.

3. After the block of code finishes, the iterator is executed.

4. The condition is then reevaluated. If the condition is still `true`, the block of code is executed once again, followed by execution of the iterator statement.

This process repeats until the condition becomes `false`, at which point the `for` loop terminates.

Here's a simple example that uses nested `for` statements to generate a simple multiplication table. The loop control variables, j and k, are declared inside their respective `for` statements. As long as the conditions in the respective `for` statements are met, the block of code following the `for` statement is executed. The ++ operator is used to increment the values of j and k each time the respective block of code is executed.

```
public class ForDemo {
    public static void main(String[] args) {
        // Compute a simple multiplication table.
        for (int j = 1; j <= 4; j++) {
            for (int k = 1; k <= 4; k++) {
                System.out.println(j + " * " + k + " = " + (j * k));
            }
        }
    }
}
```

Here's the output:

```
1 * 1 = 1
1 * 2 = 2
1 * 3 = 3
1 * 4 = 4
2 * 1 = 2
2 * 2 = 4
2 * 3 = 6
2 * 4 = 8
3 * 1 = 3
3 * 2 = 6
3 * 3 = 9
3 * 4 = 12
4 * 1 = 4
4 * 2 = 8
4 * 3 = 12
4 * 4 = 16
```

As with other flow-control structures, if only one statement is specified after the `for` condition, the braces can be omitted:

```
for (int i = 0; i < 3; i++) sum = sum + i;
```

but it's considered good programming practice to use braces regardless:

```
for (int i = 0; i < 3; i++) {
    sum = sum + i;
}
```

while Statements

A while statement is similar in function to a for statement, in that both are used to repeatedly execute an associated block of code. However, if it's impractical to predict the number of times that the code block is to be executed when the loop first begins, a while statement is the preferred choice, because a while statement continues to execute as long as a specified condition is met.

The general syntax for the while statement is as follows:

```
while (condition) {
    code to repeatedly execute while condition continues to evaluate to true
}
```

The condition can be either a simple or a complex logical expression that evaluates to a true or false value, for example:

```
int x = 1;
int y = 1;

while ((x < 20) || (y < 10)) {
    hopefully we'll do something within this loop body that increments the value of
    either x or y, to avoid an infinite loop!
}
```

When program execution reaches a while statement, the condition is evaluated first. If the condition is true, the block of code following the condition is executed. When the block of code is finished, the condition is evaluated again, and if it's still true, the process repeats itself until the condition evaluates to false, at which point the while loop terminates.

Here's a simple example illustrating the use of a while loop to print consecutive integer values from 0 to 3. A boolean variable named finished is initially set to false. The finished variable is used as a flag: as long as finished is false, the block of code following the while loop will continue to execute. When the value of i reaches 4, the finished flag will get set to true, at which point the while loop will terminate.

```
public class WhileDemo {
    public static void main(String[] args) {
        boolean finished = false;
        int i = 0;

        while (!finished) {
            System.out.println(i);
            i++;
            if (i == 4) finished = true;  // toggle the flag to terminate the loop
        }
    }
}
```

Here's the output:

```
0
1
2
3
```

As with the other flow-control structures, if only one statement is specified after the condition, the braces can be omitted:

```java
while (x < 20) x = x * 2;
```

but it's considered good programming practice to use braces regardless:

```java
while (x < 20) {
    x = x * 2;
}
```

Jump Statements

The Java language defines two **jump statements** that are used to redirect program execution to another statement elsewhere in the code. The two types of jump statement are the break and continue statements.

You've already seen break statements in action earlier in this chapter, when they were used in conjunction with switch statements. A break statement can also be used to abruptly terminate a for or while loop. When a break statement is encountered during loop execution, the loop immediately terminates, and program execution is transferred to the line of code immediately following the loop, as in the following example:

```java
// We start out with the intention of incrementing x from 1 to 4 ...
for (int x = 1; x <= 4; x++) {
    // ... but when x reaches the value 3, we prematurely terminate this
    // loop with a break statement.
    if (x == 3) break;
    System.out.println(x);
}

System.out.println("Loop finished");
```

The output produced by this code would be as follows:

```
1
2
Loop finished
```

A continue statement, on the other hand, is used to exit from the *current iteration* of a loop *without* terminating *overall* loop execution. That is, a continue statement transfers program execution back up to the top of the loop without finishing the particular iteration that is already in progress; the loop counter is incremented, in the case of a for loop, and execution continues.

Let's look at the same example as before, but we'll replace the break statement with a continue statement:

```java
// We start out with the intention of incrementing x from 1 to 4 ...
for (int x = 1; x <= 4; x++) {
    // ... but when x reaches the value 3, we prematurely terminate
    // this iteration of the loop (only) with a continue statement.
```

```
    if (x == 3) continue;
    System.out.println(x);
}

System.out.println("Loop finished");
```

The output produced by this code would be as follows:

```
1
2
4
Loop finished
```

Block-Structured Languages and the Scope of a Variable

Java (like C and C++) is a **block-structured language**. As mentioned earlier in the chapter, a "block" of code is a series of zero or more lines of code enclosed within braces { ... }.

Blocks may be nested inside one another to any arbitrary depth, as illustrated by the following code example:

```
public class SimpleProgram {
    // We're inside of the "class" block (one level deep).
    public static void main(String[] args) {
        // We're inside of the "main method" block (two levels deep).
        int x = 3;
        int y = 4;
        int z = 5;

        if (x > 2) {
            // We're now one level deeper (level 3), in an "if" block.
            if (y > 3) {
                // We're one level deeper still (level 4), in a
                // nested "if" block.
                // (We could go on and on!)
            } // We've just ended the level 4 block.
            // (We could have additional code here, at level 3.)
        } // Level 3 is done!
        // (We could have additional code here, at level 2.)
    } // That's it for level 2!
    // (We could have additional code here, at level 1.)
} // Adios, amigos! Level 1 (the "class" block) has just ended.
```

Variables can be declared in any block within a program. The **scope** of a variable is that portion of code in which the variable can be referenced by name—specifically, from the point where the variable name is first declared down to the closing (right) brace for the block of code in which it was declared. A variable is said to be **in scope** as long as the compiler recognizes its name. Once program execution exits a block of code, any variables that were declared inside that block go **out of scope** and will be inaccessible to the program; the compiler effectively forgets that the variable was ever declared.

As an example of the consequences of variable scope, let's look at a simple program called ScopeExample. This program makes use of three nested code blocks: one for the class body, one for the main method body, and one as part of an if statement inside the body of the main method. We in turn declare two variables: x, in the main code block (at level 2), and y, in the if block (level 3).

```
public class ScopeExample { // Start of block level 1.
  public static void main(String[] args) { // Start of block level 2.
    double x = 2.0;  // Declare "x" at block level 2.

    if (x < 5.0) { // Start of block level 3.
      double y = 1.0;  // Declare "y" inside block level 3.
      System.out.println("The value of x = " + x);   // x, declared at level 2, is
                                                      // still in scope at level 3.
      System.out.println("The value of y = " + y);
    } // Variable "y" goes out of scope when the "if" block (level 3) ends.

    // "y" has gone out of scope, and is no longer recognized by the compiler.
    // If we try to reference "y" in a subsequent statement, the compiler will
    // generate an error. "x", on the other hand, remains in scope until the main
    // method block (level 2) ends.

    System.out.println("The value of x = " + x);   // This will compile.
    System.out.println("The value of y = "  + y);   // This WON'T compile.
  } // Variable "x" goes out of scope when the main method block (level 2) ends.
}
```

In the preceding example, variable y goes out of scope as soon as the if block ends. If we try to access y later in the program, as we do in the bolded line of the preceding code, the compiler will generate the following error message:

```
cannot resolve symbol
symbol : variable y
System.out.println("The value of y = "  + y);
                                         ^
```

Note that a given variable is accessible to any nested *inner* code blocks that follow its declaration. For example, in the preceding ScopeExample program, variable x, declared at the main method block level (level 2), is accessible inside the if statement code block (level 3).

Printing to the Screen

Most applications communicate information to users by displaying messages via an application's GUI. However, it's also useful at times to be able to display simple text messages to the command-line window from which we're running a program as a quick and dirty way of verifying that a program is working properly. Until we discuss how to craft a Java GUI in Chapters 16 and 17, this will be our program's primary way of communicating with the outside world.

To print text messages to the screen, we use the following syntax:

```
System.out.println(expression to be printed);
```

The `System.out.println` method can accept very complex expressions and does its best to ultimately turn these into a single `String` value, which then gets displayed on the screen. Here are a few examples:

```
System.out.println("Hi!");          // Printing a String literal/constant.


String s = "Hi!";
System.out.println(s);              // Printing the value of a String variable.


String t = "foo";
String u = "bar";
System.out.println(t + u + "!");    // Using the String concatenation operator (+)
                                    // to print "foobar!".

int x = 3;
int y = 4;
System.out.println(x);              // Prints the String representation of the
                                    // integer value 3 to the screen.

System.out.println(x + y);          // Computes the sum of x and y, then prints the
                                    // String representation of the integer value 7
                                    // to the screen.
```

Note that in the last line of code the plus sign (+) is interpreted as the **addition** operator, not as the `String` **concatenation** operator, because it separates two variables that are both declared to be of type int. So, the sum of 3 + 4 is computed to be 7, which is then printed. In the next example, however, we get different (and arguably undesired) behavior:

```
System.out.println("The sum of x plus y is: " + x + y);
```

The preceding line of code causes the following to be printed:

```
The sum of x plus y is: 34
```

Why is this? Recall that we evaluate expressions from left to right, and so since the first of the two plus signs separates a `String` literal and an `int`

```
System.out.println("The sum of x plus y is: " + x + y);
```

the first plus sign is interpreted as a `String` concatenation operator, producing the intermediate `String` value "The sum of x plus y is: 3". The second plus sign separates this intermediate `String` value from an `int`, and so the second plus sign is **also** interpreted as a `String` concatenation operator, producing the final `String` value "The sum of x plus y is: 34", which is printed to the command window.

To print the **correct** sum of x and y, we must force the second plus sign to be interpreted as an integer addition operator by enclosing the addition expression in nested parentheses:

```
System.out.println("The sum of x plus y is: " + (x + y));
```

The nested parentheses cause the innermost expression to be evaluated first, thus computing the sum of x + y properly. Hence, this `println` statement displays the correct message on the screen:

```
The sum of x plus y is: 7
```

When writing code that involves complex expressions, it's a good idea to use parentheses liberally to make your intentions clear to the compiler. Extra parentheses, when used correctly, never hurt!

print vs. println

When we call the System.out.println method, whatever expression is enclosed inside the parentheses will be printed, followed by a (platform-dependent) **line terminator**. The following code snippet

```java
System.out.println("First line.");
System.out.println("Second line.");
System.out.println("Third line.");
```

produces three separate lines of output:

```
First line.
Second line.
Third line.
```

By contrast, the statement

```java
System.out.print(expression to be printed);
```

causes whatever expression is enclosed in parentheses to be printed *without* a trailing line terminator. Using print in combination with println allows us to generate a *single* line of output across a *series* of Java statements, as shown by the following example:

```java
System.out.print("J");          // Using print here.
System.out.print("AV");         // Using print here.
System.out.println("A!!!");     // Note use of println as the last statement.
```

This code snippet produces a single line of output:

```
JAVA!!!
```

When a single print statement gets too long to fit on a single line, as in this example:

```java
    // Pseudocode.
    statement;
    another statement;
    System.out.println("Here's an example of a single print statement
that is very long ... SO long that it wraps around and makes the program
listing difficult to read.");
    yet another statement;
```

we can make a program listing more readable by breaking up the contents of such a statement into multiple concatenated String expressions, and then breaking the statement along plus-sign boundaries:

```
// Pseudocode.
statement;
another statement;
System.out.println("Here's an example of how " +
                   "to break up a long print statement " +
                   "with plus signs.");
yet another statement;
```

Even though the preceding System.out.println call is broken across three lines of code, it will be printed as a single line of output:

```
Here's an example of how to break up a long print statement with plus signs.
```

Escape Sequences

Java defines a number of **escape sequences** so that we can represent special characters, such as newline and tab characters, within String or char literals. The most commonly used escape sequences are listed in Table 2-5.

Table 2-5. *Java Escape Sequences*

Escape Sequence	Description
\n	Newline
\b	Backspace
\t	Tab
\\	Backslash
\'	Single quote; used within single quotes (e.g., char singleQuote = '\'';)
\"	Double quote; used within double quotes (e.g., String doubleQuote = "\"";)

One or more escape sequences can be included in the expression that is passed to the print and println methods. For example, consider the following code snippet:

```
System.out.println("One ...");
System.out.println("\t... two ...");
System.out.println("\t\t... three ... \"WHEEE!!!\"");
```

When the preceding code is executed, the following output is displayed:

```
One ...
    ... two ...
        ... three ... "WHEEE!!!"
```

The second and third lines of output have been indented one and two tab positions, respectively, by virtue of the use of \t, and the expression "WHEEE!!!" is printed enclosed in double quotes because of our use of \".

Elements of Java Style

One of the trademarks of good programmers is that they produce *human-readable* code, so that their colleagues will be able to work with and modify their programs. The following sections present some guidelines and conventions that will help you to produce clear, readable Java code.

Proper Use of Indentation

One of the best ways to make a Java program readable is through proper use of indentation to clearly delineate its block structure. Statements within a block of code should be indented relative to the starting/ending line of the enclosing block (i.e., indented relative to the lines carrying the braces). Sun Microsystems' recommendation is to use four spaces (note that some of the examples in this book vary from that standard).

To see how indentation can make a program readable, consider the following two programs. In the first simple program, proper indentation is used:

```java
public class IndentationExample {
    public static void main(String[] args) {
        for (int i = 1; i <= 4; i++) {
            System.out.print(i);

            if ((i == 2) || (i == 4))  {
                if (i == 2) {
                    System.out.print("Two ");
                }
                else {
                    System.out.print("Four ");
                }
                System.out.println("is an even number");
            }
            else if ((i == 1) || (i == 3))  {
                if (i == 1) {
                    System.out.print("One ");
                }
                else {
                    System.out.print("Three ");
                }
                System.out.println("is an odd number");
            }
        }
    }
}
```

and it's relatively easy to see how the following output would be produced:

```
1 is an odd number
2 is an even number
3 is an odd number
4 is an even number
```

Now let's remove all indentation from the program:

```java
public class IndentationExample {
public static void main(String[] args) {
for (int i = 1; i <= 4; i++) {
System.out.print(i);

if ((i == 2) || (i == 4))  {
if (i == 2) {
System.out.print("Two ");
}
else {
System.out.print("Four ");
}
System.out.println("is an even number");
}
else if ((i == 1) || (i == 3))  {
if (i == 1) {
System.out.print("One ");
}
else {
System.out.print("Three ");
}
System.out.println("is an odd number");
}
}
}
}
```

Both versions of this program are understood by the Java compiler, and both produce the same output when executed, but the first version is much more readable to a human being.

Failure to properly indent not only makes programs unreadable, but also makes them harder to debug, particularly if a compilation error arises due to unbalanced/missing braces. In such a situation, the compilation error message often gets reported on a line much later in the program than where the problem actually exists. For example, the following program is missing an opening/left brace on line 9, but the compiler doesn't report an error until line 23:

```java
public class IndentationExample2 {
    public static void main(String[] args) {
        int x = 2;
        int y = 3;
        int z = 1;
```

```
if (x >= 0) {
    if (y > x) {
        if (y > 2) // we're missing a left brace here on line 9, but ...
            System.out.println("A");
            z = x + y;
        }
        else {
            System.out.println("B");
            z = x - y;
        }
    }
    else {
        System.out.println("C");
        z = y - x;
    }
}
else System.out.println("D");  // ... compiler first complains here!
                               // (line 23)
    }
}
```

What's even worse, the error message that the compiler generates in such a situation can be rather cryptic. In this particular example, the compiler (incorrectly) points to line 23 as the problem, with a misleading error message:

```
IndentationExample2.java:23: illegal start of type
else System.out.println("D");
^
```

This error message doesn't help us to locate the *real* problem on line 9. However, at least we've properly indented our code, and so it will likely be far easier to hunt down the missing brace than it would be if our indentation were sloppy or nonexistent.

If ever you get a compilation error that makes absolutely no sense whatsoever, consider looking earlier in the program for missing punctuation—that is, a missing brace, parenthesis, or semicolon!

Sometimes, we have so many levels of nested indentation, or individual statements are so long, that lines wrap when viewed in an editor or printed as hard copy:

```
while (a < b) {
    while (c > d) {
        for (int j = 0; j < 29; j++) {
            x = y + z + a - b + (c * (d / e) + f) -
g + h + j - l - m - n + o + p * q / r + s;
        }
    }
}
```

To avoid this, it's best to break the line in question along white space or punctuation boundaries, indenting continuation lines relative to the start of the line:

```
while (a < b) {
    while (c > d) {
        for (int j = 0; j < 29; j++) {
            // This is cosmetically preferred.  Note indentation
            // of continuation lines.
            x = y + z + a - b + (c * (d / e) + f) -
                g + h + j - l - m - n + o + p *
                q / r + s;
        }
    }
}
```

Use Comments Wisely

Another important feature that makes code more readable is the liberal use of meaningful comments. Always keep in mind when writing code that *you* may know what you're trying to do, but someone else trying to read your code may not. (Actually, we sometimes even need to remind *ourselves* of why we did what we did if we haven't looked at code that we've written in a while!)

Here are some basic rules of thumb:

- If there can be any doubt as to what a passage of code does, precede it with a comment.

- Indent each comment to the same level as the block of code or statement to which it applies.

- Make sure that all comments add value—don't state the obvious, as in the following fairly useless comment:

```
// Declare x as an integer, and assign it an initial value of 3.
int x = 3;
```

Placement of Braces

For block-structured languages that use braces to delimit the start/end of blocks (e.g., C, C++, C#, Java), there are two general schools of thought as to where the *left/opening* brace of a code block should be placed.

The first style is to place an opening brace at the *end* of the line of code that starts a given block. Each closing brace goes on its own line, aligned with the *first* character of the line containing the opening brace:

```
public class Test {
    public static void main(String[] args) {
        for (int i = 0; i < 3; i++) {
            System.out.println(i);
        }
    }
}
```

An alternative brace placement style is to place every opening brace on a line by itself, aligned with the immediately preceding line. Each closing brace goes on its own line as before, aligned with the corresponding opening brace:

```
public class Test
{
    public static void main(String[] args)
    {
        for (int i = 0; i < 3; i++)
        {
            System.out.println(i);
        }
    }
}
```

Either approach to left/opening brace placement is fine; the first of the two approaches produces code listings that are a bit more compact (i.e., contain less white space) and is the more popular of the two styles. It's a good practice to maintain consistency in your code, however, so pick whichever brace placement style you prefer and stick with it.

Descriptive Variable Names

As with indentation and comments, the goal when choosing variable names is to make a program as readable, and hence self-documenting, as possible. Avoid using single letters as variable names, except for loop control variables (or as parameters to methods, discussed later in the book).

Abbreviations should be used sparingly, and only when the abbreviation is commonly used and widely understood by developers. Consider the following variable declaration:

```
int grd;
```

It's not completely clear what the variable name grd is supposed to represent. Is the variable supposed to represent a grid, a grade, or a gourd? A better practice would be to spell out the entire word:

```
int grade;
```

At the other end of the spectrum, names that are too long—such as perhaps

```
double averageThirdQuarterReturnOnInvestment;
```

can make a code listing overwhelming to anyone trying to read it. It can sometimes be challenging to shorten a variable name while still keeping it descriptive, but do try to keep the length of your variable names within reason, for example:

```
double avg3rdQtrROI;
```

Summary

In this chapter, you've learned some of the advantages of Java as an OO programming language—namely, that

- Java is an elegant OO programming language that improves upon many languages that preceded it.

- Java was designed from the ground up to be fully object-oriented.

- Java is architecture neutral.

- All of the facilities necessary for building industrial-strength applications are integrated into the core Java language.

- Java is an open-source language.

- Java can be downloaded for free from the Sun Microsystems http://java.sun.com web site.

In addition to exploring some of the advantages of Java, you've also learned some basic elements of Java syntax. In particular, we covered

- The anatomy of a simple Java program

- The mechanics of how to compile and execute a Java program from the command line

- The eight primitive Java types and the String type

- How variables of these types are declared and initialized

- How an expression of one type can be cast into a different type, and when it's necessary to do so

- Arithmetic, assignment, logical, and relational expressions and operators

- Loops and other flow-control structures available with Java

- How to define blocks of code, and the concept of variable scope

- How to print text messages with the System.out.println and System.out.print methods

- Some basic elements of good Java programming style

There's a lot more to learn about Java—things you'll need to know in building the SRS application in Part 3 of the book—but I need to explain a number of basic object concepts first. So, on to Chapter 3!

Exercises

1. Research Java on Sun's web site, `http://java.sun.com`, and cite any advantages or features of Java not mentioned in this chapter.

2. Do some web surfing to see how various other vendors have embraced the Java language—for example, IBM, Oracle, Microsoft, and Apple.

3. Compare what you've learned about Java so far to another programming language that you're already familiar with. What is similar about the two languages? What is different?

4. [*Coding*] Create a code snippet that will print the even numbers from 2 to 10 to the command window using (a) a `for` loop and a `continue` statement and (b) a `while` loop and a `boolean` variable as a flag.

5. Given the following initial variable declarations and value assignments, evaluate the expression in the last line of code:

```
int a = 1;
int b = 1;
int c = 1;
((((c++ + --a) * b) != 2) && true)
```

CHAPTER 3

■ ■ ■

Objects and Classes

Objects are the fundamental building blocks of an object-oriented application. Just as you learned in Chapter 1 that abstraction involves producing a model of the real world, you'll see in this chapter that objects are "mini abstractions" of the various real-world elements that comprise such a model.

In this chapter, you'll learn

- The advantages of an object-oriented approach to software development as compared with the "traditional" non-OO approach

- How to use classes to specify an object's data and behavior

- How to create objects at run time

- How to declare **reference variables** to refer to objects symbolically within a program

- How objects keep track of one another in memory

Software at Its Simplest

At its simplest, every software application consists of two primary components: ***data*** and ***functions*** that operate on (i.e., input, output, calculate, store, retrieve, print, etc.) that data. (See Figure 3-1.)

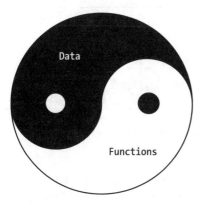

Figure 3-1. *At its simplest, software consists of data and functions that operate on that data.*

The pre-OO way of designing software was known as (**top-down**) **functional decomposition**. Let's compare the functional decomposition approach of designing software to the OO approach.

Functional Decomposition

With functional decomposition, we started with a statement of the overall function that a system was expected to perform—for example, "Student Registration." We then broke that function down into subfunctions:

- "Add a New Course to the Course Catalog"

- "Allow a Student to Enroll in a Course"

- "Print a Student's Class Schedule"

and so forth.

We next decomposed those functions into smaller subfunctions. For example, we might decompose "Allow Student to Enroll in a Course" into

- "Display List of Available Courses"

- "Allow Student to Select a Course"

- "Verify That Student Has Met All Prerequisites"

etc. We kept decomposing functions into smaller and smaller logical pieces until we could reasonably subdivide no further, as illustrated in Figure 3-2.

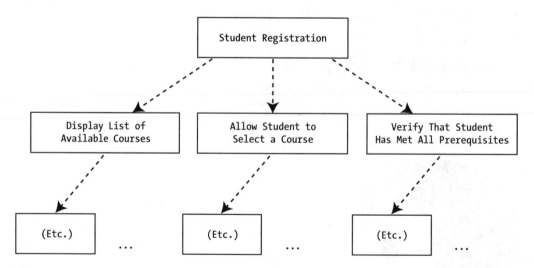

Figure 3-2. *We functionally decomposed an application from the top down ...*

We then assigned the lowest level functions to different programmers to code and **unit test** (i.e., test in isolation). Finally, we assembled these functions in modular fashion from the bottom up, testing the results of each successive stage in the integration process, until we had a complete application built, as illustrated in Figure 3-3.

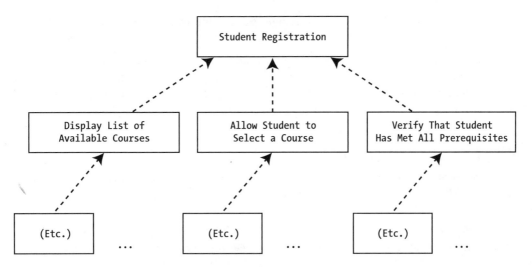

Figure 3-3. . . . *and assembled the application from the bottom up.*

With the functional decomposition approach to software development, our primary focus was on the ***functions*** that an application was to perform; ***data*** was an afterthought. That is,

- Data was passed around from one function to the next, like a car being manufactured via an assembly-line process in an automotive plant.

- Data structure thus had to be understood in ***many*** places (i.e., by many functions) throughout an application.

- If an application's data structure had to change after the application was deployed, ***major "ripple effects" often arose throughout the application.*** One of the most dramatic examples of a ripple effect due to a change in data structure was the **Y2K crisis**, wherein a seemingly simple change in date formats—from a two- to four-digit year—caused a worldwide panic! ***Billions*** of dollars were spent on trying to find and repair what were expected to be disastrous ripple effects before the clock struck midnight on January 1, 2000.

- Despite our best efforts to test an application thoroughly before deploying it, bugs always manage to creep through undetected. If data integrity errors arose as a result of faulty logic after an application had been fully integrated, it was often very difficult to pinpoint precisely where—that is, ***in which specific function(s)***—the error might have occurred, because the data had been passed from function to function so many times.

The Object-Oriented Approach

As you'll see over the next several chapters, the OO approach to software development remedies the vast majority of these shortcomings.

- With OO software development, we focus on designing the application's ***data structure*** first, and its functions second.

- Data is ***encapsulated*** inside of objects; thus, data structure has to be understood only by the object to which the data belongs.

- If an object's data structure has to change after the application has been deployed, there are virtually **no ripple effects**; only the internal logic of the affected object must change.

- **Each object is responsible for ensuring the integrity of its own data**. Thus, if data integrity errors arise within a given object's data, we can pretty much assume that it was the object **itself** that allowed this to happen, and we can therefore focus on that object's internal functional logic to isolate the "bug."

What Is an Object?

Before we talk about software objects, let's talk about real-world objects in general. According to Merriam-Webster's Collegiate Dictionary, an object is

(1) something material that may be perceived by the senses; (2) something mental or physical toward which thought, feeling, or action is directed.

The first part of this definition refers to objects as we typically think of them: as physical "things" that we can see and touch, and which occupy space. Because we intend to use the Student Registration System (SRS) case study as the basis for learning about objects throughout this book, let's think of some examples of **physical objects** that make sense in the general context of an academic setting, namely

- The **students** who attend classes

- The **professors** who teach the students

- The **classrooms** in which class meetings take place

- The **audiovisual equipment** in these classrooms

- The **buildings** in which the classrooms are located

- The **textbooks** students use

and so forth. Of course, while all of these types of objects are commonly found on a typical college campus, not all of them are relevant to registering students for courses, nor are they all necessarily called out by the SRS case study, but we won't worry about that for the time being. In Part 2 of this book, you'll learn a technique for using a requirements specification as the basis for identifying which types of objects are relevant to a particular abstraction.

Now, let's focus on the second half of the definition, particularly on the phrase *"something mental . . . toward which thought, feeling, or action is directed."* There are a great many **conceptual objects** that play important roles in an academic setting; some of these are

- The **courses** that students attend

- The **departments** that faculty work for

- The **degrees** that students receive

and, of course, many others. Even though we can't see, touch, taste, smell, or hear them, conceptual objects are every bit as important as physical objects in an overall abstraction.

From a software perspective, a (software) **object** is a software construct/module that bundles together **state** (**data**) and **behavior** (**functions**) which, taken together, represent an abstraction of a real-world (physical or conceptual) object. This is illustrated conceptually in Figure 3-4.

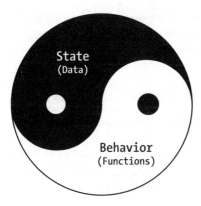

Figure 3-4. *A software object bundles state (data) and behavior (functions).*

Let's explore the two sides of objects—their state and behavior—separately, in more depth.

State/Data/Attributes

If we wish to record information about a student, what data might we require? Some examples might be

- The student's name

- His or her student ID number

- The student's birth date

- His or her address

- The student's designated major field of study

- His or her cumulative grade point average (i.e., the student's *GPA*)

- Who the student's faculty advisor is

- A list of the courses that the student is currently enrolled in this semester (i.e., the student's current *course load*)

- A history of all of the courses that the student has taken to date, the semester/year in which each was taken, and the grade that was earned for each (i.e., the student's *transcript*)

and so on. Now, how about for an academic course? Perhaps we'd wish to record

- The course number (e.g., "ART 101")

- The course name (e.g., "Introductory Basketweaving")

- A list of all of the courses that must have been successfully completed by a student prior to registering for this course (i.e., the course's *prerequisites*)

- The number of credit hours that the course is worth

- A list of the professors who have been approved to teach this course

and so on. In object nomenclature, the data elements used to describe an object are referred to as the object's **attributes**.

An object's attribute values, when taken collectively, are said to define the **state**, or condition, of the object. For example, if we wanted to determine whether or not a student is "eligible to graduate" (a *state*), we might look at a combination of the following:

- The student's transcript (an ***attribute value***)

- The list of courses the student is currently enrolled in (a second ***attribute value***)

to determine if the student indeed is expected to have satisfied the course requirements for his or her chosen major field of study (a third attribute value) by the end of the current academic year.

A given attribute may be simple—for example, "GPA," which can be represented as a simple floating-point number (perhaps a double in Java)—or complex—for example, "transcript," which represents a rather extensive collection of information with no simple representation.

Programmers new to the object paradigm often ask, "Why not represent a transcript as a String? A *long* String, no doubt, but a String nonetheless?" You'll learn over successive chapters that there is a far more elegant way to represent the notion of a student's transcript in object-oriented terms.

Behavior/Operations/Methods

Now, let's revisit the same two types of object—a student and a course—and talk about these objects' respective behaviors.

A student's behaviors (relevant to academic matters, at any rate!) might include

- Enrolling in a course

- Dropping a course

- Designating a major field of study

- Selecting a faculty advisor

- Telling us his or her GPA

- Telling us whether or not he or she has taken a particular course, and if so, when the course was taken, which professor taught it, and what grade the student received

It's a bit harder to think of an inanimate, conceptual object like a course as having behaviors, but if we were to imagine a course to be a living thing, we can envision that a course's behaviors might include

- Permitting a student to register

- Determining whether or not a given student is already registered

- Telling us how many students have registered so far, or conversely, how many seats remain before the course is full

- Telling us what its prerequisite courses are

- Telling us how many credit hours the course is worth

- Telling us which professor is assigned to teach the course this semester

and so on.

When we talk about software objects specifically, we define an object's behaviors, also known as its **operations**, as both the things that an object does to *access* its attribute values (data) and the things that an object does to *modify/maintain* its attribute values (data).

If we take a moment to reflect back on the behaviors we expect of a student as listed previously, we see that each operation involves one or more of the student's attributes; for example:

- Telling you his or her GPA involves *accessing* the value of the student's "GPA" attribute

- Choosing a major field of study involves *modifying* the value of the student's "major field of study" attribute

- Enrolling in a course involves *modifying* the value of the student's "course load" attribute

Since you recently learned that the collective set of attribute values for an object defines its state, you now can see that operations are capable of *changing an object's state*. Let's say that we define the state of a student who hasn't yet selected a major field of study as an "undeclared" student. Asking such a student object to perform its "choosing a major field of study" method will cause that object to update the value of its "major field of study" attribute to reflect the newly selected major field. This, then, changes the student's state from "undeclared" to "declared."

Yet another way to think of an object's operations are as *services* that can be requested of the object on behalf of the application. For example, one service that we might ask a course object to perform is to provide us with a list of all of the students who are currently registered for the course (i.e., a *student roster*).

When we actually get around to programming an object's behaviors in a language like Java, we refer to the programming language representation of an operation as a **method**, whereas, strictly speaking, the term "operation" is typically used to refer to a behavior conceptually.

What Is a Class?

A **class** is an abstraction describing the common features of all objects in a group of similar objects. For example, a class called "Student" could be created to describe all student objects recognized by the SRS.

A class defines

- The *data structure* (i.e., the names and types of *attributes*) of each and every object belonging to that class

- The operations/*methods* to be performed by such objects: specifically, what these operations are, how an object is formally called upon to perform them, and what behind-the-scenes actions an object has to take to actually carry them out

For example, the Student class might be designed to have the nine attributes listed in Table 3-1.

Table 3-1. *Proposed Attributes of the Student Class*

Attribute	Type
name	String
studentId	String
birthDate	Date
address	String
major	String
gpa	double
advisor	???
courseLoad	???
transcript	???

Note that many of the Student attributes can be represented by simple predefined Java types (e.g., String, double, and Date) but that a few of the attributes—advisor, courseLoad, and transcript—are too complex for built-in Java types to handle. You'll learn how to tackle such attributes a bit later on in the book.

In terms of operations, the Student class might define five methods whose names are as follows:

- registerForCourse
- dropCourse
- chooseMajor
- changeAdvisor
- printTranscript

You'll learn how to formally declare methods in Java in Chapter 4.

Note that an object can only do those things for which methods have been defined by the object's class. In that respect, an object is like an appliance: it can do whatever it was designed to do (a DVD player provides buttons to play, pause, stop, and seek a particular movie scene), and nothing more (you can't ask a DVD to toast a bagel—at least not with much chance of success!). So, an important aspect of successfully designing an object is making sure to anticipate all of the behaviors it will need to perform in order to carry out its "mission" within the system. You'll learn how to formally determine what an object's mission, data structure, and behaviors should be, based on the overall requirements for the application that it is to support, in Part 2 of the book.

The term **feature** is used informally to collectively refer to both the attributes and methods of a class. That is, a class definition that includes nine attribute declarations and five method declarations is said to have 14 features.

The Java-specific term for the notion of a feature is **member**. However, the term "feature" as we'll use it informally throughout the book and the *precise* meaning of "member" in the Java sense are not quite the same thing. We'll defer an in-depth discussion of what a Java member specifically is until Chapter 13.

A Note Regarding Naming Conventions

All object-oriented programming languages (OOPLs), including Java, uphold the following naming conventions:

- When naming classes, we begin with an ***uppercase*** letter, but use mixed case for the name overall: Student, Course, Professor, and so on. When the name of a class would ideally be stated as a multiword phrase, such as "course catalog," we start each word with a capital letter, and concatenate the words without using spaces, dashes, or underscores to separate them—for example, CourseCatalog. This style is known as **Pascal casing**.

- The convention for attribute and method names is to start with a ***lowercase*** letter, but to capitalize the first letter of any subsequent words in the name. Typical attribute names might thus be name, studentId, or courseLoad, while typical method names might thus be registerForCourse and printTranscript. This style is known as **camel casing**.

Declaring a Class, Java Style

Once we've determined what common data structure and behaviors we wish to impart to a set of similar objects, we must formally declare them as attributes and methods in the context of a Java class. For example, we'd program the Student class data structure as presented in Table 3-1 as follows:

```java
public class Student {
    // Attribute declarations typically appear first in a class declaration ...
    String name;
    String studentId;
    Date birthDate;
    String address;
    String major;
    double gpa;
    // type? advisor - we'll declare this attribute in earnest later!
    // type? courseLoad - ditto
    // type? transcript - ditto

    // ... followed by method declarations (details omitted - you'll
    // learn how to program methods in Java in Chapter 4.)
}
```

As with all Java class definitions that you've seen thus far in the book, this class definition would reside in a source file named *ClassName*.java (Student.java, to be specific) and would be subsequently compiled into bytecode form as a file named Student.class.

Note that, for the preceding code to compile, we'd need to insert the statement

```java
import java.util.Date;
```

ahead of the declaration

```java
public class Student { ... }.
```

We'll discuss import directives in Chapter 6.

Note that our Student class is not required to declare a main method. Unlike the classes shown previously in the book, which served to encapsulate a program's main method

```
public class Simple {
    public static void main(String[] args) {
        System.out.println("I love Java!!!");
    }
}
```

the Student class serves a different purpose: namely, we're defining what the data structure and behaviors of Student objects should be.

Instantiation

A class definition may be thought of as a template for creating software objects—a "pattern" used to

- Allocate a prescribed amount of memory within the JVM to house the ***attributes*** of a new object.
- Associate a certain set of ***behaviors*** with that object.

The term **instantiation** is used to refer to the process by which an object is created in memory at run time based upon a class definition. From a single class definition—for example, Student—we can create many objects with identical data structures and behaviors, in the same way that we use a single cookie cutter to make many cookies all of the same shape. Another way to refer to an object, then, is as an **instance** of a particular class—for example, "A Student object is an instance of the Student class." (We'll talk about the physical process of instantiating objects as it occurs in Java in a bit more detail later in this chapter.)

Classes may thus be differentiated from objects as follows:

- A ***class*** defines the features—attributes, methods—that every object belonging to the class must possess; a class can thus be thought of as serving as an ***object template***, as illustrated in Figure 3-5.

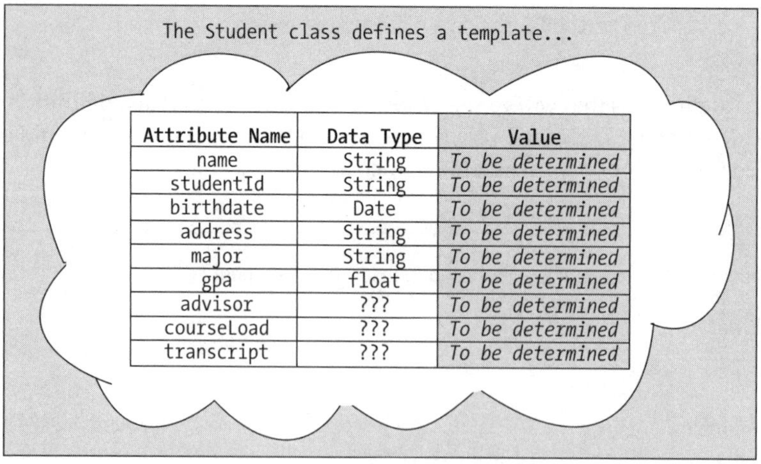

Attribute Name	Data Type	Value
name	String	*To be determined*
studentId	String	*To be determined*
birthdate	Date	*To be determined*
address	String	*To be determined*
major	String	*To be determined*
gpa	float	*To be determined*
advisor	???	*To be determined*
courseLoad	???	*To be determined*
transcript	???	*To be determined*

Figure 3-5. *A class prescribes a template for instantiating objects . . .*

- An ***object***, on the other hand, is a unique instance of a ***filled-in template*** for which attribute values have been provided, and upon which methods may be performed, as illustrated in Figure 3-6.

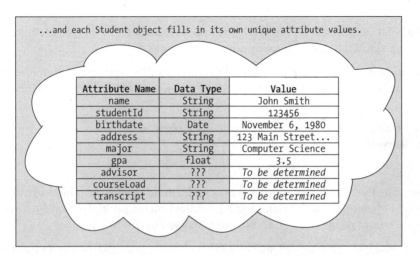

Figure 3-6. *. . . and an object then fills in its own unique attribute values.*

Encapsulation

Encapsulation is a formal term referring to the mechanism that bundles together the state and behavior of an object into a single logical unit. Everything that we need to know about a given student is, in theory, contained within the boundaries of a Student object, either

- Directly, as an attribute of that object or

- Indirectly, as a method that can answer a question or make a determination about the object's state.

Encapsulation isn't unique to OO languages, but in some senses it is perfected by them. If you're familiar with C, you know that a C struct(ure) encapsulates data:

```
struct employee {
    char name[30];
    int age;
}
```

and a C function encapsulates logic—data is passed in and operated on, and an answer is optionally returned:

```
float average(float x, float y) {
    return (x + y)/2.0;
}
```

But only with OO programming languages is the notion of encapsulating data and behavior in a single class construct, to represent an abstraction of a real-world entity, truly embraced.

User-Defined Types and Reference Variables

In a non-OO programming language such as C, the statement

```
int x;
```

is a **declaration** that variable x is an int(eger), one of several primitive data types defined to be part of the C language. What does this *really* mean? It means that

- x is a *symbolic name* that we've invented to refer to an int(eger) value that is stored somewhere in the computer's memory. We don't care where this value is stored, however, because

- Whenever we want to operate on this particular integer value in our program, we refer to it via its symbolic name x, for example:

    ```
    if (x > 17) x = x + 5;
    ```

- Furthermore, the "thing" that we've named x understands how to respond to a number of different operations, such as addition (+), subtraction (–), multiplication (*), division (/), logical comparisons (>, <, =), and so on, as defined by the int type.

In an OO language like Java, we can define a class such as Student, and then declare a variable to be of type Student, as follows:

```
Student y;
```

What does this *really* mean? It means that

- y is a symbolic name that we've invented to refer to a Student object (i.e., an instance of the Student class) that is stored somewhere in the computer's memory. We don't care where this object is stored, however, because

- Whenever we want to operate on this particular object in our program, we refer to it via its symbolic name y, for example:

    ```
    if (y.isOnAcademicProbation()) System.out.println ("Uh oh ...");
    ```

- Furthermore, the "thing" that we've named y understands how to respond to a number of different service requests—how to register for a course, drop a course, and so on—that have been defined by the Student class.

Note the parallels between y as a Student and x as an int in the preceding examples. Just as int is said to be a *predefined type* in Java (and other languages), the Student class is said to be a **user-defined type**. And, because y in the preceding example is a variable that *refers to* an instance (object) of class Student, y is known as a **reference variable**.

In contrast, variables declared to be one of the eight primitive types in Java—int, double, float, byte, short, long, char, and boolean—are *not* reference variables, because in Java, primitive types are *not* **reference types**; that is, they do not refer to *objects*.

```
// x is NOT a reference variable, because in Java,
// an int is NOT an object.
int x;
```

```
// yesNo is NOT a reference variable, because in Java,
// a boolean is NOT an object.
boolean yesNo;

// etc.
```

Various OO languages differ in their treatment of simple types. In some OO languages (e.g., Smalltalk), *all* types, including "simple" types such as int and char, are reference types, whereas in other languages (e.g., Java and C++), they are not.

The fact that Java contains a mix of reference types and nonreference types affects the way that we manipulate variables under certain circumstances, such as when we're placing primitive values into **collections**, a subject that we'll explore in Chapter 6. As we'll discuss in Chapter 6 and again in Appendix G, enhancements made to the Java language as of version 5.0 lessen the impact of this difference somewhat.

Naming Conventions for Reference Variables

Names for reference variables follow the same convention as method and attribute names—that is, they use camel casing. Some sample reference variable declarations are as follows:

```
Course prerequisiteOfThisCourse;
Professor facultyAdvisor;
Student s;
Student student;
```

The last of these, Student student;, might take some getting used to if you are new to case-sensitive programming languages. However, it is considered good programming practice to pattern reference variable names after the name of the class to which they belong if there is only one such variable within scope in a particular body of code. Because the class name starts with an uppercase "S" and the reference variable name starts with a lowercase "s," Student and student are *completely different symbols* as far as the compiler is concerned.

Instantiating Objects: A Closer Look

Different OO languages differ in terms of when an object is actually instantiated (created). In Java, when we declare a variable to be of a user-defined type, as in

```
Student y;
```

we haven't actually created an object in memory yet. Rather, we've simply declared a reference variable of type Student named y. This reference variable has the *potential* to refer to a Student object, but it doesn't refer to one just yet; rather, as with variables of the various simple types, y's value is undefined as far as the compiler is concerned until we explicitly assign it a value.

If we want to instantiate a **_brand-new_** Student object for y to refer to, we have to take the distinct step of using a special Java keyword, new, to allocate a new Student object within the JVM's memory at run time. We associate the new object with the reference variable y via an assignment statement, as follows:

```
y = new Student();
```

Don't worry about the parentheses at the end of the preceding statement. I'll talk about their significance in Chapter 4, when we discuss the notion of **constructors**.

Think of the newly created object as a helium balloon, as shown in Figure 3-7, and a reference variable as the hand that holds a string tied to the balloon so that we may access the object whenever we'd like.

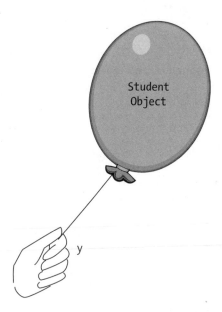

Figure 3-7. *Using a reference variable to keep track of an object in memory*

Because a reference variable is sometimes informally said to "hold onto" an object, we often use the informal term **handle**, as in the expression "Reference variable y maintains a handle on a Student object."

If you're familiar with the concept of **_pointers_** from languages such as C and C++, a reference is similar to a pointer, in that it refers behind the scenes to the memory location/address where a particular object is stored. Java references **_differ_** from pointers, however, in that references can't be manipulated arithmetically the way that pointers can.

We could also create a new object without immediately assigning it to a reference variable, as in the following line of code:

```
new Student();
```

but such an object would be like a helium balloon without a string: it would indeed exist, but we'd never be able to access this object in our program. It would, in essence, "float away" from us in memory immediately after being "inflated."

Note that we can combine the two steps—declaring a reference variable and actually instantiating an object for that variable to refer to—into a single line of code:

```
Student y = new Student();
```

Another way to initialize reference variable y is to use an assignment statement to "hand" y a reference to an ***already existing*** object: that is, an object ("helium balloon") that is already being referenced by a ***different*** reference variable x. Let's look at an example:

```
// We declare a reference variable, and instantiate our first Student object.
Student x = new Student();

// We declare a second reference variable, but do *not* instantiate
// a second Student object.
Student y;

// We assign y a reference to the SAME object that x is referring to
// (x continues to refer to it, too).  We now, in essence,
// have two "strings" tied to the same "balloon."
y = x;
```

The conceptual outcome of the preceding assignment statement is illustrated in Figure 3-8: two "strings," being held by two different "hands," tied to the same "balloon"—that is, two ***different*** reference variables referring to the ***same*** physical object in memory.

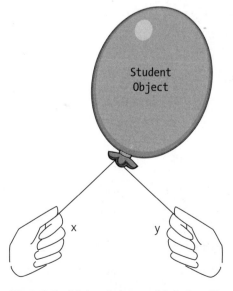

Figure 3-8. *Maintaining multiple handles on the same object*

We therefore see that *multiple* reference variables may simultaneously refer to the *same* object. However, any *one* reference variable may only hold on to/refer to *one* object at a time. Therefore, if a reference variable is already holding on to an object, it must let go of that object to reference a different object. If there comes a time when all of the handles for a particular object have been released, then that object is no longer accessible to our program, like a helium balloon that has been let loose.

Let's expand our previous example to illustrate these concepts (note the **highlighted** code that has been added):

```
// We declare a reference variable, and instantiate our first Student object.
Student x = new Student();

// We declare a second reference variable, but do not instantiate a
// second object.
Student y;

// We assign y a reference to the SAME object that x is referring to
// (x continues to refer to it, too).
y = x;

// We declare a THIRD reference variable and instantiate a SECOND
// Student object.
Student z = new Student();
```

At this point in time, we now have two references to the *first* Student object, x and y, and one reference, z, to the *second* Student object, as illustrated in Figure 3-9.

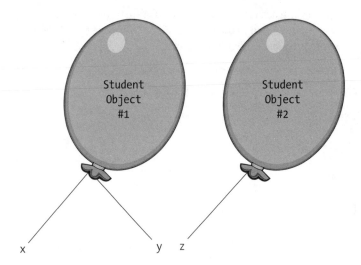

Figure 3-9. *A second object comes into existence.*

Let's expand our example yet again (note the **highlighted** code that has been added):

```
// We declare a reference variable, and instantiate our first Student object.
Student x = new Student();
```

```
// We declare a second reference variable, but do *not* instantiate
// a second object.
Student y;

// We assign y a reference to the SAME object that x is referring to
// (x continues to refer to it, too).
y = x;

// We now declare a third reference variable and instantiate a second
// Student object.
Student z = new Student();
```

// We reassign y to refer to the same object that z is referring to;
// y therefore lets go of the first Student object and grabs on to the second.
y = z;

Because we've now asked y to refer to the same object that z is referring to—namely, the ***second*** Student object—y must release its handle on the ***first*** Student object. This is illustrated in Figure 3-10. (Note that x is still holding on to the first Student object, however.)

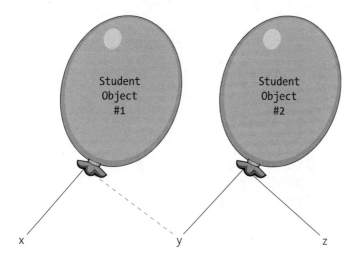

Figure 3-10. *Transferring object handles: y lets go of Student #1 to hold onto Student #2*

We'll now complete our example with the code that we've **highlighted**:

```
// We declare a reference variable, and instantiate our first
// Student object.
Student x = new Student();

// We declare a second reference variable, but do *not* instantiate
// a second object.
Student y;
```

```
// We assign y a reference to the SAME object that x is referring to
// (x continues to refer to it, too).
y = x;

// We now declare a third reference variable and instantiate a second
// Student object.
Student z = new Student();

// We reassign y to refer to the same object that z is referring to.
y = z;

// We reassign x to refer to the same object that z is referring to.
// x therefore lets go of the first Student object, and grabs on to
// the second, as well.
x = z;
```

Because we've now asked x to refer to the same object that z is referring to—namely, the *second* Student object—x must release its handle on the *first* Student object. Since we're no longer maintaining any references to the first Student object whatsoever—x, y, and z are now all referring to the *second*—the first Student object is now lost to the program, as illustrated in Figure 3-11.

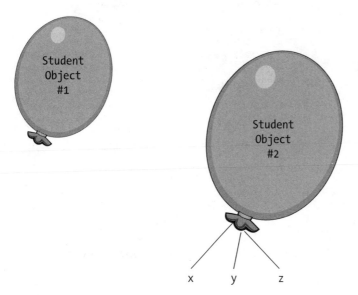

Figure 3-11. *The first Student object is now lost to our program.*

Another way to get a reference variable to release its handle on an object is to set the reference variable to the value null, which as we discussed in Chapter 2 is the Java keyword used to represent a nonexistent object. Continuing with our previous example

- Setting x to null gets x to release its handle on the second Student object, as illustrated in Figure 3-12.

  ```
  x = null;
  ```

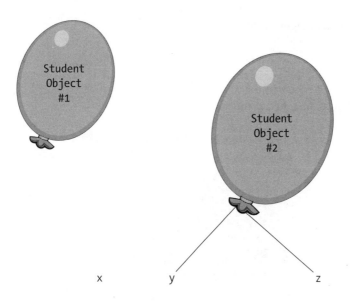

Figure 3-12. *Only two handles remain on the second Student object.*

- Setting y to null gets y to release its handle on the second Student object, as illustrated in Figure 3-13.

```
x = null;
y = null;
```

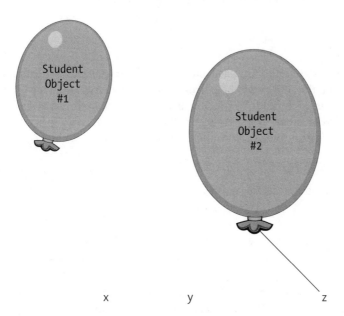

Figure 3-13. *Only one handle remains on the second Student object.*

- Ditto for z, as illustrated in Figure 3-14.

```
x = null;
y = null;
z = null;
```

Now, **both** Student objects have been lost to our program!

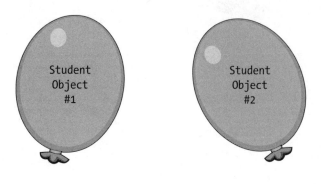

Figure 3-14. *The second Student object is now lost to our program, as well.*

Garbage Collection

As it turns out, if all of an object's handles are released, it might seem as though the memory that the object occupies within the JVM would be permanently wasted. In a language like C++, this can indeed happen if programmers don't explicitly take care to reclaim the memory of an object that is no longer needed before all of its handles are dropped. Failure to do so is a chronic source of problems in C++ programs and is commonly known as a **memory leak**.

In C++, this is accomplished via the following statement:

```
x.delete();
```

but such a statement is unnecessary in Java, for reasons that we are about to discuss.

With Java, on the other hand, the JVM periodically performs **garbage collection**, a process that automatically reclaims the memory of "lost" objects for us while an application is executing. Here's how the Java garbage collector works:

- If there are no remaining active references to an object, it becomes a ***candidate*** for garbage collection.

- The garbage collector doesn't ***immediately*** recycle the object, however; rather, garbage collection occurs whenever the JVM determines that the application is getting low on free memory, or when the JVM is otherwise idle.

- So, for some period of time, the "orphaned" object will still exist in memory—we simply won't have any handles/reference variables with which to access it.

Note that there is a way to explicitly request garbage collection to occur in Java via the following statement:

```
Runtime.getRuntime().gc();
```

Even then, however, the precise moment of *when* garbage collection occurs is out of the programmer's control, as is which and how many of the eligible objects will be collected.

The inclusion of garbage collection in Java has virtually eliminated memory leaks of the type that arose in C++. Note that it is still possible for the JVM to run out of memory, however, if we maintain handles on too many active objects simultaneously. Thus, a Java programmer cannot be totally oblivious to memory management; managing memory is just less error-prone in Java than it is in C/C++.

Objects As Attributes

When I first discussed the attributes and methods associated with the Student class, I stated that some of the attributes could be represented by predefined types provided by the Java language, whereas the types of a few others (advisor, courseLoad, and transcript) were temporarily left unspecified. Let's now put what you've learned about user-defined types to good use with respect to one of these attributes: the Student class's advisor attribute.

Rather than declaring the advisor attribute as simply a String representing the advisor's name, we'll declare it to be of user-defined type—namely, type Professor, another class that we've invented. This attribute type is reflected in Table 3-2.

Table 3-2. *Student Class Attributes Revisited*

Attribute	Type
name	String
studentID	String
birthDate	Date
address	String
major	String
gpa	double
advisor	**Professor**
courseLoad	???
transcript	???

It is also reflected in our Student class declaration:

```
public class Student {
    // Attribute declarations typically appear first ...
    String name;
    String studentId;
    Date birthDate;
    String address;
    String major;
    double gpa;
    // A class is a user-defined type, and so we may declare attributes
    // to be of such a type.
    Professor advisor;
    // type? courseLoad - we'll declare this attribute later.
    // type? transcript - ditto.

    // ... followed by method declarations (details omitted for now).
}
```

By having declared the advisor attribute to be of type Professor—that is, by having the advisor attribute serve as a ***reference variable***—we've just enabled a Student object to maintain a handle on the actual Professor object that represents the professor who is advising the student.

The Professor class, in turn, might be defined to have the attributes listed in Table 3-3.

Table 3-3. *Student Class Attributes*

Attribute	Type
name	String
employeeID	String
birthDate	Date
address	String
worksFor	String (or Department)
advisee	**Student**
teachingAssignments	???

Again, by having declared the advisee attribute to be of type Student—that is, by making the advisee attribute a reference variable—we've just given a Professor object a way to hold on to/refer to the actual Student object that represents the student whom the professor is advising.

The methods of the Professor class might be as follows:

- transferToDepartment

- adviseStudent

- agreeToTeachCourse

- assignGrades

and so forth.

Just as we did for the Student class earlier in the chapter, we'd render this Professor class design in Java code as follows:

```
public class Professor {
    // Attributes.
    String name;
    String employeeId;
    Date birthDate;
    String address;
    String worksFor;
    Student advisee;
    double gpa;
    // type? teachingAssignments - we'll declare this attribute later.

    // ... followed by method declarations (details omitted for now).
}
```

This class definition would reside in a source file named Professor.java, and would be subsequently compiled into bytecode form as a file named Professor.class.

Note that, as mentioned earlier for the Student class, we'd need to insert the declaration

```
import java.util.Date;
```

ahead of the declaration

```
public class Professor { ... }
```

in order for the code to compile properly. We'll talk about the Java Date type in Chapter 13.

The following are a few noteworthy points about the Professor class:

- It's likely that a professor will be advising several students simultaneously, so having an attribute like studentAdvisee that can reference only a ***single*** Student object is not terribly useful. We'll discuss techniques for handling this in Chapter 6, when we discuss **collections**, which we'll also see as being useful for defining the teachingAssignments attribute of Professor, and the courseLoad and transcript attributes of Student.

- The worksFor attribute represents the department to which a professor is assigned. We can choose to represent this as either a simple String representing the department name— for example, "MATH"—or as a reference variable that maintains a handle on a Department object—specifically, the Department object representing the "real-world" Math Department. Of course, to do so would require us to define the attributes and methods for a new class called Department.

  As we'll discuss further in Part 2 of this book, the decision of whether or not we need to invent a new user-defined type/class to represent a particular real-world concept/ abstraction isn't always clear-cut.

A Compilation Trick: "Stubbing Out" Classes

If we were to want to program the Student and Professor classes in Java as shown earlier, neither one could be compiled in isolation; that is, if we merely wrote the code for the Student class:

```java
// Student.java

public class Student {
    // Attribute declarations typically appear first ...
    String name;
    String studentId;
    Date birthDate;
    String address;
    String major;
    double gpa;
    Professor advisor;
    // etc.
}
```

without having yet written the code for the Professor class (Professor.java), we'd get a compilation error on Student as follows:

```
Student.java: cannot find symbol
symbol   : class Professor
location : class Student
Professor advisor;
^
```

because we haven't yet defined "Professor" as a type to the Java compiler.

We could wait until we've programmed both the Student and Professor classes before attempting to compile either one of them, but what if we were to introduce a third class into the mix:

```java
public class Student {
    String name;
    Professor advisor;
    Department major;
    // etc.
}

public class Professor {
    String name;
    Student advisee;
    Department worksFor;
    // etc.
}
```

```
public class Department {
    String name;
    Professor chairman;
    // etc.
}
```

or a fourth class, or a fifth? Must we program *all* of them before compiling any *one* of them?

Fortunately, we can use the technique of **"stubbing out"** a class to temporarily work around issues related to compiling a class X that refers to a class Y, which we haven't yet programmed. Going back to our Student class as originally written

```
// Student.java

public class Student {
    // Attribute declarations typically appear first ...
    String name;
    // etc.
    Professor advisor;
    // etc.
}
```

we can temporarily code a "bare-bones" Professor class as follows:

```
// Professor.java

// A "stub" class:  note that the body consists of a pair of empty braces!
public class Professor { }
```

Trivial as this Professor class definition may be, it is nonetheless considered to be a *legitimate* class definition by the Java compiler that, when compiled, will yield a Professor.class byte-code file.

When we now attempt to compile our Student.java file, the compiler will indeed deem "Professor" to be a valid symbol—specifically, the name of a user-defined type—and Student will compile properly, as well.

Recall that we can compile the Student.java and Professor.java ("stub") files simultaneously with the single command

```
javac *.java
```

That is, Professor.java needn't be compiled separately first.

Composition

Whenever we create a class, such as Student or Professor, in which one or more of the attributes are themselves references to other objects, we are employing an OO technique known as **composition**. The number of levels to which objects can be conceptually bundled inside one another is endless, and so composition enables us to model very sophisticated real-world concepts. As it turns out, most "interesting" classes employ composition.

With composition, it may conceptually seem as though we're physically nesting objects one inside the other, as depicted in Figure 3-15.

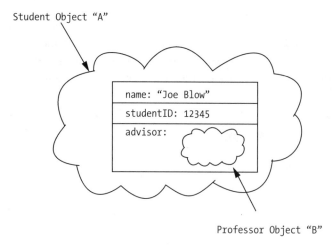

Student Object "A"

name: "Joe Blow"

studentID: 12345

advisor:

Professor Object "B"

Figure 3-15. *Conceptual object "nesting"*

Actual object nesting (i.e., declaring one class inside of another) is possible in many OO programming languages, and it does indeed sometimes make sense—namely, if an object A doesn't need to have a life of its own from the standpoint of an OO application, and it exists only for the purpose of serving the enclosing object B.

- Think of your brain, for example, as an object that exists only within the context of your body (another object).

- As an example of object nesting relevant to the SRS, let's consider a grade book used to track student performance in a particular course. If we were to define a GradeBook class, and then create GradeBook objects as attributes—one per Course object—then it might be reasonable for each GradeBook object to exist wholly within the context of its associated Course object. No other objects would need to communicate with the GradeBook directly; if a Student object wished to ask a Course object what grade the Student has earned, the Course object might internally consult its embedded GradeBook object, and simply hand a letter grade back to the Student.

We'll in fact illustrate the notion of a GradeBook when we discuss **inner classes** in Chapter 13.

However, we often encounter the situation—as with the sample Student and Professor classes—in which an object A needs to refer to an object B, object B needs to refer back to object A, and *both* objects need to be able to respond to requests independently of each other as made by the application as a whole. In such a case, handles come to the rescue!

In reality, we do *not* store whole objects as attributes inside of other objects; rather, we store *references* to objects. When an attribute of an object A is defined in terms of an object reference B, the two objects exist separately in memory and simply have a convenient way of finding one another whenever it's necessary for them to interact. Think of yourself as an object and your cellular phone number as your reference. Other people—"objects"—can reach you via your cell phone number to speak with you whenever they need to, even though they don't know where you're physically located; and conversely, if you have their cell phone numbers, you can call them whenever you like.

Memory allocation using handles might look something like Figure 3-16 conceptually.

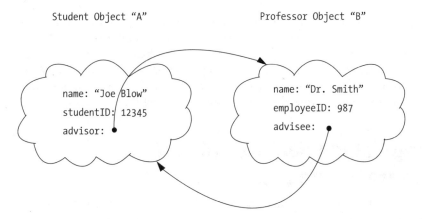

Figure 3-16. *Objects exist separately in memory and maintain handles on one another.*

With this approach, each object is allocated in memory only once:

- The Student object knows how to find and communicate with its advisor (Professor) object whenever it needs to through its advisor attribute/handle/***reference***.

- The Professor object knows how to find and communicate with its advisee (Student) object whenever it needs to through its advisee attribute/handle/***reference***.

You'll learn how to actually code such object intercommunication in Java in Chapter 4.

The Advantages of References As Attributes

What do we gain by defining the Student's advisor attribute as a reference to a Professor object, instead of merely storing the name of the advisor as a String attribute of the Student object? ***We avoid data redundancy and the associated potential loss of data integrity***. Let's see how this works.

By encapsulating the name of each professor inside of the corresponding Professor object, each name will be represented in only one place within an application: namely, ***within the object to which the name belongs***, which is ***precisely*** where it belongs! (You'll learn in Chapter 4 how to ask a Professor object for its name whenever you need to know it.) Then, if a given professor's name changes for some reason, we have only one copy of that name to change in our application—the name that is encapsulated inside of the corresponding Professor object.

If we were to instead design our application such that we redundantly stored the Professor's name both as a String attribute of the Professor object and as a String attribute of every Student object that the professor advises, we'd have a lot more work to do! We'd have to remember to update the professor's name not only in the `Professor` object, but also in potentially many different `Student` objects. If we were to forget to update all such objects, then the name of the `Professor` might wind up being inconsistent from one `Student` instance to another.

Just as important, by maintaining a handle on the `Professor` object via the `advisor` attribute of `Student`, the `Student` object can also ***request other services*** of this `Professor` object via whatever methods are defined for the `Professor` class. In addition to asking for the advisor's (`Professor`'s) name, a `Student` object may, for example, ask its advisor (`Professor`) object where the `Professor`'s office is located, or what courses the `Professor` is teaching so that the `Student` can sign up for one of them.

One final advantage of using object references from an implementation standpoint is that they also reduce memory overhead. Storing a reference to (aka memory address of) an object only requires 4 bytes (on 32-bit machines) or 8 bytes (on 64-bit machines) of memory, instead of however many bytes of storage the referenced object as a whole occupies in memory. If we were to have to make a copy of an entire object everywhere we needed to refer to it in our application, we could quickly exhaust the total amount of memory available to the JVM.

Three Distinguishing Features of an Object-Oriented Programming Language

In order to be considered truly object-oriented, a programming language must provide support for three key mechanisms:

- User-defined (reference) types

- Inheritance

- Polymorphism

You've just learned about the first of these mechanisms; we'll discuss the other two in chapters to follow.

Summary

In this chapter, you've learned that

- An ***object*** is a software abstraction of a physical or conceptual real-world object.

- A ***class*** serves as a template for creating objects. Specifically, a class defines (a) the data that an object will encapsulate, known as the object's ***attributes***, and (b) the behaviors/***services*** that an object will be able to perform, known as an object's operations/***methods***.

- An object may be thought of as ***instance*** of a class to which attribute ***values*** have been assigned—in essence, a ***filled-in*** template.

- Just as we can declare variables to be of primitive types such as `int`, `double`, and `boolean`, we can also declare variables to be of ***user-defined types*** such as `Student` and `Professor`. User-defined types are declared as classes.

- When we create a new object at run time (a process known as ***instantiation***), we typically store a reference to ("handle" on) that object in a ***reference variable***. We can then use the reference variable as a symbolic name for accessing and communicating with the object.

- We can define attributes of a class A to serve as references to objects belonging to another class B. In doing so, we allow each object to encapsulate the information that rightfully belongs to that object, but enable objects to find one another in memory at run time so that they can contact one another to share information whenever necessary.

Exercises

1. From the perspective of an academic setting (but not necessarily the SRS case study specifically), think about what the appropriate attributes and methods of the following classes might be:
   - `Classroom`
   - `Department`
   - `Degree`

2. [*Coding*] Render the `Student` and `Professor` classes as presented in this chapter in Java code. In so doing, (a) omit method declarations, (b) declare any `Date` attributes to be of type `String` instead. Finally, create a third class called `MainClass` to serve as a "wrapper" for a `main` method that instantiates one `Student` object and one `Professor` object.

3. [*Coding*] Revise the code that you wrote for exercise 2 above to include a third class, `Department`; declare whatever `Department` attributes seem reasonable but, once again, omit method declarations for now. Then, go back and modify the `major` attribute of `Student` to refer to a `Department`, and the `worksFor` attribute of `Professor` to refer to a `Department`. Finally, modify the `MainClass`'s `main` method to instantiate a `Department` object along with a `Student` and a `Professor`.

4. For the problem area whose requirements you defined for exercise 3 in Chapter 1, list the classes that you might need to create in order to model it properly.

5. List the classes that you might need to create in order to model the Prescription Tracking System (PTS) discussed in Appendix B.

6. Would `Color` be a good candidate for a user-defined type/class? Why or why not?

CHAPTER 4

Object Interactions

As you learned in Chapter 3, objects are the building blocks of an object-oriented software system. In such a system, objects collaborate with one another to accomplish common system goals, similar to the ants in an anthill, or the employees of a corporation, or the cells in your body. Each object has a specific structure and mission; these respective missions complement one another in accomplishing the overall mission of the system as a whole.

In this chapter, you'll learn

- How methods are used to specify an object's behaviors

- The various code elements that make up a method

- How objects publicize their methods as services to one another

- How objects communicate with one another to request one another's services in order to collaborate

- How objects maintain their data, and how they guard their data to ensure its integrity

- The power of an OO language feature known as **information hiding**, and how information hiding can be used to limit ripple effects on an application's code when the private implementation details of a class inevitably change

- How a special type of function known as a **constructor** can be used to initialize the state of an object when it is first instantiated

Events Drive Object Collaboration

At its simplest, the process of object-oriented software development involves the following four basic steps:

1. Properly establishing the functional requirements for, and overall mission of, an application

2. Designing the appropriate classes—their data structures, behaviors, and relationships with one another—necessary to fulfill these requirements and mission

3. Instantiating these classes to create the appropriate types and number of object instances

4. Setting these objects in motion through **external triggering events**

Think of an anthill: at first glance, you may see no apparent activity taking place. But if you drop a candy bar nearby, a flurry of activity suddenly begins as ants rush around to gather up the "goodies," as well as to repair any damage that may have been caused if you dropped the candy bar ***too close*** to the anthill!

Within an OO application (the "anthill"), the objects ("ants") may be set in motion by an external event such as

- The click of a button on the SRS graphical user interface, indicating a student's desire to register for a particular course

- The receipt of information from some other automated system, such as when the SRS receives a list of all students who have paid their tuition from the university's billing system

As soon as such a triggering event has been noted by an OO system, the appropriate objects react, performing services themselves and/or requesting services of other objects in chain-reaction fashion, until some overall goal of the application has been accomplished. For example, the request to register for a course as made by a student user via the SRS application's GUI may involve the collaboration of many different objects, as illustrated in Figure 4-1:

- A Student object (an abstraction of the ***real*** student user)

- A DegreeProgram object, to ensure that the requested course is truly required for the student to graduate

- The appropriate Course object, to make sure that there is a seat available for the student in that course

- A Classroom object, representing the room in which the course will be meeting, to verify its seating capacity

- A Transcript object—specifically, the Transcript of the Student of interest—to ensure that the student has met all prerequisites for the course

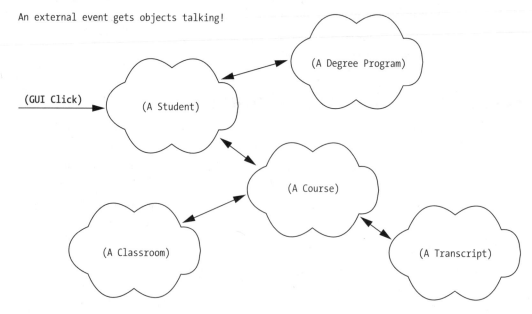

An external event gets objects talking!

Figure 4-1. *SRS objects must collaborate to accomplish the overall SRS mission.*

Meanwhile, a student user of the SRS is blissfully ignorant of all the objects that are "scurrying around" behind the scenes to accomplish his or her goal. The student merely fills in a few fields and clicks a button on the SRS GUI, and a few moments later sees a message that either confirms or rejects his or her registration request.

Once the ultimate goal of an event chain has been achieved (e.g., registering a student for a course), an application's objects effectively become idle, and may remain so until the next such triggering event occurs. An object-oriented application is in some ways similar to a game of billiards: hit the cue ball with your cue, and it (hopefully!) hits another ball, which might collide with three other balls, and so on. Eventually, however, all balls will come to a standstill until the cue ball is hit again.

Declaring Methods

Let's talk in a bit more detail about how we formally specify an object's behaviors as Java methods. Recall from Chapter 3 that an object's behaviors may be thought of as services that the object can perform. In order for an object A to request some service of an object B, A needs to know the specific language with which to communicate with B. That is,

- ***Object A needs to be clear as to exactly which of B's methods/services A wants B to perform***. Think of yourself as object A, and a pet dog as object B. Do you want your dog to sit? Stay? Heel? Fetch?

- ***Depending on the service request, object A may need to give B some additional information so that B knows exactly how to proceed***. If you tell your dog to fetch, the dog needs to know ***what*** to fetch: a ball? A stick? The neighbor's cat?

- ***Object B in turn needs to know whether object A expects B to report back the outcome of what it has been asked to do***. In the case of a command to fetch something, your dog will hopefully bring the requested item to you as an outcome. However, if your dog is in another room and you call out the command "Sit!", you won't see the result of your command; you have to trust that the dog has done what you have asked it to do.

We take care of specifying/defining these three aspects of each method by declaring a **method header**. We must then program the behind-the-scenes logic for ***how*** B will perform the requested service in the **method body**.

For readers familiar with the C programming language, a Java method declaration is virtually the same syntactically as a C function declaration. The only philosophical difference between a function in a non-OO language like C and a method in an OO language like Java is the context in which they are executed: a non-OO function is executed by the programming environment as a whole, whereas a method in an OO language is executed by a particular object. We'll explore this difference in more detail as this chapter unfolds.

Let's look at method headers first.

Method Headers

A **method header** is a formal specification (from a programming standpoint) of how that method is to be invoked. A method header, at minimum, consists of

- A method's **return type**—that is, the type of information that is going to be returned by object B to object A, if any, when B's method finishes executing.

- A method's name.

- An optional list of comma-separated **formal parameters** (specifying their types and names) to be passed to the method, enclosed in parentheses. If no parameters need be passed in, an empty set of parentheses is used; such methods are said to "take no parameters," and we'll refer to them as **parameterless**.

As an example, here is a typical method header that we might define for the Student class:

```
boolean  registerForCourse(String courseID, int secNo)
return type  method name    comma-separated list of formal parameters,
                                  enclosed in parentheses
                            (parentheses may be left empty)
```

When casually referring to a method such as registerForCourse in narrative text, some authors attach an empty set of parentheses, (), to the method name, for example, registerForCourse(). This doesn't necessarily imply that the *formal* header is parameterless, however.

Method Naming Conventions

Java method names are crafted using the ***camel casing*** style; recall from Chapter 2 that variable names are also crafted using camel casing. By way of review, with camel casing

- The first letter of the method name is in lowercase.

- The first letter of each subsequent concatenated word in the method name is in uppercase, and the remaining characters are in lowercase.

- We don't use any "punctuation" characters—dashes, underscores, etc.—to separate these words.

As an example, chooseAdvisor is an appropriate method name, whereas none of the following would be appropriate: ChooseAdvisor (uppercase "C"), chooseadvisor (lowercase "a"), choose_advisor (separating underscore).

Passing Arguments to Methods

The purpose of passing arguments into a method is twofold:

- To provide it with the (optional) "fuel" necessary to do its job

- To otherwise guide its behavior in some fashion

With the `registerForCourse` method shown previously, for example, it's necessary to tell the specific `Student` object performing the method which course we want it to register for; we'll do so by passing in two arguments, a course ID (e.g., "MATH 101") and a section number (e.g., 10, which happens to meet Monday nights from 8:00 to 10:00 p.m.), as illustrated here:

```
boolean registerForCourse(String courseID, int secNo)
```

Had we instead declared the `registerForCourse` method header with an *empty* parameter list

```
boolean registerForCourse()
```

the request would be ambiguous, because the `Student` object performing this method would have no idea as to which section it's expected to register for.

Not all methods require such "fuel," however; some methods are able to produce results solely based on the information stored internally within an object as attribute values, in which case no additional guidance is needed in the form of arguments. For example, the method

```
int getAge()
```

is designed to be parameterless because a `Student` object can presumably tell us its age without having to be given any qualifying information, perhaps by comparing the value of its `birthDate` attribute with the system date. Let's say, however, that we wanted a `Student` object to be able to report its age expressed either in years or in months; in such a case, we might wish to declare the getAge method as follows:

```
int getAge(int ageType)
```

allowing us to pass in an `int`(eger) argument to serve as a control flag for informing the `Student` object of how we want the answer to be returned. That is, we might program the getAge method so that

- If we pass in a value of 1, it means that we want the answer to be returned in terms of years.

- If we pass in a value of 2, we want the answer to be returned in terms of months (e.g., a 21-year-old student would respond that it is 252 months old).

An alternative way of handling the requirement to retrieve the age of a `Student` object in two different forms would be to define two separate methods, such as perhaps the following:

```
int getAgeInYears()
int getAgeInMonths()
```

but in object-oriented programming, it's common practice to control a method's behavior through the values (and types) of arguments.

A BIT OF TERMINOLOGY

To make sure that everyone understands the difference between "parameter" and "argument," both of which are generic terms that are equally applicable to both OO and non-OO programming languages, we'll define both terms here.

A **parameter** is a locally scoped variable, declared in a method header, that temporarily comes into existence while a method is executing. For example, when the (C language) square root method, declared as follows, is invoked:

```
// C code.
double sqrt(double x) { ... }
```

parameter x (of type double) temporarily comes into existence while the method is executing. x is initialized with the *argument* value that is passed in when the method is invoked:

```
// C code.
double y = 39.7;
```

Here, we're invoking the sqrt function, passing in an argument value of 39.7.

```
double z = sqrt(y);
```

In this case, since we are invoking the sqrt method with an *argument* value of 39.7, *parameter* x is initialized with the value 39.7.

While the method is executing, the method body can reference the variable x as it sees fit; however, the variable x ceases to exist as far as the compiler is concerned—that is, x goes *out of scope* (a concept we discussed in Chapter 2)—when the method exits.

```
double sqrt(double x) {
    // Use the value of x as appropriate.
    if (x < 0) { ... }
    else { ... }
        // Pseudocode.
        return result;
}
// "x" goes out of scope here ... it's only defined locally to the sqrt method.
```

Although the terms "parameter" and "argument" are frequently and casually used interchangeably, the bottom line is that they are different concepts—namely, *arguments are values; parameters are variables*.

Method Return Types

The registerForCourse method as previously declared is shown to have a return type of boolean, which implies that this method will return one of the following two values:

- A value of true, to signal "mission accomplished"—namely, that the Student object has successfully registered for the course that it was instructed to register for.

- A value of false, to signal that the registration request has been denied for some reason. Perhaps the desired section was full, or the student didn't meet the prerequisites of the course, or the requested course/section has been canceled, etc.

In Chapter 13, you'll learn techniques for communicating and determining precisely **why** the mission of a method has failed when we discuss **exception handling**.

Note that a method may be designed so as to not return anything—that is, it may go about its business silently, without needing to report the outcome of its efforts. If so, it is declared to have a return type of void (another of Java's keywords). As an example, consider the Student method header:

```
void setName(String newName)
```

This method requires one argument—a String representing the new name that we want this Student object to assume—and performs "silently" by setting the Student object's internal name attribute to whatever value is being passed into the method, returning no answer in response.

Here's an additional example of a method header that we might declare for the Student class with a void return type:

```
void switchMajor(String newDepartment, Professor newAdvisor)
```

This method represents a request for a Student object to change its major field of study, which involves designating both a new academic department (e.g., "BIOLOGY") as well as a reference to the Professor object that is to serve as the student's advisor in this new department.

The preceding example demonstrates that we can declare parameters to be of any type, including user-defined types such as Professor. The same is true for the return type of a method—for example, a method with the following header:

```
Professor getAdvisor()
```

could be used to ask a Student object who its advisor is. Rather than merely returning the **name** of the advisor, the Student object returns a reference to the Professor object as a whole (as recorded by the Student's internal facultyAdvisor attribute; you'll learn how to inform a Student object of **which** Professor object is to serve as its facultyAdvisor a bit later in the chapter).

Note that a method can return at most one result, which may seem limiting. What if, for example, we want to ask a Student object for a list of **all** of the Courses that the Student has ever taken—must we ask for these one by one through multiple method calls? Fortunately not: the result handed back by a method can actually be a reference to an object of arbitrary complexity, including a special type of object called a **collection** that can contain references to **multiple** other objects. We'll talk about collections in depth in Chapter 6.

An Analogy

Let's use an analogy to help illustrate what we've discussed so far about methods. With respect to household chores, let's say that a person is capable of

- Taking out the trash
- Mowing the lawn
- Washing the car

Expressing this notion in Java code, we'd perhaps declare three methods for the Person class, one for each chore (service):

- takeOutTheTrash
- mowTheLawn
- washTheCar

In the case of the takeOutTheTrash method, we needn't provide any qualifying details in the form of arguments, nor do we expect the person performing this service (method) to report back to us, so we declare the method header with a return type of void and an empty parameter list:

```
void takeOutTheTrash()
```

In the case of the mowTheLawn method, we'd like whoever is mowing the lawn to report back to us as to whether or not he or she sees any crabgrass, but again, we needn't provide any qualifying details in the form of arguments, so we declare the method header with a return type of boolean (where true means the person saw crabgrass, and false means the person did not) and an empty parameter list:

```
boolean mowTheLawn()
```

Finally, in the case of the washTheCar method, we might own several different cars, and so we'd need to specify which car is to be washed by passing in a reference to the car of interest. We needn't get any sort of response from the person doing the washing, however, and so we might craft the following method header:

```
void washTheCar(Car c)
```

We'll revisit this "chores" analogy to expand upon it later in this chapter.

Method Bodies

When we design and program a class's methods, declaring method headers alone is not enough: we must also program the internal details of how each method should behave when it's invoked. These internal programming details, known as the **method body**, are enclosed within braces { ... } immediately following the method header, as follows:

```
public class Student {
    // Attributes.
    String name;
    double gpa;
    // Other Student attribute declarations have been omitted from this example ...

    // We declare a method header ...
    boolean isHonorsStudent() {
        // ... and program the details of what this method is to do
        // within enclosing braces ... this is the method body.

        // Here, we're accessing the value of "gpa", declared as an
        // attribute of the Student class above.
```

```
    if (gpa >= 3.5) {
        // Returning the value "true" indicates "yes, this is
        // an honors student".
        return true;
    }
    else {
        // Returning the value "false" indicates "no, this isn't
        // an honors student".
        return false;
    }
}

// Other method declarations for the Student class would follow ...
// details omitted.
}
```

We can thus see that *a method is a function*—a function that is *performed by a specific object*, but a function nonetheless.

Features May Be Declared in Any Order

Note that the relative order in which features are declared within a Java class doesn't matter. That is, we're permitted to reference a feature A from within method B even though the declaration of feature A comes *after* the declaration of method B in the overall class declaration.

For example, in the following simple class, we declare two methods, foo and bar, and one attribute, x. The foo method is able to invoke the bar method, despite the fact that the declaration of bar comes *after* the declaration of foo in the class:

```
public class Simple {
    // Attributes.
    int x;

    // Methods.
    void foo() {
        // Invoke bar() from within foo.
        bar();
    }

    // bar() is declared AFTER foo().
    void bar() {
        System.out.println(x);
    }
}
```

All languages are not created equal in this regard; in C++, for example, you may only reference a feature if it has been *previously declared*. Hence, invoking bar from foo would generate a compilation error if the preceding example were a C++ versus Java example.

Similarly, attribute declarations needn't precede method declarations for a class; it is thus permissible to rewrite our Student class as follows:

```
public class Student {
    // Here, we BEGIN with method declarations ...

    void foo() {
        bar();
    }

    void bar() {
        // We are able to reference attribute 'x' despite the fact
        // that its declaration hasn't
        // been "seen" by the compiler yet.
        System.out.println(x);
    }

    // ... and END with attribute declarations.
    int x;
}
```

However, it is common practice to consolidate all attribute declarations at the beginning of a class, prior to declaring any of its methods.

return Statements

A return statement is a jump statement that is used to exit a method:

```
void doSomething() {
    // Pseudocode.
    do whatever is required by this method ...

    return;
}
```

Whenever a return statement is encountered, the method stops executing as of that line of code, and execution control immediately returns to the code that invoked the method in the first place.

For methods with a return type of void, the return keyword is used by itself, as a complete statement:

```
return;
```

However, it turns out that for methods with a return type of void, the use of a return; statement is ***optional.*** If omitted, a return; statement is implied as the last line of the method. That is, the following two versions of method doSomething are equivalent:

```
void doSomething() {
    int x = 3;
    int y = 4;
    int z = x + y;
}
```

and

```
void doSomething() {
    int x = 3;
    int y = 4;
    int z = x + y;
    return;
}
```

The bodies of methods with a ***non***-void return type, on the other hand, ***must*** include at least one explicit return statement. The return keyword in such a case must be followed by an expression that evaluates to a value compatible with the method's declared return type. For example, if a method is defined to have a return type of int, then any of the following return statements would be acceptable:

```
return 0;        // returning a constant integer value

return x;        // returning the value of x (assuming that x
                 // has previously been declared to be an int)

return x + y;    // returning the value of the expression "x + y" (here,
                 // we're assuming that "x + y" evaluates to an int value)

return (int) z;  // casting the value of z (assume z was declared as a double)
                 // to an int value
```

and so forth. As another example, if a method is defined to have a return type of boolean, then any of the following return statements would be acceptable:

```
return false;        // returning a boolean constant value

return outcome;      // returning the value of variable outcome
                     // (assuming that outcome has previously been
                     // declared to be of type boolean)

return (x < 3);      // returning the boolean value that results when
                     // the (numeric) value of x is compared to 3:
                     // if x is less than 3, this method returns a
                     // value of true; otherwise, it returns false.
```

A method body is permitted to include more than one return statement. Good programming practice, however, is to have only ***one*** return statement in a method, at the very end. Let's look once again at the isHonorsStudent method discussed previously, which has two return statements:

```
boolean isHonorsStudent() {
  if (gpa >= 3.5) {
    return true;   // first return statement
  }
  else {
    return false;  // second return statement
  }
}
```

Let's rewrite this method to use a locally declared boolean variable, result, to capture the true/false answer that is to ultimately be returned. We'll return the value of result with a single return statement at the very end of the method:

```
boolean isHonorsStudent() {
    // Declare a local variable to keep track of the outcome; arbitrarily
    // initialize it to false.
    boolean result = false;

    if (gpa >= 3.5) {
        // Instead of returning true, we record the value in our "result"
        // variable:
        result = true;
    }
    else {
        // Instead of returning false, we record the value in our "result"
        // variable:
        result = false;
    }

    // We now have a single return statement at the end of our method to return the
    // result.
    return result;
}
```

As it turns out, since we initially assigned the value false to result, setting it to false explicitly in the else clause is unnecessary; we could therefore simplify the isHonorsStudent method as follows:

```
boolean isHonorsStudent() {
    // Declare a local variable to keep track of the outcome; arbitrarily
    // initialize it to false.
    boolean result = false;

    if (gpa >= 3.5) {
      result = true;
    }
    // Note that we've removed the 'else' clause ... if the "if" test
    // fails, variable "result" already has a value of false.

    return result;
}
```

There is, however, one situation in which multiple return statements are considered acceptable, and that is when a method needs to perform a series of operations where failure at any step along the way constitutes failure as a whole. This situation is illustrated via pseudocode:

```
// Pseudocode.
boolean someMethod() {
```

```
// Perform a test ... if it fails, we wish to abort the method as
// a whole.
if (first test fails) return false;

// If we pass the first test, we do some additional processing ...
do something interesting ...

// Then, perhaps we perform a second test, where again failure of the
// test warrants immediately giving up in our "quest."
if (second test fails) return false;

// If we pass the second test, we do some additional processing ...
// details omitted.

// If we reach this point in our code, we return a value of true
// to signal that we made it to the finish line!
return true;
}
```

Note that the Java compiler will verify that ***all*** logical pathways through a method return an appropriately typed result. For example, the following method will generate a compiler error because a proper return statement will only be reached if the if test succeeds; if the if test fails, the return statement is bypassed:

```
boolean xGreaterThanThree(int x) {
    if (x <= 3) return false;
}
```

The specific compiler error message in this case would be as follows:

```
missing return statement:
        boolean xGreaterThanThree(int x) {
```

Methods Implement Business Rules

The logic contained within a method body defines the **business logic**, also known as **business rules**, for an abstraction. For example, in the isHonorsStudent method

```
boolean isHonorsStudent() {
    boolean result = false;

    if (gpa >= 3.5) {
      result = true;
    }

    return result;
}
```

a single business rule is expressed for determining whether or not a student is an honors student, namely,

If a student has a grade point average (GPA) of 3.5 or higher, then he or she is an honors student.

If the business rules underlying this method were more complex—say, if the rules were as follows:

In order for a student to be considered an honors student, the student must
(a) Have a grade point average (GPA) of 3.5 or higher
(b) Have taken at least three courses
(c) Have received no grade lower than "B" in any of these courses

then our method's logic would of necessity be more complex:

```
boolean isHonorsStudent() {
    boolean result = false;

    // Pseudocode.
    if ((gpa >= 3.5) &&
        (number of courses taken >= 3) &&
        (no grades lower than a B have been received)) {
            result = true;
    }

    return result;
}
```

In a sense, even a method ***header*** expresses a simple form of business rule/requirement; in this particular case, that there is such a notion as an "honors student" in the first place. But, the ***details*** of an application's business rule(s) are encoded in its various classes' method ***bodies***.

Objects As the Context for Method Invocation

As mentioned in passing a bit earlier in the chapter, methods in an OOPL differ from functions in a non-OOPL in that

- Functions are executed by the programming environment as a whole, whereas

- Methods are executed by specific objects

That is, we are able to invoke a C function "in a vacuum" as follows:

```
// A C program.
void main() {
    doSomething(42.0);  // invoke the doSomething function ...
    // etc.
}
```

whereas in an OOPL like Java, we typically must **qualify** the method call by prefixing it with the name of the reference variable representing the object that is to perform the method, followed by a period (**dot**). This is illustrated for the registerForCourse method as follows:

```
// Instantiate two Student objects.
Student x = new Student();
Student y = new Student();

// Invoke the registerForCourse method on Student object x, asking it to
// register for course MATH 101, section 10; Student y is unaffected.
x.registerForCourse("MATH 101", 10);
```

We refer to an expression of the form *referenceVariable.methodName(args)* as a **message**. That is, this line of code

```
x.registerForCourse("MATH 101", 10);
```

can be interpreted as either "invoking a method on object x" or as "sending a message to object x." Either way, such code should be viewed as *requesting object x to perform a method as a service, on behalf of the application to which the object belongs*.

The terminology "sending a message to an object" originated with the Smalltalk language, and is used when speaking of OOPLs generically. When talking about Java specifically, the terminology "invoking a method on an object" is preferred. Similarly, the Java-specific alternative for the generic OOPL term "message" is "method invocation." Throughout the book, I'll alternate between the generic and Java-specific forms for referring to these notions, but tend to favor the generic "message" nomenclature.

Because we use a "dot" to append a method call to a particular reference variable, we informally refer to the notation *referenceVariable.methodName(args)* as **dot notation**.

Another informal way to think of the notation x.*methodName(args)* is that we are **"talking to" object** x; specifically, that we are "talking to" object x to request it to perform a particular method/service. Let's return to the analogy of household chores introduced earlier in the chapter to illustrate this point.

Recall that a person is capable of the following household chores:

- Taking out the trash

- Mowing the lawn

- Washing the car

Here's an expression of this abstraction as Java code:

```
public class Person {
    // Attributes omitted from this snippet ...

    // Methods.
    void takeOutTheTrash() {  ... }
    boolean mowTheLawn() { ... }
    void washTheCar(Car c)  { ... }
}
```

We decide that we want our teenaged sons Larry, Moe, and Curly to each do one of these three chores. How would we ask them to do this? If we were to simply say

- "Please wash the Camry."

- "Please take out the trash."

- "Please mow the lawn, and let me know if you see any crabgrass."

chances are that **none** of the chores would get done, because we haven't tasked a **specific** son with fulfilling any of these requests! Larry, Moe, and Curly will probably all stay glued to the TV, because none of them will acknowledge that a request has been directed toward them specifically.

On the other hand, if we were to instead say

- "**Larry**, please wash the Camry."

- "**Moe**, please take out the trash."

- "**Curly**, please mow the lawn, and let me know if you see any crabgrass."

we'd be directing each request to a **specific** son; again, using Java syntax, this might be expressed as follows:

```
// We declare and instantiate three Person objects:
Person larry = new Person();
Person moe = new Person();
Person curly = new Person();

// And, while we're at it, a Car object, as well!
Car camry = new Car();

// We send a message to each son, indicating the service that we wish
// each of them to perform:
larry.washTheCar(camry);
moe.takeOutTheTrash();
boolean crabgrassFound = curly.mowTheLawn();


if (crabgrassFound) {
    // Pseudocode.
    handle the crabgrass ...
}
```

By applying each method call to a specific "son" (Person object reference), there is no ambiguity as to which object is being asked to perform which service.

Assuming that takeOutTheTrash is a method defined for the Person class as previously illustrated, the following code won't compile in Java (or, for that matter, in any OOPL) because the method call is **unqualified**—that is, the dot notation is missing:

```
public class BadCode {
  public static void main(String[] args) {
    // This next line won't compile -- where's the "dot"?  That is, which object
    // are we talking to???
    takeOutTheTrash();
  }
}
```

The following compilation error would be reported:

```
cannot find symbol
symbol   :    method takeOutTheTrash()
location:  class BadCode
```

However, in a **non**-OOPL language like C, there is no notion of objects or classes, and so functions in such languages are **always** invoked "in a vacuum" (i.e., on the programming environment as a whole):

```
// A C program.
void main() {
    doSomething(42.0);
    // etc.
}
```

Java Expressions, Revisited

When we discussed Java expressions in Chapter 2, there was one form of expression that was omitted from the list—namely, **messages**—because we hadn't yet talked about objects. I've repeated the list of what constitutes Java expressions here, adding message expressions to the mix:

- A constant: 7, false

- A char(acter) literal: 'A', '&'

- A String literal: "foo"

- The name of any variable declared to be of one of the predefined types that we've seen so far: myString, x

- Any one of the preceding that is modified by one of the Java unary operators: i++

- **A method invocation ("message")**: z.length()

- Any two of the preceding that are combined with one of the Java binary operators: z.length() + 2

- Any of the preceding simple expressions enclosed in parentheses: (z.length() + 2)

The **type** of a message expression is the type of the result that the method returns. For example, if length() is a method with a return type of int, then the expression z.length() is an expression of type int, and, if registerForCourse is a method with a return type of boolean, then the expression s.registerForCourse(...) is an expression of type boolean.

Capturing the Value Returned by a Method

Whenever we invoke a method with a non-void return type, it's up to us to choose to either ignore or react to the value that the method returns. In an earlier example, we declared the Student class's registerForCourse method to have a return type of boolean:

```
boolean registerForCourse(String courseId, int sectionNumber)
```

but we didn't pay any attention to what boolean value was returned when we invoked the method:

```
x.registerForCourse("MATH 101", 10);
```

If we wish to react to the value returned by a non-void method, we may choose to capture the value in a variable declared to be of the appropriate type, as in the following example:

```
boolean successfullyRegistered = x.registerForCourse("MATH 101", 10);

if (!successfullyRegistered) { // or:  if (successfullyRegistered == false)
    // Pseudocode.
    action to be taken if registration failed ...
}
```

However, if we only plan on using the returned value from a method once in our code, then going to the trouble of declaring an explicit variable such as successfullyRegistered to capture the result is overkill. We can instead react to the result simply by ***nesting*** a message expression within a more complex statement. For example, we can rewrite the preceding code snippet to eliminate the variable successfullyRegistered as follows:

```
if (!(x.registerForCourse("MATH 101", 10))) {
    // Pseudocode.
    action to be taken if registration failed ...
}
```

Because the registerForCourse method returns a boolean value, the message x.registerForCourse(...) is a boolean expression and can be used within the if clause of an if statement. Furthermore, we can apply the ! ("not") operator to the expression, as in the preceding example.

We often combine method calls with other types of statements when developing object-oriented applications—for example, when returning values from methods:

```
public class Student {
    Professor advisor;
    // Details omitted.

    public String getAdvisorsDepartment() {
        return advisor.getDepartment();  // a String expression
    }

    // etc.
}
```

or when printing to the command window:

```
Student s = new Student();
// Details omitted.
System.out.println("The student named " + s.getName() +
    " has a GPA of " + s.getGPA());
```

etc.

Method Signatures

You've already learned that a method header consists at a minimum of the method's return type, name, and formal parameter list:

```
void switchMajor(String newDepartment, Professor newAdvisor)
```

From the standpoint of the code used to invoke a method on an object, however, the return type and parameter names aren't immediately evident upon inspection:

```
Student s = new Student();
Professor p = new Professor();
// Details omitted ...
s.chooseMajor("MATH", p);
```

We can infer from inspecting the last line of code that

- chooseMajor is the name of a method defined for the Student class; otherwise, the compiler would reject this line.

- The chooseMajor method declares two parameters of type String and Professor, respectively, because those are the types of the arguments that we're passing in: specifically, a String literal and a reference to a Professor object.

However, what we ***cannot*** determine from inspecting this code is (a) how the formal parameters were ***named*** in the corresponding method header, or (b) what the ***return type*** of this method is declared to be; it may be void, or the method may be returning a non-void result that we've simply chosen to ignore.

For this reason, we refer to a method's **signature** as those aspects of a method header that are "discoverable" by inspecting the code used to invoke the method, namely,

- The method's ***name***

- The order, types, and number of ***parameters declared by*** the method

but ***excluding***

- The parameter names

- The method's return type

Furthermore, we'll introduce the informal terminology **argument signature** to refer to that ***subset*** of a method signature consisting of the order, types, and number of arguments, but excluding the method ***name***.

"Argument signature" isn't an industry standard term, but one that is nonetheless useful. We'll use it throughout the book.

Some examples of method headers and their corresponding method/argument signatures are as follows:

- Method header: int getAge(int ageType)

  - Method signature: getAge(int)

  - Argument signature: (int)

- Method header: void chooseMajor(String newDepartment, Professor newAdvisor)

    - Method signature: chooseMajor(String, Professor)

        - Argument signature: (String, Professor)

- Method header: String getName()

    - Method signature: getName()

        - Argument signature: ()

Choosing Descriptive Method Names

Assigning intuitive, descriptive names to our methods helps to make an application's code self-documenting. When combined with carefully crafted variable names such as those chosen in the following code example, comments are (virtually) unnecessary:

```
public class IntuitiveNames {
    public static void main(String[] args) {
        Student student;
        Professor professor;
        Course course1;
        Course course2;
        Course course3;

        // Later in the program ...

        // This code is fairly straightforward to understand!
        // A student chooses a professor as its advisor ...
        student.chooseAdvisor(professor);
        // ... and registers for the first of three courses.
        student.registerForCourse(course1);

        // etc.
```

Now, contrast the preceding code with the much "fuzzier" code that follows:

```
public class FuzzyNames {
    public static void main(String[] args) {
        Student s;
        Professor p;
        Course c1;
        Course c2;
        Course c3;

        // Later in the program ...

        // Without comments, this next bit of code is not nearly as intuitive.
        s.choose(p);
        s.reg(c1);

        // etc.
```

Method Overloading

Overloading is a language mechanism that allows two or more different methods belonging to the same class to have the *same* name as long as they have *different* argument signatures. Overloading is supported by numerous non-OO languages like C as well as by OO languages like Java.

For example, the Student class may legitimately define the following five different print method headers:

```
void print(String fileName) { ... // version #1
void print(int detailLevel) { ... // version #2
void print(int detailLevel, String fileName) { ... // version #3
int print(String reportTitle, int maxPages) { ... // version #4
boolean print() { ... // version #5
```

and hence the print method is said to be **overloaded**. Note that all five of the methods differ in terms of their argument signatures:

- The first takes a single String as an argument.

- The second takes a single int.

- The third takes two arguments—an int followed by a String.

- The fourth takes two arguments—a String followed by an int (although these are the same parameter types as in the previous header, they are in a different order).

- The fifth takes no arguments at all.

Thus, all five of these headers represent valid, different methods, and all can coexist happily within the Student class without any complaints from the compiler.

We can then choose which of these five "flavors" of print method we'd like a Student object to perform based on what form of message we send to a Student object:

```
Student s = new Student();

// Invoking the version of print that takes a single String argument.
s.print("output.rpt");

// Invoking the version of print that takes a single int argument.
s.print(2);

// Invoking the version that takes two arguments, an int followed by a String.
s.print(2, "output.rpt");

// etc.
```

The compiler is able to unambiguously match up which version of the print method is being called in each instance based on the argument signatures.

This example illustrates why overloaded methods must have unique argument signatures: if we *were* permitted to introduce the following additional print method as a sixth method of Student

```
boolean print(int levelOfDetail) { ... // version #6
```

despite the fact that its argument signature—a single int—duplicates the argument signature of one of the other five print methods

```
void print(int detailLevel) { ... // version #2
```

then the compiler would be unable to determine which version of the print method, #2 or #6, we are trying to invoke with the following line of code:

```
s.print(3);  // Which version do we want to execute:  #2 or #6?  HELP!!!
```

So, to make life simple, the compiler prevents this type of ambiguity from arising in the first place by preventing classes from declaring like-named methods with identical argument signatures. The compiler error we'd generate if we were to try to declare version #6 of the print method along with the other five versions would be as follows:

```
print(int) is already defined in Student
boolean print(int levelOfDetail) {
      ^
```

The ability to overload methods allows us to create an entire family of similarly named methods that do essentially the same job. Think back to Chapter 2 where we discussed the System.out.println method, which is used to display printed output to the command window. As it turns out, there is not one, but *many* versions of the System.out.println method; each overloaded version accepts a different argument type (println(int), println(String), println(double), etc.). Using an overloaded System.out.println method is much simpler and neater than having to use separate methods named printlnString, printlnInt, printlnDouble, and so on.

Note that there is no such thing as *attribute* overloading; that is, if a class tries to declare two attributes with the same name

```
public class Student {
  private String studentId;
  private int studentId;
  // etc.
```

the compiler will generate an error message on the second declaration:

```
studentId is already defined in Student
```

Message Passing Between Objects

Let's now look at a message-passing example involving two objects. Assume that we have two classes defined—Student and Course—and that the following methods are defined for each.

- For the Student class:

  ```
  boolean successfullyCompleted(Course c)
  ```

  Given a reference c to a particular Course object, we're asking the Student object receiving this message to confirm that the student has indeed taken the course in question and received a passing grade.

- For the Course class:

```
boolean register(Student s)
```

Given a reference s to a particular Student object, we're asking the Course object receiving this message to do whatever is necessary to register the student. In this case, we expect a Course to ultimately respond true or false to indicate success or failure of the registration request.

Figure 4-2 reflects one possible message interchange between a Course object c and a Student object s; each numbered step in the diagram is narrated in the text that follows. Solid-line arrows represent messages being passed/methods being invoked; dashed-line arrows represent values being returned from methods.

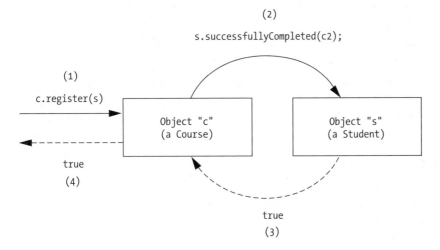

Figure 4-2. *Message passing between Student and Course objects*

(Please refer back to Figure 4-2 when reading through steps 1 through 4.)

1. A Course object c receives the message

```
c.register(s);
```

where s represents a particular Student object. (For now, we won't worry about the origin of this message; it was most likely triggered by a user's interaction with the SRS GUI. We'll see the complete code context of how all of these messages are issued later in this chapter, in the section entitled "Objects As Clients and Suppliers.")

2. In order for Course object c to officially determine whether or not s should be permitted to register, c sends the message

```
s.successfullyCompleted(c2);
```

to Student s, where c2 represents a reference to a ***different*** Course object that happens to be a prerequisite of Course c. (Don't worry about how Course c knows that c2 is one of its prerequisites; this involves interacting with c's internal prerequisites attribute, which we haven't talked about yet. Also, Course c2 isn't depicted in Figure 4-2 because, strictly speaking, c2 isn't engaged in this "discussion" between objects c and s. c2 is being talked ***about***, but isn't doing any talking itself!)

3. Student object s replies to c with the value true, indicating that s has successfully completed the prerequisite course. (We will for the time being ignore the details as to how s determines this; it involves interacting with s's internal transcript attribute, which we haven't covered the structure of just yet.)

4. Convinced that the student has complied with the prerequisite requirements for the course, Course object c finishes the job of registering the student (internal details omitted for now) and confirms the registration by responding with a value of true to the originator of the service request.

This example was overly simplistic; in reality, Course c may have had to speak to numerous other objects as well:

- A Classroom object (the room in which the course is to be held, to make sure that it has sufficient room for another student)

- A DegreeProgram object (the degree sought by the student, to make sure that the requested course is indeed required for the degree that the student is pursuing)

and so forth—before sending a true response to indicate that the request to register Student s had been fulfilled.

We'll see a slightly more complex version of this message exchange later in the chapter.

Delegation

If a request is made of an object A and, in fulfilling the request, A in turn requests assistance from another object B, this is known as **delegation** by A to B. The concept of delegation among objects is exactly the same as delegation between people in the real world: if your "significant other" asks you to mow the lawn while he or she is out running errands, and you in turn hire a neighborhood teenager to mow the lawn, then, as far as your partner is concerned, the lawn has been mowed. The fact that you delegated the activity to someone else is (hopefully!) irrelevant.

The fact that delegation has occurred between objects is often transparent to the initiator of a message, as well. In our previous message-passing example, Course c delegated part of the work of registering Student s ***back to*** s when c asked s to verify having taken a prerequisite course. However, from the perspective of the originator of the registration request—c.register(s);—this seems like a simple interaction: namely, the requestor asked c to register a student, and it did so! All of the behind-the-scenes details of what c had to do to accomplish this are hidden from the requestor (see Figure 4-3).

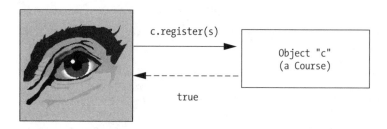

Figure 4-3. *A requestor sees only the external details of a message exchange.*

Obtaining Handles on Objects

The only way that an object A can pass a message to an object B is if A has access to a reference to/handle on B. This can happen in several different ways.

- ***Object A might maintain a reference to B as one of A's attributes***. For example, here's the example from Chapter 3 of a Student object having a Professor reference as an attribute:

```
public class Student {
    // Attributes.
    String name;
    Professor facultyAdvisor;
    // etc.
```

(Again, you'll learn how to inform a Student object of ***which*** Professor object is to serve as its facultyAdvisor a bit later in the chapter.)

By way of analogy, this is like a person A "permanently" recording the phone number for person B in his or her address book so that A can look up and call B whenever A needs to interact with B.

- ***Object A may be handed a reference to B as an argument of one of A's methods***. This is how Course object c obtained access to Student object s in the preceding message passing example, when c's register method was called:

```
c.register(s);
```

This is analogous to person A being handed a slip of paper with person B's phone number on it, so that A may call B.

- ***A reference to object B may be made "globally available" to the entire application***, such that all other objects can access it. We'll discuss techniques for doing so later in the book, and will employ such techniques in building the SRS.

This is analogous to advertising person B's phone number on a billboard for ***anyone*** to call!

- ***Object A may have to explicitly request a handle/reference to B by calling a method on some third object C***. Since this is potentially the most complex way for A to obtain a handle on B, we'll illustrate this with an example.

This is analogous to person A having to call person C to ask C for person B's phone number.

Going back to the example interaction between Course object c and Student object s from a few pages ago, let's complicate the interaction a bit.

- First, we'll introduce a third object: a Transcript object t, which represents a record of all courses taken by Student object s.

- Furthermore, we'll assume that Student s maintains a handle on Transcript t as one of s's attributes (specifically, the transcript attribute) and, conversely, that Transcript t maintains a handle on its "owner," Student s, as one of t's attributes:

```
public class Student {
    // Attributes.
    Transcript transcript;
    // etc.
}

public class Transcript {
    // Attributes.
    Student owner;
    // etc.
}
```

Figure 4-4 reflects this more elaborate message interchange between Course c, Student s, and Transcript t; each numbered step in the diagram is narrated in the text that follows. Again, solid-line arrows represent messages being passed/methods being invoked; dashed-line arrows represent values being returned from methods.

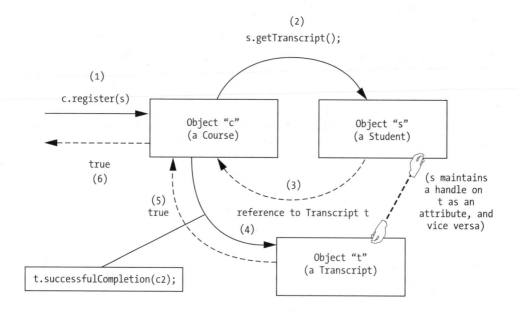

Figure 4-4. *A more complex message-passing example involving three objects*

(Please refer back to Figure 4-4 when reading through steps 1 through 6.)

1. In this enhanced object interaction, the first step is exactly as previously described: namely, a Course object c receives the message

   ```
   c.register(s);
   ```

   where s represents a Student object.

2. Now, instead of Course c sending the message s.successfullyCompleted(c2) to Student s as before, where c2 represents a prerequisite Course, Course object c instead sends the message

   ```
   s.getTranscript();
   ```

   to the Student, because c wants to check s's transcript firsthand. This message corresponds to a method on the Student class whose header is declared as follows:

   ```
   Transcript getTranscript()
   ```

   Note that this method is defined to return a Transcript object reference—specifically, a handle on the Transcript object belonging to this student.

3. Because Student s maintains a handle on its Transcript object as an attribute, it's a snap for s to respond to this message by passing a handle on t back to Course object c.

4. Now that Course c has its ***own*** temporary handle on Transcript t, object c can talk directly to t. Object c proceeds to ask t whether t has any record of c's prerequisite course c2 having successfully been completed by Student s by passing the message

   ```
   t.successfulCompletion(c2);
   ```

   This implies that there is a method defined for the Transcript class with the header

   ```
   boolean successfulCompletion(Course c)
   ```

5. Transcript object t responds with the value true to Course c, indicating that Student s has indeed successfully completed the prerequisite course in question. (Note that Student s is unaware that c is talking to t; s knows that it was asked by c to return a handle to t in an earlier message, but s has no insights as to ***why*** c asked for the handle.)

This is not unlike the real-world situation in which person A asks person C for person B's phone number, without telling C ***why*** they want to call B.

---

6. Satisfied that Student s has complied with its prerequisite requirements, Course object c finishes the job of registering the student (internal details omitted for now) and confirms the registration by responding with a value of true to the originator of the registration request that first arose in step 1. Now that c has finished with this transaction, it discards its (temporary) handle on t.

Note that, from the perspective of whoever sent the original message

```
c.register(s);
```

to Course c, this more complicated interaction appears **_identical_** to the earlier, simpler interaction, as shown in Figure 4-5. All the sender of the original message knows is that Course c eventually responded with a value of true to the request.

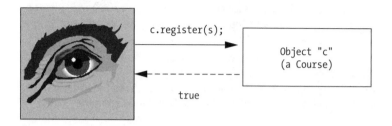

Figure 4-5. *The external details of this more complex interaction appear identical from the requestor's standpoint.*

Objects As Clients and Suppliers

In the preceding example of message passing between a Course object and a Student object, we can consider Course object c to be a **client** of Student object s, because c is requesting that s perform one of its methods—namely, getTranscript—as a **_service_** to c. This is identical to the real-world concept of **_you_**, as a client, requesting the services of an accountant, or an attorney, or an architect. Similarly, c is a client of Transcript t when c asks t to perform its successfulCompletion method. We therefore refer to code that invokes a method on an object X as **client code** relative to X because such code benefits from the services performed by X.

Let's look at a few examples of client code corresponding to the message-passing example involving a Course, Student, and Transcript object from a few pages back. This first code example, taken from the main method of an application, instantiates two objects—Course c and Student s—and invokes a method on one of them, which gets them "talking":

```
public class MyApp {
    public static void main(String[] args) {
        Course c = new Course();
        Student s = new Student();

        // details omitted ...

        // Invoke a method on Course object c.
        // (This is labeled as message (1) in the earlier figure; the returned
        // value, labeled as (6) in that figure, is being captured in boolean
        // variable "success".)
        boolean success = c.register(s);

        // etc.
    }
}
```

In this example, the main method body is considered to be ***client code*** relative to Course object c because the main method calls upon c to perform its register method as a service.

Let's now look at the code that implements the body of the register method, inside of the Course class:

```
public class Course {
  // Attribute details omitted ...

  public boolean register(Student s) {
    boolean outcome = false;

    // Request a handle on Student s's Transcript object.
    // (This is labeled as message (2) in the earlier figure.)
    Transcript t = s.getTranscript();
    // (The return value from this method is labeled as (3) in
    // the earlier figure.)

    // Now, request a service on that Transcript object.
    // (Assume that c2 is a handle on some prerequisite Course ...)
    // (This is labeled as message (4) in the earlier figure.)
    if (t.successfulCompletion(c2)) {
      // (This next return value is labeled as (5) in the earlier figure.)
      outcome = true;
    }
    else {
      outcome = false;
    }

    return outcome;
  }

  // etc.
```

We see that the register method body of the Course class is considered to be ***client code*** relative to ***both*** Student object s and Transcript object t because this code calls upon both s and t to each perform a service: s.getTranscript() and t.successfulCompletion(c2).

Whenever an object A is a client of object B, object B in turn can be thought of as a **supplier** to A. Note that the roles of client and supplier are not absolute between two objects; such roles are only relevant for the duration of a particular message-passing event. If I ask you to pass me the bread, I am your client, and you are my supplier; and if a moment later you ask me to pass you the butter, then you are my client, and I am your supplier.

The notion of objects as clients and suppliers is discussed further in *Object-Oriented Software Construction* by Bertrand Meyer (Prentice Hall, 2000).

Information Hiding/Accessibility

Just as we've been using dot notation to formulate messages to objects, we can also use dot notation to refer to an object's attributes. For example, if we declare a reference variable x to be of type Student, we can refer to any of Student x's attributes from client code via the following notation:

x.*attribute_name*

where the dot is used to qualify the name of the ***attribute*** of interest with the name of the reference variable representing the object to which it belongs: x.name, x.gpa, and so forth.

Here are a few additional examples:

```
// Instantiate two objects.
Student x = new Student();
Student y = new Student();

// Use dot notation to access attributes as variables.

// Assign student x's name ...
x.name = "John Smith";

// ... and student y's name.
y.name = "Joe Blow";

// Compare the ages of the two students.
if (x.age == y.age) { ... }
```

However, just because we ***can*** access attributes this way doesn't mean that we ***should***. There are many reasons why we'll want to ***restrict*** access to an object's data so as to give the object complete control over when and how its data is altered, and several mechanisms for how we can get the Java compiler's help in enforcing such restrictions.

In practice, objects often restrict access to some of their features (attributes or methods). Such restriction is known as **information hiding**. In a well-designed object-oriented application, a class typically publicizes ***what*** its objects can do—that is, the services the objects are capable of providing, as declared via the class's method headers—but ***hides*** the internal details both of ***how*** they perform these services as well as of the data (attributes) that they maintain internally in order to ***support*** these services.

By way of analogy, think of a Yellow Pages advertisement for a dry cleaner. Such an ad will promote the services that the dry cleaner provides—that is, ***what*** they can do for you: "We clean formal wear," "We specialize in cleaning area rugs," and so forth. However, the ad typically ***won't*** disclose the details of ***how*** they do the cleaning—for example, what specific chemicals or equipment that they use—because you, the potential customer, needn't know such details in order to determine whether a particular dry cleaner can provide the services that you need.

We use the term **accessibility** to refer to whether or not a particular feature of an object can be accessed outside of the class in which it is declared—that is, whether it is accessible from client code via dot notation. The accessibility of a feature is established by placing an **access modifier** keyword at the beginning of its declaration:

```
public class MyClass {
    // Attributes.
    access-modifier int x;
    // etc.

    // Methods.
    access-modifier void foo() { ... }
    // etc.
}
```

Java defines several different access modifiers. Let's explore the implications of using the two primary access modifiers: private and public.

There is a third access modifier, protected, that we'll defer discussing until Chapter 5.

Public Accessibility

When a feature is declared to have **public accessibility**, it's freely accessible from client code using dot notation. For example, if we were to declare the name attribute of the Student class as being publicly accessible by placing the keyword public just ahead of the attribute's type in the declaration

```
public class Student {
    public String name;
    // etc.
```

we've granted client code permission to directly access the name attribute of a Student object via dot notation; that is, it would be perfectly acceptable to write client code as follows:

```
public class MyProgram {
    public static void main(String[] args) {
        Student x = new Student();

        // Because name is a public attribute of the Student class, we may access
        // it via dot notation from client code.
        x.name = "Fred Schnurd";  // assign a value to x's name attribute
        // or:
        System.out.println(x.name);  // retrieve the value of x's name attribute

        // etc.
    }
}
```

Similarly, if we were to declare the isHonorsStudent method of Student as having public accessibility, which we do by adding the keyword public to the beginning of the method header declaration

```
public class Student {
    // Attribute details omitted from this example.

    // Methods.
    public boolean isHonorsStudent() { ... }

    // etc.
}
```

we've granted client code permission to invoke the isHonorsStudent method on a Student object via dot notation; that is, it would be perfectly acceptable to write client code as follows:

```
public class MyProgram {
    public static void main(String[] args) {
        Student x = new Student();

        // Because isHonorsStudent is a public method, we may access it
        // via dot notation from client code.
        if (x.isHonorsStudent()) { ... }

        // etc.
```

Private Accessibility

When a feature is declared to have **private accessibility**, on the other hand, it's *not* accessible outside of the class in which it's declared—that is, we may *not* use dot notation to access such a feature from client code. For example, if we were to declare the ssn attribute of the Student class to have private accessibility

```
public class Student {
    public String name;
    private String ssn;
    // etc.
```

then we are not permitted to access ssn directly via dot notation from client code. In the following code example, a compiler error would arise on the line that is **bolded**:

```
public class MyProgram {
    public static void main(String[] args) {
        Student x = new Student();

        // Not permitted from client code!  ssn is private to the
        // Student class, and so this will not compile.
        x.ssn = "123-45-6789";

        // etc.
```

The resultant error message would be

```
ssn has private access in Student
```

The same is true for ***methods*** that are declared to be private—that is, such methods can't be invoked from client code. For example, if we were to declare the printInfo method of Student as being private

```
public class Student {
    // Attribute details omitted from this example.

    // Methods.
    public boolean isHonorsStudent() { ... }
    private void printInfo() { ... }

    // etc.
}
```

then it would not be possible to invoke the printInfo method on a Student object from within client code. In the following code snippet, a compiler error would arise on the line that is **bolded**:

```
public class MyProgram {
    public static void main(String[] args) {
        Student x = new Student();

        // Because printInfo() is a private method, we may not access it
        // via dot notation from client code; this won't compile:
        x.printInfo();

        // etc.
```

The resultant error message would be

```
printInfo() has private access in Student
```

Publicizing Services

As it turns out, methods of a class are typically declared to be public because an object (class) needs to publicize its services (as in the Yellow Pages advertisement analogy) so that client code may request these services. By contrast, most attributes are typically declared to be private (and effectively "hidden"), so that an object can maintain ultimate control over its data. We'll look at several detailed examples later in this chapter of how an object goes about doing so.

Although it isn't explicitly declared as such, the internal code that implements each method (i.e., the method body) is also, in a sense, ***implicitly*** private. When a client object A asks another object B to perform one of its methods, A doesn't need to know the behind-the-scenes details of ***how*** B is doing what it's doing; object A needs simply to trust that object B will perform the "advertised" service. This is depicted conceptually in Figure 4-6, where those aspects of a class/object deemed to be private are depicted as being sealed off from client code by an impenetrable brick wall.

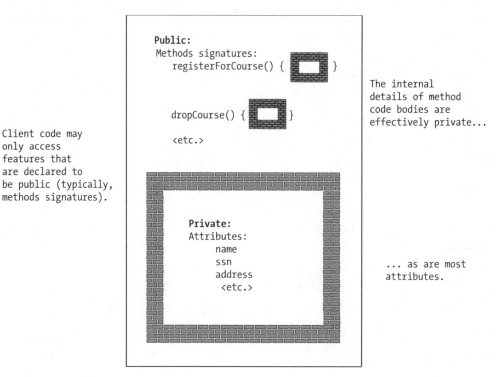

Client code may only access features that are declared to be public (typically, methods signatures).

The internal details of method code bodies are effectively private...

... as are most attributes.

Figure 4-6. *Public versus private visibility*

Method Headers, Revisited

Let's amend the definition of a method header from a bit earlier in the chapter. A method header actually consists of the following:

- *A method's access modifier*

- A method's return type—that is, the data type of the information that is going to be passed back by object B to object A, if any, when the method is finished executing

- A method's name

- An optional list of comma-separated formal parameters (specifying their types and names) to be passed to the method, enclosed in parentheses

As an example, here is a typical method header that we might define for the Student class, with the access modifier included:

```
public        boolean      registerForCourse (String courseID, int secNo)
access        return type     method name      comma-separated list of formal
modifier                                       parameters, enclosed in parentheses
                                               (parentheses may be left empty)
```

Accessing the Features of a Class from Within Its Own Methods

Note that we can access all of a given class's features, ***regardless of their accessibility***, from ***within*** any of that class's ***own*** method bodies; that is, public/private designations only affect access to a feature ***from outside the class itself*** (i.e., ***from client code***).

Let's study the following example to see how one feature of a class may be accessed from within another:

```
public class Student {
    // A few private attributes.
    private String name;
    private String ssn;
    private double totalLoans;
    private double tuitionOwed;

    // Get/set methods would be provided for all of these attributes;
    // details omitted ...

    public void printStudentInfo() {
        // Accessing attributes of the Student class.
        System.out.println("Name:  " + name);
        System.out.println("Student ID:  " + ssn);
        // etc.
    }

    public boolean allBillsPaid() {
        boolean answer = false;
        // Accessing another method of the Student class.
        double amt = moneyOwed();

        if (amt == 0.0) {
            answer = true;
        }
        else {
            answer = false;
        }

        return answer;
    }

    private double moneyOwed() {
        // Accessing attributes of the Student class.
        return totalLoans + tuitionOwed;
    }
}
```

The first thing we observe is that we needn't use dot notation to access any of the features of the Student class from within Student methods. It's automatically understood by the compiler that a class is accessing one of its own features when a **simple name**—that is, a name without a dot notation prefix, also known as an **unqualified name**—is used, for example:

```java
    public void printStudentInfo() {
        // Here, we're accessing the "name" attribute without dot notation.
        System.out.println("Name:   " + name);
        // etc.
    }
```

and

```java
    public boolean allBillsPaid() {
        boolean answer = false;
        // Here, we're accessing the "moneyOwed" method without dot notation.
        double amt = moneyOwed();
        // etc.
    }
```

That being said, the Java keyword this can be used in dot notation fashion—this.*featureName*—within any of a class's methods to emphasize the fact that we're accessing another feature of ***this same class***. I've rewritten the Student example from earlier to take advantage of the this keyword:

```java
public class Student {
    // A few private attributes.
    private String name;
    private String ssn;
    private double totalLoans;
    private double tuitionOwed;

    // Get/set methods would be provided for all of these attributes;
    // details omitted ...

    public void printStudentInfo() {
        // We've added the prefix "this.".
        System.out.println("Name:   " + this.name);
        System.out.println("Student ID:   " + this.ssn);
        // etc.
    }

    public boolean allBillsPaid() {
        boolean answer = false;
        // We've added the prefix "this.".
        double amt = this.moneyOwed();

        if (amt == 0.0) {
            answer = true;
        }
        else {
            answer = false;
        }
```

```
        return answer;
    }

    private double moneyOwed() {
        // We've added the prefix "this.".
        return this.totalLoans + this.tuitionOwed;
    }
}
```

Either approach—prefixing internal feature references with this. or omitting such a qualifying prefix—is acceptable; common practice is to forego the use of the this. prefix except when necessary to disambiguate a method parameter from a similarly-named attribute. That is, it is permissible to declare a method parameter with the same name as an attribute, as illustrated by the following code:

```
public class Student {
    private String major;
    // Other attributes omitted.

    // Note that we've used "major" as the name of a parameter
    // to the following method - this duplicates the name of
    // the "major" attribute above.  This is OK, however, if
    // we use "this." within the method body below to disambiguate
    // the two.
    public void updateMajor(String major) {
        // In the next line of code, "this.major" on the left side
        // of the assignment statement refers to the PARAMETER
        // named "major", whereas "major" on the right side of
        // the assignment statement refers to the PARAMETER
        // named "major".
        this.major = major;
    }

    // etc.
}
```

Of course, we could avoid having to use this. as a prefix simply by choosing an alternative name for our method parameter:

```
public class Student {
    private String major;
    // Other attributes omitted.

    public void updateMajor(String m) {
        // No ambiguity!
        major = m;
    }

    // etc.
}
```

It's important to avoid *accidentally* giving parameters/local variables names that duplicate the names of attributes, as this can lead to bugs that are hard to diagnose. For example, in the Student class that follows are both an *attribute* and a *local variable* named major. Please refer to the comments in the code example for an explanation of why this is problematic.

```
public class Student {
    // Attributes.
    private String major;

    public void updateMajor() {
        // We've inadvertantly declared a local variable, "major", with
        // the SAME name as an attribute of this class.  This is a BAD IDEA!
        // Note that this code will compile WITHOUT ERROR ...
        String major = null;

        // Later in the method:

        // We THINK we're updating the value of ATTRIBUTE "major" below,
        // but we're instead updating LOCAL VARIABLE "major", which will
        // go out of scope as soon as this method ends;
        // meanwhile, the value of ATTRIBUTE "major" is unchanged!
        major = major.toUppercase();
        // etc.
    }
}
```

We'll see other uses for the this keyword, involving code reuse and object self-referencing, later in the book.

Accessing Private Features from Client Code

If private features can't be accessed outside of an object's own methods, how does client code ever manipulate them? Through *public* features, of course!

Good OO programming practice calls for providing public **accessor methods** by which clients of an object can effectively manipulate selected private attributes to read or modify their values. Why is this? *So that we may empower an object to have the "final say" in whether or not what client code is trying to do to its attributes is valid*. That is, we want an object to be involved in determining whether or not any of the business rules defined by its class are being violated. Before looking at specific examples that illustrate *why* this is so important, let's first discuss the mechanics of *how* we declare accessor methods.

Declaring Accessor Methods

The following code, excerpted from the Student class, illustrates the conventional accessor methods—informally known as **"get"** and **"set" methods**—that we might write for reading/writing the value of two private attributes of the Student class called name and facultyAdvisor, respectively:

```
public class Student {
    // Attributes are typically declared to be private.
    private String name;
    private Professor facultyAdvisor;
    // other attributes omitted from this example ...

    // Provide public accessor methods for reading/modifying
    // private attributes from client code.

    // Client code will use this method to read ("get") the value of the
    // "name" attribute of a particular Student object.
    public String getName() {
        return name;
    }

    // Client code will use this method to modify ("set") the value of the
    // "name" attribute of a particular Student object.
    public void setName(String newName) {
        name = newName;
    }

    // Client code will use this method to read ("get") the value of the
    // facultyAdvisor attribute of a particular Student object.
    public Professor getFacultyAdvisor() {
        return facultyAdvisor;
    }

    // Client code will use this method to modify ("set") the value of the
    // facultyAdvisor attribute of a particular Student object.
    public void setFacultyAdvisor(Professor p) {
        facultyAdvisor = p;
    }

    // etc.
}
```

The nomenclature "get" and "set" is stated from the standpoint of *client code*: think of a "set" method as the way that *client code* stuffs a value *into* an object's attribute (see Figure 4-7).

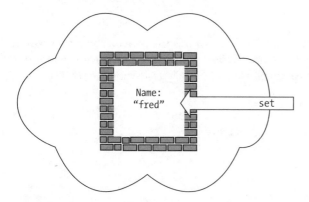

Figure 4-7. *A "set" method is used to pass data* **into** *an object.*

And think of the "get" method as the way that ***client code*** retrieves an attribute value ***from*** an object (see Figure 4-8).

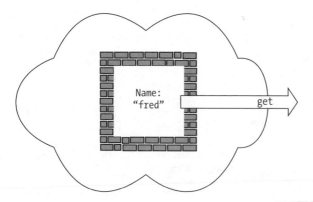

Figure 4-8. *A "get" method is used to retrieve data* **from** *an object.*

Recommended "Get"/"Set" Method Headers

For an attribute declaration of the form

```
accessibility*  attribute-type attributeName;      * typically private
```

for example,

```
private String majorField;
```

the rules for formulating conventional accessor method headers are as follows.

> ***For a "get" method, the formula is as follows***:

```
public attribute-type getAttributeName()
```

for example,

```
public String getMajorField()
```

- The name of the method is formulated by capitalizing the first letter of the attribute name in question (e.g., majorField) and sticking "get" in front (e.g., getMajorField).

- Note that we don't typically pass any arguments into a "get" method, because all we want an object to do is to hand us back the value of one of its attributes; we don't typically need to tell the object anything special for it to know how to do this.

- Also, because we're expecting an object to hand back the value of a specific attribute, the return type of the "get" method must match the type of the attribute of interest. If we're "getting" the value of an int attribute, then the return type of the corresponding "get" method must be int; if we're "getting" the value of a String attribute, then the return type of the corresponding "get" method must be String; and so forth.

- Here's a typical "get" method in its entirety, shown in the context of the Student class:

```
public class Student {
    private String majorField;
    // Other attributes omitted from this example.

    public String getMajorField {
        // Return the value of the majorField attribute.
        return majorField;
    }

    // etc.
}
```

For a "set" method, the formula is as follows:

```
 public void setAttributeName(attributeType parameterName)
```

for example,

```
public void setMajorField(String major)
```

- The name of the method is formulated by capitalizing the first letter of the attribute name in question (e.g., majorField) and sticking "set" in front (e.g., setMajorField).

- In the case of a "set" method, we must pass in the value that we want the object to use when setting its corresponding attribute value, and the type of the value that we're passing in must match the type of the attribute being set. If we're "setting" the value of an int attribute, then the argument that is passed in to the corresponding "set" method must be an int; if we're "setting" the value of a String attribute, then the argument that is passed in to the corresponding "set" method must be a String; and so forth.

- Since simple "set" methods are typically expected to perform their mission silently, without returning a value to the client, we typically declare "set" methods to have a return type of void.

- Here's a typical "set" method in its entirety, shown in the context of the Student class:

```
public class Student {
    private String majorField;
    // Other attributes omitted from this example.
```

```
        public String getMajorField {
            // Return the value of the majorField attribute.
            return majorField;
        }

        public void setMajorField(String major) {
            // Assign the value passed in as an argument as the new value of
            // the majorField attribute.
            majorField = major;
        }
    }
```

There is one exception to the "get" method naming convention: when an attribute is of type boolean, it's recommended to name the "get" method starting with the verb is instead of with get. The "set" method for a boolean attribute would still follow the standard naming convention, however, for example:

```
public class Student {
    private boolean honorsStudent;
    // other attributes omitted from this example ...

    // Get method.  For a boolean, the method name starts with "is" vs. "get".
    public boolean isHonorsStudent() {
        return honorsStudent;
    }

    // Set method.
    public void setHonorsStudent(boolean x) {
        honorsStudent = x;
    }

    // etc.
}
```

All of the "get"/"set" method bodies that we've seen thus far are simple "one-liners": we're either returning the value of the attribute of interest with a simple return statement in a "get" method, or copying the value of the passed-in argument to the internal attribute in a "set" method so as to store it. This isn't to imply that all "get"/"set" methods need be this simple; in fact, there are endless possibilities for what actually gets coded in accessor methods, because, as we discussed earlier, methods must implement business rules, not only about how an object behaves, but also what valid states its data can assume.

As a simple example, let's say that we always want to store a Student's name such as "Steve Barker" in the format "S. BARKER," where we abbreviate the first name to a single letter and represent the entire name in all uppercase. We might therefore wish to write the setName method of Student class as follows:

```
public void setName(String newName) {
    // First, reformat the newName, as necessary ...
    // Pseudocode.
```

```
  if (newName contains full first name) {
    newName = newName with first name converted to a single character
               followed by a period;
  }

  // Next, convert newName to all uppercase.
  // Pseudocode.
  newName = uppercase version of newName;

  // Only then do we update the name attribute with the (modified) value.
  name = newName;
}
```

The "Persistence" of Attribute Values

Because I haven't explicitly stated so before, and because it may not be obvious to everyone, I'd like to call attention now to the fact that an object's attribute values persist as long as the object itself persists in memory. That is, once we instantiate a Student object in our application

```
Student s = new Student();
```

then any values that we assign to s's attributes

```
s.setName("Mel");
```

will persist until such time as either the value is explicitly changed

```
// Renaming Student s.
s.setName("Klemmie");
```

or the object as a whole is garbage collected by the Java Virtual Machine (JVM), a process that we discussed in Chapter 3. So, to return to our analogy of objects as helium balloons from Chapter 3, as long as the "helium balloon" representing Student s stays "inflated," whenever we ask s for its name, it will "remember" whatever value we've *last* assigned to its name attribute.

Using Accessor Methods from Client Code

We already know how to use dot notation to invoke methods on objects from client code, and so we'll do the same when invoking accessor methods on object references:

```
Student s = new Student();

// Modify ("set") the attribute value.
s.setName("Joe");

// Read ("get") the attribute value.
System.out.println("Name: " + s.getName());
```

I promised earlier in this chapter to discuss how a given Student can be informed as to which particular Professor is its facultyAdvisor; now that you know about "set" methods, doing so is a snap! Assuming that (a) facultyAdvisor is an attribute of the Student class declared to be of type Professor, and (b) we've written a "set" method for this attribute with the "standard" header public void setFacultyAdvisor(Professor p), here's the client code for "acquainting" students with their advisors:

```
Student s1 = new Student();
Student s2 = new Student();
Student s3 = new Student();
Student s4 = new Student();
// etc.

Professor p1 = new Professor();
Professor p2 = new Professor();
// etc.

// Details omitted ...

s1.setFacultyAdvisor(p1);
s2.setfacultyAdvisor(p1);
s3.setFacultyAdvisor(p2);
s4.setFacultyAdvisor(p2);
// etc.
```

The Power of Encapsulation Plus Information Hiding

You learned earlier that encapsulation is the mechanism that bundles together the state (attribute values) and behavior (methods) of an object. Now that you've gained some insights into public/private accessibility, encapsulation warrants a more in-depth discussion.

It's useful to think of an object as a "fortress" that "guards" its data—namely, the values of all of its attributes. Rather than trying to march straight through the walls of a fortress, which typically results in death and destruction (!), we ideally would approach the guard at the gate to ask permission to enter. Generally speaking, the same is true for objects: we can't directly access the values of an object's privately declared attributes without an object's permission and knowledge—that is, without using one of an object's publicly accessible methods to access the attribute's value.

Assume that you've just met someone for the first time, and wish to know his name. One way to determine his name would be to reach into his pocket, pull out his wallet, and look at his driver's license—essentially, accessing his private attribute values without his permission! The more socially acceptable way would be to simply ask him for his name—akin to using his getName method—and to allow him to respond accordingly. He may respond with his formal name, or a nickname, or an alias, or he may say, "It's none of your business!"—but the important point is that you're giving the person (object) *control* over his response.

By restricting access to an object's private attributes through public accessors, we derive three important benefits:

- Preventing unauthorized access to encapsulated data

- Helping to ensure data integrity

- Limiting "ripple effects" that can otherwise occur throughout an application when the private implementation details of a class must change

Let's discuss each of these benefits in detail.

Preventing Unauthorized Access to Encapsulated Data

Some of the information that a Student object maintains about itself—say, the student's identification number—may be highly confidential. A Student object may choose to selectively pass along this information when necessary—for example, when registering for a course—but may not wish to hand out this information to any object that happens to casually ask for it.

Simply by making the attribute private, and intentionally omitting a public "get" method with which to request the attribute's value, there'd be no way for another object to request the Student object's identification number.

Helping to Ensure Data Integrity

As mentioned previously, one of the arguments against declaring public attributes is that the object loses control over its data, for as we saw earlier, a public attribute's value can be changed by client code without regard to any business rules that the object's class may wish to impose. On the other hand, when an accessor method is used to change the value of a private attribute, value checking can be built into the "set" method to ensure that the attribute value won't be set to an "improper" value.

As an example, let's say that we've declared a Student attribute as follows:

```
private String birthDate;
```

Our intention is to record birth dates in the format "mm/dd/yyyy". By requiring that client code invoke methods to manipulate the birthDate attribute (instead of permitting direct public access to the attribute), we can provide logic within those methods to validate the format of any newly proposed birth date, and reject those that are invalid. We'll illustrate this concept by declaring an updateBirthDate method for the Student class as shown in the following code:

```
public class Student {
    private String birthDate;
    // other attributes omitted from this example ...

    public boolean updateBirthDate(String newBirthDate) {
        boolean newDateApproved;

        // Perform appropriate validations.
        // Remember, italics represent pseudocode ...
        if (date is not in the format mm/dd/yyyy) {
            newDateApproved = false;
        }
        else if (mm not in the range 01 to 12) {
            newDateApproved = false;
        }
        else if (the day number isn't valid for the selected month) {
            newDateApproved = false;
        }
        else if (the year is NOT a leap year, but 2/29 was specified) {
            newDateApproved = false;
        }
        // etc. for other validation tests.
```

```
        else {
            // If we've gotten this far in the code, all is well with what was
            // passed in as a value to this method, and so we can go ahead and
            // update the value of the birthDate attribute with this value.
            birthDate = newBirthDate;

            // Set our flag to indicate success!
            newDateApproved = true;
        }

        return newDateApproved;
    }

    // etc.
}
```

If an attempt is made to pass an improperly formatted birth date to the method from client code, as in

```
s.updateBirthDate("foo");
```

the change will be rejected and the value of s's birthDate attribute will be unchanged. In fact, we'd probably insert the attempt to update the birth date within an "if" statement so that we could detect and react to such a rejection:

```
// Somewhere along the line, the newDate variable takes on an invalid value.
String newDate = "foo";

// Later in the application ...
if (!(s.updateBirthDate(newDate)) {
  // Pseudocode.
  do whatever we need to do if value is rejected ...
}
```

On the other hand, if birthDate had been declared to be a ***public*** attribute of the Student class, then setting the attribute directly as follows would be permitted by the compiler:

```
    s.birthDate = "foo";
```

and hence it would be possible to corrupt the attribute's value by bypassing the error checking, based on business rules, that a "set" method would normally perform for us.

Limiting "Ripple Effects" When Private Features Change

Despite our best attempts to avoid such situations, we often have a need to go back and modify the design of an application after it has been deployed, either when an inevitable change in requirements occurs, or if we unfortunately discover a design flaw that needs attention. Unfortunately, in a non-OO (or poorly designed OO) application, this can open us up to "ripple effects," wherein dozens, or hundreds, or ***thousands*** of lines of code throughout an application have to be changed, retested, etc.

One of the most dramatic examples of the negative impact of a design change was the notorious **Y2K problem**. When the need to change date formats to accommodate a four-digit year arose as the year 2000 approached, the burden to hunt through **billions** of lines of code in **millions** of applications worldwide to find all such cases—and to **fix** them without unintentionally **breaking** anything else—was mind-boggling. Many folks were convinced at the time that the world would actually melt down as a result, and in fact, it's quite amazing that it didn't!

Perhaps the most **dramatic** benefit of encapsulation combined with information hiding, therefore, is that the **hidden implementation details of a class**—that is, its private data structure and/or its (effectively private) accessor code—**can change without affecting how client code interacts with objects belonging to that class**. To illustrate this principle, we'll craft an example.

Let's say that an attribute is declared in the Student class as follows:

```
private int age;
```

and that we declare a corresponding getAge() method as follows:

```
public int getAge() {
  return age;
}
```

(We've chosen not to declare a setAge method because we've decided that we want age to be a read-only attribute.)

We then proceed to use our Student class in countless applications; so, in literally **thousands** of places within the client code of these applications, we write statements such as the following, relying on the "get" method to provide us with a student's age as an int value, for example:

```
int currentAge = s.getAge();
```

A few years later, we decide to modify the data structure of the Student class so that, instead of maintaining an age attribute explicitly, we instead use the student's birthDate attribute to compute a student's age whenever it's needed. We thus modify our Student class code as shown in Table 4-1.

Table 4-1. *Modifying Private Details of the Student Class: A Before and After View*

The "Before" Code	The "After" Code
	`import java.util.Date;`

`public class Student {`
`    // We have an explicit`
`    // age attribute.`
`    private int age;`
 	
`    public int getAge() {`
`        return age;`
`    }`
 	
`    // etc.`
`}`
	`public class Student {`
	`    // We replace age with`
	`    // birthDate.`
	`    private Date birthDate;`
	
	`    public int getAge() {`
	`        // Compute the age on demand`
	`        // (pseudocode).`
	`        return system date - birthDate;`
	`    }`
	
	`    // etc.`
	`}`

In the "after" version of Student, we're computing the student's age by subtracting their birth date (stored as an attribute value) from today's date. This is an example of what can be informally referred to as a **pseudoattribute**—to client code, the presence of a getAge() method implies that there is an attribute by the name of age, when in fact there may not be.

The beauty is that *we don't care* that the *private* details of the Student class design have changed! In all of the thousands of places within the client code of countless applications where we've used code such as

```
int currentAge = s.getAge();
```

to retrieve a student's age as an int value, this code will continue to work *as is*, without any changes to client code being necessary, because the expression

```
s.getAge()
```

still evaluates to an int value representing Student s's age. Hence, we've avoided "dreaded" ripple effects, and have *dramatically* reduced the amount of effort necessary to accommodate a design change. Such changes are said to be **encapsulated**, or limited to the internal code of the Student class only.

Of course, all bets are off if the developer of a class changes one of its *public* features—most often, a public method header—because then all of the client code that passes messages to objects of this type using this method will potentially have to change. For example, if we were to change the Student class design so that the getAge() method is now declared to return a double value, as follows:

```
public class Student {
    // We've changed the type of the age attribute from int to double ...
    private double age;

    // ... and the return type of the getAge() method accordingly.
    public double getAge() {
        return age;
    }

    // etc.
```

then much of our client code *would* indeed potentially "break," as in the following example:

```
// This will no longer compile!
int currentAge = s.getAge();
```

This particular client code will "break" because we now have a type mismatch. We are getting back a double value, but are trying to assign it to an int variable, which as we learned in Chapter 2 will generate a compiler error as follows:

```
possible loss of precision
found    : double
required : int
```

We'd have to hunt for all of the countless instances throughout potentially many applications where we are calling the getAge() method on a Student reference, and modify each such line of code to either do an explicit cast from double to int, as follows:

```
// We're now using a cast.
int currentAge = (int) s.getAge();
```

and thus we'd potentially incur a significant ripple effect. But again, this ripple effect is due to the fact that we changed a ***public*** feature of our class—a public method header, to be precise.

As long as we restrict our changes to the private features of a class, ripple effects aren't an issue; any client code that was previously written to use public Student methods will continue to work as intended.

Using Accessor Methods from Within a Class's Own Methods

Earlier in the chapter, we discussed the fact that a class is permitted to directly access its own attributes by name, as in the following printStudentInfo method:

```
public class Student {
    private String name;
    private String ssn;
    // etc.

    // Details omitted.

    public void printStudentInfo() {
        // We're accessing our own attributes directly.
        System.out.println("Name:  " + this.name);
        System.out.println("Student ID:  " + this.ssn);
        // etc.
    }

    // etc.
```

However, it's considered to be a best practice for a class to ***use its own "get"/"set" methods*** whenever it needs to access one of its own attribute values. Let's revise the printStudentInfo method to illustrate this best practice:

```
public class Student {
    private String name;
    private String ssn;
    // etc.

    // "Garden variety" accessor methods.

    public String getName() {
        return name;
    }

    public void setName(String n) {
        name = n;
    }
```

```java
public String getSsn() {
    return ssn;
}

public void setSsn(String s) {
    ssn = s;
}

public void printStudentInfo() {
    // We're now using our own "get" methods to access our own
    // attribute values.
    System.out.println("Name:  " + this.getName());
    System.out.println("Student ID:  " + this.getSsn());
    // etc.
}
```

```java
// etc.
```

Why is it important to use a class's own "get"/"set" methods rather than accessing attributes directly? Let's say that, at some future date, the getName and getSsn methods of the Student class are modified as follows:

```java
public String getName() {
    // Business rules have changed!  We now want to reformat the name
    // as stored within a Student object before returning it to
    // client code.
    // (Pseudocode.)
    String reformattedName = name reformatted in the form
        "LastName, FirstName";
    return reformattedName;
}
```

```java
public String getSsn() {
    // Business rules have changed!  We now want to reformat the
    // ssn as stored within a Student object to insert dashes
    // before returning it to client code.
    // (Pseudocode.)
    String reformattedSsn = ssn reformatted in the form "xxx-xx-xxxx";
    return reformattedSsn;
}
```

Because we've redesigned the printStudentInfo method to invoke this.getName() and this.getSsn(), we'll automatically benefit from the changes in business logic within the getName and getSsn methods:

```java
// Client code.
Student s = new Student();
s.setName("Susan Yamate");
s.setSsn("123456789");
s.printStudentInfo();
```

Here's the output:

```
Name:  Yamate, Susan
Student ID: 123-45-6789
```

On the other hand, if we had accessed the name and ssn attributes directly from within the printStudentInfo method

```
public void printStudentInfo() {
    // We're accessing private attributes directly by name rather than
    // using the corresponding get methods.
    System.out.println("Name:  " + name);
    System.out.println("Student ID:  " + ssn);
    // etc.
}
```

we would **not** benefit from changes in business logic:

```
// Client code.
Student s = new Student();
s.setName("Susan Yamate");
s.setSsn("123456789");
s.printAllAttributes();
```

Here's the output (***incorrectly*** formatted):

```
Name:  Susan Yamate
Student ID: 123456789
```

The same holds true for using a class's own **"*set*"** methods when **updating** the value of an attribute from within another method—for example, this version of the assignMajor method of Student:

```
public class Student {
    private String name;
    private String ssn;
    private String major;
    private Professor advisor;
    // etc.

    // Set/get methods provided; details omitted.

    public void assignMajor(String m, Professor p) {
        // Preferred.
        this.setMajor(m);
        this.setAdvisor(p);
    }

    // etc.
```

is preferred over this version:

```
public class Student {
    private String name;
    private String ssn;
    private String major;
    private Professor advisor;
    // etc.

    // Set/get methods provided; details omitted.

    public void assignMajor(String m, Professor p) {
        // Not as desirable.
        this.major = m;
        this.advisor = p;
    }

    // etc.
```

because the Student class's "set" methods may be simple "one-liners" today

```
public void setMajor(String m) {
    major = m;
}
```

but may be enhanced to reflect more sophisticated business logic at some point in the future:

```
public void setMajor(String m) {
    // Pseudocode.
    look up m in a database to verify that it is an "approved" major designation
    before updating the major attribute

    if (m is valid) {
        major = m;
    }
}
```

Of course, the one place where we *cannot* invoke a class's "get"/"set" methods is *within* the "get"/"set" methods themselves. To do so would result in an infinitely recursive method:

```
// This method is recursive!
public void setName(String n) {
    this.setName(n);
}
```

which will compile properly, but will produce a runtime error when invoked, as follows:

```
// Client code.
Student s = new Student();
s.setName("Fred Schnurd");
```

Here's the error:

```
Exception in thread "main" java.lang.StackOverflowError
        at Student.setName(Student.java:8)
        at Student.setName(Student.java:8)
        at Student.setName(Student.java:8)
        at Student.setName(Student.java:8)
        at Student.setName(Student.java:8)
        (repeated 1024 times!)
```

Exceptions to the Public/Private Rule

Even though it's often the case that

- Attributes are declared to be private

- Methods are declared to be public

- Private attributes are accessed through public methods

there are numerous exceptions to this rule, as explained in the sections that follow.

Exception #1: Internal Housekeeping Attributes

An attribute may be used by a class strictly for internal housekeeping purposes. (Like the dishwashing detergent you keep under the sink, guests needn't know about it!) For such attributes, we needn't bother to provide public accessors.

One example for the Student class might be an int attribute countOfDsAndFs, used to keep track of how many poor grades a student has received in order to determine whether or not the student is on academic probation. We may in turn provide a Student class method onAcademicProbation as follows:

```java
public class Student {
  private int countOfDsAndFs;
  // other attributes omitted from this example ...

  public boolean onAcademicProbation() {
    boolean onProbation = false;

    // If the student received more than three substandard grades,
    // he or she will be put on academic probation.
    if (countOfDsAndFs > 3) {
      onProbation = true;
    }

    return onProbation;
  }

  // other methods omitted from this example ...
}
```

The onAcademicProbation method uses the value of private attribute countOfDsAndFs to determine whether a student is on academic probation, but no **_client code_** need ever know that there is such an attribute as countOfDsAndFs, and so no explicit public accessor methods are provided for this attribute. Such attributes are instead set as a **_side effect_** of performing some **_other_** method, as in the following example, also taken from the Student class:

```
public void completeCourse(String courseName, int creditHours, char grade) {
    // Updating this private attribute is considered to be a
    // "side effect" of completing a course.
    if (grade == 'D' || grade == 'F') countOfDsAndFs++;

    // Other processing details omitted from this example ...
}
```

Exception #2: Internal Housekeeping Methods

Some methods may be used strictly for internal housekeeping purposes, as well, in which case these may also be declared private rather than public. (A neighbor needn't know that we have a maid who comes to clean every other week!)

An example of such a Student method might be updateGpa, which recomputes the value of the gpa attribute each time a student completes another course and receives a grade. The only time that this method may ever need to be called is perhaps from within another method of Student—for example, the public completeCourse method—as follows:

```
public class Student {
    private double gpa;
    private int totalCoursesTaken;
    private int totalQualityPointsEarned;
    private int countOfDsAndFs;
    // other details omitted ...

    public void completeCourse(String courseName,
            int creditHours, char grade) {
        if (grade == 'D' || grade == 'F') {
            countOfDsAndFs++;
        }

        // Record grade in transcript.
        // details omitted ...

        // Update an attribute ...
        totalCoursesTaken = totalCoursesTaken + 1;

        // ... and call a PRIVATE housekeeping method from within this
        // public method to adjust the student's GPA accordingly.
        updateGpa(creditHours, grade);
    }
```

```
// The details of HOW the GPA gets updated are a deep, dark
// secret! Even the EXISTENCE of this next method is hidden from
// the "outside world" (i.e., inaccessible from client code) by
// virtue of its having been declared to be PRIVATE.
private void updateGpa(int creditHours, char grade) {
  int letterGradeValue = 0;

  if (grade == 'A') letterGradeValue = 4;
  if (grade == 'B') letterGradeValue = 3;
  if (grade == 'C') letterGradeValue = 2;
  if (grade == 'D') letterGradeValue = 1;
  // For an 'F', it remains 0.

  int qualityPoints = creditHours * letterGradeValue;

  // Update two attributes.
  totalQualityPointsEarned =
      totalQualityPointsEarned + qualityPoints;
  gpa = totalQualityPointsEarned/totalCoursesTaken;
  }
}
```

Client code shouldn't be able to directly cause a Student object's gpa to be updated; this should only occur as a side effect of completing a course. By making the updateGpa method private, we've prevented any client code from explicitly invoking this method to manipulate this attribute's value out of context.

Exception #3: "Read-Only" Attributes

If we provide only a "get" method for an attribute, but no "set" method, then that attribute is rendered effectively read-only from the perspective of client code. We might do so, for example, with a student's ID number, which once set, should remain unchanged.

```
public class Student {
  private String studentId;
  // details omitted

  // We render studentId as a read-only attribute by only writing a get method
  // for it.
  public String getStudentId() {
    return studentId;
  }

  // The set method is intentionally omitted from the class.
}
```

How do we *ever* set such an attribute's value initially? We've already seen that some attributes' values get modified as a side effect of performing a method (as with the countOfDsAndFs attribute that we discussed earlier). We'll also see how to explicitly initialize such a read-only attribute a bit later in this chapter, when we talk about constructors.

By the same token, we could choose to provide only a "set" method for an attribute, in which case the attribute would be write-only. And, if we provide **neither** a "get" nor "set" method, we've effectively rendered the attribute as a private "housekeeping" data item, as previously discussed.

Exception #4: Public Attributes

On rare occasions, a class may declare selected attributes as public for ease of access; **this is only done when there is no business logic governing the attributes per se**.

One such example is the predefined Java Point class, which is used to define an (x, y) coordinate in two-dimensional space; its attributes are declared simply as

```
public class Point {
    // Both attributes are public:
    public double x;
    public double y;

    // etc.
}
```

so that, in client code, we may easily assign values as follows:

```
Point p = new Point();
p.x = 3.7;
p.y = -4.8;
```

That being said, **resist the urge** to declare attributes with public accessibility simply as a lazy way of avoiding having to write "get"/"set" methods! We've seen the many benefits that "get"/"set" methods provide in terms of enforcing business logic when appropriate. As it turns out, the vast majority of attributes will need to be governed by such business logic.

Constructors

When we talked about instantiating objects in the previous chapter, you may have been curious about the interesting syntax involved with the new keyword:

```
Student x = new Student();
```

In particular, you may have wondered why there were parentheses tacked onto the end of the statement.

It turns out that when we instantiate an object via the new keyword, we're actually invoking a special type of procedure called a **constructor**. Invoking a constructor serves as a request to the JVM to construct (instantiate) a brand-new object at run time by allocating enough program memory to house the object's attributes. Returning to our "object as helium balloon" analogy, we're asking the JVM to inflate a new helium balloon of a particular type.

Default Constructors

If we don't explicitly declare any constructors for a class, Java automatically provides a **default constructor** for that class. The default constructor is parameterless—that is, it takes no arguments—and does the "bare minimum" required to initialize a new object: namely, setting all attributes to their zero-equivalent default values.

Thus, even though we may have designed a class with no explicit constructors whatsoever, as with the following Student class:

```java
public class Student {
  // Attributes.
  private String name;
  // other details omitted ...

  // We've declared methods, but NO EXPLICIT CONSTRUCTORS.

  public String getName() {
    return name;
  }

  public void setName(String newName) {
      name = newName;
  }

  // etc.
}
```

we are still able to write client code to instantiate a "bare-bones" Student object as follows:

```java
Student s1 = new Student();
```

because the JVM uses the default constructor for the Student class.

Writing Our Own Explicit Constructors

We needn't rely on Java to provide a default constructor for each of our classes; we can instead write constructors of our own design for a particular class if we wish to do something more "interesting" to initialize an object when it is first instantiated.

Note that the header syntax for a constructor is a bit different from that of a method:

public	_____	Student()
access	*NO return type!*	*constructor name must match*
modifier		*class name, followed by*
		comma-separated list of formal
		parameters enclosed in ()

- A constructor's name must be exactly the same as the name of the class for which we're writing the constructor—we have no choice in the matter.

- A parameter list, enclosed in parentheses, is provided for a constructor header as with method headers. And, as with method headers, the parameter list may be left empty if appropriate.

- We ***cannot*** specify a return type for a constructor; by definition, a constructor returns a reference to a newly created object of the type represented by the class to which the constructor belongs. That is, a constructor of the form

```
// Note:  no return type!
public Student() { ... }
```

returns a newly instantiated Student object reference. A constructor of the form

```
// Note:  no return type!
public Professor() { ... }
```

returns a newly instantiated Professor object reference, and so forth.

Another disparity with respect to constructor syntax as compared with that of methods is that invoking a constructor does not involve dot notation:

```
Professor p = new Professor();
```

This is because we aren't requesting a service of a particular object; rather, we're requesting that a brand-new object be crafted by the JVM.

Passing Arguments to Constructors

One of the most common motivations for declaring an explicit constructor for a class is to provide a convenient way to pass in initial values for an object's attributes at the time of instantiation.

If we use a default constructor to instantiate a bare-bones object, we then must invoke the object's "set" methods one by one to initialize its attribute values, as illustrated by this next snippet:

```
// Create a bare-bones Student object.
Student s = new Student();

// Initialize the attributes one by one.
s.setName("Fred Schnurd");
s.setSsn("123-45-6789");
s.setMajor("MATH");
// etc.
```

This can be rather tedious if there are a lot of attributes to initialize.

Alternatively, if we design a constructor that accepts arguments, we can simultaneously instantiate an object and provide meaningful initial attribute values in a single line of code, for example:

```
// This single line of code replaces the previous four lines.
Student s = new Student("Fred Schnurd", "123-45-6789", "MATH");
```

In order to accomplish this, we'd of course have to declare a Student class constructor with an appropriate header, as shown here:

```
public class Student {
  // Attributes.
  private String name;
  private String ssn;
  private String major;
  // etc.
```

```
  // We've declared a constructor that accepts three arguments, to accommodate
  // passing in three attribute values.
  public Student(String s, String n, String m) {
    this.setName(n);
    this.setSsn(s);
    this.setMajor(m);
  }

  // etc.
```

Note that we're invoking the `setName`, `setSsn`, and `setMajor` methods in our constructor to set the values of the associated `name`, `ssn`, and `major` attributes rather than accessing these attributes directly, a best practice that was discussed earlier in the chapter.

Constructor arguments can also be used as control flags for influencing how a constructor behaves, as illustrated in the next example constructor:

```
public Student(String name, boolean assignDefaults) {
  setName(n);
  if (assignDefaults) {
    this.setSsn("?");
    this.setMajor("UNDECLARED");
  }
}
```

Client code for the preceding might look as follows:

```
// We DO want to assign default values to other attributes.
Student s = new Student("Cynthia Coleman", true);
```

Replacing the Default Parameterless Constructor

If we wish, we can explicitly program a parameterless constructor for our classes to do something more interesting than merely instantiating a bare-bones object, thereby *replacing* the default parameterless constructor with one of our own design. This is illustrated by the following class:

```
public class Student {
    // Attributes.
    private String name;
    private String major;
    // etc.

    // We've explicitly programmed a parameterless constructor, thus replacing
    // the default version.
    public Student() {
        // Perhaps we wish to initialize attribute values to something other than
        // their zero equivalents.
```

```
        this.setName("?");
        this.setMajor("UNDECLARED");
        // etc.
    }

    // Other methods omitted from this example.
}
```

More Elaborate Constructors

We can program a constructor to do whatever makes sense in constructing a new Student.

- We may wish to instantiate additional objects related to the Student object:

```
public class Student() {
    // Every Student maintains a handle on his/her own individual Transcript
    // object.
    private Transcript transcript;

    public Student() {
        // Create a new Transcript object for this new Student.
        transcript = new Transcript();
        // etc.
    }

    // etc.
}
```

- We may wish to access a relational database to read in the data needed to initialize the Student's attributes:

```
public class Student {
    // Attributes.
    String studentId;
    String name;
    double gpa;
    // etc.

    // Constructor.
    public Student(String id) {
        studentId = id;

        // Pseudocode.
        use studentId as a primary key to retrieve data from the Student table of a
        relational database;

        if (studentId found in Student table) {
            retrieve all data in the Student record;
            name = name retrieved from database;
```

```
            gpa = value retrieved from database;
            // etc.
        }
    }

    // etc.
    }
```

- We may wish to communicate with other already existing objects to announce a new Student's existence:

```
public class Student {
    // Details omitted.

    // Constructor.
    public Student(String major) {
        // Alert the student's designated major department that a new student has
        // joined the university.
        // Pseudocode.
        majorDept.notify(about this student ...);

        // etc.
    }

    // etc.
}
```

etc.—*whatever* is required of our application. We'll see examples of such constructors later in the book, when we craft the SRS.

Overloading Constructors

Just as we are permitted to overload methods in Java, we are permitted to overload constructors. That is, we may write as many different constructors for a given class as we wish, as long as they have different argument signatures.

Here is an example of a Student class that declares three different constructors:

```
public class Student {
  private String name;
  private String ssn;
  private int age;
  // etc.

  // Constructor #1:  takes no arguments; supercedes the default constructor.
  public Student() {
    // Assign default values to selected attributes, if desired.
    this.setSsn("?");
    // Those that aren't explicitly initialized in the constructor will
    // automatically assume the zero-equivalent value for their respective type.
  }
```

```
// Constructor #2:  takes a single String argument.
public Student(String s) {
  this.setSsn(s);
}


// Constructor #3:  takes two Strings and an int as arguments.
public Student(String s, String n, int i) {
  this.setSsn(s);
  this.setName(n);
  this.setAge(i);
}


// Other methods omitted from this example.
}
```

By overloading the constructor for a class, we make the class more versatile by giving client code a variety of constructors to choose from, depending on the circumstances. Here is an example of client code illustrating the use of all three forms of Student constructor:

```
// We don't know ANYTHING about our first student, so we use the
// parameterless constructor to instantiate s1.
Student s1 = new Student();


// We know the ssn (only) for our second student, and so we use the second
// form of constructor to instantiate s2.
Student s2 = new Student("123-45-6789");


// We know the ssn, name, and age of our third student, and so we use
// the third form of constructor to instantiate s3.
Student s3 = new Student("987-65-4321", "John Smith", 21);
```

As with overloaded methods, the compiler is able to unambiguously match up which version of constructor is being invoked in each case based on the argument signatures:

- (): No arguments tells the compiler that we are invoking constructor #1.

- ("123-45-6789"): One String argument tells the compiler that we are invoking constructor #2.

- ("987-65-4321", "John Smith", 21): Two Strings and an int as arguments tell the compiler that we are invoking constructor #3.

This example also reinforces why no two constructors may have the same argument signature. If we *were* permitted to introduce a fourth constructor whose argument signature duplicated that of constructor #2, for example:

```
// Constructor #4:  takes a single String argument, thereby duplicating the
// argument signature of constructor #2.
public Student(String n) {  // THIS WON'T COMPILE!!!
    this.setName(n);
}
```

then the compiler would not know which constructor—#2 or #4—we're trying to invoke in the following client code:

```
// Pseudocode.
Student x = new Student(aStringExpression);
```

So, to avoid such an ambiguous situation, the compiler generates an error message on the preceding declaration of constructor #4, as follows:

```
Student(java.lang.String) is already defined in Student
        public Student(String n) { }
           ^
```

An Important Caveat Regarding the Default Constructor

There is one very important caveat about default constructors in Java: if we declare *any* of our own constructors for a class, with *any argument signature*, then the default parameterless constructor is *not* automatically provided. This is by design, because it is assumed that if we've gone to the trouble to program any constructors whatsoever for a class, then we must have some special initialization requirements for that class that the default constructor could not possibly anticipate.

The implication of this language feature is as follows: if we want or need a constructor that accepts no arguments for a particular class *along with* other versions of constructors that *do* take arguments, *we must explicitly program a parameterless constructor*. To illustrate this point, let's consider a Student class that only declares one explicit constructor:

```
public class Student {
    // Details omitted.

    // Only one constructor is explicitly declared, and which takes a
    // single String argument.
    public Student(String s) {
        this.setSsn(s);
    }

    // etc.
}
```

In client code, we may instantiate a Student based on this class as follows:

```
Student s = new Student("123-45-6789");
```

but if we try to use the (what is now nonexistent) default constructor

```
Student s = new Student();
```

we'll get the following compilation error:

```
cannot find symbol
symbol  : constructor Student()
location: class Student
    Student s = new Student();
                    ^
```

Generally speaking, it is considered a best practice to always explicitly provide a parameterless constructor (to replace the lost default) if we are providing *any* constructors for a class at all. We'll revisit the importance of this practice when we discuss **inheritance** in Chapter 5.

One common mistake made by beginning Java programmers is to accidentally declare a return type in a constructor header, for example:

```
public void Student() { ... }
```

This is a particularly difficult bug to track down, because while such header declarations will *compile*, they are viewed by the compiler as *methods* and *not* as *constructors*, and cannot be used as such. What's worse, developers will *think* that they've programmed a parameterless constructor when in fact they haven't; any attempt to *use* such a constructor in their application will meet with the following seemingly cryptic compilation error message:

```
Student s = new Student();
```

This is the compiler error:

```
cannot find symbol
symbol:   constructor Student()
location:  class Student
Student s = new Student();
                ^
```

Using the "this" Keyword to Facilitate Constructor Reuse

Earlier in this chapter, we covered the this keyword, and illustrated how it can be used to option-ally qualify features of a class when accessed from within methods of the same class, as in

```
public class Student {
    // Details omitted.

    public void printAllAttributes() {
        System.out.println("Name:  " + this.getName());
        System.out.println("Student ID:  " + this.getSsn());
        // etc.
    }
}
```

We're now going to explore a second alternative use of the this keyword, related to reusing code from one constructor by another within the same class.

It's conceivable that if we've overloaded the constructor for a class, there will be some common initialization steps required of all versions. For example, let's say that, for all new students, we must

- Alert the registrar's office of this student's existence.

- Create a transcript for this student.

If we were to declare three constructors for the Student class, it would be tedious to duplicate the same logic across all three (see the **bolded** lines of code):

```java
public class Student {
    // Attribute details omitted.

    // Constructor #1.
    public Student() {
        // Assign default values to selected attributes ... details omitted.

        // Pseudocode.
        alert the registrar's office of this student's existence

        // Create a transcript for this student.
        transcript = new Transcript();
    }

    // Constructor #2.
    public Student(String s) {
        this.setSsn(s);

        // This code is duplicated from above!
        // Pseudocode.
        alert the registrar's office of this student's existence

        // Create a transcript for this student.
        transcript = new Transcript();
        // end of code duplication
    }

    // Constructor #3.
    public Student(String s, String n, int i) {
        this.setSsn(s);
        this.setName(n);
        this.setAge(i);

        // DUPLICATION YET AGAIN!!!
        // Pseudocode.
        alert the registrar's office of this student's existence

        // Create a transcript for this student.
        transcript = new Transcript();
        // end of code duplication
    }

    // etc.
}
```

Worse yet, if the logic needed to change, we'd have to change it in all three constructors! Fortunately, the this keyword comes to our rescue. From within any constructor of a class X, we can invoke any other constructor of the same class X via the following syntax:

```java
this(optional arguments);
```

Let's rewrite our previous three Student constructors so that constructor #2 takes advantage of the logic of #1, and #3 takes advantage of #2:

```
public class Student {
    // Attribute details omitted.

    // Constructor #1.
    public Student() {
        // Assign default values to selected attributes ... details omitted.

        // Do the things common to all three constructors in this first
        // constructor ...
        // Pseudocode.
        alert the registrar's office of this student's existence

        // Create a transcript for this student.
        transcript = new Transcript();
    }

    // Constructor #2.
    public Student(String s) {
        // ... then, REUSE the code of the first constructor within the second!
        this();

        // Then, do whatever else extra is necessary for constructor #2.
        this.setSsn(s);
    }

    // Constructor #3.
    public Student(String s, String n, int i) {
        // ... and REUSE the code of the first constructor within the third!
        this();

        // Then, do whatever else extra is necessary for constructor #3.
        this.setSsn(s);
        this.setName(n);
        this.setAge(i);
    }

    // etc.
}
```

By invoking this(); from within constructors #2 and #3, we were able to eliminate all duplication of code. We coded the shared logic once, in constructor #1 (the parameterless constructor), and then invoked the parameterless constructor from within the other two.

If we wanted to invoke the *second* constructor from within the third rather than invoking the *first* from within the third, we'd simply modify our use of this as follows:

```
// Constructor #3.
public Student(String s, String n, int i) {
    // Here, we're reusing the code of the SECOND constructor within the third
    // simply by changing the argument signature used with this(...).
    this(s);

    // Then, do whatever else extra is necessary for constructor #3;
    // details omitted.
}
```

Because we've modified the syntax of the this(...); statement in constructor #3 to supply a single String argument

```
this(s);
```

the compiler knows that it is the **second** constructor, which takes a single String argument, that we wish to reuse the code of.

When using the this(...); syntax to reuse code from one constructor to another, note that the statement must be the **first** statement in the constructor; that is, the following code will not compile:

```
// Constructor #3.
public Student(String s, String n, int i) {
    // Do whatever extra is necessary for constructor #3;
    // details omitted.
    ...

    // Then, attempt to reuse the code of constructor #2;
    // THIS NEXT LINE WON'T COMPILE!
    this(s);
}
```

Here's the error:

```
call to this must be first statement in constructor
    this(s);
      ^
```

We'll revisit the this keyword yet again in Chapter 13, to discuss a third context in which it can be used.

Software at Its Simplest, Revisited

As we discussed in Chapter 3, software at its simplest consists of two primary components: **data**, and **functions** that operate on that data (see Figure 4-9).

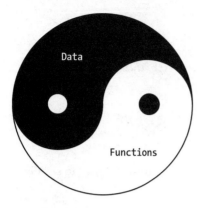

Figure 4-9. *At its simplest, software consists of data and functions that operate on that data.*

We also compared the functional decomposition approach of designing software to the object-oriented approach. By way of review,

> *With the functional decomposition approach to software development, our primary focus was on the functions that an application was to perform; data was an afterthought.*

That is,

- Data was passed around from one function to the next.

- Data structure thus had to be understood in *many* places—that is, by many functions—throughout an application.

- If an application's data structure had to change after the application was deployed, nontrivial ripple effects often arose throughout the application.

- If data integrity errors arose as a result of faulty logic after an application had been fully integrated, it was often very difficult to pinpoint precisely where—that is, *in which specific function(s)*—the error might have occurred.

We now know that by taking advantage of the mechanisms of encapsulation plus information hiding, *the object-oriented approach to software development remedies the vast majority of these shortcomings*:

- Data is *encapsulated* inside of objects as *attributes*, and, if we declare these attributes as having *private* accessibility, then the data structure has to be understood only by the object/*class* to which the data belongs.

- If the (private) attribute declarations of a class have to change after an application has been deployed—as was the case when we modified the data structure of the Student class, replacing an int age attribute with a Date birthDate attribute—there are virtually *no ripple effects*: only the internal logic of the affected class's methods must change.

(Recall that we modified the internal workings of the getAge method in one of our Student class examples, but that *none* of the client code that called getAge had to change, because we hadn't altered the *public* method signature of the method.)

- *Each class is responsible for ensuring the integrity of its object's data*. Thus, if data integrity errors arise within a given object's data, we can pretty much assume that it was the class to which the object belongs whose method logic is faulty.

  (Recall the updateBirthdate method from an earlier Student class example. This method contained all sorts of validity checks to ensure that the String being passed in as an argument represented a valid birth date. Had an *invalid* birth date somehow crept in, we'd know that there was something faulty about the validation logic of the updateBirthdate method in particular.)

If every software application consists of data and functions that operate on that data, then *an object can be thought of as a sort of "mini application"* whose methods (functions) operate on its attributes (data), as shown in Figure 4-10. You'll learn in Chapter 5 how such objects "join forces" to collaborate on accomplishing the overall mission of an application.

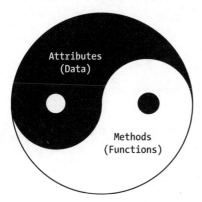

Figure 4-10. *An object is a "mini application" that encapsulates data and functions.*

Summary

In this chapter, you've learned

- How to formally specify method headers, the "language" with which services may be requested of an object, and how to formulate messages—using dot notation—to actually get an object to perform such services

- That multiple objects often have to collaborate in carrying out a particular system function, such as registering a student for a course

- That an object A can only communicate with another object B if A has a handle on B, and the various ways that such a handle/reference can be obtained

- How classes designate the public/private accessibility of their features (attributes, methods) through a mechanism known as *information hiding*

- How powerful a language feature information hiding is, both in terms of protecting the integrity of an object's data and in preventing ripple effects in client code when private implementation details of an application inevitably change

- How to declare and use accessor ("get"/"set") methods to gracefully access the private attributes of an object from client code

- How a special type of procedure called a ***constructor*** is specified and used to control what is to occur when we instantiate new objects

- How ***overloading*** enables a class to have multiple methods with the same name and/or multiple constructors as long as their argument signatures are different

Exercises

1. Given a class Book defined as having the following attributes:

```
Author author;
String title;
int noOfPages;
boolean fiction;
```

write standard "get"/"set" method headers for each of these attributes.

2. [Coding] Actually code and compile the Book class based on the attributes and "get"/"set" methods called for in exercise 1.

3. It's often possible to discern something about a class's design based on the messages that are getting passed to objects in client code. Consider the following client code snippet:

```
Student s;
Professor p;
boolean b;
String x = "Math";

s.setMajor(x);
if (!s.hasAdvisor()) {
  b = s.designateAdvisor(p);
}
```

What features—attributes, methods—are implied for the Student and Professor classes by virtue of how this client code is structured? Be as specific as possible with respect to

- The accessibility of each feature

- How each feature would be declared (e.g., the details, to the extent that you can "discover" them, of a method header)

4. [Coding] Expand the `Student` and `Professor` classes that you developed for exercise 2 of Chapter 3 (and, optionally, the `Department` class that you developed for exercise 3 of Chapter 3) as follows:

- Include accessor methods for every attribute.

- Reflect the appropriate accessibility on all features.

- Include one or more constructors per class.

- Write a method with the header `public void printAllAttributes()` that can be used to display the values of all attributes to the command prompt, for example:

```
Student Name: John Smith
Student ID: 123-45-6789
```

etc.

Then, modify the accompanying `MainClass`'s `main` method to take advantage of your new constructors to instantiate one of each of the object types.

5. What's wrong with the following code? Point out things that go against OO convention or best practices based on what you've learned in this chapter, regardless of whether or not the Java compiler would "complain" about them.

```
public class Building {
  private String address;
  public int numberOfFloors;

  void GetnumberOfFloors() {
    return numberOfFloors;
  }

  private void SetNoOfFloors(float n) {
    NumberOfFloors = n;
  }

  public void display() {
    System.out.println("Address:  " + address);
    System.out.println("No. of Floors:  " + numberOfFloors);
  }
```

CHAPTER 5

Relationships Between Objects

You learned in Chapter 4 that any two objects can have a "fleeting" relationship based on the fact that they exchange messages, in the same way that two strangers passing on the street might say "Hello!" to one another. We informally call such relationships between objects **behavioral relationships**, because they arise out of the behaviors, or actions, taken by one object X relative to another object Y.

With behavioral relationships, object X is either temporarily handed a reference to object Y as an argument in a method call, or temporarily requests a handle on Y from another object Z. However, the emphasis is on *temporary*: when X is finished communicating with Y, object X often discards the reference to Y.

In the same way that you have significant and more lasting relationships with some people (family members, friends, colleagues), there is also the notion of a more permanent relationship between objects. We informally refer to such relationships as **structural relationships** because, in order to keep track of such relationships, an object actually maintains long-term references to its related objects in the form of attributes, a technique that we discussed in Chapter 3.

In this chapter, you'll learn

- The various kinds of structural relationships that can be defined between classes, which in turn govern how individual objects may be linked together at run time

- How a powerful OOPL mechanism called **inheritance** enables us to derive new classes by describing only how they differ from existing classes

- The rules for what we can and can't do when deriving classes through inheritance

- How we must refine our understanding of (a) constructors and (b) accessibility of features when inheritance is at work

Associations and Links

The formal name for a structural relationship that exists between classes is an **association**. With respect to the Student Registration System, some sample associations might be as follows:

- A Student *is enrolled in* a Course.

- A Professor *teaches* a Course.

- A DegreeProgram *requires* a Course.

Whereas an association refers to a relationship between *classes*, the term **link** is used to refer to a structural relationship that exists between two specific *objects* (*instances*). Given the association "a Student *is enrolled in* a Course," we might have the following links:

- Chloe Shylow (a particular Student object) is enrolled in Math 101 (a particular Course object).

- Fred Schnurd (a particular Student object) is enrolled in Basketweaving 972 (a particular Course object).

- Mary Smith (a particular Student object) is enrolled in Basketweaving 972 (a particular Course object; as it turns out, the *same* Course object that Fred Schnurd is linked to).

In the same way that an object is a specific instance of a class with its attribute values filled in, a link may be conceptually thought of as a specific instance of an association with its participating objects filled in, as illustrated in Figure 5-1.

Association: _ _ _ _ _ _ _ _ _ _ is enrolled in _ _ _ _ _ _ _ _ .
                    (Some Student)   (Some Course)

    Link: _ _ _James Conroy_ _ _ is enrolled in _ Phys ED 311 _ .
              (A *Specific* Student)   (A *Specific* Course)

Figure 5-1. *An association is a template for creating links.*

Yet another way to think of the difference between an association and a link is that

- An association is a *potential* relationship between objects of a certain type/class.

- A link is an *actual* relationship between objects of those particular types.

For example, given any Student object X and any Course object Y, there is the *potential* for a link of type *is enrolled in* to exist between those two objects *precisely because* there is an *is enrolled in* association defined between the two classes that those objects belong to. In other words, *associations enable links*.

Most associations arise between two *different* classes; such associations are known as **binary associations.** The *is enrolled in* association, for example, is a binary association, because it interrelates two different classes—Student and Course. A **unary**, or **reflexive**, **association**, on the other hand, is between two instances of the *same class*, for example:

- A Course *is a prerequisite for* (another) Course(s).

- A Professor *supervises* (other) Professor(s).

Even though the two classes specified at either end of a reflexive association are the same, the *objects* are typically different instances of that class:

- Math 101 (a Course object) is a prerequisite for Math 202 (a *different* Course object).

- Professor Smith (a Professor object) supervises Professors Jones and Green (other Professor objects).

Although somewhat rare, there can be situations in which the ***same*** object can serve in both roles of a reflexive relationship. For example, with regard to the association "a Professor ***is the department chair who represents*** other Professors," the actual Professor who is the chair of a given department would be his or her own representative.

Higher order associations are also possible. A **ternary association** involves three classes—for example, "a Student takes a Course from a particular Professor," as illustrated in Figure 5-2.

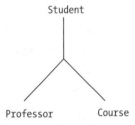

Figure 5-2. *A ternary association*

We typically decompose higher-order associations into an appropriate number of binary associations. We can, for example, represent the preceding three-way association as three binary associations instead (see Figure 5-3):

- A Student ***attends*** a Course.

- A Professor ***teaches*** a Course.

- A Professor ***instructs*** a Student.

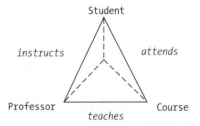

Figure 5-3. *An equivalent representation using three binary associations*

Within a given association, each participant class is said to have a **role**. In the *advises* association ("a Professor *advises* a Student"), the role of the Professor might be said to be "advisor," and the role of the Student might be said to be "advisee."

We only bother to assign names to the roles for the objects participating in an association if it helps to clarify the abstraction. In the *is enrolled in* association ("a Student *is enrolled in* a Course"), there is no need to invent role names for the Student and Course ends of the association, because such role names wouldn't add significantly to the clarity of the abstraction.

Multiplicity

For a given association type X between classes A and B, the term **multiplicity** refers to the number of objects of type A that may be associated with a given instance of type B. For example, a Student attends *multiple* Courses, but a Student has only *one* Professor in the role of advisor.

There are three basic "flavors" of multiplicity: **one-to-one**, **one-to-many**, and **many-to-many**.

One-to-One (1:1)

With a one-to-one (1:1) association, exactly one instance of class A is related to exactly one instance of class B—no fewer, no more, and vice versa. For example:

- A Student has exactly one Transcript, and a Transcript belongs to exactly one Student.

- A Professor chairs exactly one Department, and a Department has exactly one Professor in the role of chairperson.

We can further constrain an association by stating whether the participation of the class at either end is optional or mandatory. For example, we can change the preceding association to read as follows:

- A Professor *optionally* chairs exactly one Department, but it is *mandatory* that a Department has exactly one Professor in the role of chairperson.

This revised version of the association is a more realistic portrayal of real-world circumstances than the previous version. While every department in a university typically does indeed have a chairperson, not every professor is a chairperson of a department—there aren't enough departments to go around! However, it's true that, *if* a professor happens to be a chairperson of a department, then that professor is the chairperson of only *one* department.

One-to-Many (1:m)

In a one-to-many (1:m) association, there can be *many* instances of class B related to a *single* instance of class A in a particular fashion; but, from the perspective of an instance of class B, there can only be *one* instance of class A that is so related. For example:

- A Department employs *many* Professors, but a Professor works for *exactly one* Department.

- A Professor advises *many* Students, but a given Student has *exactly one* Professor as an advisor.

Note that "many" in this case can be interpreted as either "zero or more (optional)" or as "one or more (mandatory)." To be a bit more specific, we can refine the previous one-to-many associations as follows:

- A Department employs *one or more* ("many"; *mandatory*) Professors, but a Professor works for exactly one Department.

- A Professor advises *zero or more* ("many"; *optional*) Students, but a given Student has exactly one Professor as an advisor.

In addition, as with one-to-one relationships, the "one" end of a one-to-many association may also be designated as mandatory or as optional. If we're modeling a university setting in which students aren't required to select an advisor, for example, we'd most likely refine the previous association as follows:

- A Professor advises *zero or more* ("many"; *optional*) Students, but a given Student may *optionally* have *at most one* (i.e., *zero or one*) Professor as an advisor.

Many-to-Many (m:m)

With a many-to-many (m:m) association, a given single instance of class A can have many instances of class B related to it, and vice versa. For example:

- A Student enrolls in many Courses, and a Course has many Students enrolled in it.

- A given Course can have many prerequisite Courses, and a given Course can in turn *be* a prerequisite for many *other* Courses. (This is an example of a many-to-many *reflexive* association.)

As with one-to-many associations, "many" can be interpreted as *zero* or more (*optional*) or as *one* or more (*mandatory*) at either end of an (m:m) association, for example:

- A Student enrolls in *zero or more* ("many"; *optional*) Courses, and a Course has *one or more* ("many"; *mandatory*) Students enrolled in it.

Of course, the validity of a particular association—the classes that are involved, its multiplicity, and the optional or mandatory nature of participation in the association on the part of both participating classes—is wholly dependent on the real-world circumstances being modeled. If you were modeling a university in which departments could have more than one chairperson, or where students could have more than one advisor, your choice of multiplicities would differ from those used in the preceding examples.

Multiplicity and Links

Note that the concept of multiplicity pertains to associations, but not to links. *Links always exist in pairwise fashion between two objects* (or, as mentioned earlier, in rare cases between an object and itself). Therefore, multiplicity in essence defines how many links of a certain association type can originate from a given object. This is best illustrated with an example. Consider once again the many-to-many *is enrolled in* association:

- A Student enrolls in zero or more Courses, and a Course has one or more Students enrolled in it.

A *specific* Student object can have zero, one, or more links to Course objects, but any *one* of those links is between exactly *two* objects: a single Student object and a single Course object. In Figure 5-4, for example:

- Student X has one link (to Course A).

- Student Y has four links (to Courses A, B, C, and D).

- Student Z has no links to any Course objects whatsoever. (Z is taking the semester off!)

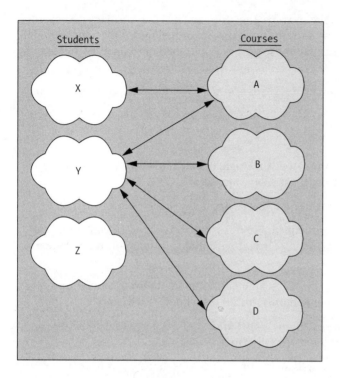

Figure 5-4. *Illustrating a many-to-many association between classes with pairwise links between objects*

Conversely, a ***specific*** Course object must have one or more links to Student objects to satisfy the mandatory nature and multiplicity of the *is enrolled in* association, but again, any ***one*** of those links is between exactly ***two*** objects: a single Course object and a single Student object. In Figure 5-4, for example:

- Course A has two links (to Students X and Y).

- Courses B, C, and D each have one link (to the same Student, Y).

This example scenario does indeed uphold the many-to-many *is enrolled in* association between the Student and Course classes; it's but one of an infinite number of possible scenarios that may exist between the classes in question.

Just to make sure that this concept is clear, let's look at another example, this time using the one-to-one association:

- A Professor ***optionally*** chairs exactly one Department, and it is ***mandatory*** that a Department has exactly one Professor in the role of chairperson.

In Figure 5-5, we see that

- `Professor` objects 1 and 4 each have one link, to `Department` objects A and B, respectively.

- `Professor` objects 2 and 3 have no such links.

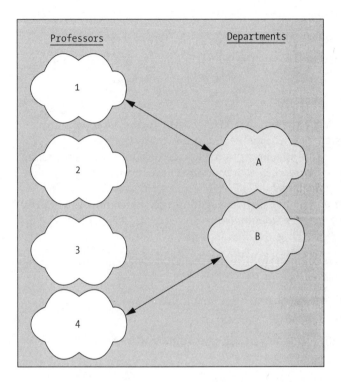

Figure 5-5. *Illustrating a one-to-one association between classes with **binary** links between objects*

Moreover, from the `Department` objects' perspective, each `Department` does indeed have exactly one link to a `Professor`. Therefore, this example upholds the one-to-one *chairs* association between `Professor` and `Department`, while further illustrating the optional nature of the `Professor` class's participation in such links. Again, it's but one of an infinite number of possible scenarios that may exist between the classes in question.

Aggregation and Composition

Aggregation is a special form of association, alternatively referred to as the "consists of", "is composed of", or "has a" relationship. Like an association, an aggregation is used to represent a relationship between two classes, A and B. But, with an aggregation, we're representing more than mere relationship: we're stating that an object belonging to class A, known as an **aggregate**, is composed of, or contains, **component objects** belonging to class B.

For example, a car is composed of an engine, a transmission, four wheels, etc., so if Car, Engine, Transmission, and Wheel were all classes, then we could form the following aggregations:

- A Car ***contains*** an Engine.

- A Car ***contains*** a Transmission.

- A Car ***is composed of*** many (in this case, four) Wheels.

Or, as an example related to the SRS, we can say that

- A University ***is composed of*** many Schools (the School of Engineering, the School of Law, etc.).

- A School ***is composed of*** many Departments.

and so forth. We wouldn't typically say, however, that a Department ***is composed of*** many Professors; instead, we'd probably state that a Department ***employs*** many Professors.

Note that these aggregation statements appear very similar to associations, where the name of the association just so happens to be *is composed of* or *contains*. That's because an aggregation *is* an association in the broad sense of the term!

Why the fuss over trying to differentiate between aggregation and association? If an aggregation is really an association, must we even ***acknowledge*** aggregation as a distinct type of relationship between classes? Strictly speaking, the answer is no.

- There are indeed distinct representations in UML for the notions of aggregation versus association, which we'll discuss in Chapter 10.

- However, as it turns out, both of these abstractions are ultimately rendered in code in precisely the same way.

Thus, it can be argued that it isn't really absolutely necessary to differentiate the notion of aggregation from association.

Nonetheless, it behooves anyone who aspires to become proficient with object modeling and UML to be aware of this subtle distinction, if for no other reason than to be able to communicate effectively with other UML practitioners who are using such notation.

Composition is a strong form of aggregation, in which the "parts" cannot exist without the "whole." As an example, given the relationship "a Book is composed of many Chapters", we could argue that a chapter cannot exist if the book to which it belongs ceases to exist; whereas given the relationship "a Car ***is composed of*** many Wheels", we know that a wheel can be removed from a car and still serve a useful purpose. Thus, we'd categorize the Book–Chapter relationship as ***composition*** and the Car–Wheel relationship as ***aggregation***.

Inheritance

Whereas many of the OO techniques that you've learned for achieving a high degree of code flexibility and maintainability—for example, encapsulation and information hiding—are arguably achievable with non-OO languages in some form or another, the **inheritance** mechanism is what truly sets OO languages apart from their non-OO counterparts.

Before we dive into an in-depth discussion of how inheritance works, let's establish a compelling case for inheritance by looking at the problems that arise in its absence.

Responding to Shifting Requirements with a New Abstraction

Let's assume that we've accurately and thoroughly modeled all of the essential features of students via our Student class, and that we've actually programmed the class in Java. A simplified version of the Student class is as follows:

```java
public class Student {
  private String name;
  private String studentId;
  // etc.

  public String getName() {
    return name;
  }

  public void setName(String n) {
      name = n;
  }

  public String getStudentId() {
    return studentId;
  }

  public void setStudentId (String i) {
      studentId = i;
  }

  // etc.
}
```

Let's further assume that our Student class has been rigorously tested, found to be bug free, and is actually being used in a number of applications: our Student Registration System, for example, as well as perhaps a student billing system and an alumni relations system for the same university.

A new requirement has just arisen for modeling graduate students as a special type of student. As it turns out, the only information about a graduate student that we need to track above and beyond that which we've already modeled for a "generic" student is

- What undergraduate degree the student previously received before entering his or her graduate program of study

- What institution the student received the undergraduate degree from

All of the other features necessary to describe a graduate student—the attributes name, studentId, and so forth, along with the corresponding accessor methods—are the same as those that we've already programmed for the Student class, because a graduate student *is* a student, after all.

How might we approach this new requirement for a GraduateStudent class? If we weren't well versed in object-oriented concepts, we might try one of the following approaches.

(Inappropriate) Approach #1: Modify the Student Class

We could add attributes to our existing Student class to reflect undergraduate degree information, along with "get"/"set" methods for these new attributes, as follows:

```
public class Student {
  private String name;
  private String studentId;
  // We've added two attributes to Student to handle the new requirements for
  // graduate students.
  private String undergraduateDegree;
  private String undergraduateInstitution;
  // etc.

  // We've also added four accessor methods.
  public String getName(...
  public void setName(...
  public String getStudentId(...
  public void setStudentId(...
  public String getUndergraduateDegree(...
  public void setUndergraduateDegree(...
  public String getUndergraduateInstitution(...
  public void setUndergraduateInstitution(...

  // etc.
}
```

Because these new features are not relevant to **all** students—only to graduate students—we'd perhaps simply allow these attributes to remain uninitialized for students who hadn't yet received an undergraduate degree. However, to keep track of whether or not these attributes were supposed to contain values for a given Student object, we'd probably also want to add a boolean attribute to serve as a flag, along with accessor methods for this attribute:

```
public class Student {
  private String name;
  private String studentId;
  private String undergraduateDegree;
  private String undergraduateInstitution;

  // We'll set this next attribute to true if this is a
  // graduate student, false otherwise.
  private boolean graduateStudent;

  // etc.
```

```
public String getName(...
public void setName(...
public String getStudentId(...
public void setStudentId(...
public String getUndergraduateDegree(...
public void setUndergraduateDegree(...
public String getUndergraduateInstitution(...
public void setUndergraduateInstitution(...
public boolean isGraduateStudent(...
public void setGraduateStudent(...

  // etc.
}
```

Finally, in any methods that we've written for this class—or those that we write for this class in the future—we'd have to take the value of this boolean attribute into account:

```
public void display() {
  System.out.println(this.getName());
  System.out.println(this.getStudentId());

  // If a particular student is NOT a graduate student, then the values
  // of the attributes "undergraduateDegree" and "undergraduateInstitution"
  // would be undefined/irrelevant, and so we only want to print them
  // if we are dealing with a GRADUATE student.
  if (this.isGraduateStudent()) {
    System.out.println(this.getUndergraduateDegree());
    System.out.println(this.getUndergraduateInstitution());
  }

  // etc.
}
```

Having to sort out whether or not a given student is a graduate student in each and every Student method (the display method being but one) results in convoluted code that is difficult to debug and maintain. Where this *really* gets messy, however, is if we have to add a third, or a fourth, or a fifth type of "specialized" Student to the mix. For example, consider how complicated the display method would become if we wanted to use it to represent a third type of student: namely, continuing education students, who don't seek a degree, but rather are just taking courses for continuing professional enrichment.

- Perhaps for such students, we'd like to track their current place of employment as an attribute.

- We'd most likely need to add yet another boolean flag as an attribute, as well, to keep track of whether or not a particular Student is a continuing education student.

We'd perhaps extend our Student class once more, as highlighted in **bold** in the following code, to reflect the newly added attributes and accessor methods:

```java
public class Student {
  private String name;
  private String studentId;
  private String undergraduateDegree;
  private String undergraduateInstitution;
  private String placeOfEmployment;
  private boolean graduateStudent;
  private boolean continuingEdStudent;
  // etc.

  public String getName(...
  public void setName(...
  public String getStudentId(...
  public void setStudentId(...
  public String getUndergraduateDegree(...
  public void setUndergraduateDegree(...
  public String getUndergraduateInstitution(...
  public void setUndergraduateInstitution(...
  public boolean isGraduateStudent(...
  public void setGraduateStudent(...
  public boolean isContinuingEdStudent(...
  public void setContinuingEdStudent(...

  // etc.
}
```

We also now must take the value of the `boolean isContinuingEdStudent` attribute into account in all of the Student methods involving the notion of `placeOfEmployment`. Take a look at how this impacts the logic of the `display` method:

```java
public void display() {
  System.out.println(this.getName());
  System.out.println(this.getStudentId());
  // etc.

  if (this.isGraduateStudent()) {
    System.out.println(this.getUndergraduateDegree());
    System.out.println(this.getUndergraduateInstitution());
  }

  if (this.isContinuingEdStudent()) {
    System.out.println(this.getPlaceOfEmployment());
  }

  // etc.
}
```

Now, imagine how much *more* "spaghetti-like" our code might become if we had *dozens* of different student types to accommodate. ***Approach #1 is clearly not the answer***! The underlying flaw with this approach is that we're trying too hard to force a *single* abstraction, Student, to represent ***multiple*** real-world object types. While graduate students, continuing education students, and "generic" students certainly have some features in common, they are nonetheless ***different*** types of object.

(Inappropriate) Approach #2: "Clone" the Student Class to Create a GraduateStudent Class

We could instead create a new GraduateStudent class by ***copying*** the code of Student.java to create GraduateStudent.java, renaming the latter class GraduateStudent, and then adding the extra features required of a graduate student to the ***copy***.

Here's the resultant GraduateStudent class:

```java
// GraduateStudent.java

public class GraduateStudent {
    // Student attributes DUPLICATED!
    private String name;
    private String birthDate;
    // etc.

    // Add the two new attributes required of a GraduateStudent.
    private String undergraduateDegree;
    private String undergraduateInstitution;

    // Student methods DUPLICATED!
    public String getName(...
    public void setName(...
    public String getBirthDate(...
    public void setBirthDate(...
    // etc.

    // Add the new accessor methods required of a GraduateStudent.
    public String getUndergraduateDegree(...
    public void setUndergraduateDegree(...
    public String getUndergraduateInstitution(...
    public void setUndergraduateInstitution(...
}
```

This would be a very poor design, since we'd have much of the same code in two places: Student.java and GraduateStudent.java. If we wanted to change how a particular method worked or how an attribute was defined later on—say, a change of the type of the birthDate attribute from String to Date, with a corresponding change to the accessor methods for that attribute—then we'd have to make the same changes in ***both*** classes. Again, this problem quickly gets compounded if we've defined three, or four, or a ***dozen*** different types of Student, all created as "clones" of the original Student class; the code maintenance burden would quickly become excessive. ***Approach #2 is clearly not the answer, either***!

Strictly speaking, either of the preceding two approaches would work, but the inherent redundancy/complexity of the resultant code would make the application prohibitively difficult to maintain. Unfortunately, with non-OO languages, such convoluted approaches would typically be our ***only*** options for handling the requirement for a new type of object. It's no wonder that applications become so complicated and expensive to maintain as requirements inevitably evolve over time. Fortunately, we do have yet another very powerful approach that we can take specific to OO programming languages: we can take advantage of the mechanism of **inheritance**.

The Proper Approach (#3): Taking Advantage of Inheritance

With an object-oriented programming language, we can solve the problem of specializing the Student class by harnessing the power of **inheritance**, a mechanism for defining a new class by stating only the differences (in terms of features) between the new class and another class that we've already established.

Using inheritance, we can declare a new class named GraduateStudent that inherits all of the features of the Student class "as is." The GraduateStudent class would then only have to specify the two extra attributes associated with a graduate student—undergraduateDegree and undergraduateInstitution—plus their accessor methods, as shown in the following GraduateStudent class. Note that inheritance is triggered in a Java class declaration using the extends keyword: public class *NewClass* extends *ExistingClass* { ....

```
public class GraduateStudent extends Student {
    // Declare two new attributes above and beyond
    // what the Student class has already declared ...

    private String undergraduateDegree;
    private String undergraduateInstitution;

    // ... and accessor methods for each of these new attributes.

    public String getUndergraduateDegree {
        return undergraduateDegree;
    }

    public void setUndergraduateDegree(String s) {
        undergraduateDegree = s;
    }

    public String getUndergraduateInstitution {
        return undergraduateInstitution;
    }

    public void setUndergraduateInstitution(String s) {
        undergraduateInstitution = s;
    }

    // That's the ENTIRE GraduateStudent class declaration!
    // Short and sweet!
}
```

That's all we need to declare in establishing our new GraduateStudent class: two attributes plus the associated four accessor methods. There is no need to duplicate any of the features of the Student class within the code of GraduateStudent, because we're automatically inheriting these. It's as if we had "plagiarized" the code for the attributes and methods of the Student class, copying this code from Student and pasting it into GraduateStudent, but without the fuss of actually having done so. The GraduateStudent class thus has $n + 6$ features: the six features that are explicitly declared within the GraduateStudent.java file plus n more that are inherited from Student.

When we take advantage of inheritance, the original class that we're starting from—Student, in this case—is called the (**direct**) **superclass.** The new class—GraduateStudent—is called a (**direct**) **subclass.** A subclass is said to **extend** its direct superclass.

The "is a" Nature of Inheritance

Inheritance is often referred to as the "is a" relationship between two classes, because if a class B (GraduateStudent) is derived from a class A (Student), then B truly *is a* special case of A. Anything that we can say about a superclass must therefore also be true about all of its subclasses; that is,

- A Student attends classes, and so a GraduateStudent attends classes.

- A Student has an advisor, and so a GraduateStudent has an advisor.

- A Student pursues a degree, and so a GraduateStudent pursues a degree.

In fact, an "acid test" for legitimate use of inheritance is as follows: *if there is something that can be said about a class A that can't be said about a proposed subclass B, then B really isn't a valid subclass of A.*

Because subclasses are special cases of their superclasses, the term **specialization** is used to refer to the process of deriving one class from another. **Generalization**, on the other hand, is a term used to refer to the opposite process: namely, recognizing the common features of several existing classes and creating a new, common superclass for them all.

Let's say we now wish to declare a Professor class to complement our Student class. Students and Professors have some features in common: attributes name, birthDate, etc., and the methods that manipulate these attributes. Yet, they each have unique features, as well:

- The Professor class might require the attributes title (a String) and worksFor (a reference to a Department).

- Conversely, the Student class's studentID, degreeSought, and majorField attributes are irrelevant for a Professor.

Because each class has attributes that the other would find useless, neither class can be derived from the other. Nonetheless, to *duplicate* their common attribute declarations and method code in two places would be very inefficient. In such a circumstance, we'd want to invent a new superclass called Person, consolidate the features common to both Students and Professors in the Person class, and then have Student and Professor inherit these common features by extending Person. The resultant code in this situation follows.

First, we'll define the Person superclass in a file named Person.java:

```java
// Person.java

public class Person {
  // Attributes common to Students and Professors.
  private String name;
  private String address;
  private String birthDate;

  // Common accessor methods.

  public String getName() {
      return name;
  }

  public void setName(String n) {
      name = n;
  }

  // etc. for the other attributes

  // Other general-purpose Person methods, if any, would go here - details omitted.
}
```

Next, we'll streamline our Student class as previously presented to remove those features that it will now inherit from Person:

```java
// Student.java

public class Student extends Person {
  // Attributes specific only to a Student; redundant attributes - i.e., those
  // that are shared with Professor, and hence are now declared by Person - have
  // been REMOVED from Student.
  private String studentId;
  private String majorField;
  private String degreeSought;

  // Student-specific accessor methods - redundant methods have been removed.

  public String getStudentId() {
      return studentId;
  }

  public void setStudentId(String i) {
      studentId = i;
  }

  // etc. for the other explicitly declared Student attributes.

  // Other Student-specific methods go here, if any; details omitted.
}
```

Finally, we'll define the second new (sub)class, Professor. This class would go into a separate Professor.java file:

```
// Professor.java

public class Professor extends Person {
  // Attributes specific only to a Professor; redundant attributes - i.e., those
  // that are shared with Student, and hence are now declared by Person - are
  // not included here.
  private String title;
  private Department worksFor;

  // Professor-specific accessor methods go here.

  public String getTitle() {
      return title;
  }

  public void setTitle(String t) {
      title = t;
  }

  // etc. for the other explicitly declared Professor attributes.

  // Other Professor-specific methods go here, if any; details omitted.
}
```

By generalizing the shared features of Students and Professors into a common superclass called Person, we'll easily be able to introduce a third type of Person, or a fourth, or a fifth, if needed in the future, and they'll all *share in these same features* through the mechanism of inheritance. Furthermore, if we wish to introduce new subtypes of these subclasses—perhaps AdjunctProfessor and TenuredProfessor as subclasses of the Professor class—they'll all derive a common set of features as a result of their shared Person "ancestry."

The Benefits of Inheritance

Inheritance is perhaps one of the most powerful and unique aspects of an OO programming language for the following reasons:

- *We dramatically reduce code redundancy*, thus lessening the burden of code maintenance when requirements change or logic flaws are detected.

- *Subclasses are much more succinct than they would be without inheritance.* A subclass contains only the essence of what differentiates it from its direct superclass. We know from looking at the GraduateStudent class definition, for example, that a graduate student is "a student who already holds an undergraduate degree from an educational institution." As a result, *the total body of code for a given OO application is significantly reduced* as compared with the traditional/non-OO version of the same application.

- *Through inheritance, we can reuse and extend code that has already been thoroughly tested without modifying it*. As you saw, we were able to invent a new class—GraduateStudent—without disturbing the Student class code in any way. We can therefore rest assured that any client code that relies on instantiating generic Student objects and passing messages to them will be unaffected by the creation of subclass GraduateStudent, and thus we avoid having to retest huge portions of our existing application(s). (Had we used a non-OO approach of "tinkering" with the Student class code to try to accommodate graduate student requirements, on the other hand, we would have had to retest our entire existing application to make sure that nothing had "broken"!)

- *Best of all, we can derive a new class from an existing class even if we don't own the source code for the latter!* As long as we have the *compiled bytecode version* of a class, the inheritance mechanism works just fine; we don't need the original source code of a class in order to extend it. *This is one of the most dramatic ways to achieve productivity with an object-oriented language*: find a class (either one written by someone else or one that is built into the language) that does much of what you need, and create a subclass of that class, adding just those features that you need for your own purposes.

We'll look at a specific example of extending one of the predefined Java collection classes in Chapter 6.

- Finally, as we discussed in Chapter 1, *classification is the natural way that humans organize information*; so, it only makes sense that we'd organize software along the same lines, making it much more intuitive and hence easier to develop, maintain, extend, and communicate with users about.

Class Hierarchies

Over time, we build up an inverted tree of classes that are interrelated through inheritance; such a tree is called a **class hierarchy**. One such class hierarchy example is shown in Figure 5-6. Note that arrows are used to point *upward* from each subclass to its direct superclass.

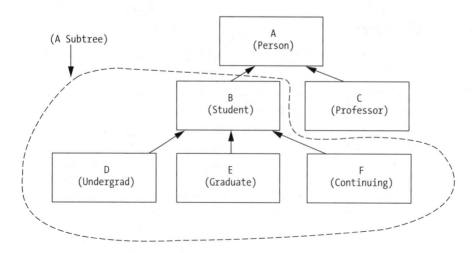

Figure 5-6. *A sample class hierarchy*

A bit of nomenclature follows:

- We may refer to each class as a **node** in the hierarchy.

- Any given node in the hierarchy is said to be (directly or indirectly) ***derived from*** all of the nodes above it in the hierarchy, known collectively as its **ancestors**.

- The ancestor that is ***immediately*** above a given node in the hierarchy is considered to be that node's direct superclass.

- Conversely, all nodes below a given node in the hierarchy are said to be its **descendants**.

- The node that sits at the top of the hierarchy is referred to as the **root node**.

- A **terminal**, or **leaf**, **node**, is one that has no descendants.

- Two nodes that are derived from the same direct superclass are known as **siblings**.

Applying this terminology to the example hierarchy in Figure 5-6,

- Class A (Person) is the root node of the entire hierarchy.

- Classes B, C, D, E, and F are all said to be derived from class A, and thus are all descendants of A.

- Classes D, E, and F can be said to be derived from class B.

- Classes D, E, and F are siblings; so are classes B and C.

- Class D has two ancestors, B (its direct superclass) and A.

- Classes C, D, E, and F are terminal nodes, in that they don't have any classes derived from them (as of yet, at any rate).

As with any hierarchy, this one may evolve over time:

- It may ***widen*** with the addition of new siblings/branches in the tree.

- It may ***expand downward*** as a result of future specialization.

- It may ***expand upward*** as a result of future generalization.

Such changes to the hierarchy are made as new requirements emerge, or as our understanding of the existing requirements improves. For example, we may determine the need for MastersStudent and PhDStudent classes as specializations of GraduateStudent, or of an Administrator class as a sibling to Student and Professor. This would yield the revised hierarchy shown in Figure 5-7.

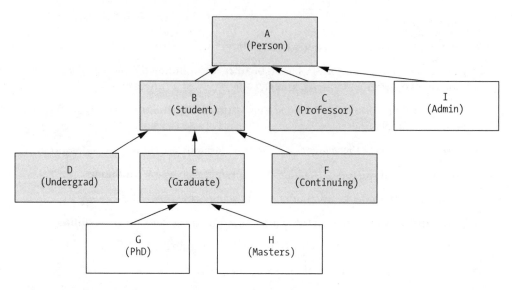

Figure 5-7. *Class hierarchies inevitably expand over time.*

The Object Class

In the Java language, the built-in `Object` class serves as the ultimate superclass for all other reference types, both user-defined as well as those built into the language. Even when a class is not explicitly declared to extend `Object`, such extension is implied. That is, when we declare a class as follows:

```
public class Person { ... }
```

it is as if we've written

```
public class Person extends Object { ... }
```

without having to explicitly do so. And, when we write

```
public class Student extends Person { ... }
```

then, because the `Person` class is derived from `Object`, `Student` is derived from `Object` as well. Thus, the ***true*** root of the hierarchy illustrated in Figure 5-5—and of ***all*** class hierarchies—is the `Object` class.

We'll talk in depth about the significance of the `Object` class, and the fact that all Java objects are ultimately descended from `Object`, in Chapter 13.

Is Inheritance Really a Relationship?

Association, aggregation, and inheritance are all said to be relationships between ***classes***. Where inheritance differs from association and aggregation is at the ***object*** level.

As you saw earlier in this chapter, association (and aggregation, as a special form of association) can be said to relate individual objects, in the sense that two different objects are linked to one another by virtue of the existence of an association between their respective classes. Inheritance, on the other hand, does *not* involve linking distinct objects; rather, inheritance is a way of describing the collective features of a *single object*. With inheritance, an object is *simultaneously* an instance of a subclass and all of its superclasses: a GraduateStudent is a Student that is a Person that is an Object, all wrapped into one!

So, in looking once again at the hierarchy of Figure 5-5, we see that

- *All* classes in the hierarchy—class A (Person) as well as all of its descendants B through I—may be thought of as yielding Person objects.

- Class B (Student), along with its descendants D through H, may all be thought of as yielding Student objects.

This notion of an object having "multiple identities" is a significant one that we'll revisit several times throughout the book.

So, getting back to the question posed as the title of this section: inheritance is indeed a relationship between *classes*, but *not* between distinct *objects*.

Avoiding "Ripple Effects" in a Class Hierarchy

Once a class hierarchy is established and an application has been coded, changes to *non*-leaf classes (i.e., those classes that have descendants) have the potential to introduce undesired ripple effects further down the hierarchy. For example, if after we've established the GraduateStudent class, we go back and add a minorField attribute to the Student class, then the GraduateStudent class will automatically inherit this new attribute. Perhaps this is what we want; on the other hand, we may not have anticipated the derivation of a GraduateStudent class when we first conceived of Student, and so this may *not* be what we want!

As the developers of the Student superclass, it would be *ideal* if we could speak with the developers of all derived classes—GraduateStudent, MastersStudent, and PhDStudent—to obtain their approval for any proposed changes to Student. But, this is typically not practical; in fact, we often don't even *know* that our class has been extended if, for example, our code is being distributed and reused on other projects. This evokes a general rule of thumb:

> *Whenever possible, avoid adding features to non-leaf classes once they have been established in code form in an application, to avoid ripple effects throughout an inheritance hierarchy.*

This is easier said than done! However, it reinforces the importance of spending as much time as possible on the requirements analysis and object modeling stages of an OO application development project before diving into the coding stage. This won't prevent new requirements from emerging over time, but we should at least do everything possible to avoid oversights regarding the *current* requirements.

Rules for Deriving Classes: The "Do's"

When deriving a new class, we can do several things to specialize the superclass that we are starting out with.

- We may **extend** the superclass by **adding features**. In our GraduateStudent example, we added six features: two attributes—undergraduateDegree and undergraduateInstitution—and four accessor methods —get/setUndergraduateDegree and get/setUndergraduateInstitution.

- We also may **specialize** the way that a subclass performs one or more of the **services** inherited from its superclass.

For example, when a "generic" student enrolls for a course, the business rules for the SRS may require us to ensure that

- The student has taken the necessary prerequisite courses.

- The course is required for the degree that the student is seeking.

When a **graduate student** enrolls for a course, on the other hand, the business rules may involve doing both of these things as well as ensuring that the student's graduate committee feels that the course is appropriate.

Specializing the way that a subclass performs a service—that is, how it responds to a given message as compared with the way that its superclass would have responded to the same message—is accomplished via a technique known as **overriding**.

Overriding

Overriding involves "rewiring" how a method works internally, without changing the client code interface to/signature of that method. For example, let's say that we've defined a print method for the Student class to print out the values of all of a Student's attributes:

```
public class Student {
  // Attributes.
  private String name;
  private String studentId;
  private String majorField;
  private double gpa;
  // etc.


  // Accessor methods for each attribute would also be provided; details omitted.

  public void print() {
    // Print the values of all of the attributes that the Student class
    // knows about.  (Remember: "\n" is a newline.)
    System.out.println("Student Name:   " + this.getName() + "\n" +
                       "Student No.:   " + this.getStudentId() + "\n" +
                       "Major Field:   " + this.getMajorField() + "\n" +
                       "GPA:   " + this.getGpa());
  }
}
```

By virtue of inheritance, all of the subclasses of Student will inherit this method.

We go on to derive the GraduateStudent subclass from Student, adding two attributes to GraduateStudent—undergraduateDegree and undergraduateInstitution. If we take the "lazy" approach of just letting GraduateStudent inherit the print method of Student as is, then whenever we invoke the print method for a GraduateStudent, all that will be printed are the values of the four attributes inherited from Student—name, studentId, major, and gpa—because these are the only attributes that the print method has been explicitly programmed to print the values of. Ideally, we would like the print method, when invoked for a GraduateStudent, to print these same four attributes *plus* the two additional attributes of undergraduateDegree and undergraduateInstitution.

With an object-oriented language, we are able to *override*, or supersede, the superclass's version of a method with a subclass-specific version. To override a superclass's method in Java rather than merely inheriting the method as is, the header of the method as declared in the superclass must be repeated in the subclass; we are then free to reprogram the *body* of that method in the subclass to specialize its behavior.

Let's look at how the GraduateStudent class would go about overriding the print method of the Student class. For your convenience, I've repeated the code of the Student class here:

```java
public class Student {
  // Attributes.
  private String name;
  private String studentId;
  private String majorField;
  private double gpa;
  // etc.

  // Accessor methods for each attribute would also be provided; details omitted.

  public void print() {
    // Print the values of all the attributes that the Student class
    // knows about; again, note the use of accessor methods.
    System.out.println("Student Name:  " + this.getName() + "\n" +
                       "Student No.:  " + this.getStudentId() + "\n" +
                       "Major Field:  " + this.getMajorField() + "\n" +
                       "GPA:  " + this.getGpa());
  }
}


//-----------------------------------------------


public class GraduateStudent extends Student {
  private String undergraduateDegree;
  private String undergraduateInstitution;

  // Accessor methods for each newly added attribute would also be provided;
  // details omitted.

  // We are overriding the Student class's print method; note that
  // we've repeated the print method header verbatim from the
  // Student class, which triggers overriding.
  public void print() {
```

```
    // We print the values of all of the attributes that the
    // GraduateStudent class knows about:  namely, those that it
    // inherited from Student plus those that it explicitly declares above.
    System.out.println("Student Name:  " + this.getName() + "\n" +
                       "Student No.:  " + this.getStudentId() + "\n" +
                       "Major Field:  " + this.getMajorField() + "\n" +
                       "GPA:  " + this.getGpa() + "\n" +
                       "Undergrad. Deg.:  " + this.getUndergraduateDegree() +
                       "\n" + "Undergrad. Inst.:  " +
                       this.getUndergraduateInstitution());
  }
}
```

The GraduateStudent class's version of print thus overrides, or supersedes, the version that would otherwise have been inherited from the Student class.

In a complex inheritance hierarchy, we often have occasion to override a given method multiple times. In the hierarchy shown in Figure 5-8,

- Root class A (Person) declares a method with the header public void print() that prints out all of the attributes declared for the Person class.

- Subclass B (Student) overrides this method, changing the internal logic of the method body to print not only the attributes inherited from Person, but also those that were added by the Student class itself.

- Subclass E (GraduateStudent) overrides this method again, to print not only the attributes inherited from Student (which include those inherited from Person), but also those that were added by the GraduateStudent class itself.

Note that, in all cases, the method signature ***must*** remain the same—print()—for overriding to take place.

The only permitted change that can be made when overriding a method is with regard to its accessibility. That is, given the following example:

```
public class Super {
    // Details omitted.
    accessibility void methodX() { ... }
}

public class Sub extends Super {
    // Details omitted.

    // Override methodX() { ... }
    accessibility void methodX() { ... }
}
```

the accessibility granted to methodX in the subclass cannot be more restrictive than the accessibility of the corresponding method in the superclass. For example, a subclass may override what was a private method in its superclass to assign it public accessibility in the subclass, but not vice versa.

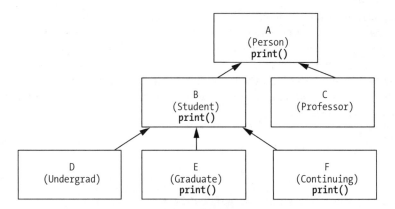

Figure 5-8. *A method may be overridden multiple times within a class hierarchy.*

Under such circumstances, any class not specifically overriding a given method itself will inherit the definition of that method used by its most immediate ancestor. Thus,

- Classes C and D in Figure 5-8 inherit the versions of print() that are defined by A and B, respectively.

- F is therefore overriding the print() method of A as inherited by C.

Reusing Superclass Behaviors: The "super" Keyword

The preceding example of overriding is less than ideal because the first four lines of the print method of GraduateStudent duplicated the code from the Student class's version of print. Here's the Student version of the method once again:

```
public void print() {
    // Print the values of all the attributes that the Student class
    // knows about; again, note the use of accessor methods.
    System.out.println("Student Name:  " + this.getName() + "\n" +
                    "Student No.:  " + this.getStudentId() + "\n" +
                    "Major Field:  " + this.getMajorField() + "\n" +
                    "GPA:  " + this.getGpa());
}
```

and here's the GraduateStudent version:

```
public void print() {
    // This code is repeated from the Student version!
    System.out.println("Student Name:  " + this.getName() + "\n" +
                    "Student No.:  " + this.getStudentId() + "\n" +
                    "Major Field:  " + this.getMajorField() + "\n" +
                    "GPA:  " + this.getGpa() + "\n" +
                    "Undergrad. Deg.:  " + this.getUndergraduateDegree() + "\n" +
                    "Undergrad. Inst.:  " + this.getUndergraduateInstitution());
}
```

Redundancy in an application is to be avoided whenever possible, because redundant code represents a maintenance headache. When we have to change code in one place in an application, we don't want to have to remember to change it in countless other places or, worse yet, forget to do so, and wind up with inconsistency in our logic.

Fortunately, Java provides a way for us to have our cake and eat it too—that is, a way for us to *override* the print method while *simultaneously reusing its code*. We'd code the print method for the GraduateStudent class as follows:

```java
public class GraduateStudent extends Student {
  // Details omitted.

  public void print() {
    // Reuse code by calling the print method as defined by the Student
    // superclass ...
    super.print();

    // ... and then go on to do something extra - namely, print this derived
    // class's specific attributes.
    System.out.println("Undergrad. Deg.:  " + this.getUndergraduateDegree() + "\n" +
                       "Undergrad. Inst.:  " + this.getUndergraduateInstitution());
  }
}
```

We use the Java keyword super as the qualifier for a method call:

```java
super.methodName(arguments);
```

whenever we wish to invoke the version of method *methodName* that was defined by our superclass. That is, in the preceding example, we're essentially saying to the compiler, "First, execute the print method the way that the superclass, Student, would have executed it, and then do something extra—namely, print out the values of the new GraduateStudent attributes."

Note that the syntax

```java
super.methodName(arguments);
```

involves *invoking* one method from within another. Let's look at a slightly more involved example to emphasize this syntax.

We'll start with this superclass declaration:

```java
public class Superclass {
    public void foo(int x, int y) { ... }
}
```

and will derive this subclass from it:

```java
public class Subclass extends Superclass {
    // We're overriding the foo method.
    // (Note that we're using a and b as parameter names here to override
    // parameters x and y in the superclass; this is perfectly fine as long
    // as their types are identical.)
```

```
    public void foo(int a, int b) {
        // Details to follow ...
    }
}
```

We have numerous options as to how we might use the super keyword within the overridden foo method of a subclass, as illustrated by the **bolded** passages (and corresponding comments) in the examples that follow:

```
public class Subclass extends Superclass {
    // We're overriding the foo method.
    public void foo(int a, int b) {
        // We can pass the argument values a and b through to our superclass's
        // version of foo ...
        super.foo(a, b);
    }
}
```

or

```
public class Subclass extends Superclass {
    // We're overriding the foo method.
    public void foo(int a, int b) {
        int x = 2;  // a local variable

        // We can pass selected argument values through to our superclass's
        // version of foo ...
        super.foo(a, x);
    }
}
```

or even

```
public class Subclass extends Superclass {
    // We're overriding the foo method.
    public void foo(int a, int b) {
        int x = 2;  // a local variable

        // Here, we're using neither a nor b as an argument.
        super.foo(x, 3);
    }
}
```

Note that our invocation of super.foo(...) can occur anywhere within the method:

```
public class Subclass extends Superclass {
    // We're overriding the foo method.
    public void foo(int a, int b) {
        // Pseudocode.
        do some stuff;
```

```
        super.foo(a, b);

        // Pseudocode.
        do more stuff;
    }
}
```

And, if foo were declared to have a non-void return type in Superclass—say, int—we could even return the result of calling super.foo(...):

```
public class Subclass extends Superclass {
    // We're overriding the foo method (here, we
    // assume that foo was declared with an int return
    // type in the superclass).
    public int foo(int a, int b) {
        int x = 3 * a;
        int y = 17 * b;
        return super.foo(x, y);
    }
}
```

The bottom line is we can use super.*methodName*(...) in whatever way makes sense in carrying out a subclass's version of the method that is being overridden.

Another important use of the super keyword has to do with reusing constructor code; we'll learn about this alternative use of super later in this chapter.

Rules for Deriving Classes: The "Don'ts"

When deriving a new class, there are some things that we should ***not*** attempt to do. (And, as it turns out, OO language compilers will actually prevent us from successfully compiling programs that attempt to do most of these things.)

We shouldn't change the semantics—that is, the intention, or meaning—of a feature. For example:

- If the print method of a superclass such as Student is intended to display the values of all of an object's attributes in the command window, then the print method of a subclass such as GraduateStudent shouldn't, for example, be overridden so that it directs all of its output to a file instead.

- If the name attribute of a superclass such as Person is intended to store a person's name in "last name, first name" order, then the name attribute of a subclass such as Student should be used in the same fashion.

We can't physically eliminate features, nor should we effectively eliminate them by ignoring them. To attempt to do so would break the spirit of the "is a" hierarchy. By definition, inheritance requires that ***all*** features of ***all*** ancestors of a class A must also apply to class A itself in order for A to truly be a proper subclass. If a GraduateStudent could eliminate the degreeSought attribute that it inherits from Student, for example, is a GraduateStudent ***really*** a Student after all? Strictly speaking, the answer is no.

Furthermore, from a practical standpoint, if we effectively disable a method by overriding it with a "do nothing" version, as illustrated in the following BadStudent example,

```
public class Student {
    // Details omitted.
    public void printStudentInfo() {
        // Pseudocode.
        print all attribute values ...
    }
}

public class BadStudent extends Student {
    // Details omitted.
    // We're overriding the printStudentInfo method of Student by
    // "stubbing it out" - that is, by providing it with an EMPTY method
    // body, so that it effectively does NOTHING.
    // (Note that this WILL compile!)
    public void printStudentInfo() { }
}
```

someone else might wish to derive a subclass from *our* subclass later on:

```
public class NaiveStudent extends BadStudent { ...
```

assuming that they'll inherit a *meaningful* version of printStudentInfo from our BadStudent superclass. This is a reasonable thing for them to assume, given the "all or nothing" nature of inheritance, especially if this other person doesn't have access to the *source code* of BadStudent to look at. Unfortunately, because we've broken the spirit of the "is a" relationship in the way that we've compromised the printStudentInfo method, we've burdened them—and anyone else who might choose to derive a class from BadStudent—with a "defective" method. *The bottom line is, never do this*!

Finally, *we shouldn't attempt to change a method's signature when we override it*. For example, if the print method inherited by the Student class from Person has the signature print(), then the Student class can't change this method's header to accept an argument, say, print(int noOfCopies). To do so is to create a different method entirely, due to another language feature known as **overloading**, a concept that we discussed in Chapter 4. That is, in the following example,

```
public class Person {
    // Details omitted.
    public void print() { ... }
}

public class Student extends Person {
    // Details omitted.
    // We're naively trying to modify the print method signature here.
    public void print(int noOfCopies) { ... }
}
```

the Student class will wind up with *two* overloaded versions of the print method: the version that it has explicitly declared to take one int argument plus the parameterless version that it has inherited from the Person class.

Private Features and Inheritance

As mentioned earlier, inheritance is an "all or nothing" proposition. That is, if class Y is declared to be a subclass of class X

```
public class Y extends X { ... }
```

then Y cannot pick and choose which features of X it will inherit. In particular, while all of the attributes declared by X will become an inherent part of the "bone structure" of all objects of type Y, some of the attributes of superclass X may not be inherited by Y, so they are not *directly referenceable* by name within subclass Y, depending on what accessibility the attributes were assigned in the superclass.

Consider the following code:

```
public class Person {
  <accessibility modifier> int age;
  // Other details omitted.
}
```

You learned about two types of accessibility in Chapter 4: public and private. As it turns out, there are actually *three* different explicit accessibility modifier keywords in Java. That is, *<accessibility modifier>* can be one of the following:

- private

- public

- protected (an accessibility modifier that is only relevant within a superclass/subclass relationship, as you'll see shortly)

If the accessibility modifier is omitted entirely, a feature has what is known as **package visibility** by default. We'll discuss this notion in Chapter 13.

Suppose that we were to derive the Student class from Person as follows:

```
public class Student extends Person {
  // Details omitted.

  // We declare a method that manipulates the age attribute.
  public boolean isOver65( ) {
    if (age > 65) return true;
    else return false;
  }

  // Other details omitted.
}
```

What will happen when we try to compile this Student class? The answer to this question depends on what accessibility was granted to the age attribute when it was declared in the Person class.

If age is declared to be private in Person, as most attributes typically are

```
public class Person {
  private int age;
  // etc.
}
```

then we'll encounter a compilation error on the line of code **highlighted** in the following code for the Student class:

```
public class Student extends Person {
  // Details omitted.

  public boolean isOver65( ) {
    if (age > 65) return true;   // this won't compile!
    else return false;
  }

  // Other details omitted.
}
```

The error message will be

```
cannot find symbol
symbol:    variable age
location:  class Student
if (age > 65) return true;
    ^
```

Why is this? Since the age attribute is declared to be private in Person, the symbol age is not inherited, so it is not in scope within the Student class. Yet, the memory allocated for a Student object when it is instantiated does indeed allow for storage of a student's age, because as mentioned earlier, it is part of the "bone structure" of a Person, and a Student *is a* Person by virtue of inheritance.

What can we do to get around this roadblock? It turns out that we have three choices in Java.

Option #1: We can change the accessibility of age to be public in Person:

```
public class Person {
  public int age;
  // etc.
}
```

thus making it inherited and directly accessible by name in the Student subclass. The line of code that previously generated a compiler error in our Student subclass, namely,

```
if (age > 65) return true;
```

would now compile without error. The downside of this approach, however, is that by making the age attribute public in Person, we'd thus be allowing ***client code*** to freely access the age attribute, as well:

```
public class Example {
    public static void main(String[] args) {
        Student s = new Student();
        // Details omitted.
        s.age = 23; // This would compile, but is undesirable.
    }
}
```

This is, generally speaking, a bad practice, for the reasons discussed at length in Chapter 4.

Option #2: We could modify the accessibility of age to be protected in Person:

```
public class Person {
    protected int age;
    // etc.
}
```

protected accessibility is a sort of "middle ground" between private and public accessibility, in that protected features are inherited by/*in scope* within subclasses; that is, age would now be recognized as a symbol in the Student class, such that

```
if (age > 65) return true;
```

would compile in Student. However, protected features are *not* accessible by classes that *aren't* derived from the superclass. For example, the following would not compile:

```
public class Example {
    public static void main(String[] args) {
        Student s = new Student();
        // Details omitted.
        s.age = 23; // This would NOT compile if age were declared to be
                    // protected in Person.
    }
}
```

This would be a step in the right direction, but unfortunately requires us to modify the source code of the Person class, which we'd like to avoid if at all possible. Furthermore, we may not even *have* the Person source code at our disposal.

Option #3: The *best* approach is to allow age to *remain* a private attribute of Person, but to use the *publicly accessible* getAge/setAge methods that we inherit from the Person class to manipulate the value of a Student's age:

```
public class Person {
    // Let's allow age to REMAIN private!
    private int age;
    // etc.

    // We assume that Person declares public
    // get/set methods for age ... details omitted.
}

public class Student extends Person {
    public boolean isOver65( ) {
```

```
    // All is well!  We're using our publicly inherited getAge
    // method to access our Student's age.
    if (this.getAge() > 65) return true;
    else return false;
  }
}
```

As we first learned in Chapter 4, it is considered a best practice to always use a class's own "get" and "set" methods to access its attribute values from within its own methods. By doing so, we take advantage of any special processing that the "get"/"set" methods might provide relative to that attribute. You've just learned yet another reason why doing so is a best practice when inheritance is involved.

And, if we **_don't_** inherit a `public` "get"/"set" method with which to access a `private` attribute declared by a superclass, then we can argue that we ought not to be "tinkering" with such an attribute in the first place!

Inheritance and Constructors

You learned about constructors as special procedures used to instantiate objects in Chapter 4. Now that you've learned about inheritance, there are a number of complexities with regard to constructors in the context of inheritance hierarchies that I'd like to alert you to.

Constructors Are Not Inherited

Constructors are not inherited. This raises some interesting challenges that are best illustrated via an example.

Let's start by declaring a constructor for the Person class that takes two arguments:

```
public class Person {
  String name;
  String ssn;

  // Other details omitted.

  public Person(String n, String s) {
    // Initialize our attributes.
    this.setName(n);
    this.setSsn(s);

    // Pseudocode.
    do other complex things related to instantiating a Person
  }
}
```

We know from our discussion of constructors in Chapter 4 that the Person class now only recognizes one constructor signature—that which takes two arguments—because the default parameterless constructor has been eliminated. (We'll return to discuss the implications of this with regard to inheritance in a moment.)

Next, let's derive the Student class from Person, declaring ***two*** constructors—one that takes two arguments and one that takes three arguments:

```
public class Student extends Person {
  private String major;

  // Other details omitted.

  // Constructor with two arguments.
  public Student(String n, String s) {
    // Note the redundancy of logic between this constructor and
    // the Person constructor - we'll come back and fix this in a
    // moment.

    // Initialize our attributes.
    this.setName(n);
    this.setSsn(s);
    this.setMajor("UNDECLARED");

    // Pseudocode.
    do other complex things related to instantiating a Person ...
    ... and still more complex things related to instantiating a Student
    specifically.

  }

  // Constructor with three arguments.
  public Student(String n, String s, String m) {
    // More redundancy!

    // Initialize our attributes.
    this.setName(n);
    this.setSsn(s);
    this.setMajor(m);

    // Pseudocode.
    do other complex things related to instantiating a Person ...
    ... and still more complex things related to instantiating a Student
    specifically.
  }
}
```

As a result of having declared explicit constructors, the Student class has also lost its default parameterless constructor.

The first thing that we notice is that we've duplicated code that was provided by the Person constructor in ***both*** of the constructors for the Student class.

```
    // Initialize our attributes.
    this.setName(n);
    this.setSsn(s);

    // Pseudocode.
    do other complex things related to instantiating a Person ...
```

As I've said numerous times before, code redundancy is to be avoided in an application whenever possible; fortunately, Java provides us with a mechanism for reusing a superclass's constructor code from within a subclass's constructor.

super(...) for Constructor Reuse

We accomplish code reuse of a superclass constructor via the same super keyword we discussed earlier in the chapter for the reuse of standard methods of a superclass. However, the syntax for reusing constructor code is a bit different. If we wish to explicitly reuse a particular parent class's constructor, we refer to it as follows in the subclass constructor body:

```
super(arguments);  // note that there is no "dot" involved
                   // when reusing CONSTRUCTOR code
```

Using super(*arguments*); to invoke a superclass constructor is similar to using this(*arguments*); to invoke one constructor from within another in the *same* class, a technique that you learned about in Chapter 4.

We select whichever of a superclass's constructors we wish to reuse, if more than one exists, by virtue of the arguments that we pass in to super(...); because constructors, if overloaded for a given class, all have unique argument signatures, the compiler has no difficulty in sorting out which superclass constructor we're invoking. This is illustrated in the following revised version of the Student class (note the **bolded** code):

```
public class Student extends Person {
    // name and ssn are inherited from Person ...
    private String major;

  // Constructor with two arguments.
  public Student(String n, String s) {
    // We're explicitly invoking the Person constructor that accepts two
    // String arguments by passing in two String arguments - namely, the
    // values of n and s.
    super(n, s);

    // Then, go on to do only those things that need to be done uniquely
    // for a Student.
    this.setMajor("UNDECLARED");
    // Pseudocode.
    do complex things related to instantiating a Student specifically.
  }
```

```
    // Constructor with three arguments.
    public Student(String n, String s, String m) {
        // See comments above.
        super(n, s);
        this.setMajor(m);
        // Pseudocode.
        do complex things related to instantiating a Student specifically.
    }
}
```

One important thing to note is that if we explicitly call a superclass constructor from a subclass constructor using the super(...) syntax, the call **must** be the **first** statement in the subclass constructor—that is, the following constructor would fail to compile:

```
public Student(String n, String s, String m) {
    this.setMajor(m);

    // This won't compile, because the call to the superclass's
    // constructor must come first in the subclass's constructor.
    super(n, s);
}
```

The following error message would arise:

```
call to super(n, s) must be first statement in constructor
```

The requirement to put a call to super(...) as the first line of code in a constructor arises by virtue of the "is a" nature of inheritance. When we create a Student object, we are in reality simultaneously creating an Object, a Person, and a Student, all rolled into one. So, whether we **explicitly** call a superclass constructor from a subclass constructor using super(...) or not, the fact is that Java will **always** attempt to execute constructors for all of the ancestor classes for a given class, from most general to most specific in the class hierarchy, before launching into that given class's constructor code. For example, if we are instantiating a Student

```
Student s = new Student("Fred", "123-45-6789");
```

then, behind the scenes, an Object constructor will automatically be executed first, followed by a Person constructor, followed by whichever Student constructor we've explicitly invoked—in this example, the one that takes two String arguments. The question is, **which superclass constructors get called if there's more than one defined for a given superclass?** Unless we explicitly invoke a particular constructor as we did in our Student constructors, for example:

```
public Student(String n, String s) {
    super(n, s);
    // etc.
```

then the parameterless constructor for the superclass is called automatically. That is, if we write a constructor without an **explicit** call to super(*args*), as follows:

```
public Student(String n, String s) {
    // NO EXPLICIT CALL TO super(...)
    this.setName(n);
```

```
    this.setSsn(s);
    this.setMajor("UNDECLARED");
    // etc.
  }
```

it is as if we've written

```
  public Student(String n, String s) {
    super(); // implied
    this.setName(n);
    this.setSsn(s);
    this.setMajor("UNDECLARED");
    // etc.
  }
```

instead. *Herein arises a potential problem*, which is described in the next section.

Replacing the Default Parameterless Constructor

If we don't bother to define any explicit constructors for a particular class, then as discussed in Chapter 4, Java will attempt to provide us with a default parameterless constructor for that class. What we've just seen is that when we invoke the default constructor for a *derived* class such as Student, the compiler will automatically try to invoke a parameterless constructor for each of the *ancestor* classes in the inheritance hierarchy in top-down fashion. So, in writing code as follows:

```
// Person.java

public class Person {
    // Attributes ... details omitted.

    // NO EXPLICIT CONSTRUCTORS PROVIDED!!!
    // We're going to be "lazy," and let Java provide us with
    // a default parameterless constructor for the Person class.

    // Methods ... details omitted.
}

//---------------------------------------

// Student.java

public class Student extends Person {
    // Attributes ... details omitted.

    // NO EXPLICIT CONSTRUCTORS PROVIDED!!!
    // We're going to be "lazy," and let Java provide us with
    // a default parameterless constructor for the Student class.

    // Methods ... details omitted.
}
```

it is as if we've designed our classes as follows:

```
// Person.java

public class Person {
    // Attributes ... details omitted.

    // The default parameterless Person constructor essentially would
    // look like this if we were to code it explicitly:
    public Person() {
        // Calling the default constructor for the Object class.
        super();
    }

    // Methods ... details omitted.
}

//---------------------------------------------

// Student.java

public class Student extends Person {
    // Attributes ... details omitted.

    // The default parameterless Student constructor essentially would
    // look like this if we were to code it explicitly:
    public Student() {
        // Calling the default constructor for the Person class.
        super();
    }

    // Methods ... details omitted.
}
```

The implication is that if we derive a class B from class A, and write no explicit constructors for B, then *the (default) parameterless constructor of B will automatically look for a parameterless constructor of A*. Thus, code such as the following example *won't compile*:

```
// Person.java

public class Person {
    private String name;

    // We've written an explicit constructor with one argument for
    // this (super)class; by having done so, we've LOST the
    // Person class's default parameterless constructor.
    public Person(String n) {
        name = n;
    }
```

```
    // Note that we haven't bothered to REPLACE the parameterless
    // constructor with one of our own design. This is going to
    // cause us problems, as we'll see in a moment.

    // Methods ... details omitted.
}

//------------------------------------

// Student.java

public class Student extends Person {
    // Attributes ... details omitted.

    // NO EXPLICIT CONSTRUCTORS PROVIDED!!!
    // We're going to be "lazy," and let Java provide us with
    // a default parameterless constructor for the Student class.

    // Methods ... details omitted.
}
```

When we try to compile this code, we'll get the seemingly *very cryptic* compiler error message regarding the following Student class:

```
Student.java: cannot find symbol
symbol:    constructor Person()
location:  class Person
public class Student extends Person {
      ^
```

This is because the Java compiler is trying to create a default parameterless constructor with no arguments for the Student class. In order to do so, the compiler knows that it is going to need to be able to invoke a parameterless constructor for Person from within the Student default constructor—however, no such constructor for Person exists!

      The best way to avoid such a dilemma is to remember to *always explicitly program a parameterless constructor* for a class X any time you program *any* explicit constructor for class X, to replace the "lost" default constructor.

A Few Words About Multiple Inheritance

All of the inheritance hierarchies that we've looked at in this chapter are known informally as **single-inheritance** hierarchies, because any particular class in the hierarchy may only have a *single* direct superclass/immediate ancestor. In the hierarchy shown in Figure 5-9, for example,

- Classes B, C, and I all have the single direct superclass A.

- Classes D, E, and F have the single direct superclass B.

- Classes G and H have the single direct superclass E.

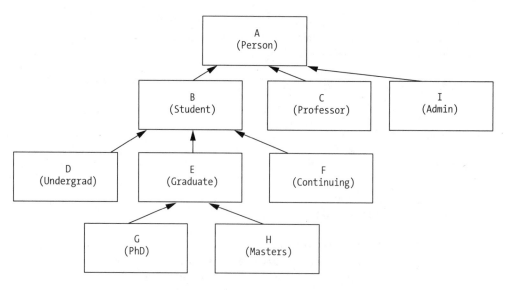

Figure 5-9. *A sample single-inheritance hierarchy*

If we for some reason find ourselves needing to meld together the characteristics of two different superclasses to create a hybrid third class, **multiple inheritance** may seem to be the answer. With multiple (as opposed to single) inheritance, any given class in a class hierarchy is permitted to have *two or more* classes as immediate ancestors. For example, we have a Professor class representing people who teach classes, and a Student class representing people who take classes. What might we do if we have a professor who wants to enroll in a class via the SRS? Or a student—most likely a graduate student—who has been asked to teach an undergraduate level course? In order to accurately represent either of these two people as objects, we would need to be able to combine the features of the Professor class with those of the Student class—a hybrid ProfessorStudent. This might be portrayed in our class hierarchy as shown in Figure 5-10.

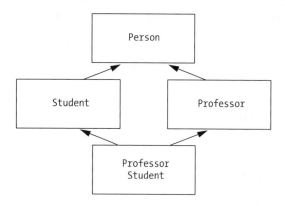

Figure 5-10. *Multiple inheritance permits a subclass to have multiple direct superclasses.*

On the surface, this seems quite handy. However, there are many complications inherent in multiple inheritance—so many, in fact, that the Java language designers chose not to support multiple inheritance. Instead, they've provided an alternative mechanism for handling the requirement of creating an object with a "split personality": that is, one that can behave like two or more different real-world entities. This mechanism involves the notion of **interfaces** and will be explored in detail in Chapter 7. Therefore, if you're primarily interested in object concepts only as they pertain to the Java language, you may wish to skip the rest of this section. If, on the other hand, you're curious as to why multiple inheritance is so tricky, then please read on.

Here's the problem with what we've done in the previous example. We discussed previously that, with inheritance, a subclass automatically inherits the attributes and methods of its superclass. What about when we have two or more direct superclasses? If these superclasses have no overlaps in terms of their features, then we are fine. But, what if the direct superclasses in question were, as an example, to have *conflicting* features—perhaps public methods with the *same* signature, but with *different* code body implementations, as illustrated in the following simple example?

We'll start with a trivially simple Person class that declares one attribute and one method:

```
public class Person {
    private String name;

    // Accessor method details omitted.

    public String printDescription() {
        System.out.println(getName());
        // e.g., "John Doe"
    }
}
```

Later on, we decide to specialize Person by creating two subclasses—Professor and Student—which each add a few attributes along with overriding the printDescription method to take advantage of their newly added attributes, as follows:

```
public class Student extends Person {
    // We add two attributes.
    private String major;
    private String studentId;

    // Accessor method details omitted.

    // Override this method as inherited from Person.
    public String printDescription() {
        return getName() + " [" + getMajor() + "; " +
            getStudentId() + "]";
        // e.g., "Mary Smith [Math; 10273]"
    }
}

//-----------------------------------
```

```
public class Professor extends Person {
    // We add two attributes.
    private String title;
    private String employeeId;

    // Accessor method details omitted.

    // Override this method as inherited from Person.
    public String printDescription() {
        return getName() + " [" + getTitle() + "; "
            + getEmployeeId() + "]";
        // e.g., "Harry Henderson [Chairman; A723]"
    }
}
```

Note that both subclasses have overridden the printDescription method differently, to take advantage of each class's own unique attributes.

At some future point in the evolution of this system, we determine the need to represent a single object as both a Student and a Professor simultaneously, and so we create the hybrid class StudentProfessor as a subclass of both Student and Professor. We don't particularly want to add any attributes or methods—we simply want to meld together the characteristics of both superclasses—and so we'd ideally like to declare StudentProfessor as follows:

```
// * * * Important Note:  this is not permitted in Java!!! * * *
public class StudentProfessor extends Professor and Student {
    // It's OK to leave a class body empty; the class itself is not
    // REALLY "empty," because it inherits the features of all of its
    // ancestors.
}
```

However, we encounter a roadblock to doing so:

- StudentProfessor cannot inherit both the Professor and Student versions of the printDescription method, because we'd then wind up with two (overloaded) methods with identical signatures in ProfessorStudent, which is not permitted by the Java compiler.

- Chances are that we'll want to inherit *neither*, because neither one takes full advantage of the other superclass's attributes. That is, the Professor version of printDescription knows nothing about the getMajor and getStudentId methods inherited from Student, nor does the Student version of printDescription know about the getTitle or getEmployeeId methods inherited from Professor.

- If we did wish to use one of the superclass's versions of the method versus the other, we'd have to invent some way of informing the compiler of which one we wanted to inherit.

This is just a simple example, but it nonetheless illustrates why multiple inheritance can be so problematic.

Three Distinguishing Features of an OOPL, Revisited

In Chapter 3, we called out three key features that are required of a programming language in order to be considered truly object-oriented. We've now discussed *two* of these three features at length:

- (Programmer creation of) User-defined types, as discussed in Chapter 3

- Inheritance, as discussed in this chapter

- Polymorphism

All that remains is to discuss **polymorphism**, one of the subjects of an upcoming chapter (Chapter 7, to be precise). We're going to take a bit of a detour first, however, to discuss what we can do to gather up and organize groups of objects as we create them through the use of a special type of object called a **collection**.

Summary

In this chapter, you've learned

- That an *association* describes a relationship between classes—that is, a potential relationship between objects of two particular types/classes—whereas a *link* describes an actual relationship between two objects belonging to these classes.

- That we define the *multiplicity* of an association between classes X and Y in terms of how many objects of type X can be linked to a given object of type Y, and vice versa. Possible multiplicities are one-to-one (1:1), one-to-many (1:m), and many-to-many (m:m). In all of these cases, the involvement of the objects at either end of the relationship may be optional or mandatory.

- That an *aggregation* is a special type of association that implies containment.

- How to derive new classes based on existing classes through *inheritance*, and what the do's and don'ts are when deriving these new classes; specifically, how we can *extend* a superclass and *specialize* it by *adding features* or *overriding methods*.

- How class hierarchies develop over time, and what we can do to try to avoid ripple effects to our application as the class hierarchy changes with evolving requirements.

- Some of the complexities of constructors with respect to inheritance.

- Why multiple inheritance can be so troublesome to implement in an OO language.

Exercises

1. Given the following pairs of classes, what associations might exist between them from the perspective of the PTS case study described in Appendix B?

   - Pharmacist–Prescription

   - Prescription–Medication

2. Go back to your solution for exercise 3 at the end of Chapter 1. For all of the classes you suggested, list the pairwise associations that you might envision occurring between them.

3. If the class FeatureFilm were defined to have the following methods:

   ```
   public void update(Actor a, String title)
   public void update(Actor a, Actor b, String title)
   public void update(String topic, String title)
   ```

   which of the following additional method headers would be allowed by the compiler?

   ```
   public boolean update(String category, String theater)
   public boolean update(String title, Actor a)
   public void update(Actor b, Actor a, String title)
   public void update(Actor a, Actor b)
   ```

4. [Coding] Try coding the FeatureFilm class discussed in exercise 3 to verify your answer for 3. (Note that you can "stub out" the Actor class by creating a file named Actor.java that contains the single line:

   ```
   public class Actor { }
   ```

   This satisfies the compiler that Actor is a legitimate type.)

5. Given the following simplistic code, which illustrates overloading, overriding, and straight inheritance of methods across four classes—Vehicle, Automobile, Truck, and SportsCar:

   ```
   public class Vehicle {
     String name;

     public void fuel(String fuelType) {
       // details omitted ...
     }

     public boolean fuel(String fuelType, int amount) {
       // details omitted ...
     }
   }

   public class Automobile extends Vehicle {
     public void fuel(String fuelType, String timeFueled) {
       // details omitted ...
     }
   ```

```
        public boolean fuel(String fuelType, int amount) {
          // ...
        }
    }

    public class Truck extends Vehicle {
      public void fuel(String fuelType) {
        // ...
      }
    }

    public class SportsCar extends Automobile {
      public void fuel(String fuelType) {
        // ...
      }

      public void fuel(String fuelType, String timeFueled) {
        // ...
      }
    }
```

How many different Fuel method signatures would each of the four classes recognize? List these.

6. Reflecting on all that you've learned about Java and OOPLs in general thus far, recount all of the language mechanisms that (a) facilitate code reuse, and (b) minimize ripple effects due to requirements changes.

7. Given the following simplistic classes, FarmAnimal, Horse, and Cow:

```
public class FarmAnimal {
  private String name;

  public String getName() {
      return name;
  }

  public void setName(String n) {
      name = n;
  }

  public void makeSound() {
    System.out.println(getName() + " makes a sound ...");
  }
}

public class Cow extends FarmAnimal {
  public void makeSound() {
    System.out.println(getName() + " goes Moooooo ...");
  }
}
```

```
public class Horse extends FarmAnimal {
  public void setName(String n) {
      super.setName(n + " [a Horse]");
  }
}
```

what would be printed by the following client code?

```
Cow c = new Cow();
Horse h = new Horse();
c.setName("Elsie");
h.setName("Mr. Ed");
c.makeSound();
h.makeSound();
```

CHAPTER 6

■ ■ ■

Collections of Objects

You learned about the process of creating objects based on class definitions, a process known as **instantiation**, in Chapter 3. When we're only creating a few objects, we can afford to declare individualized reference variables for these objects: Students s1, s2, s3, perhaps, or Professors profA, profB, profC. But, at other times, individualized reference variables are impractical.

- Sometimes, there will be too many objects, as when creating Course objects to represent the hundreds of courses in a university's course catalog.

- Worse yet, we may not even *know* how many objects of a particular type we'll need to instantiate at *run time*, and so cannot declare a predefined number of reference variables at *compile time*.

Fortunately, OOPLs solve this problem by providing a special category of object called a **collection** that is used to hold and organize references to other objects.

In this chapter, you'll learn about

- The properties of three generic collection types: **ordered lists**, **sets**, and **dictionaries**

- The specifics of several different predefined Java collection types/classes, along with how we represent and manipulate classic arrays in Java

- How logically related classes are bundled together in Java into **packages**, and how we must **import** packages if we wish to make use of the classes that they contain

- How collections enable us to model very sophisticated real-world concepts or situations

- Design techniques for inventing our own collection types

What Are Collections?

We'd like a way to gather up objects as they are created so that we can manage them as a group and operate on them collectively, along with referring to them individually when necessary, for example:

- A professor may wish to step through all Student objects registered for a particular course that the professor is teaching in order to assign their final semester grades.

- The Student Registration System (SRS) application as a whole may need to iterate through all of the Course objects in the current schedule of classes to determine if any of them should be canceled due to insufficient enrollment.

We use a special type of object called a **collection** to organize other objects. Think of a collection like an egg carton, and the objects it holds like the eggs: both the egg carton and the eggs are objects, but with decidedly different properties.

Collections Are Defined by Classes and Must Be Instantiated

The Java language predefines a number of different collection classes. As with any class, a collection object must be instantiated before it can be put to work. That is, if we merely declare a reference variable to be of a collection type:

```
CollectionType<elementType> x;
```

for example:

```
ArrayList<Student> x;  // ArrayList is one of Java's predefined collection types.
```

then until we "hand" x a *specific* collection object to *refer* to, x is said to be undefined.

We must take the distinct step of using the new operator to invoke a specific constructor for the type of collection that we wish to create:

```
x = new CollectionType<elementType>();
```

for example:

```
x = new ArrayList<Student>();
```

Think of the newly created collection object as an *empty* egg carton, and the reference variable referring to the collection as the handle that allows us to locate and access—*reference*—this "egg carton" in the JVM's memory whenever we'd like.

Collections Organize References to Other Objects

Actually, the "collection-as-egg-carton" analogy is a bit of an oversimplification, because rather than physically storing objects ("eggs") in a collection ("egg carton"), we store *references* to such objects in the collection. That is, the objects being organized by a collection live physically *outside* of the collection in the JVM's memory; only their *handles* reside inside of the collection. This notion is illustrated in Figure 6-1.

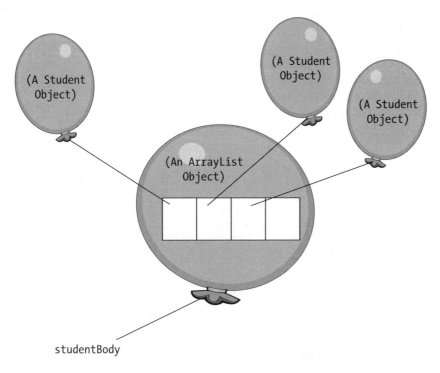

Figure 6-1. *A collection organizes references to objects that live in memory outside of the collection.*

Thus, perhaps a better analogy than that of "collection-as-egg-carton" would be that of a collection as an ***address book***: we record an entry in an address book (collection) for each of the people (objects) that we wish to be able to contact, but the people themselves are physically remote (see Figure 6-2).

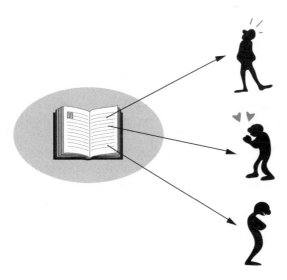

Figure 6-2. *A collection is analogous to an address book, with the people it references as the objects.*

Collections Are Encapsulated

We don't need to know the private details of how object references are stored internally to a specific type of collection in order to use the collection properly; we only need to know a collection's *public features*—in particular, its public method headers—in order to choose an appropriate collection type for a particular situation and to use it effectively.

Virtually all collections, regardless of type and regardless of the programming language in which they are implemented, provide, at a minimum, methods for

- Adding objects

- Removing objects

- Retrieving specific individual objects

- Iterating through the objects in some predetermined order

- Getting a count of the number of objects presently referenced by the collection

- Answering a true/false question as to whether a particular object's reference is in the collection or not

---

Throughout this chapter, we'll talk casually about manipulating *objects* in collections, but please remember that, with Java, what we really mean is that we're manipulating object *references.*

Three Generic Types of Collection

Before diving into the specifics of some of Java's predefined collection classes, let's talk first about the general properties of three basic collection types implemented by most OO languages:

- Ordered lists

- Dictionaries

- Sets

Ordered Lists

An **ordered list** is a type of collection that allows us to insert items in a particular order and later retrieve them in that same order. Specific objects can also be retrieved based on their position in the list (e.g., we can retrieve the first, or last, or *n*th item).

The vast majority of collection types—ordered lists included—needn't be assigned an explicit capacity (in terms of "egg-carton compartments") at the time that they are instantiated; collections automatically expand as new items are added. Conversely, when an item is removed from most collection types—including ordered lists—the "hole" that would have been left behind is automatically closed up, as shown in Figure 6-3.

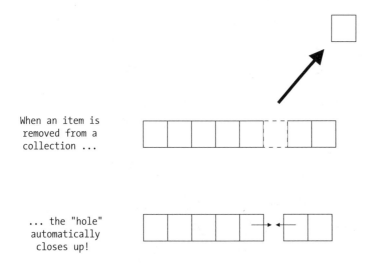

When an item is removed from a collection ...

... the "hole" automatically closes up!

Figure 6-3. *Most collections automatically shrink in size as items are removed.*

When we talk about classic arrays as a ***particular*** type of ordered list later in this chapter, we'll see that they alone have some limitations in this regard.

By default, items are added at the end of an ordered list, unless explicit instructions are given to insert an item at a different position.

An example of where we might use an ordered list in building our SRS would be to manage a wait list for a course that has become full. Because the order with which Student objects are added to such a list is preserved, we can be fair about selecting students from the wait list in first-come, first-served fashion should seats later become available in the course.

Several predefined Java classes implement the notion of ordered list collections: ArrayList, LinkedList, Stack, Vector, etc. We'll use the ArrayList class in building the SRS, and so we'll discuss the details of working with ArrayLists a bit later in this chapter.

Dictionaries

A **dictionary**—also known as a **map**—provides a means for storing each object reference along with a unique **lookup key** that can later be used to quickly retrieve the object (see Figure 6-4).

The key is often contrived based on one or more of the object's attribute values. For example, a Student object's student ID number would make an excellent key, because its value is inherently unique for each Student.

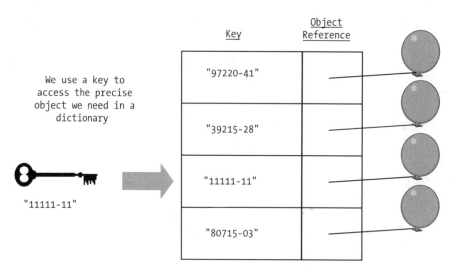

We use a key to access the precise object we need in a dictionary

"11111-11"

Figure 6-4. *Dictionary collections accommodate direct access by key.*

Items in a dictionary can typically also be iterated through one by one, in ascending key (or some other predetermined) order.

The SRS might use a dictionary, indexed on course number, to manage its course catalog. With so many course offerings to keep track of, being able to "pluck" the appropriate Course object from a collection directly (instead of having to step through an ordered list one by one to find it) adds greatly to the efficiency of the application.

Several examples of predefined Java classes that implement the notion of a dictionary are HashMap, Hashtable, and TreeMap. We'll use both the HashMap and TreeMap classes in building the SRS, and so we'll discuss the details of working with these specific collection types a bit later in this chapter.

Sets

A **set** is an ***unordered*** collection, which means that there is no way to ask for a particular item by number/position once it has been inserted into the set. Using a set is analogous to tossing an assortment of differently colored marbles into a sack (see Figure 6-5): we can reach into the sack (set) to pull out the marbles (objects) one by one, but there is no predictability as to the order with which we'll pull them out as compared with the order in which we put them in.

Placing objects in a set is like placing marbles in a sack!

Figure 6-5. *A set is an unordered collection.*

We can also perform tests on a set to determine whether or not a given specific object has been previously added to the set, just as we can answer the question "Is the blue marble in the bag?"

Note that duplicate entries aren't allowed in a set. That is, if we were to create a set of Student object references, and a reference to a particular Student object had already been placed in that set, then a second reference to the **same** Student object couldn't be subsequently added to the same set; the set would simply ignore our request. This **isn't** true of collections in general. If warranted by the requirements of our application, we can add several references to the **same** Student object to a given ordered list or dictionary instance, as illustrated in Figure 6-6.

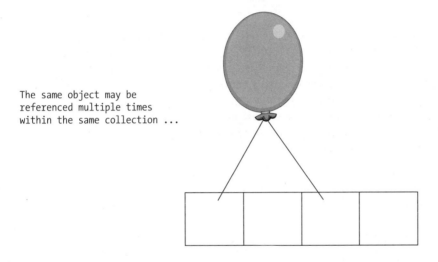

The same object may be
referenced multiple times
within the same collection ...

...UNLESS the collection is a set!

Figure 6-6. *Collections other than sets accommodate multiple references to the same object.*

An example of where we might use sets in building our SRS would be to group students according to the academic departments that they are majoring in. Then, if a particular course— say, Biology 216—requires that a student be a biology major in order to register, it would be a trivial matter to determine whether or not a particular Student is a member of the "Biology Department Majors" set.

Two predefined Java classes that implement the notion of a set are HashSet and TreeSet.

Arrays As Simple Collections

One simple type of collection that you may already be familiar with from your work with other programming languages—OO or otherwise—is an **array**.

As mentioned in passing earlier in the chapter, an array is a simple type of ordered list. We can think of an array as a series of compartments, with each compartment sized appropriately for whatever type of data the array as a whole is intended to hold. Arrays typically hold items of like type—for example, int(eger)s; or char(acter)s; or, in an OO language, object references (references to Student objects, or to Course objects, or to Professor objects, etc.).

Declaring and Instantiating Arrays

Because many newcomers to the Java language are used to programming with arrays in non-OO languages like C, the Java language supports syntax for declaring and manipulating arrays that is borrowed from C, and hence is decidedly "un-objectlike"!

The official Java syntax for declaring that a variable x will serve as a reference to an array containing items of a particular data type is as follows:

```
datatype[] x;
```

for example:

```
int[] x;
```

which is to be read "int(eger) array x" (or, alternatively, "x refers to an array of ints").

Because Java arrays are objects, they must be instantiated using the new operator. However, unlike any of the Java predefined collection classes we'll be talking about later in this chapter, we must specify how many items an array is capable of holding (i.e., its **capacity** in terms of its number of elements) when we first instantiate the array.

Here is a code snippet that illustrates the somewhat unusual syntax for constructing an array. In this particular example, we're declaring and instantiating an array designed to hold Student object references, as depicted in Figure 6-7:

```
// We declare variable x as a reference to an array object
// that will be used to store 20 Student object references.
Student[] x = new Student[20];
```

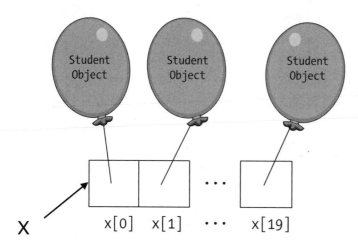

Figure 6-7. *Array* x *is designed to hold up to 20 Student references.*

This application of the new operator with arrays is unusual, in that we don't see a typical constructor call ending in parentheses (. . .) following the new keyword, the way we do when we're instantiating other types of objects. Instead, we use *square brackets* [. . .] to enclose the desired capacity of the array. Despite its unconventional appearance, however, the line of code

```
Student[] x = new Student[20];
```

is indeed instantiating an array object behind the scenes.

It turns out that there is another way to create an array in Java that looks more "objectlike," but the code isn't "pretty":

```
// Declare an array "x" of 20 Student references.
Object x  = Array.newInstance(Class.forName("Student"), 20);
```

To fully appreciate what this code is doing is beyond the scope of what you've learned about objects thus far; suffice it to say that virtually all Java programmers use the shorthand form instead:

```
Student[] x = new Student[20];
```

Accessing Individual Array Elements

Individual array elements are accessed by appending square brackets to the end of the array name, enclosing an int(eger) expression representing the **index**, or position relative to the beginning of the array, of the element to be accessed (e.g., x[3]). This syntax is known as an **array access expression**, and takes the place of using classic "get"/"set" methods to access array contents.

Note that when we refer to individual items in an array based on their index, we start counting at 0. As it turns out, the vast majority of collection types in Java, as well as in other languages, are **zero-based**. So, the items stored in Student[] x in our previous example would be referenced as x[0], x[1], ..., x[19], as was illustrated in Figure 6-7. In the following code example, we declare and instantiate a double array of size 3. We then assign the double value 4.7 to the "*zeroeth*" (*first*) element of the array. Finally, we retrieve the value of the *last* element of the array, which is referred to as data[2], because the size of the array is 3.

```
// Declare an array capable of holding three double values.
double[] data = new double[3];

// Set the FIRST (zeroeth) element to 4.7.
data[0] = 4.7;

// Details omitted ...

// Access the LAST element's value.
double temp = data[2];
```

In the next code example, we populate an array named squareRoot of type double to serve as a lookup table of square root values, where the value stored in cell squareRoot[n] represents the square root of n. We declare the array to be one element larger than we need it to be so that we may ignore the zeroeth cell—that is, for ease of lookup, we want the square root of 1 to be contained in cell 1 of the array, not in cell 0:

```
double[] squareRoot = new double[11];  // we'll ignore cell 0

// Note that we're skipping cell 0.
for (int n = 1; n <= 10; n++) {
  squareRoot[n] = Math.sqrt(n);
```

```
System.out.println("The square root of " + n + " = " +
    squareRoot[n]);
}
```

Here's the output:

```
The square root of 1 = 1.0
The square root of 2 = 1.4142135623730951
The square root of 3 = 1.7320508075688772
The square root of 4 = 2.0
The square root of 5 = 2.23606797749979
The square root of 6 = 2.449489742783178
The square root of 7 = 2.6457513110645907
The square root of 8 = 2.8284271247461903
The square root of 9 = 3.0
The square root of 10 = 3.1622776601683795
```

The `Math.sqrt` method computes the square root of a `double` argument passed to the method. We're passing in an `int` in the preceding example, which automatically gets cast to a `double`. We'll revisit the `Math` class again in Chapter 7.

Initializing Array Contents

Values can be assigned to individual elements of an array using indexes as shown earlier; alternatively, we can initialize an array with a complete set of values with a single Java statement when the array is first instantiated. In the latter case, initial values are provided as a comma-separated list enclosed in braces. For example, the following code instantiates and initializes a five-element `String` array:

```
String[] names = { "Steve", "Jacquie", "Chloe", "Shylow", "Baby Grode" };
```

Java automatically counts the number of initial values that we're providing, and sizes the array appropriately. The preceding approach is much more concise than the equivalent alternative shown here:

```
String[] names = new String[5];
names[0] = "Steve";
names[1] = "Jacquie";
names[2] = "Chloe";
names[3] = "Shylow";
names[4] = "Baby Grode";
```

although the result in both cases is the same: an array object of capacity 5 is instantiated, the zeroeth (first) element of the array will reference the `String` "Steve", the next element will reference "Jacquie";, and so on.

Note that it isn't possible to bulk load an array in this fashion *after* the array has been instantiated, as a separate line of code. That is, the following won't compile:

```
String[] names = new String[4];

// This next line won't compile.
names = {"Mike", "Cheryl", "Mickey", "Will" };
```

If a set of comma-separated initial values isn't provided when an array is first instantiated, the elements of the array are automatically initialized to their zero-equivalent values:

- An int array would be initialized to contain integer zeroes (0s).

- A double array would be initialized to contain floating-point zeroes (0.0s).

- A boolean array would be initialized to contain the value false in each cell.

and so on. And, if we declare and instantiate an array intended to hold references to objects, as in

```
Student[] studentBody = new Student[100];
```

then we'd wind up with an array object filled with null values.

Manipulating Arrays of Objects

To fill our Student array with values other than null, we'd have to individually store Student object references in each cell of the array. If we wanted to create *brand-new* Student objects to store in our array, we could write code as follows:

```
studentBody[0] = new Student("Fred");
studentBody[1] = new Student("Mary");
// etc.
```

or

```
Student s = new Student("Fred");
studentBody[0] = s;

// Reuse s!
s = new Student("Mary");
studentBody[1] = s;

// etc.
```

In the latter example, note that we're "recycling" the *same* reference variable, s, to create many *different* Student objects. This works because, after each instantiation, we store a *second* handle on each newly created object in an array element, thus allowing s to let go of *its* handle on that same object, as depicted in Figure 6-8. This technique is used frequently, with *all* collection types, in virtually all OO programming languages.

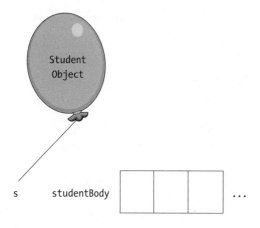

A Student object is created and handed to s ...

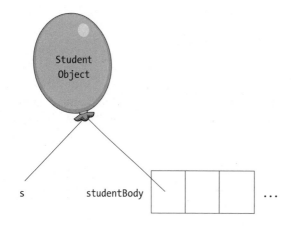

... s hands the object's handle off to the array ...

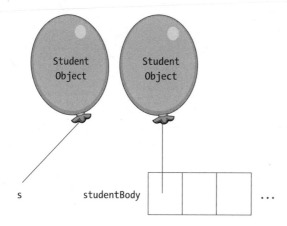

... thus freeing up s to take hold of another new Student!

Figure 6-8. *Handing new objects one by one into a collection, using a single reference variable as a temporary handle*

If we're simply using the default (parameterless) constructor to instantiate "bare-bones" Student objects, however, we'd probably populate our array using a looping construct, and eliminate the need for reference variable s entirely:

```
for (int i = 0; i < 20; i++) {
    // We're using the default constructor.
    studentBody[i] = new Student();
}
```

Assuming that we've fully populated all elements of the studentBody array, an indexed reference to any particular populated element in the array—for example, studentBody[i]—represents a Student object, and can be used accordingly. In the following line of code, for example, we're invoking the getName method on such a Student:

```
studentBody[i].getName();   // We're using dot notation to call a method on
                            // studentBody[i], the ith Student object referenced by
                            // the array.
```

Being able to reference individual objects within a collection in this fashion enables us to step through a collection using a looping construct to process its objects one by one. As an example, let's use a for loop to iterate through all of the Students in our studentBody array to print their names—in essence, we're printing a student roster:

```
// Step through all elements of the array.
for (int i = 0; i < studentBody.length; i++) {
    System.out.println(studentBody[i].getName());
}
```

Note the stopping condition on the for loop:

```
i < studentBody.length
```

It turns out that arrays have a **public attribute** named length whose value represents the capacity of the array in terms of the number of elements that it may accommodate. Since we count starting with 0 for the first element, we must stop one short of the value of length to avoid stepping past the end of the array.

If ever we accidentally try to step beyond the end of an array at run time, as in the following example:

```
// Array x contains 3 elements, indexed as 0, 1, and 2.
int[] x = new int[3];

// However, rather than stopping at element 2, we accidentally try to step
// to (nonexistent) element 3 in our loop:
for (int i = 0; i <= 3; i++) {
    System.out.println(x[i]);
}
```

we'll get the following **run-time** error message:

```
Exception in thread "main" java.lang.ArrayIndexOutOfBoundsException: 3
```

We'll discuss in Chapter 13 how these types of run-time failures—known as **exceptions**—can be programmatically anticipated and handled through a mechanism known as **exception handling**.

Note that the length attribute is a ***read-only*** attribute—that is, we cannot assign a value to it explicitly, perhaps in an attempt to enlarge an array at run time (recall that this isn't possible: an array, once sized, cannot be expanded). If we try to do so, as in the following snippet:

```
int[] x = new int[3];

// Let's naively try to enlarge array x!
x.length = 10;
```

we'd get the following compilation error:

```
cannot assign a value to final variable length
```

We'll revisit **final** variables in Chapter 7.

We also have to take care when stepping through an array of object references to avoid "land mines" due to empty/null elements. That is, if we're iterating through an array, but the array isn't completely filled with Student object references, then our invocation of the getName method will fail as soon as we reach the first empty/null element, because in essence we'd be trying to talk to a nonexistent object. Let's look at an example:

```
// When we first instantiate an array of object references, all cells contain the
// value null.
Student[] students = new Student[3];

// Store a Student object reference in cells 0 and 1, but leave
// cell 2 empty (i.e., it retains its default value of null).
students[0] = new Student("Elmer");
students[1] = new Student("Klemmie");

// Try to step through the array, printing each Student's name.
// There's a "land mine" lurking at element 2!!!
for (int i = 0; i < studentBody.length; i++) {
    System.out.println(studentBody[i].getName());
}
```

If this code were executed, we'd get the following ***run-time*** error message as soon as the value of i reached the value 2:

```
Exception in thread "main" java.lang.NullPointerException
```

because the value of studentBody[2] is null; we cannot invoke a method on (i.e., "talk to") a nonexistent object.

Again, we'll cover how to handle run-time exceptions in Chapter 13.

There's a simple way to avoid such "land mines" in an array: simply test the value of a given array element to see if it's null before attempting to address the object at that location:

```
// Step through all elements of the array.
for (int i = 0; i < studentBody.length; i++) {
    // Check for the presence of a valid object reference before trying to
    // "talk to" it via dot notation.
    if (studentBody[i] != null) {
        System.out.println(studentBody[i].getName());
    }
}
```

A More Sophisticated Type of Collection: The ArrayList Class

Arrays are ideal for organizing a fixed number of like-typed elements—for example, a String array containing the abbreviated names of the days of the week:

```
String[] daysOfWeek = { "Mon.", "Tue.", "Wed.", "Thu.", "Fri.", "Sat.", "Sun." };
```

However, as mentioned earlier, it's often difficult—if not impossible—for us to predict in advance the number of objects that a collection will need to hold (e.g., how many courses a given student is going to register for when he or she is logged on to the SRS). When using an Array as a collection type, however, we're required to make such a determination when we first instantiate the array and, once sized, an array can't be expanded. To use an array under such unpredictable circumstances, we'd therefore have to ensure that it was big enough to handle the worst-case scenario, which isn't very efficient.

Fortunately, OO languages provide a wide variety of collection types besides arrays for us to choose from; each has its own unique properties and advantages. As mentioned earlier in the chapter, one important differentiating feature of ***all*** Java collection types ***besides*** arrays is that they needn't be sized in advance: when we add items to a nonarray collection, it automatically ***grows*** in size, and as we remove items, the collection will ***shrink*** accordingly (recall Figure 6-3).

Let's now take a look at one of the most commonly used predefined Java collection classes, ArrayList, to see how it implements the notion of an ordered list collection.

IMPORTANT!

Sun Microsystems introduced some important new features with J2SE 5.0 that significantly increased the power and versatility of Java as an object-oriented programming language. These improvements were particularly noteworthy with respect to the improved ease with which collections are created and managed. I've thus adopted the J2SE 5.0 approach to collections as of this (second) edition of *Beginning Java Objects*.

Note that the code examples presented through the end of this chapter will ***not*** compile with an earlier (pre-5.0) version of the Java compiler. For readers who are still working with an earlier version of the Java language, please refer to Appendix G for a discussion of how collections were handled in Java version 1.4.*x* and earlier.

Using the ArrayList Class: An Example

Here is a simple program that illustrates the use of an ArrayList collection to hold on to references to Student objects. We'll look at the program in its entirety first, and we'll then step through it to examine key points one by one.

```java
import java.util.*;

public class ArrayListExample {
    public static void main(String[] args) {
        // Instantiate a collection.
        ArrayList<Student> students = new ArrayList<Student>();

        // Create a few Student objects.
        Student a = new Student("Herbie");
        Student b = new Student("Klem");
        Student c = new Student("James");

        // Store references to all three Students in the collection.
        students.add(a);
        students.add(b);
        students.add(c);

        // ... and then iterate through them one by one,
        // printing each student's name.
        for (Student s : students) {
            System.out.println(s.getName());
        }
    }
}
```

Import Directives and Packages

Our example program starts out with an **import directive**, which precedes the ArrayListExample class declaration:

import java.util.*;

```java
public class ArrayListExample { ... }
```

When we originally discussed Java program anatomy in Chapter 2, we skipped this optional yet key element. I've revised the anatomy figure from Chapter 2 to include import directives, as shown in Figure 6-9.

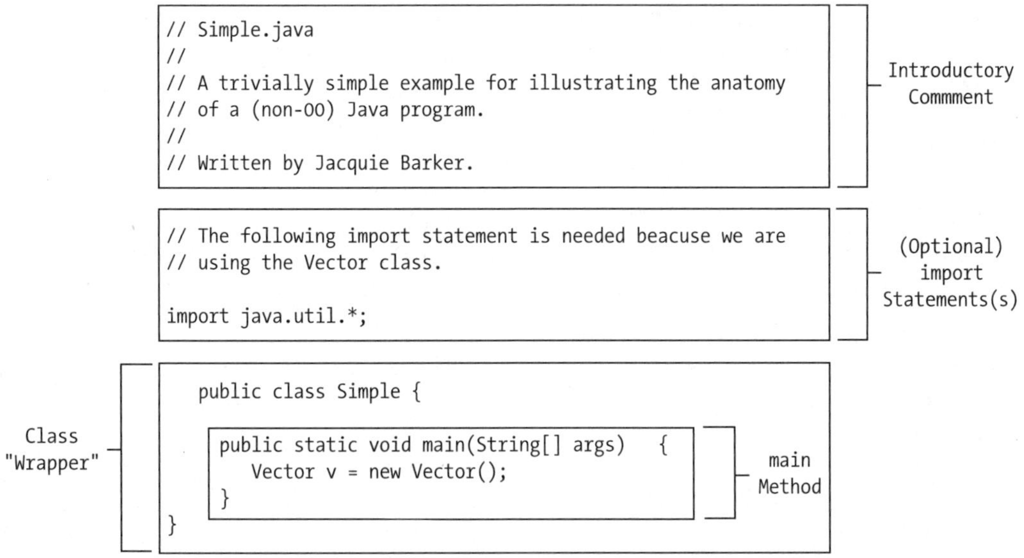

```
// Simple.java
//
// A trivially simple example for illustrating the anatomy
// of a (non-OO) Java program.
//
// Written by Jacquie Barker.
```
Introductory Commment

```
// The following import statement is needed beacuse we are
// using the Vector class.

import java.util.*;
```
(Optional) import Statements(s)

Class "Wrapper"
```
public class Simple {

    public static void main(String[] args)    {
        Vector v = new Vector();
    }
}
```
main Method

Figure 6-9. *Revisiting anatomy, now with* import *directives*

To appreciate import directives, you first must understand the notion of Java **packages**. Because the Java language is so extensive, its various predefined classes are organized into logical groupings called packages. For example, we have

- java.io: This package contains classes related to file input/output, which we'll discuss in depth in Chapter 15.

- java.util: This package contains a number of utility classes, such as the Java collection classes that you're learning about in this chapter.

- java.awt and javax.swing: These two packages contain classes related to Java GUI development, which we'll discuss in depth in Chapter 16.

and so forth.

Most built-in Java package names start with "java", but there are some that start with other prefixes, like "javax" and, if we acquire Java classes from a third party, they typically come in a package that starts with the organization's (unique) domain name, reversed. For example, an organization with a domain name of xyz.com would typically name their packages com.xyz.*packagename*, where *packagename* describes the logical purpose of the classes included in the package (e.g., com.xyz.accounting). By using unique domain names as the basis for package names, we ensure that no two organizations' package names will ever duplicate one another; this is important whenever we incorporate packages from more than one organization in the *same* application.

The built-in package named java.lang contains the absolute *core* of the Java language, and the classes contained within that package—for example, Math, System, and String—are always available to both the Java compiler and the JVM whenever we compile/run Java programs, so we needn't worry about importing java.lang. However, if we wish to reference the name of any other predefined class that isn't contained within the java.lang package—ArrayList, for example—then we must *import* the package to which the class belongs, as we did with the java.util package in our example program:

```
// Our code needs to refer to the predefined ArrayList class as a type, and since
// the ArrayList class isn't included in the "core" java.lang package, we must
// import the package that defines what an ArrayList is.

import java.util.*;

public class ArrayListExample { ... }
```

The asterisk (*) at the end of the import directive informs the Java compiler that we wish to import *all* of the classes contained within the java.util package. As an alternative, we can import individual classes from within a package, as follows:

```
// We can import individual classes by name, to better document where each class
// that we are using originates.
import java.util.ArrayList;
import java.util.Date;
import java.io.PrintWriter;
// etc.

public class SomeClass { ... }
```

This approach, of course, requires more typing, but provides better traceability of where each class that we are using in our program originates. Either approach—listing individual classes to be imported one by one, or using wildcards to import all classes in a package as a whole—is equally acceptable.

As you'll learn when we discuss the mechanics of the JVM in more detail in Chapter 13, neither approach is less efficient than the other at run time.

If we were to accidentally omit the import directive our ArrayListExample program, we'd get the following compilation error once for every occurrence of the symbol ArrayList in our code:

```
cannot find symbol
symbol: class ArrayList
```

That is, our output from compiling the following code:

```
// WHOOPS!  We've forgotten our import directive.

public class ArrayListExample {
    public static void main(String[] args) {
        // Instantiate a collection.
        ArrayList<Student> students = new ArrayList<Student>();

        // Create a few Student objects.
        Student a = new Student("Herbie");
        Student b = new Student("Klem");
        Student c = new Student("James");
```

```
        // etc.
    }
}
```

would be as follows:

```
ArrayListExample.java:6: cannot find symbol
symbol  : class ArrayList
location: class ArrayListExample
        ArrayList<Student> students = new ArrayList<Student>();
        ^
ArrayListExample.java:6: cannot find symbol
symbol  : class ArrayList
location: class ArrayListExample
        ArrayList<Student> students = new ArrayList<Student>();
                                          ^
2 errors
```

This is because the symbol ArrayList is not automatically in the **namespace** of the class that we're compiling—that is, it's not one of the names/symbols that the Java compiler recognizes in the context of that class.

The Namespace of a Class

Generally speaking, the namespace for a given class contains the following categories of names, among others:

1. The name of the class itself (e.g., Student)

2. The names of all of the features (attributes, methods, etc.) declared by the class

3. The names of any local variables declared within any methods of the class (including parameters being passed in)

4. The names of all classes belonging to the *same* package that the class we're compiling belongs to

5. The names of all *public* classes in the java.lang package: String, Math, System, etc.

You'll learn what constitutes a public (versus a nonpublic) class in Chapter 13.

---

6. The names of all *public* classes in any *other* package that has been *imported* by the class that we're compiling

7. The names of all *public* features (attributes, methods) of the classes listed in points 5 and 6

and so forth. As a simple example, when compiling the following class:

```
// Simple.java

public class Simple {
    private int foo;

    public void bar(double x) {
        boolean maybe;
        if (x < 0) maybe = true;
        else maybe = false;
    }
}
```

the compiler would recognize the following names/symbols:

1. Simple (the class name).

2. foo, bar (names of features of the Simple class).

3. x, maybe (local variables of Simple's methods).

4. The names of all classes belonging to the *default* (unnamed) package, since Simple is *in* the default package.

5. The names of all public classes in the java.lang package: String, Math, System, etc.

6. The names of all public classes in any other package that has been imported. Since Simple contains no import directives, there are no symbols in this category in Simple's namespace.

7. The names of all public features (attributes, methods) of the classes listed in points 4 and 5.

The Java compiler compiles classes one by one, and "resets" its notion of what is within scope for each new class that it compiles. Therefore, importing a package is only effective for the particular .java source code file in which the import directive resides. If, for example, you have three separate classes, each stored in its own .java file, that all need to manipulate ArrayLists, then all three .java files must include an appropriate import directive, either

```
import java.util.*;
```

or

```
import java.util.ArrayList;
```

We can avoid importing a package/class by **fully qualifying** the names of any classes, methods, etc. that we use from such a package. That is, we can prefix the name of the class, method, etc. with the name of the package from which it originates every time that we use it in our code, as shown in the next example:

```
// Note:  NO import directive!

public class Simple {
  public static void main(String[] args) {
    java.util.ArrayList<Student> x = new java.util.ArrayList<Student>();
    java.util.ArrayList<Professor> y = new java.util.ArrayList<Professor>();
    // etc.
```

This, of course, requires a lot more typing, and impairs the readability of our code. By importing a package, on the other hand, we're telling the compiler how to resolve *simple/unqualified* names—the *real* (*qualified*) name of the ArrayList class is java.util.ArrayList, but we're able to refer to it by the simple name ArrayList because of the import directive.

Although most built-in Java packages have names that consist of two terms separated by a period (dot)—for example, java.awt—some built-in Java package names consist of three or more dot-separated terms—for example, java.awt.event. There's really no limit to the number of terms that can be concatenated to form a package name.

When one package name is a subset of another package name—as in the case of java.awt and java.awt.event—*both* must be imported separately if *both* are needed in the same class scope. That is, an asterisk at the end of an import directive

```
import nameA.nameB.*;
```

only serves to import *members* of the specified package, not to extend the package name per se:

```
// This first import directive is not sufficient to import java.awt.event members;
// it only imports members of the java.awt package.
import java.awt.*;

// We'd need to include this second import directive, as well.
import java.awt.event.*;
```

User-Defined Packages and the Default Package

Java also provides programmers with the ability to logically group their *own* classes into packages. For example, if we wanted to, we could invent a package such as com.objectstart.srs to house all classes related to our SRS application. Then, anyone else wishing to incorporate our SRS classes within an application that they were going to write could include the directive

```
import com.objectstart.srs;
```

in their code.

A detailed discussion of how to create our own packages is beyond the scope of this book. But, as it turns out, if we do nothing in particular to take advantage of programmer-defined packages, then as long as all of the compiled .class files for an application reside in the *same* directory on our computer system, they are automatically considered to be in the same package, known as the **default package**. This is what enables us to write code such as the following:

```
public class SRS {
  public static void main(String[] args) {
    Student s = new Student();
    Professor p = new Professor();
    // etc.
```

without using import directives, because the class definitions for all of the classes that we've written and compiled—Student, Professor, and SRS—all coexist within the *same* (default) package.

The bottom line is that import directives as a building block of a .java source code file are only needed if we are using classes that are neither found in the package java.lang nor coexist in our own (default) package.

Generics

Let's return to our examination of the `ArrayListExample` program from earlier in the chapter, which is repeated in its entirety here for your convenience:

```
import java.util.*;

public class ArrayListExample {
    public static void main(String[] args) {
        // Instantiate a collection.
        ArrayList<Student> students = new ArrayList<Student>();

        // Create a few Student objects.
        Student a = new Student();
        Student b = new Student();
        Student c = new Student();

        // Store references to all three Students in the collection.
        students.add(a);
        students.add(b);
        students.add(c);

        // ... and then iterate through them one by one,
        // printing each student's name.
        for (Student s : students) {
            System.out.println(s.getName());
        }
    }
}
```

The next bit of "unusual" syntax occurs on the line of code that declares and instantiates our `ArrayList`:

```
ArrayList<Student> students = new ArrayList<Student>();
```

Prior to release 5.0 of the Java language, all predefined collection types were ***untyped***; that is, they were all designed to hold generic `Object` references, or any subtype thereof. This led to some complications with regard to the manner in which we retrieved objects from a collection, which I review in Appendix G.

As of Java release 5.0, Sun Microsystems introduced the notion of **generics**. Simply put, Sun designed the predefined Java collection classes to operate ***generically*** on object references of any type, but then provided a syntactic means of ***constraining*** the type of element that a particular collection is to manage. Now, whenever we want to instantiate a collection such as an `ArrayList`, we can indicate the type of element that the collection is intended to hold by enclosing the type name in angle brackets <...> immediately after the class name:

```
ArrayList<Professor> faculty = new ArrayList<Professor>();
ArrayList<String> names = new ArrayList<String>();
```

and so forth. In essence, `ArrayList<xxx>` becomes the type of the collection that we're instantiating.

Note that there is a trick to inserting *primitive* types (int, double, boolean, etc.) into a collection. We'll discuss this when the notion of **autoboxing** is introduced a bit later in the chapter.

ArrayList Features

In our ArrayListExample program, we use the add method to insert Student references into the collection:

```
// Store references to all three Students in the collection.
students.add(a);
students.add(b);
students.add(c);
```

The ArrayList class supports a total of 38 public methods—many of which are common to all collection types—and three overloaded public constructors. Some of the more commonly used ArrayList methods, which we'll use in building the SRS, are as follows:

- boolean add(E element): Appends the specified element to the end of the list. E refers to whatever type was specified inside of angle brackets <...> when the ArrayList was first declared/instantiated—for example, Student in the following declaration:

  ```
  ArrayList<Student> students = new ArrayList<Student>();
  Student s = new Student();
  students.add(s);
  // or:
  students.add(new Student());
  ```

  With this (and any other) method, we are permitted to pass in an argument of type E *or of any subtype thereof*:

  ```
  ArrayList<Student> students = new ArrayList<Student>();

  // As long as GraduateStudent is derived from Student, all is well!
  students.add(new GraduateStudent());
  ```

- void add(int n, E element): *Inserts* the specified element at the *n*th position in the list, shifting all subsequent items over to make room for the newly added element, for example:

  ```
  Student s = new Student();
  students.add(0, s);
  // As of the preceding line of code, whatever reference was previously
  // in the first (0th) position will now be in the SECOND position (i.e.,
  // in position #1), because we've inserted a NEW Student reference
  // in the first (0th) position.
  ```

- boolean addAll(Collection<? extends E> c): Appends all of the elements in the specified collection c to the end of this list. The items continue to be referenced by the original collection, as well, so this is an effective way to *copy* an existing collection of virtually any type into an existing ArrayList.

Note that the rather cryptic-looking syntax Collection<? extends E> is simply meant to indicate that whatever type of collection c we wish to copy into the ArrayList must be of a type that is **compatible** with the type of the ArrayList. That is, c must have been declared to hold either the **same** type of element as the ArrayList was declared to hold, or c must have been declared to hold elements that are a **subtype** of the elements that the ArrayList was declared to hold.

For example, we can addAll elements from an arbitrary collection of GraduateStudents to an ArrayList designed to hold Student references as long as GraduateStudent is a subtype of Student, but we **cannot** addAll elements from an arbitrary collection of Professors to an ArrayList designed to hold Student references (assuming that Professor is a **sibling** class to Student).

Here is an example to illustrate the use of the addAll method:

```
// Create two collections, x and y; x needn't be an ArrayList.
// Pseudocode.
CollectionType<Student> x = new CollectionType<Student>();
ArrayList<Person> y = new ArrayList<Person>();

// Instantiate two Students, and add them to x.
Student s1 = new Student();
Student s2 = new Student();
x.add(s1);
x.add(s2);

// Instantiate two more Students, and add them to y.
Student s3 = new Student();
Student s4 = new Student();
y.add(s3);
y.add(s4);

// Add all of the references in x to y.
y.addAll(x);
// y now contains references to FOUR Students:  s1, s2, s3, and s4;
// x still contains its original references to s1 and s2.
```

- void clear(): Removes all elements from the collection, rendering it empty.

Whether or not these elements subsequently get **garbage collected** as a result of eliminating their handles from the collection will depend on whether any **other** handles are being maintained on these objects. We'll revisit this topic later in this chapter.

- boolean contains(Object element): Returns true if the specific object referenced by the argument is also referenced by the ArrayList, and false otherwise:

```
// Create a collection.
ArrayList<Student> x = new ArrayList<Student>();

// Instantiate two Students, but only add the FIRST of them
// to ArrayList x.
Student s1 = new Student();
Student s2 = new Student();
x.add(s1);

// Declare a third reference variable of type Student, and have it refer to
// the SAME student as s1:  that is, a Student whose reference has already been
// added to collection x.
Student s3 = s1;
```

The situation with regard to objects x, s1, s2, and s3 can be thought of conceptually as illustrated in Figure 6-10.

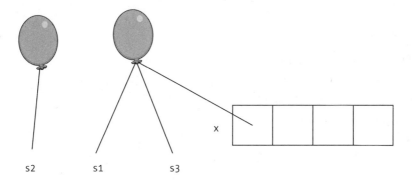

Figure 6-10. *Student* s1 *was placed into collection x, and because* s1 *and* s3 *reference the* **same** *Student, x* **contains** s3.

Continuing with our example, the following first if test will return a value of false, while the second will return true, because s3 refers to the *same* Student object that s1 refers to:

```
// Tests for containment:  the first test will return false ...
if (x.contains(s2)) { ... }

// ... while the second will return true.
if (x.contains(s3)) { ... }
```

- int size(): Returns a count of the number of elements currently referenced by the ArrayList. An empty ArrayList will report a size of 0.

- boolean isEmpty(): Returns true if the ArrayList in question contains no elements, and false otherwise.

- boolean remove(Object element): Locates and ***removes*** a single instance of the ***specific object*** referred to by the argument from the ArrayList, closing up the hole that would otherwise be left behind. It returns true if such an object was found and removed, or false if the object wasn't found.

```
// Create a collection.
ArrayList<Student> x = new ArrayList<Student>();

// Instantiate two Students, and add both to x.
Student s1 = new Student();
Student s2 = new Student();
x.add(s1);
x.add(s2);

// Remove s1.
x.remove(s1);
// x now only contains one reference, to s2.
```

and so forth.

Iterating Through ArrayLists

The for loop syntax that we use for iterating through an ArrayList (such as the students ArrayList in our ArrayListExample program) was newly introduced as of J2SE 5.0:

```
for (type referenceVariable : collectionName) {
    // Pseudocode.
    manipulate the referenceVariable as desired
}
```

for example:

```
for (Student s : students) {
    System.out.println(s.getName());
}
```

This for statement is to be interpreted as follows: "for every Student object (which we'll temporarily refer to as s) in the students collection, perform whatever logic is specified within the body of the loop." We are then able to refer to s within the body of the for loop to manipulate it as desired, thus processing the items in the ArrayList one by one.

For a discussion of how we iterated through collections prior to J2SE 5.0, please refer to Appendix G.

Copying the Contents of an ArrayList into an Array

From time to time, we'll have a need to copy the contents of a collection into an array. We'll discuss the motivations for doing so when we build the SRS in Part 3 of this book, but I'd like to explain the mechanism for doing so now.

We'll use a method declared by the ArrayList class with the following header:

type[] toArray(*type*[] *arrayRef*)

That is, we'll invoke the toArray method on an ArrayList object, passing in an array of the desired *type* as an argument, and the method will in turn hand us back an array that contains a copy of the contents of the ArrayList, as follows:

- If the array that we pass in is of sufficient capacity to hold the contents of the ArrayList, that **same** array object is filled and returned.

- Otherwise, a **brand-new** array of the appropriate type and size is **created**, filled, and returned, and the one that we pass in as an argument is ignored.

Since it's easy to create an array whose size matches that of an existing ArrayList—we'll see how to do so in just a moment—we'll do so whenever we have occasion to invoke the toArray method on an ArrayList within the SRS application.

Let's look at an example. First, we'll create an ArrayList named students, "stuffing" it with three Student references:

```
ArrayList<Student> students = new ArrayList<Student>();
students.add(new Student("Herbie"));
students.add(new Student("Klemmie"));
students.add(new Student("James"));
```

Next, we'll declare and instantiate an array named copyOfStudents that's designed to be just the right size to hold the contents of the students ArrayList—note the use of a nested call to students.size() to accomplish this:

```
Student[] copyOfStudents = new Student[students.size()];
```

Then, to copy the contents of the ArrayList into the copyOfStudents array, we simply have to invoke the toArray method on students, passing in copyOfStudents as an argument:

```
students.toArray(copyOfStudents);
```

Let's verify that the copy works by iterating first through the ArrayList, then through the array, printing the names of the Student objects referenced by each:

```
System.out.println("The ArrayList contains the following students:");

for (Student s : students) {
    System.out.println(s.getName());
}

System.out.println();

System.out.println("The array contains the following students:");

for (int i = 0; i < copyOfStudents.length; i++) {
    System.out.println(copyOfStudents[i].getName());
}
```

Here's the output:

```
The ArrayList contains the following students:
Herbie
Klemmie
James

The array contains the following students:
Herbie
Klemmie
James
```

Success! Both the array and the ArrayList now refer to the same three Students, as depicted conceptually in Figure 6-11.

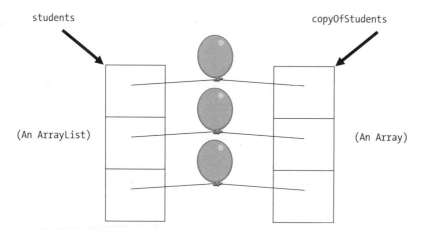

Figure 6-11. *Using the toArray method of the ArrayList class, we copy the contents of an ArrayList to an array.*

The HashMap Collection Class

As mentioned earlier in the chapter, a Java HashMap is a dictionary type collection—that is, a HashMap gives us direct access to a given object based on a unique key value. Both the key and the object itself can be declared to be of any type.

Let's look at a simple example program called HashMapExample that illustrates the basics of manipulating HashMaps. This program involves

- Creating and populating a HashMap with Student object references, using the value of their idNo attribute (a String) as the key

- Attempting to retrieve several individual Students based on specific idNo values

- Iterating through the entire collection of Students

For purposes of this example, we'll use the following simplified Student class declaration:

```java
public class Student {
    private String idNo;
    private String name;

    // Constructor.
    public Student(String i, String n) {
        idNo = i;
        name = n;
    }

    public String getName() {
        return name;
    }

    public String getIdNo() {
        return idNo;
    }
}
```

and we'll use the value of each Student's idNo attribute as the key.

Let's look at the program in its entirety first, and we'll walk through selected passages afterward:

```java
import java.util.HashMap;

public class HashMapExample {
    public static void main(String[] args) {
        // Instantiate a HashMap with String as the key type and Student as
        // the value type.
        HashMap<String, Student> students = new HashMap<String, Student>();

        // Instantiate three Students; the constructor arguments are
        // used to initialize Student attributes idNo and name,
        // respectively, which are both declared to be Strings.
        Student s1 = new Student("12345-12", "Fred");
        Student s2 = new Student("98765-00", "Barney");
        Student s3 = new Student("71024-91", "Wilma");

        // Insert all three Students into the HashMap, using their idNo
        // as a key.
        students.put(s1.getIdNo(), s1);
        students.put(s2.getIdNo(), s2);
        students.put(s3.getIdNo(), s3);

        // Retrieve a Student based on a particular (valid) ID.
        String id = "98765-00";
        System.out.println("Let's try to retrieve a Student with ID = " + id);
        Student x = students.get(id);
```

```java
    // If the value returned by the get method is non-null, then
    // we indeed found a matching Student ...
    if (x != null) {
        System.out.println("Found!  Name = " + x.getName());
    }
    // ... whereas if the value returned was null, then we didn't find
    // a match on the id that was passed in as an argument to get().
    else {
        System.out.println("Invalid ID:   " + id);
    }

    System.out.println();

    // Try an invalid ID.
    id = "00000-00";
    System.out.println("Let's try to retrieve a Student with ID = " + id);
    x = students.get(id);

    if (x != null) {
        System.out.println("Found!  Name = " + x.getName());
    }
    else {
        System.out.println("Invalid ID:   " + id);
    }

    System.out.println();
    System.out.println("Here are all of the students:");
    System.out.println();

    // Iterate through the HashMap to process all Students.
    for (Student s : students.values()) {
        System.out.println("ID:   " + s.getIdNo());
        System.out.println("Name:  " + s.getName());
        System.out.println();
    }
  }
}
```

Here's the output:

```
Let's try to retrieve a Student with ID = 98765-00
Found!  Name = Barney

Let's try to retrieve a Student with ID = 00000-00
Invalid ID:  00000-00

Here are all of the students:

ID:  12345-12
Name:  Fred

ID:  98765-00
Name:  Barney

ID:  71024-91
Name:  Wilma
```

The first point of interest is that when we declare and instantiate a HashMap, we must specify types for *two* elements: the **key**, which is of type String in our example, and the **value** that this key represents, which is of type Student in our example.

```
HashMap<String, Student> students = new HashMap<String, Student>();
```

We use the put method to insert an object into a HashMap:

```
students.put(s1.getIdNo(), s1);
```

This method inserts the object represented by the **second** argument (s1, in the preceding example) into the collection with a retrieval key value represented by the **first** argument (the idNo of s1, retrieved by calling the getIdNo method, in the preceding example).

If we attempt to insert a second object into a HashMap with a key value that duplicates the key of an object that is already referenced by the HashMap, the put method will silently **replace** the original object reference with the new reference. If we want to **avoid** such inadvertent object replacement in a HashMap, we can use the containsKey method, which returns a value of true if a particular key already exists in the HashMap, and false otherwise. Here's an example of this method's use:

```
// If it is NOT the case that the students HashMap already contains
// a key value matching the idNo of student s1 ...
if (!(students.containsKey(s1.getIdNo()))) {
    // ... then it is safe to add such a reference.
    students.put(s1.getIdNo(), s1);
}
else {
    // Another Student reference with the same idNo value is already in the HashMap.
    System.out.println("ERROR:  Duplicate student ID found in HashMap:  " +
        s1.getIdNo());
}
```

The get method is used to retrieve an object reference from the HashMap whose key value matches the value passed in as an argument to the method:

```
Student x = students.get(id);
```

If no match is found, a value of null is returned.

The syntax that we've used for iterating through the students HashMap in our HashMapExample program is very similar to the code that we used to iterate through ArrayLists earlier in the chapter:

```
// Iterate through the HashMap to process all Students.
for (Student s : students.values()) {
    ...
}
```

The only subtle difference is that we are invoking the values method on the students collection to access the (Student) objects contained within the HashMap, bypassing their **keys**, as illustrated in Figure 6-12.

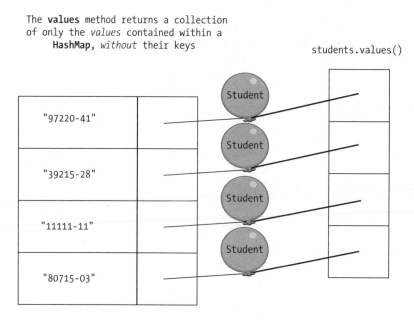

Figure 6-12. *The values method returns a collection of values (only) from a HashMap.*

Some of the other commonly used methods declared by the HashMap class are as follows:

- Object remove(Object key): Removes the reference to the object represented by the given key from the HashMap.

- boolean contains(Object value): Returns true if the specific object passed in as an argument to the method is already referenced by the HashMap, **regardless of what its key value might be**; otherwise, returns false. Here's an example:

```
// Instantiate a new HashMap and two Students.
HashMap<String, Student> x = new HashMap<String, Student>();
Student s1 = new Student("12345-12", "Fred");
Student s2 = new Student("98765-00", "Barney");

// Insert only the first Student into the HashMap.
x.put(s1.getIdNo(), s1);

// Maintain a second handle on each of the two Students.
Student s3 = s1;   // s1, and hence s3, is in the HashMap.
Student s4 = s2;   // s2, and hence s4, are NOT in the HashMap.
```

The situation with regard to objects x, s1, s2, s3, and s4 can be thought of conceptually as illustrated in Figure 6-13.

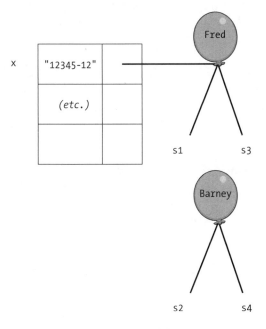

Figure 6-13. *Two Student objects, only one of which is referenced by* HashMap x

and the results of calling x.contains(...) with respect to s3, then s4, are as follows:

```
// This first test will evaluate to true ...
if (x.contains(s3)) { ...

// ... while this second test will evaluate to false.
if (x.contains(s4)) { ...
```

- int size(): Returns a count of the number of key/object pairs currently stored in the HashMap.

- void clear(): Empties out the HashMap of all key/object pairs, as if it had just been newly instantiated.

- boolean isEmpty(): Returns true if the HashMap contains no entries; otherwise, returns false.

The TreeMap Class

The Java TreeMap class is another dictionary type collection. TreeMaps are very similar to HashMaps, with one notable difference:

- When we iterate through a TreeMap, objects are automatically retrieved from the collection in *ascending key (sorted) order*.

- When we iterate through a HashMap, on the other hand, there's no guarantee as to the order in which items will be retrieved.

Let's write a program to demonstrate this difference between HashMaps and TreeMaps. In our program, we'll instantiate one of each of these two types of collection. This time, we'll insert Strings into the collections rather than Students; we'll let the same String serve as *both* the key and the value.

```java
import java.util.*;

public class TreeHash {
    public static void main(String[] args) {
    // Instantiate two collections -- a HashMap and a TreeMap -- with
    // String as both the key type and the object type.
    HashMap<String, String> h = new HashMap<String, String>();
    TreeMap<String, String> t = new TreeMap<String, String>();

    // Insert several Strings into the HashMap, where the String serves
    // as both the key and the value.
    h.put("FISH", "FISH");
    h.put("DOG", "DOG");
    h.put("CAT", "CAT");
    h.put("ZEBRA", "ZEBRA");
    h.put("RAT", "RAT");

    // Insert the same Strings, in the same order, into the TreeMap.
    t.put("FISH", "FISH");
    t.put("DOG", "DOG");
    t.put("CAT", "CAT");
    t.put("ZEBRA", "ZEBRA");
    t.put("RAT", "RAT");

    // Iterate through the HashMap to retrieve all Strings ...
    System.out.println("Retrieving from the HashMap:");
    for (String s : h.values()) {
        System.out.println(s);
    }

    System.out.println();
```

```
    // ... and then through the TreeMap.
    System.out.println("Retrieving from the TreeMap:");
        for (String s : t.values()) {
            System.out.println(s);
        }
    }
}
```

Here's the output:

```
Retrieving from the HashMap:
ZEBRA
CAT
FISH
DOG
RAT

Retrieving from the TreeMap:
CAT
DOG
FISH
RAT
ZEBRA
```

Note that the TreeMap did indeed sort the Strings, whereas the Strings were retrieved in an arbitrary order—neither in the order in which they were inserted, nor in sorted order—from the HashMap.

All of the other methods that we discussed for the HashMap class work in the same fashion for TreeMaps.

If TreeMaps are effectively identical to HashMaps with the added benefit of sorted iteration, why don't we simply ignore the HashMap class and always use the TreeMap class to create dictionary collections instead? The answer lies in the fact that dictionaries can use **any object type** as a key.

If we use Strings as keys, as we've done in all of our examples thus far, a TreeMap has no trouble determining how to sort them, because the String class defines a compareTo method that the TreeMap class takes advantage of. However, if we use a **user-defined type** as a key, the burden is on us to programmatically define what it means to sort that object type.

Let's say, for example, that we create a dictionary collection where a Department object serves as the key, and the Professor who chairs the department is the value referenced by a given key. If we declare the collection to be a TreeMap, we must define what it means for one Department to "come before" another in sorted fashion if we plan on iterating through the collection. The code required to do so is rather advanced—certainly beyond the scope of what we've learned about Java thus far. Suffice it to say that if we don't truly **need** to iterate through a dictionary in sorted key order, it's not worth the extra trouble of using TreeMap when HashMap will do quite nicely.

The Same Object Can Be Simultaneously Referenced by Multiple Collections

As mentioned earlier, when we talk about inserting an object into a collection, what we really mean is that we're inserting a reference to the object, not the object itself. This implies that the *same* object can be referenced by *multiple* collections simultaneously.

Think of a person as an object, and his or her telephone number as a reference for reaching that person. Now, as I proposed earlier in this chapter, think of an address book as a collection: it's easy to see that the *same* person's phone number (reference) can be recorded in many *different* address books (collections) simultaneously.

Let's consider an example relevant to the SRS. Given the students who are registered to attend a particular course, we may simultaneously maintain the following:

- An ordered list of these students for purposes of knowing who registered first for a follow-on course

- A dictionary that allows us to retrieve a given Student object based on the student's name

- Perhaps even a second SRS-wide dictionary that organizes *all* students at the university based on their student ID numbers

This is depicted conceptually in Figure 6-14.

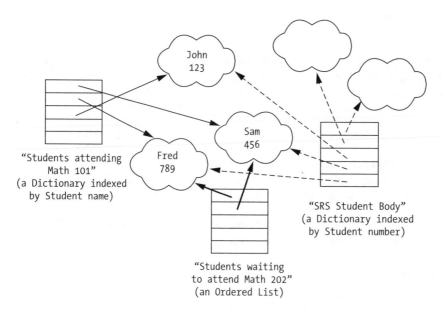

Figure 6-14. *A given object may be referenced by multiple collections simultaneously.*

One common mistake made by beginning OO programmers is to assume that if a given collection is emptied (perhaps via an explicit call to its clear method), then the objects that the collection was previously referencing will be garbage collected. Recall our discussion of garbage collection from Chapter 3: only when there are no longer *any* handles on a given object will its memory will be recycled by the JVM. Given that objects are often referenced by multiple collections simultaneously, we cannot assume that clearing a single collection will free up the objects that it is referencing. For example, if we were to clear the contents of the "Students waiting to attend Math 202" collection of Figure 6-14, the "John", "Fred", and "Sam" Student objects would still be referenced by two other collections. Unless these Student objects were subsequently removed from those other collections, as well, they would not be garbage collected.

Inventing Our Own Collection Types

As mentioned earlier, different types of collections have different properties and behaviors. You must therefore familiarize yourself with the various predefined collection types available for your OO language of choice, and choose the one that is the most appropriate for what you need in a given situation. Or, if none of them suits you, invent your own! This is where we start to get a real sense of the power of an OO language. Since we have the ability to invent our own user-defined types, it of course follows that we have free rein to define our own *collection* types.

We have several ways to create our own collection types:

- *Approach #1*: We can design a brand-new collection class from scratch.

- *Approach #2*: We can use the techniques that we learned in Chapter 5 to extend a predefined collection class.

- *Approach #3*: We can create a "wrapper" class that encapsulates one of the built-in collection types, to "abstract away" some of the details involved with manipulating the collection.

Let's discuss each of these three approaches in turn.

Approach #1: Designing a New Collection Class from Scratch

Creating a brand-new collection class from scratch is typically quite a bit of work. Since most OO languages provide such a wide range of predefined collection types, it's almost always possible to find a preexisting collection type to use as a starting point, in which case one of the other two approaches would almost always be preferred.

If we *were* to want to create a new collection class from scratch, however, we'd almost certainly want such a class to take advantage of the predefined Collection **interface**. We'll discuss the notion of interfaces in general, and of the Collection interface specifically, in Chapter 7.

Note that, despite the fact that an array serves as a simple sort of ordered list collection, it is not formally a Java Collection in the "capital C" sense of the word.

Approach #2: Extending a Predefined Collection Class (MyIntCollection)

To illustrate this approach, let's extend the ArrayList class to create a collection class called MyIntCollection. An object of type MyIntCollection will be able to, at a minimum, respond to all of the same service requests that an ArrayList can respond to, because by virtue of inheritance,

MyIntCollection *is* an ArrayList. However, we want our MyIntCollection class to do some extra work: we want it to keep track of the smallest and largest int values stored within a given MyIntCollection instance. To accomplish this, we'll add a few new features, along with overriding the add method that we'd otherwise inherit as is from ArrayList.

We'll look at the code for the MyIntCollection class in its entirety first, and we'll walk through it step by step afterward.

```java
import java.util.ArrayList;

public class MyIntCollection extends ArrayList<Integer> {
    // We inherit all of the attributes and methods of a standard ArrayList
    // as is, then define a few extra attributes and methods of our own:
    // two ints to keep track of the smallest and largest values
    // added to the collection, plus another int to keep a running
    // total of all values added to the collection.
    private int smallestInt;
    private int largestInt;
    private int total;

    // Replace the default constructor.
    public MyIntCollection() {
     // Do everything defined by the constructor of the ArrayList
        // base class first - we needn't know what those things are, simply
        // that we ought to do them!
        super();

        // Initialize the total.
        total = 0;
    }

    // Override the add() method as inherited from ArrayList.
    public boolean add(int i) {
        // Remember this int as the largest/smallest, if appropriate.
        // (The FIRST time we add a value, that value will, by definition,
        // be BOTH the smallest AND the largest that we've seen so far!)
        if (this.isEmpty()) {
            smallestInt = i;
            largestInt = i;
        }
        else {
            if (i < smallestInt) smallestInt = i;
            if (i > largestInt) largestInt = i;
        }

        // Include this value in the running total.
        total = total + i;

        // Insert the int into the collection using the add method as implemented
        // by the ArrayList base class.  Again, we needn't understand
```

```
        // the inner workings of HOW this method does so ...
        return super.add(i);
    }

    // Several new methods.

    public int getSmallestInt() {
        return smallestInt;
    }

    public int getLargestInt() {
        return largestInt;
    }

    public double getAverage() {
        // Note that we must cast ints to doubles to avoid
        // truncation when dividing.
        return ((double) total) / ((double) this.size());
    }
}
```

Now, let's walk through selected portions of the MyIntCollection code.

Wrapper Classes for Primitive Types

The first unusual bit of syntax that we notice is with regard to the class that we're extending:

```
public class MyIntCollection extends ArrayList<Integer> {
```

If we are going to be placing int values in our collection, why are we designating Integer as the type of element to be inserted?

Unlike arrays, whose elements may be either primitive or reference types, Java collections are designed to hold only *reference types*. An int is not an object, and so if we wish to store primitive values in collections, we must "box" them *inside* of objects, as illustrated conceptually in Figure 6-15.

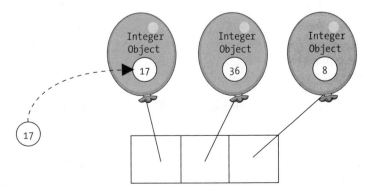

Figure 6-15. *We must "box" primitive values in objects in order to insert them into a collection.*

The Java language provides a different "wrapper" class to serve as a "box" for each of the eight distinct primitive types: `Integer`, `Float`, `Double`, `Byte`, `Short`, `Long`, `Boolean`, and `Character`. All of these classes are included in the core `java.lang` package.

Prior to J2SE 5.0, programmers were responsible for writing the explicit code necessary to "wrap" primitive values inside of corresponding wrapper objects before inserting them into a collection, as well as the code to "unwrap" them when retrieving them from a collection; an example of how this was done is provided in Appendix G.

As of J2SE 5.0, the **autoboxing** feature was introduced to save us the trouble of having to do this explicitly. Simply by declaring a collection as containing the appropriate wrapper type, we are free to insert and retrieve primitive values as is:

```
ArrayList<Integer> x = new ArrayList<Integer>();

// Directly add a primitive (int) value to the ArrayList;
// it automatically gets "boxed" inside of an Integer object.
x.add(17);

// Details omitted ...

// Directly retrieve a primitive (int) value from the
// ArrayList; it automatically gets "unboxed" from its
// enclosing Integer object.
int y = x.elementAt(0); // y now has the value 17
```

We'll revisit the wrapper classes for primitive types several more times in the book, as they serve many useful purposes.

Reusing a Base Class Constructor

The constructor that we've provided for the `MyIntCollection` class takes advantage of the `super` keyword to reuse the constructor code of the base `ArrayList` class, a technique that we discussed in Chapter 5:

```
public MyIntCollection() {
    // Do everything defined by the constructor of the ArrayList
    // base class first - we needn't know what those things are, simply
    // that we ought to do them!
    super();
```

It isn't necessary for us to know the behind-the-scenes details that take place when an instance of an `ArrayList` is created. Simply by including

```
super();
```

as the first line of code in our constructor, we ensure that such details are taken care of for us.

Strictly speaking, you could omit the preceding line of code, for as you learned in Chapter 5, a call to `super()` is **implied** as the first line of code of a derived class's constructor. However, inserting this line of code explicitly doesn't hurt, and in fact clarifies what is actually happening when this constructor is executed.

Overriding the add Method

We override the add method of the MyIntCollection class as inherited from ArrayList so that we may continuously monitor values as we add them to our custom collection to keep track of what the smallest and largest values have been.

```java
public boolean add(int i) {
    // Remember this int as the largest and/or the smallest,
    // as appropriate.  (The FIRST time we add a value, it by default
    // will be BOTH the smallest AND the largest!)
    if (this.isEmpty()) {
        smallestInt = i;
        largestInt = i;
    }
    else {
        if (i < smallestInt) smallestInt = i;
        if (i > largestInt) largestInt = i;
    }

    // Include this value in the running total.
    total = total + i;
```

Finally, by invoking super.add(i) from our overridden add method, we're ensuring that we do everything that the ArrayList base class does when adding an item to its internal collection—again without having to know the details of what is happening behind the scenes. And, because we must return a boolean value from our add method per the (overridden) method header, we can accomplish this by simply returning the value that results from this base class method call:

```java
    // Insert the int into the collection using the add method as implemented
    // by the ArrayList base class.  Again, we needn't understand
    // the inner workings of HOW this method does so ...
    return super.add(i);
}
```

The remainder of the code for the MyIntCollection class as shown earlier in this section is self-explanatory, except perhaps for the final method:

```java
public double getAverage() {
    return ((double) total) / ((double) this.size());
}
```

Since both total and this.size() are int(eger) expressions, we must explicitly cast at least one of them to be a double value before performing the division. If we were to simply return the result of total / this.size(), we'd be dividing an int by an int, which would cause the fractional part of the answer to be truncated.

Putting MyIntCollection to Work

Here's sample client code to demonstrate how our new MyIntCollection collection type can be put to good use:

```java
public class MyIntCollectionExample {
    public static void main(String[] args) {
        // Instantiate one of our newly designed collections.
        MyIntCollection mic = new MyIntCollection();

        // Add four random integers to our "special" collection.
        mic.add(3);
        mic.add(6);
        mic.add(1);
        mic.add(9);

        // Take advantage of the size method as inherited from ArrayList ...
        System.out.println("The collection contains " + mic.size() +
            " int values");

        // ... and then ask mic "specialized" questions about its contents that a
        // garden-variety ArrayList couldn't easily answer.
        System.out.println("The smallest value is:  " + mic.getSmallestInt());
        System.out.println("The largest value is:  " + mic.getLargestInt());
        System.out.println("The average is:  " + mic.getAverage());
    }
}
```

Here's the output:

```
The collection contains 4 int values
The smallest value is:  1
The largest value is:  9
The average is:  4.75
```

Approach #3: Encapsulating a Standard Collection (MyIntCollection2)

Let's now take a look at an alternative way of inventing a custom collection class such as MyIntCollection. Instead of **_extending_** the ArrayList class as we did with MyIntCollection, we'll design a custom class to **_encapsulate_** an instance of an ArrayList collection.

We'll design a class called MyIntCollection2 to illustrate this approach, using the code for MyIntCollection as a starting point; as you'll see, the differences between the two approaches are rather subtle.

- The first change would, of course, be to eliminate the extends ArrayList clause from the class declaration:

  ```java
  // We're no longer extending the ArrayList class.
  public class MyIntCollection2 {
  ```

- Instead, we'll encapsulate an ArrayList as an **_attribute_**:

  ```java
  ArrayList<Integer> numbers;
  ```

along with retaining the other attributes that we declared for MyIntCollection: smallestInt, largestInt, and total.

- In the constructor for our new class, we'll instantiate the embedded numbers ArrayList whenever we instantiate MyIntCollection2 as a whole:

```java
public MyIntCollection2() {
    // Instantiate the embedded ArrayList.
    numbers = new ArrayList<Integer>();

    // Initialize the total.
    total = 0;
}
```

- Since we aren't extending the ArrayList class any longer, we won't inherit a size method automatically, and so we'll declare one of our own. Our size method will simply delegate the task of determining collection size to the embedded numbers ArrayList:

```java
// Since we don't INHERIT a size() method any longer, let's add one!
public int size() {
    // DELEGATION!
    return numbers.size();
}
```

- Recall that we overrode the add method in our MyIntCollection class to specialize its behavior as compared with the generic ArrayList version that we'd otherwise have inherited. Since we aren't extending the ArrayList class in designing MyIntCollection2, we won't inherit an add method, and so we'll declare one of our own. The code for this add method is virtually identical to that of the MyIntCollection class's version of add, except for two minor syntactical changes that are necessary to delegate work to the encapsulated numbers collection—these changes are **bolded** in the following code:

```java
// Since we don't INHERIT an add() method any longer, let's add one!
public boolean add(int i) {
    // Remember this int as the largest/smallest,
    // if appropriate.  (The FIRST time we add a value, it by default
    // will be BOTH the smallest AND the largest!)
    // DELEGATE to the embedded collection.
    if (numbers.isEmpty()) {
        smallestInt = i;
        largestInt = i;
    }
    else {
        if (i < smallestInt) smallestInt = i;
        if (i > largestInt) largestInt = i;
    }

    // Increase the total.
    total = total + i;
```

```
        // Add the int to the numbers collection.
        // DELEGATE to the embedded collection.
        return numbers.add(i);
    }
```

- All remaining methods as declared for MyIntCollection—getSmallestInt, getLargestInt, and getAverage—remain unchanged for MyIntCollection2.

Here is the code for MyIntCollection2 in its entirety—changes as compared to MyIntCollection are **bolded**:

```
import java.util.ArrayList;

// We're no longer extending the ArrayList class.
public class MyIntCollection2 {
    // Instead, we're encapsulating a ArrayList inside of this class.
    ArrayList<Integer> numbers;

    // We define a few extra attributes and methods beyond those that the
    // encapsulated ArrayList will provide -- the SAME attributes and methods
    // that we declared for the MyIntCollection class:
    private int smallestInt;
    private int largestInt;
    private int total;

    public MyIntCollection2() {
        // Instantiate the embedded ArrayList.
        numbers = new ArrayList<Integer>();

        // Initialize the total.
        total = 0;
    }

    // Since we don't INHERIT a size() method any longer, let's add one!
    public int size() {
        // DELEGATION!
        return numbers.size();
    }

    // Since we don't INHERIT an add() method any longer, we can't override it;
    // so, let's add one instead!
    public boolean add(int i) {
        // Remember this int as the largest/smallest,
        // if appropriate.  (The FIRST time we add a value, it by default
        // will be BOTH the smallest AND the largest!)
        // DELEGATE to the encapsulated collection.
        if (numbers.isEmpty()) {
            smallestInt = i;
            largestInt = i;
        }
```

```
        else {
            if (i < smallestInt) smallestInt = i;
            if (i > largestInt) largestInt = i;
        }

    // Increase the total.
    total = total + i;

    // Add the int to the numbers collection.
    // DELEGATE to the encapsulated collection.
    return numbers.add(i);
    }

    // All remaining methods are identical to those of MyIntCollection.

    public int getSmallestInt() {
        return smallestInt;
    }

    public int getLargestInt() {
        return largestInt;
    }

    public double getAverage() {
        return ((double) total)/this.size();
    }
}
```

Putting MyIntCollection2 to Work

The client code needed to manipulate this "flavor" of custom int collection is *identical* to the client code that we used to manipulate the first version of MyIntCollection—*a testimonial to the power of encapsulation*! The client code is repeated here, substituting all references to MyIntCollection with references to MyIntCollection2—but that's all that had to change!

```
public class MyIntCollection2Example {
  public static void main(String[] args) {
    // Instantiate one of our newly designed collections!
    MyIntCollection2 mic = new MyIntCollection2();

    // Add four random integers to our "special" collection.
    mic.add(3);
    mic.add(6);
    mic.add(1);
    mic.add(9);

    // Take advantage of the size method ...
    System.out.println("The collection contains " + mic.size() +
        " int values");
```

```
    // ... and then ask mic "specialized" questions about its contents.
    System.out.println("The smallest value is:  " + mic.getSmallestInt());
    System.out.println("The largest value is:  " + mic.getLargestInt());
    System.out.println("The average is:  " + mic.getAverage());
  }
}
```

and the output would be the same as before.

Trade-offs of Approach #2 vs. Approach #3

As illustrated with the MyIntCollection and MyIntCollection2 examples, the coding effort required with either of the two approaches to creating a custom collection—extending a predefined collection class versus encapsulating an instance of such a collection—is comparable. What are the advantages, then, of one approach versus the other?

An advantage of extending a predefined collection class (approach #2) is that when we instantiate such a class at run time, we create only one object in memory—an instance of MyIntCollection, which is *simultaneously* an ArrayList by virtue of inheritance. By comparison, when we create an instance of MyIntCollection2, we wind up creating two objects, as illustrated in Figure 6-16. Thus, approach #2 is a bit more economical in terms of memory usage.

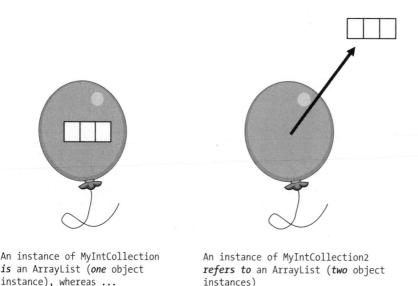

An instance of MyIntCollection *is* an ArrayList (*one* object instance), whereas ...

An instance of MyIntCollection2 *refers to* an ArrayList (*two* object instances)

Figure 6-16. *Instantiating one versus two objects at run time*

Alternatively, an advantage of encapsulating a predefined collection class instance (approach #3) is that we can choose to expose as few of the encapsulated collection's public behaviors as we wish to our client code.

- MyIntCollection, as an ArrayList, inherits all 30 public behaviors of the ArrayList class. Even if we see relevance only in the size and add methods of MyIntCollection, the other 28 features are exposed to/accessible by client code, as well.

- Based on the way that we designed the MyIntCollection2 class, on the other hand, it exposes only ***two*** of these public behaviors—size and add—thus simplifying the task of using our class from the perspective of client code. Furthermore, if we wanted to, we could ***disguise*** these methods by giving them entirely different names in MyIntCollection2, as follows:

```
public class MyIntCollection2 {
    // details omitted ...

    // This was formerly the size() method ...
    public int getIntCount() {
        // DELEGATION!
        return numbers.size();
    }

    // This was formerly the add() method ...
    public boolean insertAnInt(int i) {
        // Remember this int as the largest/smallest,
        // if appropriate.  (The FIRST time we add a value, it by default
        // will be BOTH the smallest AND the largest!)
        // DELEGATE to the encapsulated collection.
        if (numbers.isEmpty()) { ...

    // etc.
```

thus taking full advantage of the power of encapsulation and information hiding.

The bottom line is that neither approach #2 nor approach #3 is dramatically better than the other. By understanding the subtle differences between the two, you'll be able to choose between them on a case-by-case basis.

Collections As Method Return Types

Collections provide a way to overcome the limitation noted in Chapter 4 about methods being able to return only a single result. If we define a method as having a return type that is a ***collection*** type, we can return an arbitrarily sized collection of object references to client code.

In the following code snippet for the Course class, a getRegisteredStudents method is provided to enable client code to request a reference to the entire collection of Student objects that are registered for a particular course:

```
public class Course {
    private ArrayList<Student> enrolledStudents;

    // Details omitted ...
```

```
// The following method returns a reference to an entire collection
// containing however many Students are registered for the Course in question.
public ArrayList<Student> getRegisteredStudents() {
    return enrolledStudents;
}

// etc.
```

Here's an example of how client code might then use such a method:

```
// Instantiate a course and several students.
Course c = new Course();
Student s1 = new Student();
Student s2 = new Student();
Student s3 = new Student();

// Enroll the students in the course.
c.enroll(s1);
c.enroll(s2);
c.enroll(s3);

// Now, ask the course to give us a handle on the collection of
// all of its registered students and iterate through the collection,
// printing out a grade report for each student.
for (Student s : c.getRegisteredStudents()) {
    s.printGradeReport();
}
```

Note the use of a nested method call in the for statement; since c.getRegisteredStudents() is an expression of type ArrayList, this expression can be used in the for statement to designate the collection that we wish to iterate through.

In Chapter 7, when we discuss interfaces in general and the Collection interface in particular, we'll look at an alternative way of returning a collection from a method that makes our code more versatile.

Collections of Derived Types

As mentioned previously, arrays, as simple collections, contain items (either primitive values or object references) that are all of the same type: all int(egers), for example, or all (references to) Student objects. As it turns out, regardless of what type of collection we're using, we'll typically want to constrain it to contain similarly typed objects, for reasons that we'll explore in Chapter 7 when we discuss *polymorphism*. However, the power of inheritance steps in to make collections quite flexible in terms of what they contain.

It turns out that if we declare a collection to hold objects of a given superclass—for example, Person—then we're free to insert objects explicitly declared to be of type Person *or of any type derived from* Person—for example, UndergraduateStudent, GraduateStudent, and Professor.

This is due to the "is a" nature of inheritance; UndergraduateStudent, GraduateStudent, and Professor objects, as subclasses of Person, are simply special cases of Person objects. The Java compiler would therefore be perfectly happy to see code such as the following:

```
Person[] people = new Person[100];

Professor p = new Professor();
UndergraduateStudent s1 = new UndergraduateStudent();
GraduateStudent s2 = new GraduateStudent();

// Add a mixture of professors and students in random order to the array.

people[0] = s1;
people[1] = p;
people[2] = s2;
// etc.
```

or, for an ArrayList:

```
ArrayList<Person> people = new ArrayList<Person>();

Professor p = new Professor();
UndergraduateStudent s1 = new UndergraduateStudent();
GraduateStudent s2 = new GraduateStudent();

// Add a mixture of professors and students in random order to the ArrayList.

people.add(s1);
people.add(p);
people.add(s2);
// etc.
```

Revisiting Our Student Class Design

You may recall that when we talked about the attributes of the Student class back in Chapter 3, we held off on assigning types to the courseLoad and transcript attributes, as shown in Table 6-1.

Table 6-1. *Proposed Data Structure for the Student Class*

Attribute Name	Data Type
name	String
studentID	String
birthDate	Date
address	String
major	String
gpa	double
advisor	Professor
courseLoad	???
transcript	???

Armed with what we now know about collections, we can now complete our Student class design.

The courseLoad Attribute of Student

The courseLoad attribute is meant to represent a list of all Course objects that the Student is presently enrolled in. So, it makes perfect sense that this attribute be declared as simply a standard collection of Course object references—an ArrayList, perhaps:

```java
import java.util.ArrayList;

public class Student {
  private String name;
  private String studentId;
  private ArrayList<Course> courseLoad;
  // etc.
```

The transcript Attribute of Student

The transcript attribute is a bit more challenging. What is a transcript, in real-world terms? It's a report of all of the courses that a student has taken since he or she was first admitted to this university, along with the semester in which each course was taken, the number of credit hours that each course was worth, and the letter grade that the student received for the course. A typical transcript entry, when printed, might look as follows:

```
CS101       Beginning Objects       3.0          A
```

If we think of each line item on a printed transcript as an *object*, we can declare a TranscriptEntry class to describe them, as follows:

```java
public class TranscriptEntry {
    // One TranscriptEntry object represents a single line item on a printed
    // transcript.
    private Course courseTaken;
    private String semesterTaken;  // e.g., "Fall 2006"
    private String gradeReceived;  // e.g., "B+"

    // Constructor.
    public TranscriptEntry(Course c, String semester, String grade) {
        // Details omitted ...
    }

    // Accessor method details omitted ...

    public void printTranscriptEntry() {
        // We "talk to" the courseTaken object/attribute to obtain the
        // majority of the required information (an example of
        // delegation). Reminder: \t is a tab character.
        System.out.println(
            this.getCourseTaken().getCourseNo() + "\t" +
            this.getCourseTaken().getTitle() + "\t" +
```

```
            this.getCourseTaken().getCreditHours() + "\t" +
            this.getGradeReceived());
    }


    // Other methods TBD ...
}
```

Since each TranscriptEntry object maintains a handle on a Course object, the TranscriptEntry object can avail itself of the Course object's course number, title, or credit hour value (needed for computing the GPA)—all privately encapsulated in the Course object as attributes—by calling the appropriate accessor methods on that Course object as needed.

Back in the Student class, we can now define the Student's transcript attribute to be a *collection* of TranscriptEntry objects:

```
import java.util.ArrayList;

public class Student {
    private String name;
    private String studentId;
    private ArrayList<TranscriptEntry> transcript;
    // etc.
```

We can then equip the Student class with an addTranscriptEntry method for use in inserting a new TranscriptEntry into the transcript collection:

```
    public void addTranscriptEntry(TranscriptEntry te) {
        // Store the TranscriptEntry in our ArrayList.
        transcript.add(te);
    }
```

along with a printTranscript method for iterating through this collection:

```
    // This method merely iterates through the collection,
    // delegating the work of printing to the individual
    // TranscriptEntry objects.
    public void printTranscript() {
        // Print header information on the transcript:
        // Student's name, name of the university, date
        // printed, etc.
        System.out.println("Academic transcript for " +
            this.getName());
        // Other transcript header details omitted ...

        // Print individual transcript line items.
        for (TranscriptEntry t : transcript) {
            t.printTranscriptEntry();
        }
    }


    // etc.
}
```

Figure 6-17 illustrates how Student, ArrayList, TranscriptEntry, and Course objects would thus be "wired together" in memory at run time.

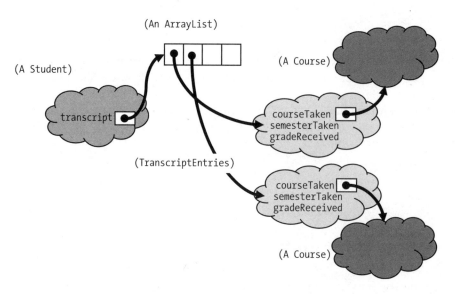

Figure 6-17. *As "wired together" in memory, a Student references an ArrayList, which in turn references TranscriptEntry objects. These in turn each reference a Course object.*

Finally, let's look at the client code that might be involved in putting these classes to work:

```
Student s = new Student("1234567", "James Huddleston");
Course c = new Course("LANG 800", "Advanced Language Studies");
s.registerForCourse(c);

// Time passes ... details omitted.

// Semester is finished!  Assign a grade to this student (he's brilliant!).
TranscriptEntry te = new TranscriptEntry(c, "Spring 2006", "A+");
s.addTranscriptEntry(te);

// Additional grades assigned for other courses ... details omitted.

s.printTranscript();
```

The manner in which we're assigning a grade to a student for a course that she or he has completed (namely, by instantiating a TranscriptEntry object, and then calling the Student's addTranscriptEntry method)

```
TranscriptEntry te = new TranscriptEntry(c, "Spring 2006", "A+");
s.addTranscriptEntry(te);
```

is not as intuitive as it could be to someone reading this client code. Let's see if we can improve upon our design with a goal of rendering client code that is a bit more straightforward.

The transcript Attribute, Take 2

We'll add a bit more sophistication to our abstraction by declaring a class called `Transcript` to encapsulate a standard type of collection, the technique that we employed when creating the `MyIntCollection2` class earlier in this chapter.

```java
public class Transcript {
    // The Transcript class ENCAPSULATES a garden variety ArrayList
    // of TranscriptEntry references.
    private ArrayList<TranscriptEntry> transcriptEntries;

    // Maintain a handle on the Student to whom this
    // transcript belongs.
    Student owner;

    // Constructor/accessor details omitted.

    // Rather than having client code manufacture a TranscriptEntry object
    // to pass in as an argument, we'll "disguise" what we are doing a bit.
    public void courseCompleted(Course c, String semester, String grade) {
        // Instantiate and insert a brand-new TranscriptEntry object into the
        // ArrayList - details hidden away!
        transcriptEntries.add(new TranscriptEntry(c, semester, grade);
    }

    // We've transferred the logic of the Student class's printTranscript
    // method into the Transcript class's print method.
    public void print() {
        for (TranscriptEntry te : transcript) {
            te.printTranscriptEntry();
        }
    }

    // etc.
}
```

Of particular note is the fact that we've effectively hidden our use of `TranscriptEntry` objects from client code by providing a `courseCompleted` method. This method accepts the "raw materials" necessary to create a `TranscriptEntry` object—namely, a `Course` reference plus `Strings` representing the semester in which the course was completed and the grade received—and ***invokes the*** `TranscriptEntry` ***constructor from within the privacy of the*** `courseCompleted` ***method body***. As you'll see shortly, this relieves client code from having to deal with the `TranscriptEntry` class; `TranscriptEntry` is now strictly a "helper" class that exists to serve the `Transcript` class behind the scenes.

Chapter 13 introduces the notion of **inner classes**, a construct used to "bury" the declaration of one class, such as `TranscriptEntry`, wholly within another so that it truly is a ***private type***.

We'll now go back to the Student class and change our declaration of the transcript attribute from an ArrayList to a Transcript:

```
public class Student {
  private String name;
  private String studentId;
  // This used to be declared as an ArrayList.
  private Transcript transcript;
  // etc.
```

We can in turn simplify the printTranscript method of the Student class, to take advantage of delegation—it's now a one-liner!

```
  public void printTranscript() {
    // We now DELEGATE the work of printing all entries to
    // the Transcript itself!
    transcript.print();
  }

  // etc.
```

Finally, let's look at the client code that might be involved in putting these ***new and improved*** classes to work. I've repeated the client code example used before, **bolding** the subset of client code that has changed as a result of our improved design:

```
Student s = new Student("1234567", "James Huddleston");
Course c = new Course("LANG 800", "Advanced Language Studies");
s.registerForCourse(c);

// Time passes ... details omitted.

// Semester is finished!  Assign a grade to this student (he's brilliant!).
// It's now accomplished as a single line of arguably more intuitive code.
s.courseCompleted(c, "Spring 2006", "A+");

// Additional grades assigned for other courses ... details omitted.

s.printTranscript();
```

The manner in which we're assigning a grade to a student for a course that she or he has completed—namely, by calling the courseCompleted method of Student—is arguably much clearer and more self-documenting to anyone reading this client code than the previous version of client code. Here's the code before:

```
TranscriptEntry te = new TranscriptEntry(c, "Fall 2006", "B+");
s.addTranscriptEntry(te);
```

And here's the code after:

```
s.courseCompleted(c, "Spring 2006", "A+");
```

This "take 2" approach of introducing **two** new classes/abstractions—TranscriptEntry and Transcript—is a bit more sophisticated than the first approach, where we only introduced TranscriptEntry as an abstraction.

- We've simplified the Student class considerably. Student code needn't be complicated by the details of **how** transcripts are represented or managed internally, or even that there is such a thing as a TranscriptEntry object—those details are hidden inside of the Transcript class, as they should be.

- **More significantly, we've simplified our client code**. The Student class need be designed and coded only once, but **client code** written to **manipulate** Student objects will potentially occur in countless places across numerous applications.

Whenever possible, it's desirable to bury implementation details inside of a class rather than exposing client code to such details; this lessens the burden on developers/maintainers of client code by lessening the likelihood of logic errors in such code.

Figure 6-18 illustrates how Student, Transcript, ArrayList, TranscriptEntry, and Course objects would be "wired together" at run time, and Table 6-2 provides a side-by-side comparison of the code used in our two "takes" on representing the notion of student transcripts.

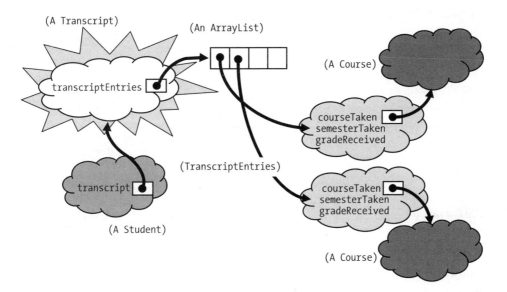

Figure 6-18. *Introducing another level of abstraction in the form of a* Transcript *class ultimately simplifies client code, which is an important design goal.*

Table 6-2. *Comparing the "Take 1" and "Take 2" Code Versions*

Code for "Take 1"	*Code for "Take 2"*

The TranscriptEntry **Class**

| ```java
public class TranscriptEntry {
  private Course courseTaken;
  private String semesterTaken;
  private String gradeReceived;

  // Details omitted ...


  // Constructor.
  public TranscriptEntry(Course c,
    String semester, String grade) {
    // Details omitted ...
}


  public void printTranscriptEntry() {
    System.out.println((
      courseTaken.getCourseNo() +
      "\t" +
      courseTaken.getTitle() +
      "\t" +
      courseTaken.getCreditHours() +
      "\t" +
      getGradeReceived()));
  }


  // etc.
}
``` | *(The* TranscriptEntry *class code for "Take 2" is the same as for "Take 1.")* |

The Transcript **Class**

| *("Take 1" did not involve the* Transcript *class.)* | ```java
public class Transcript {
    private ArrayList<TranscriptEntry>
        transcriptEntries;

    // Details omitted ...

    public void courseCompleted(Course c,
        String semester, String grade) {
        transcriptEntries.add(
            new TranscriptEntry(c,
                semester, grade);
    }

    public void print() {
        print header info. ...
        for (TranscriptEntry te :
            transcript) {
            te.printTranscriptEntry();
        }
    }

    // etc.
}
``` |

Code for "Take 1"	*Code for "Take 2"*

The Student *Class*

```
import java.util.ArrayList;
```

```public class Student {```
 ``` private String name;```
 ``` private String studentId;```
	```public class Student {```
	 ``` private String name;```
	 ``` private String studentId;```

Here, we use an ArrayList.	*Here, we use a* Transcript.
``` private ArrayList<TranscriptEntry>``` ``` transcript;```	``` private Transcript transcript;```
``` // etc.```	``` // etc.```

	This method hides more "gory details," and is hence easier for client code to use. But, it serves the same purpose as the addTranscriptEntry *method in "Take 1."*
Client code has to be aware of the notion of a TranscriptEntry.	

``` public void addTranscriptEntry(```
 ```   TranscriptEntry te) {```
 ```   transcript.add(te);```
 ``` }```
	``` public void courseCompleted(Course c,```
	 ``` String semester, String grade) {```
	 ``` Transcript.courseCompleted(```
	 ``` c, semester, grade);```
	 ``` }```

``` public void printTranscript() {```
 ```   print header information ...```
 ```   for (TranscriptEntry t : transcript) {```
 ```   t.printTranscriptEntry();```
 ```   }```
 ``` }```
	``` public void printTranscript() {```
	 ``` // Delegation !```
	 ``` transcript.print();```
	 ``` }```

``` // etc.```	``` // etc.```
```}```	```}```

Sample Client Code

```Student s = new Student(...);```
 ```Course c = new Course(...);```
 ```s.registerForCourse(c);```
 ```// etc.```
	```Student s = new Student(...);```
	 ```Course c = new Course(...);```
	 ```s.registerForCourse(c);```
	 ```// etc.```

Client code is somewhat "ugly."	*Client code is more streamlined and intuitive!*

```TranscriptEntry te =```
 ```   new TranscriptEntry(c,```
 ```   "Fall 2006", "B+");```
 ```s.addTranscriptEntry(te);```
	```s.courseCompleted(c, "Fall 2006", "B+");```

```s.printTranscript();```	```s.printTranscript();```

Our Completed Student Data Structure

Table 6-3 illustrates how we've taken full advantage of collections to round out our Student class definition.

Table 6-3. *Rounding Out the* Student *Class's Data Structure with Collections*

Attribute Name	Data Type
name	String
studentID	String
birthDate	Date
address	String
major	String
gpa	double
advisor	Professor
courseLoad	**ARRAYLIST<COURSE>**
transcript	**Transcript**

Summary

In this chapter, you've learned

- Collections are special types of objects used to gather up and manage references to other objects.

- Most OO languages support three generic types of collection:

  - Ordered lists

  - Sets

  - Dictionaries (aka maps)

- Arrays are a simple type of collection that have some limitations, but we also have other more powerful collection types to draw upon with OO languages, such as Java's ArrayLists, HashMaps, TreeMaps, etc.

- It's important to familiarize yourself with the unique characteristics of whatever collection types are available for a particular OO language, so as to make the most informed selection of which collection type to use for a particular circumstance.

- You can invent your own collection types by either ***extending*** predefined collection classes or creating "wrapper classes" to ***encapsulate*** an instance of a predefined collection class, and the subtle differences between the two approaches.

- You can work around the limitation that a method can return only one result by having that result be a collection.

- You can create very sophisticated composite classes through the use of collections as attributes.

- "Burying" increasing levels of detail within layers of abstraction serves to simplify client code.

There's a bit more to appreciate about collections, but we must first cover some additional Java topics. We'll revisit collections in Chapter 7.

Don't forget to review Appendix G if you are working with a version of Java prior to version 5.0.

Exercises

1. Given the following abstraction:

   A book is a collection of chapters, each of which is a collection of pages.

   sketch out the code for the Book, Chapter, and Page classes.

   - Invent whatever attributes you think would be relevant, taking advantage of collections as attributes where appropriate.

   - Include methods in the Chapter class for adding pages, and for determining how many pages a chapter contains.

   - Include methods in the Book class for adding chapters, for determining how many chapters the book contains, for determining how many pages the book contains (hint: use delegation!), and for printing out a book's table of contents.

2. [*Coding*] Code the Book, Chapter, and Page classes that you specified in exercise 1, and write a simple driver program to put them through their paces.

3. What generic type(s) of collection(s)—ordered list, sorted ordered list, set, dictionary—might you use to represent each of the following abstractions? Explain your choices.

   - A computer parts catalog

   - A poker hand

   - Trouble calls logged by a technical help desk

4. What collections do you think it would be important to maintain for the SRS, based on the requirements presented in the Introduction to this book?

5. What collections do you think it would be important to maintain for the Prescription Tracking System (PTS) described in Appendix B?

6. What collections do you think it would be important to maintain for the problem area that you described for exercise 3 in Chapter 1?

7. [*Coding*] Modify the MyIntCollection class as presented in this chapter to add a method called printSortedContents that, when invoked, prints the contents of the collection in sorted order. You may make whatever changes you wish to the private details of the class in accommodating this new behavior.

   Then, modify the MyIntCollection2 version of the class to accommodate a printSortedContents method, as well.

   Was accommodating this new requirement significantly easier with one version of the custom collection than with the other?

CHAPTER 7

■ ■ ■

Some Final Object Concepts

By now, you've hopefully gained a solid appreciation for how powerful object-oriented languages are for modeling complex real-world situations. By way of review,

- We can create our own user-defined types, also known as classes, to model objects of arbitrary complexity, as we discussed in Chapter 3.

- We can arrange these types into class hierarchies to take advantage of the inheritance mechanism of OO languages, as we discussed in Chapter 5.

- Through encapsulation and information hiding, we can shield client code from changes that we make to the private implementation details of our classes, making objects responsible for ensuring the integrity of their own data, as we discussed in Chapter 4.

- We can design relationships between classes into their very "bone structure" so that collaborating objects can be linked together in memory at run time, as we discussed in Chapter 5.

- Classes can model the most complex of real-world concepts, particularly when we take advantage of collections, as we did when modeling the `transcript` attribute of the `Student` class in Chapter 6.

You might wonder how there could possibly be anything left in our OO bag of tricks! However, as powerful as all of the preceding OO language features are, there are still a few more important features of objects to be discussed.

In this chapter, we'll discuss

- How a *single* line of code, representing a message—for example, `x.foo();`—can exhibit a variety of different behaviors at run time

- How we can specify *what* an object's mission should be without going to the trouble of specifying the details of *how* the object is to carry out that mission, and also under what circumstances we'd want to be able to do so

- How an object can have a "split personality" by exhibiting the behaviors of two or more different types of object

- Creative ways for an entire class of objects to easily and efficiently share data without breaking the spirit of encapsulation

- How features can be defined that are associated with a class as a whole rather than with an instance of a class, and how we can take advantage of this capability to design *utility classes*

- How we may declare variables whose values, once assigned, remain constant while an application is executing

Polymorphism

The term **polymorphism** refers to the ability of two or more objects belonging to *different* classes to respond to exactly the *same* message (method call) in different class-specific ways.

As an example, if we were to instruct three different people—a surgeon, a hair stylist, and an actor—to "Cut!", then

- The surgeon would begin to make an incision.

- The hair stylist would begin to cut someone's hair.

- The actor would abruptly stop acting out the current scene, awaiting directorial guidance.

These three different professionals may be thought of as Person objects belonging to different professional subclasses: Surgeon, HairStylist, and Actor. Each was given the same message—"Cut!"—but carried out the operation differently as prescribed by the subclass that each belongs to.

Let's now turn to a software example relevant to the SRS. Assume that we've defined a Student superclass and two subclasses, GraduateStudent and UndergraduateStudent. In Chapter 5, we discussed the fact that a print method designed to print the values of all of a Student's attributes wouldn't necessarily suffice for printing the attribute values for a GraduateStudent, because the code as written for the Student superclass wouldn't know about any attributes that may have been added to the GraduateStudent subclass. We then looked at how to *override* the print method of Student to create specialized versions of the method for all of its subclasses. The syntax for doing so, which was first introduced in Chapter 5 with the GraduateStudent class, is repeated again here for your review. I've added the UndergraduateStudent class code, as well.

```
//-------------
// Student.java
//-------------

public class Student {
    private String name;
    private String studentId;
    private String major;
    private double gpa;

    // Public get/set methods would also be provided (details omitted) ...

    public void print() {
        // We can print only the attributes that the Student class
        // knows about.
        System.out.println("Student Name:  " + getName() + "\n" +
            "Student No.:  " + getStudentId()  + "\n" +
```

```
                    "Major Field:  " +  getMajor()  + "\n" +
                    "GPA:  " + getGpa());
        }
}


//--------------------
// GraduateStudent.java
//--------------------

public class GraduateStudent extends Student {
        // Adding several attributes.
        private String undergraduateDegree;
        private String undergraduateInstitution;

        // Public get/set methods would also be provided (details omitted) ...

        // Overriding the print method.
        public void print() {
            // Reuse code from the Student superclass ...
            super.print();

            // ... and then go on to print this subclass's specific attributes.
            System.out.println("Undergrad. Deg.:  " + getUndergraduateDegree() +
                "\n" + "Undergrad. Inst.:  " +
                getUndergraduateInstitution() + "\n" +
                "THIS IS A GRADUATE STUDENT ...");
        }
}


//-------------------------
// UndergraduateStudent.java
//-------------------------

public class UndergraduateStudent extends Student {
        // Adding an attribute.
        private String highSchool;

        // Public get/set methods would also be provided (details omitted) ...

        // Overriding the print method.
        public void print() {
            // Reuse code from the Student superclass ...
            super.print();

            // ... and then go on to print this subclass's specific attributes.
            System.out.println("High School Attended:  " + getHighSchool() +
                "\n" + "THIS IS AN UNDERGRADUATE STUDENT ...");
        }
}
```

In our main SRS application, we'll declare an ArrayList called studentBody to hold references to Student objects. We'll then populate the ArrayList with Student object references—some GraduateStudents and some UndergraduateStudents, randomly mixed—as shown here:

```
// Declare and instantiate an ArrayList of Students.
ArrayList<Student> studentBody = new ArrayList<Student>();

// Instantiate various types of Student object.
UndergraduateStudent u1 = new UndergraduateStudent();
UndergraduateStudent u2 = new UndergraduateStudent();
GraduateStudent g1 = new GraduateStudent();
GraduateStudent g2 = new GraduateStudent();
// etc.

// "Stuff" them into the ArrayList in random order.
studentBody.add(u1);
studentBody.add(g1);
studentBody.add(g2);
studentBody.add(u2);
// etc.
```

Since we're storing both GraduateStudent and UndergraduateStudent objects in this ArrayList, we've declared the ArrayList to be of a base type common to all objects that the collection is intended to contain, namely Student. By virtue of the "is a" nature of inheritance, an UndergraduateStudent object *is a* Student, and a GraduateStudent object *is a* Student, and so the compiler won't complain when we insert either type of object into this ArrayList.

Note that the compiler *would* object, however, if we tried to insert a Professor object into the same ArrayList, because a Professor isn't a Student, at least not in terms of the class hierarchy that we've defined for the SRS. If we wanted to include Professors in our ArrayList along with various types of Students, we'd have to declare the ArrayList as holding a base type common to *both* the Student and Professor classes, namely Person (or Object, which as we discussed in Chapter 5 is the implied superclass for all inheritance hierarchies in Java).

Perhaps we'd like to print the attribute values of all of the Students in our studentBody collection. We'd want each Student object—whether it's a GraduateStudent or an UndergraduateStudent instance—to use the version of the print method appropriate for its (sub)class. The following code will accomplish this nicely:

```
// Step through the ArrayList (collection) ...
for (Student s : studentBody) {
  // ... invoking the print method of each Student object.
  s.print();
}
```

Variable s is declared in the for statement to be a reference to a *generic* Student object, because that's the type of reference that we declared studentBody to hold. As we step through this collection of Student objects at *run time*, however, each object will *automatically* know which version of the print method it should execute, based on its own internal knowledge of the *specific* type/(sub)class that it belongs to (GraduateStudent versus UndergraduateStudent, in this example). We'd wind up with a report similar to the following, where the **bolded** lines emphasize the differences in output between the GraduateStudent and UndergraduateStudent versions of the print method:

```
Student Name:  John Smith
Student No.:  12345
Major Field:  Biology
GPA:  2.7
```
High School Attended: Rocky Mountain High
THIS IS AN UNDERGRADUATE STUDENT ...

```
Student Name:  Paula Green
Student No.:  34567
Major Field:  Education
GPA:  3.6
```
Undergrad. Deg.: B.A. English
Undergrad. Inst.: UCLA
THIS IS A GRADUATE STUDENT ...

```
Student Name:  Dinesh Prabhu
Student No.:  98765
Major Field:  Computer Science
GPA:  4.0
```
Undergrad. Deg.: B.S. Computer Engineering
Undergrad. Inst.: Case Western Reserve University
THIS IS A GRADUATE STUDENT ...

```
Student Name:  Jose Rodriguez
Student No.:  82640
Major Field:  Math
GPA:  3.1
```
High School Attended: James Ford Rhodes High
THIS IS AN UNDERGRADUATE STUDENT ...

The term ***polymorphism*** is defined in Merriam-Webster's dictionary as "the quality or state of being able to assume different forms." The line of code

```
    s.print();
```

in the preceding example is said to be ***polymorphic*** because the logic performed in response to the message can take many different forms, depending on the class identity of the object at run time.

Of course, this approach of iterating through a collection to ask each object, one by one, to do something in its own class-specific way won't work unless all objects in the collection understand the message being sent. That is, all objects in the studentBody collection ***must*** have defined a method with the signature print(). However, we've ***guaranteed*** that every object in the studentBody collection at run time ***will*** have such a method, as follows:

- First of all, we declared the studentBody ArrayList to hold objects of type Student (or subclasses thereof), so the compiler will therefore not allow us to put non-Student object references into the ArrayList. That is, any attempt to add a non-Student reference to the studentBody collection will be rejected at compile time:

```
ArrayList<Student> studentBody = new ArrayList<Student>();
Professor p = new Professor();

// This next line won't compile.
studentBody.add(p);
```

Here's the compilation error:

```
cannot find symbol
symbol: method add(Professor)
location: class java.util.ArrayList<Student>
```

- Second, we provided the Student superclass with a parameterless print method. Had we not done so, then the Java compiler would have objected to the line of code contained within the for loop:

```
// Step through the ArrayList (collection) ...
for (Student s : studentBody) {
    // This next line won't compile if the Student class doesn't define a
    // method with the signature "print()".
    s.print();
}
```

Here's the compilation error:

```
cannot find symbol
symbol: method print()
location: class Student
```

This error arises because the compiler checks the Student class (of which s is declared to be a member) for the presence of a parameterless print method. At **run time**, s might actually be referring to a generic Student, or to a GraduateStudent, or to an UndergraduateStudent, or to any other type derived from the Student class; however, the compiler has no way of predicting at **compile time** what the true **run-time** type of the object referred to by s will be. (The compiler doesn't have a crystal ball at its disposal!)

- Finally, by virtue of inheritance, any **subclass** of Student is guaranteed to either **inherit** the Student's version of the parameterless print method or to optionally **override** it with one of its own. Either way, all classes derived from Student will have such a method.

The bottom line is that all objects inserted into the studentBody ArrayList are **guaranteed** to be "print savvy" at run time.

Reflecting for a moment, you can now see that you'd previously learned about everything that's needed to facilitate polymorphism in a programming language before this discussion of polymorphism even began. ***Inheritance combined with overriding facilitates polymorphism***.

Polymorphism Simplifies Code Maintenance

To appreciate the power of polymorphism, let's look at how we might have to approach this same challenge—handling different objects in different type-specific ways—with a programming language that *doesn't* support polymorphism.

In the absence of polymorphism, we'd typically handle scenarios having to do with a variety of different kinds of students using a series of if tests:

```
for (Student s : studentBody) {
    // Process the next student.
    // Pseudocode.
    if (s is an undergraduate student)
        s.printAsUndergraduateStudent();
    else if (s is a graduate student)
        s.printAsGraduateStudent();
    else if ...
}
```

As the number of cases grows, so too does the "spaghetti" nature of the resultant code. And, keep in mind that this sort of if test would arise in *countless* places throughout an application, namely wherever we are iterating through a collection declared to hold Students of various types.

Let's now contrast this with our *polymorphic* iteration through the studentBody collection:

```
// Step through the ArrayList (collection) ...
for (Student s : studentBody) {
    // ... invoking the print method of the next Student object.
    s.print(); // polymorphism at work!
}
```

Thanks to polymorphism, a single line of code—s.print();—can handle all types of Students, thus making our code much more concise. Better still, polymorphic client code is *robust to change*. For example, let's say that, long after our SRS application has been coded, tested, and deployed, we derive classes called PhDStudent and MastersStudent from GraduateStudent, each of which in turn overrides the print method of GraduateStudent to provide its own "flavor" of print functionality. We're now free to randomly insert MastersStudents and PhDStudents into our studentBody collection, along with GraduateStudents and UndergraduateStudents, and our polymorphic code for iterating through the collection *doesn't have to change*! The following code illustrates this:

```
// Declare and instantiate an ArrayList.
ArrayList<Student> studentBody = new ArrayList<Student>;

// Instantiate various types of Student object.  We're now dealing with FOUR
// different derived types!
UndergraduateStudent u1 = new UndergraduateStudent();
PhDStudent p1 = new PhDStudent();
GraduateStudent g1 = new GraduateStudent();
MastersStudent m1 = new MastersStudent();
// etc.
```

```
// Insert them into the ArrayList in random order.
studentBody.add(u1);
studentBody.add(p1);
studentBody.add(g1);
studentBody.add(m1);
// etc.

// Then, later in our application ...

// This is the EXACT SAME CODE that we've seen before!
// Step through the ArrayList (collection) ...
for (Student s : studentBody) {
    // ... and invoke the print method of the next Student object.
    // Because of the polymorphic nature of Java, this next line didn't require
    // any changes!
    s.print();
}
```

The for loop in our client code didn't have to change to accommodate the new subclasses—MastersStudent and PhDStudent—because, as subclasses of Student, these new types of object are once again **guaranteed** to understand the **same** print message by virtue of inheritance plus (optional) overriding.

The story is quite different, however, with the nonpolymorphic example that we crafted earlier. That version of client code would indeed have to change to accommodate these new student types; specifically, we'd have to hunt through our application to find every situation where we were trying to differentiate among the various subclasses of Student, and complicate our if tests even further by adding additional cases as follows:

```
for (Student s : studentBody) {
    // Process each student.
    // Pseudocode.
    if (s is an undergraduate student)
        s.printAsUndergraduateStudent();
    else if (s is a Masters student)
        s.printAsMastersStudent();
    else if (s is a PhD student)
        s.printAsPhDStudent();
    else if (s is a generic graduate student)
        s.printAsGraduateStudent();
    else if ...
}
```

causing the "spaghetti piles" to grow ever taller. Maintenance of nonpolymorphic applications quickly becomes a **nightmare**!

As we saw with encapsulation and information hiding earlier, polymorphism is another extremely effective mechanism for minimizing ripple effects on an application if requirements change after the application has been deployed. We're able to introduce new subclasses to an application's class hierarchy in order to meet such requirements, and our existing client code won't "break."

Three Distinguishing Features of an Object-Oriented Programming Language

We've now defined all three of the features required to make a language truly object oriented:

- (Programmer creation of) user-defined types

- Inheritance

- Polymorphism

By way of review, let's look at the benefits of each of these language features.

The Benefits of User-Defined Types

The following are among the benefits of user-defined types:

- User-defined types provide an intuitive way to represent real-world objects, resulting in *easier-to-verify requirements*.

- Classes are convenient units of reusable code, which means *less code to write from scratch when building an application*.

- Through encapsulation, we *minimize data redundancy*—each item of data is stored once, in the object to which it belongs—thereby *lessening the likelihood of data integrity errors* across an application.

- Through information hiding, we *insulate our application against ripple effects* if private details of a class must change after deployment, thereby *dramatically reducing maintenance costs*.

- Objects are responsible for ensuring the integrity of their own data, making it *easier to isolate errors in an application's (business) logic*; we know to inspect the method(s) of the class to which a corrupted object belongs.

The Benefits of Inheritance

The following are among the benefits of inheritance:

- We can extend already deployed code without having to change and then retest it, resulting in *dramatically reduced maintenance costs*.

- Subclasses are much more succinct, which means *less code overall to write/maintain*.

The Benefits of Polymorphism

The following is one of the benefits of polymorphism:

- It *minimizes "ripple effects"* on client code when new subclasses are added to the class hierarchy of an existing application, resulting in *dramatically reduced maintenance costs*.

ONE VERY IMPORTANT CAVEAT

A common misconception is that switching to object technology will dramatically reduce the time required to develop a given application. Anecdotes abound of managers who have expected that a team using an object-oriented approach should be able to craft an application in a fraction of the time that it would take them to build its non-OO counterpart—**despite the fact that team in question might be using OO techniques for the first time ever**! Unfortunately, due to the learning curve involved in switching to the OO paradigm—particularly for software developers who've been entrenched in non-OO techniques for many years—it will typically take **longer** for a team inexperienced with objects to develop their first OO application.

Where economies of scale **do** come into play for a properly designed OO application, however, is during the **maintenance phase** of the application's life cycle. The maintenance phase of an application—OO or otherwise—is typically much longer, and hence more costly, than the development phase. A general rule of thumb is that most application lifetimes are split between 20 percent development and 80 percent maintenance. By dramatically reducing ripple effects through the thoughtful application of (a) encapsulation/information hiding and (b) inheritance/polymorphism, we stand to reduce maintenance costs—and hence overall software life-cycle costs—significantly.

And, once we become adept in the OO paradigm, we should indeed be able to shorten application **development** time, as well. By virtue of the fact that classes can readily be reused and optionally extended/specialized via inheritance—**including the vast number of predefined classes that are provided as an integral part of an OOPL framework**—we'll have less code to write overall for a given application. If in turn we embrace the philosophy of code sharing and reuse across projects, we can gain significant productivity in terms of development as well as maintenance across the life cycles of **multiple** applications.

Abstract Classes

We discussed in Chapter 5 how beneficial it is to consolidate common features of two or more classes into a common superclass, a process known as **generalization**. For example, we noticed similarities between the Student and Professor classes (e.g., both declared a name attribute and methods to get/set its value), and so we created the Person class after the fact to serve as a generalization of both Students and Professors.

Let's now assume that we know at the very outset of an application development effort that we're going to want to take advantage of specialization. For example, with regard to the SRS, perhaps we're going to want to model various types of Course objects: lecture courses, lab courses, independent study courses, etc. We therefore want to start out on the right foot by designing a Course superclass first, to handle all of the common features of these various types of courses before we set out to derive specialized subclasses.

We might determine up front that all Courses, regardless of type, are going to need the following common attributes:

- String courseName

- String courseNumber

- int creditValue

- *CollectionType* enrolledStudents

- Professor instructor

as well as the following common behaviors:

- enrollStudent
- assignInstructor
- establishCourseSchedule

Some of these behaviors may be generic enough so that we can afford to program them in detail for the Course class, knowing that it's a pretty safe bet that any subclasses of Course will be able to inherit these methods as is, without needing to override them. For example, the enrollStudent and assignInstructor methods could be written generically as follows:

```
import java.util.ArrayList;

public class Course {
    private String courseName;
    private String courseNumber;
    private int creditValue;
    private ArrayList enrolledStudents;
    private Professor instructor;

    // Accessor methods would also be provided; details omitted ...

    public void enrollStudent(Student s) {
        enrolledStudents.add(s);
    }

    public void assignInstructor(Professor p) {
        setInstructor(p);
    }

    // etc.
```

When we attempt to program a generic version of the establishCourseSchedule method, however, we realize that the business rules governing how to establish a course schedule differ significantly for different types of courses:

- A lecture course may meet only once a week for three hours at a time.
- A lab course may meet twice a week for two hours each time.
- An independent study course may meet on a custom schedule that has been jointly negotiated by a given student and professor.

It would be a waste of time for us to bother trying to program a generic, "one-size-fits-all" version of the establishCourseSchedule method within the Course class, because no matter what generic logic we'd attempt to provide, *all three subclasses*—LectureCourse, LabCourse, and IndependentStudyCourse—would wind up having to replace such logic by overriding the method to make it meaningful for them.

What other options do we have, then? Can we afford to simply *omit* the establishCourseSchedule method from the Course class entirely, adding such a method to each of the subclasses of Course as a *new* feature instead? Not if we want to take advantage of polymorphism with respect to this method. Consider the following example:

```
ArrayList<Course> courses = new ArrayList<Course>();

// Add a variety of different Course types to the collection.
courses.add(new LectureCourse());
courses.add(new LabCourse());
courses.add(new IndependentStudyCourse());
// etc.

for (Course c : courses) {
    // This next line of code is polymorphic.
    c.establishCourseSchedule("1/24/2005", "5/10/2005");
}
```

As we discussed earlier in the chapter, the polymorphic expression
c.establishCourseSchedule(...) will be deemed valid by the Java compiler only if the Course
class has defined such a method signature. Well, then, is it possible to "trick" the compiler by
adding a "dummy" establishCourseSchedule method to the Course class that has the required
method header, but that does nothing meaningful? If we program the method with an empty
body

```
// This method does NOTHING!  Its method body is empty.
public void establishCourseSchedule(String startDate, String endDate) { }
```

it would indeed compile, and we could then allow each subclass to override the "do-nothing"
version of this method with a meaningful version. While it's *possible* to do so, it's *not* considered
good programming practice to do so, for the following reasons:

- By providing the Course class with an establishCourseSchedule method, we're declaring
  that Course objects will be able to provide such a service on behalf of an application.

- However, if client code were to ever call upon a generic Course object to *perform* this
  service

  ```
  Course c = new Course();

  // We believe that we're calling upon c to perform the indicated service,
  // but behind the scenes, nothing is happening.
  c.establishCourseSchedule("1/24/2005", "5/10/2005");
  ```

  the method as implemented doesn't do what its name *implies* that it will do; for that
  matter, it doesn't do anything at all!

- Furthermore, there's no guarantee that any classes derived from Course will override this
  method to do something meaningful, either, so we could wind up with an entire hierarchy
  of Course types that are incapable of performing the establishCourseSchedule service in
  a meaningful way.

This is seemingly a dilemma! We *know* we'll need a type-specific establishCourseSchedule
method to be programmed for all subclasses of Course. We *don't* want to go to the trouble of
programming a *meaningless* version of this method in the superclass, but we must nonetheless
equip the Course class to recognize such a method header in order to facilitate polymorphism.
How do we communicate the requirement for an establishCourseSchedule method in all subclasses of Course and, more important, *enforce its future implementation*?

OO languages such as Java come to the rescue with the concept of **abstract classes**. An abstract class is used to define ***what*** behaviors a class is required to perform without having to provide an explicit implementation of ***how*** each and every such behavior will be carried out. We program an abstract class in much the same way that we program a nonabstract class (aka a **concrete class**), with one exception: for those behaviors for which we can't (or care not to) program a generic implementation (e.g., the establishCourseSchedule method in the preceding example), we're permitted to specify method ***headers*** without having to program the corresponding method ***bodies***. We refer to a "bodiless," or header-only, method declaration as an **abstract method**. And, to differentiate such methods from methods with bodies, we'll refer to the latter as **implemented methods**.

Let's go back to our Course class definition to add an abstract establishCourseSchedule method:

```
// Note the use of the "abstract" keyword in the class declaration.
public abstract class Course {
    private String courseName;
    private String courseNumber;
    private int creditValue;
    private ArrayList enrolledStudents;
    private Professor instructor;

    // Other details omitted.

    public void enrollStudent(Student s) {
        enrolledStudents.add(s);
    }

    public void assignInstructor(Professor p) {
        setInstructor(p);
    }

    // Note the use of the "abstract" keyword and the terminating
    // semicolon.
    public abstract void establishCourseSchedule(String startDate,
                                                 String endDate);
}
```

The establishCourseSchedule method is declared to be abstract by adding the abstract keyword to its header, just before the return type. Note that the header of an abstract method has no braces following the closing parenthesis of the parameter list. Instead, the header is followed by a semicolon (;)—that is, it's missing its code body, which normally contains the detailed logic of how the method is to be performed. The method must therefore be explicitly labeled as abstract to inform the compiler that we didn't accidentally forget to program this method; rather, we knew what we were doing when we ***intentionally*** omitted the body.

Whenever a class contains one or more abstract methods, then we must declare the class abstract as a whole by inserting the abstract keyword ahead of the class keyword in the class declaration:

```
public abstract class Course { ... }
```

If we forget to designate as abstract a class that contains one or more abstract methods, a compilation error such as the following will arise:

```
Course should be declared abstract; it does not define
establishCourseSchedule(String, String)
```

Note that it isn't necessary for all of the methods in an abstract class to be abstract; an abstract class can also declare implemented methods. For example, in our abstract Course class, both the enrollStudent and assignInstructor methods are implemented.

By providing an abstract establishCourseSchedule method in the Course class, we've specified a service that all types of Course objects must be able to perform, but without pinning down the private details of *how* the service should be performed by a given subclass. We're instead leaving it up to each of the subclasses—LectureCourse, LabCourse, and IndependentStudyCourse— to specify its own class-appropriate way of performing the service. This is accomplished by requiring each of the subclasses to *override* the *abstract* method with an *implemented* version; stated simply, it is accomplished by having each subclass *implement the abstract method*.

Implementing Abstract Methods

When we derive a class from an abstract superclass, the subclass will inherit all of the superclass's features, including all of its *abstract* methods. To replace an inherited abstract method with a concrete version, the subclass need merely override it; in so doing, we drop the abstract keyword from the method header and replace the terminating semicolon with a method body (i.e., code enclosed in braces).

Let's illustrate this approach by deriving a class called LectureCourse from the Course class:

```
// Deriving a concrete subclass from an abstract superclass.
public class LectureCourse extends Course {
    // Details omitted.

    // Override the abstract establishCourseSchedule method with a concrete
    // version by (a) removing the abstract keyword from the method header
    // and (b) providing a method body.
    public void establishCourseSchedule(String startDate,
                                        String endDate) {
        // Logic specific to the business rules for a LectureCourse
        // would be provided here ... pseudocode.
        determine what day of the week the startDate falls on;
        determine how many weeks there are between startDate and endDate;
        schedule one three-hour class meeting per week on the appropriate
            day of the week;
    }
}
```

Note that in overriding the establishCourseSchedule method, we've dropped the abstract keyword from the method header because the method is no longer abstract; we've implemented it by providing it with a method body. In so doing, we're also able to drop the abstract keyword from the LectureCourse class declaration:

```
// No need for the "abstract" keyword here!
public class LectureCourse extends Course { ... }
```

because LectureCourse no longer contains any abstract methods; it is a ***concrete*** class.

Unless a class derived from an abstract class implements ***all*** of the abstract methods that it inherits, the subclass must also be declared to be abstract. For example, say that in deriving a class named IndependentStudyCourse from our abstract Course class, we neglect to implement the abstract establishCourseSchedule method. If we were to try to compile IndependentStudyCourse, we'd get the following compilation error:

```
IndependentStudyCourse should be declared abstract; it does not define
establishCourseSchedule(String, String) in Course
```

To get our IndependentStudyCourse class to compile properly, we have two options for how to amend it:

- We have to implement the abstract establishCourseSchedule method inherited from Course, as we did for the LectureCourse subclass.

- We have to declare the IndependentStudyCourse class as a whole to be abstract:

  ```
  public abstract class IndependentStudyCourse extends Course { ... }
  ```

Note that allowing a subclass to remain abstract isn't necessarily a mistake, as we'll discuss a bit later in this chapter.

Abstract Classes and Instantiation

Abstract classes ***cannot be instantiated***. That is, if the Course class is declared to be abstract, then we can't ever instantiate generic Course objects in our application—an attempt to do so will result in a compilation error:

```
Course c = new Course();  // Impossible!
```

Here's the error message:

```
Course is abstract; cannot be instantiated
```

Why does the compiler prevent us from creating Course objects? The answer lies in the fact that the Course class declares an establishCourseSchedule method ***header***, thus implying that Courses are able to perform this service by providing no body to explain ***how*** the method is to be performed. If we ***were*** able to instantiate a Course object, it would therefore be expected to know how to respond to a service request such as the following:

```
c.establishCourseSchedule("01/24/2005", "05/10/2005");  // Behavior undefined!
```

But because there is no executable method body associated with the abstract establishCourseSchedule method, the Course object in question wouldn't know how to behave in response to such a message at run time. So, the compiler is actually doing us a favor by preventing us from creating this impossible run-time situation to begin with.

We've just hit upon the mechanism for how abstract methods serve to enforce implementation requirements! Declaring an abstract method in a superclass ultimately ***forces*** all subclasses to provide implementations of all inherited abstract methods; otherwise, the subclasses themselves will also be abstract, and we won't be able to instantiate them either. Therefore, somewhere along the line in a derivation hierarchy, a class derived from an abstract class must provide concrete implementations for all of its inherited abstract methods if we wish to "break the spell of abstractness"—that is, if we wish to instantiate objects of that particular derived type. Referring to Figure 7-1,

- Class A is abstract because it declares an abstract method foo; objects of type A therefore **cannot** be instantiated.

- Class X is derived from A, and is a concrete class because it concretely implements the abstract method foo as inherited from A. Thus, we **can** instantiate objects of type X.

- Class B is abstract because it inherits the abstract method foo from A without implementing it. Note that B also introduces a second abstract method, bar, of its own. Objects of type B therefore **cannot** be instantiated.

- Class Y is concrete because it implements all of the abstract methods that it has inherited from its various ancestors—foo from A and bar from B. Thus, we **can** instantiate objects of type Y.

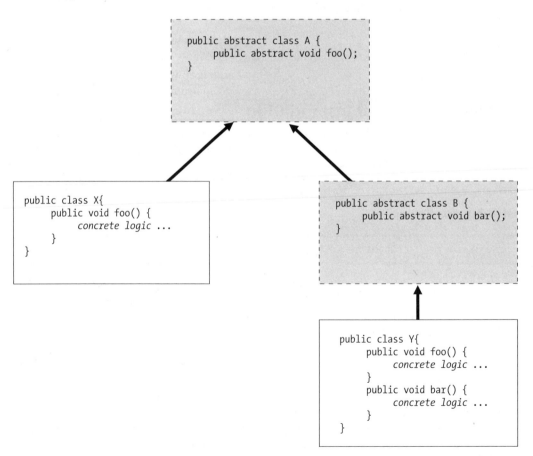

Figure 7-1. *"Breaking the spell of abstractness" by implementing abstract methods*

As mentioned earlier, allowing a subclass (e.g., IndependentStudyCourse from the earlier example) to remain an abstract class isn't necessarily a mistake. It's perfectly acceptable to have multiple layers of abstract classes in an inheritance hierarchy; we simply need a terminal/leaf class to be concrete in order for it to be useful in creating objects.

Declaring Reference Variables of Abstract Types

Despite the fact that we're prevented from instantiating an abstract class, we're nonetheless permitted to declare *reference variables* to be of an abstract type; this is necessary to facilitate polymorphism, as in the following code:

```
for (Course c : courses) {
    c.establishCourseSchedule(...);
}
```

Here, we're declaring c to be of type Course at compile time, knowing that, at *run time*, c will actually be referring to an object belonging to a *specific concrete subclass* of Course, for reasons that we discussed earlier.

An Interesting Twist on Polymorphism

Let's now explore an interesting polymorphic phenomenon specific to abstract classes: it's possible for a *concrete* method in an abstract class to invoke an *abstract* method in the *same* class. This is illustrated in the following code, where the concrete initializeCourse method invokes the abstract establishCourseSchedule method:

```
public abstract class Course {
    // Details omitted.

    // An abstract method ...
    public abstract void establishCourseSchedule(String startDate,
                                                 String endDate);

    // ... and a concretely implemented method that INVOKES the
    // abstract method.
    public void initializeCourse(Professor p, String s, String e) {
        // We assume that both assignInstructor and reserveClassroom are
        // implemented methods of the Course class ... details omitted.
        this.assignInstructor(p);
        this.reserveClassroom();

        // Here, we're invoking an abstract method -- HOW IS THIS POSSIBLE???
        establishCourseSchedule(s, e);
    }
}
```

How can this be possible? That is, how will we ever be able to invoke the initializeCourse method if there is no *body* defined for the establishCourseSchedule method upon which initializeCourse depends? The fact of the matter is that the compiler will never let us get into this predicament, for the following reasons:

- First of all, recall that it's impossible to invoke initializeCourse on a Course object specifically because we cannot ***instantiate*** a Course object in the first place—Course is abstract!

- Then, for any class ***derived*** from Course (e.g., LectureCourse) one of two sets of circumstances will be true:

  - LectureCourse will provide implementations of ***all*** abstract methods that it has inherited—establishCourseSchedule included—such that, at run time, there will be no ambiguity as to what the initializeCourse method is to do behind the scenes:

    ```
    LectureCourse l = new LectureCourse();

    // This next line of code is perfectly fine, because behind the
    // scenes, initializeCourse will invoke the establishCourseSchedule
    // method that LectureCourse has implemented.
    l.initializeCourse(p, s, e);
    ```

  - Alternatively, if LectureCourse ***doesn't*** implement establishCourseSchedule, then LectureCourse will by definition be an abstract class, such that we won't be able to instantiate a LectureCourse object in the first place:

    ```
    // Now THIS line of code won't compile, because LectureCourse is abstract ...
    LectureCourse l = new LectureCourse();

    // ... and so we'll never reach this ambiguous situation at run time!
    l.initializeCourse(p, s, e);
    ```

We thus see that implementing a method X that in turn relies on an ***abstract*** method Y is a "safe" thing to do, because by the time we're ever able to ***invoke*** method X on an object, the fact that the object exists means that all of its methods have been implemented. Thus, in writing X, we can count on the ***future*** availability of a method Y that hasn't been implemented yet.

Interfaces

Recall that a class is an abstraction of a real-world object from which some of the unessential details have been omitted. We can therefore see that an ***abstract*** class is ***more*** abstract than a ***concrete*** class, because with an abstract class we've omitted the details for how one or more particular services are to be performed.

Now, let's take the notion of abstractness one step further. With an abstract class, we are able to avoid programming the bodies of methods that are declared to be abstract. But what about the ***data structure*** of such a class? In our abstract Course class example, we went ahead and prescribed the attributes that we thought would be needed generically by all types of courses, so that a common data structure would be inherited by all subclasses:

```
private String courseName;
private String courseNumber;
private int creditValue;
private ArrayList enrolledStudents;
private Professor instructor;
```

Suppose we only wanted to specify common ***behaviors*** of Courses, and not even ***bother*** with declaring attributes? Attributes are, after all, typically declared to be private; we may not wish to mandate the private data structure that a subclass must use in order to achieve the desired public behaviors, instead leaving it up to the designer of the subclass to ultimately make this determination.

As an example, say that we wanted to define what it means to teach at a university. Perhaps, in order to teach, an object would need to be able to perform the following services:

- Agree to teach a particular course.

- Designate a textbook to be used for the course.

- Define a syllabus for the course.

- Approve the enrollment of a particular student in the course.

Each of these behaviors could be formalized by specifying a method header, representing how an object that is ***capable of teaching*** would be asked to perform each behavior:

```
public boolean agreeToTeach(Course c)
public void designateTextbook(TextBook b, Course c)
public Syllabus defineSyllabus(Course c)
public boolean approveEnrollment(Student s, Course c)
```

We could then declare an abstract class called Teacher that prescribes no data structure and only ***abstract*** methods:

```
public abstract class Teacher {
    // We omit attribute declarations entirely, allowing subclasses to establish
    // their own class-specific data structures.

    // We declare only abstract methods.
    public abstract boolean agreeToTeach(Course c);
    public abstract void designateTextbook(TextBook b, Course c);
    public abstract Syllabus defineSyllabus(Course c);
    public abstract boolean approveEnrollment(Student s, Course c);
}
```

We then proceed to create Professor as a concrete derivation of Teacher:

```
public Professor extends Teacher {
    // Declare relevant attributes.
    private String name;
    private String employeeID;
    private ArrayList teachingAssignments; // of Section objects
    // etc.

    // Provide concrete implementations of all inherited abstract methods.
    public boolean agreeToTeach(Course c) { ... }
    public void designateTextbook(TextBook b, Course c) { ... }
    public Syllabus defineSyllabus(Course c) { ... }
    public boolean approveEnrollment(Student s, Course c) { ... }

    // Additional methods can also be declared - details omitted.
}
```

However, if our intention is to declare a set of abstract method headers to define what it means to assume a certain *role* within an application (such as teaching) without imposing either data structure or concrete behavior on the subclasses, then the preferred way to do so in Java is with an **interface**.

Here's how we'd render the abstract Teacher class with an equivalent interface:

```
// Note use of "interface" vs. "class" keyword.
public interface Teacher {
    boolean agreeToTeach(Course c);
    void designateTextbook(TextBook b, Course c);
    Syllabus defineSyllabus(Course c);
    boolean approveEnrollment(Student s, Course c);
}
```

Here are some observations about interface syntax:

- We use the keyword interface rather than class when declaring them:

  ```
  public interface Teacher { ... }
  ```

- Because all of an interface's methods are implicitly public and abstract, we needn't specify either of those two keywords when declaring them (although doing so will not generate a compiler error). We *will* get an error, however, if we attempt to assign something other than public accessibility to a method within an interface:

  ```
  public interface teacher {
      // This won't compile - interface methods must all be public.
      private void takeSabbatical();
      // etc.
  ```

  Here's the compiler error:

  ```
  modifier private not allowed here
  private void takeSabbatical();
  ^
  ```

- Because all of the methods prescribed by an interface are abstract, *none* of them have bodies.

As with classes, the source code for each interface typically goes into its own .java file, whose external name matches the name of the interface contained within (e.g., the Teacher interface would go into a file named Teacher.java). Interfaces are then compiled into bytecode in the same way that classes are compiled. For example, the command

```
javac Teacher.java
```

will produce a bytecode file named Teacher.class.

Note that interfaces may not declare variables (with one exception that we'll discuss later in the chapter), and they may not declare any implemented methods. They are, simply put, a collection of abstract method headers. Therefore, in terms of the "abstractness spectrum," *an interface is more abstract than an abstract class* (which is in turn more abstract than a concrete class) because an interface leaves even more details to the imagination.

Implementing Interfaces

Once we've defined an interface such as Teacher, we can set about designating various classes of objects as being teachers—for example, Professors, or Students, or generic Person objects—simply by declaring that the class of interest *implements* the Teacher interface, using the following syntax:

```
// Implementing an interface ...
public class Professor implements Teacher { ... }
```

That is, rather than using the extends keyword, as we do when one class is derived from another, we use the implements keyword.

Recall our discussion of packages from Chapter 6, and in particular the fact that we aren't going to be "packaging" any of our SRS code, thereby relegating it to the default (unnamed) package. Similarly, if we are implementing an interface of our own design (e.g., Teacher) that belongs to the default package, we needn't use an import directive to make that interface visible to the compiler. On the other hand, if we wish to implement a predefined Java interface type (the Java language provides many of these), we must use an import directive to make that interface type known to the compiler, for example:

```
import packagename.PredefinedInterfaceType;
```

```
public class MyClass implements PredefinedInterfaceType { ... }
```

You'll see import directives in use when we discuss the java.util.Collection interface a bit later in this chapter.

Once a class declares that it's implementing an interface, the implementing class *must* implement all of the (implicitly abstract) methods declared by the interface in question in order to satisfy the compiler. As an example, let's say that we were to code the Professor class as follows, implementing three of the four methods called for by the Teacher interface but neglecting to code the approveEnrollment method:

```
public class Professor implements Teacher {
    private String name;
    private String employeeId;
    // etc.

    // We implement three of the four methods called for by the
    // Teacher interface, to provide method bodies.

    public boolean agreeToTeach(Course c) {
        logic for the method body goes here; details omitted ...
    }

    public void designateTextbook(TextBook b, Course c) {
        logic for the method body goes here; details omitted ...
    }
```

```
    public Syllabus defineSyllabus(Course c) {
        logic for the method body goes here; details omitted ...
    }

    // However, we FAIL to provide an implementation of the
    // approveEnrollment method.

    // Other miscellaneous methods of Professor unrelated to the Teacher
    // interface could also be declared ... details omitted.
}
```

If we were to try to compile the Professor class as just shown, we'd get the following compiler error:

```
Professor should be declared abstract; it does not define
approveEnrollment(Student, Course) in Teacher
```

Recall that this is the ***exact same type*** of compiler error message that is generated if we are deriving a class from an abstract class and fail to override one of the inherited abstract methods. Here's the result from an earlier example, involving the abstract superclass Course and the subclass IndependentStudyCourse:

```
IndependentStudyCourse should be declared abstract; it does not implement
establishCourseSchedule(String, String) in Course
```

Thus, implementing an interface is conceptually similar to extending an abstract class, in that both interfaces and abstract classes are alternative constructs for prescribing abstract behaviors that implementing/subclasses must be able to carry out.

When should we use one versus the other?

- If we wish to impart a particular data structure to go along with these prescribed behaviors, or if we need to provide some concrete behaviors along with abstract behaviors, we'll create an abstract class.

- Otherwise, we'll create an interface.

Tables 7-1 and 7-2 summarize the syntactical differences between interfaces and abstract classes.

Table 7-1. *Syntactical Differences for Declaring Abstract Classes vs. Interfaces*

Example Using an Abstract Class	Example Using an Interface
Declaring the Teacher Type As an Abstract Class	Declaring the Teacher Type As an Interface

```
public abstract class Teacher {
    // Abstract classes may prescribe
    // data structure.
    private String name;
    private String employeeId;
    // etc.



    // We declare abstract methods using
    // the "abstract" keyword; these
    // must also be declared "public".
    public abstract void agreeToTeach(
        Course c);

    // etc.




    // Abstract classes may also declare
    // concrete methods.
    public void print() {
        System.out.println(name);
    }

    // etc.
}
```

```
public interface Teacher {
    // Interfaces may NOT prescribe
    // data structure.




    // We needn't use the "public" or
    // "abstract" keywords - all methods
    // declared by an interface are
    // automatically public and
    // abstract by default.
    void agreeToTeach(Course c);


    // etc.




    // Interfaces may NOT declare
    // concrete methods.
}
```

Table 7-2. *Syntactical Differences for Extending Abstract Classes vs. Implementing Interfaces*

Example Using an Abstract Class	Example Using an Interface
Professor *Extends* Teacher	Professor *Implements* Teacher

```
public class Professor extends Teacher {
    // Professor inherits attributes, if
    // any, from the abstract
    // superclass, and optionally
    // adds additional attributes.
    private Department worksFor;
    // etc.




    // We override abstract methods
    // inherited from the Teacher class
    // to provide a concrete
    // implementation.

    public void agreeToTeach(Course c) {
        logic for the method body goes
        here; details omitted ...
    }

    // etc. for other abstract methods.

    // Additional methods may be added;
    // details omitted.
}
```

```
public class Professor implements
    Teacher {
    // Professor must provide ALL of
    // its own data structure, as an
    // interface cannot provide this.
    private String name;
    private String employeeId;
    private Department worksFor;
    // etc.




    // We implement methods required by
    // the Teacher interface.

    public void agreeToTeach(Course c) {
        logic for the method body goes
        here; details omitted ...
    }

    // etc. for other abstract methods.

    // Additional methods may be added;
    // details omitted.
}
```

Another Form of the "Is A" Relationship

You learned in Chapter 5 that inheritance is often referred to as the "is a" relationship. As it turns out, implementing an interface is another form of "is a" relationship; that is,

- If the Professor class *extends* the Person *class*, then a Professor *is a* Person.

- If the Professor class *implements* the Teacher *interface*, then a Professor *is a* Teacher.

When a class A implements an interface X, all of the classes that are subsequently derived from A may also be said to implement that same interface X. For example, if we derive a class called AdjunctProfessor from Professor, then since Professor implements the Teacher interface, an AdjunctProfessor is a Teacher, as well:

```
public class Professor implements Teacher {
    // Attribute details omitted.

    // The Professor class must implement all four of the methods called for by
    // the Teacher interface.
    public boolean agreeToTeach(Course c) { ... }
    public void designateTextbook(TextBook b, Course c) { ... }
    public Syllabus defineSyllabus(Course c) { ... }
    public boolean approveEnrollment(Student s, Course c) { ... }

    // Other details omitted.
}

// Even though AdjunctProfessor isn't explicitly declared to implement Teacher,
// it does so IMPLICITLY, because it inherits all of a Teacher's behaviors from
// the Professor class.
public class AdjunctProfessor extends Professor { ... }
```

This makes intuitive sense, because AdjunctProfessor will either inherit all of the methods called for by the Teacher interface from Professor as is, or optionally override one or more of them. Either way, an AdjunctProfessor will be "equipped" to perform *all* of the services required to serve in the role of a Teacher; that is, an AdjunctProfessor will be able to perform the following services on behalf of an application:

- Agree to teach a particular course.

- Designate a textbook to be used for the course.

- Define a syllabus for the course.

- Approve the enrollment of a particular student in the course.

Recall that this is the *precise* purpose for having declared the Teacher interface in the first place: to define a behavioral role in an application. So, even though AdjunctProfessor isn't explicitly declared to implement Teacher, it does so *implicitly*.

Interfaces and Casting

Note that the compiler is perfectly happy for us to assign a Professor object to a Teacher reference variable:

```
Teacher t = new Professor();
```

because the compiler generally allows assignments to occur if the type of the expression to the right of the equal sign (=) is a type that is compatible with the variable to the left of the equal sign. Since Professor **implements** Teacher, a Professor **is a** Teacher, and so this assignment is permitted.

The opposite is **not** permitted, however: we cannot directly assign a Teacher reference to a Professor reference variable, because not all Teachers are necessarily Professors—many different classes can implement the same interface. For example, assuming that both the Student and Professor classes implement the Teacher interface, the last line of the following code will generate a compiler error:

```
Professor p = new Professor();
Student s = new Student();
Teacher t;

// Details omitted.

// The compiler won't allow this.
p = t;
```

Here's the compiler error:

```
incompatible types
found:    Teacher
required: Professor
p = t;
    ^
```

However, if we know that t will be referring to an object of an appropriate type at run time, we may **force** such an assignment to occur through use of a cast. Recall from Chapter 2 that we use casting to convince the compiler that an assignment should occur even though precision is lost in doing so (e.g., when assigning a double value to an int variable):

```
int x;
double y;

// Cast the double value into an int before assigning it to x.
x = (int) y;
```

Recall that this was referred to as a **narrowing conversion**. In a sense, attempting to assign a Teacher reference to a Professor reference variable is also a narrowing conversion: we're trying to narrow down all of the possible types of object that a Teacher variable could possibly be referencing at run time to a ***single*** type, Professor. In the preceding example, since both the Professor and Student classes implement the Teacher interface, t could, at run time, be referring to a Student object or a Professor object, as illustrated in Figure 7-2.

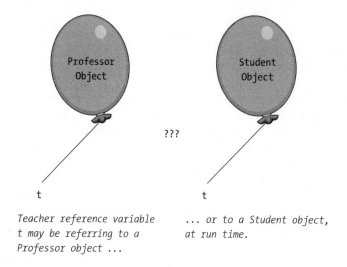

???

t

t

Teacher reference variable t may be referring to a Professor object ...

... or to a Student object, at run time.

Figure 7-2. *A Teacher reference variable can refer to multiple types of object at run time.*

However, if we ***know*** that, based on the way we've written our code, t will be referring to a Professor object at run time, we may force the assignment through the use of a cast as follows:

```
Professor p1 = new Professor();
Teacher t;

// We assign a Professor reference to t.
t = p1;

// Details omitted.

// Later in our application, we are confident that t is still referring
// to the same Professor, and so we assign t to p2 by using a cast.
Professor p2 = (Professor) t;
```

The resultant situation in memory is depicted in Figure 7-3. Our use of a cast in the last line of code

```
Professor p2 = (Professor) t;
```

is effectively telling the compiler "Trust me, I know that t1 will be referring to a Professor object at run time, so doing this assignment makes sense."

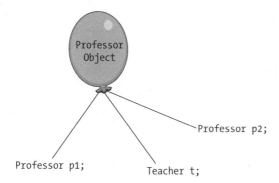

Figure 7-3. *Because* t *refers to a* Professor *object at run time, we force an assignment of* t *to* p2 *via a cast.*

If we force a cast, but we're ***wrong***—that is, if the run-time type of t is ***not*** compatible with the Professor type—then we'll get a ClassCastException type of error at run time. (We'll talk about how to deal with such an error, a technique known as ***exception handling***, in Chapter 13.) Returning to our previous example, let's change the code a bit so that a cast would be inappropriate:

```
// We instantiate both a Professor and a Student object; recall that
// in this example, both classes implement the Teacher interface.
Professor p = new Professor();
Student s = new Student();
Teacher t;

// We assign a Student reference to t.  This is permitted, because a Student
// is a Teacher.
t = s;

// Details omitted ...

// Later on, we mistakenly try to cast t as a Professor, but t is really
// referring to a Student.
p = (Professor) t;
```

The last line of code will compile, because the compiler trusts that we know what we are doing, but since the actual situation at run time is as depicted in Figure 7-4, such a cast is ***invalid***—there's no way to transform a Student into a Professor object at run time—and so we get the following error message when ***executing*** this code:

```
Exception in thread "main" java.lang.ClassCastException: Student
at classname.main(classname.java:line#)
```

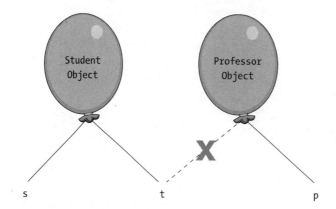

t refers to a Student object at run time, and so trying to cast
t as a Professor generates a ClassCastException.

Figure 7-4. *A ClassCastException arises at run time when trying to refer to a Student object as a Professor.*

We'll revisit the use of casts with object references later in this chapter and again in Chapter 13.

Implementing Multiple Interfaces

Another important distinction between extending an abstract class versus implementing an interface is that whereas a given class may only be derived from ***one*** direct superclass, a class may implement as ***many*** interfaces as desired. If a class is to implement multiple interfaces, we must name all such interfaces as a comma-separated list after the implements keyword in the class declaration:

```
public class ClassName implements Interface1, Interface2, ..., InterfaceN { ... }
```

In so doing, the implementing class would then need to implement all of the methods prescribed by ***all*** of these interfaces collectively.

As an example, if we were to invent a second interface called Administrator, which in turn specified the following method headers:

```
public interface Administrator {
    boolean approveNewCourse(Course c);
    boolean hireProfessor(Professor p);
    void cancelCourse(Course c);
}
```

we could then declare that the Professor class implements ***both*** the Teacher and Administrator interfaces as follows:

```
// The Professor class implements two interfaces.
public class Professor implements Teacher, Administrator {
    // Details omitted.
```

```
    // The Professor class must implement all four of the methods called for by
    // the Teacher interface ...
    public boolean agreeToTeach(Course c) { ... }
    public void designateTextbook(TextBook b, Course c) { ... }
    public Syllabus defineSyllabus(Course c) { ... }
    public boolean approveEnrollment(Student s, Course c) { ... }

    // ... as well as all three of the methods called for by
    // the Administrator interface.
    public boolean approveNewCourse(Course c) { ... }
    public boolean hireProfessor(Professor p) { ... }
    public void cancelCourse(Course c) { ... }

    // Details omitted.
}
```

If a class implements two or more interfaces that call for methods with identical signatures, we need only implement one such method in the implementing class—that method will do "double duty" in satisfying both interfaces' implementation requirements as far as the compiler is concerned.

When a class implements more than one interface, its objects are capable of assuming multiple identities or roles in an application; such objects can therefore be "handled" by various types of reference variables. Based on the preceding definition of a Professor as both a Teacher and an Administrator, the following client code would be possible:

```
// Instantiate a Professor object, and maintain a handle on it via
// a reference variable of type Professor.
Professor p = new Professor();

// We then declare reference variables of the two types of interfaces that the
// Professor class implements.
Teacher t;
Administrator a;

t = p;  // We store a second handle on the same Professor in a reference variable of
        // type Teacher; this is possible because a Professor IS A Teacher!

a = p;  // We store a third handle on the same Professor in a reference variable of
        // type Administrator; this is possible because a Professor IS AN
        // Administrator!
```

This code is illustrated conceptually in Figure 7-5.

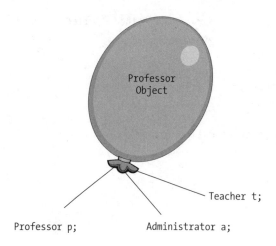

Professor
Object

Teacher t;

Professor p;   Administrator a;

A Professor object can be "handled" by Professor,
Teacher, and Administrator references, because a Professor
is a Teacher, and a Professor is an Administrator!

Figure 7-5. *A Professor object has three different identities/roles in our application.*

This is conceptually the same thing as you, as a person, being viewed as having different roles by different people: you're viewed as an employee by your manager, as a son or daughter by your parents, and perhaps as a partner by your significant other and/or as a parent by your children, etc.

We may then command the *same* object at run time as either a Professor

```
// setDepartment is a method defined by the Professor class ...
p.setDepartment("Computer Science");
```

or as a Teacher

```
// agreeToTeach is a method defined by the Teacher interface ...
t.agreeToTeach(c);
```

or as an Administrator

```
// approveNewCourse is a method defined by the Administrator interface ...
a.approveNewCourse(c);
```

because it's all three, rolled into one!

A class may simultaneously extend a *single* superclass and implement *one or more* interfaces, as follows:

```
public class Professor extends Person implements Teacher, Administrator { ... }
```

Under such circumstances, extends *className* should always precede implements *interfaceNameList* in the declaration.

Interfaces and Casting, Revisited

Continuing with the previous example, note that, despite the fact that t would, at *run time*, be referring to a Professor object, we *cannot* ask t to perform a method declared by the Professor class:

```
Professor p = new Professor();
Teacher t = p;

// setDepartment is a method defined for the Professor class, but t is
// declared to be of type Teacher ... this won't compile!
t.setDepartment("Computer Science");
```

The compiler will check the type of t, determining that t is *declared* to be of type Teacher and, since the Teacher interface doesn't declare a setDepartment method, the compiler will reject the last line of the preceding code with the following compilation error:

```
cannot find symbol
symbol:  method setDepartment(String)
location:  interface Teacher
```

Thus, even if the code that we've written *guarantees* that t would be referring to a Professor at *run time*, we may only command t at *compile* time as a Teacher, because not all Teachers are necessarily Professors as far as the compiler is concerned.

Once again, casting comes to our rescue: if we are *certain* that t will indeed be referring to a Professor object at run time, we may invoke the setDepartment method on that object by casting the reference to t as follows:

```
Professor p = new Professor();
Teacher t = p;

// setDepartment is a method defined for the Professor class; since we know
// that t will refer to a Professor at run time, we use a cast so that
// this will compile.
((Professor) t).setDepartment("Computer Science");
```

Note the use of nested parentheses: ((Professor) t).setDepartment(...). We use nested parentheses to force the cast to occur *before* we attempt to invoke the setDepartment method on t. If we were to write the line of code *without* nested parentheses, as follows:

```
(Professor) t.setDepartment("Computer Science");
```

then the compiler would interpret this as saying, "First, invoke the setDepartment method on t, and *then* cast the result that is *returned* from this method invocation to be a Professor," which is not what we want. (And, in fact, since a set method typically is declared to have a return type of void, the preceding line won't even compile.)

Interfaces and Instantiation

As with abstract classes, interfaces cannot be instantiated. That is, if we define Teacher to be an interface, we may not instantiate it directly:

```
Teacher t = new Teacher();  // Impossible!
```

because interfaces don't have constructors—only classes do, as templates for instantiating objects—and so we'd encounter the following compilation error:

```
Teacher is abstract; cannot be instantiated
```

Recall that this is the ***exact same type*** of compiler error message that is generated if we attempt to instantiate an abstract class. Here's the result from an earlier example:

```
Course is abstract; cannot be instantiated
```

While we're indeed prevented from instantiating an interface, we're nonetheless permitted to declare reference variables to be of an interface type, as we were able to do with abstract classes:

```
Teacher t;  // This is OK.
```

This is necessary to facilitate polymorphism, as discussed in the next section.

Interfaces and Polymorphism

Let's look at an example of polymorphism as it applies to interfaces. We'll assume that

- The Professor and Student classes are both derived from the Person class.

- Professor and Student are sibling classes—neither derives from the other.

- Person implements the Teacher interface, and thus by virtue of inheritance, both Professor and Student ***implicitly*** implement the Teacher interface.

We may declare a collection to hold Teacher references, and then populate it with a mixture of Student and Professor object references as follows:

```
ArrayList<Teacher> teachers = new ArrayList<Teacher>();
teachers.add(new Student("Becky Elkins"));
teachers.add(new Professor("Bobby Cranston"));
// etc.
```

We may then iterate through the teachers collection in polymorphic fashion, referring to all of its elements as Teachers:

```
for (Teacher t : teachers) {
    // This line of code is polymorphic.
    t.agreeToTeach(c);
}
```

because we constrained the collection to contain only Teacher type object references when we first declared it.

The Importance of Interfaces

Interfaces are one of the most poorly understood, and hence underused, features of the OO programming languages that support them. This is quite unfortunate, as interfaces are extremely powerful if used properly.

Whenever possible/feasible when designing classes, if we use *interface* types rather than specific class types in declaring

- (Private) attributes

- Formal parameters to methods

- Method return types

our classes will be more flexible in terms of how client code can use them. Let's explore two different examples to see why this is so.

Example #1

In this example, let's assume that

- The Professor and Student classes are both immediate subclasses of Person, along with a third subclass, Janitor.

- In this example, Person does *not* implement the Teacher interface, because we don't wish to designate either Janitors or Students as Teachers; instead, we have the Professor class (only) *explicitly* implement the Teacher interface.

The four class declarations are as follows:

```
public class Person { ... }


// Only Professors are Teachers in this example.
public class Professor extends Person implements Teacher { ... }


public class Student extends Person { ... }


public class Janitor extends Person { ... }
```

Next, we'll design a class called Course with a private attribute of type Professor called instructor, along with accessor methods for this attribute:

```
public class Course {
    private Professor instructor;
    // Other attributes omitted from this example ...

    public Professor getInstructor() {
        return instructor;
    }

    public void setInstructor(Professor p) {
        instructor = p;
    }

    // Other methods omitted from this example ...
}
```

We'd then perhaps use this class from client code as follows to assign a specific Professor to teach a specific Course:

```
// Client code.
Course c = new Course("Math 101");
Professor p = new Professor("John Smith");
c.setInstructor(p);
```

Let's say that at some future date the university decides to permit selected students to teach courses. To implement this new business rule, we derive a new subclass of Student called StudentInstructor, and have it implement the Teacher interface. Our classes are thus as follows:

```
public class Person { ... }

// Professors are Teachers ...
public class Professor extends Person implements Teacher { ... }

public class Student extends Person { ... }

// ... and now selected Students are Teachers, as well!
public class StudentInstructor extends Student implements Teacher { ... }

public class Janitor extends Person { ... }
```

We would not be able to assign a StudentInstructor to teach a Course given the current design of our Course class, however, because a StudentInstructor is not a Professor in terms of our class hierarchy; that is, the following client code would not compile:

```
Course c = new Course("Math 101");
StudentInstructor si = new StudentInstructor("Mary Jones");

// An attempt to assign a student as an instructor won't compile.
c.setInstructor(si);
```

We'd get the following compilation error:

```
setInstructor(Professor) in Course cannot be applied to StudentInstructor
```

Now, let's look at an improvement to our original Course class design. Instead of declaring the instructor attribute of Course to be of type Professor (a specific *class* type), let's declare it to be of type Teacher (an ***interface*** type) instead. We'll also adjust the return type of the "get" method and the parameter type of the "set" method for this attribute accordingly:

```
public class Course {
    // We've changed our declaration of the instructor attribute to take
    // advantage of an interface type.
    private Teacher instructor;
    // Other attributes omitted from this example ...
```

```
    // We make a corresponding change to the return type of our get method ...
    public Teacher getInstructor() {
        return instructor;
    }

    // ... and to the type of the parameter that we pass into the set method.
    public void setInstructor(Teacher t) {
        instructor = t;
    }

    // Other methods omitted from this example ...
}
```

We're thus opening up more possibilities for client code. Using our improved Course class design, we can assign a Professor as an instructor for a Course:

```
// Client code.
Course c = new Course("Math 101");
Professor p = new Professor("John Smith");
c.setInstructor(p);
```

or a StudentInstructor as an instructor for a Course:

```
// Client code.
Course c = new Course("Math 101");
StudentInstructor si = new StudentInstructor("George Jones");
c.setInstructor(si);
```

or a reference x to any other *future* type of object as yet to be invented:

```
c.setInstructor(x);
```

as long as x is an instance of a class that implements the Teacher interface.

We can therefore see that using an interface type when declaring

- (Private) instructor attribute of Course

- The parameter passed into the setInstructor method of Course

results in a much more flexible design for our application overall.

Example #2

The Java language provides many predefined interfaces. One such example is the Collection interface of the java.util package. The Collection interface enforces implementation of 14 methods, many of which—add, addAll, clear, contains, isEmpty, remove, size, etc.—we discussed when talking about various collection classes in Chapter 6. These 14 methods collectively define the services that an object has to be able to provide in order to perform in the role of a proper Collection in a Java application.

The Collection interface is implemented by numerous predefined Java Collection classes, including the ArrayList class. In fact, the **collections framework**, introduced with Java version 1.2 (aka Java 2), is based on a total of *six* interfaces: Map, SortedMap, Collection, Set, List, and SortedSet. The relationships between these interfaces and the various collection classes are illustrated in Figure 7-6.

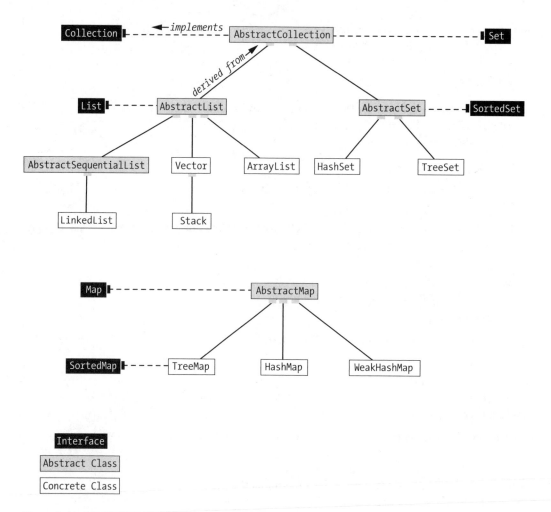

Figure 7-6. *The "family tree" of Java's predefined collection classes*

ALL JAVA COLLECTIONS ARE NOT CREATED EQUAL!

Figure 7-6 points out an interesting phenomenon regarding the TreeMap and HashMap classes, two of the predefined collection types that we discussed in Chapter 6. While TreeMaps and HashMaps are indeed collections in the ***generic*** sense, in that they organize references to other objects, these classes do ***not*** implement the Collection interface. Hence, client code such as the following will ***not*** compile:

```
Collection c = new TreeMap<String, String>();
```

because a TreeMap, while being a collection (in the lowercase "c" sense of the word), is not truly a Collection (in the formal, uppercase "C" sense). The following compilation error message would be generated:

```
incompatible types:
found:    java.util.TreeMap<java.lang.String, java.lang.String>
required: java.util.Collection
```

Similarly, an array is not truly a `Collection` in the uppercase "C" sense of the term either, and so the following won't compile either:

```
Collection c = new Student[20];
```

Here's the compilation error:

```
incompatible types:
found:    Student[]
required: java.util.Collection
```

On the other hand, the following client code **will** compile:

```
Collection c = new ArrayList<String>;
```

because the `ArrayList` class is derived from the `AbstractCollection` class, which implements the `Collection` interface; hence, an `ArrayList` **is a** `Collection` (uppercase "C") in the true uppercase "C" sense.

If we design methods that are to operate on collections of objects to accept a **generic** `Collection` reference as an argument (rather than requiring that a **specific** type of collection be passed in), such methods will be much more versatile; client code will be free to pass in whatever `Collection` type it wishes.

By way of example, let's say that we wish to design an `enrollStudents` method for the `Course` class so that client code can pass in a collection of `Students` to enroll them all at once. If we were to specify a particular collection type as a parameter to the method—say, an `ArrayList`

```
import java.util.ArrayList;

public class Course {
    // Details omitted ...

    // Accept a specific collection type as an argument.
    public void enrollStudents(ArrayList x) {
        for (Student s : x) {
            this.enroll(s);
        }
    }

    // etc.
}
```

then client code would be forced to pass in an `ArrayList` as an argument. However, if we design the method to accept a **generic** `Collection` as an argument instead

```
import java.util.Collection;

public class Course {
    // details omitted ...

    // Accept a generic Collection reference as an argument.
    public void enrollStudents(Collection c) {
        for (Student s : x)  {
            this.enroll(s);
        }
    }
}
```

then client code using this method will be able to pass in an ArrayList of Student references:

```
Course c = new Course();
ArrayList al = new ArrayList();
// Populate al with Students ... details omitted.

// Pass in an ArrayList ...
c.enrollStudents(al);
```

or a Vector of Student references:

```
// Client code.
Course c = new Course();
Vector v = new Vector();
// Populate v with Students ... details omitted.

// Pass in a Vector ...
c.enrollStudents(v);
```

or any other type of Collection desired.

The same is true for methods that *return* collections of objects: if we design them to return generic Collections instead of specific collection types, then we are free to change the internal details of what type of collection we're crafting. Recall our discussion from Chapter 6 of the getRegisteredStudents method of the Course class. I've repeated that code here for your convenience:

```
import java.util.ArrayList;

public class Course {
    private ArrayList enrolledStudents;

    // Details omitted ...

    // The following method returns a reference to an entire collection -
    // specifically, an ArrayList - containing however many Students are
    // registered for the course in question.
    public ArrayList getRegisteredStudents() {
```

```
        return enrolledStudents;
    }

    // etc.
}
```

Because we declared getRegisteredStudents to have a return type of ArrayList (a specific collection type), we're going to run into problems later on if we decide to change the type of the encapsulated enrolledStudents collection from ArrayList to some other collection type. In essence, we've exposed client code to what should be a ***private*** detail of the Course class: namely, the type of collection that we're using ***internally*** to manage Student references.

If we instead declare getRegisteredStudents to return a ***generic*** Collection as follows:

```
import java.util.ArrayList;
import java.util.Collection;

public class Course {
    // We're still maintaining an ArrayList internally.
    private ArrayList enrolledStudents;

    // Details omitted ...

    // However, we've now "hidden" the fact that we're using an ArrayList
    // internally by returning it as a generic Collection instead.
    public Collection getRegisteredStudents() {
        // We're allowed to do this, because enrolledStudents is an ArrayList,
        // and an ArrayList IS A Collection.
        return enrolledStudents;
    }

    // etc.
}
```

we're now free to change the type of internal collection that we're using (a ***private*** detail) without impacting the signature of the getRegisteredStudents method (a ***public*** detail). For example, we may wish to switch from an ArrayList to a TreeSet to take advantage of a set's inherent elimination of duplicate entries (recall our discussion of this aspect of set type collections from Chapter 6):

```
import java.util.TreeSet;
import java.util.Collection;

public class Course {
    // We've switched to a different Collection type internally.
    private TreeSet enrolledStudents;

    // Details omitted ...

    // This method signature needn't change!!!
    public Collection getRegisteredStudents() {
        // We're allowed to do this, because enrolledStudents is a TreeSet,
```

```
        // and a TreeSet IS A Collection.
        return enrolledStudents;
    }

    // etc.
}
```

In fact, given this improved design, we could even switch to a type of collection that ***doesn't*** implement the Collection interface, as long as we transform it into a proper Collection prior to returning it—for example, a Student array:

```
public class Course {
    // We've switched to a non-Collection type of collection internally.
    private Student[] enrolledStudents;

    // Details omitted ...

    // This method signature needn't change!!!
    public Collection getRegisteredStudents() {
        // We have to do a bit more work to convert the array to a
        // proper Collection of some sort; we're using an ArrayList
        // constructor that accepts an array as an argument,
        // prepopulating the ArrayList with a copy of the array's
        // contents.
        return new ArrayList(enrolledStudents);
    }

    // etc.
}
```

Here's another example, this time involving a TreeMap versus an array:

```
public class Course {
    // We've switched to TreeMap, another a non-Collection type of
    // collection, this time.
    private TreeMap<String, Student> enrolledStudents;

    // Details omitted ...

    // This method signature needn't change!!!
    public Collection getRegisteredStudents() {
        // We have to do a bit more work to convert the TreeMap to a
        // proper Collection of some sort; we're extracting the
        // elements stored in the TreeMap (versus the keys to these
        // elements, which we don't care about) via the "values"
        // method declared by the TreeMap class.
        return enrolledStudents.values();
    }

    // etc.
}
```

Once again, we've illustrated the flexibility to be gained by using interface types (`Collection`, in this case) as

- Formal parameters to methods

- Return types of methods

Be certain to master the notion of interfaces—both predefined as well as user defined—to harness their power in your code!

In Chapter 6, our discussion of creating custom collections started out by mentioning that we could, if desired, invent a custom collection type from scratch, but that the Java language provides so many predefined collection types that doing so is not usually necessary. However, should you ever find yourself wanting to invent a brand-new collection type without extending one of the ***predefined*** collection types, be certain that your collection type implements the predefined `Collection` interface, at a minimum:

```
import java.util.Collection;
```

```
public class MyBrandNewCollectionType implements Collection { ... }
```

so that your collection type will be usable in any context where a generic `Collection` is required.

Static Features

Up until this point, all of the attributes that we've discussed have been associated with an individual instance of a class. Every `Student` object has its own copy of the `String` name attribute, for example, and can manipulate its value independently of what other `Student` objects are doing with ***their*** copies of the same attribute (see Figure 7-7).

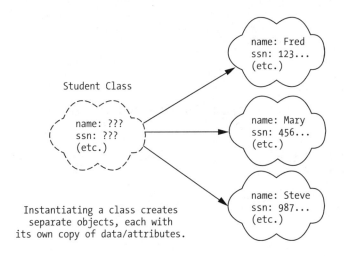

Figure 7-7. *Objects manage their individual attribute values.*

Circumstances can arise in an application where we'll want all objects belonging to a particular class to **share** a single value of a particular variable instead of having each object maintain its own copy of that variable as an attribute. The Java language satisfies this need through **static variables** that are associated with classes as a whole rather than with individual objects.

As we'll discuss in more depth in Chapter 13, Java uses different nomenclature for the notion of static features than that used when discussing objects generically. I've chosen to stick with the generic (and somewhat informal) object terminology in this chapter, but I'll disclose the Java-specific terminology in Chapter 13.

Static Variables

Suppose there were some piece of general information—say, the count of the total number of students enrolled at the university—that we wanted **all** Student objects to have shared knowledge of. We could implement this as a simple attribute of the Student class, int totalStudents, along with code for manipulating the attribute as shown here:

```java
public class Student {
    private int totalStudents;
    // Other attribute details omitted.

    // Accessor methods.

    public int getTotalStudents() {
        return totalStudents;
    }

    public void setTotalStudents(int x) {
        totalStudents = x;
    }

    // Other miscellaneous methods.

    public int reportTotalEnrollment() {
        System.out.println("Total Enrollment:  " + getTotalStudents());
    }

    public void incrementEnrollment() {
        setTotalStudents(getTotalStudents() + 1);
    }

    // etc.
}
```

This would be a less-than-desirable design approach, however, because client code would have to invoke the incrementEnrollment method on **every** Student object in the system any time a **new** Student were instantiated, to ensure that **all** Students were in agreement on the total student count:

```
// Client code.

// Create a Student ...
Student s1 = new Student();

// ... and increment the enrollment count.
s1.incrementEnrollment();

// Details omitted ...

// Later, we create another Student ...
Student s2 = new Student();

// ... and have to remember to increment the enrollment count for BOTH.
s1.incrementEnrollment();
s2.incrementEnrollment();

// More details omitted ...

// Still later, we create yet another Student ...
Student s3 = new Student();

// ... and have to remember to increment the enrollment count for ALL THREE!
s1.incrementEnrollment();
s2.incrementEnrollment();
s3.incrementEnrollment();
// Phew!
```

Fortunately, there is a simple solution: we can designate totalStudents to be what is known as a **static variable** of the Student class through use of the static keyword.

```
public class Student {
    // totalStudents is now declared to be a static attribute.
    private static int totalStudents;
    // Other attribute details omitted.

    // The next four methods are unchanged from the previous version of Student.

    public int getTotalStudents() {
      return totalStudents;
    }

    public void setTotalStudents(int x) {
      totalStudents = x;
    }

    public int reportTotalEnrollment() {
        System.out.println("Total Enrollment:  " + getTotalStudents());
    }
```

```
    public void incrementEnrollment() {
        setTotalStudents(getTotalStudents() + 1);
    }
}
```

Static variables are also casually referred to as "static attributes," but since I prefer the notion of an "attribute" as "a data item belonging to an individual object," I generally favor the nomenclature of "static variables" instead.

This causes the totalStudents variable to be associated with the Student class as a whole, as represented conceptually in Figure 7-8.

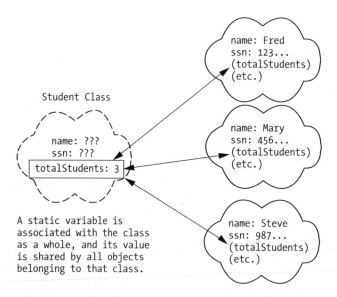

Figure 7-8. *Static variables are associated with a class as a whole.*

This enables us to simplify our client code as follows:

```
// Client code.

// Create three Students, incrementing the enrollment each time
// FOR THAT STUDENT ONLY.

Student s1 = new Student();
s1.incrementEnrollment();

// Later ...
Student s2 = new Student();
s2.incrementEnrollment();
```

```
// Still later ...
Student s3 = new Student();
s3.incrementEnrollment();
```

Each time we invoke incrementEnrollment for *one* Student, the others will benefit, because they all share the *same* totalStudents value. To demonstrate this, let's ask each Student object to report on total enrollment:

```
s1.reportTotalEnrollment();
s2.reportTotalEnrollment();
s3.reportTotalEnrollment();
```

Here's the output (all Students agree!):

```
Total Enrollment:  3
Total Enrollment:  3
Total Enrollment:  3
```

In fact, since this variable is effectively associated with the Student class as a whole, we can even ask the Student *class* to reportTotalEnrollment, and we'll get the same output:

```
Student.reportTotalEnrollment();
```

Here's the output:

```
Total Enrollment:  3
```

Note that we're using dot notation to talk to a class as a whole versus talking to individual objects. This is only possible, however, if the method in question—in this case, reportTotalEnrollment— is declared to be a **static method**. Before we discuss static methods, however, let's look at one final improvement to the design of our Student class.

A Design Improvement: Burying Implementation Details

Since we want to increment totalStudentCount whenever we create a new Student, we can insert such logic into the Student class's constructor(s) to do so automatically:

```
public class Student {
    private static int totalStudents;
    // Other details omitted.

    // Constructor.
    public Student(...) {
        // Details omitted.
        // Automatically increment the student count every time we
        // instantiate a new Student.
        totalStudents++;
    }

    // etc.
}
```

thereby eliminating the need for an incrementEnrollment method. This makes our client code much more concise:

```
// Client code.
// Create three Students, AUTOMATICALLY incrementing the totalStudents value
// each time.
Student s1 = new Student();
Student s2 = new Student();
Student s3 = new Student();

s1.reportTotalEnrollment();
s2.reportTotalEnrollment();
s3.reportTotalEnrollment();
Student.reportTotalEnrollment();
```

Here's the output:

```
Total Enrollment:  3
Total Enrollment:  3
Total Enrollment:  3
Total Enrollment:  3
```

It also makes our client code ***foolproof***: we no longer run the risk of forgetting to invoke incrementEnrollment explicitly after creating each Student. As mentioned before, ***whenever possible, it's desirable to bury such implementation details inside of a class, to lessen the burden on—and hence to lessen the likelihood for logic errors in—client code.***

Static Methods

Just as static variables are associated with a class as a whole versus with a specific individual object, **static methods** are in turn methods that may be ***invoked*** on a class as a whole.

Let's declare all of the methods related to the totalStudents variable—namely, getTotalStudents, setTotalStudents, and reportTotalEnrollment—to be static:

```
public class Student {
    private static int totalStudents;
    // Other details omitted.

    // Constructor.
    public Student(...) {
        // Details omitted.
        // Automatically increment the student count every time we
        // instantiate a new Student.
        totalStudents++;
    }

    // The following three methods are now static methods; note, however, that
    // the method BODIES are UNCHANGED from when these were nonstatic methods.
```

```
    public static int getTotalStudents() {
        return totalStudents;
    }

    public static void setTotalStudents(int x) {
        totalStudents = x;
    }

    public static int reportTotalEnrollment() {
        System.out.println("Total Enrollment:   " + getTotalStudents());
    }

    // etc.
}
```

Static methods can either be invoked on a ***class as a whole***

```
Student.reportTotalEnrollment();
```

or on an ***object belonging to the class*** for which it is defined

```
s.reportTotalEnrollment();
```

and the effect will be the same.

Restrictions on Static Methods

Note that there is an important restriction on static methods: such methods are not permitted to access ***non***static features of the class to which the methods belong. Before we discuss the rationale for this, let's consider a specific example.

If we were to attempt to write a static `print` method for our `Student` class that in turn accessed the ***non***static `getName` method of `Student`, the compiler would prevent us from doing so. Here's the proposed code:

```
public class Student {
  // Two variables -- one nonstatic, one static.
  private String name;
  private static int totalStudents;
  // etc.

  // We declare accessor methods for both variables:
  // STATIC get/set methods for STATIC variable "totalStudents" ...
  public static int getTotalStudents() { ... }
  public static void setTotalStudents(int x) { ... }
  // ... and NONstatic get/set methods for NONstatic attribute "name".
  public String getName() { ... }
  public void setName(String n) { ... }

  // Another static method.
  public static void print() {
    // A static method may NOT access NONstatic features
```

```
      // such as "getName()" -- the following line won't compile.
      System.out.println(getName() + " is one of " + getTotalStudents() +
                         "students.");
  }
}
```

The compiler would generate the following error message regarding the println statement in the static print method:

```
non-static method getName() cannot be referenced from a static context
```

Why is this? As we discussed in Chapter 3, classes are empty templates as far as attributes are concerned; it's not until we instantiate an object that its attribute values get filled in. If a static method is invoked on a class as a whole, and that method were in turn to try to access the value of an attribute, the value of that attribute would be undefined for the class, as illustrated conceptually in Figure 7-9. Since our static print method invokes the nonstatic getName method, which in turn accesses the (nonstatic) variable name, we're precluded from calling the getName method from print.

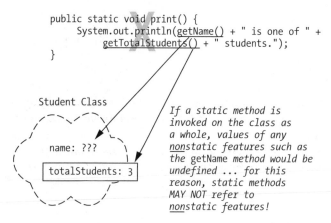

Figure 7-9. *Nonstatic attribute values are undefined in the context of a class.*

Another restriction on static methods is that they may not be declared to be abstract:

```
public class Student {
  // This won't compile.
  public abstract static void incrementEnrollment();
}
```

The following compiler error would result:

```
illegal combination of modifiers: abstract and static
```

Revisiting the Syntax of Print Statements

We've been using the syntax

```
System.out.println(expression);
```

throughout the book to display messages to the command window. Now that we have explored the notion of static features, we are in a position to understand the syntax of this statement.

As it turns out,

- `System` is a class built into the core Java language (i.e., it's defined within the `java.lang` package).

- `out` is a `public static` attribute of the `System` class, declared to be of type `PrintStream`. Thus, the expression `System.out` refers to an object of type `PrintStream`.

- The (overloaded) `println` method of the `PrintStream` class accepts an expression as an argument and displays it in `String` form to the standard output window (i.e., the command-line window from which the program was invoked).

We therefore needn't ever instantiate a `System` object to print messages to the screen; we simply call the `println` method on the `System` class's `public static PrintStream` attribute, `out`.

Utility Classes

We can take advantage of static features to design **utility classes**, which are classes that provide convenient ways of performing frequently used behaviors without having to instantiate an object to perform such behaviors. Such classes are often comprised wholly of static methods and public static variables.

The Java language includes several predefined utility classes. One example of such a class is the `Math` class of the `java.lang` package. The `Math` class declares a variety of static methods to compute trigonometric, exponential, logarithmic, and power functions; to round numeric values; and to generate random numbers. We saw the use of one such static method—`Math.sqrt`—in an example in Chapter 6:

```
squareRoot[i] = Math.sqrt(i);
```

The mathematical constant π is declared as a `public static` attribute of the `Math` class named `Math.PI`, and can be accessed from client code as follows:

```
// Compute the area of a circle.
double area = Math.PI * radius * radius;
```

In order to prevent client code from ***modifying*** the values of such "constants"

```
Math.PI = 0.0;  // Whoops!  This isn't good!
```

utility classes make use of **final variables**, as discussed in the following section.

Chapter 6 mentioned that the Java language provides a different class to serve as a "wrapper" for each of the eight distinct primitive types: `Integer`, `Float`, `Double`, `Byte`, `Short`, `Long`, `Boolean`, and `Character`. We'll talk about their roles as ***utility classes*** in Chapter 13.

The final Keyword

The Java final keyword can be applied to variables, methods, and classes as a whole. A **final variable** is a variable that can be assigned a value only once in a program; after that first assignment, the variable's value cannot be changed. We declare such a variable by placing the final keyword just before the type of the variable, as follows:

```
public class Example {
    // A static variable can be declared to be final ...
    public static final int x;

    // ... as can a (nonstatic) attribute.
    private final int y;

    public void someMethod() {
        // Even a local variable may be declared to be final.
        final int z;
        // etc.
```

Whereas a *local* final variable can be assigned a value separately from its declaration, we cannot do so for other final *variables*; that is, in the following expanded example, we'll get compilation errors on the lines so marked:

```
public class Example {
    // A static variable can be declared to be final ...
    public static final int x;

    // ... as can a (nonstatic) attribute.
    private final int y;

    public void someMethod() {
        // Even a local variable may be declared to be final.
        final int z;

        // However, whereas we ARE permitted to assign a local
        // final variable a value in a method separately from its
        // declaration ...
        z = 3;

        // .. we CANNOT do so for final static variables or for attributes.
        x = 1;  // Compilation error!
        y = 2;  // Compilation error!
    }

    // etc.
```

The compiler will generate the following error messages:

```
cannot assign a value to final variable x
x = 1;
  ^

cannot assign a value to final variable y
y = 2;
  ^
```

To avoid such a problem, we must assign values to ***class and instance*** final variables at the time that we declare them:

```
public class Example {
    // Assign values to static final variables/final attributes at the
    // same time that we declare them.
    public static final int x = 1;
    private final int y = 2;
    // etc.
```

Going back to our Math class example, we can now see that if Math.PI is declared to be a ***final*** static variable, client code will be prohibited from modifying its value, as it should be.

As another example, recall from our discussion of arrays in Chapter 6 that arrays have a public length attribute whose value represents the capacity of the array:

```
int[] x = new int[9];
for (int i = 0; i < x.length; i++) { ... }
```

As it turns out, the length attribute is declared to be final so that we are prevented from changing its value programmatically. Continuing the preceding example, the following won't compile:

```
// Let's try to enlarge the array!
x.length = 12;  // this won't compile
```

The compilation error that is produced is as follows:

```
cannot assign value to final variable length
x.length = 12;
    ^
```

Public Static Final Variables and Interfaces

As stated earlier in the chapter, interfaces are not permitted to declare variables, but for one exception: as it turns out, interfaces are allowed to declare public static final variables to serve as ***global constants***—that is, constant values that are in scope and hence accessible throughout an entire application.

Let's say, for example, that when a university administrator hires a new professor, she or he must designate whether the professor is going to be working full-time or part-time. If we wish, we can declare public static final variables of the Administrator interface to symbolically represent these two values, as shown in the following code, to be passed in as argument values to the hireProfessor method:

```
public interface Administrator {
    // Defining symbolic values to use as argument values for the second parameter of
    // the hireProfessor method.
    public static final int FULL_TIME = 1;
    public static final int PART_TIME = 2;

    // Valid values for workStatus are FULL_TIME (1) or PART_TIME (2).
    public boolean hireProfessor(Professor p, int workStatus);

    // Other method headers declared; details omitted.
}
```

This enables client code to take advantage of such values when invoking the hireProfessor method, as follows:

```
// Client code.
Administrator pAdmin = new Professor();
Professor p = new Professor();

// Hire p as a full-time faculty member.
pAdmin.hireProfessor(p, Administrator.FULL_TIME);
```

The naming convention for a public static final variable of either a class or an interface is rather unusual: we traditionally use all uppercase to name them, and hence use underscore characters (_) to visually separate words in multiword names—for example, FULL_TIME and PART_TIME. This explains why the Math class's public static final PI attribute is written in all uppercase—Math.PI versus Math.pi, for example.

In Chapter 13, you'll learn about **enum**(eration)s, a language feature introduced with J2SE 5.0 that provides a more elegant way to accomplish the same purpose.

As mentioned earlier, the final keyword may also be applied to methods and to classes as a whole:

- A method declared to be final cannot be overridden in a subclass:

```
public class Person {
    // Details omitted.

    public final int computeAge() { ... }

    // etc.
}
```

- A class declared to be final cannot be subclassed:

```
// No subclasses may be derived from this class.
public final class PhDStudent extends GraduateStudent { ... }
```

Numerous predefined Java classes are declared to be `final`. One such example is the `java.lang.String` class.

The Static Import Facility

Note that in the previous code example, we had to prefix the FULL_TIME variable name with the name of the interface that it belongs to—Administrator.FULL_TIME—in order for the Java compiler to recognize this symbol. As of J2SE 5.0, we are able to selectively import *specific static members* of a class or interface, rather than importing the class or interface as a whole, using an import static statement. That is, we could rewrite the previous example's client code (shown this time in the context of a main method) as follows:

```
// Note the insertion of the keyword "static" in the following import
// directive - we're not importing the Administrator interface as a whole;
// rather, we're importing all STATIC features of that interface:  namely,
// the FULL_TIME and PART_TIME constants.
import static Administrator.*;
// These can also be imported individually, e.g.:
// import static Administrator.FULL_TIME;

public class StaticImportExample {
    public static void main(String[] args) {
        // Client code.
        Administrator pAdmin = new Professor();
        Professor p = new Professor();

        // Hire p as a full-time faculty member.
        // Note that we no longer have to prefix the FULL_TIME variable
        // name, thanks to our static import directive above.
        pAdmin.hireProfessor(p, FULL_TIME);

        // etc.
```

Custom Utility Classes

We can take advantage of the same techniques used to create predefined Java utility classes like the Math class to create our own *custom* utility classes. For example, suppose that we are going to have a frequent need to do temperature conversions from degrees Fahrenheit to degrees Centigrade and vice versa. We could invent a utility class called Temperature as follows:

```
// A utility class to provide F=>C and C=>F conversions.
public class Temperature {
  public static double FahrenheitToCentigrade(double tempF) {
    return (tempF - 32.0) * (5.0/9.0);
  }

  public static double CentigradeToFahrenheit(double tempC) {
    return tempC * (9.0/5.0) + 32.0;
  }
}
```

Then, to use this class, we'd simply write client code as follows:

```
double degreesF = 212.0;
double degreesC = Temperature.FahrenheitToCentigrade(degreesF);
System.out.println("A temperature of " + degreesF + " degrees F = " +
                   degreesC + "degrees C");
```

This would give us the following output:

```
A temperature of 212.0 degrees F = 100.0 degrees C
```

We might even wish to include some commonly used constants—say, the boiling and freezing points of water in both F and C terms—as public static final variables in our utility class:

```
// A utility class to provide F=>C and C=>F conversions.
public class Temperature {
  // We've added some public static final variables.
  public static final double FAHRENHEIT_FREEZING = 32.0;
  public static final double CENTIGRADE_FREEZING = 0.0;
  public static final double FAHRENHEIT_BOILING = 212.0;
  public static final double CENTIGRADE_BOILING = 100.0;

  public static double FahrenheitToCentigrade(double tempF) {
    // We can utilize our new attributes in our method code.
    return (tempF - FAHRENHEIT_FREEZING) * (5.0/9.0);
  }

  public static double CentigradeToFahrenheit(double tempC) {
    // Ditto.
    return tempC * (9.0/5.0) + FAHRENHEIT_FREEZING;
  }
}
```

We could then take advantage of these constants in our client code, as well:

```
Soup s = new Soup("chicken noodle");

// Bring the soup to a boil.
if (s.getTemperature() < Temperature.FAHRENHEIT_BOILING) {
  s.cook();
}
```

Because all of the features of the Temperature class are static, we need never instantiate a Temperature object in our application.

Summary

Congratulations! You've made it through all of the major object technology concepts that you'll need to know for the rest of the book, and you've learned a great deal of Java syntax in the process. Please make sure that you're comfortable with these concepts before proceeding, as they form the foundation for the rest of your object learning experience:

- These same concepts will be reinforced when you learn how to model a problem in Part 2.

- They will be reinforced yet again when you learn how to render a model as Java code in Part 3.

In this chapter, you've learned that

- Different objects can respond to the same exact message in different class-specific ways, thanks to an OO language feature known as ***polymorphism***.

- ***Abstract classes*** are useful if you want to prescribe common behaviors among a group of (derived) classes without having to go into details about ***how*** those behaviors should be performed. That is, you specify ***what*** services an object must be able to perform—the messages that an object must be able to respond to, as defined by method headers—without programming method bodies.

- ***Interfaces*** are an even more abstract way to prescribe behaviors, in that they may only declare abstract methods (and constants).

- By implementing multiple interfaces, a class of objects may take on multiple roles in an application.

- Using interface types when declaring attributes, method return types, and parameters to methods make user-defined classes much more versatile and robust to requirements changes.

- ***Static variables*** may be used to enable an entire class of objects to share data, and can be manipulated on a class versus on specific objects/instances of that class via ***static methods***.

- You can take advantage of static methods along with public static final variables to create ***custom utility classes***.

Reflecting back on the home construction example from the Introduction to this book, you now know all about the unique properties of "blue stars" (objects), and why they are superior construction materials. But, you still need to learn how to lay out a blueprint for how to use them effectively in building an application—you'll learn how to do so in Part 2.

Exercises

1. Test yourself. Run through the following list of OO terms—some formal, some informal—and see if you can define each in your own words without referring back to the text:

Abstract class	Final variable	Overloading
Abstract method	Generalization	Overriding
Abstraction	"Get" method	Polymorphism
Accessor method	Handle	Predefined type
Aggregation	Implemented method	Primitive type
Ancestor class	Information hiding	Private accessibility
Attribute signature	Inheritance	Protected accessibility
Association	Instance	Public accessibility
Attribute	Instantiation	Reference type
Behavioral relationship	Interface	Reference variable
Binary association	Local variable	Root (of a class hierarchy)
Class	Link	Service
Class hierarchy	Message	Set (type of collection)
Classification	Method	"Set" method
Client code	Method header	Sibling class
Collection	Method signature	Specialization
Collections framework	Modeling	State (of an object)
Composite class	Multiple inheritance	Static attribute
Concrete class	Multiplicity	Static method
Constructor	Object (in the software sense)	Static variable
Delegation		Subclass
Dictionary (type of collection)	Operation	Superclass
Encapsulation	Ordered list	User-defined type

2. Which attributes, belonging to which SRS classes, might be well suited to being declared as static?

3. Which attributes, belonging to which Prescription Tracking System classes (as described in Appendix B), might be well suited to being declared as static?

4. It has been argued that the ability to implement multiple interfaces in the Java language eliminates the need for multiple inheritance support. Do you agree or disagree? Why or why not? Can you think of any ways in which implementing multiple interfaces "falls short" as compared with true multiple inheritance?

5. The following client code scenarios would each cause compilation errors. Can you explain why this is so in each case? Try answering this question *without* compiling the code. Be as precise as possible as to the reasons—they may not be as obvious as first meets the eye!

Assume that `Professor` and `Student` are both classes that implement the `Teacher` interface.

Scenario #1:

```
Professor p;
Student s = new Student();
Teacher t;

t = s;
p = t;
```

Scenario #2:

```
Professor p = new Professor();
Student s;
Teacher t = new Student();

s = t;
```

Scenario #3:

```
Professor p = new Professor();
Student s = new Student();
Teacher t;

p = t;
```

6. [*Coding*] Test your answers to question 5 by coding simple versions of the `Professor`, `Student`, and `Teacher` types plus a `main` class/method to house your client code.

PART 2

▪▪▪

Object Modeling 101

CHAPTER 8

The Object Modeling Process in a Nutshell

Let's look in on the homebuilder whom we met in the Introduction to this book. He's just returned from a seminar entitled "Blue Stars: A Builder's Dream Come True." He now knows all about the unique properties of blue stars, and he appreciates why they are superior construction materials—just as you've learned about the unique properties of software objects as application "construction materials" earlier in the book. But he is still inexperienced with actually using blue stars in a construction project; in particular, he doesn't yet know how to develop a blueprint suitable for a home that is to be built from blue stars. And we still need to see how to develop a "blueprint" for a software system that is to be constructed from objects. This is the focus of Part 2 of this book.

In this chapter, you'll learn

- The goals and philosophy behind object modeling

- How much flexibility we have in terms of selecting or devising a modeling methodology

- The pros and cons of object modeling software tools

The "Big Picture" Goal of Object Modeling

Our goal in object modeling is to render a precise, concise, understandable object-oriented model, or "blueprint," of the system to be automated. This model will serve as an important tool for communication:

- ***To the future users of the system that we are about to build, an object model communicates our understanding of the system requirements***. Having the users review and "bless" the model will ensure that we get off on the right foot with a project, for a mistake in judgment at the requirements analysis stage can prove much more costly to fix—by orders of magnitude—than if such a misunderstanding is found and corrected when the system is still just a "gleam in the user's eye."

- *To the software development team, an object model communicates the structure and function of the software that needs to be built in order to satisfy those requirements.* This benefits not only the software engineers themselves, but also the folks who are responsible for quality assurance, testing, and documentation.

- Long after the application is operational, an object model lives on as a schematic diagram to help the myriad folks responsible for supporting and maintaining an application understand its structure and function.

Of course, this last point is true only if the object model accurately reflects the system as it was actually built, not just as it was originally conceived. The design of complex systems invariably changes during their construction, so care should be taken to keep the object model up-to-date as the system is built.

Modeling Methodology = Process + Notation + Tool

According to Webster's dictionary, a **methodology** is

A set of systematic procedures used by a discipline [to achieve a particular desired outcome].

A modeling methodology, OO or otherwise, ideally involves three components:

- A **process**: The "how to" steps for gathering the requirements and determining the abstraction to be modeled

- A **notation**: A graphical "language" for communicating the model

- A **tool**: An automated way of rendering the notation, typically in drag-and-drop fashion

Although these constitute the ideal components of a modeling methodology, they are not all of equal importance.

- Adhering to a sound *process* is certainly critical.

- However, we can sometimes get by with a narrative text description of an abstraction without having to resort to portraying it with formal graphical *notation*.

- And, when we *do* choose to depict an abstraction formally via a graphical notation, it isn't mandatory that we use a specialized *tool* for doing so.

In other words, following an organized process is the most critical aspect of object modeling; using a particular notation is important, but less so; and our choice of a particular tool for rendering the model is the least important aspect of the three (see Figure 8-1).

Figure 8-1. *Of the three aspects of a methodology, a sound process is by far the most important.*

Many important contributions in the form of new processes, notations, and tools have been made in the OO methodology arena over the years by numerous well-known methodologists. In some sense, if you're just getting into objects for the first time now, you're fortunate, because you managed to avoid the "methodology wars" that raged for many years as methodologists and their followers argued about what were in some cases esoteric details.

Here is a partial list of contributions made in the object methodology arena over the past few decades; the list is in no particular order.

- *James Rumbaugh et al.*: The Object Modeling Technique (OMT)

- *Grady Booch*: The Booch Method

- *Sally Shlaer and Stephen Mellor*: Emphasis on state diagrams

- *Rebecca Wirfs-Brock et al.*: Responsibility-driven design; Class-Responsibilities-Collaborators (CRC) cards

- *Bertrand Meyer*: The Eiffel programming language; the notion of programming by contract

- *James Martin and James Odell*: Retooling of their functional decomposition methodologies for use with OO systems

- *Peter Coad and Edward Yourdon*: As in the preceding entry

- *Ivar Jacobson*: Use cases as a means of formalizing requirements

- *Derek Coleman et al. (HP)*: The Fusion Method

- *Erich Gamma, Richard Helm, Ralph Johnson, and John Vlissides (the "Gang of Four")*: Design pattern reuse

In recent years, there was a major push in the industry to meld the best ideas of competing methodologies into a single approach, with particular emphasis placed on coming up with a universal modeling notation. The resultant notation, known as the **Unified Modeling Language (UML)**, represents the collaborative efforts of three of the leaders in the OO methodology field—James Rumbaugh, Grady Booch, and Ivar Jacobson—and has become the industry standard object-modeling notation. (You'll learn the basics of UML in Chapters 10 and 11.)

Along with UML, these three gentlemen—known affectionately in the industry as the "Three Amigos"—have also contributed heavily to the evolution of an overall methodology known as the **Rational Unified Process (RUP)**, a full-blown software development methodology encompassing modeling, project management, and configuration management workflows. But I'm not going to dwell on the details of this particular methodology in this book, because as mentioned in the Introduction, it isn't my intention to teach you any one *specific* methodology in great detail. By learning a sound, *generic* process for object modeling, you'll be armed with the knowledge you need to read about, evaluate, and select a specific methodology such as RUP, or to craft your own hybrid approach by mixing and matching the processes, notations, and tool(s) from various methodologies that make the most sense for your organization.

As for modeling tools, you don't need one, strictly speaking, to appreciate the material presented in this book. But, I've anticipated that you'll likely want to get your "hands dirty" with a modeling tool. Because of this, I include a general discussion of modeling tool pros and cons a bit later in this chapter.

It's important to keep in mind that a methodology is but a means to an end, and it's the *end*—a usable, flexible, maintainable, reliable, and functionally correct software system, along with thorough, clear supporting documentation—that we care most about when all is said and done.

To help illustrate this point, let's use a simple analogy. Say that our goal is to cheer people up. We decide to hand draw (process) a smiley face (an abstraction of the desired behavior, rendered with a graphical notation) with a pencil (tool), as shown in Figure 8-2.

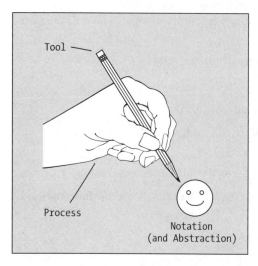

Figure 8-2. *A methodology encompasses process, notation, and tools.*

After we're done, we put our pencil away, hang our smiley face picture on the wall, and go about our business. A few days go by, and we note that people are indeed cheered up by our picture, and so our original goal has been achieved. In hindsight, we could have accomplished this same goal using

- A variety of different "processes"—hand drawing, rubber stamping, cutting pictures from a magazine

- A variety of different "notations"—the graphical notation of a smiley face or a cartoon, or the narrative text of a joke or sign

- A variety of different "tools"—a pen, a pencil, a paintbrush, a crayon

Now, back to our homebuilding analogy. Long after the architect and construction crew have left a building site, taking their equipment and tools with them, the house that they have built will remain standing as a testimonial to the quality of the materials they used, how sound a construction approach they employed, and how elegant a blueprint they had to start with. The blueprint will come in handy later on when the time comes to remodel or maintain the home, so we certainly won't throw it away; but, the "livability" and ease/affordability of maintaining the home will be the primary measure of success.

The same is true for software development: the real legacy of a software development project is the resultant software system, which is, after all, the reason for using a methodology to produce a model in the first place. We must take care to avoid getting so caught up in debating the relative merits of one methodology versus another that we fail to produce useful software. As you can see in Figure 8-3, there are ***many*** paths to the same destination.

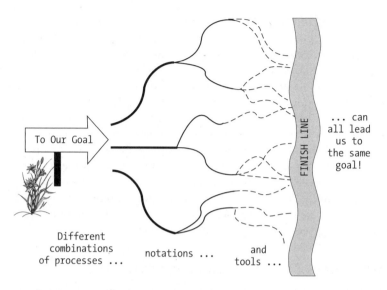

To Our Goal

FINISH LINE

... can
all lead
us to
the same
goal!

Different
combinations
of processes ...   notations ...   and
                                            tools ...

Figure 8-3. *Many different approaches can serve us well when building software.*

Jacquie's Recommended Object Modeling Process, in a Nutshell

I present here a basic preview of the modeling process that I advocate, and which I'm going to illustrate in depth throughout the remainder of Part 2 of the book.

- Begin by obtaining or writing a narrative problem statement, similar to the Student Registration System (SRS) problem statement presented in the Introduction, or the alternative case study problem statements included as Appendix B. Think about the different categories of users that will be interacting with the system, and the various situations in which they'll each use it, to make sure that you uncover any not-so-obvious requirements that may have been missed. (I'll discuss a technique for doing this—known as **use case analysis**—in Chapter 9.)

- Handle the data side of the application by identifying the different classes of "real-world" objects that your application will need to be concerned with, and determine how these interrelate. (I'll illustrate the process of creating a **class diagram** in Chapter 10.)

- Handle the functional side of the application by studying how objects need to collaborate to accomplish the system's mission, determining what behaviors/responsibilities will be required of each class. (I'll illustrate the process of modeling the behavioral aspects of an OO system in Chapter 11.)

- Test the model to ensure that it does indeed meet all of the original requirements. (I'll discuss testing in Chapter 12.)

You'll see plenty of examples of each of these techniques in the chapters to follow, and you'll get an opportunity to practice these techniques based on the hands-on exercises suggested at the end of each chapter. Armed with a solid model of the SRS, you'll then be ready to render the model into Java code, which is the subject of Part 3 of the book.

Note that these process steps need not be performed in strictly sequential fashion. In fact, as you become comfortable with each of the steps, you may find yourself carrying some of them out in parallel, or in shuffled order. For example, contemplating the behavioral aspects of a model may bring to light new data requirements. In fact, for all but the most trivial models, it's commonplace to iterate through these steps multiple times, "dialing in" increased levels of understanding, hence more detail in the model and supporting documentation, with each iteration.

It's also important to note that the formality of the process should be adjusted to the size of the project team and the complexity of the requirements. If we separate the *form* of using a methodology from the *substance* of what that methodology produces in the way of **artifacts**—models, documentation, code, and so on—then a good rule of thumb is that a project team should spend no more than 10 to 20 percent of its time on *form*, and 80 to 90 percent on *substance*. If the team finds itself spending so much time on form that little or no progress is being made on substance, it's time to reevaluate the methodology and its various components to see where simplifying adjustments or improvements to efficiency may be made.

Thoughts Regarding Object Modeling Software Tools

It's worthwhile to spend a little bit of time talking about the pros and cons of using an object modeling software tool. For purposes of learning how to produce models, a generic drawing tool such as PowerPoint may be good enough; for that matter, you may simply want to sketch your models using paper and pencil. But, getting some hands-on experience with using a tool specifically designed for object modeling will better prepare you for your first "industrial-strength" project, so you may wish to acquire one before embarking upon the next chapter. You'll find information about various object modeling software tools, including links to free or evaluation copies of software, on my web site: `http://objectstart.com`.

I make it a practice not to mention specific tools, vendors, versions, etc., in this book, as they change much too rapidly. As soon as a software product is mentioned in print, it's virtually guaranteed that it will either change names, change vendors who market it, or disappear completely!

Object modeling tools fall under the general heading of **Computer-Aided Software Engineering**, or **CASE**, **tools**. CASE tools afford us many advantages, but aren't without their drawbacks.

Advantages of Using CASE Tools

There are many arguments in favor of using CASE tools; several of the more compelling are as follows.

Ease of Use

CASE tools provide a quick drag-and-drop way to create visual models. Rather than trying to render a given notation with a generic drawing tool, where your basic drawing components are simple lines, arrows, text, boxes, and other geometric shapes, CASE tools provide one or more palettes of prefabricated graphical components specific to the supported notation. For example, you can drag and drop the graphical representation for a class rather than having to painstakingly fabricate it from simpler drawing components.

Added Information Content

CASE tools produce "intelligent" drawings that enforce the syntax rules of a particular notation. This is in contrast to a generic drawing package, which will pretty much let you draw whatever you like, whether it adheres to the notational syntax or not.

The controls imposed by a CASE tool can be a mixed blessing: on the plus side, they will prevent you from making syntactic errors, but as I discuss a little later, they may also prevent you from making desired adjustments to the notation.

Also, information about the classes reflected in a diagram—their names, attributes, methods, and relationships—is typically stored in a repository that underlies the diagram. Most CASE tools provide documentation-generation features based upon this repository, enabling you to automatically generate project documentation such as a **data dictionary report**, a type of report that I'll discuss in Chapter 10. Some tools even allow you to tap into this repository programmatically, should you find a need to do so.

Automated Code Generation

Most CASE tools provide code-generation capabilities, enabling you to transition from a diagram to skeletal Java code with the push of a button. You may or may not wish to avail yourself of this feature, however, for the following reasons:

- Depending on how much control the CASE tool gives you as to the structure that the generated code takes, the code that is generated will potentially not meet team/corporate standards.

- With most tools, you're unable to edit the generated code externally to the tool, because the tool will then be unaware of the changes that you've made, meaning that the next time the code is generated, your changes will be overwritten and obliterated.

- This has implications for reusing code from other projects, as well: make sure that your tool of choice allows you to import and introduce software components that didn't originate within the tool.

It's sometimes better in the end to write your code from scratch, for even though it may take a bit longer at the outset, it often is much easier to manage such code over the lifetime of the project, and you avoid become "enslaved" to a particular modeling tool for ongoing code maintenance. In the worst-case scenario, the tool vendor goes out of business, and you're left with an unsupported product and perhaps unsupportable project.

Project Management Aids

Many CASE tools provide some sort of version control, enabling you to maintain different generations of the same model. If you make a change to your model, but then after reviewing the change with your users decide that you'd prefer to return to the way things were previously, it's trivial to do if version control is in place.

CASE tools also often provide configuration management/team collaboration capabilities, to enable a group of modelers to easily share in the creation of a single model.

Flexibility

Some CASE tools support multiple graphical notations, enabling you to initially create a diagram in one notation (say, OMT) but to then convert the diagram to another notation (such as UML) quickly and effortlessly.

This doesn't always occur flawlessly, however; things can get lost in the translation if the two notations don't have a one-for-one match in terms of notational components. It's not unusual to have to do some minor cleanup after the fact.

Some tools even support customizable or "do it yourself" notational paradigms, should you wish either to embellish a standard notation such as UML or to invent a new notation from scratch.

Some Drawbacks of Using CASE Tools

CASE tools aren't without their drawbacks, however:

- ***CASE tools can be expensive***. It's not unusual for a high-end CASE tool to cost hundreds or even thousands of dollars per "seat." The ***good news*** is that, in recent years, many shareware/free UML modeling tools have become available, as mentioned earlier in this chapter.

- ***CASE tools can sometimes be inflexible***. I talk about adapting processes, notations, and tools to suit your own needs throughout Part 2 of the book, but tools don't always cooperate! I'll point out in upcoming chapters some specific examples of situations where you might want to bend the notation a little bit, if your CASE tool will accommodate it.

- ***You run the risk of getting locked into a particular vendor's product*** if the CASE tool in question can't export your model in a vendor-neutral fashion (e.g., as XML).

- ***It's easy to get caught up with form over substance***! This is true of any automated tool—even a word processor tends to lure people into spending more time on the cosmetics of a document than is warranted, long after the substantive content is rock solid.

Generally speaking, however, the pros of using an OO CASE tool significantly outweigh the cons—consider the cons as "words to the wise" on how to successfully apply such a tool to your modeling efforts.

A Reminder

Although I've said it several times already in this book, it's important to remind you that the process of object modeling is ***language neutral***. I presented Java syntax in Part 1 of the book because the ultimate goal is to make you comfortable with both object modeling and Java programming. In Part 2 of the book, however, we're going to drift away from Java, because we truly are at a point where the concepts you'll be learning are just as applicable to Java as they are to C++, or C#, any other OO programming language. But, never fear—we'll return to Java "big time" in Part 3!

Summary

By far, the most important lesson to take away from this chapter is the following:

> **Don't get caught up in form over substance!**

The model that you produce is only a means to an end . . . and the process, notation, and tools that you use to produce the model are but a *means* to the means to this end. If you get too hung up on which notation to use, or which process to use, or which tool to use, you may wind up spinning your wheels in "analysis paralysis." Don't lose sight of your ultimate goal: to build *usable, flexible, maintainable, reliable, functionally correct software systems*.

Exercises

1. Briefly describe the methodology—process, notation, and tool(s)—that you used on a recent software development project. What aspects of this methodology worked well for you and your teammates, and what, in hindsight, do you think could have been approached more effectively?

2. Research one of the object modeling technologies/techniques mentioned in the "Modeling Methodology = Process + Notation + Tool" section earlier in this chapter, and report briefly on the process, notation, and tools involved.

■ ■ ■

CHAPTER 9

Formalizing Requirements Through Use Cases

When you get ready to leave on a vacation, you may run through a mental or written checklist to make sure that you've properly prepared for your departure. Did you pack everything you need to take? Did you pack **_too much_**? Did you arrange to have the appropriate services (newspaper, mail delivery, etc.) stopped? Did you arrange for someone to water the plants and feed your pet rat? Once you depart on your trip, you want to enjoy yourself and know that when you arrive home again, you won't find any disasters waiting for you.

This isn't unlike a software development project: we need to organize a checklist of the things that must be provided for by the system before we embark on its development, so that the project runs smoothly and so that we don't create a disaster (in the form of unmet requirements and dissatisfied customers/users) when the system is delivered.

The art and science of requirements analysis—for it truly is both!—is so extensive a topic that an entire book could be devoted to this subject alone. There is one technique in particular for discovering and rounding out requirements known as **use case modeling**, which is a cornerstone of the Rational Unified Process (RUP) and which warrants your consideration. Use cases aren't strictly an artifact of OO methodologies; they can be prepared for any software system, regardless of the development methodology to be used. However, they made their debut within the software development community in the context of object systems, and have gained widespread popularity in that context.

In this chapter, you'll learn

- How we must anticipate all of the different roles that users will play when interacting with our future system

- That we must assume each of the users' viewpoints in describing the services that a software application as a whole is to provide

- How to prepare use cases as a means of documenting all of the preceding requirements

I'll also give you enough general background about requirements analysis to provide an appropriate context for use case modeling.

What Are Use Cases?

In determining what the desired functionality of a system is to be, we must seek answers to the following questions:

- *Who* will want to use our system?

- What *services* will the system need to provide in order to be of value to the users?

- When users interact with the system for a particular purpose, what is their expectation as to the *desired outcome*?

Use cases are a natural way to express the answers to these questions. Each use case is a simple statement, narrative or graphical in fashion, that describes a particular goal or outcome of the system, and who expects that outcome. For example, one goal of the SRS is to "enable a student user to register for a course," and thus we've just expressed our first use case! (Yes, use cases really are that straightforward. In fact, we *need* for them to be that straightforward, so that they are understandable by the users/sponsors of the system, as we'll discuss further in a moment.)

Functional vs. Technical Requirements

The purpose of thinking through all of the use cases for a system is to explore the system's functional requirements thoroughly, so as to make sure that a particular category of user, or potential purpose for the system, isn't overlooked. We differentiate between functional requirements and technical requirements as follows.

Functional requirements are those aspects of a system that have to do with how it is to operate or function from the perspective of someone using the system. Functional requirements may in turn be subdivided into

- **"Goal-oriented" functional requirements:** These provide a statement of a system's purpose without regard to how the requirement will "play out" from the user's vantage point— for example, "The system must be able to produce tailorable reports." Avoid discussing implementation details when specifying goal-oriented requirements.

- **"Look and feel" requirements:** These requirements get a bit more specific in terms of what the user expects the system to look like externally (e.g., how the GUI will be presented), and how the user expects it to behave, again from the user's perspective. For example, we might have as a requirement "The user will click a button on the main GUI, and a confirmation message will appear . . .". A good practice is to write a **concept of operations** document to serve as a "paper prototype" describing how you envision the future system will look and behave, to stimulate discussion with intended users of the as-yet-to-be-built system before you even begin modeling.

We emphasize goal-oriented functional requirements when preparing use cases.

I present a sample concept of operations for the SRS application in Chapter 16.

Technical requirements, on the other hand, have more to do with *how* a system is to be built internally in order to *meet* the functional requirements; for instance, "The system will use the TCP/IP protocol . . ." or "We will use a dictionary collection as the means for tracking students . . .". We can think of these as requirements for how programmers should tackle the *solution*, in contrast to functional requirements, which are a statement of what the *problem to be tackled* actually is.

Technical requirements such as these don't play a role in use case analysis. Although it's certainly conceivable that the users of our system may be technically sophisticated, it's best to express functional requirements in such a way that even a user who knows nothing about the inner workings of a computer will understand them. This helps to ensure that technical requirements don't creep into the functional requirements statement, a common mistake made by many inexperienced software developers. When we allow technical requirements to color the functional requirements, they artificially constrain the solution to a problem too early in the development life cycle.

Involving the Users

Because the intended users of a system are the ultimate experts in what they need the system to do, it's essential that they be involved in the use case definition process. If the intended users haven't (as individuals) been specifically defined or recruited (as with a software product that is to be sold commercially), their anticipated needs nonetheless need to be taken into account by identifying people with comparable experience to serve as "user surrogates." Ideally, the users or user surrogates will write some or all of the use cases themselves; at a minimum, you'll interview such people, write the use cases on their behalf, and then get their confirmation that what you've written is indeed accurate.

Use cases are one of the first deliverables/artifacts to emerge in a software development project's life cycle, but also one of the last things to be put to good use in making sure that the system is a success. They turn out to be quite useful as a basis for writing testing scripts, to ensure that all functional threads are exercised during system and user acceptance testing.

Use cases also lend themselves to the preparation of a **requirements traceability matrix**— that is, a final checklist against which the users can verify that all of their initial requirements have indeed been met when the system is delivered.

Note that a requirements traceability matrix must take into account all of the requirements for a system— functional as well as technical—of which use cases represent only a subset.

Returning to the questions posed at the outset of this section, let's answer the first question— namely, "Who will want to use our system?"—which in use case nomenclature is known as identifying **actors**.

Actors

Actors represent anybody or anything that will interact with the system after it's built; actors drive use cases. Actors generally fall into two broad categories:

- Human users

- Other computer systems

"Interaction" is generally defined to mean using the system to achieve some result, but can also be thought of as simply (a) providing/contributing information to the system, and/or (b) receiving/consuming information from the system.

By *providing* information, I mean whether or not the actor inputs substantive information that adds to the collective data stored by the system—for example, a department chairperson defining a new course offering, or a student registering his or her plan of study. This doesn't include the relatively trivial information that users have to provide to look things up—for example, typing in a student ID to request their transcript.

By *consuming* information, I mean whether or not the actor uses the system to obtain information—for example, a faculty user printing out a student roster for a course that he or she will be teaching, or a student viewing his or her course schedule online.

Identifying Actors and Determining Their Roles

We must create an actor for every different role that will be assumed by various categories of user relative to the system. To identify such roles, we typically turn first to the **narrative requirements specification**, if one exists—that is, a statement of the functional requirements, such as the Student Registration System specifications as presented in the Introduction to this book. The only category of user explicitly mentioned by that specification is a student user. So, we would definitely consider Student to be one of the actor types for the SRS.

If we think beyond the specification, however, it isn't difficult to come up with other potential categories of user who might also benefit from using the SRS:

- Faculty may wish to get a headcount of how many students are registered for one of the upcoming classes that they are going to be teaching, or they may use the system to post final grades, which in turn are reflected by a student's transcript.

- Department chairpersons may wish to see how popular various courses are or, conversely, whether or not a course ought to be canceled due to lack of interest on the part of the student body.

- Personnel in the Registrar's Office may wish to use the SRS to verify that a particular student is projected to have met the requirements to graduate in a given semester.

- Alumni may wish to use the SRS to request copies of their transcripts.

- Prospective students—that is, those who are thinking about applying for admission but who haven't yet done so—may wish to browse the courses that are going to be offered in an upcoming semester to help them determine whether or not the university has a curriculum that meets their interests.

and so on. Similarly, since other computer systems can be actors, we might have to build interfaces between the SRS and other existing automated systems at the university, such as

- The Billing System, so that students can be billed accurately based on their current course load

- The Classroom Scheduling System, to ensure that classes to be taught are assigned to rooms of adequate capacity based on the student headcount

- The Admissions System, so that the SRS can be notified when a new student has been admitted and is eligible to register for courses

Of course, we have to make a decision early on as to what the scope of the system we're going to build should be, to avoid "requirements inflation" aka "scope creep." To try and accommodate *all* of the actors hypothesized earlier would result in a massive undertaking that may simply be too costly for the sponsors of the system. For example, does it make sense to provide for potential students to use the SRS to preview what the university offers in the way of courses, or is there a different system—say, an online course catalog of some sort—that is better suited to this purpose? Through in-depth interviews with all of the intended user groups, the scope of the system can be appropriately bounded, and some of the actors that we conceived of may be eliminated as a result.

In our particular case, we'll assume that the sponsors of the SRS have decided that we needn't accommodate the needs of alumni or prospective students in building the system; that is, that we needn't recognize alumni or prospective students as actors. A key point here is that the *sponsors* decide such things, *not the programmers*! One responsibility of a software engineer is indeed to identify requirements, and certainly part of that responsibility may include suggesting functional enhancements that the software engineer feels will be of benefit to the user. But, the sponsors of the system rightfully have the final say in what actually gets built.

Many software engineers get into trouble because they assume that they "know better" than their clients as to what the users really need. You may indeed have a brilliant idea to suggest, but think of it simply as that— a *suggestion*—and consider your task as one of either convincing the sponsors/users of its merit, or of graciously accepting their decision to decline your recommendation.

Note that the same user may interact with the system on different occasions in different roles. That is, a professor who chairs a department may assume the role of a Department Chair actor when he or she is trying to determine whether or not a course should be canceled. Alternatively, the same professor may assume the role of a Faculty actor when he or she wishes to query the SRS for the student headcount for a particular course that he or she is teaching.

Diagramming a System and Its Actors

Once we've settled on the actors for our system, we may wish to optionally diagram them. UML notation calls for representing all actors—whether a human user or a computer system—as stick figures, and then connecting these via straight lines to a rectangle representing the system, as you see in Figure 9-1.

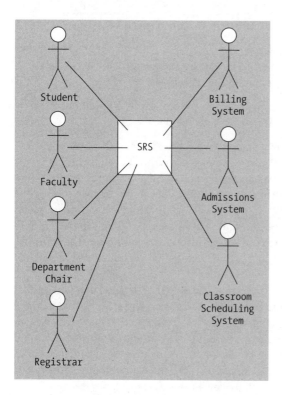

Figure 9-1. *A proper UML use case diagram*

This figure appears rather simplistic, and yet, this is a legitimate diagram that might be produced for a project such as the SRS development effort.

I prefer to use a slightly modified version of UML notation, as follows:

- I've extended the use of a rectangle to represent not only the core system but also all actors that are external systems, rather than representing the latter as human stick figures.

- I find that using arrowheads to reflect a directional flow of information—that is, whether an actor provides and/or consumes information—is a bit more communicative. For example, in the amended version of the notation as follows, I represent a student as both providing and consuming information, whereas a registrar only consumes information.

Note that the registrar does indeed provide information, but not to the SRS directly. He or she provides information to the Admissions System as to which students are registered at the university; this information then gets fed into the SRS by the Admissions System. So, the Admissions System is shown as providing information as an actor to the SRS; but, from the standpoint of the SRS, the registrar is simply a consumer.

With these slight changes in notation, as reflected in Figure 9-2, the use case diagram becomes a much more communicative instrument.

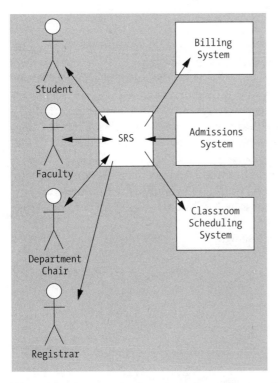

Figure 9-2. *A customized version of use case notation*

Of course, if you do decide to deviate from a widely understood notational standard such as UML, you'll need to follow these steps:

1. Reach consensus among your fellow software developers, to ensure that the team as a whole is speaking the same language.

2. Document and communicate such deviations (along with the notation as a whole) to your customers/users, so that they, too, understand your particular "dialect."

3. Make sure that such documentation is incorporated into the full documentation set for the project, so that future reviewers of the documentation will immediately understand your notational "embellishments."

If you make these enhancements intuitive enough, however, they may just speak for themselves!

Of course, as pointed out in Chapter 8, you'll also need to consider whether the CASE tool you're using, if any, will support such alterations.

Time and again throughout Part 2 of this book, I'll remind you that it's perfectly acceptable to adapt or extend any process, notation, or tool that you care to adopt to best suit your company's or project's purposes; none of these methodology components is "sacred."

Specifying Use Cases

Having made a first cut at what the SRS actors are, we'll next enumerate in what ways the system will be used by these actors—in other words, the use cases themselves.

A use case represents a logical thread, or a series of cause-and-effect events, beginning with an actor's first contact with the system and ending with the achievement of that actor's goal for using the system in the first place. Note that an actor always initiates a use case; actions initiated by a system on its own behalf don't warrant the development of a use case (although they do warrant expression as either a functional or technical requirement, as defined earlier in the chapter).

Use cases emphasize "what" the system is to do—functional requirements—without concern for "how" such things will be accomplished internally; they aren't unlike method signatures in this regard. In fact, you can think of a use case as a "behavioral signature" for the system as a whole.

Some example high-level use cases for the SRS might be

- Register for a Course

- Drop a Course

- Determine a Student's Course Load

- Choose a Faculty Advisor

- Establish a Plan of Study

- View the Schedule of Classes

- Request a Student Roster for a Given Course

- Request a Transcript for a Given Student

- Maintain Course Information (e.g., change the course description, reflect a different instructor for the course, and so on)

- Determine a Student's Eligibility for Graduation

- Post Final Semester Grades for a Given Course

Remember that a use case is initiated by an actor, which is why I didn't list other functionality called out by the SRS requirements specification, such as "Notify Student by Email," as use cases.

We may decompose any one of the use cases into steps, with each step representing a more detailed use case. For example, "Register for a Course" may be decomposed into these steps:

1. Verify that a student has met the prerequisites.

2. Check student's plan of study to ensure that this course is required.

3. Check for availability of a seat in the course.

4. (Optionally) Place student on a wait list.

and so forth. Use cases may be interrelated in parent-child fashion, with more detailed use cases being shared by more than one general use case. For example, the "Request a Student Roster" and "Post Final Semester Grades" general use cases may both involve the more detailed "Verify That Professor Is Teaching the Course in Question" use case.

Unfortunately, as is true of all requirements analysis, there is no magical formula to apply in order to determine whether or not you've identified all of the important use cases or all of the actors, and/or whether you've gone into sufficient depth in terms of sub use cases. The process of use case development is iterative; when subsequent iterations fail to yield substantial changes, you're probably finished! Copious interviews and reviews with users, along with periodic team walk-throughs of the use case set as a whole, go a long way in ensuring that nothing important has been missed.

Matching Up Use Cases with Actors

Another important step is to match up use cases with actors. The relationship between actors and use cases is potentially many-to-many, in that the same actor may initiate many different use cases, and a single use case may be relevant to many different actors. By cross-referencing actors with use cases, we ensure that

- We didn't identify an actor who, in the final analysis, really has no use for the system after all.

- Conversely, that we didn't specify a use case that nobody really cares about.

For each use case–actor combination, it's useful to determine whether the actor consumes information and/or provides information. Another way to view this aspect of a system is whether actors need write access (providing) to the system's information resources versus having read-only access (consuming).

If the number of actors and/or use cases isn't prohibitive, a simple table such as Table 9-1 can be used to summarize all of the preceding information.

Table 9-1. *A Simple Actor/Use Case Cross-Referencing Technique*

Initiating Actor ==> Use case:	Student	Faculty	Billing System	Etc.
Register for a Course	Provides info	N/A	N/A	
Post Final Grades	Consumes info	Provides info	N/A	
Request a Transcript	Consumes info	Consumes info	N/A	
Determine a Student's Course Load	Consumes info	Consumes info	Consumes info	
Etc.				

To Diagram or Not to Diagram?

The use case concept is fairly straightforward, and hence simple narrative text as we've seen thus far in the chapter is often sufficient for expressing use cases. UML does, however, provide a formal means for diagramming use cases and their interactions with actors. As mentioned earlier, actors (whether people or systems) are represented as stick figures; use cases are represented as ovals labeled underneath with a brief phrase describing the use case; and the box surrounding the oval(s) represents the system boundaries.

Figure 9-3 shows a sample UML use case diagram. Here, we depict three actors—Student, Faculty, and Registrar—as having occasion to participate individually in the Request Transcript use case.

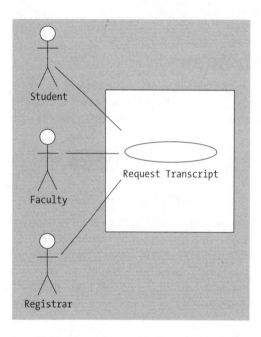

Figure 9-3. *A sample UML use case diagram*

When deciding whether or not to go to the trouble of diagramming your use cases rather than merely expressing them in narrative form, think back to the rationale for producing use cases in the first place: namely, to think through, and to then communicate, the software development team's understanding of the system requirements to the users/sponsors in order to obtain consensus. It's up to you, your project team, and your users/sponsors to determine whether diagrams enhance this process or not. If they do, use them; if they don't, go with narrative use case documentation instead.

Once you've documented a system's actors and use cases, whether in text alone or with accompanying diagrams, these become part of the core documentation set defining the problem to be automated. In the next chapter, we'll examine how to use such documentation as a starting point for determining what classes we'll need to create and instantiate as our system "building blocks."

UML spells out some additional formalism with regard to use case modeling; for more details on use case diagrams, including advanced diagramming techniques, please see the recommended reading list in Chapter 18.

Summary

In this chapter, you've seen that

- Use case analysis is a simple yet powerful technique for specifying the requirements for a system more precisely and completely.

- Use cases are based upon the goal-oriented functional requirements for a system.

- Use cases are used to describe

  - The desired behavior/functionality of the system to be built

  - The external users or systems (known as actors) who avail themselves of these services

  - The interactions between the two

Exercises

1. Determine the actors that might be appropriate for the Prescription Tracking System (PTS) case study discussed in Appendix B.

2. For the problem area whose requirements you defined for exercise 3 in Chapter 1, determine who the appropriate actors might be.

3. Based on the PTS specification in Appendix B, list (a) the use cases that are explicitly called for by the specification, and (b) any additional use cases that you suspect might be worth exploring with the future users of the system.

4. Repeat exercise 3 above, but in the context of the problem area whose requirements you defined for exercise 3 in Chapter 1.

5. Create a table mapping the actors you identified for the PTS in exercise 1 above to the use cases you listed for the PTS in exercise 3 above, indicating whether a particular actor's participation in a use case is as an information provider or a consumer.

6. Create a table mapping the actors you identified in exercise 2 above to the use cases you listed in exercise 4 above, indicating whether a particular actor's participation in a use case is as an information provider or an information consumer.

CHAPTER 10

■ ■ ■

Modeling the Static/Data Aspects of the System

Having employed use case analysis techniques in Chapter 9 to round out the Student Registration System (SRS) requirements specification, we're ready to tackle the next stage of modeling, which is determining how we're going to meet those requirements in an object-oriented fashion.

We saw in Part 1 of the book that objects form the building blocks of an OO system, and that classes are the templates used to define and instantiate objects. An OO model, then, must specify the following:

- ***What types of objects we're going to need to create and instantiate in order to represent the proper abstraction***: In particular, their attributes, methods, and structural relationships with one another. Because these elements of an OO system, once established, are fairly static—in the same way that a house, once built, has a specific layout, a given number of rooms, a particular roofline, and so forth—we often refer to this process as preparing the **static model**.

  We can certainly change the static structure of a house over time by undertaking remodeling projects, just as we can change the static structure of an OO software system as new requirements emerge by deriving new subclasses, inventing new methods for existing classes, and so forth. However, if a structure—whether a home or a software system—is properly designed from the outset, then the need for such changes should arise relatively infrequently over its lifetime and shouldn't be overly difficult to accommodate.

- ***How these objects will need to collaborate in carrying out the overall requirements, or "mission," of the system***: The ways in which objects interact can change literally from one moment to the next based upon the circumstances that are in effect. One moment, a Course object may be registering a Student object, and the next, it might be responding to a query by a Professor object as to the current student headcount. We refer to the process of detailing object collaborations as preparing the **dynamic model**. Think of this as all of the different day-to-day activities that go on in a home: same structure, different functions.

The static and dynamic models are simply two different sides of the same coin: they jointly comprise the object-oriented "blueprint" that we'll work from in implementing an object-oriented Student Registration System application in Part 3 of the book.

In this chapter, we'll focus on building the static model for the SRS, leaving a discussion of the dynamic model for Chapter 11. You'll learn

- A technique for identifying the appropriate classes and their attributes

- How to determine the structural relationships that exist among these classes

- How to graphically portray this information as a **class diagram** using UML notation

Identifying Appropriate Classes

Our first challenge in object modeling is to determine what classes of objects we're going to need as our system building blocks. Unfortunately, the process of class identification is rather "fuzzy"; it relies heavily on intuition, prior modeling experience, and familiarity with the subject area, or **domain**, of the system to be developed. So, how does an object-modeling *novice* **ever** get started? One tried and true (but somewhat tedious) procedure for identifying candidate classes is to use the "hunt and gather" method: that is, to hunt for and gather a list of all nouns/noun phrases from the project documentation set and to then use a process of elimination to whittle this list down into a set of appropriate classes.

In the case of the SRS, our documentation set thus far consists of the following:

- The requirements specification

- The use case model that we prepared in Chapter 9

Noun Phrase Analysis

Let's perform noun phrase analysis on the SRS requirements specification first, which was originally presented in the Introduction to the book, a copy of which is provided in the following sidebar. All noun phrases have been **bolded**.

HIGHLIGHTING NOUN PHRASES IN THE SRS SPECIFICATION

We have been asked to develop an *automated Student Registration System* (*SRS*) for the *university*. This *system* will enable *students* to register online for *courses* each *semester*, as well as track their *progress* toward *completion* of their *degree*.

When a *student* first enrolls at the *university*, he/she uses the *SRS* to set forth a *plan of study* as to which *courses* he/she plans on taking to satisfy a particular *degree program*, and chooses a *faculty advisor*. The *SRS* will verify whether or not the proposed *plan of study* satisfies the *requirements of the degree* that the *student* is seeking.

Once a *plan of study* has been established, then, during the *registration period* preceding each *semester*, *students* are able to view the *schedule of classes* online, and choose whichever *classes* they wish to attend, indicating the *preferred section* (*day of the week* and *time of day*) if the *class* is offered by more than one *professor*. The *SRS* will verify whether or not the *student* has satisfied the necessary *prerequisites* for each *requested course* by referring to the *student*'s online *transcript* of *courses completed* and *grades received* (the *student* may review his/her *transcript* online at any time).

Assuming that (a) the *prerequisites* for the *requested course(s)* are satisfied, (b) the *course(s)* meet(s) one of the *student*'s *plan of study requirements*, and (c) there is *room* available in each of the *class(es)*, the *student* is enrolled in the *class(es)*.

If (a) and (b) are satisfied, but (c) is not, the *student* is placed on a *first-come, first-served wait list*. If a *class/section that he/she was previously waitlisted for* becomes available (either because some other *student* has dropped the *class* or because the *seating capacity* for the *class* has been increased), the *student* is automatically enrolled in the *waitlisted class*, and an *email message* to that effect is sent to the *student*. It is the student's *responsibility* to drop the *class* if it is no longer desired; otherwise, he/she will be billed for the *course*.

Students may drop a *class* up to the *end* of the *first week of the semester in which the class is being taught*.

A simple spreadsheet serves as an ideal tool for recording our initial findings; we enter noun phrases as a single-column list in the order in which they occur in the specification. Don't worry about trying to eliminate duplicates or consolidating synonyms just yet; we'll do that in a moment. The resultant spreadsheet is shown in part in Figure 10-1.

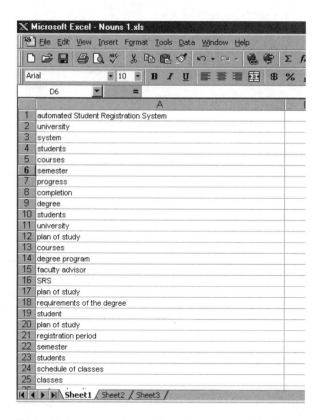

Figure 10-1. *Noun phrases found in the SRS specification*

We're working with a very concise requirements specification (approximately 350 words in length), and yet this process is already proving to be very tedious! It would be impossible to carry out an exhaustive noun phrase analysis for anything but a trivially simple specification. If you're faced with a voluminous requirements specification, start by writing an "executive summary" of no more than a few pages to paraphrase the system's mission, and then use your summary version of the specification as the starting point for your noun survey. Paraphrasing a specification in this fashion provides the added benefit of ensuring that you have read through the system requirements and understand the "big picture." Of course, you'll need to review your summary narrative with your customers/future users to ensure that you've accurately captured all key points.

After we've typed all of the nouns/noun phrases into the spreadsheet, we sort the spreadsheet and eliminate duplicates; this includes eliminating plural forms of singular terms (e.g., eliminate "students" in favor of "student"). We want all of our class names to be singular in the final analysis, so if any plural forms remain in the list after eliminating duplicates (e.g., "prerequisites"), we make these singular, as well. In so doing, our SRS list shrinks to 38 items in length, as shown in Figure 10-2.

	A
1	automated Student Registration System
2	class
3	class that he/she was previously waitlisted for
4	completion
5	course
6	courses completed
7	day of the week
8	degree
9	degree program
10	email message
11	end
12	faculty advisor
13	first week of the semester in which the class is being taught
14	first-come, first-served wait list
15	grades received
16	plan of study
17	plan of study requirements
18	preferred section
19	prerequisites
20	professor
21	progress
22	registration period
23	requested course
24	requirements of the degree
25	responsibility
26	room
27	schedule of classes
28	seating capacity
29	section
30	section that he/she was previously waitlisted for
31	semester
32	SRS
33	student
34	system
35	time of day
36	transcript
37	university
38	waitlisted class

Sheet1 / Sheet2 / Sheet3 /

Figure 10-2. *Removing duplicates streamlines the noun phrase list.*

Remember, we're trying to identify both physical and conceptual objects: as stated in Chapter 3, "*something mental or physical toward which thought, feeling, or action is directed*." Let's now make another pass to eliminate the following:

- References to the system itself ("automated Student Registration System," "SRS," "system").

- References to the university. Because we're building the SRS within the context of a single university, the university in some senses "sits outside" and "surrounds" the SRS; we don't need to manipulate information about the university within the SRS, and so we may eliminate the term "university" from our candidate class list.

    Note, however, that if we were building a system that needed to span multiple universities—say, a system that compared graduate programs of study in information technology across the top 100 universities in the country—then we would indeed need to model each university as a separate object, in which case we'd keep "university" on our candidate class list.

- Other miscellaneous terms that don't seem to fit the definition of an object are "completion," "end," "progress," "responsibility," "registration period," and "requirements of the degree." Admittedly, some of these are debatable, particularly the last two; to play it safe, you may wish to create a list of rejected terms to be revisited later on in the modeling life cycle.

The list shrinks to 27 items as a result, as shown in Figure 10-3—it's starting to become manageable now!

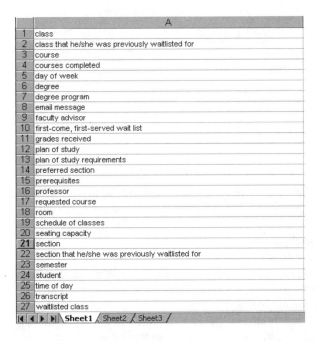

	A
1	class
2	class that he/she was previously waitlisted for
3	course
4	courses completed
5	day of week
6	degree
7	degree program
8	email message
9	faculty advisor
10	first-come, first-served wait list
11	grades received
12	plan of study
13	plan of study requirements
14	preferred section
15	prerequisites
16	professor
17	requested course
18	room
19	schedule of classes
20	seating capacity
21	section
22	section that he/she was previously waitlisted for
23	semester
24	student
25	time of day
26	transcript
27	waitlisted class

Figure 10-3. *Further streamlining the SRS noun phrase list*

The next pass is a bit trickier. We need to group apparent synonyms, to choose the one designation from among each group of synonyms that is best suited to serve as a class name. Having a subject matter expert on your modeling team is important for this step, because determining the subtle shades of meaning of some of these terms so as to group them properly isn't always easy.

We group together terms that seem to be synonyms, as shown in Figure 10-4, **bolding** the term in each synonym group that we're inclined to choose above the rest. *Italicized* words represent those terms for which no synonyms have been identified.

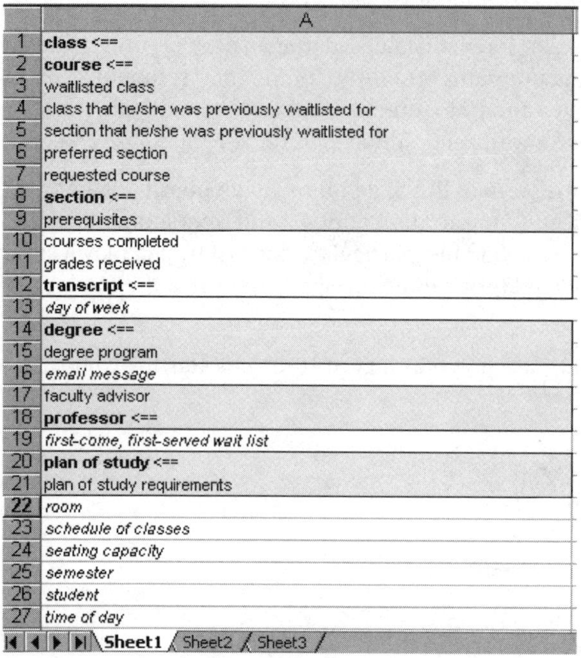

	A
1	**class <==**
2	**course <==**
3	waitlisted class
4	class that he/she was previously waitlisted for
5	section that he/she was previously waitlisted for
6	preferred section
7	requested course
8	**section <==**
9	prerequisites
10	courses completed
11	grades received
12	**transcript <==**
13	*day of week*
14	**degree <==**
15	degree program
16	*email message*
17	faculty advisor
18	**professor <==**
19	*first-come, first-served wait list*
20	**plan of study <==**
21	plan of study requirements
22	*room*
23	*schedule of classes*
24	*seating capacity*
25	*semester*
26	*student*
27	*time of day*

Sheet1 / Sheet2 / Sheet3 /

Figure 10-4. *Grouping synonyms*

Let's now review the rationale for our choices.

We choose the shorter form of equivalent expressions whenever possible—"degree" instead of "degree program" and "plan of study" instead of "plan of study requirements"—to make our model more concise.

Although they aren't synonyms as such, the notion of a "transcript" implies a record of "courses completed" and "grades received," so we'll drop the latter two noun phrases for now.

When choosing candidate class names, we should avoid choosing nouns that imply **roles** between objects. As you learned in Chapter 5, a role is something that an object belonging to class A possesses by virtue of its relationship to/association with an object belonging to class B. For example, a professor holds the role of "faculty advisor" when that professor is associated with a student via an *advises* association. Even if a professor were to lose all of his or her advisees, thus losing the role of faculty advisor, he or she would still be a professor by virtue of being employed by the university—it's inherent in the person's nature relative to the SRS.

If a professor were to lose his or her job with the university, one might argue that he or she is no longer a professor; but then, this person would have no dealings with the SRS, either, so it's a moot point.

For this reason, we prefer "Professor" to "Faculty Advisor" as a candidate class name, but make a mental note to ourselves that faculty advisor would make a good potential association when we get to considering such things later on.

Regarding the notion of a course, we see that we've collected numerous noun phrases that all refer to a course in one form or another: "class," "course," "preferred section," "requested course," "section," "prerequisite," "waitlisted class," "class that they were previously waitlisted for," "section that they were previously waitlisted for." Within this grouping, several roles are implied:

- "Waitlisted class" in its several different forms implies a role in an association between a Student and a Course.

- "Prerequisite" implies a role in an association between two Courses.

- "Requested course" implies a role in an association between a Student and a Course.

- "Preferred section" implies a role in an association between a Student and a Course.

Eliminating all of these role designations, we're left with only three terms: "class," "course," and "section." Before we hastily eliminate all but one of these as synonyms, let's think carefully about what real-world concepts we're trying to represent.

- The notion that we typically associate with the term "course" is that of a semester-long series of lectures, assignments, exams, etc., that all relate to a particular subject area, and which are a unit of education toward earning a degree. For example, Beginning Math is a course.

- The terms "class" and "section," on the other hand, generally refer to the offering of a ***particular*** course in a ***given*** semester on a given day of the week and at a given time of day. For example, the course Beginning Math is being offered this coming Spring semester as three classes/sections:

    - Section 1, which meets Tuesdays from 4:00 to 6:00 p.m.

    - Section 2, which meets Wednesdays from 6:00 to 8:00 p.m.

    - Section 3, which meets Thursdays from 3:00 to 5:00 p.m.

    There is thus a one-to-many association between Course and Class/Section. The same course is offered potentially many times in a given semester and over many semesters during the "lifetime" of the course.

Therefore, "course" and "class/section" truly represent different abstractions, and we'll keep ***both*** concepts in our candidate class list. Since "class" and "section" appear to be synonyms, however, we need to choose one term and discard the other. Our initial inclination would be to keep "class" and discard "section," but in order to avoid confusion when referring to a class named Class (!) we'll opt for "section" instead.

Refining the Candidate Class List

A list of candidate classes has begun to emerge from the fog! Here is our remaining "short list" (please disregard the trailing symbols [*, +] for the moment—I'll explain their significance shortly):

- Course

- Day of week*

- Degree*

- Email message+

- Plan of study

- Professor

- Room*

- Schedule of classes+

- Seating capacity*

- Section

- Semester*

- Student

- Time of day*

- Transcript

- (First-come, first-served) Wait list

Not all of these will necessarily survive to the final model, however, as we're going to scrutinize each one very closely before deeming it worthy of implementation as a class. One classic test for determining whether or not an item can stand on its own as a class is to ask these questions:

- Can we think of any ***attributes*** for this class?

- Can we think of any ***services*** that would be expected of objects belonging to this class?

One example is the term "room." We could invent a Room class as follows:

```
public class Room {
  // Attributes.
  int roomNo;
  String building;
  int seatingCapacity;
  // etc.
}
```

or we could simply represent a room location as a String attribute of the Section class:

```
public class Section {
  // Attributes.
  Course offeringOf;
  String semester;
  char dayOfWeek;  // 'M', 'T', 'W', 'R', 'F'
  String timeOfDay;
```

```
    String classroomLocation; // building name and room name:  e.g.,
                              // "Innovation Hall Room 333"
   // etc.
}
```

Which approach to representing a room is preferred? It all depends on whether or not a room needs to be a focal point of our application. If the SRS were meant to also do "double duty" as a Classroom Scheduling System, then we may indeed wish to instantiate `Room` objects so as to be able to ask them to perform such services as printing out their weekly usage schedules or telling us their seating capacities. However, since these services weren't mentioned as requirements in the SRS specification, we'll opt for making a room designation a simple `String` attribute of the `Section` class. We reserve the right, however, to change our minds about this later on; it's not unusual for some items to "flip flop" over the life cycle of a modeling exercise between being classes on their own versus being represented as simple attributes of other classes.

Following a similar train of thought for all of the items marked with an asterisk (*) in the preceding candidate class list, we'll opt to treat them all as attributes rather than making them classes of their own:

- "Day of week" will be incorporated as either a `String` or `char` attribute of the `Section` class.

- "Degree" will be incorporated as a `String` attribute of the `Student` class.

- "Seating capacity" will be incorporated as an `int` attribute of the `Section` class.

- "Semester" will be incorporated as a `String` attribute of the `Section` class.

- "Time of day" will be incorporated as a `String` attribute of the `Section` class.

When we're first modeling an application, we want to focus exclusively on functional requirements to the exclusion of technical requirements, as defined in Chapter 9; this means that we need to avoid getting into the technical details of how the system is going to function behind the scenes. Ideally, we want to focus solely on what are known as **domain classes**—that is, abstractions that an end user will recognize, and which represent "real-world" entities—and to avoid introducing any extra classes that are used solely as behind-the-scenes "scaffolding" to hold the application together, known alternatively as **implementation classes** or **solution space classes**. Examples of the latter would be the creation of a collection object to organize and maintain references to all of the `Professor` objects in the system, or the use of a dictionary to provide a way to quickly find a particular `Student` object based on the associated student ID number. We'll talk more about solution space objects in Part 3 of the book; for the time being, the items flagged with a plus sign (+) in the candidate class list earlier—"email message," "schedule of classes"—seem arguably more like implementation classes than domain classes.

- An email message is typically a transient piece of data, not unlike a pop-up message that appears on the screen while using an application. An email message gets sent out of the SRS system, and after it's read by the recipient, we have no control over whether the email is retained or deleted. It's unlikely that the SRS is going to archive copies of all email messages that have been sent—there certainly was no requirement to do so—so we won't worry about modeling them as objects at this stage in our analysis.

- Email messages will resurface in Chapter 11, when we talk about the behaviors of the SRS application, because sending an email message is definitely an important *behavior*; but, emails don't constitute an important *structural* piece of the application, so we don't want to introduce a class for them at this stage in the modeling process. When we actually get to programming the system, we might indeed create an EmailMessage class in Java, but it needn't be modeled as a domain class. (If, on the other hand, we were modeling an email messaging system in anticipation of building one, then EmailMessage would indeed be a key domain class in our model.)

- We could go either way with the schedule of classes—include it as a candidate class, or drop it from our list. The schedule of classes, as a single object, may not be something that the user will manipulate directly, but there will be some notion behind the scenes of a schedule of classes collection controlling which Section objects should be presented to the user as a GUI pick list when he or she registers in a given semester. We'll omit ScheduleOfClasses from our candidate class list for now, but we can certainly revisit our decision as the model evolves.

Determining whether or not a class constitutes a domain class instead of an implementation class is admittedly a gray area, and either of the preceding candidate class "rejects" could be successfully argued into or out of the list of core domain classes for the SRS. In fact, this entire exercise of identifying classes hopefully illustrates a concept that was first introduced in Chapter 1; because of its importance, it is repeated again in the following sidebar.

THE CHALLENGES OF OBJECT MODELING

Developing an appropriate model for a software system is perhaps the most difficult aspect of software engineering, because

There are an unlimited number of possibilities. Abstraction is to a certain extent in the eye of the beholder: several different observers working independently are almost guaranteed to arrive at different models. Whose is the best? Passionate arguments have ensued!

To further complicate matters, *there is virtually never only one "best" or "correct" model*, only "better" or "worse" models relative to the problem to be solved. The same situation can be modeled in a variety of different, equally valid ways.

Finally, there is no "acid test" to determine if a model has *adequately captured all of a user's requirements.*

As we continue along with our SRS modeling exercise, and particularly as we move from modeling to implementation in Part 3 of the book, we'll have many opportunities to rethink the decisions that we've made here. The key point to remember is that the model isn't "cast in stone" until we actually begin programming, and even then, if we've used objects wisely, the model can be fairly painlessly modified to handle most new requirements. Think of a model as being formed out of modeling clay: we'll continue to reshape it over the course of the analysis and design phases of our project until we're satisfied with the result.

Meanwhile, back to the task of coming up with a list of candidate classes for the SRS. The terms that have survived our latest round of scrutiny are as follows:

- Course

- PlanOfStudy

- Professor

- Section

- Student

- Transcript

- WaitList

Let's examine WaitList one last time. There is indeed a requirement for the SRS to maintain a student's position on a first-come, first-served wait list. But, it turns out that this requirement can actually be handled through a combination of an association between the Student and Section classes, plus something known as an **association class**, which you'll learn about later in this chapter. This would not be immediately obvious to a beginning modeler, and so we'd fully expect that the WaitList class might make the final cut as a suggested SRS class. But, we're going to assume that we have an experienced object modeler on the team, who convinces us to eliminate the class; we'll see that this was a suitable move when we complete the SRS class diagram at the end of the chapter.

So, we'll settle on the following list of classes, based on our noun phrase analysis of the SRS specification:

- Course

- PlanOfStudy

- Professor

- Section

- Student

- Transcript

Revisiting the Use Cases

One more thing that we need to do before we deem our candidate class list good to go is to revisit our use cases—in particular, the actors—to see if any of *these* ought to be added as classes. You may recall that we identified seven potential actors for the SRS in Chapter 9:

- Student

- Faculty

- Department Chair

- Registrar

- Billing System

- Admissions System

- Classroom Scheduling System

Do any of these deserve to be modeled as classes in the SRS? Here's how to make that determination: if any user associated with any actor type A is going to need to manipulate (access or modify) information concerning an actor type B when A is logged on to the SRS, then B needs to be included as a class in our model. This is best illustrated with a few examples.

- When a student logs on to the SRS, might he or she need to manipulate information about faculty? Yes; when a student selects an advisor, for example, he or she might need to view information about a variety of faculty members in order to choose an appropriate advisor. So, ***the Faculty actor role must be represented as a class in the SRS***; indeed, we have already designated a `Professor` class, so we're covered there. But, student users are not concerned with department chairs per se.

- Following the same logic, ***we'd need to represent the Student actor role as a class*** because when professors log on to the SRS, they will be manipulating `Student` objects when printing out a course roster or assigning grades to students, for example. Since `Student` already appears in our candidate class list, we're covered there, as well.

- When ***any*** of the actors—Faculty, Students, the Registrar, the Billing System, the Admissions System, or the Classroom Scheduling System—access the SRS, will there be a need for any of them to manipulate information about the registrar? No, at least not according to the SRS requirements that we've seen so far. Therefore, ***we needn't model the Registrar actor role as a class.***

- ***The same holds true for the Billing, Admissions, and Classroom Scheduling Systems***: they require "behind the scenes" access to information managed by the SRS, but nobody logging on to the SRS expects to be able to manipulate any of these three systems directly, so ***they needn't be represented by domain classes in the SRS***.

Again, when we get to implementing the SRS in code, we may indeed find it appropriate to create "solution space" Java classes to represent interfaces to these other automated systems; but, such classes don't belong in a ***domain*** model of the SRS.

Therefore, our proposed candidate class list remains unchanged after revisiting all actor roles:

- `Course`
- `PlanOfStudy`
- `Professor`
- `Section`
- `Student`
- `Transcript`

Is this a "perfect" list? No—there is no such thing! In fact, before all is said and done, the list may—and in fact probably will—evolve in the following ways:

- We may ***add classes*** later on: terms we eliminated from the specification, or terms that don't even appear in the specification, but which we'll unearth through continued investigation.

- We may see an opportunity to ***generalize***—that is, we may see enough commonality between two or more classes' respective attributes, methods, or relationships with other classes to warrant the creation of a common base class.

- In addition, as mentioned earlier, we may ***rethink our decisions*** regarding representing some concepts as simple attributes (semester, room, etc.) instead of as full-blown classes, and vice versa.

The development of a candidate class list is, as illustrated in this chapter thus far, fraught with uncertainty. For this reason, it's important to have someone experienced with object modeling available to your team when embarking on your first object modeling effort. Most experienced modelers don't use the rote method of noun phrase analysis to derive a candidate class list; such folks can pretty much review a specification and directly pick out significant classes, in the same way that a professional jeweler can easily choose a genuine diamond from among a pile of fake gemstones. Nevertheless, what does "significant" really mean? That's where the "fuzziness" comes in! It's impossible to define precisely what makes one concept significant and another less so. I've tried to illustrate some rules of thumb by working through the SRS example, but you ultimately need a qualified mentor to guide you until you develop—and trust—your own intuitive sense for such things.

The bottom line, however, is that even expert modelers can't really confirm the appropriateness of a given candidate class until they see its proposed use in the full context of a class diagram that also reflects associations, attributes, and methods, which we'll explore later in this chapter as well as in Chapter 11.

Producing a Data Dictionary

Early on in our analysis efforts, it's important that we clarify and begin to document our use of terminology. A **data dictionary** is ideal for this purpose. For each candidate class, the data dictionary should include a simple definition of what this item means in the context of the model/system as a whole; include an example if it helps to illustrate the definition.

The following sidebar shows our complete SRS data dictionary so far.

THE SRS DATA DICTIONARY, TAKE 1: CLASS DEFINITIONS

- **Course**: A semester-long series of lectures, assignments, exams, etc., that all relate to a particular subject area, and which are typically associated with a particular number of credit hours; a unit of study toward a degree. For example, Beginning Objects is a required **course** for the Master of Science degree in Information Systems Technology.

- **PlanOfStudy**: A list of the **courses** that a student intends to take to fulfill the **course** requirements for a particular degree.

- **Professor**: A member of the faculty who teaches **sections** or advises **students**.

- **Section**: The offering of a particular **course** during a particular semester on a particular day of the week and at a particular time of day (for example, **course** Beginning Objects as taught in the Spring 2005 semester on Mondays from 1:00 to 3:00 p.m.).

- **Student**: A person who is currently enrolled at the university and who is eligible to register for one or more **sections**.

- **Transcript**: A record of all of the **courses** taken to date by a particular **student** at this university, including which semester each **course** was taken in, the grade received, and the credits granted for the **course**, as well as a reflection of an overall total number of credits earned and the **student's** grade point average (GPA).

Note that it's permissible, and in fact encouraged, for the definition of one term to include one or more of the other terms; when we do so, we highlight the latter in **bold text.**

The data dictionary joins the set of other SRS narrative documents as a subsequent source of information about the model. As our model evolves, we'll expand the dictionary to include definitions of attributes, associations, and methods.

It's a good idea to also include the dictionary definition of a class as a header comment in the Java code representing that class. Make sure to keep this inline documentation in sync with the external dictionary definition, however.

Determining Associations Between Classes

Once we've settled on an initial candidate class list, the next step is to determine how these classes are interrelated. To do this, we go back to our narrative documentation set (which has grown to consist of the SRS requirements specification, use cases, and data dictionary) and study *verb* phrases this time. Our goal in looking at verb phrases is to choose those that suggest structural relationships, as were defined in Chapter 5—associations, aggregations, and inheritance—but to eliminate or ignore those that represent (transient) actions or behaviors. (We'll focus on behaviors, but from the standpoint of use cases, in Chapter 11.)

For example, the specification states that a student "chooses a faculty advisor." This is indeed an action, but the result of this action is a lasting structural relationship between a professor and a student, which can be modeled via the association "a Professor *advises* a Student."

As a student's advisor, a professor also meets with the student, answers the student's questions, recommends courses for the student to take, approves the student's plan of study, etc.—these are behaviors on the part of a professor acting in the role of an advisor, but don't directly result in any new links being formed between objects.

Let's try the verb phrase analysis approach on the requirements specification. All relevant verb phrases are highlighted in the sidebar that follows (note that I omitted such obviously irrelevant verb phrases as "We've been asked to develop an automated SRS . . .").

HIGHLIGHTING VERB PHRASES IN THE SRS SPECIFICATION

We have been asked to develop an automated Student Registration System (SRS) for the university. This system will **enable students to register** online **for courses** each semester, as well as **track their progress toward completion of their degree**.

When a student first **enrolls at the university**, he/she uses the SRS to **set forth a plan of study** as to which **courses he/she plans on taking** to **satisfy a particular degree program**, and **chooses a faculty advisor**. The SRS will **verify whether or not the proposed plan of study satisfies the requirements of the degree that the student is seeking**.

Once a **plan of study has been established**, then, during the registration period preceding each semester, a student is able to **view the schedule of classes** online, and **choose whichever classes he/she wishes to attend, indicating the preferred section** (day of the week and time of day) if the **class is offered by more than one professor**. The SRS will **verify whether or not the student has satisfied the necessary prerequisites** for each requested course by **referring to the student's online transcript** of courses completed and grades received (the **student may review his/her transcript** online at any time).

Assuming that (a) the **prerequisites for the requested course(s) are satisfied**, (b) the **course(s) meet(s) one of the student's plan of study requirements**, and (c) **there is room available** in each of the class(es), the **student is enrolled in the class(es)**.

If (a) and (b) are satisfied, but (c) is not, the **student is placed on a first-come, first-served wait list**. If a **class/section that he/she was previously waitlisted for becomes available** (either because some other **student has dropped the class** or because the **seating capacity for the class has been increased**), the **student is automatically enrolled in the waitlisted class,** and an **email message** to that effect **is sent** to the student. It is the student's responsibility to **drop the class** if it is no longer desired; otherwise, **he/she will be billed for the course**.

Students may **drop a class** up to the end of the first week of the semester in which the **class is being taught**.

Let's scrutinize a few of these:

- **"Students [...] register [...] for courses"**: Although the act of registering is a behavior, the end result is that a static relationship is created between a Student and a Section, as represented by the association "a Student *registers* for a Section." Note that the specification mentions registering for "courses," not "sections," but as we stated in our data dictionary, a Student registers for concrete Sections as embodiments of Courses. Keep in mind when reviewing a specification that natural language is often imprecise, and that as a result we have to read between the lines as to what the author really meant in every case. (If we're going to be the ones to write the specification, here is an incentive to keep the language as clear and concise as possible!)

- **"[Students track] their progress toward completion of their degree"**: Again, this is a behavior, but it nonetheless implies a structural relationship between a Student and a Degree. However, recall that we didn't elect to represent Degree as a class—we opted to reflect it as a simple String attribute of the Student class—and so this suggested relationship is immaterial with respect to the candidate class list that we've developed.

- ***"Student first enrolls at the university"***: This is a behavior that results in a static relationship between a Student and the University; but, we deemed the notion of "university" to be external to the system and so chose not to create a University class in our model. So, we disregard this verb phrase, as well.

- ***"[Student] sets forth a plan of study"***: This is a behavior that results in the static relationship "a Student *pursues/observes* a Plan of Study."

- ***"Students are able to view the schedule of classes online"***: This is strictly a transient behavior of the SRS; no lasting relationship results from this action, so we disregard this verb phrase.

and so on.

Association Matrices

Another complementary technique for both determining and recording what the relationships between classes should be is to create an ***n × n* association matrix,** where *n* represents the number of candidate classes that we've identified. Label the rows and the columns with the names of the classes, as shown for the empty matrix represented by Table 10-1.

Table 10-1. *An "Empty" Association Matrix for the SRS*

	Section	Course	PlanOfStudy	Professor	Student	Transcript
Section						
Course						
PlanOfStudy						
Professor						
Student						
Transcript						

Then, complete the matrix as follows.

In each cell of the matrix, list all of the associations that you can identify between the class named at the head of the row and the class named at the head of the column. For example, in the cell in Table 10-2 at the intersection of the Student "row" and the Section "column," we have listed three potential associations:

- A Student *is waitlisted for* a Section.

- A Student *is registered for* a Section. (This could be alternatively phrased as "a Student *is currently attending* a Section.")

- A Student *has previously taken* a Section. This third association is important if we plan on maintaining a history of all of the classes that a student has ever taken in his or her career as a student, which we must do if we are to prepare a student's transcript online. (As it turns out, we'll be able to get by with a single association that does "double duty" for the latter two of these, as you'll see later on in this chapter.)

Mark a cell with an × if there are no known relationships between the classes in question, or if the potential relationships between the classes are irrelevant. For example, in Table 10-2 the cells representing the intersection between Professor and Course are marked with an ×, even though there is an association possible—"a Professor *is qualified to teach* a Course"— because it isn't relevant to the mission of the SRS.

As mentioned in Chapter 4, all associations are inherently bidirectional. This implies that if a cell in row *j*, column *k* indicates one or more associations, then the cell in row *k*, column *j* should reflect the reciprocal of these relationships. For example, since the intersection of the PlanOfStudy "row" and the Course "column" indicates that "a PlanOfStudy *calls for* a Course," then the intersection of the Course "row" and the PlanOfStudy "column" must indicate that "a Course *is called for by* a PlanOfStudy."

It's not always practical to state the reciprocal of an association; for example, our association matrix shows that "a Student *plans to take* a Course," but trying to state its reciprocal—"a Course *is planned to be taken by* a Student"—is quite awkward. In such cases where a reciprocal association would be awkward to phrase, simply indicate its presence with the symbol ✔.

Table 10-2. *Our Completed Association Matrix*

	Section	Course	PlanOfStudy	Professor	Student	Transcript
Section	×	*instance of*	×	*is taught by*	✔	*included in*
Course	✔	*prerequisite for*	*is called for by*	×	✔	×
PlanOfStudy	×	*calls for*	×	×	*observed by*	×
Professor	*teaches*	×	×	×	*advises; teaches*	×
Student	*registered for; waitlisted for; has previously taken*	*plans to take*	*observes*	*is advised by; studies under*	×	*owns*
Transcript	*includes*	×	×	×	*belongs to*	×

We'll be portraying these associations in graphical form shortly! For now, let's go back and extend our data dictionary to explain what each of these associations means. The following sidebar shows one such example.

ADDITIONS TO THE SRS DATA DICTIONARY

Calls for (a Plan of Study calls for a Course): In order to demonstrate that a **student** will satisfy the requirements for his or her chosen degree program, the **student** must formulate a **plan of study**. This **plan of study** lays out all of the **courses** that a **student** intends to take, and possibly specifies in which semester the **student** hopes to complete each **course**.

Identifying Attributes

To determine what the attributes for each of our domain classes should be, we make yet another pass through the requirements specification looking for clues. We already stumbled upon a few attributes earlier, when we weeded out some nouns/noun phrases from our candidate class list:

- For the Section class, we identified "day of week," "room," "seating capacity," "semester," and "time of day" as attributes.

- For the Student class, we identified "degree" as an attribute.

We can also bring any prior knowledge that we have about the domain into play when assigning attributes to classes. Our knowledge of the way that universities operate, for example, suggests that all students will need some sort of student ID number as an attribute, even though this isn't mentioned anywhere in the SRS specification. We can't be sure whether this particular university assigns an arbitrary student ID number, or whether the policy is to use a student's Social Security number (SSN) as his or her ID; these are details that we'd have to go back to our users for clarification on.

Finally, we can also look at how similar information has been represented in existing legacy systems for clues as to what a class's attributes should be. For example, if a Student Billing System already exists at the university based on a relational database design, we might wish to study the structure of the relational database table housing student information. The columns that have been provided in that table—name, address, birthdate, etc.—are logical attribute choices.

UML Notation: Modeling the Static Aspects of an Abstraction

Now that we have a much better understanding about the static aspects of our model, we're ready to portray these in graphical fashion to complement the narrative documentation that we've developed for the SRS. We'll be using the UML to produce a **class diagram.** Here are the rules for how various aspects of the model are to be portrayed.

Classes, Attributes, and Operations

We represent classes as rectangles. When we first conceive of a class—before we know what any of its attributes or methods are going to be—we simply place the class name in the rectangle, as illustrated in Figure 10-5.

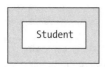

Figure 10-5. *UML depiction of the* Student *class*

An ***abstract*** class is denoted by presenting the class name in *italics*, as shown in Figure 10-6.

Figure 10-6. *UML depiction of an abstract class*

When we're ready to reflect the attributes and operations of a class, we divide the class rectangle into three **compartments**—the class name compartment, the attributes compartment, and the operations compartment—as shown in Figure 10-7. Note that UML favors the nomenclature of "operations" versus "methods" to reinforce the notion that the diagram is intended to be programming language independent.

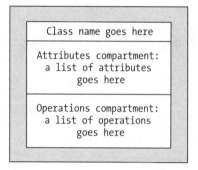

Figure 10-7. *Class rectangles are divided into three compartments.*

Some CASE tools automatically portray all three (empty) compartments when a class is first created, even if we haven't specified any attributes or operations yet, as shown in Figure 10-8.

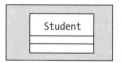

Figure 10-8. *Alternative UML class depiction as rendered by some CASE tools*

As we begin to identify what the attributes and/or operations need to be for a particular class, we can add these to the diagram in as much or as little detail as we care to.

We may choose simply to list attribute names (see Figure 10-9), or we may specify their names along with their types (see Figure 10-10).

Student
name
ssn
birthdate
gpa

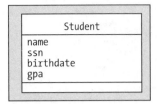

Figure 10-9. *Sometimes just attribute names are presented.*

Student
name: string
ssn: string
birthdate: Date
gpa: double

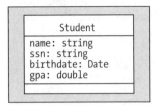

Figure 10-10. *Sometimes both attribute names and types are shown.*

We may even wish to specify an initial starting value for an attribute, as in `gpa : double = 0.0`, although this is less common.

Static attributes are identified as such by underlining their names (see Figure 10-11).

Student
totalStudents
name
ssn
birthdate

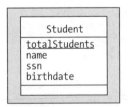

Figure 10-11. *Identifying static attributes by underlining*

We may choose simply to list operation names in the operations compartment of a class rectangle, as shown in Figure 10-12, or we may optionally choose to use an expanded form of operation definition, as we have for the `registerForCourse` operation in Figure 10-13.

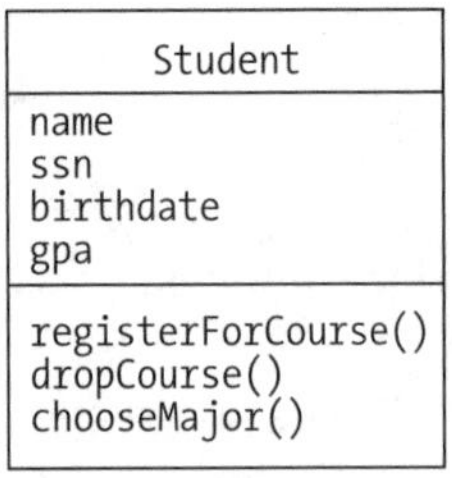

Student
name
ssn
birthdate
gpa
registerForCourse()
dropCourse()
chooseMajor()

Figure 10-12. *Sometimes just method names are presented.*

```
           Student
------------------------------------
name
ssn
birthdate
gpa
------------------------------------
registerForCourse(Course x) : boolean
dropCourse()
chooseMajor()
```

Figure 10-13. *Sometimes argument signatures and return types are also reflected.*

Note that the formal syntax for operation specifications in a UML class diagram:

[*visibility*] *name* [*(parameter list)*] [*: return type*]

for example,

registerForCourse(Course x) : boolean

differs from the syntax that we're used to seeing for Java method headers:

returnType methodName(parameter list)

for example,

boolean registerForCourse(Course x)

Note in particular that the UML refers to the combination of operation name, parameters, and return type as the **operation signature**, but that in Java the return type is part of the method header but *not* part of the *method signature*.

The rationale for making these operation signatures generic versus language specific is so that the same model may be rendered in any of a variety of target programming languages. It can be argued, however, that there is nothing inherently better or clearer about the first form versus the second. Therefore, if you know that you're going to be programming in Java, it might make sense to reflect standard Java method headers in your class diagram, if your object modeling tool will accommodate this.

It's often impractical to show all of the attributes and operations of every class in a class diagram, because the diagram will get so cluttered that it will lose its "punch" as a communications tool. Consider the data dictionary to be the official, complete source of information concerning the model, and reflect in the diagram only those attributes and operations that are particularly important in describing the mission of each class. In particular, "get" and "set" operations are implied for all attributes, and shouldn't be explicitly shown.

Also, just because the attribute or operation compartment of a class is empty, don't assume that there are no features of that type associated with a class; it may simply mean that the model is still evolving.

Relationships Between Classes

Chapter 4 defined several different types of structural relationship that may exist between classes: associations, aggregations (a specific type of association), and inheritance. Let's explore how each of these relationship types is represented graphically.

Associations

Binary associations—in other words, relationships between two different classes—are indicated by drawing a line between the rectangles representing the participating classes, and labeling the line with the name of the association. Role names can be reflected at either end of the association line if they add value to the model, but should otherwise be omitted.

We also mark each end of the line with the appropriate **multiplicity designator**, to reflect whether the relationship is one-to-one, one-to-many, or many-to-many (see Figure 10-14); we'll look at how to do this a bit later in the chapter.

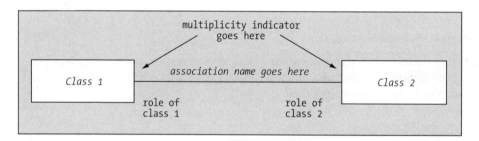

Figure 10-14. *Representing associations between classes*

All associations are assumed to be bidirectional at this stage in the modeling effort, and it doesn't matter in which order the participating classes are arranged in a class diagram. So, to depict the association "a Professor *advises* a Student," the graphical notations in Figure 10-15 are all considered equivalent.

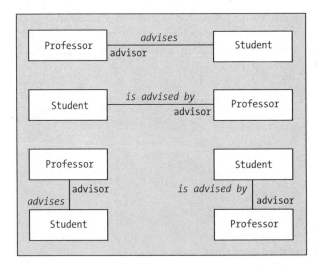

Figure 10-15. *Equivalent depictions of the advises association between the* `Professor` *and* `Student` *classes*

Achieving an optimal placement of classes for purposes of simplifying all of the association names in a diagram is often not possible in an elaborate diagram. Therefore, UML has introduced the simple convention of using a small arrowhead (▶) to reflect the direction in which the association name is to be interpreted, giving us a lot more freedom in how we place our class rectangles in a diagram, as shown in Figure 10-16.

Figure 10-16. *Using an arrowhead to indicate the direction of an association label*

With UML, no matter how the preceding two rectangles are situated, we can still always label the association "*advises*".

It's easy to get caught up in the trap of trying to make diagrams "perfect" in terms of how classes are positioned, to minimize crossed lines, etc. Try to resist the urge to do so early on, because the diagram will inevitably get changed many times before the modeling effort is finished.

Unary (reflexive) associations—that is, relationships between two different objects belonging to the same class—are drawn with an association line that loops back to the same class rectangle from which it originates. For example, to depict the association "a `Course` *is a prerequisite for* a (different) `Course`," we'd use the notation shown in Figure 10-17.

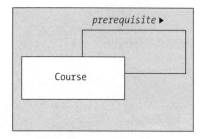

Figure 10-17. *A reflexive association involving the* `Course` *class*

Aggregation

Aggregation, which as you learned in Chapter 5 is a specialized form of association that happens to imply containment, is differentiated from a "normal" association by placing a diamond at the end of the association line that touches the "containing" class. For example, to portray the fact that a university is comprised of schools—School of Engineering, School of Law, School of Medicine, etc.—we'd use the notation shown in Figure 10-18.

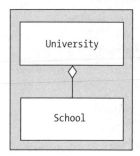

Figure 10-18. *Indicating aggregation with a diamond*

An aggregation relationship can actually be oriented in any direction, as long as the diamond is properly anchored on the "containing" class as shown in Figure 10-19.

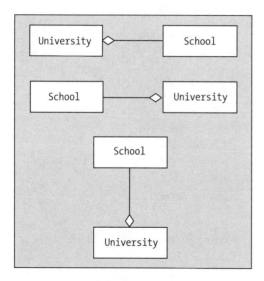

Figure 10-19. *Aggregations can be oriented in any direction.*

As mentioned in Chapter 5, however, we can get by without ever using aggregation! To represent the preceding concept, we could have just created a simple association between the University and School classes, and labeled it "*is composed of*" as shown in Figure 10-20.

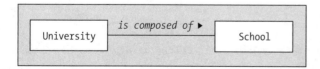

Figure 10-20. *A simple association as an alternative to an aggregation*

The decision of whether to use aggregation versus plain association is subtle, because it turns out that both can be rendered in code in essentially the same way, as you'll see in Part 3 of the book.

Unlike association lines, which should always be labeled with the name of the association that they represent, aggregation lines are typically not labeled, since an aggregation by definition implies containment.

When two or more different classes represent "parts" of some other "whole," each "part" is involved in a separate aggregation with the "whole," as shown in Figure 10-21.

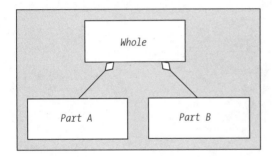

Figure 10-21. *Two aggregations, drawn using two diamonds*

However, we often join such aggregation lines into a single structure that looks something like an organization chart, as shown in Figure 10-22.

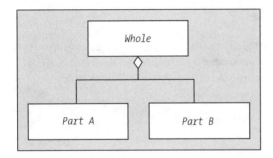

Figure 10-22. *Two aggregations involving the same "whole" class, drawn using a single diamond*

Doing so is not meant to imply anything about the relationship of Part A to Part B; it's simply a way to clean up the diagram.

Composition, which as you learned in Chapter 5 is a strong form of aggregation in which the "parts" cannot exist without the "whole," uses a ***filled-in***/black diamond rather than an open/white diamond, as illustrated in Figure 10-23.

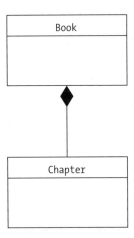

Figure 10-23. *A filled diamond signals composition, a strong form of aggregation.*

Inheritance

Inheritance (generalization/specialization) is illustrated by connecting a derived class to its base class with a line, and then marking the line with a triangle that touches the base class (see Figure 10-24).

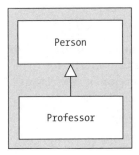

Figure 10-24. *Inheritance is designated with a triangle.*

As with aggregation, the classes involved in an inheritance relationship can be portrayed in any orientation, as long as the triangle points to/touches the base class.

Inheritance lines should ***not*** be labeled, as they unambiguously represent the "is a" relationship.

As with aggregation, when two or more different classes represent derived classes of the same parent class, each derived class is involved in a separate inheritance relationship with the parent, as shown in Figure 10-25, but we often join the inheritance lines into a single structure, as illustrated in Figure 10-26.

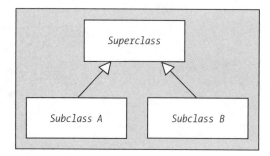

Figure 10-25. *Depicting two derived classes with two different triangles*

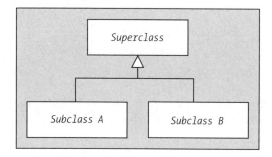

Figure 10-26. *Depicting two derived classes with a single triangle*

Doing so isn't meant to imply anything different about the relationship of derived class A to derived class B as compared with the previous depiction—these classes are considered to be sibling classes with a common parent class in both cases. It's simply a way to clean up the diagram.

Reflecting Multiplicity

You learned in Chapter 5 that for a given association type X between classes A and B, the term "multiplicity" refers to the number of instances of objects of type A that must/may be associated with a given instance of type B, and vice versa. When preparing a class diagram, we mark each end of an association line to indicate what its multiplicity should be from the perspective of an object belonging to the class at the other end of the line. In other words,

- We mark the number of instances of B that can relate to a single instance of A at B's end of the line.

- We mark the number of instances of A that can relate to a single instance of B at A's end of the line.

This is depicted in Figure 10-27.

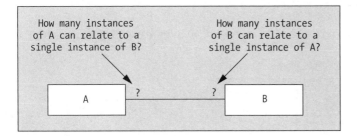

Figure 10-27. *Indicating multiplicity between classes*

By way of review, given a single object belonging to class A, there are four different scenarios for how object(s) of type B may be related to it:

- The A type object may be related to ***exactly one*** instance of a B type object, as in the situation "a Student (A) *has* a Transcript (B)." Here, the existence of an instance of B for every instance of A is ***mandatory***.

- The A type object may be related to ***at most one*** instance of a B type object, as in the situation "a Professor (A) *chairs* a Department (B)." Here, the existence of an instance of B for every instance of A is ***optional***.

- The A type object may be related to ***one or more*** instances of a B type object, as in the situation "a Department (A) *employs **many*** Professors (B)." Here, the existence of at least one instance of B for every instance of A is ***mandatory***.

- The A type object may be related to ***zero or more*** instances of a B type object, as in the situation "a Student (A) *is attending **many*** Sections (B)." (At our hypothetical university, a student is permitted to take a semester off.) Here, the existence of at least one instance of B for every instance of A is ***optional***.

In UML notation, multiplicity symbols are as follows:

- "Exactly one" is represented by the notation "1".

- "At most one" is represented by the notation "0..1", which is alternatively read as "zero or one."

- "One or more" is represented by the notation "1..*".

- "Zero or more" is represented by the notation "0..*".

- We use the notation "*" when we know that the multiplicity should be "many" but we aren't certain (or we don't care to specify) whether it should be "zero or more" or "one or more."

- It's even possible to represent an arbitrary range of explicit numerical values *x..y*, such as using "3..7" to indicate, for example, that "a Department employs no fewer than three, and no more than seven, Professors."

Here are some UML examples:

"A Student *has* exactly one Transcript, and a Transcript *belongs to* exactly one Student." (See Figure 10-28.)

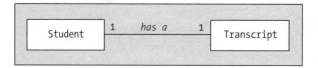

Figure 10-28. *An example of mandatory one-to-one multiplicity*

"A Professor *works for* exactly one Department, but a Department *has* many (one or more) Professors as employees." (See Figure 10-29.)

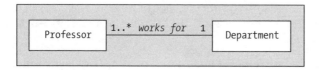

Figure 10-29. *An example of mandatory one-to-many multiplicity*

"A Professor optionally *chairs* at most one Department, while a Department *has* exactly one Professor in the role of chairman." (See Figure 10-30.)

Figure 10-30. *An example of optional one-to-many multiplicity*

"A Student *attends* many (zero or more) Sections, and a Section *is attended by* many (zero or more) Students." (See Figure 10-31.)

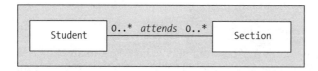

Figure 10-31. *An example of optional many-to-many multiplicity*

A Section that continues to have zero Students signed up to attend will most likely be canceled; nonetheless, there is a period of time after a Section is first made available for enrollment via the SRS that it will have zero Students enrolled.

"A Course *is a prerequisite for* many (zero or more) Courses, and a Course *can have* many (zero or more) *prerequisite* Courses." (See Figure 10-32.)

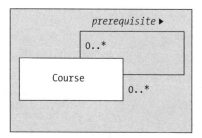

Figure 10-32. *An example of optional many-to-many multiplicity on a reflexive association*

We reflect multiplicity on aggregations as well as on simple associations. For example, the UML notation shown in Figure 10-33 would be interpreted as follows: "A (Student's) Plan of Study *is composed of* many Courses; any given Course *can be included in* many different (Students') Plans of Study."

Figure 10-33. *Reflecting multiplicity on an aggregation*

It makes no sense to reflect multiplicity on inheritance relationships, however, because as discussed in Chapter 4, inheritance implies a relationship between *classes*, but *not* between *objects*. That is, the notation shown in Figure 10-34 implies that any object belonging to *Subclass B* is also *simultaneously* an instance of *Superclass A* by virtue of the "is a" relationship.

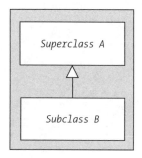

Figure 10-34. *Multiplicity adornments are inappropriate for inheritance relationships.*

If we wanted to illustrate some sort of relationship between different objects of types A and B, for example, "a Manager *supervises* Employees," we'd need to introduce a separate association between these classes independent of their inheritance relationship, as shown in Figure 10-35.

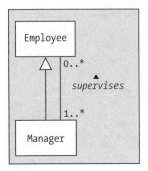

Figure 10-35. *Indicating both inheritance and an association between the* Employee *and* Manager *classes*

Object Diagrams

When describing how objects can interact, we sometimes find it helpful to sketch out a scenario of specific objects and their linkages, and for that we create an **object diagram**. An instance, or object, looks much the same as a class in UML notation, the main differences being that

- We typically provide both the name of the object and its type, separated by a colon. We underline the text to emphasize that this is an object, not a class (see Figure 10-36).

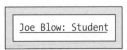

Figure 10-36. *Representing an object*

- The object's type may be omitted if it's obvious from the object's name; for example, the name "Student x" implies that the object in question belongs to the Student class (see Figure 10-37).

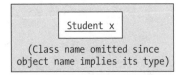

Figure 10-37. *We omit the class name if it's otherwise obvious.*

- Alternatively, the object's name may be omitted if we want to refer to a "generic" object of a given type; such an object is known as an **anonymous object**. Note that we must precede the class name with a colon (:) in such a situation (see Figure 10-38).

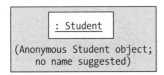

Figure 10-38. *Representing an anonymous object*

Therefore, if we wanted to indicate that Dr. Brown, a Professor, is the advisor for three Students, we could create the object diagram shown in Figure 10-39.

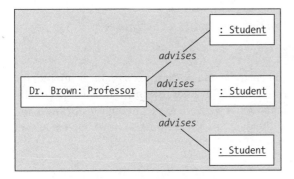

Figure 10-39. *Dr. Brown advises three students.*

To reflect that a Student by the name of Joe Blow is attending two Sections this semester, one of which is also attended by a Student named Mary Green, we could create the diagram in Figure 10-40.

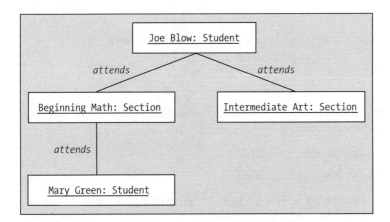

Figure 10-40. *An instance diagram involving numerous objects*

Object diagrams do ***not*** reflect multiplicity, because lines represent ***links***, and links are always ***pairwise*** between two objects/instances.

Associations As Attributes

Given Figure 10-41, which shows the association "a Course *is offered as* a Section," we see that a Course object can be related to many different Section objects, but that any one Section object can be related to a ***single*** Course object.

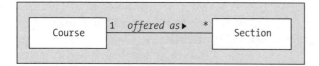

Figure 10-41. *A one-to-many association between the Course and Section classes*

By way of review, what does it mean for two objects to be related? It means that they maintain "handles" on one another so that they can easily find one another to communicate and collaborate, a concept that we covered in detail in Chapter 4. If we were to sketch out the attributes of the Course and Section classes based solely on the diagram in Figure 10-41, we'd need to allow for these handles as reference variables, as follows:

```
public class Section {
  // Attributes.
  private Course represents;   // A handle on a single related Course
                               // object.

  // etc.
}

public class Course {
  // Attributes.
  private Collection offeredAs;   // A collection of related Section
                                  // object handles.
  // etc.
}
```

So we see that the presence of an association between two classes A and B in a class diagram implies that class A ***potentially*** has an attribute declared to be either

- A reference to a ***single*** instance/object of type B

- A ***collection*** of references to ***many*** objects of type B

depending on the multiplicity involved, and vice versa. I say "potentially" because, when we get to the point of actually programming this application, we may or may not wish to code this relationship bidirectionally, even though at the analysis stage all associations are presumed to be bidirectional. We'll look at the pros and cons of coding bidirectional relationships in Chapter 14.

Because the presence of an association line implies attributes as object references in both related classes, it's inappropriate to additionally list such attributes in the attribute compartment of the respective classes (see Figure 10-42).

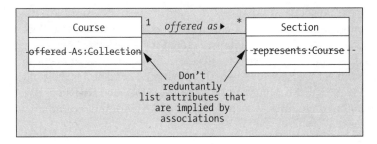

Figure 10-42. *Redundantly reflecting references as attributes is inappropriate; the presence of an association implies these.*

This is a mistake commonly made by beginners. The biggest resultant problem with doing so arises when using the code generation capability of a CASE tool: if the attribute is listed explicitly in a class's attributes compartment, and is also implied by an association, it may appear in the generated code ***twice***, as shown in the following snippet representing code that might be generated from the erroneous UML diagram shown in Figure 10-42:

```
public class Course {
  // Redundant attributes are generated in the code.
 Collection offeredAs;   // by virtue of an explicit attribute
 Collection offered_as;  // by virtue of the association
  // etc.
}
```

Information "Flows" Along an Association "Pipeline"

Beginning modelers also tend to make the mistake of introducing undesired redundancy when it comes to attributes in general. In the association portrayed in Figure 10-43, we see that the name attribute of the Professor class is inappropriately mirrored by the chairmanName attribute of the Department class.

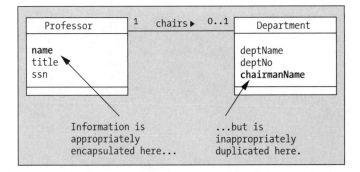

Figure 10-43. *The name and chairmanName attributes are redundant.*

While it's true that a Professor object needs to know the name of the Professor object that chairs that Department, it's inappropriate to explicitly create a chairmanName attribute to reflect this information. Because the Department object maintains a reference to its associated Professor object as an attribute, the Department has ready access to this information any time it needs it, simply by invoking the Professor object's getName method. This piece of information is rightfully encapsulated in the Professor class, where it belongs, and shouldn't be duplicated anywhere else. A corrected version of the preceding diagram is shown in Figure 10-44, with the redundancy eliminated.

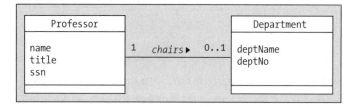

Figure 10-44. *The redundancy of Figure 10-43 has been eliminated.*

In essence, whenever you see an association/aggregation line in a diagram, you can think of this as a conceptual "pipeline" across which information can "flow" between related objects as needed.

UNIDIRECTIONAL VS. BIDIRECTIONAL ASSOCIATION

At the analysis stage, we don't typically worry about the accessibility (public, private) of attributes, or about the directionality of associations—we usually assume that the values of all of the attributes reflected in a diagram are obtainable by calling the appropriate "get" methods on an object.

That being said, UML notation supports the notion of a *uni*directional association by placing an arrowhead at the end of an association line as follows:

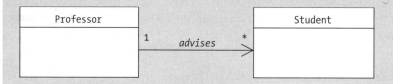

The implication of doing so is that a Professor object would be "aware of" (maintain a reference to) its Student advisee, but that a Student object would be "unaware of" (would *not* maintain a reference to) its Professor advisor.

Decisions of whether or not to bidirectionally link classes boils down to whether or not two linked objects X and Y will **both** need to **initiate** conversations with one another. That is, does X need to be able to **initiate** contact with Y and does Y need to be able to **initiate** contact with X? If only **one** of the objects needs to be able to **initiate** contact with (by sending a message to/invoking a method on) the other (e.g., if Professors need to initiate contact with Student advisees but not vice versa), then a unidirectional association is appropriate.

Some modelers represent all associations as being bidirectional, deferring a decision of whether to **code** the association bidirectionally until they are actually implementing the application in an OOPL.

Sometimes, the association pipeline extends across **multiple** objects, as illustrated by the next example.

In Figure 10-45, we have a diagram involving three classes.

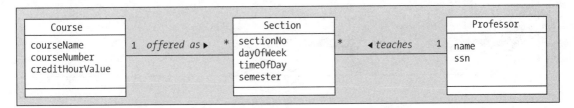

Figure 10-45. *An association "pipeline" between the* Course, Section, *and* Professor *classes.*

Let's say that someone wishes to obtain a list of all of the Professors who have ever taught the Course entitled "Beginning Objects." Because each Course object maintains a handle on all of its Section objects, past and present, the Course object representing Beginning Objects can ask each of its Section objects the name of the Professor who previously taught, or is currently teaching, that Section. The Section objects, in turn, each maintain a handle on the Professor object who taught/teaches the Section, and can use the Professor object's getName method to retrieve the name. So, information flows along the association "pipeline" from the Professor objects to their associated Section objects and from there back to the Course object that we started with (see Figure 10-46).

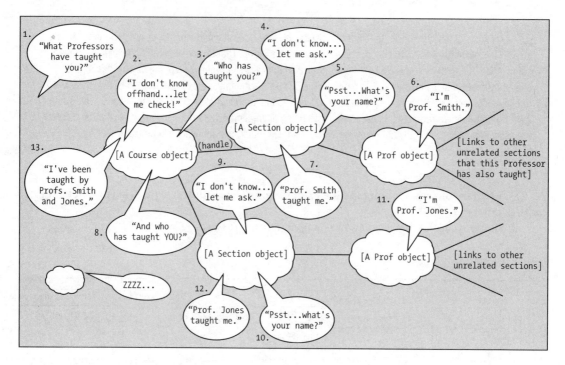

Figure 10-46. *Association "pipelines" can be quite elaborate!*

You'll learn a formal, UML-appropriate way to analyze and depict such "object conversations" in Chapter 11.

These three classes' attributes are modeled in the code that follows, highlighting all of the association-driven attributes:

```
public class Course {
  // Attributes.

  private Collection offeredAs;    // a collection of Section object
                                   // handles
  private String courseName;
  private int courseNumber;
  private double creditHourValue;
  // etc.
}

public class Section {
  // Attributes.
  private Course represents;       // a handle on the related Course
                                   // object
  private int sectionNo;
  private String dayOfWeek;
```

```
    private String timeOfDay;
    private String semester;
    private Professor taughtBy;   // a handle on the related Prof. object

    // etc.
}

public class Professor {

    private Collection sectionsTaught; // a collection of Section obj.
                                       // handles
    private String name;
    private String ssn;

    // etc.
}
```

If we knew that the Course class was going to regularly need to know who all the Professors were that had ever taught the Course, we might decide to introduce the redundant association "a Professor *has taught* a Course" into our diagram, as illustrated in Figure 10-47.

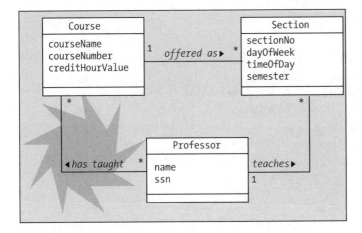

Figure 10-47. *We add redundant associations when objects frequently need a more direct "pipeline" for communication.*

This has the advantage of improving the speed with which a Course object can determine who has ever taught it: with the addition of the redundant association in Figure 10-47, Course objects can now talk ***directly*** to Professor objects without using Section objects as "go-betweens"— but the cost of this performance improvement is that we've just introduced additional complexity to our application, reflected by the highlighted additions to the following code:

```
public class Course {
    // Attributes.
```

```
    private Collection offeredAs;        // a collection of Section object
                                         // handles

    private String courseName;
    private int courseNumber;
    private float creditHourValue;

    private Collection professors;       // a collection of Professor obj.
                                         // handles

    // etc.
}

public class Section {
    // Attributes.
    private Course represents;     // a handle on the related Course
                                   // object
    private int sectionNo;
    private String dayOfWeek;
    private String timeOfDay;
    private String semester;
    private Professor taughtBy;    // a handle on the related Prof. object

    // etc.
}

public class Professor {
    // Pseudocode.
    private Collection coursesTaught;      // a collection of Course obj.
                                           // handles
    private Collection sectionsTaught;     // a collection of Section obj.
                                           // handles
    private String name;
    private String ssn;

    // etc.
}
```

By adding the redundant association, we now have extra work to do in terms of maintaining referential integrity. That is, if a different Professor is assigned to teach a particular Section, we have **two** links to update rather than one: the link between the Professor and the Section, and the link between the Professor and the related Course.

The bottom line is that deciding which associations to include, and which to eliminate as derivable from others, is similar to the decision of which web pages you might wish to create a bookmark for in your web browser: you bookmark those that you visit frequently, and type out the URL longhand, or alternatively traverse a **chain** of links, for those that you only occasionally need to access. The same is true for object linkages: the decisions of which to implement in code depends on which "communication pathways" through the application you're going to want to use most frequently. You'll get a much better sense of what these communication patterns are when we move on to modeling object **behaviors** in Chapter 11.

"Mixing and Matching" Relationship Notations

It's possible to intertwine the various relationship types in some rather sophisticated ways. To appreciate this fact, let's study the model in Figure 10-48 to see what it's telling us.

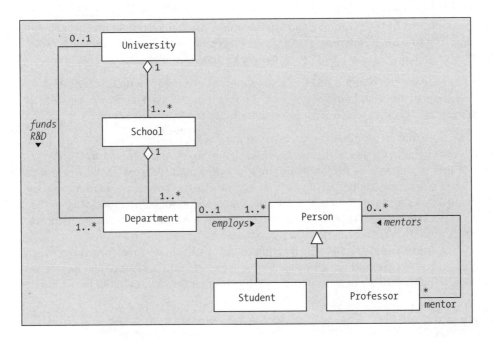

Figure 10-48. *A sample UML model*

First of all, we see some familiar uses of aggregation and inheritance.

- The use of aggregation in the upper-left corner of the diagram—a two-tier aggregation—communicates the facts that a University is comprised of one or more Schools, and that a School is comprised of one or more Departments, but that any one Department is associated with only a single School and any one School is associated with only a single University.

- The use of inheritance in the lower-right corner of the diagram indicates that Person is the common base class for both Student and Professor. Stated another way, a Student *is a* Person, and a Professor *is a* Person.

The first "interesting" use of the notation that we observe is that an association can be used to relate classes at differing levels in an aggregation, as in the use of the *funds R&D (Research & Development)* association used to relate the University and Department classes. The multiplicity on this association indicates that the University funds one or more Departments for research and development purposes, but that a **given** Department may or may not be funded for R&D.

Next, we note the use of the *employs* association to relate the Department and Person classes, indicating that a Department *employs* one or more Persons, but that a given Person *may work for* only one Department, if indeed that Person works for **any** Department at all.

Because Person is the superclass of both the Student and Professor subclasses, then by virtue of the "is a" relationship, anything we can say about a Person must also be true of its derived classes. Therefore,

- ***Associations/aggregations that a base class participates in are inherited by its derived classes.*** (This makes sense, because we now know that associations are rendered as reference variable attributes.) Thus, a given Student may optionally *work for* one Department, perhaps as a teaching assistant, and a given Professor may optionally *work for* one Department, because Student and Professor are derived from Person.

- Also, because we can deduce (via the aggregation relationship) which School and University a given Department belongs to, the fact that a Person *works for* a given Department also implies which School and University the Person *works for*.

Finally, we note that an association can be used to relate classes at differing levels in an inheritance hierarchy, as in the use of the *mentors* association to relate the Person and Professor classes. Here, we're stating that a Professor optionally *mentors* many Persons—Students and/or Professors—and conversely that a Person—either a Student or a Professor—is mentored by optionally many Professors specifically. We label the end of the association line closest to the Professor class with the role designation "mentor" to emphasize that Professors are mentors at the University, but that Persons in general (i.e., Students) are not.

What if we instead wanted to reflect the fact that ***both*** Students and Professors may serve in the capacity of a mentor? We could substitute a reflexive association on the Person class, as shown in Figure 10-49, which, by virtue of inheritance, actually implies four relationship possibilities:

- A Professor mentoring a Student

- A Professor mentoring another Professor

- A Student mentoring another Student

- A Student mentoring a Professor (which is not very likely!)

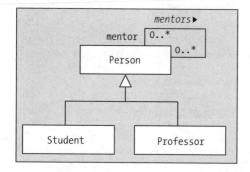

Figure 10-49. *Various possible "mentorship" associations are implied.*

If we wanted to reflect that only the first three of these are possible, we'd have to resort to the rather more complex version shown in Figure 10-50, where the three relationships of interest are all reflected as separate association lines (two reflexive, one binary).

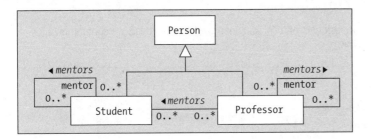

Figure 10-50. *Specific mentor associations made explicit.*

As cumbersome as it is to change the diagram to reflect these refinements in our understanding, it would be orders of magnitude more painful to change the software once the application has been coded.

Association Classes

We sometimes find ourselves in a situation where we identify an attribute that is critical to our model, but which doesn't seem to fit nicely into any one class. As an example, let's revisit the (many-to-many) association "a Student *attends* a Section," as shown in Figure 10-51. (Note that we're using the "generic" ***many*** multiplicity symbol this time, a single asterisk (*), at each end of the association line.)

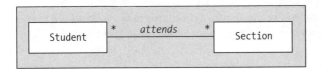

Figure 10-51. *A many-to-many association between* Student *and* Section

At the end of every semester, a student receives a letter grade for every section that he or she attended during that semester. We decide that the grade should be represented as a String attribute (e.g., "A-", "C+"). However, where does the "grade" attribute belong?

- It's not an attribute of the Student class, because a student doesn't get a single overall grade for all of his or her coursework, but rather an individual grade for each course attended.

- It's not an attribute of the Section class, either, because not all students attending a section typically receive the same letter grade.

If we think about this situation for a moment, we realize that the grade is actually an attribute of the ***pairing*** of a given Student object with a given Section; that is, it's an attribute of the ***link*** that exists between these two objects.

With UML, we create a separate class, known as an **association class**, to house attribute(s) belonging to the link between objects, and attach it with a ***dashed*** line to the association line, as shown in Figure 10-52.

Because association classes represent attributes of a link between two objects, these are sometimes informally referred to as **link attributes**.

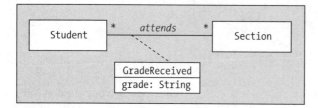

Figure 10-52. *Placing an association class on a many-to-many association*

Any time you see an association class in a class diagram, realize that there is an alternative equivalent way to represent the same situation ***without*** using an association class.

- In the case of a ***many-to-many association*** involving an association class, we can split the many-to-many association into two one-to-many associations, inserting what was formerly the association class as a "standard" class between the other two classes. Doing this for the preceding *attends* association, we wind up with the alternative equivalent representation in Figure 10-53.

  One important point to note is that the "many" ends of these two new associations reside with the newly inserted class, because a Student *receives* many Grades and a Section *issues* many Grades.

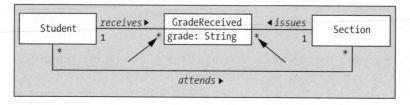

Figure 10-53. *An alternative representation for Figure 10-52*

- If we happen to have an association class for a ***one-to-many association***, as in the *works for* association between Professor and Department in Figure 10-54, then the association class's attribute(s) can, in theory, be "folded into" the class at the "many" end of the association instead, and we can do away with the association class completely as shown in Figure 10-55.

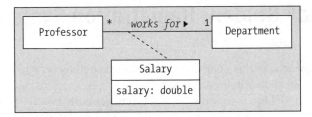

Figure 10-54. *Placing an association class on a one-to-many association*

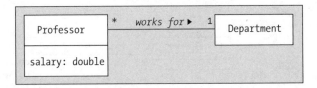

Figure 10-55. *An alternative representation for Figure 10-54*

- With a ***one-to-one association***, we can fold the association class's attributes into ***either*** of the two classes.

That being said, this practice of folding association class attributes into one end of a one-to-many or one-to-one association is discouraged, however, because it reduces the amount of information communicated by the model. In the preceding example, the only reason that a Professor has a salary attribute is because he or she *works for* a Department; knowledge of this "cause and effect" connection between employment and salary is lost if the association class is eliminated as such from the model.

Note that association classes may themselves participate in relationships with other classes. The diagram in Figure 10-56, for example, shows the association class Role participating in a one-to-many association with the class USPresident; an example illustrating this model would be "Film Star Anthony Hopkins starred in the movie *Nixon* in the role of Richard M. Nixon, thus portraying the ***real*** former U.S. President Richard M. Nixon."

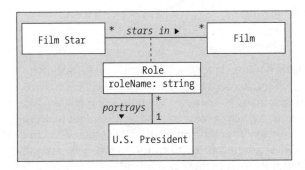

Figure 10-56. *Association classes themselves can participate in associations with other classes.*

Our "Completed" Student Registration System Class Diagram

By applying all that we've covered in this chapter about static modeling, we can produce the UML class diagram for the SRS shown in Figure 10-57. Of course, as I've said repeatedly, this isn't the only correct way to model the requirements, nor is it necessarily the "best" model that we could have produced; but it is an accurate, concise, and correct model of the static aspects of the problem to be automated.

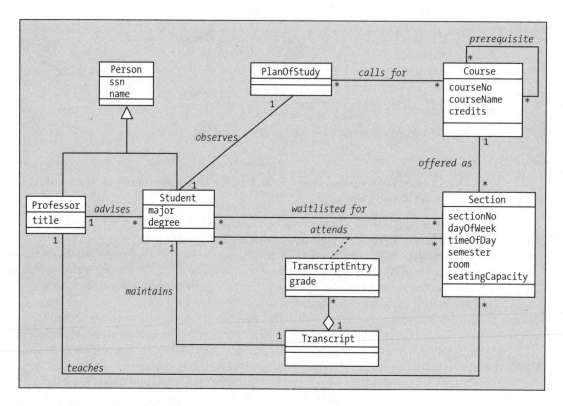

Figure 10-57. *Our "completed" SRS class diagram*

There are a few things worth noting.

We opted to use the "generic" **many** notation (* for the UML) rather than specifying 0..* or 1..*; this is often adequate during the initial modeling stages of a project.

Note that we've reflected two separate many-to-many associations between the Student and Section classes: *waitlisted for* and *attends*. A given Student may be waitlisted for many different Sections, and he or she may be registered for/attending many **other** Sections. What this model doesn't reflect is the fact that a Student is not permitted to simultaneously be attending and waitlisted for the **same** Section. Constraints such as these can be reflected as textual notes on the diagram, enclosed in curly braces, or omitted from the diagram but spelled out in the data dictionary. In the diagram excerpt in Figure 10-58, we use the annotation { xor } to represent an "exclusive or" situation between the two associations: a Student can either be *waitlisted* for or *attending* a given Section, but not both.

As mentioned earlier in this chapter, we're able to get by with a single *attends* association to handle both the Sections that a Student is currently attending, as well as those that he or she has attended in the past. The date of attendance—past or present—is reflected by the "semester" attribute of the Section class; also, for any courses that are currently in progress, the value of the "grade" attribute of the TranscriptEntry association class would be as of yet undetermined.

We could have also reflected an association class on the *waitlisted for* association representing a given Student's position in the wait list for a particular Section, and then we could have gone on to model the notion of a WaitList as an aggregation of WaitListEntry objects (see Figure 10-58).

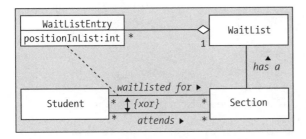

Figure 10-58. *A* WaitList *can be modeled as an aggregation of* WaitListEntry *objects.*

Since we're going to want to use the object model to gain user confirmation that we understand his or her primary requirements, we needn't clutter the diagram with such behind-the-scenes implementation details, however.

We've renamed the association class for the *attends* relationship; it was introduced earlier in this chapter as GradeReceived, but is now called TranscriptEntry. We've also introduced an aggregation relationship between the TranscriptEntry class and another new class called Transcript (see Figure 10-59).

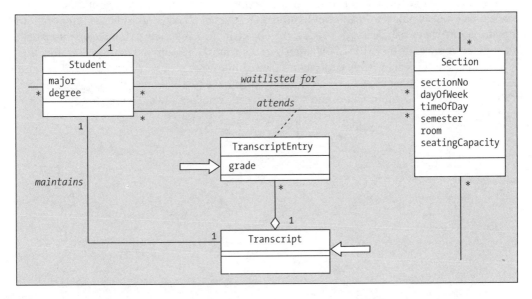

Figure 10-59. *A* Transcript *is an aggregation of* TranscriptEntry *objects.*

Let's explore how all of this evolved.

When the *attends* association was first introduced earlier in this chapter, we portrayed it as shown in Figure 10-60.

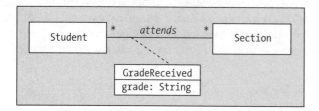

Figure 10-60. *Initial portrayal of the attends association*

We then realized that it could equivalently be represented as a ***pair*** of one-to-many associations *issues* and *receives* (see Figure 10-61).

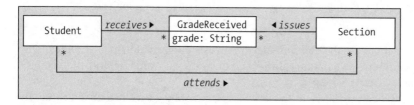

Figure 10-61. *The attends association may be portrayed alternatively as issues and receives.*

In this alternative form, it's clear that any individual GradeReceived object maintains one handle on a Student object and another handle on a Section object, and can ask either of them for information whenever necessary. The Section object, in turn, maintains a handle on the Course object that it represents by virtue of the *offered as* association. It's a trivial matter, therefore, for the GradeReceived object to request the values of attributes semester, courseNo, courseName, and credits from the Section object (which would in turn have to ask its associated Course object for the last three of these four values); this is illustrated conceptually in Figure 10-62.

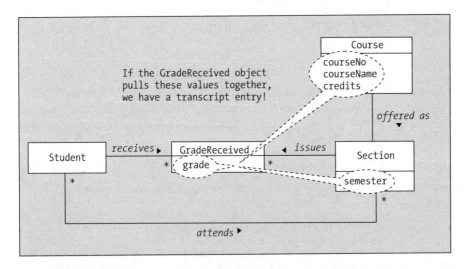

Figure 10-62. *GradeReceived has access to all of the makings of a* TranscriptEntry*.*

If the GradeReceived object pulls these values together, we have everything that we need for a line item entry on a student's transcript, as shown in Figure 10-63.

```
Transcript For: Joe Blow                              Semester: Spring 2005


Course No.      Credits      Course Name      Grade Received      Credits Earned*

MATH 101          3          Beginning Math          B                  9
OBJECTS 101       3          Intro to Objects        A                 12
ART 200           3          Clay Modeling           A                 12

* 'Credits Earned' is computed by multiplying the credit value of a course-
  say, 3—by 4 if student earned an A grade, 3 if he/she earned a B, and so forth.
```

Figure 10-63. *A sample transcript report*

Therefore, we see that renaming the association class from GradeReceived to TranscriptEntry makes good sense. It was then a natural step to aggregate these into a Transcript class.

Our SRS diagram is a little "light" in terms of attributes; we've reflected only those that we'll minimally need when we build an automated SRS in Part 3.

Of course, we now need to go back to the data dictionary to capture definitions of all of the new attributes, relationships, and classes that we've identified in putting together this model. The following sidebar shows our revised SRS data dictionary.

THE REVISED SRS DATA DICTIONARY

Classes

- **Course**: A semester-long series of lectures, assignments, exams, etc., that all relate to a particular subject area, and which are typically associated with a particular number of credit hours; a unit of study toward a degree. For example, Beginning Objects is a required **course** for the Master of Science degree in Information Systems Technology.

- **Person**: A human being associated with the university.

- **PlanOfStudy**: A list of the **courses** that a student intends to take to fulfill the **course** requirements for a particular degree.

- **Professor**: A member of the faculty who teaches **sections** or advises **students**.

- **Section**: The offering of a particular **course** during a particular semester on a particular day of the week and at a particular time of day. (For example, **course** Beginning Objects is taught in the Spring 2005 semester on Mondays from 1:00 to 3:00 p.m.)

- **Student**: A person who is currently enrolled at the university and who is eligible to register for one or more **sections**.

- **Transcript**: A record of all of the **courses** taken to date by a particular **student** at this university, including which semester each **course** was taken in, the grade received, and the credits granted for the **course**, as well as reflecting an overall total number of credits earned and the **student's** grade point average (GPA).

- **TranscriptEntry**: A single line item from a **transcript**, reflecting the **course** number and name, semester taken, value in credit hours, and grade received.

Relationships

- **advises: a professor advises a student**: A professor is assigned to oversee a student's academic pursuits for the student's entire academic career, leading up to his or her attainment of a degree. An advisor counsels his or her advisees regarding course selection, professional opportunities, and any academic problems the student might be having.

- **attends: a student attends a section**: A student registers for a section, attends class meetings for a semester, and participates in all assignments and examinations, culminating in the award of a letter grade representing the student's mastery of the subject matter.

- **calls for: a plan of study calls for a course**: A student may take a course only if it's called out by his or her plan of study. The plan of study may be amended, with a student's advisor's approval.

- **maintains: a student maintains a transcript**: Each time a student completes a course, a record of the course and the grade received is added to the student's transcript.

- **observes: a student observes a plan of study**: See notes for the *calls for* association.

- **offered as: a course is offered as a section**: The same course can be taught numerous times in a given semester, and of course over numerous semesters for the "lifetime" of a course—that is, until such time as the subject matter is no longer considered to be of value to the student body, or there is no qualified faculty to teach the course.

- **prerequisite: a course is a prerequisite for another course**: If it's determined that the subject matter of a course A is necessary background to understanding the subject matter of a course B, then course A is said to be a prerequisite of course B. A student typically may not take course B unless he or she has either successfully completed course A, or can otherwise demonstrate mastery of the subject matter of course A.

- **teaches: a professor teaches a section**: A professor is responsible for delivering lectures, assigning thoughtful homework assignments, examining students, and otherwise ensuring that a quality treatment of the subject matter of a course is made available to students.

- **waitlisted for: a student is waitlisted for a section**: If a section is "full"—for example, the maximum number of students have signed up for the course based on either the classroom capacity or the student group size deemed effective for teaching—then interested students may be placed on a wait list, to be given consideration should seats in the course subsequently become available.

  - (aggregation between Transcript and TranscriptEntry)

  - (specialization of Person as Professor)

  - (specialization of Person as Student)

Attributes

- **Person.ssn**: The unique Social Security number (SSN) assigned to an individual.

- **Person.name**: The person's name, in "last name, first name" order.

- **Professor.title**: The rank attained by the professor (e.g., "Adjunct Professor").

- **Student.major**: A reflection of the department in which a student's primary studies lie (e.g., Mathematics). (We assume that a student may designate only a single major.)

- **Student.degree**: The degree that a student is pursuing (e.g., Master of Science degree).

- **TranscriptEntry.grade**: A letter grade of A, B, C, D, or F, with an optional +/- suffix, such as A+ or C-.

- **Course.courseNo**: A unique ID assigned to a course, consisting of the department designation plus a unique numeric ID within the department (e.g., MATH 101).

- **Course.courseName**: A full name describing the subject matter of a course (e.g., Beginning Objects).

- **Course.credits**: The number of units or credit hours a course is worth, roughly equating to the number of hours spent in the classroom in a single week (typically, 3 credits for a full-semester lecture course).

- **Section.sectionNo**: A unique number assigned to distinguish one section/offering of a particular course from another offering of the same course in the same semester (e.g., MATH 101, section no. 1).

- **Section.dayOfWeek**: The day of the week on which the lecture course meets.

- **Section.timeOfDay**: The time (range) during which the course meets (e.g., 2:00 to 4:00 p.m.).

- **Section.semester**: An indication of the scholastic semester in which a section is offered (e.g., Spring 2005).

- **Section.room**: The building and room number where the section will be meeting (e.g., Innovation Hall, Room 333).

- **Section.seatingCapacity**: The maximum number of students permitted to register for a section.

Metadata

One question that is often raised by beginning modelers is why we don't use an inheritance relationship to relate the Course and Section classes, rather than using a simple association as we've chosen to do. On the surface, it does indeed seem tempting to want Section to be a derived class of Course, because all of the attributes listed for a Course—courseNo, courseName, and creditValue—also pertain to a Section; so, why wouldn't we want Section to *inherit* these, in the same way that Student and Professor inherit all of the attributes of Person? A simple example should quickly illustrate why inheritance isn't appropriate.

Let's say that because "Beginning Object Concepts" is such a popular course, the university is offering three sections of the course for the Spring 2005 semester. We therefore instantiate one Course object and three Section objects. If Section were a derived class of Course, then all *four* objects would carry courseNo, courseName, and creditValue attributes. Filling in the attribute values for these four objects, as shown in Table 10-3, we see that there is quite a bit of repetition in the attribute values across these four objects: we've *repeated* the same courseNo, courseName, and creditValue attribute values four times! That's because the information contained within a Course object is common to, and hence describes, *numerous* Section objects.

Table 10-3. *Duplication of Data Across Four Object Instances*

Attribute Name	Attribute Values for the Course Object
courseName	Beginning Object Concepts
courseNo	OBJECTS 101
creditValue	3

Attribute Name	Attr. Values for Section Object #1	Attr. Values for Section Object #2	Attr. Values for Section Object #3
courseName	Beginning Object Concepts	Beginning Object Concepts	Beginning Object Concepts
courseNo	OBJECTS 101	OBJECTS 101	OBJECTS 101
creditValue	3	3	3
studentsRegistered	(To be determined)	(To be determined)	(To be determined)
instructor	Reference to professor X	Reference to professor Y	Reference to professor Z
semesterOffered	Spring 2005	Spring 2005	Spring 2005
dayOfWeek	Monday	Tuesday	Thursday
timeOfDay	7:00 p.m.	4:00 p.m.	6:00 p.m.
classroom	Hall A, Room 123	Hall B, Room 234	Hall A, Room 345

To reduce redundancy and to promote encapsulation, we should eliminate *inheritance* of these attributes, and instead create only one instance of a Course object for *n* instances of its related Section objects. We can then have each Section object maintain a handle on the common Course object so as to retrieve these shared values whenever necessary. This is precisely what we've modeled via the one-to-many *offered as* association.

Whenever an instance of some class A encapsulates information that describes numerous instances of some other class B (such as Course does for Section), we refer to the information contained by the A object (Course) as **metadata** relative to the B objects (Sections).

Summary

Our object model has started to take shape! We have a good idea of what the static structure needs to be for the SRS—the classes, their attributes, and their relationships with one another—and are able to communicate this knowledge in a concise, graphical form. There are many more embellishments to the UML notation that we haven't covered in this chapter, but we've examined the core concepts that will suffice for most "industrial-strength" modeling projects. Once you've mastered these, you can explore the "Other Recommended Reading" section in Chapter 18 of the book if you'd like to learn more about these embellishments.

There is an obvious "hole" in our class diagram, however: all of our classes have empty operations compartments. We'll address this deficiency by learning some complementary modeling techniques for determining the *dynamic behavior* of our objects in Chapter 11.

In this chapter, you learned

- The noun phrase analysis technique for identifying candidate domain classes

- The verb phrase analysis technique for determining potential relationships among these classes

- That coming up with candidate classes is a bit subjective, and hence that we must remain flexible revisiting our model numerous times until we—and our users—are satisfied with the outcome

- The importance of producing a data dictionary as part of a project's documentation set

- How to graphically portray the static structure of a model as a class diagram using UML notation

- The importance of having an experienced object modeling mentor available to a project team

Exercises

1. Come up with a list of candidate classes for the Prescription Tracking System (PTS) case study presented in Appendix B, as well as an association matrix.

2. Develop a class diagram for the PTS case study, using UML notation. Reflect all significant attributes and relationships among classes, including the appropriate multiplicity. Ideally, you should use an object modeling software tool if you have one available to you.

3. Prepare a data dictionary for the PTS, to include definitions of all classes, attributes, and associations.

4. Devise a list of candidate classes for the problem area whose requirements you defined for exercise 3 in Chapter 1, as well as an association matrix.

5. Develop a class diagram for the problem area whose requirements you defined for exercise 3 in Chapter 1, using UML notation. Reflect all significant attributes and relationships among classes, including the appropriate multiplicity. Ideally, you should use an object modeling software tool if you have one available to you.

6. Prepare a data dictionary for the problem area whose requirements you defined for exercise 3 in Chapter 1 to include definitions of all classes, attributes, and associations.

CHAPTER 11

■ ■ ■

Modeling the Dynamic/Behavioral Aspects of the System

Thus far, we've been focused on the ***static structure*** of the problem being modeled—the floor plan for our custom home, as it were. As you learned in Chapter 10, this static structure is communicated via a class diagram plus supporting documentation. The building blocks of a class diagram are

- Classes.

- Associations/aggregations.

- Attributes.

- Generalization/specialization hierarchies (also known as inheritance relationships).

- Operations/methods. ***These are conspicuously absent from our class diagram***. Why? Because they aren't part of the static structure, and so we haven't discussed how to determine these yet; doing so is the focus of this chapter.

As I've said many times already, an OO software system is a set of collaborating objects, each with a "life" of its own. If each object went about its own business without regard to what any other object needed it to do, however, utter chaos would reign! The only way that objects can collaborate to perform some overall system mission, such as registering a student for a course, is if each class defines the appropriate methods—*services*—that will enable its instances to fulfill their respective roles in the collaboration.

In order to determine what these methods/services must be, we must complement our knowledge of the static structure of the system to be built by also modeling the ***dynamic*** aspects of the situation: that is, the ways in which concurrently active objects interact over time, and how these interactions affect each object's state. Producing a **dynamic model** to complement the static model will not only enable us to determine the methods required for each class, but also give us new insights into ways to improve upon the static structure.

In this chapter, you'll learn about the building blocks of a dynamic model:

- Events

- Scenarios

- Sequence diagrams

- Communication diagrams

and how to use the knowledge gleaned from these modeling artifacts to identify the operations/methods that are needed to complete our class diagram.

How Behavior Affects State

Back in Chapter 3, we defined the *state* of an object as the collective set of all of the object's attribute values at a given point in time, including

- The values of all of the "simple" attributes for that object—in other words, attributes that don't represent other domain objects

- The values of all of the reference variable attributes representing links to other domain objects

Table 11-1 repeats our list of Student attributes from Chapter 6, with an additional column to indicate which category each attribute falls into.

Table 11-1. Student *Class Attributes*

Attribute Name	Data Type	Represents Link(s) to an SRS Domain Object?
name	String	No
studentID	String	No
birthdate	DateTime	No
address	String	No
major	String	No
gpa	double	No
advisor	Professor	Yes
courseLoad	Collection of Course objects	Yes
transcript	Collection of TranscriptEntry objects, or Transcript	Yes

In Chapter 10, you learned about UML object diagrams as a way of portraying a "snapshot" of the links between specific individual objects. Let's use an object diagram to reflect the state of a few hypothetical objects within the SRS domain.

Figure 11-1 shows that Dr. Smith (a Professor) works for the Math Department; Dr. Green (another Professor) works for the Science Department; and Bill and Mary, both Students, are majoring in Math and Science, respectively.

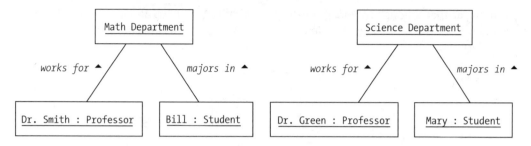

Figure 11-1. *The state of an object includes the links it maintains with other objects.*

Bill is dissatisfied with his choice of majors, and calls Dr. Green, a professor whom he admires, to make an appointment. Bill wants to discuss the possibility of transferring to the Science Department. After meeting with Dr. Green and discussing his situation, Bill indeed decides to switch majors. I've informally reflected these object interactions using arrows on the object diagram, shown in Figure 11-2; as this chapter progresses, you'll learn the "official" way to portray object interactions in UML notation.

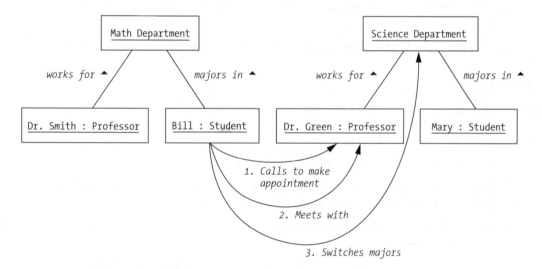

Figure 11-2. *Objects' interactions can affect their state.*

When the dust settles from all of this activity, we see that the resultant state of the system has changed, as reflected in the revised object diagram in Figure 11-3. In particular

- Bill's state has changed, because his link to the Math Department object has been replaced with a link to the Science Department object.

- The Math Department object's state has changed, because it no longer has a link to Bill.

- The Science Department's state has changed, because it now has an additional link (to Bill) that wasn't previously there.

Note, however, that although Dr. Green collaborated with Bill in helping him to make his decision to switch majors, the state of the "Dr. Green" (Professor) object *has not changed* as a result of the collaboration.

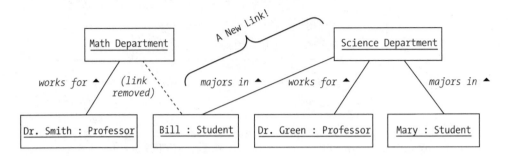

Figure 11-3. *Some interacting objects **don't** experience a change of state.*

So, we see that

- Objects' dynamic activities can result in changes to the **static structure of a system**—that is, the states of all of its objects taken collectively.

- However, such activities needn't affect the state of ***all*** objects involved in a collaboration.

Events

You saw in Chapter 4 that object collaborations are triggered by events. By way of review, an ***event*** is an external stimulus to an object, signaled to the object in the form of a ***message*** (method call). An event can be

- ***User initiated*** (e.g., the result of clicking a button on a GUI)

- ***Initiated by another computer system*** (e.g., the arrival of information being transferred from the Student Billing System to the Student Registration System)

- ***Initiated by another object within the same system*** (e.g., a Course object requesting some service of a Transcript object)

When an object receives notification of an event via a message, it may react in one or more of the following ways:

- An object may change its state.

- An object may direct an event (message) toward another object.

- An object may return a value.

- An object may react with the external boundaries of its system.

- An object may seemingly ignore an event.

Let's discuss these five types of reaction in detail, one by one.

An Object May Change Its State

An object may change its state (the values of its "simple" attributes and/or links to other objects), as in the case of a Professor object receiving a message to take on a new Student advisee, illustrated by the following code snippet:

```
Professor p = new Professor();
Student s = new Student();
// Details omitted.
p.addAdvisee(s);
```

Let's look at the code for the Professor class's addAdvisee method to see how the Professor will respond to this message. We see that the Professor object is inserting the reference to Student object s that it is being handed as an argument into a Collection of Student object references called advisees:

```
public class Professor {
  // Attributes.
  Collection advisees;   // Holds Student object references.

  // Other details omitted.

  public void addAdvisee(Student s) {
    // Insert s into the advisees collection.
    advisees.add(s);
  }
}
```

In so doing, Professor object p will have formed a new link of type *advises* with Student object s (see Figure 11-4).

Figure 11-4. *Revisiting the UML diagram for the* advises *association.*

Typical "set" methods fall into this category of event response.

An Object May Direct an Event (Message) Toward Another Object

An object may direct an event (message) toward another object (including, perhaps, the sender of the original message), as in the case of a Section object receiving a message to register a Student, illustrated by the following code snippet:

```
Section x = new Section();
Student s = new Student();
// Details omitted.
x.register(s);
```

If we next look at the code for the Section class's register method to see how it will respond to this message, we see that the Section object in turn sends a message to the Student to be enrolled, to verify that the Student has completed a necessary prerequisite course:

```java
public class Section {
  // Details omitted.

  public boolean register(Student s) {
    // Verify that the student has completed a necessary
    // prerequisite course. (We are delegating part
    // of the work to another object, Student s.)
    // Pseudocode.
    boolean completed = s.successfullyCompleted(some prerequisite);
    if (completed) {
      // Pseudocode.
      register the student and return a value of true;
    }
    else {
      // Pseudocode.
      return a value of false to signal that the registration
        request has been rejected;
    }
  }
}
```

This happens to be an example of ***delegation***, which we discussed in Chapter 4: namely, another object (a Student, in this case) helping to fulfill a service request originally made of the Section object.

An Object May Return a Value

An object may return a value. The returned value may be one of the following:

- The value of one of the object's attributes

- Some computed value (i.e., a "pseudoattribute," as we discussed in Chapter 4)

- A value that was obtained from some ***other*** object through delegation

- A status code (as in true/false responses, signaling success or failure of boolean methods)

Typical "get" methods fall into this category of event response.

An Object May React with the External Boundaries of Its System

An object may react with the external boundaries of its system; that is, it may display some information on a GUI, or cause information to be printed to a printer. As you'll learn in Chapters 15 and 16, however, what appears to be an external system boundary is often implemented in Java as yet another object.

An Object May Seemingly Ignore an Event

Finally, an object may seemingly ignore an event, as would be the case if a Professor object received the message to add an advisee, but determined that the Student whom it was being asked to take on as an advisee was ***already*** an advisee:

```
Student s = new Student();
Professor p = new Professor();
// Details omitted.
// Professor p will seemingly "ignore" this next message.
p.addAdvisee(s);
```

Let's look at slightly different version of the addAdvisee method than we saw previously:

```
public class Professor {
  Collection advisees;  // Holds Student object references.
  // Details omitted.

  public void addAdvisee(Student s) {
    // ONLY insert s into the 'advisees' collection IF IT
    // ISN'T ALREADY IN THERE.
    // Pseudocode.
    if (s is already in collection) return;  // do nothing
    else advisees.add(s);
  }
}
```

Actually, to say that the Professor object is doing nothing is an oversimplification: at a minimum, the object is executing the appropriate method code, which is performing some internal state checks ("Is this student already one of my advisees?"). It's just that, when the dust settles, the Professor object has neither changed state nor fired off any messages to other objects, so it ***appears*** as if nothing has happened.

Scenarios

Events originating externally to an application occur randomly: we can't predict, for example, when a user is going to click a button on a GUI. In order for an application to perform useful functions, however, the ***internal*** events that arise in ***response*** to these external events—in other words, the messages that objects exchange in carrying out some system function—***can't*** be left to occur randomly. Rather, they must be orchestrated in such a way as to lead, in cause-and-effect fashion, to some desired result. In the same way that a musical score indicates which notes must be played by various instruments to produce a melody, a **scenario** prescribes the sequence of internal messages (events) that must occur in carrying out some system function from beginning to end.

I introduced use cases in Chapter 9 as a way to specify all of the goals for an application from the standpoint of external actors—users or other computer systems. *Merriam-Webster's Collegiate Dictionary, Eleventh Edition*, defines the term **scenario** as

> *A sequence of events esp. when imagined; esp : an account or synopsis of a possible course of action or events.*

which is precisely how the term is used in the object modeling sense.

A scenario is one hypothetical instance of how a particular use case might play out. Just as an object is an instance of a class, and a link is an instance of an association, *a scenario may be thought of as an instance of a use case*. Or, stated another way, just as a class is a template for creating objects, and an association is a template for creating links, *a use case is a template for creating scenarios*. A single use case thus inspires many different scenarios, in the same way that planning a driving trip from one city to another can involve many different routes.

We describe scenarios in narrative fashion, as a series of steps observed from the standpoint of a hypothetical observer who is able to see not only what is happening outwardly as the system carries out a particular request, but also what is going on behind the scenes, internally to the system. (Note, however, that even though we're now concerned with internal system processes, we're still only interested in *functional* requirements as defined in Chapter 9, not in the "bits and bytes" of how the computer works.)

The following is a sample scenario representing the "Register for a Course" use case, one of several use cases that we identified for the SRS in Chapter 9.

Scenario #1 for the "Register for a Course" Use Case

In this first scenario, a student by the name of Fred successfully registers for a course. The specific sequence of events is as follows:

1. Fred, a student, logs on to the SRS.

2. He views the schedule of classes for the current semester to determine which section(s) he wishes to register for.

3. Fred requests a seat in a particular section of a course entitled "Beginning Computer Concepts," course number CMP101, section 1.

4. Fred's plan of study is checked to ensure that the requested course is appropriate for his overall degree goals. (We assume that students are not permitted to take courses outside of their plans of study.)

5. His transcript is checked to ensure that he has satisfied all of the prerequisites for the requested course, if there are any.

6. Seating availability in the section is confirmed.

7. The section is added to Fred's current course load.

From Fred's vantage point (sitting in front of a computer screen!), here's what he perceives to be occurring: after logging on to the SRS, he indicates that he wishes to register for CMP101, section 1 by choosing it from the available course list, and then clicks the Add button (see Figure 11-5).

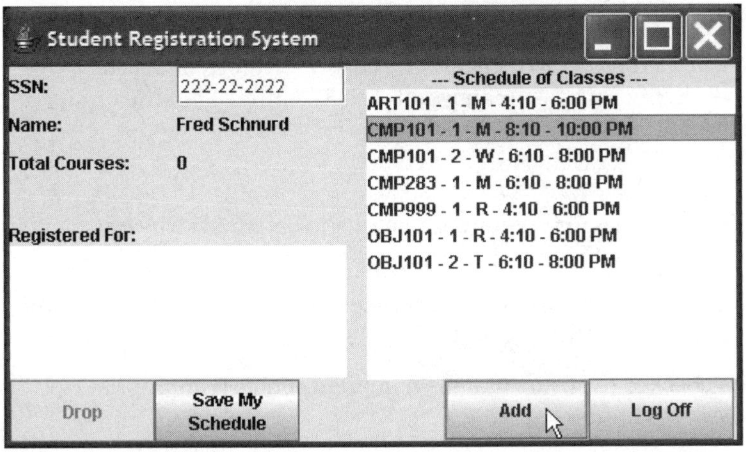

Figure 11-5. *Fred's view of things, part 1*

A few moments later, Fred receives a confirmation message, as shown in Figure 11-6.

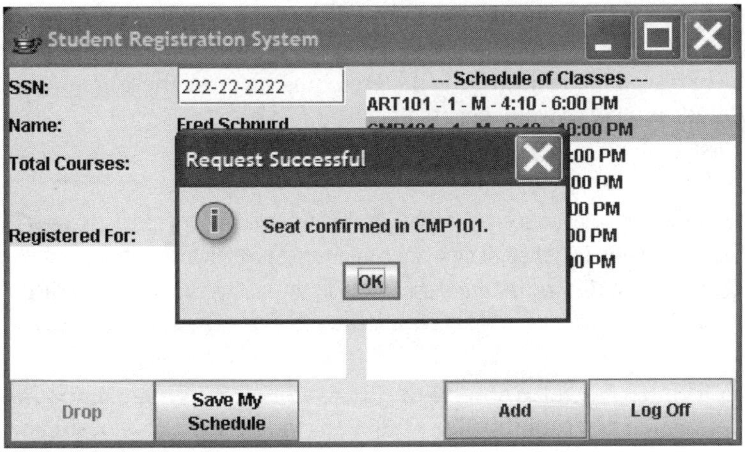

Figure 11-6. *Fred's view of things, part 2*

Fred is unaware (for the most part) of all of the "behind the scenes" processing steps that are taking place on his behalf!

The preceding scenario represents a "best case" scenario, where everything goes smoothly and Fred ends up being successfully registered for the requested course. But, as we know all too well, things don't always work out this smoothly, as evidenced by the following alternative scenario for the *same* use case. Everything is the same between Scenario #1 and Scenario #2 except for the steps that are shown in ***bold***.

Scenario #2 for the "Register for a Course" Use Case

In this scenario, Fred once again attempts to register for a course. While he meets all of the requirements, the requested section is unfortunately full. The SRS offers Fred the option of putting his name on a wait list. The specific sequence of events is as follows:

1. Fred, a student, logs on to the SRS.

2. Fred views the schedule of classes for the current semester to determine which section(s) he wishes to register for.

3. Fred requests a seat in a particular section of a course entitled "Beginning Computer Concepts," course number CMP101, section 1.

4. Fred's plan of study is checked to ensure that the requested course is appropriate for his overall degree goals.

5. His transcript is checked to ensure that he has satisfied all of the prerequisites for the requested course, if any.

6. *Seating availability in the section is checked, but the section is found to be full.*

7. *Fred is asked if he wishes to be put on a first come, first served wait list.*

8. *Fred elects to be placed on the wait list.*

With a little imagination, you can undoubtedly think of numerous other scenarios for this use case, involving such circumstances as Fred having requested a course that isn't called for by his plan of study, or a course for which he hasn't met the prerequisites. And, there are many other *use cases* to be considered, as well, as were discussed in Chapter 9.

Are there practical limits to the number of alternative scenarios that we should consider for a given use case? As with all requirements analysis, the criteria for when to stop are somewhat subjective: we stop when it appears that we can no longer generate *significantly different* scenarios; trivial variations are to be avoided.

When devising scenarios, it's often helpful to observe the future users of the system that we're modeling as they go about performing the same business functions today. In the case of student registration, for example, what manual or automated steps does a student have to go through presently to register for a course? What steps does the university take before deeming a student eligible to register? Whether the registration process is 100 percent manual at present, or is based on an automated system that you're going to be replacing or augmenting, observing the steps that are involved today in carrying out a particular business goal can serve as the basis for one or more useful scenarios.

Scenarios, once written, should be added to our project's use case documentation; generally, we pair all scenarios with their associated use cases in that document.

Why are scenarios so important? Because they're the means by which we start to gain insight into the *behaviors* that will be required of our objects. We'll need a way to formalize these scenarios so that the actual methods needed for each of our classes become apparent; UML **sequence diagrams** are the means by which we do so, so let's now discuss how to prepare these.

Sequence Diagrams

Sequence diagrams are one of two types of UML **interaction diagrams** (we'll explore the second type, **communication diagrams**, a bit later in this chapter). Sequence diagrams are a way of graphically portraying how messages should flow from one object to another in carrying out a given scenario.

We'll illustrate the process of creating a sequence diagram by creating one for Scenario #1 of the "Register for a Course" use case.

Determining Objects and External Actors for Scenario #1

To prepare a sequence diagram, we must first determine

- Which classes of objects (from among those that we specified in our static model [class diagram] in Chapter 10) are involved in carrying out a particular scenario

- Which external actors are involved

Looking back at Scenario #1 for the "Register for a Course" use case, we determine that the following objects are involved:

- One Student object (representing Fred)

- One Section object (representing the course entitled "Beginning Computer Concepts," course number CMP101, section number 1)

- One PlanOfStudy object, belonging to Fred

- One Transcript object, also belonging to Fred

The scenario also mentions that the student "views the schedule of classes for the current semester to determine which section(s) he wishes to register for." You may recall that when we were determining what our candidate classes should be back in Chapter 10, we debated whether or not to add ScheduleOfClasses as a candidate class to our model, and we elected to leave it out at that time. In order to fully represent the details of Scenario #1, we're going to reverse that decision and retrofit ScheduleOfClasses into our UML class diagram now as follows:

- We'll show ScheduleOfClasses participating in a one-to-many aggregation with the Section class because one ScheduleOfClasses object will be instantiated per semester to represent all of the sections that are being taught that semester. (It's an abstraction of the paper booklet or online schedule that students look at in choosing which classes they wish to register for in a given semester.)

- We'll also transfer the semester attribute from the Section class to ScheduleOfClasses. Since each Section object will now be maintaining a handle on its associated ScheduleOfClasses object by virtue of the aggregation relationship between them, a Section object will be able to request semester information whenever it is needed.

The results of these changes to our class diagram are highlighted in Figure 11-7.

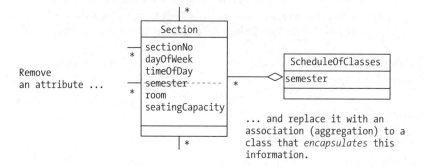

Figure 11-7. *Fine-tuning the UML diagram*

Acknowledging ScheduleOfClasses as a class in our model allows us to now reference a ScheduleOfClasses object in our sequence diagram, as we'll see in a moment. Scenarios often unearth new classes, attributes, and relationships, thus contributing to our structural "picture" of the system; this is a common occurrence, and is a ***desirable*** side effect of dynamic modeling.

Of course, we must remember to add a definition of ScheduleOfClasses to our data dictionary:

Schedule of Classes: A list of all classes/**sections** that are being offered for a particular semester; **students** review the **schedule of classes** to determine which **sections** they wish to register for.

Finally, since the scenario explicitly mentions interactions between the student user and the system, we'll reflect Fred the ***actor*** separately from Fred the ***object***. Doing so will allow us to represent the SRS interacting externally with the user, as well as showing the system's internal object-to-object interactions. We refer to an object that represents an abstraction of an actor as an instance of a **boundary class**.

Our adjusted list of object/actor participants is now as follows:

- One Student object (representing Fred)

- One Section object (representing the course entitled "Beginning Computer Concepts," course number CMP101, section number 1)

- One PlanOfStudy object, belonging to Fred

- One Transcript object, also belonging to Fred

- One ScheduleOfClasses object

- One Student actor (Fred again!)

Preparing the Sequence Diagram

To prepare a sequence diagram for Scenario #1, we do the following:

- We draw vertical dashed lines, one per object or actor that participates in the scenario; these are referred to as the objects' **lifelines**. Note that the objects/actors can be listed in any order from left to right in a diagram, although it's common practice to place the external user/actor at the far left.

- At the top of each lifeline, as appropriate, we place either an **instance icon**—that is, a box containing the (optional) name and class of an object participant—or a stick figure symbol to designate an actor. (For rules governing how an instance icon is to be formed, please refer back to the section on creating object diagrams in Chapter 10.)

- Then, for each event called out by our scenario, we reflect its corresponding message as a horizontal **solid-line** arrow drawn from the lifeline of the sender to the lifeline of the receiver.

- Responses back from messages (in other words, return values from methods, or simple `return;` statements in the case of methods declared to have a `void` return type) are shown as horizontal **dashed-line** arrows drawn from the lifeline of the **receiver** of the original message **back to** the lifeline for the **sender** of the message.

- Message arrows appear in chronological order from top to bottom in the diagram.

The completed sequence diagram for Scenario #1 is shown in Figure 11-8.

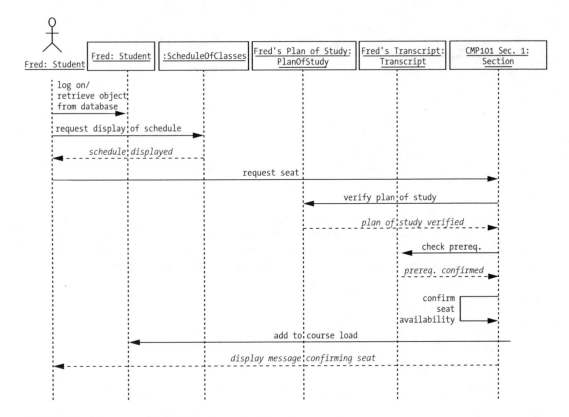

Figure 11-8. *Sequence diagram for Scenario #1*

Note that I've intentionally omitted one element of sequence diagram notation from this example: namely, the use of **focus of control bars** to illustrate the period of time over an object's lifeline that the object is actually engaged in processing a request. For more details on sequence diagram notation, please see the recommended reading list in Chapter 17.

Let's step through the diagram to make sure you understand all of the activities that are reflected in the diagram.

1. When Fred logs on to the system, his "alter ego" as an object is activated (see Figure 11-9).

Presumably, information representing each Student—in other words, the Student object's attribute values—is maintained offline in persistent storage, such as a DBMS or file, until such time as the student logs on, at which time the information is used to instantiate a Student object in memory, mirroring the user who has just logged on. We'll talk about reconstituting objects from persistent storage in Chapter 15.

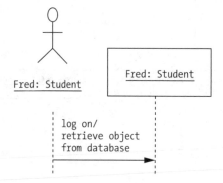

Figure 11-9. *When Fred logs on, a* Student *object is instantiated.*

2. When Fred the user/actor requests that the semester class schedule be displayed, we reflect the message "request display of schedule" being sent to an anonymous ScheduleOfClasses object. The dashed-line-arrow response from the ScheduleOfClasses object indicates that the schedule is being displayed to the user, strictly speaking, via a GUI (see Figure 11-10).

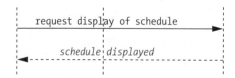

Figure 11-10. *As requested, a schedule of classes is displayed.*

I've chosen to label the response arrows with *italic* instead of regular font, a slight departure from official UML notation.

3. The next message shown in our diagram is a message from the user to the Section object, requesting a seat in the class.

This message is shown originating from the user. In reality, it originates from a GUI component object of the SRS GUI, but we aren't worrying about such implementation details at this stage in the analysis effort. We'll talk about the OO aspects of GUI design and event processing in depth in Chapters 16 and 17.

Note that there is no immediate reply to this message; that's because the Section object has a few other objects that it needs to consult with before it can grant a seat to this student, namely

- The Section sends a message to the object representing Fred's plan of study, asking that object to confirm that the course that Fred has requested is one of the courses required of Fred in completing his degree program.

- The Section next sends a message to the object representing Fred's transcript, asking that object to confirm that a prerequisite course—say CMP001—has been satisfactorily completed by this student.

4. Assuming that both of these other objects respond favorably, as they are expected to do by virtue of how this scenario was written, the Section object then performs some internal processing to verify that there is indeed room for Fred in this section. We reflect internal processing within a single object as an arrow that loops back to the same lifeline that it starts with, as shown in Figure 11-11.

Figure 11-11. *Availability of the requested section is confirmed.*

Of course, if we were to reflect ***all*** of the internal processing that is performed by every one of the objects in our sequence diagram, it would be ***flooded*** with such loops! The only reason that we've chosen to show this particular loop is because it's explicitly called out as a step in Scenario #1; if we had omitted it from our diagram, it might appear that we had accidentally overlooked this step.

5. Finally, with all checks having been satisfied, the Section object has two remaining responsibilities:

- First, it sends a new message to the "Fred" Student object, requesting that the Student object add this Section to Fred's course load.

- Next, the Section object sends a response back to Fred the user/actor (via the GUI) confirming his seat in the section. This is the response to the original "request seat" message that was sent by the user toward the beginning of the scenario! All of the extra behind the scenes processing necessary to fulfill the request—involving a Section object collaborating with a PlanOfStudy object, a Transcript object, and a Student object—is transparent to the user. As we saw earlier in the chapter, Fred merely selected a section from the schedule of classes that was displayed on the SRS GUI, clicked the Add button, and, a few moments later, saw a confirmation message appear on his screen.

Of course, as with all modeling, this particular sequence diagram isn't necessarily the ***best***, or ***only***, way to portray the selected scenario. And, for that matter, we can argue the relative merits of one scenario as compared with another. It's important to keep in mind that preparing sequence diagrams is but a means to an end: namely, discovering the dynamic aspects of the system to be built—that is, the ***methods***—to complement our static/structural knowledge of the system. Recall that our ***ultimate*** goal for Part 2 of the book is to produce an OO blueprint that we can use as the basis for coding the SRS as a Java application in Part 3. But, as already pointed out, the class diagram that we created in Chapter 10 had a noticeable deficiency: all of its classes' operations compartments were empty. Fortunately, sequence diagrams provide us with the missing pieces of information, as we'll discuss next.

Using Sequence Diagrams to Determine Methods

Now that we've prepared a sequence diagram, how do we put the information that it contains to good use? In particular, how do we "harvest" information from such diagrams concerning the methods that the various classes need to implement?

The process is actually quite simple. We step through the diagram, one lifeline at a time, and study all arrows ***pointing into*** that line.

- Arrows representing a new request being made of an object—solid-line arrows—signal methods that the receiving object must be able to perform. For example, we see a solid line arrow labeled "check prerequisite" pointing into the lifeline representing a Transcript object. This tells us that the Transcript class needs to define a method that will allow some client object to pass in a particular course object reference, and receive back a response indicating whether or not the Transcript contains evidence that the course was successfully completed.

- We're free to name our methods in whatever intuitive way makes the most sense, consistent with the method naming conventions discussed in Chapter 4. We're using the method in this particular scenario to check completion of a prerequisite course, so we could declare the method as follows:

```
boolean checkPrerequisite(Course c)
```

but this name is unnecessarily restrictive; what we're *really* doing with this method is checking the successful completion of some Course c; the fact that it happens to be a prerequisite of some other course is immaterial to how this method will perform. So, by naming the method

```
boolean verifyCompletion(Course c)
```

instead, we'll be able to use it anywhere in our application that we need to verify successful completion of a course—for example, when we check whether a student has met all of the course requirements necessary to graduate. (Of course, we could have still used the method in this fashion even if it had been named checkPrerequisite, but then our code would be less accurately self-documenting.)

- Arrows representing responses from an operation that some other object has performed— dashed-line arrows—don't get modeled as methods/operations. These do, however, hint at the return type of the method from which this response is being issued. For example, since the response to the "verify plan of study" message is "plan of study verified," this would imply that the method is returning a boolean result, hence we'd declare a method header as follows:

```
boolean verifyPlan(Course c)
```

- Loops also represent method calls, performed by an object on itself; these may either represent private "housekeeping" methods or public methods that other client objects may avail themselves of.

Table 11-2 summarizes all of the arrows reflected by the sequence diagram for Scenario #1 from a few pages back.

Table 11-2. *Determining the Methods Implied by Scenario #1*

Arrow Labeled	Drawn Pointing into Class X	A New Request or a Response to a Previous Request?	Method to Be Added to Class X
log on	Student	Request	(A method to reconstitute this object from persistent storage, such as a file or database; perhaps a special form of constructor—we'll discuss this in Part 3 of the book.)
request display of schedule	ScheduleOfClasses	Request	void display()
schedule displayed	Student	*Response*	*N/A*
request seat	Section	Request	boolean enroll(Student s)
verify plan of study	PlanOfStudy	Request	boolean verifyPlan (Course c)
plan of study verified	Section	*Response*	*N/A*
check prerequisite	Transcript	Request	boolean verifyCompletion(Course c)

(Continues)

Table 11-2. *Determining the Methods Implied by Scenario #1 (Continued)*

Arrow Labeled	Drawn Pointing into Class X	A New Request or a Response to a Previous Request?	Method to Be Added to Class X
prerequisite confirmed	Section	*Response*	*N/A*
confirm seat availability	Section	Request	boolean confirmSeatAvailability() (perhaps a private housekeeping method)
add to course load	Student	Request	void addSection(Section s)
display message confirming seat	*(actor/user)*	*Response*	*N/A (will eventually involve calling upon some method of a user interface object—we'll worry about this in Part 3 of the book)*

Thus we have identified six new "standard" methods plus one constructor that will need to be added to our class diagram, which we'll do shortly.

Repeating this process of sequence diagram production and analysis for various other use case/scenario combinations will flush out most of the methods that we'll need to implement for the SRS. Despite our best efforts, however, a few methods may not surface until we've begun to *program* our classes—this is to be expected.

Communication Diagrams

The UML notation introduced a second type of interaction diagram, called a **communication diagram**, as an alternative to sequence diagrams. Both types of diagram present essentially the same information, but portray it in a different manner.

In a communication diagram, we eliminate the lifelines used to portray objects and actors. Rather, we lay out instance icons representing objects and stick figures representing actors in whatever configuration is most visually appealing. We then use lines and arrows to represent the flow of messages and responses back and forth between these objects/actors. Because we lose the top-to-bottom chronological sense of message flow that we had with the sequence diagrams, we compensate by numbering the arrows in the order that they would occur during execution of a particular scenario.

The communication diagram in Figure 11-12 is equivalent to the sequence diagram that we produced for Scenario #1.

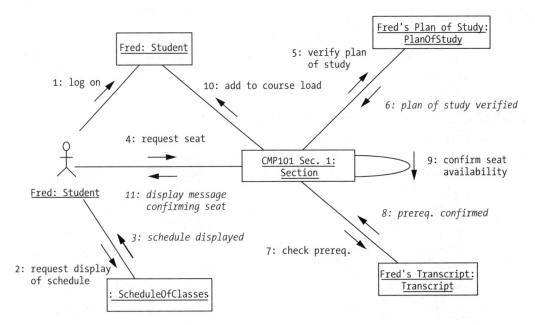

Figure 11-12. *Communication diagram for Scenario #1*

Again, from Fred's vantage point, he observes only a few of these actions, as shown in Figure 11-13.

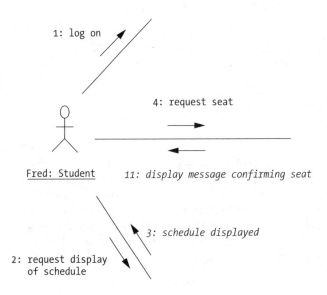

Figure 11-13. *Fred sees only a small subset of the SRS collaborations.*

Because sequence and communication diagrams reflect essentially the same information, many object modeling software tools automatically enable us to produce one diagram from the other with the push of a button.

Revised SRS Class Diagram

Going back to the SRS class diagram that we produced in Chapter 10, let's reflect all of the new insights—some behavioral, some structural—that we've gained from analyzing one scenario/ sequence diagram (see Figure 11-14).

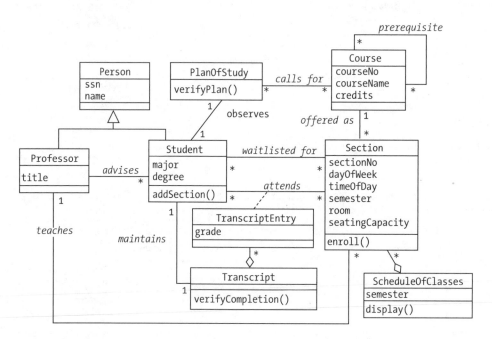

Figure 11-14. *Revised SRS class diagram*

Note that we've decided not to reflect the confirmSeatAvailability housekeeping method at this time, as we suspect that it will be a private method and don't wish to clutter our diagram. The decision of whether to reflect private methods on a class diagram—or, for that matter, to reflect *any* feature of a class—is up to the modeler, because again, the purpose of the diagram is to communicate, and too much detail can actually lessen a diagram's effectiveness in this regard.

We must remember to update the SRS data dictionary any time we add classes, attributes, relationships, or methods to our model. Here's a suggested format for how we might wish to describe a method in the dictionary:

Method: `enroll`

Defined for class: `Section`

Header: `boolean enroll(Student s)`

Description: This method enrolls the designated person in the section, unless (a) the section is already full, (b) the student's plan of study doesn't call for this course, or (c) the student hasn't met the prerequisites. It returns a `boolean` value to indicate success (`true`) or failure (`false`) of the enrollment.

Summary

In this chapter, you've seen how the process of dynamic modeling is a complementary technique to the static modeling that enriches our overall understanding of the problem to be automated, hence enabling us to improve our object "blueprint," also known as a class diagram. In particular, you've seen

- How events trigger state changes

- How to develop scenarios, based on use cases

- How to represent these as UML interaction diagrams: sequence diagrams or, alternatively, communication diagrams

- How to glean information from sequence diagrams concerning the behaviors expected of objects—that is, the methods that our classes will need to implement—so as to round out our class diagram

- How sequence diagrams can also yield additional knowledge about the structural aspects of a system

Exercises

1. Prepare a sequence diagram for Scenario #2 as presented earlier in this chapter.

2. Prepare a sequence diagram to represent the following scenario for the SRS case study:

    a. Mary, a student, logs on to the SRS.

    b. She indicates that she wishes to drop ART 222, Section 1.

    c. ART 222, Section 1 is removed from Mary's course load.

    d. The system determines that Joe, another student, is waitlisted for this section.

    e. The section is added to Joe's current course load.

    f. An email is sent to Joe notifying him that ART 222 has been added to his course load.

3. Provide a list of all of the method headers that you would add to each of your classes based on the sequence diagram that you prepared for exercise 2. Also, note any new classes, attributes, or relationships that would be needed.

4. Prepare a second sequence diagram for the SRS case study, representing a scenario of your own choosing based upon any of the SRS use cases identified in Chapter 9. This scenario should be significantly different from those presented in this chapter and from the scenario in exercise 2. You must also narrate the scenario as was done for exercise 2.

5. Provide a list of all of the method headers that you would add to each of your classes based on the sequence diagram that you prepared for exercise 4. Also, note any new classes, attributes, or relationships that would be needed.

6. Prepare a sequence diagram to represent the following scenario for the Prescription Tracking System (PTS) case study presented in Appendix B:

   a. Mary Jones, an existing customer of the pharmacy, brings in a prescription for eye drops to have it filled.

   b. The pharmacist checks to see if Ms. Jones has previously had a prescription filled for this item.

   c. The pharmacist discovers that she has, and furthermore that the last time it was refilled was less than a month ago.

   d. Knowing that her insurance won't authorize payment for this same prescription so soon, the pharmacist informs Ms. Jones, and she decides to wait to have it filled at a later date.

7. Devise an "interesting" scenario, and prepare the corresponding sequence diagram, for the problem area whose requirements you defined for exercise 3 in Chapter 1.

8. Provide a list of all of the method headers that you would add to each of your classes based on the sequence diagram that you prepared for exercise 7. Also, note any new classes, attributes, or relationships that would be needed.

■ ■ ■

CHAPTER 12

Wrapping Up Our Modeling Efforts

Having used the techniques for static and dynamic modeling presented in Chapters 10 and 11, respectively, we've arrived at a fairly thorough object model of the SRS—or so it seems! Before we embark upon implementing our class diagram as Java code in Part 3 of the book, however, we need to make sure that our model is as accurate and representative of the goal system as possible.

In this chapter, we'll

- Explore some simple techniques for testing our model

- Talk about the notion of reusing models

Testing the Model

Testing a model doesn't involve "rocket science"; rather, it calls for some common sense measures designed to identify errors and/or omissions.

- First of all, revisit all requirements-related project documentation—the original problem statement and the supporting use cases—to ensure that no requirements were overlooked. We'll do so for our SRS model in a moment.

- Conduct a minimum of two separate formal walk-throughs of the model: one with the development team members, and a second with the future users of the system. Prior to each walk-through, make sure to distribute copies of the following documentation to each of the participants far enough in advance to allow them adequate time to review these, if they so desire (but be prepared to discuss significant aspects of these at the meeting in case the participants haven't reviewed them):

  - "Executive summary" problem statement, if available

  - Class diagram

  - Data dictionary

  - Use case documentation

  - Significant scenarios and corresponding message trace diagrams

By this stage in the project, you'll have hopefully already educated your users on how to read UML diagrams, and they'll have informally seen numerous iterations of the evolving models. If any of the participants in the upcoming walk-throughs aren't familiar with any of the notation, however, take time in advance to tutor them in this regard. (The information contained in Chapters 10 and 11 of this book should be more than adequate as the basis for such a tutorial.)

When conducting the walk-through, designate someone to be the narrator and discussion leader, and a different person to be responsible for recording significant discussion content, particularly changes that need to be made. Having one person trying to do both is too distracting, and important notes may be missed as a result. If appropriate, you may even arrange to tape record the discussion.

Remain open-minded throughout the review process. It's human nature to want to defend something that we've worked hard on putting together, but remember that it's far better to find and correct shortcomings now, when the SRS is still a paper skeleton, than after it has been rendered as code.

Revisiting Requirements

In revisiting the SRS case study problem statement, we find that we've indeed *missed* one requirement, namely

> *The SRS will verify whether or not the proposed plan of study satisfies the requirements of the degree that the student is seeking.*

We didn't model Degree as a class—recall that we debated whether or not to do so back in Chapter 10, and ultimately decided against it. Nor, for that matter, do we reflect the requirements of a particular degree program in our model. Let's look at what it would take to do so properly at this time.

Researching the way in which our university specifies degree program requirements, we learn the following:

- Every degree program specifies five "core" courses—that is, courses that a student *must* take. For example, for the degree of Master of Science in Information Technology (MSIT), students are required to complete the following five core courses:

  - Analysis of Algorithms

  - Application Programming Design

  - Computer Systems Architecture

  - Data Structures

  - Information Systems Project Management

- Students are also expected to select an area of specialization, known as a **concentration**, within their degree program. For the MSIT degree, our university offers three different concentrations:

  - Object Technology

  - Database Management Systems

  - Networking and Communications

- Each concentration in turn specifies three mandatory, concentration-specific courses. For the MSIT degree with a concentration in Object Technology, the required concentration-specific courses are

  - Object Methods for Software Development

  - Advanced Java Programming

  - Object Database Management Systems

- Finally, the student must take two additional electives to bring his or her course total to ten.

Phew! To model all of these interdependencies would require a fairly complex class diagram structure, as shown in Figure 12-1.

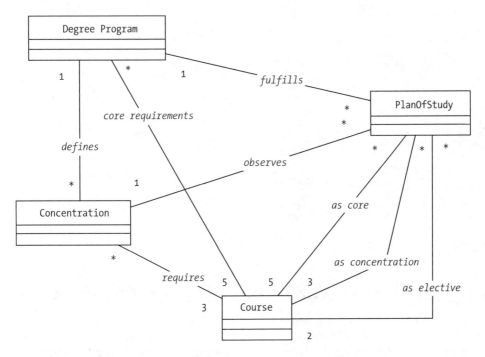

Figure 12-1. *Modeling degree program requirements proves to be rather complicated!*

We go back to our project sponsors—the future users of the SRS—and break the news to them that we've just uncovered a previously missed requirement that is going to significantly increase the complexity and cost of our automation effort. The sponsors decide that having the SRS verify the correctness of a student's plan of study is too ambitious a goal; they instead decide that a student will use the SRS to submit a ***proposed*** plan of study, but that his or her advisor will then be responsible for ***manually*** verifying and approving it. So, all we wind up having to do to correct our SRS class diagram as last presented is to add one attribute to the PlanOfStudy class, reflecting the date on which it was approved, and a new *approves* association connecting the Professor class to the PlanOfStudy class, and we're good to go!

Note that we don't need to add an approvePlan method to the PlanOfStudy class, because as discussed in Chapter 10 we may assume the presence of "set" methods for all attributes; the setDateApproved method would suffice for marking a plan as approved. And, the *approves* association between the PlanOfStudy and Professor classes (see the diagram excerpt in Figure 12-2) ensures us that each PlanOfStudy object will maintain a handle on the Professor object who actually approved the plan on the date indicated.

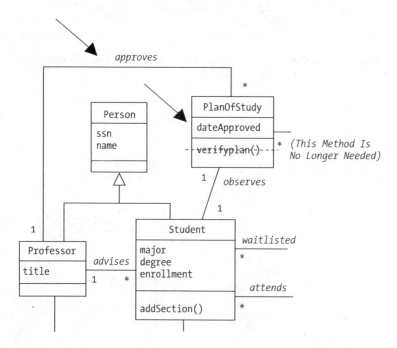

Figure 12-2. *Making minor adjustments to the SRS class diagram*

Reusing Models: A Word About Design Patterns

As we discussed in Chapter 2, when learning about something new, we automatically search our "mental archive" for other abstractions/models that we've previously built and mastered, to look for similarities that we can build upon. This technique of comparing features to find an abstraction that is similar enough to be reused effectively is known as **pattern reuse**. As it turns out, pattern reuse is an important technique for object-oriented software development.

Let's say that after we finish up our SRS class diagram, we're called upon to model a system for a small travel agency, Wild Blue Yonder (WBY). As a brand-new travel agency, WBY wishes to offer a level of customer service above and beyond their well-established competitors, and so they decide to enable their customers to make travel reservations online via the Web (most of WBY's competitors take such requests over the phone).

For any given travel package—let's say a ten-day trip to Ireland—WBY offers numerous trips throughout the year. Each trip has a maximum client capacity, so if a client can't get a confirmed seat for one of the trips, he or she may request a position on a first-come, first-served wait list.

In order to keep track of each client's overall experience with WBY, the travel agency plans on following up with each client after a trip to conduct a satisfaction survey, and will ask the client to rate his or her experience for that trip on a scale of 1 to 10, with 10 being outstanding. By doing so, WBY can determine which trips are the most successful, so as to offer them more frequently in the future, as well as perhaps eliminating those that are less popular. WBY will also be able to make more informed recommendations for future trips that a given client is likely to enjoy by studying that client's travel satisfaction history.

In reflecting on the requirements for this system, we experience déjà vu! We recognize that many aspects of the WBY system requirements are similar to those of the SRS. In fact, we're able to reuse the overall structure, or ***pattern***, of the SRS object model by making the following class substitutions:

- Substitute TravelPackage for Course

- Substitute Trip for Section

- Substitute Client for Student

- Substitute TripRecord for TranscriptEntry

- Substitute TravelHistory for Transcript

Note that all of the relationships among these classes—their names, types, and even their multiplicities—remain unchanged from the SRS class diagram (see Figure 12-3).

Such an exact match is exceptionally rare when reusing design patterns; don't be afraid to change some things (eliminate classes or associations, change multiplicities, and so forth) in order to facilitate reuse of a similar, but not identical, pattern.

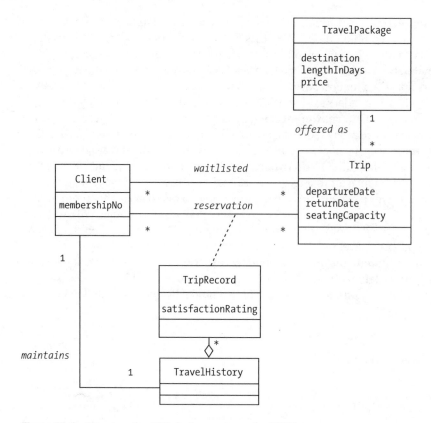

Figure 12-3. *Reusing the SRS design pattern for WBY*

Having recognized the similarities between these two designs, we're poised to take advantage of quite a bit of reuse with regard to the code of these two systems, as well. In fact, had we anticipated the need for developing these two systems prior to developing either one, we could have taken steps up front to develop a ***generic*** pattern that could have been used as the basis for both systems, as well as any future reservation systems we might be called upon to model, as illustrated in Figure 12-4.

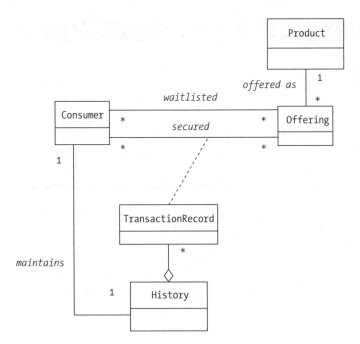

Figure 12-4. *A general-purpose class diagram for reservation systems*

Many useful, reusable patterns have been studied and documented; before embarking on a new object modeling project, it's worth exploring whether any of these may be a suitable starting point. The "Other Recommended Reading" section in Chapter 18 suggests some references that you might wish to explore on this topic.

Summary

Learning to model a problem from the perspective of objects is a bit like learning to ride a bicycle. You can read all the books ever published on the subject of successful bicycle riding, but until you actually sit on the seat, grab the handlebars, and start pedaling, you won't get a real sense of what it means to ride. You'll probably wobble at first, but with a bit of a boost from training wheels or a friendly hand to steady you, you'll be riding off on your own with time. The same is true of object modeling: with practice, you'll get an intuitive feel for what makes a good candidate class, a useful scenario, and so on.

In this chapter, we

- Discussed techniques for verifying the accuracy and completeness of a class diagram

- Looked at how object models can be reused/adapted to other problems with similar requirements

Exercises

1. Conduct a walk-through of one of the class diagrams that you prepared as an exercise for Chapter 10—either the Prescription Tracking System (PTS) case study presented in Appendix B or the problem area whose requirements you defined for exercise 3 in Chapter 1—with a classmate or coworker. Report on any insights that you gained as a result of doing so.

2. Think of two other problem areas where the Reservation pattern that we identified for the Wild Blue Yonder travel agency might also apply. What adjustments, if any, would you need to make to the Reservation pattern in order to use it in those situations?

PART 3

■■■

Translating an Object Blueprint into Java Code

CHAPTER 13

Rounding Out Your Java Knowledge

You received a solid introduction to Java syntax in Part 1 of this book, particularly as it pertains to illustrating fundamental object concepts. Before diving into the specifics of coding the Student Registration System (SRS), however, I'd like to round out your knowledge with a few more details about the Java language that we'll subsequently take advantage of when coding the SRS.

In this chapter, you'll learn about

- The architecture of a typical Java application

- The nature and purpose of Java Archive (JAR) files

- The mechanics of Java documentation comments

- The object nature of `Strings`

- A special type of class called an `enum` that can be used to enumerate the explicit values that a particular variable is allowed to assume

- How we can form highly complex expressions by chaining messages

- How objects refer to themselves from within their own methods

- The nature of Java run-time exceptions, and how to gracefully handle them, including defining and using custom exception types

- Several approaches for providing input to command line–driven "GUI-less" programs

- Some important features of the Java `Object` class

- Behind-the-scenes details of JVM operation

- The nature and use of inner classes

Java-Specific Terminology

As mentioned previously, the purpose of this book is to educate you about object principles that are, for the most part, language neutral, and so I've favored generic (and sometimes informal) OO terminology over Java-specific terminology as used by Sun Microsystems. That being said,

I'd now like to expose you to *Java-specific terminology* for a number of basic object concepts as used by Sun in their reference documentation (in particular, in the formal Java Language Specification [JLS]). Table 13-1 compares generic OO terminology with Java-specific terminology.

Table 13-1. *Comparing Generic OO vs. Java Terminology*

Generic OO Terminology Used in this Book	Formal Java-Specific Terminology Used by Sun Microsystems	Used to Describe the Following Notion
attribute	field, instance variable	A variable that is created once per object—that is, per each instance of a class. Each object has its own separate set of instance variables.
static variable (informal: static attribute)	static field, class variable	A variable that exists only once per class.
method	instance method	A function that is invoked on an object.
static method	class method	A function that can be called on a class as a whole, without reference to a specific object. Class methods can neither call instance methods nor access instance variables.
feature	member	Those components of a class that can potentially be inherited—for example, instance/class variables and instance/class methods, but *not* constructors.

To round out this terminology, the term **local variable** refers to a variable that is declared inside of a method, and hence is locally scoped relative to that method. (Method parameters are also local to the method, but Java distinguishes them from "local variables.") Local variables are neither static nor instance variables.

Here's a code snippet that illustrates all three variable types:

```
public class Student {
  // Attributes.
  private String name;  // <== name is an instance variable
  private static int totalStudents;  // <== totalStudents is a
                                     //      class variable

  // Methods.
  public void foo(int y) { // <== parameter y is local to the method
    int x;  // <== x is a local variable
    // etc.
  }

  // etc.
}
```

CLARITY OF TERMINOLOGY

I personally find some of the Java-specific terminology as set forth within the JLS to not be as intuitive as the generic OO terminology for a given concept—for example, the manner in which the term "inheritance" is formally used in the JLS versus in general OO discussion.

In general OO terms, if a class A declares three attributes (instance variables), one constructor, and two (instance) methods with the accessibilities indicated here:

```java
public class A {
    private int x;
    protected int y;
    public int z;

    public A() { ... }

    private void foo() { ... }

    public void bar() { ... }

    // etc.
}
```

and we were to then derive a subclass B from this class as follows:

```java
public class B extends A {
    // Add one new attribute ...
    private int w;

    // ... and one new method.
    public void whatever() { ... }
}
```

then, as you learned in Chapter 5, the "bone structure" of an instance of B will indeed consist of *four* data elements—int x, int y, int z, and int w—but x will not be referenceable as a symbol within the scope of B because it has private accessibility in A. Thus, we'll use the public accessor methods for x that we inherited from A whenever we want to access the value of x in B.

```java
public class B extends A {
    // Add one new attribute ...
    private int w;

    // ... and one new method.
    public void whatever() {
        // Access our own value of x.
        System.out.println(getX());
        // etc.
    }
}
```

Generally speaking, we can describe this OO phenomenon as follows: "Class B inherits all attributes of A, but can only directly refer to an inherited attribute by name if that attribute is not declared to have `private` accessibility in A." However, in the formal nomenclature of the JLS, we would instead observe that "Class B does **not** inherit attribute x, because x has `private` accessibility in A." Yet, the JLS acknowledges that x does indeed become part of the "bone structure" of an instance of B—unfortunately, however, the JLS simply provides no alternative terminology to refer to this phenomenon. Therefore, I prefer to use the term "inheritance" in the *general OO sense*, to refer to anything that becomes part of the "bone structure" of an instance of a subclass B based on its presence in superclass A, *whether or not it is directly accessible by name in B*—that is, whether or not its name, as a symbol, is in scope as far as the compiler is concerned when B is being compiled.

Returning to Sun's definition of the term "member" to refer to (among other things) "a variable or function that can potentially be inherited by subclasses," I've labeled those items in class A that would or would not be considered to be a member:

```
public class B extends A { ... }

public class A {
    private int x;   // x is a member of A, but not of B
    protected int y; // y is a member of both A and B
    public int z;    // z is a member of both A and B

    public A() { ... } // not a member of A; and, since
                       // constructors are NOT members,
                       // they cannot be inherited by B,
                       // hence this is not a member of B

    private void foo() { ... } // a member of A but not B

    public void bar() { ... }  // a member of both A and B

    // etc.
}
```

In summary, my preference is to *favor the use of terminology that is clear and intuitive*, whether such terminology is formal ("class"); informal, but widely accepted ("attribute," "feature"); or terminology that I've crafted myself ("argument signature"). The key in each such case is to clearly communicate how the terminology that I am using may differ from formal—albeit less intuitive—terminology, so that my students and readers are well versed in both.

Java Application Architecture

In Part 1 of this book, we examined the anatomy of a trivially simple Java program, which consisted of a main method—containing the logic of our program—encapsulated within a class declaration:

```
public class Simple {
    public static void main(String[] args) {
        System.out.println("I LOVE Java!!!");
    }
}
```

We discussed that

- The source code to declare such a class resides in a file by the name of *Classname*.java (Simple.java, in this example).

- We compile this source code via the command

  ```
  javac Simple.java
  ```

  to produce a bytecode file named Simple.class.

- We run this program by launching the JVM to interpret/execute this bytecode via the command

  ```
  java Simple
  ```

A nontrivial Java application, such as the one we are about to build for the SRS, consists of *many* Java source files that, when compiled, yield *many* bytecode files, as follows:

- We typically have one .java/source code file for each of the *model classes* that we define in our UML class diagram. For the SRS application, for example, we'll have ten files:

  ```
  Course.java
  CourseCatalog.java
  Faculty.java
  Person.java
  Professor.java
  ScheduleOfClasses.java
  Section.java
  Student.java
  Transcript.java
  TranscriptEntry.java
  ```

  We'll review the code for each of these SRS model classes in detail in Chapters 14 and 15.

- We typically need one or more classes to be involved with *establishing connectivity to persistent data storage* of some form (e.g., record-oriented ASCII files, or XML files, or a relational database). We'll have one such class for the SRS—SRSDataAccess—and we'll discuss this class in detail in Chapter 15, within the context of *model–data access layer separation*.

- We also typically craft a separate .java source code file to house the class declaration for each of the primary windows comprising the *graphical user interface (GUI)* of an application, if any. For the SRS application, we'll declare two such classes—MainFrame and PasswordPopup—which we'll review in detail in Chapter 16 when we discuss the importance of *model–view separation*.

- We'll typically have a separate `.java` source code file to house the class that encapsulates the official `main` method, which as we know serves as the application's starting point.

  - One of the primary responsibilities of the `main` method is to instantiate the core objects needed to fulfill a system's mission (the user's subsequent interactions with the application may cause additional objects to come to life as the application executes).

  - The `main` method may also be responsible for displaying the startup window of a GUI, if our application has one; establishing connections with persistent storage, if needed; and other application-initialization sorts of things.

  Our driver class for the SRS application will be named SRS, and so of course its declaration will be housed in a file named `SRS.java`.

- Finally, we often have additional "helper" classes to provide behind-the-scenes application support. With the SRS, we'll have a need for four such source code files:

  ```
  EnrollmentStatus.java
  InvalidStudentException.java
  SRSInitializationException.java
  StudentPersistenceException.java
  ```

  All told, by the time we reach the end of Chapter 16, we will have created a total of 18 source code (`.java`) *files, compiling them into bytecode and integrating them into a single SRS application* with a GUI and a way to persist the state of our objects from one SRS application session to the next.

Java Archive (JAR) Files

The Java bytecode comprising an application is commonly bundled and delivered in the form of a **Java Archive (JAR) file**. Let's use a simple application as an example, consisting of the following:

- Three user-defined types: the classes Person, Student, and Professor

- A `main` method wrapper class called MyApp

to illustrate the use of JAR files. The code for our simple example is as follows:

```java
public class Person {
    private String name;

    public void setName(String n) {
        name = n;
    }
}

public class Student extends Person {
    private Professor advisor;

    public void setAdvisor(Professor p) {
```

```
        advisor = p;
    }
}

public class Professor extends Person {
    private String title;

    public void setTitle(String t) {
        title = t;
    }
}
```

This code supports the following program:

```
public class MyApp {
    public static void main(String[] args) {
        Professor p = new Professor();
        Student s = new Student();
        s.setAdvisor(p);
    }
}
```

Creating a JAR File

We start by compiling our code:

javac *.java

Then, to create a JAR file, we type

jar <u>cvf</u> *jarfilename*.jar *list_of_files_to_be_included_in_jar_file*

where the command-line argument cvf indicates that

- We wish to c*reate* a JAR file.

- We wish the command to be v*erbose*—that is, we want the command to display everything that is going on as the JAR file is created.

- We are designating the (f*ile)name* of the JAR file that is to be created.

For example, to place our simple application's bytecode into a JAR file named MyJar.jar, we'd type

jar cvf MyJar.jar Person.class Student.class Professor.class MyApp.class

(Note that the bytecode files can be listed in any order.) Alternatively, we could use a wildcard character to include multiple files at once:

jar cvf MyJar.jar *.class

Because of our use of the v(erbose) command option, the following output would be displayed by the jar utility:

```
added manifest
adding: Person.class(in = 222) (out= 178)(deflated 19%)
adding: Student.class(in = 419) (out= 287)(deflated 31%)
adding: Professor.class(in = 219) (out= 176)(deflated 19%)
adding: MyApp.class(in = 1751) (out= 1021)(deflated 41%)
```

Note that we can include any type of file that we wish in a JAR file, not only bytecode files. For example, if we want to archive our source code along with our bytecode, we can type the command

```
jar cvf MyJar.jar *.class *.java
```

A JAR file is a `.zip` file in disguise. While we'll create, inspect, and (occasionally) extract individual bytecode files from a JAR file via the command line `jar` utility that comes with the Java Software Development Kit (SDK), most standard *Zip* utilities are also able to read/extract files from JAR files. Thus, as with `.zip` files, we can store literally any file type within a JAR file: source code, bytecode, image files—even other JAR files!

Inspecting the Contents of a JAR File

To inspect and list the contents of a JAR file without "unjarring" (extracting) files, we use the command

```
jar tvf jarfilename.jar
```

where the t command-line argument indicates that we wish to see a *table of contents* for the named JAR file, for example:

```
jar tvf MyJar.jar
```

Here's the output:

```
   0 Sun Feb 20 13:55:34 EST 2005 META-INF/
  71 Sun Feb 20 13:55:34 EST 2005 META-INF/MANIFEST.MF
 222 Mon Feb 07 16:07:16 EST 2005 Person.class
 419 Fri Feb 18 10:06:02 EST 2005 Student.class
 219 Mon Feb 07 16:07:16 EST 2005 Professor.class
1751 Wed Feb 06 07:36:44 EST 2002 MyApp.class
```

Once our JAR file is created, it is a simple matter to share that file with a user or another developer, perhaps by sending it to him or her as an email attachment or by storing it in a shared location on a network file system.

Using the Bytecode Contained Within a JAR File

To inform the JVM that we want to *use* the bytecode within a JAR file, we use a command-line option to set an environment variable called the **CLASSPATH** as follows:

```
java -cp path_to_jar_file class_containing_main_method
```

For example, if we store our `MyJar.jar` file in a shared directory by the name of `S:\applications`, then to execute the `MyApp` program that is stored *within* that JAR file, we would type

```
java -cp S:\applications\MyJar.jar MyApp
```

If more than one JAR file is to be referenced at the same time, the references are separated by semicolons under DOS and colons under Unix. For instance, here's an example under DOS:

```
java -cp S:\applications\MyJar.jar;T:\stuff\AnotherJar.jar SomeApp
```

The CLASSPATH can also be set globally for all applications run by a particular user on a given computer system. Please see Appendix C for details.

Extracting Content from a JAR File

Note that we need *not* extract bytecode from a JAR file in order to use it; the JVM is able to retrieve individual bytecode files from *within* JAR files as needed. However, should we ever wish to extract selected files from a JAR file—say that Java source files were included, and we'd like to work with individual source files—we'd type the command

```
jar xvf jarfilename.jar space_separated_list_of_files_to_be_extracted
```

for example:

```
jar xvf MyJar.jar Student.java Professor.java
```

where the x command option indicates that we wish to *extract* files. To extract *all* source code in a JAR file, we'd type

```
jar xvf MyApp.jar *.java
```

To extract *everything* from a JAR file, we'd type

```
jar xvf MyApp.jar
```

Note that if you extract the contents of a JAR file into a directory that contains files with the same names as those you are extracting, the extracted files will automatically *overwrite* similarly named files—and you will *not* be warned beforehand! So, it's a good idea to make a backup copy of the files in a directory before "unjarring" a JAR file there or, alternatively, to always "unjar" a file in a separate empty directory.

"Jarring" Entire Directory Hierarchies

It's possible to incorporate the contents of an entire directory hierarchy (all subfolders) into a single JAR file via the command

```
jar cvf jarFileName topLevelDirectoryName
```

For example, the SRS code examples that accompany this book are stored within a hierarchy of directories on my computer under a parent directory named C:\My Documents\BJO Second Edition\Code. To create a JAR file containing all of the code, I'd type the command

```
jar cvf BJOcode.jar "C:\My Documents\BJO Second Edition\Code"
```

(Note that you use double quotes to surround a path if it contains blank spaces.) Or, alternatively, I could type

```
cd "C:\My Documents\BJO Second Edition"
jar cvf BJOcode.jar Code
```

The resultant output, excerpted here, illustrates how all of the subdirectories are traversed so as to include their contents in the JAR file:

```
added manifest
adding: Code/(in = 0) (out= 0)(stored 0%)
adding: Code/Ch14/(in = 0) (out= 0)(stored 0%)
adding: Code/Ch14/SRS/(in = 0) (out= 0)(stored 0%)
adding: Code/Ch14/SRS/Course.java(in = 2784) (out= 953)(deflated 65%)
adding: Code/Ch14/SRS/EnrollmentStatus.java(in = 872) (out= 438)(deflated 49%)
adding: Code/Ch14/SRS/Person.java(in = 1223) (out= 513)(deflated 58%)
adding: Code/Ch14/SRS/Professor.java(in = 2967) (out= 1122)(deflated 62%)
etc.
adding: Code/Ch15/(in = 0) (out= 0)(stored 0%)
adding: Code/Ch15/SRS/(in = 0) (out= 0)(stored 0%)
adding: Code/Ch15/SRS/Course.java(in = 2784) (out= 953)(deflated 65%)
adding: Code/Ch15/SRS/CourseCatalog.java(in = 1640) (out= 713)(deflated 56%)
etc.
adding: Code/Ch16/(in = 0) (out= 0)(stored 0%)
adding: Code/Ch16/BeanExample.java(in = 668) (out= 378)(deflated 43%)
adding: Code/Ch16/BorderLayoutLayout.java(in = 1272) (out= 470)(deflated 63%)
adding: Code/Ch16/BorderLayoutLayout2.java(in = 1279) (out= 476)(deflated 62%)
adding: Code/Ch16/Calculator1.java(in = 2449) (out= 966)(deflated 60%)
adding: Code/Ch16/Calculator2.java(in = 2462) (out= 921)(deflated 62%)
adding: Code/Ch16/Calculator3.java(in = 3514) (out= 1229)(deflated 65%)
etc.
adding: Code/Ch16/SRS/(in = 0) (out= 0)(stored 0%)
adding: Code/Ch16/SRS/Course.java(in = 2784) (out= 953)(deflated 65%)
adding: Code/Ch16/SRS/CourseCatalog.java(in = 1640) (out= 713)(deflated 56%)
etc.
```

Javadoc Comments

In Chapter 2, I briefly mentioned the notion of *Java documentation comments* (aka *javadoc comments*), a special type of comment from which we can automatically generate HTML documentation for an application. Let's explore how this is accomplished.

Java documentation comments, like traditional comments, can span multiple lines of code. However, javadoc comments start with a slash followed by *two* asterisks (/**) and end with an asterisk followed by slash (*/). Within the body of a javadoc comment, we are able to use a number of predefined **javadoc tags** (whose names start with @) to control how the resultant HTML will look.

Here's a simple `Person` class that incorporates javadoc comments (**bolded**):

```
// Person.java

/**
 * A person is a human being. We might use a Person to represent a student
 * or a professor in an academic setting.
 */
public class Person {
    //------------
    // Attributes.
    //------------

    /**
     * A person's legal name. Typically represented as
     * "FirstName I. LastName".
     */
    public String name;

    /**
     * A person's age in years. No matter how imminent a person's next birthday
     * is, the person's age will always reflect how old he/she was at his/her
     * most recent birthday.
     */
    private int age;

    //-------------
    // Constructor.
    //-------------
    /**
     * This constructor initializes attributes name and age.
     * @param n the Person's name, in first name - middle initial -
     * last name order.
     * @param a the Person's age.
     */
    public Person(String n, int a) {
        name = n;
        age = a;
    }

    /**
     * This method is used to determine a person's age in dog years.
     */
    public double dogYears() {
        return age/7.0;
    }
}
```

Here are some observations about the preceding example:

- public features automatically appear in javadoc-generated documentation; private features, by default, do not. Thus, despite the fact that we've documented the private age attribute in javadoc style, age will not be reflected in the resultant HTML documentation, as we'll see in a moment.

- @param is a javadoc-specific tag used to define the purpose of a particular parameter to a method. The general syntax for its use is @param *parameterName description*.

- Intervening blank lines and/or non-javadoc comments, if present, are ignored by the javadoc utility:

```
/**
 * A person's legal name. Typically represented as
     "FirstName I. LastName".
 */
// Having a non-javadoc comment here won't hurt; neither will
// intervening blank lines.

public String name;
```

To generate HTML documentation for this class, we use the command line javadoc utility that comes standard with the Java Development Kit (JDK). We can type the command

```
javadoc Person.java
```

to generate documentation for a single class, or we may type

```
javadoc *.java
```

if documentation is to be generated for more than one .java file at the same time.

A number of files are automatically generated as a result of typing a javadoc command, as illustrated by the following output:

```
C:\> javadoc Person.java
Loading source file Person.java...
Constructing Javadoc information...
Standard Doclet version 1.5.0-beta2
Building tree for all the packages and classes...
Generating Person.html...
Generating package-frame.html...
Generating package-summary.html...
Generating package-tree.html...
Generating constant-values.html...
Building index for all the packages and classes...
Generating overview-tree.html...
Generating index-all.html...
Generating deprecated-list.html...
Building index for all classes...
Generating allclasses-frame.html...
Generating allclasses-noframe.html...
Generating index.html...
Generating help-doc.html...
Generating stylesheet.css...
```

To view the resultant documentation, use a web browser to load the `index.html` file, which will bring up the "home page" for our documentation, as shown in Figure 13-1.

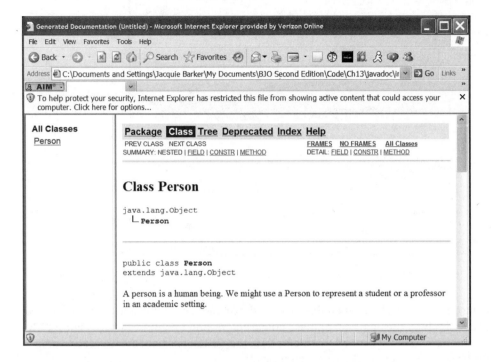

Figure 13-1. *Viewing the index.html page for our Person class*

Let's explore this page:

- At the top of the page is the inheritance hierarchy to which the `Person` class belongs (in this case, `Person` is shown as being directly derived from the `Object` class of the `java.lang` package).

- Next is the narrative description of the class from the javadoc comment that precedes the `public class Person { ...` declaration.

Scrolling down a bit further on the page, as illustrated in Figure 13-2, are lists of all `public` attributes, constructors, and methods belonging to this class under the headings Field Summary, Constructor Summary, and Method Summary, respectively. Recall that since `age` was declared to be a `private` attribute, it is omitted by default. To include ***all*** features in the generated documentation, whether `public` or not, simply include the `–private` flag on the `javadoc` command:

```
javadoc –private Person.java
```

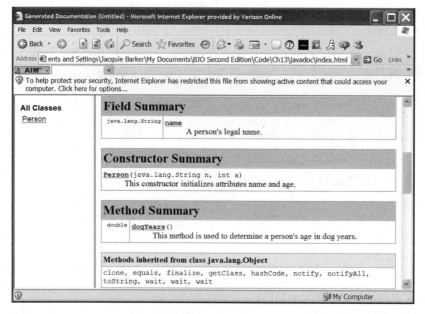

Figure 13-2. *Viewing the field, constructor, and method summaries for the* Person *class*

Scrolling down a bit further yet on the page, as shown in Figures 13-3 and 13-4, we can see additional details about the fields (attributes), constructors, and methods. Note in Figure 13-3 that our use of the @param tag in our constructor documentation has paid off: we see an explanation of each parameter under the Parameters heading.

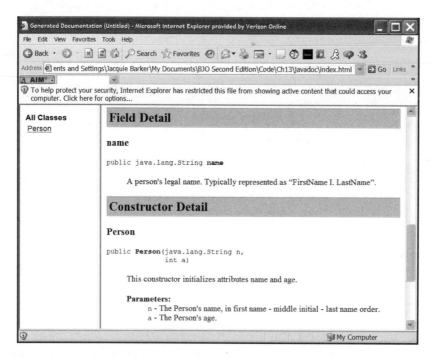

Figure 13-3. *Additional details (field and constructor related) concerning the* Person *class*

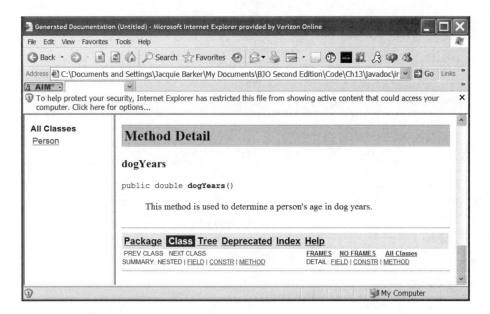

Figure 13-4. *Additional details (method related) concerning the* Person *class*

Clicking the Index link at the top of the page, as shown in Figure 13-5, brings up an alternative view of our documentation, as shown in Figure 13-6. Here, we are able to navigate through an alphabetical list of all class, attribute, constructor, and method names. Had we generated javadoc documentation for multiple classes—say, for all of the classes comprising the SRS—then *all* of these classes' *combined* features would be navigable via this *consolidated* index view.

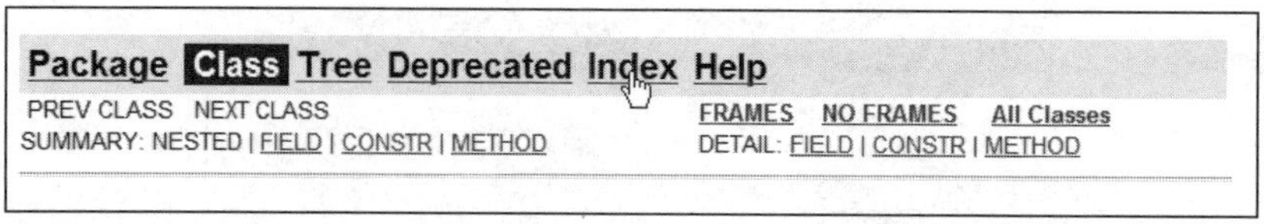

Package Class Tree Deprecated In**d**ex Help
PREV CLASS   NEXT CLASS   FRAMES   NO FRAMES   All Classes
SUMMARY: NESTED | FIELD | CONSTR | METHOD   DETAIL: FIELD | CONSTR | METHOD

Figure 13-5. *Clicking the Index link . . .*

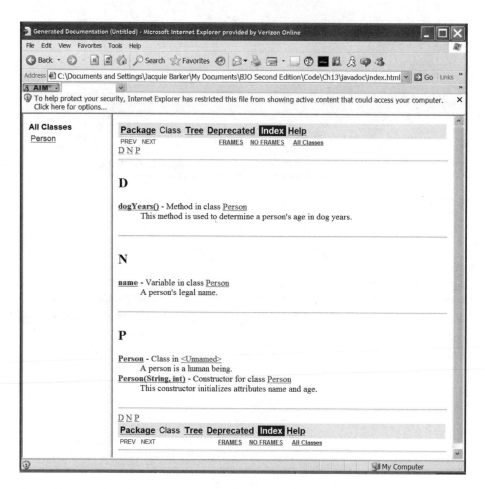

Figure 13-6. *. . . displays an alphabetical listing of all symbols*

Please visit Sun's web site (http://java.sun.com/j2se/1.5.0/docs/guide/javadoc/ index.html) for an in-depth tutorial on how to use javadoc comments. And, for tips on viewing the standard Java documentation for all of Java's predefined classes, which is similarly browser-friendly, please see Appendix C.

The Object Nature of Strings

Chapter 2 introduced the String type along with eight other primitive Java types: int, double, char, boolean, float, byte, short, and long. At that time, I emphasized the fact that the symbol String must be capitalized, whereas the other eight type names are expressed in all lowercase. What I ***didn't*** make clear at the time is that String is a ***reference type***—that is, variables declared to be of type String refer to ***objects***. (Recall from our discussion in Chapter 3 that variables declared to be one of the primitive types in Java do ***not*** refer to objects.)

```
// s refers to an OBJECT of type String.
String s = "Java";
```

Thus, String is said to be a reference type whose structural and behavioral characteristics are defined by the String class, one of the classes defined within the core java.lang package.

Operations on Strings

As you learned in Chapter 2, the plus sign (+) operator is used to concatenate String values:

```
String x = "foo";
String y = "bar";
String z = x + y + "!";   // z assumes the value "foobar!"
```

But now that you appreciate the object nature of Strings, you can also take advantage of the numerous methods that are declared by the String class for manipulating Strings:

- int length(): When applied to a String reference, returns the length of the String as an integer:

  ```
  // Continuing the previous example, where z equals "foobar!":
  int len = z.length();   // len now equals 7
  ```

- boolean startsWith(String s): Returns true if the String to which this method is applied starts with the String provided as an argument to the method, and false otherwise:

  ```
  String s = "foobar";

  // This will evaluate to true.
  if (s.startsWith("foo")) ...
  ```

- boolean endsWith(String s): Returns true if the String to which this method is applied ends with the String provided as an argument to the method, and false otherwise:

  ```
  String s = "foobar";

  // This will evaluate to true.
  if (s.endsWith("bar")) ...
  ```

- boolean contains(String s): Returns true if the String to which this method is applied contains the String provided as an argument to the method, and false otherwise:

  ```
  String s = "foobar";

  // This will evaluate to true.
  if (s.contains("oo")) ...
  ```

- `int indexOf(String s)`: Returns a non-negative integer value indicating the starting character position (counting from 0) at which the `String` provided as an argument is found within the `String` to which this method is applied, or a negative value (typically –1) if the `String` argument is not found:

```
String s = "foobar";
int i = s.indexOf("bar");  // i will equal 3
int j = s.indexOf("cat");  // j will equal -1
int k = s.indexOf("f");    // k will equal 0
```

- `String replace(char old, char new)`: Creates a brand-new `String` object in which all instances of the `old` character are replaced with the `new` character—the original `String`'s value is unaffected:

```
String s = "o1o2o3o4";
// Note use of single quotes around characters
// vs. double quotes around Strings.
String p = s.replace('o', 'x');  // p assumes the value "x1x2x3x4", while
                                  // s retains the value "o1o2o3o4"
```

- `String substring(int i)`: Creates a brand-new `String` object by copying a substring of an existing `String` object starting at the ith position through the end of the existing `String`:

```
String s = "foobar";
String p = s.substring(3); // p assumes the value "bar"
```

- `String substring(int i, int j)`: Creates a brand-new `String` object by copying a substring of an existing `String` object starting at the ith and stopping just *before* the jth position:

```
String s = "foobar";
String p = s.substring(1, 5);  // p assumes the value "ooba";
```

- `char charAt(int index)`: Returns the char(acter) value located at the ith position within the `String`:

```
String s = "foobar";

// Iterate through a String character by character.
for (int i = 0; i < s.length(); i++) {
    System.out.println(s.charAt(i));
}
```

Here's the output:

```
f
o
o
b
a
r
```

- boolean equals(String): Compares the value of the String object to which this method is applied with the value of the String object whose reference is passed in as an argument; returns true if the values are the same, and false if they are not.

```
String s = "dog";
String t = "cat";
String u = "dog";

// This will evaluate to true ...
if (s.equals(u)) { ...

// ... and this, to false.
if (s.equals(t)) { ...
```

Note that we generally should ***avoid*** using the double equal sign (==) operator to test the equality of two String objects' values—that is, the following can yield seemingly inconsistent results, depending on how we've instantiated String objects s1 and s2:

```
// We generally want to AVOID doing this ...
if (s1 == s2) { ...
```

This is because the == operator, when used to compare reference types such as Strings, or Persons, or generic Objects, is actually comparing their ***addresses in memory*** to see if the two variables are referring to the ***same exact object***, as illustrated in Figure 13-7.

x = = y ? true

x = = y ? false

Figure 13-7. *The result of evaluating* x == y *can vary depending on how many* String *instances are involved.*

We'll revisit this notion for objects in general, and for Strings specifically, a bit later in the chapter.

Strings Are Immutable

Strings are said to be **immutable**—that is, the value of a particular String object cannot be changed once it has first been assigned at the time of instantiation. When we *seem* to be programmatically modifying an existing String object's value, we are actually creating a *new* String object with the desired value.

Let's look at an example of how this works. The following line of code would result in a String object with the value "Foo" being created somewhere in memory, as illustrated in Figure 13-8:

```
String x = "Foo";
```

Figure 13-8. *A String object has been instantiated with the literal value "Foo".*

Continuing our example, this next line of code would result in a *second* String object with the value "Foobar!" being created somewhere else in memory:

```
// We're not really CHANGING the value of the specific String object
// originally referenced by x; rather, we're creating a new String
// object with the desired value for x to reference.
x = x + "bar!";
```

The original "Foo" String would still exist for some period of time, but it is no longer directly accessible to us by reference and will soon be garbage collected (see Figure 13-9).

Figure 13-9. *When we assign a new value to String reference x, we're actually instantiating a new String object.*

The net result is the same from the programmer's perspective—namely, that the value of x will now be "Foobar!" as far as we're concerned:

```
System.out.println(x);
```

Here's the output:

Foobar!

The implication of this behind-the-scenes phenomenon is that building up long String values through iterative String concatenation can be quite inefficient. As an example, consider the following code:

```java
// Initialize s to an empty String.
String s = "";

for (int x = 0; x < 10; x++) {
    // Append another digit to s.
    s = s + x;
}

System.out.println(s);
```

Here's the output:

0123456789

With each successive iteration of the preceding for loop, we "change" the value of s by creating yet another String object: "0" in the first iteration, "01" in the second iteration, and so forth. By the time the loop is finished, we'll have created ***ten separate* String *objects, nine*** of which are waiting around to be garbage collected! This is illustrated in Figure 13-10.

For this reason, the java.util package provides a special-purpose class for iteratively building up the value of a single String instance: the StringBuffer class.

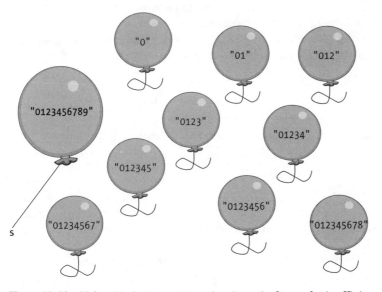

Figure 13-10. *Using* String *concatenation iteratively can be inefficient.*

The StringBuffer Class

Let's rewrite our previous example of concatenating digits using the StringBuffer class instead. Remember that we have to include the import directive:

```
import java.util.StringBuffer;
```

in whatever class this code is found:

```
// Instantiate an empty StringBuffer.
StringBuffer sb = new StringBuffer();

for (int x = 0; x < 10; x++) {
    // Append another digit to sb.
    sb.append(x);
}

// Extract the new String value from the StringBuffer.
String result = sb.toString();

// Let's see what we got!
System.out.println(result);
```

Our output will be the same as with the previous example:

```
0123456789
```

However, by switching to the StringBuffer approach of incremental String concatenation, we've instantiated only one object—a single StringBuffer—rather than creating ten String objects, nine of which are effectively wasted, as was the case with the previous version of this code (recall Figure 13-10). When the number of iterations increases—say, from 10 to 10,000— the performance improvement in using a StringBuffer can be dramatic.

Note that once we've finished "assembling" the String value of interest in a StringBuffer, we use the toString method of the StringBuffer class to extract the value as a String object:

```
String result = sb.toString();
```

We may use the add method of the StringBuffer class to append expressions of literally any type to a StringBuffer instance, because the add method is overloaded: there's a version that accepts a String expression as an argument, a version that accepts an int expression, and so forth.

The StringTokenizer Class

Another handy String-related class provided by the java.util package is the StringTokenizer class. With this class, we're able to **parse** (break apart) a String into **tokens** (segments/substrings) based on arbitrary delimiters.

The easiest way to learn how to use this class is with an example. Again, we need to include the directive

```
import java.util.StringTokenizer;
```

in whatever class this code is found. I'll present the example in its entirety first, and then we'll walk through it step by step:

```java
String s = "This is a test.";
StringTokenizer st = new StringTokenizer(s);

while (st.hasMoreTokens()) {
    System.out.println(st.nextToken());
}
```

Here's the output:

```
This
is
a
test.
```

In the preceding example,

- The default StringTokenizer constructor takes one argument—the String value to be parsed—and parses along **white space** boundaries (blank spaces, tab characters, and the like).

  ```java
  String s = "This is a test.";
  StringTokenizer st = new StringTokenizer(s);
  ```

- We use the boolean hasMoreTokens method of the StringTokenizer class to ascertain whether or not we've reached the end of the particular String instance being parsed. This method returns true if there are more tokens remaining or false if the String being parsed has been exhausted.

  ```java
  while (st.hasMoreTokens()) {
  ```

- The String nextToken method is used to pluck out the next token/segment of the String.

  ```java
      System.out.println(st.nextToken());
  }
  ```

A second overloaded form of the constructor, StringTokenizer(String s, String delimiter) can be used if we want to specify a **specific** delimiter to be used when parsing a String example, to parse along slash (/) boundaries, as when perhaps parsing a date, we'd write as follows (observe that we enclose the delimiter, which can be **one or more** character within **double** quotes):

```java
String date = "11/17/1985";

// Note use of double quotes below.
StringTokenizer st = new StringTokenizer(date, "/");

while (st.hasMoreTokens()) {
    System.out.println(st.nextToken());
}
```

Here's the output:

```
11
17
1985
```

Note that the delimiter—/, in this example—is stripped off of each token.

As another example, to parse on the three-character delimiter, -#-, we'd write

```
String fruit = "apple-#-banana-#-cherry";
StringTokenizer st = new StringTokenizer(fruit, "-#-");

while (st.hasMoreTokens()) {
    System.out.println(st.nextToken());
}
```

Here's the output:

```
apple
banana
cherry
```

As our final example, let's assume that we're reading records one by one from a file, and we want to parse on tab characters only versus on all white space. We'd write code as follows:

```
// Pseudocode.
String record = read a record from a file;

// Parse on tabs only, not on all white space.
StringTokenizer st = new StringTokenizer(record, "\t");

while (st.hasMoreTokens()) {
    System.out.println(st.nextToken());
}
```

Assuming that record contains the following text (where *<tab>* indicates the presence of an invisible tab character):

Bill Jost*<tab>*123-45-6789*<tab>*Cleveland, Ohio

we'd observe the following output:

```
Bill Jost
3-45-6789
eland, Ohio
```

t the blank spaces between words have been left intact. Had we instead parsed this
h the default StringTokenizer, which parses on all white space,

```
// Pseudocode.
String record = read a record from a file;

// Parse on any/all white space.
StringTokenizer st = new StringTokenizer(record);

while (st.hasMoreTokens()) {
    System.out.println(st.nextToken());
}
```

we'd have gotten the following as output instead:

```
Bill
Jost
123-45-6789
Cleveland,
Ohio
```

StringTokenizers are particularly useful when reading and parsing structured records from data files. We'll use this technique in building our SRS application in Chapter 15.

Instantiating Strings and the String Literal Pool

There are two ways to instantiate String objects in Java. The first, which we've seen in use many times before, allows us to simply assign a literal value to a String variable:

```
String s = "I am a String!";
```

But, because Strings are objects, we may also use the new keyword to formally invoke an explicit String constructor, as follows:

```
String t = new String("I am a String, too!");
```

I'll refer to the first way of instantiating Strings—the way that ***doesn't*** use the new operator—as the ***shortcut method*** of String instantiation, and the second way as the ***formal method***.

There is a subtle difference in terms of what happens behind the scenes with these two methods of String instantiation. When we use the shortcut method of String instantiation

```
String x = "Foo"; // shortcut method
```

the JVM checks its String **literal pool**—a special place in the JVM's memory that enables automatic shared access to String objects—to see if there is already a String object in the literal pool with that exact same value. If there is already a String object in the literal pool with that exact same value, the JVM ***reuses*** that existing instance without creating a second. Conversely, if a matching instance is ***not*** found in the literal pool, the JVM creates one and places it in the literal pool. This is illustrated conceptually in Figure 13-11.

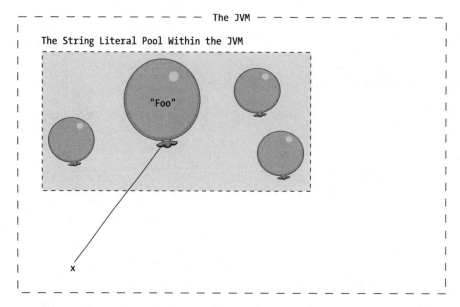

Figure 13-11. *Using the shortcut method of* String *instantiation inserts a newly created* String *object into the* String *literal pool.*

Let's now use the shortcut method a second time in the same program, in an attempt to instantiate another String object y with the same value as x:

```
String x = "Foo";
String y = "Foo"; // shortcut method again
```

This time, since the JVM finds an instance of a String with the value "Foo" in the literal pool from when we instantiated x, the JVM assigns y as a *second* handle to the *same* String object. This is illustrated conceptually in Figure 13-12.

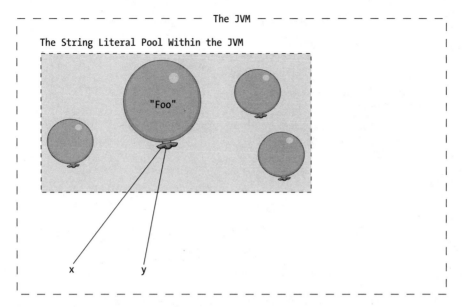

Figure 13-12. *Two shortcut instantiations of* String *with the same value wind up sharing the same* String *object within the* String *literal pool.*

Now, let's declare and instantiate a third String variable z in the same program, giving it the same value as x and y. However, rather than using the shortcut method for String instantiation with z, we'll use the new keyword to explicitly invoke a String constructor:

```
String x = "Foo";
String y = "Foo";
String z = new String("Foo");  // formal method this time
```

Our use of new instructs the JVM to ***bypass*** the literal pool—that is, a ***brand-new*** instance of a String object with the value "Foo" will be created ***outside*** of the literal pool, as illustrated in Figure 13-13.

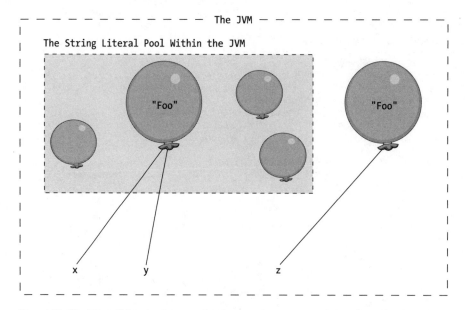

Figure 13-13. *Use of the new keyword to instantiate a* String, *on the other hand, explicitly creates a new* String *instance every time.*

Figure 13-14 completes our example, wherein we create a fourth, similarly valued String, w, again using the formal method:

```
String x = "Foo";
String y = "Foo";
String z = new String("Foo");
String w = new String("Foo");  // formal method again
```

As expected, our use of new once again circumvents the literal pool, and another distinct String object is created.

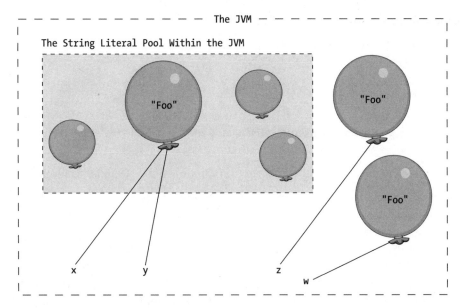

Figure 13-14. *Another distinct String object is created.*

Because we used a combination of formal and shortcut String instantiation in our example, we wound up with three different String objects in memory—one in the literal pool and two in the general memory of the JVM—all with the same value "Foo". Had we consistently used the shortcut approach when instantiating all four String objects, we'd have created only one such instance, and hence our JVM's memory would have been less cluttered. For this reason, the shortcut form of String instantiation is the preferred String construction technique in most situations.

Testing the Equality of Strings

I mentioned earlier that testing the equality of Strings using the == operator

```
String s1;
String s2;
// Instantiation details omitted ...
```

```
if (s1 == s2) { ...
```

rather than using the String class's equals method

```
String s1;
String s2;
// Instantiation details omitted ...
```

```
if (s1.equals(s2)) { ...
```

can yield seemingly puzzling results, if you don't understand the difference between the ***formal*** and ***shortcut*** methods for instantiating Strings. Using the four String references w, x, y, and z as represented in Figure 13-14, we get the following results from various tests of equality:

- Both of these first two tests, comparing x and y, evaluate to true:

```
// Are the VALUES of x and y the same?
if (x.equals(y)) { ... // true

// Are x and y referring to the SAME OBJECT?
if (x == y) { ... // true
```

because x and y not only have the same *value* "Foo", but also refer to the *same specific* String *object*.

- Where we see a difference is when we attempt to compare w and z in similar fashion:

```
// Are the VALUES of w and z the same?
if (w.equals(z)) { ... // true

// Are w and z referring to the SAME OBJECT?
if (w == z) { ... // FALSE!!!
```

The first test evaluates to true, because the *values* of w and z are equivalent, but the second test evaluates to false, because w and z refer to two *different* objects.

In the vast majority of cases, when we say we wish to compare two Strings, we typically mean that we want to compare their *values*, *not* their unique identities as objects. Thus, we virtually always compare Strings for equality using the equals method rather than the == operator.

We'll revisit this distinction between the == operator and the equals method once more, when we talk about generic Objects later in this chapter.

Message Chains

When we discussed Java expressions in Part 1 of this book, there was one form of expression omitted: **message chains**. The following is a repeat of the list of what constitutes Java expressions from Chapter 4, *highlighting* this latest addition:

- A constant: 7, false

- A char(acter) literal: 'A', '&'

- A String literal: "foo", ""

- The name of any variable declared to be of one of the predefined types that we've seen so far: myString, x

- Any one of the preceding that is modified by one of the Java unary operators: i++

- A message/method invocation on an object reference: z.length()

- Any two of the preceding that are combined with one of the Java binary operators: z.length() + 2

- *A "chain" of two or more messages concatenated by periods ("dots"):* p.getName().length()

- Any of the preceding types of expression enclosed in parentheses: (p.getName().length() + 2)

With Java (and other OOPLs), it is commonplace to form complex expressions by concatenating (and sometimes nesting) method calls. As with all expressions, we evaluate complex method expressions from innermost to outermost parentheses, left to right. So, based on the following code example:

```
// Instantiate three objects.
Student s = new Student();
Professor p = new Professor();
Department d = new Department();

// Set various of their attribute values.
d.setName("MATH");
p.setDepartment(d);
s.setAdvisor(p);
```

let's evaluate the following line of code:

```
s.setMajor(s.getAdvisor().getDepartment().getName());
```

- There are two levels of parentheses nesting in this example, but the inner sets of parentheses represent the argument signatures of the various methods being invoked, so we'll focus on evaluating the expression within the **outer** set of parentheses:

  ```
  s.getAdvisor().getDepartment().getName()
  ```

- Evaluating this expression from left to right, the first subexpression, s.getAdvisor(), returns a reference to a Professor object. It's as if we've simplified our original line of code as follows:

  ```
  // From:
  s.setMajor(s.getAdvisor().getDepartment().getName());

  // To:
  s.setMajor(p.getDepartment().getName());
  ```

- Next, we apply the getDepartment method to this Professor, which returns a reference to a Department; it's as if we've simplified the original line of code even further, as follows:

  ```
  // From:
  s.setMajor(p.getDepartment().getName());

  // To:
  s.setMajor(d.getName());
  ```

- Next, we apply the getName method to this Department, which returns a reference to a String object whose value is "Math". It's as if we've simplified the original expression further still, as follows:

  ```
  // From:
  s.setMajor(d.getName());

  // To:
  s.setMajor("Math");
  ```

- Finally, we evaluate the statement as a whole, which assigns the String value "Math" as the major field for Student s.

We'll see many such concatenated method calls in the SRS code.

The *type* of a chained message expression is the type of the result that the *last* method in the chain returns. For example, if

- s is a Student reference.

- getAdvisor is a Student method that returns a Professor reference.

- getName is a Professor method that returns a String reference.

- length is a String method that returns an int value.

then s.getAdvisor().getName().length() is an int(eger) expression.

Object Self-Referencing with "this"

We've previously seen the this keyword used in two different ways:

- In Chapter 4, we learned that the syntax this.*featureName* can be used within any (non-static) method to emphasize the fact that we're accessing another feature of *this same object*.

```java
public class SomeClass {
    // Details omitted.

    public void foo() {
        // Call method bar (declared below) from within foo.
        this.bar();
        // etc.
    }

    public void bar() {
        // ...
    }
}
```

- In that same chapter, we also learned that, from within any *constructor* of a class X, we can invoke any other constructor of the same class X via the syntax

  ```java
  this(optional arguments);
  ```

  so as to reuse code from one constructor to another.

We'll now explore a third context in which the this keyword may be used.

In client code, such as the main method of a program, we declare reference variables so as to assign symbolic names to objects:

```java
Student s = new Student();  // s is a reference variable of type Student.
```

We can then conveniently manipulate the objects that these reference variables refer to by manipulating the reference variables themselves:

```java
s.setName("Fred");
```

When we are executing the code that comprises the body of one of an object's own methods, we sometimes need the object to be able to refer to *itself*—that is to **self-reference**, as in this next bit of code (please read the inline comments carefully):

```java
public class Student {
  Professor facultyAdvisor;
  // Other details omitted.

  public void selectAdvisor(Professor p) {
    // We're down in the "bowels" of the selectAdvisor method,
    // executing this method for a particular Student object/instance.
    // We save the handle on our new advisor as one of our attributes ...
    this.setFacultyAdvisor(p);

    // ... and now we want to turn around and tell this Professor object to
    // reflect us as its student advisee. The Professor class has a
    // method with the header:  public void addAdvisee(Student s)
    // and so all we need to do is invoke this method on our advisor object,
    // passing in a reference to ourselves as a Student; but, who the heck
    // are we? That is, how do we refer to ourselves?
    facultyAdvisor.addAdvisee(???);
  }
}
```

Within the body of a method, when we need a way to refer to the object whose method we are executing, we use the reserved word this to self-reference. So, with respect to our previous example, the following **bolded** line of code would do the trick nicely:

```java
public class Student {
  Professor facultyAdvisor;
  // Other details omitted.

  public void selectAdvisor(Professor p) {
    this.setFacultyAdvisor(p);
    p.addAdvisee(this); // passing a reference to THIS Student
  }
}
```

Specifically, it would pass a reference to *this* Student—the Student object whose selectAdvisor method we are executing—as an argument to the addAdvisee method as invoked on Professor facultyAdvisor.

Java Exception Handling

Unexpected problems can arise as the JVM interprets/executes a Java program, for example:

- A program may be unable to open a data file due to inappropriate permissions.

- A program may have trouble establishing a connection to a database management system (DBMS) because a user has supplied an invalid password.

- A user may supply inappropriate data via an application's user interface—for example, a non-numeric value where a numeric value is expected.

- The problem may be something as simple as a logic error that the compiler wasn't able to detect.

Say we write the following simple program:

```java
public class Problem {
    public static void main(String[] args) {
        // Declare two Student object references and initialize them
        // to the value null, which is the "zero-equivalent" value
        // for object references; that is, null indicates that the variable
        // does not currently reference an object.
        Student s1 = null;
        Student s2 = null;

        // Details omitted ...

        // Later on, we instantiate an object for s1 to refer to, but forget
        // to do so for s2.
        s1 = new Student();

        // More details omitted ...

        // Still later in our program, we attempt to assign names to both Students.
        // This line of code is fine ...
        s1.setName("Fred");

        // ... but this next line of code causes a run-time problem, because we
        // are trying to invoke a method on -- i.e., "talk to" -- a
        // nonexistent object.
        s2.setName("Mary");
    }
}
```

The preceding code will compile without error, but if we execute this program, the JVM will report the following run-time error:

```
Exception in thread "main" java.lang.NullPointerException
        at Problem.main(Problem.java:22)
```

We refer to (recoverable) Java run-time errors as **exceptions**, and we refer to the process whereby the JVM reports that a run-time error has arisen as **throwing an exception**. With respect to this example specifically, the JVM threw a NullPointerException on line 22 of the Problem class:

```
s2.setName("Mary");   // this is line 22
```

A NullPointerException arises whenever we try to invoke a method on an object reference (s2, in this example) whose value is null or, in plain English, whenever we try to "talk to" a nonexistent object.

When the JVM throws an exception, it's as if the JVM is shooting off a signal flare to notify an application that something has gone wrong, in order to give the application a chance to *recover* from the problem if we've equipped it to do so (see Figure 13-15). Through a technique known as **exception handling**, we can design our applications so that they may anticipate and gracefully recover from such exceptions at run time.

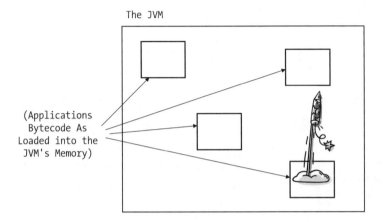

The JVM

(Applications
Bytecode As
Loaded into the
JVM's Memory)

Figure 13-15. *When the JVM throws an exception, it is effectively shooting off a signal flare to notify an application of a problem that has arisen.*

The Mechanics of Exception Handling

The basics of the exception handling mechanism are as follows.

The try Block

We enclose code that is likely to throw an exception inside of a pair of braces to form a code block, and precede the opening brace with the keyword try. This indicates our intention to **catch**—that is, to detect and respond to—any exceptions that might by thrown by the JVM while executing the code within that try **block**.

Going back to our previous example, we might amend our code as highlighted here in **bold**:

```
public class Problem2 {
    public static void main(String[] args) {
        Student s1 = null;
        Student s2 = null;

        // Details omitted ...

        // Later on, we instantiate an object for s1 to refer to, but
        // forget to do so for s2.
        s1 = new Student();

        // More details omitted ...
```

```
    // We've added a try statement to enclose the code likely to
    // generate an exception.
    try {
        s1.setName("Fred");
        s2.setName("Mary");
    }
    // There's more to follow ... stay tuned!
```

In order for the preceding code to compile, the try block must be immediately followed by at least one catch or finally block.

The catch Block

Each catch block begins with a declaration of the form

```
catch (ExceptionType variableName) { ...
```

where the keyword catch is followed by parentheses enclosing a specific type of exception that is to be caught. The braces that follow the closing parenthesis enclose the code to be used in recovering from the exception:

```
catch (ExceptionType variableName) {
    // Pseudocode.
    recovery code for an ExceptionType exception goes here ...
}
```

(For now, don't worry about the *variableName* that is also declared within these parentheses— we'll discuss its purpose shortly.)

One *or more* catch blocks can be associated with the same try block, as follows:

```
try {
    code liable to throw exception(s) goes here ...
}
catch (ExceptionType1 variableName1) {
    recovery code for ExceptionType1 goes here ...
}
catch (ExceptionType2 variableName2) {
    recovery code for ExceptionType2 goes here ...
}
// etc.
```

There are many different exception types built into the Java language, each one defined by a different predefined Java class derived from a common ancestor class called Exception. Before we discuss some of the more important Java exception types, however, let's finish amending our previous example involving Student references by adding several catch clauses (**bolded** in the following code) to the try statement. (Depending on what type of exceptions we're catching, we may need import directives; we do not need to import NullPointerException, however, as it is within the core java.lang package.)

```
public class Problem3 {
    public static void main(String[] args) {
        Student s1 = null;
        Student s2 = null;
```

```
    // Details omitted ...

    // Later on, we instantiate an object for s1 to refer to, but
    // forget to do so for s2.
    s1 = new Student();

    // More details omitted ...

    // We've added a try block to enclose the code likely to
    // generate an exception.
    try {
        s1.setName("Fred");
        s2.setName("Mary");
    } // end of try block
    // Here are our catch clauses (three in total).
    catch (ArithmeticException e) {
        // Pseudocode.
        recovery code for an ArithmeticException goes here ...
    }
    catch (NullPointerException e2) {
        // Here's where we write the code for what the program should do if
        // a NullPointerException occurred.
        System.out.println("Darn!  We forgot to initialize " +
            "all of the students!");
        // etc.
    }
    catch (ArrayIndexOutOfBoundsException e3) {
        // Pseudocode.
        recovery code for an ArrayIndexOutOfBoundsException goes here ...
    }

    // etc. ...
    }
}
```

Note that the code within the `try` block of the preceding example doesn't throw either `ArithmeticExceptions` or `ArrayIndexOutOfBoundsExceptions`; these are merely included for purposes of illustration.

With regard to exception handling, there are two possible paths through this `main` method's logic. As long as the code in the `try` block executes without error, all of the `catch` blocks are **bypassed**, and execution of our program continues after the end of the last `catch` block, as illustrated in Figure 13-16.

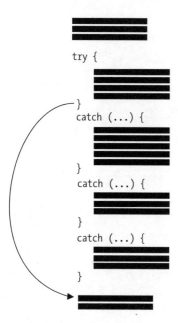

Figure 13-16. *If no exceptions are thrown in the try block, all catch blocks are bypassed.*

If, on the other hand, an exception *is* thrown by the JVM while executing the try block, execution of the try block abruptly terminates as of the line on which the exception occurred. The JVM then examines the catch clauses in order from top to bottom, looking for a catch clause whose declared exception type addresses the type of exception that was thrown.

- If a match is found, the JVM executes the associated catch block; in the case of multiple matches, only the *first* such match is executed. Then execution resumes after the *end* of the *last* catch block. This is illustrated in Figure 13-17.

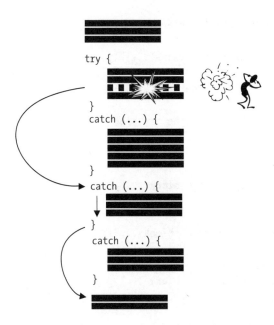

Figure 13-17. *If an exception arises, the first matching* catch *block, if any, is executed, and the rest are skipped.*

- If no matching catch clause is found, the exception is said to be ***uncaught*** and, in the case of the earlier example, it would be reported to the command window:

```
Exception in thread "main" java.lang.NullPointerException
        at Problem.main(Problem.java: ...)
```

To help illustrate this flow of control, let's insert print statements into our previous Problem*x* example to produce a trace of our program's execution:

```java
public class Problem4 {
    public static void main(String[] args) {
        Student s1 = null;
        Student s2 = null;

        // Details omitted ...

        // Later on, we instantiate an object for s1 to refer to, but
        // forget to do so for s2.
        s1 = new Student();

        // More details omitted ...
```

```
        System.out.println("We're about to enter the try block ...");
        try {
            System.out.println("We're about to call s1.setName(...)");
            s1.setName("Fred");
            System.out.println("We're about to call s2.setName(...)");
            s2.setName("Mary");
            System.out.println("We've reached the end of the try block ...");
        }
        // Here are our catch blocks (three in total).
        catch (ArithmeticException e) {
            System.out.println("Executing the first catch block ...");
        }
        catch (NullPointerException e2) {
            System.out.println("Executing the second catch block ...");
        }
        catch (ArrayIndexOutOfBoundsException e3) {
            System.out.println("Executing the third catch block ...");
        }

        System.out.println("We're past the last catch block ...");
    }
}
```

When this is executed, the following messages would be printed:

```
We're about to enter the try block ...
We're about to call s1.setName(...)
We're about to call s2.setName(...)
Executing the second catch block ...
We're past the last catch block ...
```

The finally Block

A try block may optionally have a finally block associated with it. If provided, a finally block follows any catch blocks associated with that same try block.

The code within a finally block is **_guaranteed_** to execute no matter what happens in the try/catch code that precedes it—that is, whether any of the following happen:

- The try block executes to completion without throwing any exceptions whatsoever.

- The try block throws an exception that is handled by one of the catch blocks.

- The try block throws an exception that is **_not_** handled by **_any_** of the catch blocks (a situation that we'll explore a bit later in this chapter).

Let's add a finally block to our evolving Problemx program example. We'll use the version that included print statements, so that we may once again trace our code's execution:

```
public class Problem5 {
    public static void main(String[] args) {
        Student s1 = null;
        Student s2 = null;
```

```
    // Details omitted ...

    // Later on, we instantiate an object for s1 to refer to, but
    // forget to do so for s2.
    s1 = new Student();

    // More details omitted ...

    System.out.println("We're about to enter the try block ...");
    try {
        System.out.println("We're about to call s1.setName(...)");
        s1.setName("Fred");
        System.out.println("We're about to call s2.setName(...)");
        s2.setName("Mary");
        System.out.println("We've reached the end of the try block ...");
    }
    // Here are our catch blocks (three in total).
    catch (ArithmeticException e) {
        System.out.println("Executing the first catch block ...");
    }
    catch (NullPointerException e2) {
        System.out.println("Executing the second catch block ...");
    }
    catch (ArrayIndexOutOfBoundsException e3) {
        System.out.println("Executing the third catch block ...");
    }
    finally {
        System.out.println("Executing the finally block ...");
    }

    System.out.println("We're past the last catch block ...");
    }
}
```

When executed, this version of the program would produce the following output:

```
We're about to enter the try block ...
We're about to call s1.setName(...)
We're about to call s2.setName(...)
Executing the second catch block ...
Executing the finally block ...
We're past the last catch block ...
```

Let's now *repair* the code in our try block so that it doesn't throw any exceptions, to see what output our program will produce:

```
public class NoProblemo {
    public static void main(String[] args) {
```

```
        Student s1 = null;
        Student s2 = null;

        // Details omitted ...

        // Later on, we instantiate objects for both s1 and s2
        // to refer to, thus alleviating the NullPointerException
        // in the try block below.
        s1 = new Student();
        s2 = new Student();

        // More details omitted ...

        System.out.println("We're about to enter the try block ...");
        try {
            System.out.println("We're about to call s1.setName(...)");
            s1.setName("Fred");
            System.out.println("We're about to call s2.setName(...)");
            s2.setName("Mary");
            System.out.println("We've reached the end of the try block ...");
        }
        // Here are our catch blocks (three in total).
        catch (ArithmeticException e) {
            System.out.println("Executing first catch block ...");
        }
        catch (NullPointerException e2) {
            System.out.println("Executing second catch block ...");
        }
        catch (ArrayIndexOutOfBoundsException e3) {
            System.out.println("Executing third catch block ...");
        }
        finally {
            System.out.println("Executing finally block ...");
        }

        System.out.println("We're past the last catch block ...");
    }
}
```

When executed, this version of the program would produce the following output (note that all catch blocks are *bypassed*):

```
We're about to enter the try block ...
We're about to call s1.setName(...)
We're about to call s2.setName(...)
We've reached the end of the try block ...
Executing the finally block ...
We're past the last catch block ...
```

A final variation on our Problemx program once again throws a NullPointerException, but does ***not*** catch the appropriate type of exception in any of the catch blocks:

```java
public class Problem6 {
    public static void main(String[] args) {
        Student s1 = null;
        Student s2 = null;

        // Details omitted ...

        // Later on, we instantiate an object for s1 to refer to, but
        // forget to do so for s2.
        s1 = new Student();

        // More details omitted ...

        System.out.println("We're about to enter the try block ...");
        try {
            System.out.println("We're about to call s1.setName(...)");
            s1.setName("Fred");
            System.out.println("We're about to call s2.setName(...)");
            s2.setName("Mary");
            System.out.println("We've reached the end of the try block ...");
        }
        // Here are our catch blocks (two in total) - note that we
        // are *not* catching NullPointerException this time.
        catch (ArithmeticException e) {
            System.out.println("Executing first catch block ...");
        }
        catch (ArrayIndexOutOfBoundsException e2) {
            System.out.println("Executing second catch block ...");
        }
        finally {
            System.out.println("Executing finally block ...");
        }

        System.out.println("We're past the last catch block ...");
    }
}
```

When executed, this version of the program would produce the following output:

```
We're about to enter the try block ...
We're about to call s1.setName(...)
We're about to call s2.setName(...)
Executing the finally block ...
```

Note that we never make it to the final print statement:

```
System.out.println("We're past the last catch block ...");
```

because an ***uncaught*** exception causes the overall code block in which it occurs—in our example, the main method—to terminate abnormally.

We thus see that no matter what happens in the try/catch code, a finally block, if present, is ***always*** executed.

Note that we may omit catch clauses for a try block if a finally block is present:

```
// Catch blocks are unnecessary if a finally block is present.
try { ... }
finally { ... }
```

Catching Exceptions

If the method in which an exception arises does not catch the exception, then the client code that called that method is given a chance to catch it.

Consider the following three-class example:

- In our main method, we invoke methodX on a Student object:

```
public class MainProgram {
    public static void main(String[] args) {
        Student s = new Student();
        s.methodX();
    }
}
```

- In the Student's methodX code, we in turn invoke methodY on a Professor object:

```
public class Student {
    // Details omitted.
    public void methodX() {
        Professor p = new Professor();
        p.methodY();
    }
}
```

- Finally, here's the Professor class:

```
public class Professor {
    // Details omitted.
    public void methodY() {
        // Details omitted ...
    }
}
```

When the JVM executes our MainProgram, its main method is invoked, which in turn invokes s.methodX(), which in turn invokes p.methodY();—this produces what is known as a **call stack** at run time, illustrated in Figure 13-18.

| p.methodY(...) |
| s.methodX(...) |
| MainProgram.main(...) |

Figure 13-18. *The JVM keeps track of the order in which methods are called one from another by creating a call stack.*

A **stack** is a **last-in, first-out** (**LIFO**) data structure; the most recent method call is **pushed** onto the top of the call stack, and when that method exits, it is removed from (**popped** off of) the call stack. So, as an example, when methodY finishes executing, and execution control is returned to methodX, methodY is popped off, as illustrated conceptually in Figure 13-19.

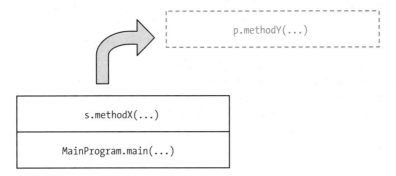

Figure 13-19. *When a method exits, it is removed from the call stack.*

Let's now assume that a NullPointerException is thrown while executing methodY. If the appropriate try/catch logic is incorporated ***within the body of*** methodY to handle/resolve such a NullPointerException, as follows:

```
public class Professor {
    // Details omitted.
    public void methodY() {
        try { ... }
        catch (NullPointerException e) { ... }
    }
}
```

then neither the Student nor MainProgram classes will be aware that such an exception was ever thrown. From the perspective of the call stack, awareness of the exception is contained within the current level of the stack, as illustrated in Figure 13-20.

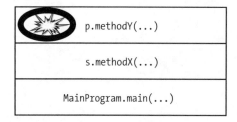

Figure 13-20. *The try/catch logic within methodY limits awareness of the exception to the current level in the call stack.*

Let's assume instead that methodY does ***not*** catch/handle NullPointerExceptions:

```
public class Professor {
    // Details omitted.
    public void methodY() {
        // A NullPointerException is thrown here, but
        // is NOT caught/handled.
        // (Details omitted.)
    }
}
```

If a NullPointerException is thrown while executing ***this*** version of methodY, it will travel down the call stack one level to the Student class's methodX, which is where the call to p.methodY() originated. If the Student class's methodX code happens to include the necessary exception handling code, as follows:

```
public class Student {
    // Details omitted.
    public void methodX() {
        Professor p = new Professor();

        // Exception handling is performed here.
        try {
            p.methodY();
        }
        catch (NullPointerException e) { ... }
    }
}
```

then the exception is contained by methodX in the Student class, and the MainProgram will thus be unaware that such an exception was ever thrown. This is illustrated in terms of the call stack in Figure 13-21.

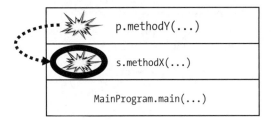

Figure 13-21. *The exception "escapes" the* methodY *level of the call stack, but is contained/handled by* methodX.

Now, let's assume that ***neither*** methodY of Professor ***nor*** methodX of Student handle NullPointerExceptions, but that our main method is written to do so:

```java
public class Professor {
    // Details omitted.
    public void methodY() {
        // A NullPointerException is thrown here, but
        // is NOT caught/handled.
        // (Details omitted.)
    }
}


//----------------------------


public class Student {
    // Details omitted.
    public void methodX() {
        Professor p = new Professor();

        // We're not doing any exception handling
        // here, either.
        p.methodY();
    }
}


//----------------------------


public class MainProgram {
    public static void main(String[] args) {
        Student s = new Student();

        // Exception handling introduced here.
        try {
            s.methodX();
        }
        catch (NullPointerException e) { ... }
    }
}
```

In this case, a `NullPointerException` thrown in `methodY` would make its way through the call stack to the `main` method, where it would be contained as shown in Figure 13-22. In this case, the ***user*** of this application is unaware that an exception has occurred.

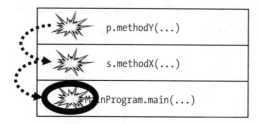

Figure 13-22. *The `NullPointerException` makes its way to the `main` method.*

As a final variation, let's assume that even the `main` method omits explicit exception handling. If a `NullPointerException` were to arise in `methodY`, we'd see the following **stack trace** appear in the command window:

```
java PSExample
Exception in thread "main" java.lang.NullPointerException
    at Professor.methodY(Professor.java: ...)
    at Student.methodX(Student.java: ...)
    at MainProgram.main(MainProgram.java: ...)
```

From the perspective of the call stack, the situation is as shown in Figure 13-23.

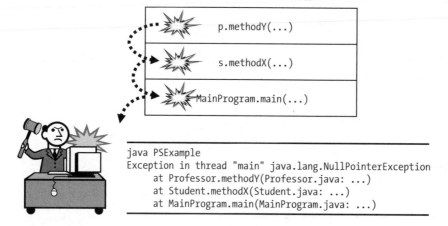

Figure 13-23. *If our application as a whole omits exception handling, the JVM terminates the application and reports the exception to the command window for the user to observe.*

We'll learn a bit later in the chapter that the Java compiler will force us to catch selected types of exceptions, but not `NullPointerException`s in particular.

Interpreting Exception Stack Traces

As detailed in the previous section, when an exception arises that we haven't properly handled, a **stack trace**—that is, a report by the JVM of where things went wrong, and how we got there—is displayed in the command window. Interpreting an exception stack trace is quite easy. Let's use a code example that will generate such a trace to illustrate how this is done.

Please read the inline comments carefully in the following three-class example to see where a potential `NullPointerException` problem is lurking:

```
public class Professor {
    // Our simplistic Professor class has only one attribute.
    private Student advisee;

    public void setAdvisee(Student s) {
        advisee = s;
    }

    public void printAdviseeInfo() {
        // A bit of delegation.
        advisee.print();
    }
}

// ---------------------------------

public class Student {
    // Our Student class has only one attribute, and no way to set its value.
    // Thus, the name attribute of a Student will be initialized to the value
    // null, and will REMAIN null.
    private String name;

    public void print() {
        // Since the name attribute is guaranteed to be null here,
        // this line will generate a NullPointerException at run time.
        if (name.length() > 5) System.out.println(name);
    }
}

// ---------------------------------

public class PSExample {
    public static void main(String[] args) {
        Student s = new Student();
        Professor p = new Professor();
```

```
        // Link the objects together.
        p.setAdvisee(s);

        // This next line of code will in turn invoke the print
        // method of p's Student advisee, which as we saw above is
        // going to generate a NullPointerException at run time.
        p.printAdviseeInfo();
    }
}
```

When we run this program, we'd see the following stack trace:

```
java PSExample
Exception in thread "main" java.lang.NullPointerException
    at Student.print(Student.java:10)
    at Professor.printAdviseeInfo(Professor.java:11)
    at PSExample.main(PSExample.java:12)
```

Reading the stack trace from top to bottom:

- The actual NullPointerException arose on line 10 of the Student class:

  ```
  if (name.length() > 5) System.out.println(name); // line 10 of Student
  ```

- *That* line of code is within the body of the print method of the Student class, which was invoked from line 11 of the Professor class:

  ```
  advisee.print(); // line 11 of Professor
  ```

- And, *that* line of code is within the body of the printAdviseeInfo method of the Professor class, which was in turn invoked from the PSExample class's main method on line 12:

  ```
  p.printAdviseeInfo(); // line 12 of PSExample
  ```

Whenever a stack trace arises from an exception, the *first* place we should look to diagnose and repair the problem is the line of code that is reported as the *first* item in the stack trace: line 10 of the Student class, in this particular example. If in inspecting this line, we cannot understand why the exception arises, we look to the second item in the stack trace, then the third, and so on, until we have looked far enough back in the call history to determine why things went awry.

The Exception Class Hierarchy

As mentioned in passing earlier in the chapter, the generic Exception class, included in the java.lang package, is the superclass of all exception types in Java. As illustrated in Figure 13-24 (taken from Sun's online Java documentation), there are *many* direct subclasses of the Exception class.

```
java.lang.Object
  └ java.lang.Throwable
      └ java.lang.Exception
```

All Implemented Interfaces:
Serializable

Direct Known Subclasses:
AclNotFoundException, ActivationException, AlreadyBoundException,
ApplicationException, AWTException, BackingStoreException,
BadAttributeValueExpException, BadBinaryOpValueExpException,
BadLocationException, BadStringOperationException, BrokenBarrierException,
CertificateException, ClassNotFoundException, CloneNotSupportedException,
DataFormatException, DatatypeConfigurationException, DestroyFailedException,
ExecutionException, ExpandVetoException, FontFormatException,
GeneralSecurityException, GSSException, IllegalAccessException,
IllegalClassFormatException, InstantiationException, InterruptedException,
IntrospectionException, InvalidApplicationException, InvalidMidiDataException,
InvalidPreferencesFormatException, InvalidTargetObjectTypeException,
InvocationTargetException, IOException, JMException, LastOwnerException,
LineUnavailableException, MidiUnavailableException, MimeTypeParseException,
NamingException, NoninvertibleTransformException, NoSuchFieldException,
NoSuchMethodException, NotBoundException, NotOwnerException, ParseException,
ParserConfigurationException, PrinterException, PrintException,
PrivilegedActionException, PropertyVetoException, RefreshFailedException,
RemarshalException, RuntimeException, SAXException, ServerNotActiveException,
SQLException, TimeoutException, TooManyListenersException, TransformerException,
UnmodifiableClassException, UnsupportedAudioFileException,
UnsupportedCallbackException, UnsupportedFlavorException,
UnsupportedLookAndFeelException, URISyntaxException, UserException,
XAException, XMLParseException, XPathException

Figure 13-24. *The java.lang.Exception class has **many** "offspring"!*

A catch clause for a given exception type X will catch that specific type of exception *or any of its subtypes*, by virtue of the "is a" nature of inheritance. For this reason, it's important to list catch clauses in most specific to least specific order after a try block; that is, from lowest level subclass to highest superclass. Let's use a specific example to illustrate why this is so.

For our example, we'll perform a database access operation (as pseudocode). Operations against databases, including possible exceptions that result from such operations, are governed by classes belonging to the java.sql package. We'll deal in this example with three types of successively more general exceptions:

- DataTruncation is the most specific type of exception that we'll concern ourselves with in this example. As its name implies, a DataTruncation exception occurs if data that is being written to a database happens to get **truncated**, as for example when a particularly long String value is written to a database field that can accommodate only 255 characters.

- DataTruncation exceptions are a special case/subtype of more general SQLWarning exception type. SQLWarning exceptions are thrown whenever any sort of database access problem occurs that, while not fatal, is significant enough to warrant alerting an application about.

- SQLWarning exceptions, in turn, are a special case/subclass of the more general SQLException class of exceptions. SQLExceptions are thrown when anything at all of concern arises in the course of interacting with a database, ranging from attempting to log on using an invalid password, to trying to access a nonexistent table, to attempting to submit a poorly formed SQL query.

- Finally, SQLWarning is a direct subclass of the generic Exception class.

This inheritance "lineage" is illustrated in Figure 13-25 (taken from Sun Microsystems' online Java documentation).

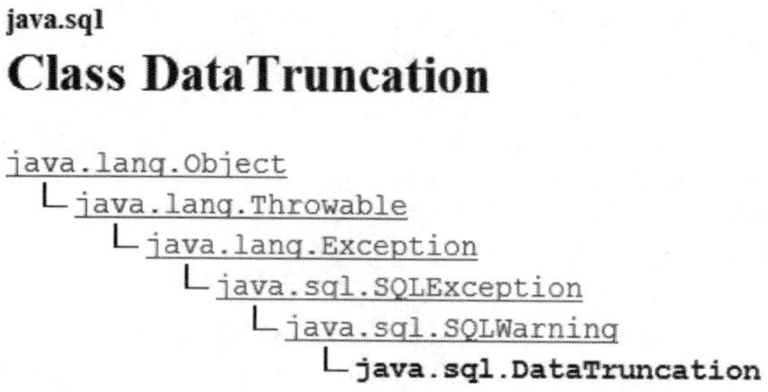

java.sql

Class DataTruncation

```
java.lang.Object
  └ java.lang.Throwable
      └ java.lang.Exception
          └ java.sql.SQLException
              └ java.sql.SQLWarning
                  └ java.sql.DataTruncation
```

Figure 13-25. *The inheritance "lineage" of the java.sql.DataTruncation exception type*

The following code snippet presents one way for us to write the try/catch code for handling DataTruncation (and other sorts of database-related) exceptions. Note that we'd need to include the appropriate import directive(s) to either import all of the java.sql classes, or just those we're referencing in our code.

```
try {
    // Pseudocode.
    attempt to write data to a database
}
catch (DataTruncation e1) {
    // Catch the most specific exception type first;
    // details omitted ...
}
catch (SQLWarning e2) {
    // ... then, the next most specific ...
    // Details omitted.
}
catch (SQLException e3) {
    // ... working our way up to the most general.
    // Details omitted.
}
```

Since a DataTruncation exception is a type of SQLException by virtue of inheritance, we could alternatively choose to write this code with a *single* catch clause, as follows:

```
try {
    // Pseudocode.
    database access operation ...
}
catch (SQLException e) {
    // This will catch DataTruncation exceptions along with
    // all other (sub)types of SQLException.
    // Details omitted.
}
```

Why would we ever bother to use **three** catch clauses when one will suffice? Because the more specific an exception we catch, the more specific our recovery code can be:

```
try {
    // Pseudocode.
    database access operations that are liable to throw, among other
    types of exceptions, DataTruncation exceptions ...
}
catch (DataTruncation e1) {
    // Pseudocode.
    respond SPECIFICALLY to data truncation issues ...
}
catch (SQLWarning e2) { ... }
catch (SQLException e3) { ... }
```

The following alternative version would **not** be appropriate because the three catch clauses are listed in least specific to most specific order; thus, the **first** catch clause would always catch all forms of SQLException, and the latter two catch clauses would never be reached:

```
try {
    // Pseudocode.
    database access operation ...
}
catch (SQLException e1) {
    // This catch clause will catch any/all SQLExceptions, including
    // SQLWarnings and DataTruncations ... details omitted.
}
catch (SQLWarning e2) {
    // This catch clause is wasted - it can never be reached!
}
catch (DataTruncation e3) {
    // This catch clause is also wasted - it can never be reached!
}
```

Catching the Generic Exception Type

Some programmers use the "lazy" approach of catching the most generic Exception type and then doing **nothing** to recover, just to silence the compiler:

```
try {
    // Pseudocode.
    do anything!!!
}
catch (Exception e) { } // Empty braces => do NOTHING to recover!!!
```

This is not a good practice! By doing so, we're masking the fact that an exception has occurred. Our program may be in a serious state of dysfunction, perhaps coming to a screeching halt (!), but it will remain *silent* as to why because the preceding catch clause suppresses the typical stack trace that would otherwise typically be displayed.

This is not to say that we should never catch generic Exceptions; one legitimate case in which we might wish to do so is if we are writing a special-purpose error-handling subsystem for an application, as suggested by the following pseudocode:

```
public class Example {
    public static void main(String[] args) {
        try {
            // Pseudocode.
            all of our main application logic is here ...
        }
        catch (Exception e) {
            // Invoke a static method on the
            // MyExceptionHandler class that we've written.
            MyExceptionHandler.handleException(e);
        }
    }
}
```

Here we assume that the static handleException method of a custom MyExceptionHandler class that we've developed encapsulates logic for handling all exceptions generated throughout our application in a central, consistent fashion (perhaps by recording them in an application log file or alerting a system administrator to the issue in real time).

Compiler Enforcement of Exception Handling

Generally speaking, the Java compiler will force us to enclose code that is liable to throw an exception in a try block with an appropriate catch block(s). For example, if we were attempting to read data from a file, as we'll do in earnest in Chapter 15:

```
public class FileIOExample {
    public static void main(String[] args) {
        // Pseudocode.
        open the file of interest;
        while (end of file not yet reached) {
            read next line from file;
            // etc.
        }
    }
}
```

we'd get compiler errors complaining that our attempts to open a file, read from a file, etc. must be handled:

```
Unreported exception java.io.FileNotFoundException; must be caught or
declared to be thrown
```

In such a situation, we have two choices:

- Ideally, we'd enclose the code in question in a try block with an appropriate catch block (or blocks):

```
import java.io.FileNotFoundException;

public class FileIOExample {
    public static void main(String[] args) {
      try {
        // Pseudocode.
        open the file of interest;
        while (end of file not yet reached) {
            read next line from file;
            // etc.
        }
      }
      catch (FileNotFoundException e) { ...
      // etc.
```

- Alternatively, we may add a throws clause to the header of the method in which the uncaught exception might arise, as follows:

```
import java.io.FileNotFoundException;

public class FileIOExample {
    // By adding the throws clause to the main method declaration, we avoid
    // having to worry about catching FileNotFoundExceptions.
    public static void main(String[] args) throws FileNotFoundException {
        // Pseudocode.
        open the file of interest;
        while (end of file not yet reached) {
            read next line from file;
            // etc.
        }
    }
}
```

The only exception types that the compiler doesn't mandate catching are those derived from the RuntimeException class, which is a direct subclass of the Exception class. Several of the more commonly encountered RuntimeException types are NullPointerException, ArithmeticException (which arises when we attempt an illegal arithmetic operation, such as dividing by zero), and ClassCastException (which, as we discussed in Chapter 7, arises if we try to incorrectly cast an object reference to an inappropriate type). Typically, these types of exceptions represent design flaws that we should "bulletproof" our application against as we are building it, before it ever goes into production.

Taking Advantage of the Exception That We've "Caught"

Note that the declaration of a catch clause looks somewhat like a method header declaration, in that we declare a parameter of type Exception (or one of its subtypes) to be passed in as an argument to the catch block:

```
catch (SomeExceptionType variableName) { ... }
```

However, we don't explicitly invoke a catch block from our program the way we directly invoke a method. Instead, as mentioned earlier, the JVM automatically transfers control to a catch block if an exception arises at run time; as it does so, the JVM also passes the catch block a reference to an object representing the type of exception that has occurred. We can therefore invoke methods on the exception object to help in diagnosing the problem, for example:

- We can invoke the String getMessage() method on the exception object to obtain a text message describing the problem that has arisen:

```
try {
    // Pseudocode.
    try to open a nonexistent file named Foo.dat ...
}
catch (FileNotFoundException e) {
    System.out.println("Error opening file " + e.getMessage());
}
```

Here's the output:

```
Error opening file Foo.dat (The system cannot find the file specified)
```

- We can invoke the void printStackTrace() method to display a traditional stack trace in the command window (recall that stack traces only occur ***automatically*** if we ***don't*** handle an exception):

```
try {
    // Pseudocode.
    try to open a nonexistent file named Foo.dat ...
}
catch (FileNotFoundException e) {
    e.printStackTrace();
}
```

This method is overloaded, such that we may also pass in a reference to a PrintWriter object to cause the stack trace to be printed to a file (we'll discuss file I/O in Chapter 15).

Nesting of try/catch Blocks

A try statement may be nested inside either the try or catch block of another try statement. We frequently have a need to nest an inner try within an outer catch block, in particular, because the recovery code that we write within a catch block may pose a risk of throwing additional exceptions of its own.

As an example, consider the following code snippet. We are attempting to open a user-specified file, and so must stand ready to catch `FileNotFoundExceptions`:

```
try {
    // Pseudocode.
    open a user-specified file
}
catch (FileNotFoundException e) {
    // Pseudocode.
    recovery code goes here ...
}
```

Our recovery plan, should a `FileNotFoundException` arise, is to open a default file instead. But, since the attempt to open a default file can also potentially throw a `FileNotFoundException` of its own, we must wrap the recovery code in its ***own*** nested try block, as follows:

```
try {
    // Pseudocode.
    open a user-specified file
}
catch (FileNotFoundException e) {
    // If we were unable to find the user-specified file, perhaps our way of
    // recovering will be to open a DEFAULT file ... but what if the DEFAULT
    // file cannot be found, either?
    try {
        // Pseudocode.
        open a DEFAULT file instead ...
    }
    catch (FileNotFoundException e2) {
        // Pseudocode.
        attempt to recover ...
    }
}
```

User-Defined Exception Types

If we think of exceptions as signal flares that are thrown by the JVM to report issues, it's natural to want to extend this notion so as to allow our application to do the same—that is, to perhaps define our own ***custom*** exception types to signal various application-specific types of errors, and to then ***programmatically*** throw them as needed when something goes awry. This is indeed possible in Java; let's explore the basics of declaring and using user-defined exception types.

To invent a custom exception type, we harness the power of inheritance to extend one of the predefined Java exception classes. Frequently, we'll extend the generic `Exception` class directly:

```
public class MissingValueException extends Exception { ... }
```

Of course, we'd store this class definition in a `.java` file—`MissingValueException.java` in this particular case—and compile it into a bytecode file named `MissingValueException.class`.

As to what we program in the body of our custom exception, we have several options. The simplest of all user-defined exceptions is a class with an ***empty body***:

```
public class MissingValueException extends Exception { }
```

As trivial as this class is, we've nonetheless accomplished an important goal: we've defined a new exception type, MissingValueException, which can be explicitly thrown and caught by our application. We'll walk through how this is done shortly, but before we do so, let's improve upon our custom exception class design a bit by introducing a constructor:

```java
public class MissingValueException extends Exception {
    // We've added a constructor ...
    public MissingValueException(String message) {
        // ... which simply invokes the base class constructor.
        super(message);
    }
}
```

Why might we want to do this?

- Recall that the generic Exception class declares a method with the header String getMessage() that can be used to extract an informative message from an exception when we catch it.

- The text of this message is originally fed into an Exception instance as an argument via the constructor: public Exception(String message).

The getMessage method will, of course, be inherited by the MissingValueException class. However, as we discussed previously, constructors are not inherited, and so if we want to initialize the message of a MissingValueException instance in a similar fashion, we must explicitly declare such a constructor for our MissingValueException class. We may then reuse the code of the Exception superclass constructor via the syntax

```java
super(message);
```

Let's make one final enhancement to our MissingValueException class. With a subclass, we are free to add whatever features make sense above and beyond those that are inherited from the superclass, so we'll add one attribute, Student student, plus a get method for this attribute— the purpose for doing so will become clear in a moment. We'll also modify the constructor header to accommodate *two* parameters—a String message and a Student:

```java
public class MissingValueException extends Exception {
    // We've added an attribute ...
    private Student student;

    // ... modified our constructor to take two arguments so
    // that we can pass in a value for both the Student attribute
    // and the message that this exception will carry with it ...
    public MissingValueException(Student s, String message) {
        super(message);
        student = s;
    }

    // ... and added a get method for our Student attribute.
    public Student getStudent() {
        return student;
    }
}
```

This is about as elaborate as a custom exception needs to be in order to give us maximum versatility.

Let's now look at how we'd go about using our new exception type to signal an error condition back to client code. First, let's put this exception type to work in the Student class. I'll present the code for the Student class in its entirety first, and then I'll narrate it in detail afterward.

```
public class Student {
    private String name;
    private String ssn;
    // Other details omitted.

    // Accessor methods.

    public String getSsn() { ... }
    public void setSsn() { ... }
    public String getName() { ... }

    public void setName(String n) throws MissingValueException {
        // We want to report an error if the String that has been
        // passed in is blank.
        if (n.equals("")) {
            throw new MissingValueException(this,
                "A student's name cannot be blank");
        }
        else {
            name = n;
        }
    }

    // etc.
}
```

The first bit of unusual syntax that we notice in the preceding code is in the method header declaration for the setName method:

```
public void setName(String n) throws MissingValueException {
```

Since we have the potential to throw a MissingValueException from within this method, we must declare that the setName method throws MissingValueException.

Then, inside the body of the setName method, we wish to throw a MissingValueException if we detect that client code has passed in an empty String ("") as the proposed name for this Student. We do so via the syntax

```
throw new MissingValueException(this, "A student's name cannot be blank");
```

That is, the keyword throw is followed by the new keyword, which in turn is followed by a call to our MissingValueException constructor. Thus, we've just "shot off a signal flare," carrying both a reference to the Student object in question and an informative message as to *why* we've shot off the flare—namely, because "A student's name cannot be blank".

Now, let's see how client code *reacts* to this "signal flare." If we were to attempt to write client code as follows:

```
public class Example {
    public static void main(String[] args) {
        // Pseudocode.
        String name = read value from GUI;
        Student s = new Student();
        s.setName(name);
        // etc.
```

the following compiler error would arise on the line that attempts to invoke the setName method of Student s:

```
Unreported exception MissingValueException; must be caught or declared to be thrown
    s.setName(name);
```

Because we included the throws MissingValueException clause on our setName method declaration in the Student class, we are **_forced_** by the Java compiler to catch this type of exception in our client code! That is, we must place our attempt to invoke the setName method on s in a try block, and follow it with an appropriate catch block:

```
public class Example {
    public static void main(String[] args) {
        // Pseudocode.
        String name = read value from GUI;
        Student s = new Student();
        try {
            s.setName(name);
        }
        catch (MissingValueException e) {
            System.out.println(e.getMessage());
            System.out.println("ID of affected student:  " +
                e.getStudent().getSsn());
        }
        // etc.
```

In our catch block, we've taken advantage of both the inherited getMessage method and the custom getStudent method of the MissingvalueException class to produce output as follows:

```
A student's name cannot be blank
ID of affected student:  123-45-6789
```

Throwing Multiple Types of Exceptions

Note that we can throw more than one type of exception from the same method. In the following example, it's assumed that we've declared a custom InvalidCharacterException in addition to MissingValueException:

```
public class Student {
    // Details omitted.
```

```
    public void setName(String s) throws MissingValueException,
        InvalidCharacterException {
        if (s.equals("")) {
            throw new MissingValueException(this,
                "A student's name cannot be blank");
        }
        // Pseudocode.
        else if (s contains an invalid character) {
            throw new InvalidCharacterException(this, s +
                " contains a non-alphabetic character");
        }
        else name = s;
    }

    // etc.
}
```

We'll take advantage of user-defined exceptions in Chapter 15 when building the SRS application's data access layer, as there are many things that can potentially go wrong when we're reaching outside of our application to access an external file system or a database.

Enum(eration)s

IMPORTANT!
As I first mentioned in the collections discussion in Chapter 6, Sun Microsystems introduced some important new features with J2SE 5.0 that significantly increased the power and versatility of Java as an object-oriented programming language. *Enums are another such feature that was introduced as of J2SE 5.0; hence, the code examples involving enums will not compile with an earlier (pre-5.0) version of the Java compiler.*

Situations often arise in an application where we wish to constrain the value that a variable can assume to a finite set of valid choices. For example, let's say that SRS University offers degrees in the following five major fields:

- Mathematics

- Biology

- Chemistry

- Computer science

- Physical education

We design our Student class so that one of its attributes, String major, reflects the discipline that a given student is majoring in. Then, to ensure that client code doesn't pass in an inappropriate value for the student's major field of study, we invent a custom exception called InvalidMajorException and use it to signal issues in this regard, as follows:

```java
public class Student {
    private String name;
    private String major;
    // etc.

    // Constructor.
    public Student(String name, String major) throws InvalidMajorException {
        this.setName(name);

        // Pseudocode.
        if (major not one of the five approved majors) {
            throw new InvalidMajorException();
        }
        else {
            this.setMajor(major);
        }
    }

    // Accessor methods.

    public void setName(String n) {
        name = n;
    }

    public void setMajor(String m) {
        major = m;
    }

    // etc.
}
```

In so doing, we cannot prevent detect-errors in client code at *compile* time:

```java
// Client code.

// The compiler forces us to place Student constructor calls in
// an appropriate try block ...
try {
    // ... but we nonetheless have WRITTEN code that is
    // guaranteed to throw a run-time exception, because the
    // COMPILER has no way to determine the error.
    Student s = new Student("Dorothy Jost", "Culinary Arts");
}
catch (InvalidMajorException e) { ... }
```

because the InvalidMajorException doesn't arise until this code is *executed*. However, we *know* that there are five—and *only* five—valid String values for a student's major. Is there perhaps a way to constrain the major attribute so that we can prevent misassignment at *compile time*? As of J2SE 5.0, the answer is *yes!* We use a construct called an **enum**—short for **enumeration**—to define/*enumerate* a finite set of values that a given variable may assume.

Along with classes and interfaces, an enum is another form of user-defined type in Java that lives in its own .java source code file and is compiled into bytecode:

```
// EnumName.java

public enum EnumName { ... }
```

More specifically, an enum is a very simplistic sort of class, consisting of only

- A single attribute, named value, declared to be of whatever (primitive or reference) type we wish for it to be:

  ```
  // A single attribute.
  // (Pseudocode.)
  private final type value;
  ```

  Note that value is declared to be both private and final. As you learned in Chapter 7, the keyword final indicates that an enum instance's value attribute may be assigned a value only ***once*** in its "lifetime," after which the value cannot be changed.

- A list (enumeration) of values that the value attribute is permitted to assume, represented as a comma-separated list of ***symbolic name/value pairs***:

  ```
  // Comma-separated list of name/value pairs.
  // (Pseudocode.)
  symbolicName1(value1),
  symbolicName2(value2),
  <...>
  symbolicNameN(valueN);
  ```

- A simple constructor, used to initialize the value attribute:

  ```
  // Constructor.
  // (Pseudocode.)
  EnumName(type v) {
      value = v;
  }
  ```

  Note that an enum's constructor ***isn't*** declared to be public, because it is not invoked from client code; rather, it is used internally to the enum (in declaring the preceding list of symbolic name/value pairs).

- A single accessor method, value(), used by client code to retrieve the value of the enum's lone attribute.

Putting this all together, the general template for declaring an enum is as follows, where the *italicized* items are those that we can customize:

```
public enum EnumName {
    // Comma-separated list of name/value pairs.
    // (Pseudocode.)
    symbolicName1(value1),
    symbolicName2(value2),
    <...>
    symbolicNameN(valueN);
```

```
// A single attribute.
// (Pseudocode.)
private final type value;

// A (nonpublic) constructor.
// (Pseudocode.)
EnumName(type v) {
    value = v;
}

// Accessor method.
// (Pseudocode.)
public type value() {
    return value;
}
}
```

Let's go back to our example involving students' majors and retrofit an enum called Major to control the assignment of valid major fields *at compile time*.

- Behind the scenes, the five values that Major can assume will be declared as Strings:

```
// Major.java

public enum Major {
    // Comma-separated list of symbolic name/value pairs, where the
    // values (enclosed in parentheses) are all String literals.
    Math("Mathematics"),
    Bio("Biology"),
    Chem("Chemistry"),
    CS("Computer Science"),
    PhysEd("Physical Education");
```

- Hence, the type of the value attribute, the type of the parameter passed to the Major constructor, and the return type of the value() method are all declared to be String to match:

```
// We declare the value attribute to be of type String.
private final String value;

// The constructor takes a String argument.
Major(String v) {
    value = v;
}

// The accessor method has a return type of String.
public String value() {
    return value;
}
}
```

Now, let's reengineer our Student class to take advantage of the new Major enum/type. In particular, we'll

- Change the declaration of the Student class's major attribute to be of type Major instead of String.

- Change the type of the second parameter that we're passing into our Student constructor accordingly.

- Eliminate our use of the InvalidMajorException.

- Change the setMajor method to accept an argument of type Major versus String.

And, while we're at it, let's add a display method for use in testing our improvements to the Student class. The new and improved Student class code is thus as follows (changes are **bolded**):

```
public class Student {
    private String name;
    // We've changed the type of this attribute from String to Major.
    private Major major;

    // Other details omitted.

    // Constructor.
    // We've changed the type of the second constructor parameter from
    // String to Major, and have eliminated the "throws
    // InvalidMajorException" clause.
    public Student(String name, Major major) {
        this.setName(name);
        this.setMajor(major);
    }

    // Accessor methods.

    public void setName(String n) {
        name = n;
    }

    // We've changed the type of the parameter on this method
    // from String to Major.
    public void setMajor(Major m) {
        major = m;
    }

    // etc.

    // We've added a display method.
    public void display() {
        // Note that we are taking advantage of the enum's value()
        // method in the print statement below.
```

```
        System.out.println(name + " is a " + major.value() + " major.");
    }
}
```

Let's now demonstrate how our newly designed Student class might be used from client code:

```
public class EnumExample {
    public static void main(String[] args) {
        // Instantiate a Student, using our newly created Major enum to
        // assign one of the five valid values for a student's major
        // (note the syntax -- Major.CS -- for referring to such a value).
        Student s = new Student("Fred Schnurd", Major.CS);
        s.display();
    }
}
```

When executed, this program produces the following output:

```
Fred Schnurd is a Computer Science major.
```

where the symbolic name Major.CS has been translated to its behind-the-scenes String equivalent, "Computer Science", courtesy of our call to the value() method from within the Student's display method. Had we instead written the display method as follows:

```
    public void display() {
        // We've dropped the call to major.value(), and are printing
        // major directly instead.
        System.out.println(name + " is a " + major + " major.");
    }
```

then the symbolic name of the enum would be printed instead:

```
Fred Schnurd is a CS major.
```

It is now ***physically impossible*** to assign any value as a Student's major other than one of the five ***enum-approved values***—Major.Math, Major.Bio, Major.Chem, Major.CS, or Major.PhysEd—anything else simply won't compile!

- The following line of code won't compile—a String is not a Major:

```
    Student s = new Student("Fred Schnurd", "Basketweaving");
```

    Here's the compiler error:

```
Student.java: cannot find symbol
symbol  : constructor Student(java.lang.String,java.lang.String)
location: class Student
    Student s = new Student("Fred Schnurd", "Basketweaving");
```

- This next line won't compile either—our `Major` enum doesn't define `Basketweaving` as a valid value:

```
Student s = new Student("Fred Schnurd", Major.Basketweaving);
```

Here's the compiler error:

```
Student.java: cannot find symbol
symbol  : variable Basketweaving
location: class Major
    Student s = new Student("Fred Schnurd", Major.Basketweaving);
                                                 ^
```

Here's another example of an `enum` called `Grade` that renders a `double` value:

```
public enum Grade {
    // Enumerate the values that a Grade can assume.
    // The values are all double constants in this case.
    A(4.0),
    B(3.0),
    C(2.0),
    D(1.0),
    F(0.0);

    // Our value attribute is declared to be of type double.
    private final double value;

    Grade(double v) { // double parameter type
        value = v;
    }

    public double value() { // double return type
        return value;
    }
}
```

And here's a bit of client code to illustrate its use:

```
public class GradeDemo {
    public static void main(String[] args) {
        // Declare a variable of type Grade.
        Grade grade;

        // We only may assign one of the "approved" values.
        grade = Grade.A;

        // Display it symbolically ...
        System.out.println(grade);
```

```
        //... and display its equivalent value as a double.
        System.out.println(grade.value());
    }
}
```

Here's the output:

```
A
4.0
```

Here's a final example of an enum called StudentBody that uses a reference type, Student, as the encapsulated enum type:

```
public enum StudentBody {
        // Assign symbolic names to actual Student instances.
    fred(new Student("Fred")),
    mary(new Student("Mary"));

    private final Student value;

    StudentBody(Student value) {
        this.value = value;
    }

    public Student value() {
        return value;
    }
}
```

plus a bit of client code to illustrate its use:

```
public class EnumExample {
    public static void main(String[] args) {
        Student x = StudentBody.fred;
        // etc.
    }
}
```

Enumerations were a powerful addition to J2SE 5.0. Be certain to take advantage of them in designing your applications, as we will in building the SRS.

Enumerating Choices Prior to J2SE 5.0

Prior to J2SE 5.0, the best we could do to enumerate possible values for a variable was to declare public static final variables for a class, assigning a different symbolic name to each permitted value. For example, to address the example of students' majors from earlier, we'd perhaps declare the Student class as follows:

```
public class Student {
    private String name;
    private String major;
```

```
// We've added some public static final variables to enumerate possible values.
public static final String BIO = "Biology";
public static final String CHEM = "Chemistry";
public static final String MATH = "Mathematics";
public static final String CS = "Computer Science";
public static final String PHYS_ED = "Physical Education";

public Student(String name, String major) {
    this.name = name;
    this.major = major;
}
}
```

We could then take advantage of these symbolic constants in our client code as follows:

```
Student s = new Student("Bobby Cranston", Student.CS);
```

However, since the second argument to the Student constructor is declared to be a String, there is no way to prevent client code from disregarding all of our carefully crafted symbolic values to assign an invalid String value as a student's major:

```
// This will compile, given the Student class declaration above,
// but it violates our business rule concerning valid major designations.
Student s = new Student("Lee Neville", "Literature");
```

Thus, prior to J2SE 5.0, we could at best provide a list of preferred values as a convenience for client code, but could not enforce their use at compile time.

Providing Input to Command Line–Driven Programs

Virtually all applications require input of some sort, in either of the following forms:

- Data to be processed by the application

- Configuration information to control the manner in which the application operates

With a classic information system like the SRS, such input is typically acquired in one of two ways:

- From users, through their interactions with an application's GUI, as we'll discuss in Chapter 16

- By retrieving information from persistent storage—a file or database—as we'll discuss in Chapter 15

On occasion, we also have a need to write command line–driven utility programs in Java. It's handy to know how to guide such programs' behavior in one of two additional ways:

- Through the use of command-line arguments when the program is first launched

- By prompting the user for textual inputs via the command window

Let's explore both of these latter techniques.

Accepting Command-Line Arguments: The args Array

You learned in Chapter 2 that to invoke a Java program from the command line, you type the command java (to launch the JVM), followed by the name of the class/bytecode file containing the official main method, for example:

```
java Simple
```

You also learned that it's possible to control certain aspects of the JVM's behavior through the use of command-line options; such flags go between the java command and the class name. For example, you learned earlier in this chapter that you can establish the ***classpath*** of a program—that is, inform the JVM of where to search for bytecode files—by using the -cp option:

```
java -cp C:\Foo\A.jar;D:\Bar\B.jar Simple
```

We can also initialize our own programs by passing in command-line information of our own design when we invoke the programs. Such data comes ***after*** the name of the program on the command line:

```
java ClassFileName arg1 arg2 [...] argN
```

For example:

```
java ComputeTotal 123 456 789
```

or

```
java AnalyzeWords -sort DOG GUPPY GIRAFFE HIPPOPOTAMUS CAT
```

Such so-called **command-line arguments** get passed to the main method of the Java program as a String array called args (or whatever else we wish to name it), as declared by the main method header:

```
public static void main(String[] args) { ...
```

Inside the main method, we can do with args whatever we'd do with any other array—for example, determine the array's length, access individual String items within the array, and so forth, as we discussed in Chapter 6.

Let's look at a few example programs that take advantage of command-line arguments. This first example is quite simple; it simply prints out information about the arguments that it has received.

```java
public class FruitExample {
    public static void main(String[] args) {
        System.out.println("The args array contains " + args.length + " entries." );

        for (int i = 0; i < args.length; i++) {
            System.out.println("Argument #" + i + " = |" + args[i] + "|");
        }
    }
}
```

If we run the program as follows:

```
java FruitExample apple banana cherry
```

we get the following output:

```
The args array contains 3 entries.
Argument #0 = |apple|
Argument #1 = |banana|
Argument #2 = |cherry|
```

If we want to provide arguments that contain spaces, we enclose them in double quotes, as follows:

```
java FruitExample "green apple" "yellow banana" "black cherry"
```

Here's the output:

```
The args array contains 3 entries.
Argument #0 = |green apple|
Argument #1 = |yellow banana|
Argument #2 = |black cherry|
```

And, if we were to run our program with no command-line arguments whatsoever, as follows:

```
java FruitExample
```

it would report the following:

```
The args array contains 0 entries.
```

Introducing Custom Command-Line Flags to Control a Program's Behavior

Let's look at a second example that is a bit more elaborate. In this program, called AnalyzeWords, we introduce a custom command-line option of our own invention, -sort, to control the program's behavior.

- At a minimum, AnalyzeWords will inspect however many command-line arguments are provided by the user to determine the length of the shortest and longest of them.

- Optionally, based on the presence of the -sort option as a command-line argument, the program will also print out a list of the words in sorted order, eliminating duplicates.

I'll present the code in its entirety first and discuss it afterward:

```java
import java.util.TreeSet;

public class AnalyzeWords {
    public static void main(String[] args) {
        // Let's start with a bit of error checking.
        // If the user forgot to provide command-line input, let's
        // report this as an error.
```

```java
if (args.length == 0) {
    System.out.println("Usage:   java AnalyzeWords [-sort] list_of_words");
    System.out.println("e.g.:    java AnalyzeWords -sort ZEBRA " +
        "ELEPHANT RAT MONKEY");
    System.exit(0);
}

// Initialize a few items.
boolean sort = false;
TreeSet<String> sortedWords = new TreeSet<String>();
String shortest = null;
String longest = null;

for (int i = 0; i < args.length; i++) {
    // Watch for the presence of the -sort option.
    if (args[i].equals("-sort")) {
        sort = true;
        continue;
    }

    // If we haven't yet recorded a shortest or longest word, then by
    // definition this is the first, and hence both the shortest
    // and longest, word!
    if (shortest == null) {
        shortest = args[0];
        longest = args[0];
    }
    // Otherwise, compare this word to the shortest/longest seen so far.
    else {
        if (args[i].length() > longest.length()) longest = args[i];
        if (args[i].length() < shortest.length()) shortest = args[i];
    }

    // Add the word to the TreeSet so as to sort them automatically,
    // whether the user asked for them to be sorted or not; if the
    // user didn't ask for them to be sorted, we'll simply suppress
    // displaying this information.
    sortedWords.add(args[i]);
}

if (sort) {
    System.out.println("Sorted words:");
    for (String s : sortedWords) {
        System.out.println("\t" + s);
    }
}
```

```
        System.out.println("The shortest word was " + shortest.length() +
            " characters long.");
        System.out.println("The longest word was " + longest.length() +
            " characters long.");
    }
}
```

Let's now review noteworthy sections of the program in detail.

Because this program requires command-line input in order for it to do anything mean-ingful, we're going to check the length of (number of command-line arguments found within) the args array. If the length is 0, we're going to inform the user of how the program is to be used:

```
// If the user forgot to provide command-line input, let's
// report this as an error.
if (args.length == 0) {
    System.out.println("Usage:  java AnalyzeWords [-sort] list_of_words");
    System.out.println("e.g.:   java AnalyzeWords -sort ZEBRA " +
        "ELEPHANT RAT MONKEY");
```

and then we're going to terminate the program—there's no need to go any further if there's no input to process:

```
    System.exit(0);
}
```

Next, we declare a few variables:

- A boolean flag, sort, that we'll set later in the program if we detect that the user has provided the optional –sort command-line argument:

```
// Keep track of whether the user wants to optionally sort the words,
// in addition to analyzing them.
boolean sort = false;
```

- A TreeSet collection. Recall from our discussion of collections in Chapter 6 that sets have the property of eliminating duplicates; TreeSets, in particular, automatically sort their contents:

```
TreeSet<String> sortedWords = new TreeSet<String>();
```

- Two Strings that will maintain handles on the shortest and longest word that we've seen as of every new argument that we process:

```
// We'll keep track of the shortest and longest words as we go.
String shortest = null;
String longest = null;
```

We then iterate through the args array. If we discover the –sort option in the command-line input, we set the our boolean sort flag to true, and then use the continue statement to jump to the next word in the args array—we don't want to process the –sort option as a true "word" with respect to our analysis.

```
for (int i = 0; i < args.length; i++) {
    // Watch for the presence of the -sort flag.
```

```
        if (args[i].equals("-sort")) {
            sort = true;
            continue;
        }
```

If we haven't yet recorded any words as being either the shortest or the longest, we'll record this (first) word as ***both*** the shortest and the longest that we've seen thus far:

```
// If we haven't yet recorded a shortest or longest word, then by
// definition this is the first, and hence both the shortest
// and longest, word!
if (shortest == null) {
    shortest = args[0];
    longest = args[0];
}
```

Otherwise, if we have already assigned values to the shortest and longest Strings, we compare ***this*** word to each of them, to see if it is either longer than the longest word or shorter than the shortest word:

```
else {
    // If the current word that we're processing is longer
    // than the longest that we've seen so far, remember IT
    // as the longest.
    if (args[i].length() > longest.length()) longest = args[i];

    // If the current word that we're processing is shorter
    // than the shortest that we've seen so far, remember IT
    // as the shortest.
    if (args[i].length() < shortest.length()) shortest = args[i];
}
```

Then, ***whether or not the user has asked for us to sort the words***, we'll add this word to the sortedWords TreeSet. We do so for two primary reasons:

- The -sort flag may appear ***later*** in the argument list—for example, java AnalyzeWords DOG MONKEY ELEPHANT -sort—and we want to be prepared to respond if it does.

- It's so ***easy*** to sort the words, simply by adding them to a TreeSet, that there's no point in having to iterate through the args array a second time later on.

```
        // Add the word to the TreeSet so as to sort them automatically.
        // whether the user asked for them to be sorted or not; if the
        // user didn't ask for them to be sorted, we'll simply suppress
        // displaying this information.
        sortedWords.add(args[i]);
    }
```

We optionally display the sorted contents of the TreeSet:

```
if (sort) {
    System.out.println("Sorted words:");
```

```
        for (String s : sortedWords) {
            System.out.println("\t" + s);
        }
    }
}
```

Finally, we display the results of our "shortest/longest" analysis:

```
    System.out.println("The shortest word was " + shortest.length() +
        " characters long.");
    System.out.println("The longest word was " + longest.length() +
        " characters long.");
    }
}
```

Let's look at a few different ways to invoke this program, and the output that each way will produce. First, we'll omit the -sort option:

```
java AnalyzeWords ZEBRA ELEPHANT RAT MONKEY
```

Here's the output:

```
The shortest word was 3 characters long.
The longest word was 8 characters long.
```

Next, we'll include the -sort option:

```
java AnalyzeWords -sort ZEBRA ELEPHANT RAT MONKEY
```

Here's the output:

```
Sorted words:
    ELEPHANT
    MONKEY
    RAT
    ZEBRA
The shortest word was 3 characters long.
The longest word was 8 characters long.
```

The same output results if the -sort option is at the ***end*** of the argument list:

```
java AnalyzeWords ZEBRA ELEPHANT RAT MONKEY -sort
```

Here's the output:

```
Sorted words:
    ELEPHANT
    MONKEY
    RAT
    ZEBRA
The shortest word was 3 characters long.
The longest word was 8 characters long.
```

As we discussed earlier, we must enclose multiword arguments in double quotes:

```
java AnalyzeWords -sort "LITTLE BO PEEP" RUMPELSTILTSKIN "EENY MEENY MINEY MOE"
```

Here's the output:

```
Sorted words:
    EENY MEENY MINEY MOE
    LITTLE BO PEEP
    RUMPELSTILTSKIN
The shortest word was 14 characters long.
The longest word was 20 characters long.
```

Using the Wrapper Classes for Input Conversion

Recall the introduction in Chapter 6 to Java's predefined *wrapper classes* for each of the eight distinct primitive Java types—Integer, Float, Double, Byte, Short, Long, Boolean, and Character—all within the core java.lang package. Our previous discussion of these classes centered on their use in "wrapping" primitive types for purposes of storing them in a Java collection. We're now going to explore an alternative use of these classes, as *utility classes*, for performing data conversions.

One such example of when we might need to perform a data conversion operation is when obtaining data via a user interface. Whether we use a GUI to acquire user input, as we'll do for the SRS in Chapter 16, or a command-line interface, as we're exploring in this chapter, data is always acquired from a user in String format. We often need to convert this data into one of the Java numeric types (int, double, etc.) in order to be able to manipulate it mathematically.

Each of the wrapper classes declares a number of static methods that are useful when we need to perform data conversions. For example, the Integer class defines a static method with the header

```
static int parseInt(String s)
```

Pass in a String as an argument to this method, and the Integer class will convert it to an int(eger) for us if it represents a valid integer, or will throw a NumberFormatException if it does not. Similarly, the Double class declares a static parseDouble method, the Float class declares a static parseFloat method, and so forth.

Here's a simple example to illustrate how the Integer.parseInt method might be used:

```java
public class IntegerTest {
    public static void main(String[] args) {
        String[] ints = { "123", "foobar", "456", "789" };
        int i = 0;

        for (i = 0; i < ints.length; i++) {
            try {
                int test = Integer.parseInt(ints[i]);
                System.out.println(test + " converted just fine!");
            }
            catch (NumberFormatException e) {
                System.out.println("Whoops!  " + ints[i] +
```

```
                " is an invalid integer.");
            }
        }
    }
}
```

This program, when run, produces the following output:

```
123 converted just fine!
Whoops!  foobar is an invalid integer.
456 converted just fine!
789 converted just fine!
```

Note that we inserted the try statement *inside of* the for loop, so that it would take effect once per loop iteration. If we had inserted the whole for loop into the try block instead, as follows:

```
public class IntegerTest {
    public static void main(String[] args) {
        String[] ints = { "123", "foobar", "456", "789" };
        int i = 0;

        try {
            // Now, the entire for loop is within the try block.
            for (i = 0; i < ints.length; i++) {
                int test = Integer.parseInt(ints[i]);
                System.out.println(test + " converted just fine!");
            }
        }

        catch (NumberFormatException e) {
            System.out.println("Whoops!   " + ints[i] + " is an invalid integer.");
        }
    }
}
```

then the first occurrence of a NumberFormatException would have *terminated* the for loop, producing the following alternate output:

```
123 converted just fine!
Whoops!  foobar is an invalid integer.
```

Another static method defined by the Integer class (and the other wrapper classes, as well) is used to do the reverse:

```
static String toString(int)
```

This method accepts an int(eger) value as an argument, converting it into a proper String, as the following example illustrates:

```
int i = 56;
String s = Integer.toString(i);      // s now has a String value of "56"
```

There is a shortcut for doing the same thing, however. We simply need to concatenate the value of i to an empty String ("") as follows:

```
int i = 56;
String s = "" + i;    // s now has a String value of "56"
```

Accepting Keyboard Input

You learned in Part 1 of this book that Java provides a special OutputStream object called System.out, which in turn provides both println and print methods for displaying messages to the command-line window. Java also provides a special InputStream object called System.in to **read** inputs from the command-line window as typed by a user via the keyboard. There is only one minor annoyance with acquiring keyboard input using System.in: the primary method provided by the InputStream class for doing so, read, reads only one character at a time, and this character is actually returned to client code as an int(eger) value. Thus, the burden is on us to

- Cast these int values into char values.

- Buffer these values in some fashion as we read them one by one.

- Monitor for end-of-line characters, signaling the user's press of the Enter key on the keyboard.

- And, while we're at it, handle any IOExceptions that might arise.

This is illustrated in the following code:

```
        StringBuffer line = new StringBuffer();

        try {
            // Read the first integer, and cast it into a character.
            char in = (char) System.in.read();

            // Keep going until we detect a newline character (\n), which is
            // generated when a user presses the Enter key on the keyboard.
            while (in != '\n') {
                line.append(in);

                // Read the next character.
                in = (char) System.in.read();
            }
        }
        catch (IOException e) {
            throw new IOException("Something went wrong with the keyboard!");
        }

        System.out.println("Line read:  |" + line.toString() + "|");
```

Rather than writing such low-level code time and time again, let's put what we've learned about information hiding to work by encapsulating all of these details in a utility class of our own making called KeyboardInput, as follows:

```
import java.io.*;

/** A utility class that provides a single static method for reading keyboard
 ** input from the command-line window (via System.in).
 **
 ** Each call to the static method KeyboardInput.readLine() returns a
 ** String representing a line's worth of input (up until the user
 ** pressed the Enter key).
 */
public class KeyboardInput {
    /** Returns a single line typed via the keyboard. */
    public static String readLine() throws IOException {
        // We'll gather up individual characters one by one using a StringBuffer.
        StringBuffer input = new StringBuffer();

        try {
            // Read the first integer, and cast it into a character.
            char in = (char) System.in.read();

            // Keep going until we detect a newline character (\n), which is
            // generated when a user presses the Enter key on the keyboard.
            while (in != '\n') {
                input.append(in);

                // Read the next character.
                in = (char) System.in.read();
            }
        }
        catch (IOException e) {
            // We aren't going to do anything special to respond to these.
        }

        // Strip off any leading/trailing white space.
        return input.toString().trim();
    }
}
```

Here's a simple example of how we might use the KeyboardInput class from within client code:

```
import java.io.*;

// A sample main program that prompts the user for command-line keyboard input.

public class KeyboardInputExample {
    public static void main(String args[]) throws IOException {
        // Note use of print vs. println.
        System.out.print("Please enter your name:  ");
```

```
        String name = KeyboardInput.readLine();
        System.out.println("Hello, " + name + "!");
    }
}
```

Running this program from the command line would produce the following results (<u>underlining</u> reflects what was typed by the user):

```
C:\> java KeyboardInputExample
Please enter your name:  Jacquie
Hello, Jacquie!
C:\>
```

Let's combine our knowledge of prompting for keyboard input with what we learned earlier about converting String input to numeric values to write a simple command line–driven calculator:

```
import java.io.*;

public class SimpleCalc {
    public static void main(String args[]) throws IOException {
        // We'll ask the user to input two numeric values to be
        // mathematically combined.
        // These will come in as Strings, however.
        double first = 0.0;
        double second = 0.0;

        for (int i = 1; i <= 2; i++) {
            System.out.print("Please enter a number:  ");
            String sNumber = KeyboardInput.readLine();

            // Let's try to convert the String input into a numeric value.
            double number = 0.0;

            try {
                number = Double.parseDouble(sNumber);
            }
            catch (NumberFormatException e) {
                System.out.println("Invalid number:  " + sNumber);
                System.out.println("Please try again!");
                System.exit(0);
            }

            // Remember the number;
            if (i == 1) first = number;
            else second = number;
        }

        System.out.print("Please choose an operation (+, -, *, /):  ");
        String operation = KeyboardInput.readLine();
```

```
        // Let's try to compute an answer.
        double answer = 0.0;

        if (operation.equals("+"))  answer = first + second;
        else if (operation.equals("-")) answer = first - second;
        else if (operation.equals("*")) answer = first * second;
        else if (operation.equals("/")) answer = first / second;
        else {
            System.out.println("Invalid operation:  " + operation);
            System.out.println("Please try again!");
            System.exit(0);
        }

        System.out.println(first + " " + operation + " " + second + " = " + answer);
    }
}
```

Here are a few observations:

- We declare two double variables, first and second, to represent the user's two numeric inputs; we use double as the more precise numeric type, as it will also handle int(eger) values just fine.

- Similarly, we use the Double.parseDouble method in lieu of Integer.parseInt, because the former will tolerate optional decimal points in the input, whereas the latter will not.

Let's look at several different outcomes from running the program as java SimpleCalc.

```
Please enter a number:  1
Please enter a number:  1
Please choose an operation (+, -, *, /):  +
1.0 + 1.0 = 2.0
```

```
Please enter a number:  2
Please enter a number:  4.5
Please choose an operation (+, -, *, /):  *
2.0 * 4.5 = 9.0
```

```
Please enter a number:  X
Invalid number:  X
Please try again!
```

```
Please enter a number:  1
Please enter a number:  1
Please choose an operation (+, -, *, /):  #
Invalid operation:  #
Please try again!
```

Features of the Object Class

We discussed in Chapter 5 that the Object class, provided in the core java.lang package, is the ultimate superclass for all classes in Java, user-defined or otherwise. Thus, all Java objects, regardless of type, inherit a common set of interesting features from the Object class, which we'll explore in this section.

Determining the Class That an Object Belongs To

Every Java object inherits a method from the Object class with the header

```
Class getClass()
```

This method, when invoked on an object reference—for example, x.getClass();—returns a reference to an object of type Class representing an abstraction of the class that object x belongs to.

The Class class, in turn, defines a method with the header

```
String getName()
```

This method, when invoked on a Class reference, returns the ***fully qualified name*** of the class for classes that belong to a ***named*** package (*packagename.Classname*—for example, java.util. ArrayList), or a simple class name—for example, Professor—for classes that belong to the default (unnamed) package (as will be the case for our SRS classes).

Chaining these two methods together, we can ask any object reference to identify which class the object it references belongs to, as follows:

```
reference.getClass().getName();
```

For example:

```
Professor pr = new Professor();
System.out.println(pr.getClass().getName());
```

Here's the output:

```
Professor
```

or

```
// Test to see if x is referring to a Professor object.
// Note that if x were null, we'd get a NullPointerException, so we've
// inserted a test for "nullness" before calling the getClass method on x.
if (x != null && x.getClass().getName().equals("Professor")) { ...
```

Returning to our discussion of exception handling from earlier in this chapter, we can also use the getClass().getName() approach within a catch block to determine what sort of exception has occurred:

```
try { ... }
catch (SomeExceptionType e) {
    System.out.println("Drat!  An exception of type " +
        e.getClass().getName() + " has occurred.");
}
```

Here's sample output:

```
Drat!  An exception of type java.lang.NullPointerException has occurred.
```

Another way to test whether a given object reference belongs to a particular class is via the `instanceof` operator. This is a `boolean` operator that allows us to determine if some reference variable x is referring to an object of class/type Y. Here's a simple code example to illustrate the use of this operator. In this example, we assume that `Person` is an abstract class, and that both `Student` and `Professor` are concrete classes derived from `Person`:

```
Person x;

// Later in the program ...
x = new Professor();

// Still later in the program ...
// Determine the precise run-time identity of x.
if (x instanceof Student) {
    System.out.println("x is a Student");
}

if (x instanceof Professor) {
    System.out.println("x is a Professor");
}

if (x instanceof Person) {
    System.out.println("x is a Person");
}
```

Here's the output:

```
x is a Professor
x is a Person
```

Testing the Equality of Objects

What does it mean when we say that two objects are "equal"? When speaking of generic `Objects`, we say that two objects (or, more precisely, two object *references*) are equal if they both refer to precisely the same object in memory (i.e., if the references both point to the same exact memory location in the JVM). Java provides two ways for determining the equality of two `Object` references x and y:

- The double equal sign operator (==), which you've seen used several times previously in this book, first to compare the values of simple data types in Chapter 2, as follows:

  ```
  int x = 3;
  int y = 3;
  if (x == y) { ...
  ```

and then to compare the identities of String references earlier in Chapter 13, as follows:

```
String x = "foo";
String y = "foo";
// Do x and y refer to the same String object?
if (x == y) { ...
```

- The boolean equals method, which is inherited by all objects from the Object class. We used this method with the String class earlier in this chapter.

As defined for Objects generically, the == operator and the equals method can be used interchangeably to test whether two references refer to exactly the same Object. Here's some example code to illustrate these two alternative approaches:

```
public class EqualsTest1 {
  public static void main(String[] args) {
    // We'll create one generic Object...
    Object o1 = new Object();

    // ... and maintain two handles on it (o1 and o2).
    Object o2 = o1;

    // We'll create a second different Object object, and
    // use variable o3 to maintain a handle on it.
    Object o3 = new Object();
```

This is illustrated conceptually in Figure 13-26.

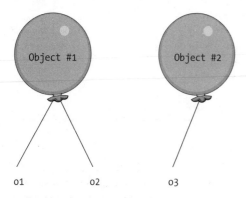

Figure 13-26. *We've created two generic Objects.*

Then, if we execute the following code (note our use of nested boolean expressions within the println statements):

```
// Are o1 and o2 "equal"?
System.out.println("The expression o1 == o2 evaluates to: " + (o1 == o2));
System.out.println("The expression o1.equals(o2) evaluates to: " +
    (o1.equals(o2)));
```

```
    // Are o1 and o3 "equal"?
    System.out.println("The expression o1 == o3 evaluates to: " + (o1 == o3));
    System.out.println("The expression o1.equals(o3) evaluates to: " +
        (o1.equals(o3)));
```

the following output results:

```
The expression o1 == o2 evaluates to: true
The expression o1.equals(o2) evaluates to: true
The expression o1 == o3 evaluates to: false
The expression o1.equals(o3) evaluates to: false
```

because o1 and o2 are truly referring to exactly the same Object, whereas p3 is referring to a different Object.

Let's repeat the example, this time using Person objects:

```
public class EqualsTest2 {
  public static void main(String[] args) {
    // We'll create one Person object ...
    Person p1 = new Person("222-22-2222", "Fred");

    // ... and maintain two handles on it (p1 and p2).
    Person p2 = p1;

    // We'll create a second different Person object with exactly the same
    // attribute values as the first Person object that we created, and
    // use variable p3 to maintain a handle on this second object.
    Person p3 = new Person("222-22-2222", "Fred");
```

When we execute the following code:

```
    // Are p1 and p2 "equal"?
    System.out.println("The expression p1 == p2 evaluates to: " + (p1 == p2));
    System.out.println("The expression p1.equals(p2) evaluates to: " +
        (p1.equals(p2)));

    // Are p1 and p3 "equal"?
    System.out.println("The expression p1 == p3 evaluates to: " + (p1 == p3));
    System.out.println("The expression p1.equals(p3) evaluates to: " +
        (p1.equals(p3)));
```

we get the same sort of result as we did for generic Objects:

```
The expression p1 == p2 evaluates to: true
The expression p1.equals(p2) evaluates to: true
The expression p1 == p3 evaluates to: false
The expression p1.equals(p3) evaluates to: false
```

Even though p1 and p3 are referring to Person objects with ***identical attribute values***, they are nonetheless physically distinct Person instances, and so p1 is not considered to be "equal to" p3.

Let's repeat this example once more, this time using Strings. We'll formally instantiate the Strings to avoid the String literal pool, ensuring that we truly do create physically separate instances of String objects:

```java
public class EqualsTest3 {
  public static void main(String[] args) {
    // We'll create one String object, using the formal method of
    // String instantiation ...
    String s1 = new String("hello");

    // ... and maintain two handles on it (s1 and s2).
    String s2 = s1;

    // We'll explicitly instantiate a second String object,
    // with EXACTLY THE SAME VALUE as the first String object -
    // "hello" -  and use variable s3 to maintain a handle
    // on this second String.
    String s3 = new String("hello");
```

This is illustrated conceptually in Figure 13-27.

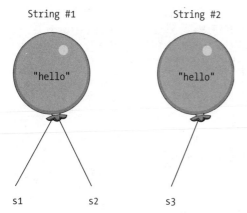

Figure 13-27. *We've created two physically distinct String instances with the same value, "hello".*

When we execute the following client code:

```java
// Are s1 and s2 "equal"?
System.out.println("The expression s1 == s2 evaluates to: " + (s1 == s2));
System.out.println("The expression s1.equals(s2) evaluates to: " + (s1.equals(s2)));

// Are s1 and s3 "equal"?
System.out.println("The expression s1 == s3 evaluates to: " + (s1 == s3));
System.out.println("The expression s1.equals(s3) evaluates to: " + (s1.equals(s3)));
```

the following output results:

```
The expression s1 == s2 evaluates to: true
The expression s1.equals(s2) evaluates to: true
The expression s1 == s3 evaluates to: false
The expression s1.equals(s3) evaluates to: true
```

Note that when comparing Strings with the equals method, the equals method behaves ***differently*** than it did for generic Objects and for Person objects—that is, s1 and s3 are deemed to be "equal" ***despite the fact that they refer to physically different*** String ***instances***! Compare the preceding last line of output

```
The expression s1.equals(s3) evaluates to: true
```

with the corresponding lines of output from our Object and Person examples

```
The expression o1.equals(o3) evaluates to: false
```

and

```
The expression p1.equals(p3) evaluates to: false
```

How is it that the equals method behaves differently for Strings than it does for other object types? As it turns out, the String class ***overrides*** the equals method as defined by the Object class so that it compares String ***values*** rather than String ***identities***. In fact, many of the predefined Java classes have overridden the equals method as inherited from Object to perform a relevant, class-specific comparison—for example, the wrapper classes (Boolean, Integer, Double, etc.), the Date class, and others. And, of course, we can override the equals method for our own classes, as well—let's see how this is accomplished.

Overriding the equals Method

Let's say we want the equals method, when used to compare two Person instances, to deem them "equal" if they have the same value for their SSN (ssn) attribute. To accomplish this, we override the equals method as in the following code. I'll present the code in its entirety first, and I'll explain some of the details afterward.

```
public class Person {
    private String ssn;
    private String name;
    // etc.

    // Constructor.
    public Person(String s, String n) {
        this.setSsn(s);
        this.setName(n);
    }
```

```
    // Accessor methods.

    public String getSsn() {
        return ssn;
    }

    // etc.

    // Overriding the equals method that we inherited from the Object class.
    public boolean equals(Object o) {
        boolean isEqual;

        // Try to cast the Object reference into a Person reference.
        // If this fails, we'll get a ClassCastException.
        try {
            Person p = (Person) o;

            // If we make it to this point in the code, we know we're
            // dealing with a Person object; next, we'll compare ssn's.
            if (this.getSsn().equals(p.getSsn())) {
                // We'll deem p equal to THIS person.
                isEqual = true;
            }
            else {
                isEqual = false;
            }
        }
        catch (ClassCastException e) {
            // They're not equal - o isn't even a Person!
            isEqual = false;
        }

        return isEqual;
    }
}
```

Let's explore the equals method in detail:

- The equals method header as declared by the Object class accepts a generic Object as an argument; when overriding this method for Person, we may not change this signature to accept a Person reference explicitly. Rather, we'll attempt to *cast* o to be a reference to a Person to determine if, at run time, o really *is* referring to a Person. If the cast attempt succeeds, we'll wind up with two handles on the same object: Object o and Person p.

```
    // Overriding the equals method that we inherited from the Object class.
    public boolean equals(Object o) {
        boolean isEqual;
```

```
        // Try to cast the Object reference into a Person reference.
        // If this fails, we'll get a ClassCastException.
        try {
            Person p = (Person) o;
```

- If a ClassCastException is ***not*** thrown by the previous line of code, then we know that o is indeed referring to a Person. Our next step is to then compare the ssn attribute value of p (aka o) to the ssn attribute value of ***this*** Person—that is, the Person whose equals method we've invoked to begin with.

```
            // If we make it to this point in the code, we know we're
            // dealing with a Person object; next, we'll compare ssn's.
            if (this.getSsn().equals(p.getSsn())) {
```

- If the ssn values are equal, then the Person referred to by p (and o) is deemed "equal to" ***this*** Person; otherwise, they are not equal:

```
                // We'll deem p equal to THIS person.
                isEqual = true;
            }
            else {
                isEqual = false;
            }
        }
```

- Conversely, if a ClassCastException arose when we tried to cast o as a Person, then we know that o doesn't "equal" this Person to whom we're comparing—after all, o isn't even a Person!

```
        catch (ClassCastException e) {
            // They're not equal - o isn't even a Person!
            isEqual = false;
        }
```

Now that we've overridden the equals method for the Person class, let's return to our earlier example program where we were testing the equality of Person objects. We'll rerun the code exactly as it was written before (the code is repeated here for your convenience):

```
public class EqualsTest2 {
  public static void main(String[] args) {
    // We'll create one Person object ...
    Person p1 = new Person("222-22-2222", "Fred");

    // ... and maintain two handles on it (p1 and p2).
    Person p2 = p1;

    // We'll create a second different Person object with exactly the same
    // attribute values as the first Person object that we created, and
    // use variable p3 to maintain a handle on this second object.
    Person p3 = new Person("222-22-2222", "Fred");
```

```
// Are p1 and p2 "equal"?
System.out.println("The expression p1 == p2 evaluates to: " + (p1 == p2));
System.out.println("The expression p1.equals(p2) evaluates to: " +
    (p1.equals(p2)));

// Are p1 and p3 "equal"?
System.out.println("The expression p1 == p3 evaluates to: " + (p1 == p3));
System.out.println("The expression p1.equals(p3) evaluates to: " +
    (p1.equals(p3)));
```

However, because we've overridden the equals method for the Person class, we'll now get a different result when we execute the code. The output is as follows:

```
The expression p1 == p2 evaluates to: true
The expression p1.equals(p2) evaluates to: true
The expression p1 == p3 evaluates to: false
The expression p1.equals(p3) evaluates to: true
```

Note that even though p1 and p3 are referring to two physically distinct Person objects, these objects have ***identical values*** for their ssn attribute, and so they are now deemed to be "equal."

Consider overriding the equals method of any class for which you have a frequent need to test the equivalence of objects.

Overriding the toString Method

Recall that the (overloaded) print and println methods do their best to render whatever expression is passed in as an argument into an equivalent String representation. This is relatively straightforward for simple data types:

```
int x = 7;
double y = 3.8;
boolean z = false;
System.out.println(x);
System.out.println(y);
System.out.println(z);
```

Here's the output:

```
7
3.8
false
```

Here's the code for expressions that ***resolve*** to one of these types:

```
int x = 7;
double y = 3.8;
boolean z = false;
System.out.println(x + y);
System.out.println(x == y);
```

Here's the output:

```
10.8
false
```

If we were to try to print the value of an expression that resolves to an ***object reference***, on the other hand, as follows:

```
Student s = new Student("Harvey", "123-45-6789");
```

```
// Try to print the object reference directly.
System.out.println(s);
```

we'd most likely get a rather cryptic-looking result, similar to the following:

```
Student@71f71130
```

where `Student@71f71130` represents an internal object ID relevant only to the JVM. ***Why is this?***

It just so happens that all objects inherit a method from the `Object` class with the header

```
String toString();
```

As inherited from the `Object` class, the `toString` method is defined to print the name of the class to which an object belongs, followed by an "at" sign (@), followed by an internal object ID (*Classname@internalID*), as we saw with the preceding `Student` example.

Note that for expressions that resolve to an object reference, the `println` and `print` methods ***automatically*** invoke that object's `toString` method—that is, the following two lines of code are equivalent:

```
System.out.println(s.toString());
```

and

```
System.out.println(s);
```

What we probably meant to do was to print one or more of the `Student` object's attributes as a ***representation*** of the object—for example, perhaps the student's `name`, followed by his or her `ssn` in parentheses:

```
John Smith (123-45-6789)
```

We can accomplish this by ***overriding*** the `toString` method for the `Student` class to define what it is that we wish to have printed as a representation of a `Student`. For example, the `Student` class may override the `toString` method as follows:

```
public String toString() {
  return this.getName() + " (" + this.getSsn() + ")");
}
```

As a result, the following code:

```
Student s = new Student("Harvey", "123-45-6789");
System.out.println(s);
```

would now produce the alternative output

```
Harvey (123-45-6789)
```

---

as desired.

It's generally a good idea to routinely override the `toString` method for all user-defined classes.

A Deeper Look Behind the Scenes of the JVM

You learned in Chapter 2 that when you type the command

```
java bytecode_filename
```

for example:

```
java SimpleProgram
```

to run a Java program, you're actually launching the JVM, which in turn goes through the following process:

1. The JVM searches for the specified bytecode file in its classpath.

2. If the file is found, the JVM loads the bytecode into its memory.

3. The JVM searches the bytecode for the official `main` method header: `public static void main(String[] args)`.

4. If the file is found, the JVM executes the `main` method to launch the application.

Now that you understand the typical multiple-class architecture of a Java application like the SRS, let's look at the mechanism of the JVM—in particular, the JVM's **class loader**—in a bit more depth.

The JVM's Class Loader

When the JVM is launched via the `java` command to execute a particular application X, a fixed amount of memory is allocated to the JVM by the host operating system. The JVM then goes about loading the bytecode definitions of all classes referenced by application X into this memory as they are needed—that is, when application X explicitly attempts to use them for the first time. This can occur in a variety of ways:

- Whenever application X instantiates an object, the bytecode to be used as the template for creating that object (i.e., its class definition) must be loaded if it isn't already in the JVM's memory:

  ```
  // The use of the new keyword below to instantiate a Student causes the
  // bytecode for the Student class to be loaded into the JVM's memory if
  // it hasn't been previously loaded.
  Student s1 = new Student();
  ```

```
// Then, when this second Student is instantiated in the same
// application, the student class bytecode will already be in the
// JVM's memory, and needn't be loaded a second time.
Student s2 = new Student();
```

- Whenever application X attempts to invoke a static method on a class, the bytecode for that class must be loaded if it isn't already in the JVM's memory:

```
// The following line of code would cause the TempUtility class
// (a user-defined type that we discussed in Chapter 7) to be
// loaded into the JVM's memory if it hadn't already been loaded.
freezingC = TempUtility.convertFtoC(32.0);
```

- Finally, application X can explicitly request the JVM to load the bytecode for a particular class via the syntax

```
Class.forName(name of class whose bytecode is to be loaded);
```

for example:

```
// When connecting to a Sybase DBMS, we must load the driver class into
// the JVM, effectively as a "plug-in".
Class.forName(com.sybase.jdbc2.jdbc.SybDriver);
```

(Note that the name of the class to be loaded is ***not*** enclosed in double quotes.)

Recall our discussion of exception handling earlier in this chapter. Whenever we use the Class.forName(...) syntax to attempt to load bytecode into memory, the compiler will force us to enclose such code in a try block with an accompanying catch block to catch ClassNotFoundExceptions, because it's possible that our classpath is misconfigured such that the JVM cannot find the bytecode in question:

```
try {
    // When connecting to a Sybase DBMS, we must load a Sybase-specific
    // driver class into the JVM, effectively as a "plug-in".
    Class.forName(com.sybase.jdbc2.jdbc.SybDriver);
}
catch (ClassNotFoundException e) { ... }
```

Note that some class definitions are used so regularly, and by so many applications, that their bytecode definitions are ***automatically*** loaded when the JVM starts up, whether or not a given application X explicitly calls for their use. For example, the many core classes defined within the java.lang package (String, Math, System, and so forth) are automatically loaded upon JVM startup.

Once a particular class's bytecode is loaded into the JVM, it remains in the JVM's memory until the application that the JVM is executing terminates. At that point, all of the memory allocated to the JVM is released back to the operating system, and the JVM itself stops running.

The -verbose Option

We can use the -verbose command-line flag of the java command to "eavesdrop" on what is happening behind the scenes when the JVM executes a particular application. Let's do so for several different programs.

First, we'll execute the following simple program:

```java
public class Simple {
    public static void main(String[] args) {
        System.out.println("I LOVE Java!!!");
    }
}
```

Typing the command

```
java -verbose Simple
```

causes the following output to be displayed:

```
[Opened C:\Program Files\Java\jdk1.5.0\jre\lib\rt.jar]
[Opened C:\Program Files\Java\jdk1.5.0\jre\lib\jsse.jar]
[Opened C:\Program Files\Java\jdk1.5.0\jre\lib\jce.jar]
[Opened C:\Program Files\Java\jdk1.5.0\jre\lib\charsets.jar]
[Loaded java.lang.Object from C:\Program Files\Java\jdk1.5.0\jre\lib\rt.jar]
[Loaded java.io.Serializable from C:\Program Files\Java\jdk1.5.0\jre\lib\rt.jar]
[Loaded java.lang.Comparable from C:\Program Files\Java\jdk1.5.0\jre\lib\rt.jar]
[Loaded java.lang.CharSequence from C:\Program Files\Java\jdk1.5.0\jre\lib\rt.jar]
[Loaded java.lang.String from C:\Program Files\Java\jdk1.5.0\jre\lib\rt.jar]
< ... etc. ... >
[Loaded java.lang.System from C:\Program Files\Java\jdk1.5.0\jre\lib\rt.jar]
< ... etc. ... >
[Loaded Simple from file:/C:/MyCode/Java]
I LOVE Java!!!
[Loaded java.lang.Shutdown from C:\Program Files\Java\jdk1.5.0\jre\lib\rt.jar]
[Loaded java.lang.Shutdown$Lock from C:\Program Files\Java\jdk1.5.0\jre\lib\rt.jar]
```

Let's examine this output in detail.

First, the JVM accesses a number of JAR files found within the Java Runtime Environment (JRE) "home" directory ([Opened ...]) to obtain and load ([Loaded ...]) the bytecode for a number of predefined core classes from various packages. These *same* core classes are loaded automatically whenever the JVM is launched, regardless of what program we've asked it to execute.

After loading these core class definitions, the JVM finally gets around to loading the class that we *asked* it to load in the first place, Simple:

```
[Loaded Simple from file:/C:/MyCode/Java]
```

Next, the JVM executes the main method found within the Simple bytecode, to produce the following output:

```
I LOVE Java!!!
```

Finally, the JVM does some wrap-up before shutting down:

```
[Loaded java.lang.Shutdown from C:\Program Files\Java\jdk1.5.0\jre\lib\rt.jar]
[Loaded java.lang.Shutdown$Lock from C:\Program Files\Java\jdk1.5.0\jre\lib\rt.jar]
```

The only class that we *explicitly* asked the JVM to load for us was `Simple`:

```
java -verbose Simple
```

However, we also took advantage of the `System` class—one of the core classes automatically loaded by the JVM upon startup—when we invoked the `System.out.println` method:

```
System.out.println("I LOVE Java!!!");
```

And, since `out` is a `public static` attribute of the `System` class declared to be of type `PrintStream`, then we also implicitly took advantage of the `PrintStream` class, etc. When all is said and done, we may have unwittingly taken advantage of *many* of the automatically loaded core classes, even with such a trivially simple program.

Let's now look at a slightly more elaborate second example, this time involving three simple user-defined classes:

```
public class Person {
    private String name;

    // Method details omitted.
}

public class Student extends Person {
    private Professor advisor;

    // Method details omitted.
}

public class Professor extends Person {
    private String title;

    // Method details omitted.
}
```

to support the following program:

```
public class MyApp {
    public static void main(String[] args) {
        // Declare a Professor reference.
        Professor p;

        // Declare a Student reference ...
        Student s;

        // ... and instantiate a Student object.
        s = new Student();
```

```
            // Note that we are NOT instantiating a
            // Professor object.

            // Print a message right before exiting.
            System.out.println("That's all, folks!");
        }
    }
```

Note that MyApp declares two reference variables—of type Professor and Student, respectively—but only instantiates *one* object: a Student.

After compiling all of the preceding code, if we type

```
java -verbose MyApp
```

we observe the following output:

```
[Opened C:\Program Files\Java\jdk1.5.0\jre\lib\rt.jar]
[Opened C:\Program Files\Java\jdk1.5.0\jre\lib\jsse.jar]
[Opened C:\Program Files\Java\jdk1.5.0\jre\lib\jce.jar]
[Opened C:\Program Files\Java\jdk1.5.0\jre\lib\charsets.jar]
[Loaded java.lang.Object from C:\Program Files\Java\jdk1.5.0\jre\lib\rt.jar]
< ... etc. ... >
[Loaded MyApp from file:/C:/MyCode/Java/]
[Loaded Person from file:/C:/MyCode/Java/]
[Loaded Student from file:/C:/MyCode/Java/]
That's all, folks!
[Loaded java.lang.Shutdown from C:\Program Files\Java\jdk1.5.0\jre\lib\rt.jar]
[Loaded java.lang.Shutdown$Lock from C:\Program Files\Java\jdk1.5.0\jre\lib\rt.jar]
```

Let's examine this output in detail.

First, the *same* core classes that were initially loaded in our previous Simple example, and which are *always* loaded upon JVM startup, are loaded.

Next, the JVM loads the MyApp class and begins to execute its main method:

```
[Loaded MyApp from file:/C:/MyCode/Java/]
```

As the main method executes, we see the JVM loading the following two user-defined classes:

```
[Loaded Person from file:/C:/MyCode/Java/]
[Loaded Student from file:/C:/MyCode/Java/]
```

Finally, the main method prints the desired message:

```
That's all, folks!
```

and then the main method ends and the JVM shuts down in the same manner as before.

Here are some interesting observations:

- Note that the Professor class was never loaded, because we don't ever instantiate a Professor object anywhere in our program. While the Java **compiler** does indeed need proof—in the form of a Professor.class bytecode file—that Professor is a valid user-defined type when the statement Professor p; is **compiled**, the JVM needn't bother to load the bytecode "blueprint" for a Professor object while our application **executes** unless we actually ask the JVM to instantiate a Professor, which we never did.

- Why, then, did the JVM load the Person class bytecode if we didn't explicitly instantiate a Person? By virtue of inheritance, a Student is a Person and, as you learned in Chapter 5, the "Personness" of a Student must be established based on a Person class constructor before the "Studentness" of a Student can be established. So, to instantiate a Student object, the JVM needed the bytecode definition for both the Person and Student classes (and, for that matter, the bytecode for the Object class, as well; note that Object is the **first** class that is automatically loaded into the JVM upon startup, because every other object to be instantiated depends on Object for purposes of establishing its "Objectness").

The Static Nature of main(...)

Ever since Chapter 2, we've been typing the official main method header as follows:

```
public static void main(String[] args) { ...
```

We are now in a position to understand why the main method of an application must be declared to be static.

When the JVM first starts running, no objects yet exist; objects are created only **after** the main method begins to execute, as it is the main method that creates the first objects for an application. So, in order to invoke the main method, the JVM must be permitted to invoke it on a **class**—in particular, on the class to which the main method belongs, and whose bytecode we've explicitly asked the JVM to load. Think back to our discussion of static methods in Chapter 7: a static method is one that can be invoked on a class as a whole, without first instantiating an object of that class. Hence, the main method must be static.

Import Directives, Revisited

When I first introduced the notion of import directives in Chapter 6, I mentioned in passing that whether we use a wildcard character (*) to import all of the classes in a given package

```
// Import all classes in the javax.swing package using a wildcard.
import javax.swing.*;
```

or we import individual classes one by one

```
// Import the JFrame and JDialog classes only.
import javax.swing.JFrame;
import javax.swing.JDialog;
```

neither approach is more or less efficient than the other at run time. Let's use the –verbose command-line flag to substantiate this claim.

We'll write three different programs called SwingExample1, SwingExample2, and SwingExample3. In these programs, we're importing several classes from the javax.swing package which, as you'll learn in Chapter 16, is involved with building GUIs. (I've chosen to craft this example around these `javax.swing` classes in particular because they are not among the core classes that automatically get loaded by the JVM upon startup. Thus, they'll be loaded only if necessary based on how we've written our SwingExample*x* programs.)

All three SwingExample*x* programs have the exact same `main` method body, and differ only in their `import` directives (**bolded** in the following code):

```java
// SwingExample1.java

// Import all classes in the javax.swing package using the wildcard syntax.
import javax.swing.*;

public class SwingExample1 {
    public static void main(String[] args) {
        // This is the same exact main method logic as found in the
        // other two SwingExample programs.
        JFrame f = new JFrame("sample frame");
        JDialog d = new JDialog(f, "sample dialog");
    }
}


//-------------------------------------------------------------


// SwingExample2.java

// Explicitly import the JFrame and JDialog classes only.
import javax.swing.JFrame;
import javax.swing.JDialog;

public class SwingExample2 {
    public static void main(String[] args) {
        // This is the same exact main method logic as found in the
        // other two SwingExample programs.
        JFrame f = new JFrame("sample frame");
        JDialog d = new JDialog(f, "sample dialog");
    }
}

//-------------------------------------------------------------


// SwingExample3.java

// Import two classes that we need -- JFrame and JDialog -- plus
// two that we DON'T need/reference in our program.
import javax.swing.JFrame;
import javax.swing.JDialog;
import javax.swing.JOptionPane;
import javax.swing.JMenu;
```

```
public class SwingExample3 {
    public static void main(String[] args) {
        // This is the same exact main method logic as found in the
        // other two SwingExample programs.
        JFrame f = new JFrame("sample frame");
        JDialog d = new JDialog(f, "sample dialog");
    }
}
```

If we were to execute these three programs using the –verbose command-line option

```
java -verbose Swing1
java -verbose Swing2
java -verbose Swing3
```

(output not shown), we'd discover that all three invocations cause ***the exact same classes to be loaded***—that is, the JFrame and JDialog bytecode would be loaded, whereas other extraneous javax.swing classes would ***not*** be loaded. Thus, the determination by the JVM at run time as to which classes should be loaded is based strictly on the logic of the main method that we are executing (which happens to be identical in all three example programs), ***without regard to the manner in which the*** import ***directives were crafted***.

Static Initializers

You learned in Chapter 5 that constructors are used to initialize an object's state when it is first instantiated:

```
public class Student {
    private String name;
    private String major;
    // etc.

    // Constructor.
    public Student(String n) {
        setName(n);
        setMajor("TBD"); // default value
        // etc.
    }

    // etc.
}
```

The initialization code contained within a constructor is executed each time a new object of a given type is instantiated; thus, we wouldn't want to include code to initialize a static variable in such a constructor:

```
public class Student {
    private String name;
    private String major;
    private int studentIDNo;
    private static int nextAvailableStudentIDNo;
    // etc.
```

```java
    // Constructor.
    public Student(String n) {
        setName(n);
        setMajor("TBD"); // default value
        // etc.

        // This would be a problem - we'd be resetting
        // the value of totalStudents to 0 with each
        // new Student object that we create.
        nextAvailableStudentIdNo = 10000;
        setStudentIDNo(nextAvailableStudentIdNo++);
        // etc.
    }

    // etc.
}
```

It's possible to define initialization code that will get performed only *once* in a given application invocation—specifically, when the class's bytecode of which it is a part is first loaded into the JVM—by enclosing it in what is known as a `static` code block, thus creating a **static initializer**. The general syntax for doing so is as follows:

```java
public class Student {
    private String name;
    private String major;
    private int studentIDNo;
    private static int nextAvailableStudentIDNo;
    // etc.

    // A static initializer.
    static {
        // Whatever code is enclosed within this block
        // will be executed once, when the enclosing
        // class (Student, in this case) is loaded into
        // the JVM's memory.
        nextAvailableStudentIDNo = 10000;
    }

    // Constructor.
    public Student(String n) {
        setName(n);
        setMajor("TBD"); // default value
        // etc.

        setStudentIDNo(nextAvailableStudentIdNo++);
        // etc.
    }

    // etc.
}
```

We can, of course, do anything that makes good sense within a static initializer; in addition to initializing static variables, we can establish resources for an application, such as a file or database connection, that need only be performed once per application session. We'll use this technique in Chapter 15 in building the SRS.

I frequently see code written as follows, wherein variables are initialized at the time they are declared:

```
public class Student {
    // Initializing an instance variable.
    private String name = "TBD";

    // Initializing a static/class variable.
    private static int nextAvailableStudentIDNo = 10000;
    // etc.
```

The preceding code is equivalent to the following:

```
public class Student {
    // Declaring an instance variable.
    private String name;

    // Declaring a static/class variable.
    private static int nextAvailableStudentIDNo;

    static {
        // Initializing a static/class variable
        // within a static code block.
        nextAvailableStudentIDNo = 10000;
    }

    public Student {
        // Initializing an instance variable
        // within a constructor.
        setName("TBD");
        // or:  name = "TBD";
        // etc.
    }

    // etc.
```

My personal preference is to use the latter style, as it's more readily apparent when such initialization takes place.

The Date Class

Throughout the examples presented thus far in the book, whenever we've needed to represent the notion of a date, we've done so as a String variable. I'd now like to introduce three predefined Java classes:

- `java.util.Calendar`

- `java.text.SimpleDateFormat`

- `java.util.Date`

as formal types to be used when declaring dates.

The `Calendar` class's `static getInstance` method can be used to obtain a reference to a `Calendar` object representing the *current* date and time:

```
Calendar rightNow = Calendar.getInstance();
```

We can also use a variety of overloaded set*xxx* methods defined by the `Calendar` class to craft a custom date/time of our liking, for example:

```
Calendar cal = Calendar.getInstance();

// Happy new year!
cal.set(2006, Calendar.JANUARY, 1); // year, month, date
```

We may then obtain a `Date` rendition of such a `Calendar` instance by invoking its `getTime` method:

```
Calendar cal = Calendar.getInstance();

// Happy new year!
cal.set(2006, Calendar.JANUARY, 1); // year, month, date
Date newYearsDay = cal.getTime();
```

Note that a `Date` is actually represented internally as a `long` integer value that encodes the current date and time converted to milliseconds that have elapsed since a standard base time known as "the epoch"—namely, January 1, 1970, 00:00:00 Greenwich Mean Time (GMT).

Two `Dates` can be compared via the `Date` class's `before`, `after`, and `equals` methods:

```
if (date1.before(date2)) { ...
if (date1.after(date2)) { ...
if (date1.equals(date2)) { ...
```

Once we have a handle on a `Date` instance of interest, we can format it as a `String` in a wide variety of ways through the use of a `SimpleDateFormat` object. First, we instantiate a `SimpleDateFormat` by passing in a pattern that we want the `Date`'s `String` representation to conform to:

```
// We'd like dates to appear in the format "January 1, 2006".
SimpleDateFormat sdf = new SimpleDateFormat("MMMM d, yyyy");
```

Then, we invoke the `format` method on the `SimpleDateFormat` instance, passing in the `Date` whose value is to be formatted as a `String`:

```
// We'll reuse the Date instance, "newYearsDay", from
// our earlier example.
String s = sdf.format(newYearsDay);

System.out.println(s);
```

Here's the output:

January 1, 2006

In formulating the pattern for a `SimpleDateFormat`, we may use standard white space and punctuation characters, plus any of the following **pattern letters** (from Sun Microsystems' online Java documentation).

The following pattern letters are defined (all other characters from `'A'` *to* `'Z'` *and from* `'a'` *to* `'z'` *are reserved):*

Letter	Date or Time Component	Presentation	Examples
G	Era designator	Text	AD
y	Year	Year	1996; 96
M	Month in year	Month	July; Jul; 07
w	Week in year	Number	27
W	Week in month	Number	2
D	Day in year	Number	189
d	Day in month	Number	10
F	Day of week in month	Number	2
E	Day in week	Text	Tuesday; Tue
a	Am/pm marker	Text	PM
H	Hour in day (0–23)	Number	0
k	Hour in day (1–24)	Number	24
K	Hour in am/pm (0–11)	Number	0
h	Hour in am/pm (1–12)	Number	12
m	Minute in hour	Number	30
s	Second in minute	Number	55
S	Millisecond	Number	978
z	Time zone	General time zone	Pacific Standard Time; PST; GMT–08:00
Z	Time zone	RFC 822 time zone	–0800

© Sun Microsystems, Inc.

We ***repeat*** pattern letters to control how we want a given item to be represented. Once again, the following information comes from Sun's online Java documentation.

Pattern letters are usually repeated, with the number of repetitions influencing the exact presentation:

- *Text: For formatting, if the number of pattern letters is 4 or more, the full form is used (e.g., if "MMMM" is used to indicate a month, the month's full name will be spelled out); otherwise a short or abbreviated form is used if available (e.g., if "M" is used to indicate a month, its numeric value [from 1 to 12] will be produced). (...)*

- *Number: For formatting, the number of pattern letters is the minimum number of digits, and shorter numbers are zero-padded to this amount. (...)*

- *Year: For formatting, if the number of pattern letters is 2, the year is truncated to 2 digits; otherwise it is interpreted as a number.*

© Sun Microsystems, Inc.

Here is an example program that demonstrates the various forms of date manipulation that we've discussed:

```java
// DateExamples.java

// Downloadable from the Apress web site.

import java.util.Calendar;
import java.util.Date;
import java.text.SimpleDateFormat;

public class DateExamples {
    public static void main(String[] args) {
        //-------------------------------------------------------------------
        // Example #1:  Get the current date and time, and print it out in
        // a default format.

        // Use the Calendar class to get a snapshot of this precise moment.
        Calendar thisInstant = Calendar.getInstance();

        // Convert to a Date.
        Date rightNow = thisInstant.getTime();

        // Convert to a String.
        String ex1 = rightNow.toString();

        System.out.print("Example #1:  ");
        System.out.println("Current time and date (default format):  " + ex1);
        System.out.println();


        //-------------------------------------------------------------------
        // Example #2:  Get the current date and time, and print it out in
        // specified way as described by the SimpleDateFormat that we've
        // designated below.
```

```java
// An alternative way to get the current date and time that doesn't
// involve the Calendar class.
Date now = new Date(System.currentTimeMillis());

SimpleDateFormat sdfEx2 = new SimpleDateFormat(
    "EEEE, MMM d, yyyy hh:mm aaa");
String ex2 = sdfEx2.format(now);

System.out.print("Example #2:  ");
System.out.println("Current time and date (custom format):  " + ex2);
System.out.println();

//-------------------------------------------------------------------------
// Example #3:  Print today's date (only) in a specified way as described by
// the alternative SimpleDateFormat that we've designated.

SimpleDateFormat sdfEx3 = new SimpleDateFormat("MMMM d, yyyy");

// We'll reuse the Date instance, "now", from above.
String ex3 = sdfEx3.format(now);

System.out.print("Example #3:  ");
System.out.println("Today's date (custom format):  " + ex3);
System.out.println();

//-------------------------------------------------------------------------
// Example #4:  Print today's date (only) in yet another format.

SimpleDateFormat sdfEx4 = new SimpleDateFormat("MM/dd/yyyy");
String ex4 = sdfEx4.format(now);

System.out.print("Example #4:  ");
System.out.println("Today's date (alternative custom format):  " + ex4);
System.out.println();

//-------------------------------------------------------------------------
// Example #5:  Craft a specific date as a Date object.

Calendar cal = Calendar.getInstance();
cal.set(2005, Calendar.NOVEMBER, 17); // year, month, date
Date specialDate = cal.getTime();

// We'll reuse the SimpleDateFormat from above.
String ex5 = sdfEx4.format(specialDate);

System.out.print("Example #5:  ");
System.out.println("A special date:  " + ex5);
System.out.println();
```

```
        //---------------------------------------------------------------------
        // Example #6:  Compare two dates.

        // We'll reuse the Calendar instance from Example #5 to craft two
        // different Dates.

        cal.set(2005, Calendar.JUNE, 1);
        Date bjo2EpublicationDate = cal.getTime();

        cal.set(2005, Calendar.JULY, 1);
        Date jjbVacationDate = cal.getTime();

        System.out.print("Example #6:  ");

        // We'll use the before() method to compare the dates (note that there's
        // also an after() method and an equals() method ...).

        if (jjbVacationDate.before(bjo2EpublicationDate)) {
            System.out.println("Jacquie can't take vacation yet ..." +
                " the book isn't finished!");
        }
        else {
            System.out.println("Have a safe and relaxing trip, Steve and Jacquie!");
        }
    }
}
```

Here's the output:

```
Example #1:
Current time and date (default format):  Sat Apr 09 12:48:20 GMT-05:00 2005

Example #2:
Current time and date (custom format):  Saturday, Apr 9, 2005 12:48 PM

Example #3:
Today's date (custom format):  April 9, 2005

Example #4:
Today's date (alternative custom format):  04/09/2005

Example #5:
A special date:  11/17/2005

Example #6:
Have a safe and relaxing trip, Steve and Jacquie!
```

Take time to explore Sun's online Java documentation for all of the many other versatile things that can be accomplished with the Calendar, Date, and SimpleDateFormat classes.

For assistance with installing and using the online Java documentation, please see Appendix C.

Accessibility, Revisited

In this section, we revisit the concept of accessibility, and round off your introduction to it by looking at the default accessibility of a feature and accessibility in the context of public or non-public classes.

Default Accessibility of a Feature

If we accidentally or intentionally omit an accessibility modifier for a feature of a class X, the default accessibility of that feature with respect to client code in another class Y depends on the relationship between X and Y with respect to which packages they each belong to.

- If X and Y are in the *same* package, the default visibility is effectively public.

- If X and Y are in *different* packages, the default visibility is effectively private.

Since all of the code that we'll be writing for the SRS is going to fall within the same (unnamed) default package, failing to declare a feature as private effectively makes it public to the code of other classes within the package.

```
public class Student {
    private String ssn;
    String name; // accessibility modifier omitted
    // etc.
}
```

Here's the client code:

```
Student s = new Student();

// As we know from earlier discussions, the next line WON'T
// compile - ssn has private accessibility Student.
s.ssn = "123-45-6789";  // won't compile

// However, the next line WILL compile - "name" is
// PACKAGE ACCESSIBLE by default.
s.name = "Fred";
```

Public vs. Nonpublic Classes

We've been dutifully declaring all of our classes as public classes:

```
// Transcript.java

public class Transcript { ... }
```

Is there any other type of class accessibility *besides* public?

As it turns out, there is only one other option for a top-level (as opposed to nested) class declaration, and that is to omit an accessibility modifier keyword completely:

```
// No accessibility specified.

class TranscriptEntry { ... }
```

Such classes are said to have **package access**; we encountered this terminology in the previous section, when we discussed what happens when the accessibility of a feature is omitted. Let's look at the implications of making a class public versus allowing it to have package access by default.

As you learned in Chapter 2, public classes must be housed in files whose names match the name of the class—for example, public class Transcript { ... } resides in a file named Transcript.java, etc. A nonpublic class (such as TranscriptEntry), on the other hand, need *not* reside in a file whose name matches the class name:

- The declaration of TranscriptEntry could be housed in a file named *anyname*.java.

- Alternatively, TranscriptEntry's declaration could be *included* with another class in a *single* *.java file—for example, with a public class:

```
//------------------------------------------------
// Transcript.java

public class Transcript {
    // Details omitted.
}

// This second class definition is in the same
// Transcript.java source code file.
class TranscriptEntry {
    // Details omitted.
}

// End of the Transcript.java file.
//------------------------------------------------
```

For that matter, we can place as many class declarations as we wish into a single *.java source file. The only restrictions are as follows:

- At most, one public class declaration can be in a given file, along with as many package accessible class declarations as desired.

- If a public class is in a file, the file name must match that class's name.

- If, on the other hand, a file contains assorted package accessible class declarations but *no* public classes

```
// SomeFile.java

class Foo { ... }
```

```
class Bar { ... }

class ZipideeDooDah { ... }

// End of file SomeFile.java
```

then the file name needn't match **_any_** of the enclosed class names.

Whenever a file containing more than one class declaration is compiled, a separate bytecode file will be generated for each class, whether public or not. For example, for the preceding SomeFile.java example, three bytecode files will be generated: Foo.class, Bar.class, and ZipideeDooDah.class.

Let's now explore the implications of declaring a class as public versus allowing it to default to package accessibility. For this discussion, assume the following hypothetical situation (illustrated in Figure 13-28):

- We have created two packages named A and B.

- Package A contains two classes, a public class named W and a package accessible class called X. (We know from our previous discussion that W would be declared in a file named W.java; X could be in a file named X.java, *anything*.java, or collocated with W in W.java—it doesn't matter.) Let's assume that both W and X are stored in the file W.java:

  ```
  // W.java

  package A;

  public class W { ... }

  class X { ... }

  // End of file W.java.
  ```

- Package B contains two classes: a public class named Y and a package accessible class named Z. Assume that both are declared in Y.java:

  ```
  // Y.java

  package B;

  public class Y { ... }

  class Z{ ... }

  // End of file Y.java.
  ```

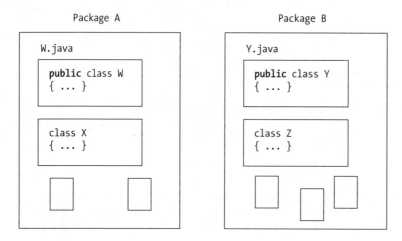

Figure 13-28. *Two packages, A and B, each contain one public and one package accessible class.*

If neither file W.java nor Y.java contain explicit import directives, then it is as if a brick wall exists between the two packages. That is, ***within file*** W.java,

- We may reference symbols W and X as valid types, because they both coexist within package A.

- However, we cannot reference symbols Y or Z from within W.java—without the benefit of an import directive, these are undefined symbols as far as the Java compiler is concerned.

This is represented conceptually in Figure 13-29.

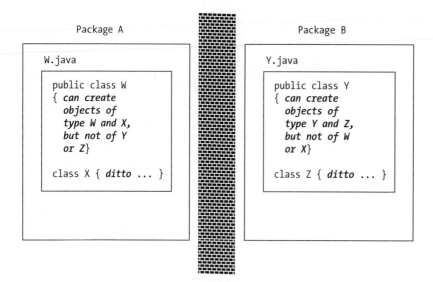

Figure 13-29. *Without the use of import directives, the classes in package A are unaware of the existence of the classes in package B, and vice versa.*

If we amend the code of W.java to include an import directive, as shown in **bold** in the following code, but do ***not*** amend the code of Y.java

```
// W.java

package A;

import B.*;

public class W { ... }

class X { ... }

// End of file W.java.
```

then it is conceptually as if we've "punched" a one-way viewing port through the brick wall—that is, the classes within package A will now be aware of, and will be able to use, the types declared as public in package B, namely type/class Y. Type Z, as a ***package accessible*** class within B, will ***remain unknown/undefined*** to the classes within A, however. And, of course, since we haven't included a directive to import A.*; in source file Y.java, then both W and X remain unknown as symbols/types to the classes in B. This is depicted in Figure 13-30.

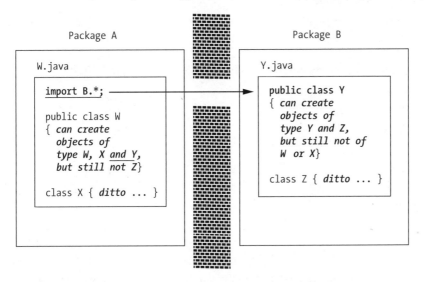

Figure 13-30. *Including an* import B.*; *directive in* W.java *makes the public classes of B visible to the classes within A.*

The bottom line is that when we bundle together classes in logical groupings/packages,

- We declare those classes that are likely to have utility outside of the "walls" of a given package—for example, Transcript—as having public visibility.

- We allow those classes that are only of utility within a package's own classes—for example, TranscriptEntry, which is only of utility to the Transcript class—to default to package accessibility.

Variable Initialization, Revisited

Recall our discussion of variable initialization earlier in this book:

> *In Java, most variables aren't automatically assigned an initial value when they are declared; we must explicitly assign a value to a variable before the variable's name is referenced in a subsequent Java expression in order to avoid compilation errors.*

For example, this next bit of code:

```
1   public class Problem {
2       public static void main(String[] args) {
3           // Declare several local variables within the main() method.
4           int i;  // not automatically initialized
5           int j;  // ditto
6           j = i;  // compilation error!
7       }
8   }
```

was shown to produce the following compilation error on line 6:

```
Variable i may not have been initialized
```

We thus learned that it's best to explicitly initialize such variables, for example:

```
public class NotAProblem {
    public static void main(String[] args) {
        // Declare several local variables within the main method and
        // explicitly initialize them all.
        int i = 0;
        double x = 0.0;
        boolean test = false;
        Student student = null;
        // etc.
    }
}
```

Out of necessity, we oversimplified the explanation of variable initialization when we first discussed this topic in Chapter 2 because we hadn't yet introduced the notion of objects and attributes. To properly discuss initialization in Java, we must distinguish among

- *Local variables*—that is, variables declared *within a method*, and whose scope is therefore only the extent of the enclosing method

- *Attributes* of a class—otherwise known as *instance variables* in Java (because they are variables whose values are associated with an object/class *instance*, as we discussed in Chapter 7)

- *Static variables* (informally referred to as "static attributes") of a class

As it turns out,

- All *local variables*, whether declared to be of one of the eight primitive Java types or of a reference type, are considered by the compiler to be *uninitialized* until they have been explicitly initialized within a program.

- All *instance/static variables*, on the other hand, whether declared to be of a simple Java type or of a reference type, are *automatically initialized to the default zero-equivalent value for the type in question*.

Thus, in the following code example, variables would be initialized as described in Table 13-2:

```java
public class Student {
  // Attributes/instance variables.
  private int age;
  private boolean isHonorsStudent;
  private double gpa;
  private Professor advisor;

  // A static/class variable.
  private static int totalStudents;

  void someMethod() {
    // Local variables.
    int x;
    boolean flag;
    double y;
    Professor p;
    // etc.

    // Details of method body omitted.
  }
  // etc.
```

Table 13-2. *The State of Automatic Initialization of the Features of Class Student*

Variable	Initialized?
age	Yes, to 0
isHonorsStudent	Yes, to false
gpa	Yes, to 0.0
advisor	Yes, to null
totalStudents	Yes, to 0
x	No
flag	No
y	No
p	No

Therefore, when first instantiated, an object has the appropriate data structure as prescribed by its class, but all of its attributes will be initialized to their zero-equivalent values.

Inner Classes

An **inner class** X is a class whose declaration is nested within the declaration of another class Y. The syntax of an inner class declaration is as follows:

```java
public class OuterClassX {
    // Declare outer class features, as desired ... details omitted.

    // We declare an INNER class wholly within the BODY of the OUTER class.
    // Note:  inner classes are NOT declared to be public - they are only
    // "visible" as a type to the outer class in which they are declared.
    class InnerClassY {
        // Declare the inner class's features ...
        // details omitted.
    } // end of inner class declaration

    // Declare outer class features, as desired ... details omitted.
} // end of outer class declaration
```

The purpose of declaring a class as an inner class is to conceal the fact that the class exists from the application as a whole—in essence, to invent a ***private type*** that ***only*** the enclosing outer class knows about. We may thus use an inner class as a type when declaring variables of the enclosing outer class, but we may ***not*** use the inner class as a type anywhere else in our application. Attempting to do so will produce a "cannot find symbol" compiler error, as we'll see in a moment.

Let's look at a specific example of an inner class called GradeBook, declared within the Course class. First, we'll look at the code of the inner class in isolation; aside from the fact that we don't declare it as a public class, it otherwise looks like a typical class.

```java
class GradeBook {
    // For every Student, we store his/her grade as
    // a String value:  e.g., "B+".
    private HashMap<Student, String> grades;

    // Constructor.
    public GradeBook() {
        grades = new HashMap<Student, String>();
    }

    // Accessor methods.

    public void setGrade(Student s, String grade) {
        // Delegation.
        grades.put(s, grade);
    }
```

```
        public String getGrade(Student s) {
            // Delegation.
            return grades.get(s);
        }
    }
```

Now, let's look at the GradeBook class in the context of its enclosing outer class, Course:

```
import java.util.*;

public class Course {
    private String name;
    private ArrayList<Student> enrolledStudents;

    // We're using "GradeBook" as a type for one of
    // the Course's attributes.
    private GradeBook gradeBook;

    public Course(String name) {
        this.name = name;
        enrolledStudents = new ArrayList<Student>();

        // We're instantiating a GradeBook object.
        gradeBook = new GradeBook();
    }

    public void assignGrade(Student s, String grade) {
        // Delegation.
        gradeBook.setGrade(s, grade);
    }

    public String lookUpGrade(Student s) {
        // Delegation.
        return gradeBook.getGrade(s);
    }

    // Our inner class.  The symbol "GradeBook" is only
    // recognized by the compiler within the scope of
    // the Course class; we can't reference GradeBook
    // as a type anywhere else.
    class GradeBook {
        // For every Student, we store a grade as
        // a String value:  e.g., "B+".
        private HashMap<Student, String> grades;
```

```
            // Constructor.
            public GradeBook() {
                grades = new HashMap<Student, String>();
                // etc.
            }

            // Other methods.

            public void setGrade(Student s, String grade) {
                grades.put(s, grade);
            }

            public String getGrade(Student s) {
                return grades.get(s);
            }
        } // end inner class declaration
    } // end outer class declaration
```

We may write client code as follows:

```
public class MyApp {
    public static void main(String[] args) {
        Course c = new Course("MATH 101");
        Student s1 = new Student("Fred");
        c.assignGrade(s1, "B-");
        Student s2 = new Student("Cynthia");
        c.assignGrade(s2, "A+");
        // etc.

        // Later on:
        System.out.println(s1.getName() +
            " received a grade of " + c.lookUpGrade(s1));
        System.out.println(s2.getName() +
            " received a grade of " + c.lookUpGrade(s2));

        // etc.
    }
}
```

Here's the output:

```
Fred received a grade of B-
Cynthia received a grade of A+
```

However, if we were to try to reference GradeBook as a type anywhere outside of the Course class

```
public class MyApp {
    public static void main(String[] args) {
        // This won't compile!  GradeBook is not known as a type outside of the
        // Course class boundaries.
        GradeBook gb = new GradeBook();
        // etc.
```

we'd get the following compiler error:

```
cannot find symbol
symbol  : class GradeBook
location: class MyApp
```

The bottom line is that the application as a whole doesn't know that GradeBook objects exist, nor does the application ***need*** to know; the existence of the GradeBook type is a ***private*** implementation detail of the Course class.

When a class containing an inner class definition is compiled, we wind up with ***separate*** bytecode files named *OuterClass*.class and *OuterClass$InnerClass*.class, respectively—for example, Course.class and Course$GradeBook.class, in the case of our preceding example.

Because the inner class in the preceding example has an explicit name, GradeBook, we actually refer to it as a ***named*** inner class. In Chapter 16, we'll see the use of another type of inner class—an unnamed inner class (aka an ***anonymous*** inner class)—when we build the SRS GUI.

Additional J2SE 5.0 Enhancements

IMPORTANT!

As with enums earlier in this chapter, the language features covered in this section were introduced as of J2SE 5.0; hence, the code examples that follow will ***not*** compile with an earlier (pre-5.0) version of the Java compiler.

Although we don't take advantage of these additional features in building the SRS, it's worth noting that J2SE 5.0 also introduces

- Formatted output

- Formatted input

- Variable-argument method signatures

I'd like to briefly introduce each of these features in turn.

Formatted Output

As of version 5.0, J2SE incorporated the ability to format output in a way that is comparable to the printf function of the C programming language. The Java syntax for doing so is as follows:

```
System.out.printf("format_string", comma_separated_list_of_expressions_to_print);
```

where "*format_string*" defines the pattern/**format** that the output should take. The format string consists of literal text to be printed interspersed with **format tags** that begin with the symbol %.

While a complete discussion of the rich variety of formatting options is beyond the scope of this book, let's look at one of the most frequently requested formatting transformations: transforming a double into a price, in U.S. dollars, with a leading $ and two digits after the decimal point. I'll present the example first, and I'll discuss details of the format string afterward:

```
double price = 1.0; // this represents $1.00
String productName = "Gizmo";
System.out.printf("Price of %s:  $%.2f", productName, price);
```

Here's the output:

```
Price of Gizmo:  $1.00
```

The format string used in this example:

```
Price of %s:  $%.2f
```

consists of

- Some literal text—"Price of "—followed by

- The formatting expression %s, which indicates that the first argument passed in after the format string—productName—is to be output as a String (s), followed by

- More literal text—": $"—followed by

- The formatting expression %.2f, which indicates that the second argument passed in after the format string—price—is to be output as a floating-point number (f), with two digits to appear after the decimal point (.2)

Some of the more commonly used conversion symbols are as follows:

- b: Boolean

- s: String

- c: Unicode character

- d: Decimal integer

- f: Decimal floating-point number

- e: Decimal floating-point number in scientific notation

- n: Platform-specific line separator

For detailed information concerning format string syntax, please refer to Sun's online documentation for the java.util.Formatter class, which serves as the basis for how System.out.printf works. Or, consider referring to a classic C language reference such as *The C Programming Language,* Second Edition by Brian W. Kernighan and Dennis M. Ritchie (Prentice Hall, 1988).

Formatted Input

As of J2SE 5.0, the java.util.Scanner class provides a convenient means of reading formatted data from input streams, such as that typed by a user in response to command-line prompts, which is made available to a Java program via the **standard input stream**, System.in.

The Scanner class provides numerous overloaded constructors. The one that we'll use in our examples takes an InputStream as an argument, for example:

```
Scanner sc = new Scanner(System.in);  // reading from the keyboard
```

We then invoke various forms of next*Type*() method on the Scanner instance—nextBoolean(), nextInt(), nextDouble(), etc.—to read the next (white space–delimited) token from the input stream and automatically convert it to the type specified. The method next() reads and returns the token as a String.

In the example program that follows, we prompt the user to enter three values: a String, an int(eger), and a double, respectively. We provide exception-handling logic for java.util. InputMismatchException, in case the user types the wrong sort of data for a given prompt.

```java
import java.util.Scanner;
import java.util.InputMismatchException;

public class ScannerExample {
    public static void main(String[] args) {
        Scanner sc = new Scanner(System.in);

        try {
            // Prompt the user for his/her first name.
            System.out.print("Please enter your FIRST name (only):  ");

            // Because we want to read the name as a String, we can use
            // the simple next() method.
            String name = sc.next();

            System.out.print("Please enter your age as an integer:  ");
            int age = sc.nextInt();

            System.out.print("Please enter your GPA as a double:  ");
            double gpa = sc.nextDouble();

            System.out.println();
            System.out.println(name + " is " + age + " years old.");
            System.out.println(name + "'s GPA is " + gpa + ".");
```

```
        }
        catch (InputMismatchException e) {
                System.out.println();
                System.out.println("Whoops!  You didn't follow the instructions " +
                        "properly; please try again.");
        }
    }
}
```

Here's the output:

```
Please enter your first name:  Herbie
Please enter your age as an integer:  32
Please enter your GPA as a double:  3.75

Herbie is 32 years old.
Herbie's GPA is 3.75.
```

Using the Scanner class's nextLine() method as illustrated in the next example would serve as an alternative to using the KeyboardInput class as presented earlier in this chapter.

```
import java.util.Scanner;

public class KeyboardInputExample2 {
    public static void main(String args[]) {
        Scanner sc = new Scanner(System.in);

        System.out.print("Please enter your name:  ");
        String name = sc.nextLine();
        System.out.println("Hello, " + name + "!");
    }
}
```

Here's the output:

```
Please enter your name:  Cathy McCabe
Hello, Cathy McCabe!
```

Variable Arguments (Varargs)

The **varargs**, or **variable arguments**, feature of J2SE 5.0 allows us to declare methods that can accept a *variable* number of *similarly typed* arguments. To declare a method as accepting a variable number of arguments, the syntax is as follows:

```
accessibility returnType methodName(argType ... args) {
    // Iterate through the args array; details omitted.
}
```

where args is the name of a parameter representing an ***array*** of type *argType*, and ***the explicit inclusion of an ellipsis*** "..." between *argType* and args signals that args is actually to be treated as an array of zero or more elements of type *argType*.

Within a so-called **varargs method**, we iterate through the args array in similar fashion to the way that we iterated through the args array of the main method earlier in this chapter to read command-line arguments. Whereas the main method of an application can accept only an array of String values as arg(ument)s, however

```java
public static void main(String[] args) { // etc.
```

a varargs method in general may declare its args parameter to be of ***any*** type:

- A predefined reference type, such as String: `public void foo(String ... args) {`

- A primitive type, such as int: `public void foo(int ... args) {`

- A user-defined type, such as Person: `public void foo(Person ... args) {`

(Note that square brackets [ ] are ***not*** needed for args to serve as an array; this happens automatically by virtue of our inclusion of an ellipsis "...".)

The following example illustrates the use of varargs methods to accept String, int, Person, and Object arguments, respectively; for purposes of this example, assume that Student and Professor are subclasses of the Person (super)class, and that Pineapple, Bicycle, and Cloud are three unrelated classes all derived directly from Object.

```java
import java.util.ArrayList;

public class VarargsExample {
    public static void main(String[] args) {
        // Invoking methods that define variable argument
        // signatures, where the type of argument(s)
        // to be passed in is designated by the name
        // of the method.

        stringExample("foo", "bar");
        stringExample("eeny", "meeny", "miney", "mo");

        intExample(1, 3, 9, 27);
        intExample();

        Student student = new Student("Fred");
        Professor professor = new Professor("Dr. Carson");
        personExample(student, professor);

        ArrayList<String> arrayList = new ArrayList<String>();
        arrayList.add("Hello!");
        arrayList.add("How are you?");
        arrayList.add("Goodbye ...");
        objectExample(student, arrayList);
```

```java
        objectExample2(new Pineapple(), new Bicycle(), new Cloud());
    }

    //-----------------------------
    // Here are our varargs methods.
    //-----------------------------

    private static void stringExample(String ... args) {
        System.out.println("In stringExample, there were " +
            args.length + " arguments.");

        for (int i = 0; i < args.length; i++) {
            System.out.println("    " + args[i] + " is a " +
                args[i].getClass().getName());
        }

        System.out.println();
    }

    private static void intExample(int ... args) {
        System.out.println("In intExample, there were " +
            args.length + " arguments.");

        for (int i = 0; i < args.length; i++) {
            System.out.println("    " + args[i] +
                " is an int");
        }

        System.out.println();
    }

    private static void personExample(Person ... args) {
        System.out.println("In personExample, there were " +
            args.length + " arguments.");

        for (int i = 0; i < args.length; i++) {
            System.out.println("    " + args[i] + " is a " +
                args[i].getClass().getName());
        }

        System.out.println();
    }

    private static void objectExample(Object ... args) {
        System.out.println("In objectExample, there were " +
            args.length + " arguments.");
```

```java
        for (int i = 0; i < args.length; i++) {
            System.out.println("    " + args[i] + " is a " +
                args[i].getClass().getName());
        }

        System.out.println();
    }

    private static void objectExample2(Object ... args) {
        // Here, we assume that we know that the args array will contain
        // an assortment of Pineapples, Bicycles, and Clouds.
        for (int i = 0; i < args.length; i++) {
            // Note casts.
            if (args[i] instanceof Pineapple) {
                ((Pineapple) args[i]).eat();
            }
            else if (args[i] instanceof Bicycle) {
                ((Bicycle) args[i]).ride();
            }
            else if (args[i] instanceof Cloud) {
                ((Cloud) args[i]).paint();
            }
        }

        System.out.println();
    }
}
```

Here's the output:

```
In stringExample, there were 2 arguments.
    foo is a java.lang.String
    bar is a java.lang.String

In stringExample, there were 4 arguments.
    eeny is a java.lang.String
    meeny is a java.lang.String
    miney is a java.lang.String
    mo is a java.lang.String

In intExample, there were 4 arguments.
    1 is an int
    3 is an int
    9 is an int
    27 is an int

In intExample, there were 0 arguments.
```

```
In personExample, there were 2 arguments.
    Fred is a Student
    Dr. Carson is a Professor

In objectExample, there were 2 arguments.
    Fred is a Student
    [Hello!, How are you?, Goodbye ...] is a java.util.ArrayList

Eating a pineapple ...
Riding a bicycle ...
Painting a cloud ...
```

Summary

In this chapter, you learned

- How formal Java-specific terminology differs from the informal terminology commonly used to describe object concepts

- The anatomy of a nontrivial Java application consisting of many separate classes driven by one "official" main method

- The object nature of Strings, and some of the methods provided to manipulate them

- How to form highly complex expressions by chaining messages

- How Java exceptions arise, and how to gracefully handle them, including the ability to define custom exception types

- How to read input from the command line when a Java application is invoked, as well as how to prompt the user for keyboard inputs—useful techniques when running a command line–driven application

- Using the this keyword to self-reference an object from within one of its methods

- The utility features of the wrapper classes—Integer, Double, etc.—to convert String data to numeric values and vice versa

- The nature of object identities in Java, how to discover the true class that an object belongs to, and how to test the equality of two Java objects

- The importance of overriding the toString method for all user-defined classes, and how the equals method may similarly be overridden

- The nature of inner classes

With all of this Java knowledge at your fingertips, you are now ready to proceed to building the SRS application.

Exercises

1. [*Coding*] Write a Java program that will accept a series of individual characters, separated by one or more spaces, as command-line input, and will then "glue" them together to form a word. For example, if we were to invoke the program as follows:

   ```
   java Glue B A    N A    N    A
   ```

   then the program should output the following:

   BANANA

   ---

   with no spaces.

2. [*Coding*] Write a Java program that accepts a sentence as command-line input and outputs statistics about this sentence. For example, if we were to invoke the program as follows:

   ```
   java SentenceStatistics this is my sample sentence
   ```

   then the program should output the following results:

   ```
   number of words:          5
   longest word(s):              sentence
   length of longest word(s):  8
   shortest word(s):          is my
   length of shortest word(s): 2
   ```

   (To keep things simple, do not use any punctuation in your sentence.)

3. [*Coding*] Practice declaring enums by declaring

   - An enum called Weekday that represents the seven days of the week as Strings.

   - An enum called SolarSystem that represents the nine planets in our solar system as Planet objects: Mercury, Venus, Earth, Mars, Jupiter, Saturn, Uranus, Neptune, and Pluto. In support of this enum, declare a simple Planet class that has the following features: a single String attribute representing the planet's name, a constructor that takes the planet's name as an argument, and a toString method that returns the phrase "Planet: *planetName*".

4. [*Coding*] Practice with javadoc comments by retrofitting such comments into any Java code that you've previously written.

5. [*Coding*] Modify the SimpleCalc program presented in this chapter so that it will loop, continuing to prompt users for input until they type the command

   ```
   EXIT
   ```

6. [*Coding; Advanced*] Use the KeyboardInput class presented in this chapter (and downloadable from the Apress web site) as the basis of a simple program called GuessIt that asks a user to guess a number between 1 and 10 (program the "answer" to be guessed as a local int variable in the GuessIt main method).

A sample interactive scenario using the GuessIt program follows. For this example, assume that the correct answer is 6:

```
C:\Programs> java GuessIt
Please type a number between 1 and 10, and press Enter:  3
Too low; please try again:  7
Too high; please try again:  6
Correct!
C:\Programs>
```

■ ■ ■

CHAPTER 14

Transforming Your Model into Java Code

It's now time to turn our attention back to the UML class diagram that we produced in Part 2 of the book in order to develop a Java application based on that object-oriented "blueprint." We'll step through all of the Java code necessary to automate a simple command-line version of the SRS application first, focusing solely on what it takes to accurately model the SRS domain information in an OO programming language. Then, in the next two chapters, we'll round out our application by adding

- A means of persisting the state of our objects from one SRS session to the next

- A graphical user interface, by which users will be able to "drive" the SRS model

Meanwhile, in this chapter, you'll learn how to represent all of the following object-oriented constructs in Java code:

- Associations of varying multiplicities (one-to-one, one-to-many, and many-to-many), including aggregations

- Inheritance relationships

- Association classes

- Reflexive associations

- Abstract classes

- Metadata

- Static attributes and methods

along with practical guidelines as to when to use these various constructs. We'll also cover a technique for testing your core classes via a command line–driven application.

Suggestions for Getting the Maximum Value from This and Subsequent Chapters

One of the **best** ways to master a language is to start with code that works, and to experiment with it. A good approach is to get some hands-on experience with Java by actually compiling and running the SRS application; studying it, so as to familiarize yourself with the techniques that we've used; and finally, modifying it yourself. As you know, exercises provided at the end of each chapter provide specific suggestions for experiments that you may wish to try. Therefore, before you dive into this chapter, *I encourage you to download the Java source code for Chapters 14, 15, and 16 from the Downloads area of the Apress website* (http://www.apress.com) *if you haven't already done so*; instructions are included in Appendix D. You'll also want to install Sun's free Java 2 Software Development Kit (SDK) now, if you haven't already done so; please see Appendix C for details.

The primary goal of this book is to show you how to take the same SRS case study through a complete object-oriented software development life cycle, from requirements definition via use cases, to object modeling, and from there into Java code as a working application. To do so required me to develop a nontrivial application that was complex enough to be able to demonstrate as many "real-world" issues surrounding OO development as possible within the scope of a single book.

The code that I've written for the SRS application is sizeable; to have included the complete code listing for each and every Java class intact in every chapter would have been prohibitive. So, to make this as effective a learning experience as possible for you, I've chosen to feature just those portions of code in each chapter that are particularly critical to your understanding of object concepts as they translate into the Java language.

I realize that you will, of course, need access to the complete source code to round out your understanding of the SRS application as it's been implemented, which is another compelling reason for you to download the SRS source code at this time. I recommend printing a copy of the SRS source code and putting it into a loose-leaf binder, so that you can jot down notes on the printouts as you read through this and the next two chapters.

IMPORTANT!

As mentioned several times previously, Sun Microsystems introduced some important new features with J2SE 5.0 that significantly increased the power and versatility of Java as an object-oriented programming language. I've thus adopted the J2SE 5.0 approach to collections as of this (second) edition of *Beginning Java Objects*.

Note that the SRS code as presented in Chapters 14, 15, and 16 will *not* compile with an earlier (pre-5.0) version of the Java compiler. For readers who are still working with an earlier version of the Java language, please visit the Downloads section of the Apress website (http://www.apress.com) for a version of the SRS code that will compile with these earlier language versions.

The SRS Class Diagram Revisited

Let's turn our attention back to the SRS class diagram that we produced in Part 2 of the book. In speaking with our sponsors for the SRS system, we learn that they've decided to cut back on a few features in the interest of reducing development costs:

- First of all, they have decided not to automate students' Plans of Study via the SRS. Instead, it will be up to each student to make sure that the courses that they register for are appropriate for the degree that they are seeking.

- Since automated Plans of Study are being eliminated, there will no longer be a need to track who a student's faculty advisor is. The only reason for modeling the *advises* relationship between the Professor and Student classes in the first place was so that a student's advisor could be called upon to approve a tentative Plan of Study when a student had first posted it via the SRS.

- Finally, our sponsors have decided that maintaining a wait list for a section once it becomes full is a luxury that they can live without, since most students, upon learning that a section is full, immediately choose an alternative course anyway.

We've thus pared down the SRS class diagram accordingly, to eliminate these unnecessary features. Also, to keep the diagram from getting too cluttered, we've chosen not to reflect attribute types or full method signatures in the UML. The resultant diagram is shown in Figure 14-1.

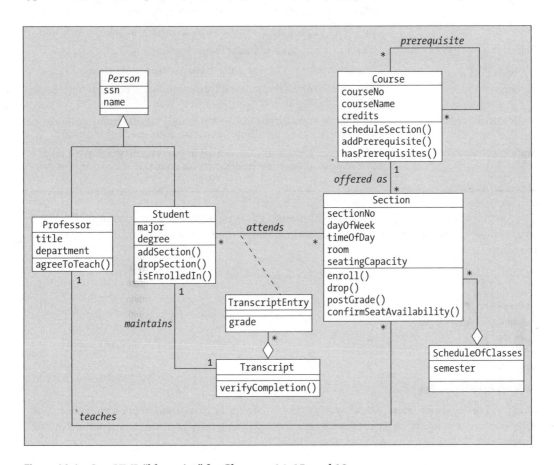

Figure 14-1. *Our UML "blueprint" for Chapters 14, 15, and 16*

Fortunately for us, the resultant model still provides examples of all of the key object-oriented elements that we need to learn how to program, as listed in Table 14-1.

Table 14-1. *Key Object-Oriented Features for SRS Class Diagram*

OO Feature	Embodied in the SRS Class Diagram As Follows:
Inheritance	The Person class serves as the base class for the Student and Professor subclasses.
Aggregation	We have two examples of this: the Transcript class represents an aggregation of TranscriptEntry objects, and the ScheduleOfClasses class represents an aggregation of Section objects.
One-to-one association	The *maintains* association between the Student and Transcript classes.
One-to-many association	The *teaches* association between Professor and Section; the *offered as* association between Course and Section.
Many-to-many association	The *attends* association between Student and Section; the *prerequisite* (reflexive) association between instances of the Course class.
Association class	The TranscriptEntry class is affiliated with the *attends* association.
Reflexive association	The *prerequisite* association between instances of the Course class.
Abstract class	The Person class will be implemented as an abstract class.
Metadata	Each Course object embodies information that is relevant to multiple Section objects.
Static attributes	Although not specifically illustrated in the class diagram, we'll take advantage of static attributes when we code the Section class.
Static methods	Although not specifically illustrated in the class diagram, we'll take advantage of static methods when we code the TranscriptEntry class.

As mentioned earlier, we're going to implement a command line–driven version of the SRS in this chapter; in particular, we're going to code the eight model classes called for by the SRS class diagram:

```
Course.java
Person.java
Professor.java
ScheduleOfClasses.java
Section.java
Student.java
Transcript.java
TranscriptEntry.java
```

along with a "wrapper" class, SRS, that will encapsulate the main method of our application, and a supporting enum(eration), EnrollmentStatus, the purpose for which will be explained in due time.

The Person Class (Specifying Abstract Classes)

Let's start with writing the code for the Person class (see Figure 14-2).

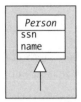

Figure 14-2. *The Person class*

The first thing that we notice in the UML diagram is that the name of the class is italicized, which as you learned in Chapter 10 means that Person is to be implemented as an abstract class. By including the keyword abstract in the class declaration, we prevent client code from ever being able to instantiate a Person object directly.

```
public abstract class Person {
```

Attributes of Person

The Person class icon specifies two simple attributes. We'll make *all* of our attributes private throughout the SRS application unless otherwise stated:

```
//------------
// Attributes.
//------------

private String name;
private String ssn;
```

Person Constructors

We'll provide a constructor for the Person class that accepts two arguments, so as to initialize our two attributes:

```
//----------------
// Constructor(s).
//----------------

public Person(String name, String ssn) {
    this.setName(name);
    this.setSsn(ssn);
}
```

Note that we use the Person class's own set methods to set the values of the name and ssn attributes, a best practice that was recommended in Chapter 4.

And, because the creation of any constructor for a class eliminates that class's default constructor, as we discussed in Chapter 4, we'll program a replacement for the default constructor, as well, to avoid some of the issues related with constructors and inheritance that we discussed in Chapter 5.

```java
public Person() {
    this.setName("?");
    this.setSsn("???-??-????");
}
```

Person Accessor Methods

Next, we provide accessor methods for all of the attributes, observing proper accessor method signature syntax as recommended in Chapter 4. All of our accessor methods, in all classes, will be declared with public accessibility:

```java
//------------------
// Accessor methods.
//------------------

public void setName(String n) {
    name = n;
}

public String getName() {
    return name;
}

public void setSsn(String s) {
    ssn = s;
}

public String getSsn() {
    return ssn;
}
```

toString()

We'd like for all subclasses of the Person class to override the version of the toString method that would normally be inherited from the Object class, a practice that we discussed in Chapter 13. However, we don't want to bother coding the details of such a method for Person; we'd prefer to let each subclass handle the details of how the toString method will work in its own class-appropriate way.

The best way to enforce this requirement for a toString method is to declare an ***abstract method*** for this method in Person, as we discussed in Chapter 7:

```java
//----------------------------
// Miscellaneous other methods.
//----------------------------

// We'll let each subclass determine how it wishes to be
// represented as a String value.

public abstract String toString();
```

This will ensure that all classes derived from Person override this abstract method with a concrete version of their own.

Note that since the Person class itself would normally have inherited a *generic* version of toString from the Object class, we're in essence overriding the *concrete* toString of Object with an *abstract* version in Person—this is a perfectly fine thing to do.

---

display()

We also want all subclasses of Person to implement a display method, to be used for printing the values of a Person object's attributes to the command window. We'll use the display method solely for testing our application, to verify that an object's attributes have been properly initialized. But, rather than making this method abstract, as well, we'll go ahead and actually program the body of this method, since we know how we'd like the attributes of Person to be displayed when these are inherited, at a minimum.

```java
public void display() {
    System.out.println("Person Information:");
    System.out.println("\tName:  " + this.getName());
    System.out.println("\tSoc. Security No.:  " + this.getSsn());
}
```

By doing so, we are facilitating code reuse: subclasses of Person (Student, Professor) will be able to use the super keyword to incorporate this logic in their own display methods without having to duplicate it, as we discussed in Chapter 5. As an example, here is a preview excerpt from the Student class's display method:

```java
public void display() {
  // First, let's display the generic Person info.
  super.display();
  // etc.
```

Again, note that we are invoking the Person class's get methods from within the println calls, versus accessing attributes directly. Also observe that we are inserting a tab character (\t) in the second and third println calls so that those two lines of printed output will be indented by one tab stop.

That's all there is to programming the Person class—it's pretty straightforward! We'll tackle the Student and Professor subclasses of Person next.

The Student Class (Reuse Through Inheritance, Abstract Class Extension, Delegation)

Figure 14-3 shows the UML representation of the Student class.

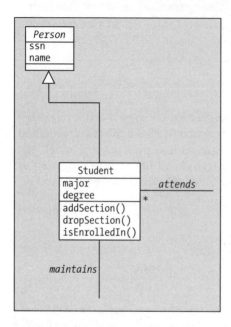

Figure 14-3. *The Student class*

We indicate that Student is a subclass of Person by using the extends keyword.

```
public class Student extends Person {
```

Attributes of Student

There are two attributes explicitly called out for the Student class in our UML diagram: major and degree. However, we learned in Chapter 10 that we must also encode associations as attributes. Student participates in two associations:

- *attends*, a many-to-many association with the Section class

- *maintains*, a one-to-one association with the Transcript class

and so we must allow for each Student to maintain handles on a single Transcript object and on many Section objects.

Of the various types of Java collection covered in Chapter 6, an ArrayList seems like the best choice for managing multiple Section handles:

- An Array is a bit too rigid; we'd have to size the Array in advance to be large enough to accommodate references to all of the Sections that a Student will ever attend over the course of his or her studies at the university. An ArrayList, on the other hand, can start out small and automatically grow in size as needed.

- The decision of using an ArrayList versus a dictionary type of collection comes down to whether or not we'll need to retrieve an object reference from the collection based on some key value. We don't anticipate the need for such a lookup capability as it pertains to the Sections that a Student has attended; we *will* need the ability to verify if a Student has taken a particular Section or not, but this can be accomplished by using the ArrayList class's contains method. That is, if attends is declared to be of type ArrayList, then we can use the statement

```
if (attends.contains(someSection)) { ...
```

to verify whether or not a Student has taken a particular Section. For most other uses of the attends collection, we'll need to step through the entire collection anyway, as when printing out a Student's course schedule. So, an ArrayList should serve our purposes quite nicely.

The attributes for the Student class thus turn out as follows:

```
//------------
// Attributes.
//------------

private String major;
private String degree;
private Transcript transcript;
private ArrayList<Section> attends;
```

Of course, by virtue of inheritance, Student also inherits the attributes declared by Person—namely, name and ssn—but with *private* accessibility. Hence, as we discussed in Chapter 5, these attributes do indeed become part of the "bone structure" of a Student object, but the symbols name and ssn are not within the *namespace* of the Student class. Thus, we'll use the associated *public* accessor ("get"/"set") methods, also inherited from Person, to access them as needed.

Since we are using the ArrayList class, we'll need to remember to include the following import directive at the beginning of the Student class, ahead of the class declaration:

```
import java.util.ArrayList;
```

Student Constructors

We'll provide two constructors for convenience of initializing attributes.

```
//----------------
// Constructor(s).
//----------------

public Student(String name, String ssn, String major, String degree) {
```

In the first Student constructor, we use the construct super(*arguments*) to reuse the code of one of the Person class constructors from our Student constructor, to establish the "Personness" of a Student. Recall from our discussion of the super keyword in Chapter 5 that any invocation of super(...) must be the *first* such line in a subclass's constructor.

```
// Reuse the code of the parent's constructor.
super(name, ssn);
```

After setting the values of the major and degree attributes based on arguments passed into the constructor

```
this.setMajor(major);
this.setDegree(degree);
```

we set about to instantiate the transcript attribute as follows:

```
// Create a brand new Transcript to serve as this Student's
// transcript.
this.setTranscript(new Transcript(this));
```

Let's evaluate the preceding line of code from the inside out:

- First, we instantiate a brand-new ***unnamed*** Transcript object, passing a reference to ***this*** Student in as the lone argument to the Transcript constructor:

```
new Transcript(this)
```

(Since we haven't discussed the structure of the Transcript class yet, the signature of its constructor may seem a bit puzzling, but it will make sense once we get a chance to review the Transcript class in its entirety later in this chapter.)

- We then nest this instantiation request inside of a call to setTranscript:

```
this.setTranscript(new Transcript(this));
```

Note that we ***could*** have accomplished this with ***two*** lines of code instead of one:

```
Transcript t = new Transcript();
this.setTranscript(t);
```

but there is no point in going to the trouble of declaring a variable t to serve as a reference to a Transcript object if we're only going to reference the variable one time, and then discard it when it goes out of scope as soon as the constructor exits. As we discussed in Chapter 13, it is commonplace to chain together/nest method calls in a single Java statement.

Finally, as we discussed in Chapter 6, we routinely instantiate collection attributes such as the attends ArrayList in a constructor to guarantee that we have an empty "egg carton" ready for us when it is time to add "eggs":

```
// Note that we're instantiating empty support Collection(s).
attends = new ArrayList<Section>();
}
```

We choose to overload the Student constructor by providing a second constructor, shown in the following code, to be used if we wish to create a Student object for which we don't yet know the name, major field of study, or degree sought. As discussed in Chapter 4, we use the syntax this(*arguments*) to reuse the code from the first Student constructor within the second, passing in the String value "TBD" to serve as a temporary value for the name, major, and degree attributes:

```
// A second simpler form of constructor.

public Student(String ssn) {
    // Reuse the code of the first Student constructor.
    this("TBD", ssn, "TBD", "TBD");
}
```

Student Accessor Methods

We provide accessor methods for all of the simple (noncollection attributes):

```
//------------------
// Accessor methods.
//------------------

public void setMajor(String major) {
    this.major = major;
}

public String getMajor() {
    return major;
}

public void setDegree(String degree) {
    this.degree = degree;
}

public String getDegree() {
    return degree;
}

public void setTranscript(Transcript t) {
    transcript = t;
}

public Transcript getTranscript() {
    return transcript;
}
```

And, as mentioned previously, Student inherits the accessor methods of the Person class, as well.

For the attends collection attribute, we will provide the methods addSection and dropSection in lieu of traditional accessor methods, to be used for adding and removing Section objects from the ArrayList; we'll talk about these methods momentarily.

display()

As we did for Person, we choose to provide a display method for Student for use in testing our command-line version of the SRS. Because a Student is a Person, and because we've already gone to the trouble of programming a display method for the attributes inherited from Person, we'll reuse that method code by making use of the super keyword before going on to additionally display attribute values specific to a Student object:

```
public void display() {
    // First, let's display the generic Person info.
    super.display();

    // Then, display Student-specific info.
    System.out.println("Student-Specific Information:");
    System.out.println("\tMajor:  " + this.getMajor());
    System.out.println("\tDegree:  " + this.getDegree());
    this.displayCourseSchedule();
    this.printTranscript();

    // Finish with a blank line.
    System.out.println();
}
```

Note that we are calling two of the Student class's other methods, displayCourseSchedule and printTranscript, from within the Student's display method. We chose to program these as separate methods versus incorporating their code into the body of the display method to keep the display method from getting too cluttered.

toString()

By extending an abstract class, as we are in deriving the Student subclass from Person, we implicitly agree to override any abstract method(s) specified by the parent class with concrete methods. In the case of the Person class, we have one such method, toString:

```
// We are forced to program this method because it is specified
// as an abstract method in our parent class (Person); failing to
// do so would render the Student class abstract, as well.
//
// For a Student, we wish to return a String as follows:
//
//      Joe Blow (123-45-6789) [Master of Science - Math]

public String toString() {
    return this.getName() + " (" + this.getSsn() + ") [" + this.getDegree() +
        " - " + this.getMajor() + "]";
}
```

displayCourseSchedule()

The displayCourseSchedule method is a more complex example of delegation; we'll defer a discussion of this method until we've discussed a few more of the SRS classes.

addSection()

When a Student enrolls in a Section, this method will be used to pass a reference to that Section to the Student object so that the Section reference may be stored in the attends ArrayList:

```
public void addSection(Section s) {
    attends.add(s);
}
```

This is yet another example of delegation: the Student object is delegating the work of organizing Section references to its encapsulated collection.

dropSection()

When a Student withdraws from a Section, this method will be used to pass a reference to the "dropped" Section to the Student object. The Student object in turn delegates the work of removing the Section to the attends ArrayList by invoking its remove method:

```java
public void dropSection(Section s) {
    attends.remove(s);
}
```

isEnrolledIn()

This method is used to determine whether a given Student is already enrolled in a particular Section—that is, whether that Student's attends collection is already referring to the Section in question—by taking advantage of the ArrayList class's contains method:

```java
// Determine whether the Student is already enrolled in THIS
// EXACT Section.
public boolean isEnrolledIn(Section s) {
    if (attends.contains(s)) return true;
    else return false;
}
```

As you can see, there is a lot of delegation going on within the Student class's methods! The ArrayList that we've encapsulated as an attribute of Student does a lot of behind-the-scenes work for the Student object to which it belongs.

isCurrentlyEnrolledInSimilar()

Although not specified by our model, I've added another version of the isEnrolledIn method called isCurrentlyEnrolledInSimilar, because I found a need for such a method when coding the Section class (coming up later in this chapter). No matter how much thought you put into the object modeling stage of an OO software development project, you will inevitably determine the need for additional attributes and methods for your classes once coding is under way, because coding causes you to think at a very fine-grained level of detail about the "mechanics" of your application.

Because this method is somewhat complex, the method code is shown in its entirety first, followed by an in-depth explanation.

```java
// Determine whether the Student is already enrolled in ANY
// Section of this SAME Course.
public boolean isCurrentlyEnrolledInSimilar(Section s1) {
    boolean foundMatch = false;

    Course c1 = s1.getRepresentedCourse();
```

```
        for (Section s2 : attends) {
            Course c2 = s2.getRepresentedCourse();
            if (c1 == c2) {
                // There is indeed a Section in the attends()
                // ArrayList representing the same Course.
                // Check to see if the Student is CURRENTLY
                // ENROLLED (i.e., whether or not he or she has
                // yet received a grade).  If there is no
                // grade, he/she is currently enrolled; if
                // there is a grade, then he/she completed
                // the course sometime in the past.
                if (s2.getGrade(this) == null) {
                    // No grade was assigned!  This means
                    // that the Student is currently
                    // enrolled in a Section of this
                    // same Course.
                    foundMatch = true;
                    break;
                }
            }
        }

        return foundMatch;
    }
```

The details of this method are as follows.

In coding the enroll method of the Section class (to be discussed later in this chapter), I realized that we needed a way to determine whether a particular Student is enrolled in *any* Section of a given Course. That is, if a Student is attempting to enroll for Math 101 Section 1, we want to reject this request if that student is already enrolled in Math 101 Section 2.

```
// Determine whether the Student is already enrolled in ANY
// Section of this SAME Course.
public boolean isCurrentlyEnrolledInSimilar(Section s1) {
```

We initialize a local boolean variable to false, with the intention of resetting it to true later on if we do indeed discover that the Student is currently enrolled in a Section of the same Course:

```
boolean foundMatch = false;
```

Next, we obtain a handle on the Course object that the Section of interest represents, assigning it to reference variable c1:

```
Course c1 = s1.getRepresentedCourse();
```

We then use the technique discussed in Chapter 6 for iterating through a collection via a for loop, using the variable s2 to maintain a temporary handle on each Section in the attends collection, one by one:

```
        for (Section s2 : attends) {
```

Within the for loop, we obtain a handle on a second Course object, c2—the Course object that Section s2 is a Section of—and test the equality of the two Course objects:

```
        Course c2 = s2.getRepresentedCourse();
        if (c1 == c2) {
```

Note that we use the == test for equality, because as we discussed in Chapter 13, we do indeed wish to know if the two Course references c1 and c2 are indeed referring to the ***exact same object***.

If we find a match, we're not quite done yet, however, because the attends ArrayList for a Student holds on to all Sections that the Student has ***ever*** taken. To determine if Section s2 is truly a Section that the Student is ***currently*** enrolled in, we must check to see if a grade has been issued for this Section. A missing grade—that is, a grade value of null—indicates that the Section is currently in progress.

```
            if (s2.getGrade(this) == null) {
                // No grade was assigned!  This means
                // that the Student is currently
                // enrolled in a Section of this
                // same Course.
```

As soon as we have found the ***first*** such match, we can set our boolean flag accordingly, break out of the enclosing while loop, and return a value of true to the caller:

```
                foundMatch = true;
                break;
            }
        }
    }

    return foundMatch;
}
```

getEnrolledSections()

The getEnrolledSections method used previously is a simple one-liner:

```
public Collection<Section> getEnrolledSections() {
    return attends;
}
```

Note the return type of the method: we're returning what is actually an ArrayList reference as a ***generic*** Collection reference instead. As you learned in Chapter 7, Collection is a predefined interface within the java.util package and, since the ArrayList class ***implements*** the Collection interface, an ArrayList ***is a*** Collection. By returning an interface type—Collection—rather than an explicit class type—ArrayList—from this method, we reserve the right to change the type of collection that we use internally to the Student in the future without subjecting client code to a ripple effect, a benefit of interfaces that we discussed at length in Chapter 7.

We must also remember to include the following import directive at the beginning of our Student class declaration:

```
import java.util.Collection;
```

printTranscript()

The printTranscript method is a straightforward example of ***delegation***. We use the Student's getTranscript method to retrieve a handle on the Transcript object that belongs to this Student, and then invoke the display method for that Transcript object (you'll see the details of this later in the chapter, when we discuss the Transcript class):

```
public void printTranscript() {
    this.getTranscript().display();
}
```

Note that, once again, we could have accomplished this with two lines of code instead of one:

```
public void printTranscript() {
  Transcript t = this.getTranscript();
  t.display();
}
```

but the "chained" version is more concise.

Next, we'll turn our attention to the Professor class.

The Professor Class (Bidirectional Relationships)

Figure 14-4 shows the UML representation of the Professor class.

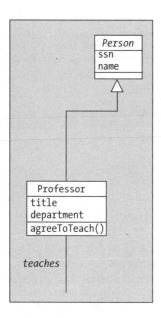

Figure 14-4. *The Professor class*

Because the code that is necessary to implement the Professor class of Person is so similar to that of Student, I'll comment only on those features of Professor that are particularly noteworthy. I encourage you to look at the full code of the Professor class, however, to reinforce your ability to read and interpret Java syntax.

Professor Attributes

The Professor class is involved in one association—the one-to-many *teaches* association with the Section class—and so we must provide a means for a Professor object to maintain multiple Section handles, which we do by creating a teaches attribute of type ArrayList:

```
//------------
// Attributes.
//------------

private String title;
private String department;
private ArrayList<Section> teaches;
```

agreeToTeach()

Our class diagram calls for us to implement an agreeToTeach method. This method accepts a Section object reference as an argument, and begins by storing this reference in the teaches ArrayList:

```
public void agreeToTeach(Section s) {
  teaches.add(s);
```

Associations, as modeled in a UML class diagram, are assumed to be bidirectional. When implementing associations in *code*, however, we must think about whether or not bidirectionality is important on a case-by-case basis for each association.

- Can we think of any situations in which a Professor object would need to know which Sections it is responsible for teaching? Yes—for example, when we ask a Professor object to print out its teaching assignments.

- How about the reverse? That is, can we think of any situations in which a Section object would need to know who is teaching it? Yes—for example, when we print out a Student's course schedule.

So, not only must we store a reference to the Section object in the Professor's teaches ArrayList, but also we must make sure that the Section object is somehow notified that this Professor is going to be its instructor. We accomplish this by invoking the Section object's setInstructor method, passing in a handle on the Professor object whose method we are in the midst of executing via the this keyword, a technique for object self-referencing that we discussed in Chapter 13:

```
// We want to link these objects bidirectionally.
  s.setInstructor(this);
}
```

displayTeachingAssignments()

The displayTeachingAssignments method is very similar in concept to the displayCourseSchedule method of Student. We'll hold off on discussing the latter until later in this chapter, but once we've discussed displayCourseSchedule in detail, you'll be in a position to revisit the displayTeachingAssignments method of Professor, as well.

We'll turn our attention next to the Course class.

The Course Class (Reflexive Relationships, Unidirectional Relationships)

Figure 14-5 shows the UML representation of the Course class. The sections that follow provide more detail about this class.

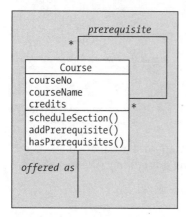

Figure 14-5. *The Course class*

Course Attributes

Referring back to the SRS class diagram, we see that Course has three simple attributes and participates in two associations:

- ***offered as***, a one-to-many association with the Section class

- ***prerequisite***, a many-to-many reflexive association

for a total of five attributes:

```
//------------
// Attributes.
//------------

private String courseNo;
private String courseName;
private double credits;
private ArrayList<Section> offeredAsSection;
private ArrayList<Course> prerequisites;
```

Note that a reflexive association is handled in exactly the same way that any other association is handled—that is, we've provided the Course class with a ArrayList attribute called prerequisites that enables a given Course object to maintain handles on *other* Course objects.

We have chosen not to encode this reflexive association bidirectionally. That is, a given Course object X will know which other Course objects A, B, C, etc. serve as *its* prerequisites, but it will *not* know which Course objects L, M, N, etc. consider X to be one of *their* prerequisites, as illustrated in Figure 14-6.

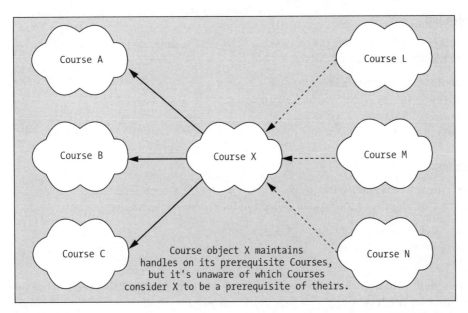

Course object X maintains handles on its prerequisite Courses, but it's unaware of which Courses consider X to be a prerequisite of theirs.

Figure 14-6. *The reflexive* prerequisites *association is not implemented bidirectionally.*

Our rationale for implementing this association unidirectionally is as follows. A given Course X has reason to know which courses are its prerequisites, so that when a Student S attempts to enroll in X, X can inquire of S whether S has completed all such prerequisites. X doesn't need to know about courses that require X as a prerequisite—it's up to ***those*** courses to worry about X!

Had we wanted this association to be bidirectional, we would have had to include a ***second*** ArrayList of Course references as an attribute in the Course class, as shown in **bold**:

```
//------------
// Attributes.
//------------

private String courseNo;
private String courseName;
private double credits;
private ArrayList<Section> offeredAsSection;
private ArrayList<Course> prerequisites;
private ArrayList<Course> prerequisiteOf;
```

so that Course object X could hold on to this latter group of Course objects separately.

Course Methods

Most of the Course methods use techniques that should already be familiar to you, based on our discussions of the Person, Professor, and Student classes. I'll highlight a few of the more interesting Course methods here, and leave it for you as an exercise to review the rest.

hasPrerequisites()

This method inspects the size of the prerequisites ArrayList to determine whether or not a given Course has any prerequisite Courses:

```java
public boolean hasPrerequisites() {
    if (prerequisites.size() > 0) return true;
    else return false;
}
```

getPrerequisites()

This method returns a reference to the prerequisites ArrayList as a generic Collection reference, hiding the true identity of the type of collection that we've encapsulated:

```java
public Collection<Course> getPrerequisites() {
    return prerequisites;
}
```

We see this method in use within the Course display method, and we'll also see it in use by the Section class a bit later on.

scheduleSection()

This method illustrates several interesting techniques.

```java
public Section scheduleSection(char day, String time, String room,
    int capacity) {
    // Create a new Section (note the creative way in
    // which we are assigning a section number) ...
    Section s = new Section(offeredAsSection.size() + 1,
            day, time, this, room, capacity);

    // ... and then remember it!
    this.addSection(s);

    return s;
}
```

First, note that this method invokes the Section class constructor to instantiate a new Section object, s, storing **one** handle on this Section object in the offeredAsSection ArrayList before returning a **second** handle on the object to client code.

Second, we are generating the first argument to the Section constructor—representing the section number—as a "one-up" number by adding 1 to the size of the offeredAsSection ArrayList. The first time that we invoke the scheduleSection method for a given Course object, the ArrayList will be empty, and so the expression

offeredAsSection.size() + 1

will evaluate to 1, and hence we'll be creating Section number 1. The second time that this method is invoked for the same Course object, the ArrayList will already contain a handle on the first Section object that was created, so the expression

```
offeredAsSection.size() + 1
```

will evaluate to 2, and hence we'll be creating Section number 2, and so forth.

There is, however, a flaw with this approach: if we were to create, then ***delete***, Section objects, the size of the ArrayList would expand and contract, and we could wind up with duplicate Section numbers.

Now, let's turn our attention to the Section class.

The Section Class (Representing Association Classes, Public Static Final Attributes, Enums)

Figure 14-7 shows the UML representation of the Section class. The sections that follow provide more detail about this class.

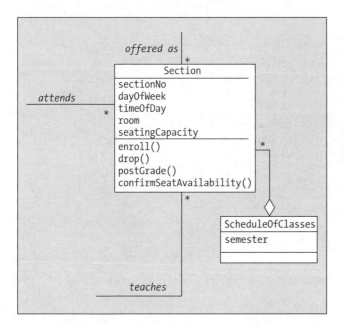

Figure 14-7. *The Section class*

Section Attributes

In addition to the following handful of relatively simple attributes:

```
//------------
// Attributes.
//------------
```

```
private int sectionNo;
private char dayOfWeek;
private String timeOfDay;
private String room;
private int seatingCapacity;
```

the Section class participates in numerous relationships with other classes:

- ***offered as***, a one-to-many association with Course

- An unnamed, one-to-many aggregation with ScheduleOfClasses

- ***teaches***, a one-to-many association with Professor

- ***attends***, a many-to-many association with Student

The *attends* association is in turn affiliated with an association class, TranscriptEntry. You learned in Chapter 10 that an association class can alternatively be depicted in a class diagram as having direct relationships with the classes at either end of the association, as shown in Figure 14-8.

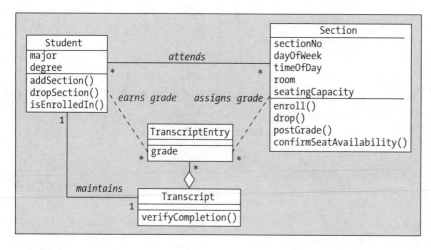

Figure 14-8. *An alternative UML representation of the TranscriptEntry association class*

And so we'll encode a fifth relationship for the Section class, namely,

- ***assigns grade***, a one-to-many association with the TranscriptEntry class.

  (You may be wondering whether we should now go back and adjust the Student class to reflect the *earns grade* association with the TranscriptEntry class as a Student class attribute. The decision of whether or not to implement a particular relationship in code depends in part on what we anticipate our usage patterns to be, as discussed in Chapter 10. We'll defer the decision of what to do with *earns grade* until we talk about the TranscriptEntry class in a bit more depth later in this chapter.)

We'll represent these five relationships in terms of Section attributes as follows:

- A Section object need only maintain a handle on one other object for those one-to-many relationships in which Section occupies the "many" end, namely,

```
private Course representedCourse;
private ScheduleOfClasses offeredIn;
private Professor instructor;
```

- For the two situations in which Section needs to maintain handles on **collections** of objects—Students and TranscriptEntrys—we are going to employ HashMaps instead of ArrayLists this time. We do so because it is conceivable that we'll have a frequent need to "pluck" a given item from the collection directly, and a HashMap—as a dictionary type collection—provides a key-based lookup mechanism that is ideal for this purpose.

  - For the HashMap of Student object references, we'll use a String representing the Student's social security number (ssn) as a key for looking up a Student:

```
// The enrolledStudents HashMap stores Student object references,
// using each Student's ssn as a String key.
private HashMap<String, Student> enrolledStudents;
```

  - For the HashMap of TranscriptEntry object references, on the other hand, we'll use a Student object as a whole as a key for looking up that particular Student's TranscriptEntry as issued by this Section:

```
// The assignedGrades HashMap stores TranscriptEntry object
// references, using a reference to the Student to whom it belongs
// as the key.
private HashMap<Student, TranscriptEntry> assignedGrades;
```

The Use of an Enum(eration) Type

In the Section class, we encounter our first use of an enum(eration), which as you learned in Chapter 13 is an excellent means of defining a finite list of symbolic values. In this particular situation, we want to define some status codes that the Section class can use when signaling the outcome of an enrollment attempt.

We discussed the syntax of an enum type in detail in Chapter 13. The following code defines four symbolic values to represent four different outcomes of an enrollment attempt—success, secFull, prereq, and prevEnroll—each of which correlates to a String value as indicated:

```
public enum EnrollmentStatus {
    // Enumerate the values that the enum can assume.
    success("enrollment successful!  :o)"),
    secFull("enrollment failed:  section was full.  :op"),
    prereq("enrollment failed; prerequisites not satisfied.  :op"),
    prevEnroll("enrollment failed; previously enrolled.  :op");

    // This represents the value of an enum instance.
    private final String value;

    // A "constructor" of sorts (used above).
    EnrollmentStatus(String value) {
        this.value = value;
    }
```

```
        // Accessor for the value of an enum instance.
    public String value() {
        return value;
    }
}
```

Let's look at how these values are put to use by studying the enroll method of Section.

enroll()

This is a very complex method; I'll list the code in its entirety first without discussing it, and then I'll explain it in detail.

```
    public EnrollmentStatus enroll(Student s) {
        // First, make sure that this Student is not already
        // enrolled for this Section, and that he/she has
        // NEVER taken and passed the course before.

        Transcript transcript = s.getTranscript();

        if (s.isCurrentlyEnrolledInSimilar(this) ||
            transcript.verifyCompletion(this.getRepresentedCourse()))) {
            return EnrollmentStatus.prevEnroll;
        }

        // If there are any prerequisites for this course,
        // check to ensure that the Student has completed them.

        Course c = this.getRepresentedCourse();
        if (c.hasPrerequisites()) {
            for (Course pre : c.getPrerequisites()) {
                // See if the Student's Transcript reflects
                // successful completion of the prerequisite.

                if (!transcript.verifyCompletion(pre)) {
                    return EnrollmentStatus.prereq;
                }
            }
        }

        // If the total enrollment is already at the
        // the capacity for this Section, we reject this
        // enrollment request.

        if (!this.confirmSeatAvailability()) {
            return EnrollmentStatus.secFull;
        }

        // If we made it to here in the code, we're ready to
        // officially enroll the Student.
```

```
    // Note bidirectionality:  this Section holds
    // on to the Student via the HashMap, and then
    // the Student is given a handle on this Section.

    enrolledStudents.put(s.getSsn(), s);
    s.addSection(this);

    return EnrollmentStatus.success;
  }
```

Note that the return type of this method is declared to be EnrollmentStatus—that is, we are going to return an instance of the EnrollmentStatus enum as a symbolic value representing the outcome of this enrollment attempt.

We begin by verifying that the Student seeking enrollment (represented by argument s) hasn't already enrolled for this Section, and furthermore that the student has ***never*** taken and successfully completed this Course (any Sections) in the past. We obtain a handle on the Student's transcript and store it in a locally declared reference variable called transcript, because we are going to need to consult with the Transcript object twice in this method.

```
public EnrollmentStatus enroll(Student s) {
    // First, make sure that this Student is not already
    // enrolled for this Section, and that he/she has
    // NEVER taken and passed the course before.

    Transcript transcript = s.getTranscript();
```

We then use an if statement to test for either of two conditions: (a) is the Student currently enrolled in this Section or another Section of the same Course, and/or (b) does the Student's Transcript indicate successful prior completion of the Course that is represented by this Section?

```
    if (s.isCurrentlyEnrolledInSimilar(this) ||
        transcript.verifyCompletion(this.getRepresentedCourse())) {
```

Because we have need to use this Course object only once in this method, we don't bother to save the handle returned to us by the getRepresentedCourse method in a variable; we just nest the invocation of this method within the call to verifyCompletion, so that the Course object can be retrieved by the former and immediately passed along as an argument to the latter.

Whenever we encounter a return statement midway through a method as we have here, the method's execution will immediately terminate without running to completion.

```
        return EnrollmentStatus.prevEnroll;
    }
```

Note our use of EnrollmentStatus.prevEnroll, one of the symbolic values defined by the EnrollmentStatus enum, as a return value. Declaring and using such standardized values is a great way to communicate status back to client code.

Next, we check to see if the Student has satisfied the prerequisites for this Section, if there are any. We use the Section's getRepresentedCourse method to obtain a handle on the Course object that this Section represents, and then invoke the hasPrerequisites method on that Course object. If the result returned is true, then we know that there are prerequisites to be checked.

```
// If there are any prerequisites for this course,
// check to ensure that the Student has completed them.

Course c = this.getRepresentedCourse();
if (c.hasPrerequisites()) {
```

If there are indeed prerequisites for this Course, we use the getPrerequisites method defined by the Course class to obtain a collection of all prerequisite Courses, and iterate through this collection via a for loop:

```
for (Course pre : c.getPrerequisites()) {
```

For each Course object reference pre that we extract from the collection, we invoke the verifyCompletion method on the Student's Transcript object, passing in the prerequisite Course object reference pre. We haven't taken a look at the inner workings of the Transcript class yet, so for now, all we need to know about verifyCompletion is that it will return a value of true if the Student has indeed successfully taken and passed the Course in question; otherwise, it will return a value of false. We want to take action in situations where a prerequisite was *not* satisfied, so we use the unary negation operator (!) in front of the expression to indicate that we want the if test to succeed if the method call returns a value of false:

```
        // See if the Student's Transcript reflects
        // successful completion of the prerequisite.
        if (!transcript.verifyCompletion(pre)) {
            return EnrollmentStatus.prereq;
        }
    }
```

If the student is found to have not satisfied any one of the prerequisites, the return statement is triggered, and we return the status value EnrollmentStatus.prereq. If, on the other hand, we make it through the prerequisite check without triggering the return statement, the next step in this method is to verify that there is still available seating in the Section. We return the status value EnrollmentStatus.secFull value if there is not.

```
        // If the total enrollment is already at the
        // the capacity for this Section, we reject this
        // enrollment request.
        if (!this.confirmSeatAvailability()) {
            return EnrollmentStatus.secFull;
        }
```

Finally, if we've made it through *both* of the tests unscathed, we're ready to officially enroll the Student. We use the HashMap class's put method to insert the Student reference into the enrolledStudents HashMap, invoking the getSsn method on the Student to retrieve the String value of its ssn attribute, which we pass in as the key value.

```
        enrolledStudents.put(s.getSsn(), s);
```

To achieve bidirectionality of the link between a Student and a Section, we then turn around and invoke the addSection method on the Student object reference, passing it a handle on *this* Section. We then return the value EnrollmentStatus.success to signal successful enrollment.

```
        s.addSection(this);
        return EnrollmentStatus.success;
    }
```

drop()

The `drop` method of `Section` performs the reverse operation of `enroll`. We start by verifying that the `Student` in question is indeed enrolled in this `Section`, since we can't drop a `Student` who isn't enrolled in the first place:

```
public boolean drop(Student s) {
    // We may only drop a student if he/she is enrolled.
    if (!s.isEnrolledIn(this)) return false;
```

If the student truly is enrolled, we use the `HashMap` class's `remove` method to locate and delete the `Student` reference, again via its `ssn` attribute value:

```
    else {
        // Find the student in our HashMap, and remove it.
        enrolledStudents.remove(s.getSsn());
```

In the interest of bidirectionality, we invoke the `dropSection` method on the `Student`, as well, to get rid of the handles at ***both*** ends of the link.

```
        // Note bidirectionality.
        s.dropSection(this);

        return true;
    }
}
```

postGrade()

The `postGrade` method is used to assign a grade to a `Student` by creating a `TranscriptEntry` object to link this `Section` to the `Student` being assigned a grade.

We begin by validating that the proposed grade to be assigned to `Student` s (both s and grade are passed in as arguments to the `postGrade` method) is properly formed by calling a `static` utility method, `validateGrade`, that is defined by the `TranscriptEntry` class. The business rules that govern what constitutes a "valid" grade representation are encoded within that method; these business rules will be revealed when we explore the `TranscriptEntry` class later in this chapter. For the time being, all we need know is that, if the `validateGrade` method rejects the proposed grade by returning a value of `false`, we in turn exit the `postGrade` method, returning a value of `false` to client code to indicate that the request to post a grade for `Student` s has been rejected.

```
public boolean postGrade(Student s, String grade) {
    // First, validate that the grade is properly formed by calling
    // a utility method provided by the TranscriptEntry class.

    if (!TranscriptEntry.validateGrade(grade)) return false;
```

Next, to ensure that we aren't inadvertently trying to assign a grade to a particular `Student` more than once, we first check the `assignedGrades` `HashMap` to see if it already contains an entry for this `Student`. If the `get` method call on the `HashMap` returns anything but `null`, then we know a grade has already been posted for this `Student`, and we terminate execution of the method, once again returning a value of `false`.

```
// Make sure that we haven't previously assigned a
// grade to this Student by looking in the HashMap
// for an entry using this Student as the key.  If
// we discover that a grade has already been assigned,
// we return a value of false to indicate that
// we are at risk of overwriting an existing grade.
// (A different method, eraseGrade(), can then be written
// to allow a Professor to change his/her mind.)

if (assignedGrades.get(s) != null) return false;
```

Assuming that a grade was not previously assigned, we invoke the appropriate constructor to create a new TranscriptEntry object. As you will see when we study the inner workings of the TranscriptEntry class, this object will maintain handles on both the Student to whom a grade has been assigned and on the Section for which the grade was assigned.

```
// First, we create a new TranscriptEntry object.  Note
// that we are passing in a reference to THIS Section,
// because we want the TranscriptEntry object,
// as an association class ..., to maintain
// "handles" on the Section as well as on the Student.
// (We'll let the TranscriptEntry constructor take care of
// linking this T.E. to the correct Transcript.)

TranscriptEntry te = new TranscriptEntry(s, grade, this);
```

To enable this latter link to be bidirectional, we also store a handle on the TranscriptEntry object in the Section's assignGrades HashMap for this purpose.

```
// Then, we "remember" this grade because we wish for
// the connection between a T.E. and a Section to be
// bidirectional.
assignedGrades.put(s, te);

return true;
}
```

getGrade()

The getGrade method uses the Student reference passed in as an argument to this method as a lookup key for the assignedGrades HashMap, to retrieve the TranscriptEntry stored therein for this Student.

```
public String getGrade(Student s) {
        String grade = null;

        // Retrieve the associated TranscriptEntry object for this specific
        // student from the assignedGrades HashMap, if one exists, and in turn
        // retrieve its assigned grade.

        TranscriptEntry te = assignedGrades.get(s);
```

If a TranscriptEntry is found, we use its getGrade method to retrieve the actual grade (as a String value) so that it may be returned by this method.

```
if (te != null) {
    grade = te.getGrade();
}
```

Otherwise, we return a value of null to signal that no grade has yet been assigned for the Student of interest.

```
// If we found no TranscriptEntry for this Student, a null value
// will be returned to signal this.

return grade;
}
```

confirmSeatAvailability()

The confirmSeatAvailability method called from within enroll is an internal "housekeeping" method. By declaring it to have private versus public visibility, we restrict its use so that only other methods of the Section class may invoke it.

```
private boolean confirmSeatAvailability() {
    if (enrolledStudents.size() < this.getSeatingCapacity()) return true;
    else return false;
}
```

Delegation Revisited

In discussing the Student class, I briefly mentioned the displayCourseSchedule method as a complex example of delegation, and promised to come back and discuss it further.

What are the "raw materials"—data—available for an object to use when it is responding to a service request by executing one of its methods? By way of review, an object has at its disposal the following data sources:

- Simple data and/or object references (handles) that have been ***encapsulated as attributes*** within the object itself

- Simple data and/or object references that are ***passed in as arguments*** in the method signature

- Data that is made available ***globally*** to the application as public static attributes of some other class

- Data that ***can be requested*** from any of the objects that this object has a handle on

It is this last source of data—data available by ***collaborating with other objects***—that is going to play a particularly significant role in implementing the displayCourseSchedule method for the Student class.

Let's say we want the displayCourseSchedule method to display the following information for each Section that a Student is currently enrolled in:

```
Course No.:
Section No.:
Course Name:
Meeting Day and Time Held:
Room Location:
Professor's Name:
```

for example:

```
Course Schedule for Fred Schnurd
    Course No.:  CMP101
    Section No.:  2
    Course Name:  Beginning Computer Technology
    Meeting Day and Time Held:  W - 6:10 - 8:00 PM
    Room Location:  GOVT202
    Professor's Name:  Claudio Cioffi
    -----
    Course No.:  ART101
    Section No.:  1
    Course Name:  Beginning Basketweaving
    Meeting Day and Time Held:  M - 4:10 - 6:00 PM
    Room Location:  ARTS25
    Professor's Name:  Snidely Whiplash
    -----
```

Let's start by looking at the attributes of the Student class, to see which of this information is readily available to us. Student inherits from Person:

```
private String name;
private String ssn;
```

and adds

```
private String major;
private String degree;
private Transcript transcript;
private ArrayList<Section> attends;
```

Let's begin to write the method. By stepping through the attends ArrayList, we can gain access to Section objects one by one:

```
public void displayCourseSchedule() {
    // Display a title first.
    System.out.println("Course Schedule for " + this.getName());

    // Step through the ArrayList of Section objects,
    // processing these one by one.
    for (Section s : attends) {
        // Now what goes here????
        // We must create the rest of the method ...
    }
}
```

Now that we have the beginnings of the method, let's determine how to fill in the gap in the preceding code.

Looking at all of the method headers declared for the Section class as evidence of the services that a Section object can perform, we see that several of these can immediately provide us with useful pieces of information relative to our mission of displaying a Student's course schedule—namely, those that are flagged (***) in the following code:

```java
public void setSectionNo(int no)
public int getSectionNo() ***
public void setDayOfWeek(char day)
public char getDayOfWeek() ***
public void setTimeOfDay(String time)
public String getTimeOfDay() ***
public void setInstructor(Professor prof)
public Professor getInstructor()
public void setRepresentedCourse(Course c)
public Course getRepresentedCourse()
public void setRoom(String r)
public String getRoom() ***
public void setSeatingCapacity(int c)
public int getSeatingCapacity()
public void setOfferedIn(ScheduleOfClasses soc)
public ScheduleOfClasses getOfferedIn()
public String toString()
public int enroll(Student s)
public boolean drop(Student s)
public int getTotalEnrollment()
public void display()
public void displayStudentRoster()
public String getGrade(Student s)
public boolean postGrade(Student s, String grade)
public boolean successfulCompletion(Student s)
public boolean isSectionOf(Course c)
```

Let's put the four designated methods to use, and where we can't yet fill the gap completely, we'll insert "???" as a placeholder:

```java
public void displayCourseSchedule() {
  // Display a title first.
  System.out.println("Course Schedule for " + this.getName());

  // Step through the ArrayList of Section objects,
  // processing these one by one.
  for (Section s : attends) {
    // Since the attends ArrayList contains Sections that the
    // Student took in the past as well as those for which
    // the Student is currently enrolled, we only want to
    // report on those for which a grade has not yet been
    // assigned.
```

```
    if (s.getGrade(this) == null) {
      System.out.println("\tCourse No.:   " + ???
      System.out.println("\tSection No.:  " + s.getSectionNo());
      System.out.println("\tCourse Name:  " + ???
      System.out.println("\tMeeting Day and Time Held:  " +
        s.getDayOfWeek() + " - " + s.getTimeOfDay());
      System.out.println("\tRoom Location:  " + s.getRoom());
      System.out.println("\tProfessor's Name:  " + ???
      System.out.println("\t-----");
    }
  }
}
```

Now, what about the remaining "holes"? Two of the Section methods

```
public Professor getInstructor()
public Course getRepresentedCourse()
```

will each hand us yet another object that we can "talk to"—namely, the Professor who teaches this Section, and the Course that this Section represents. Let's now look at what *these* objects can perform in the way of services.

- A Professor object can perform the following services (the first four are inherited from Person). Again, those that seem relevant to the mission we're trying to accomplish with the displayCourseSchedule method of the Student class are flagged (***):

```
        public void setName(String n)
        public String getName()        ***
        public void setSsn(String ssn)
        public String getSsn()
        public void display()
        public void setTitle(String title)
        public String getTitle()
        public void setDepartment(String dept)
        public String getDepartment()
        public void display()
        public String toString()
        public void displayTeachingAssignments()
        public void agreeToTeach(Section s)
```

- A Course object can perform these services (the relevant methods are flagged [***]):

```
        public void setCourseNo(String cNo)
        public String getCourseNo() ***
        public void setCourseName(String cName)
        public String getCourseName() ***
        public void setCredits(double c)
        public double getCredits()
        public void display()
        public String toString()
        public void addPrerequisite(Course c)
```

```
public boolean hasPrerequisites()
public Collection<Course> getPrerequisites()
public Section scheduleSection(char day, String time, String room,
    int capacity)
```

If we bring all of the flagged (***) methods to bear, we can wrap up the displayCourseSchedule method of the Student class as follows:

```
public void displayCourseSchedule() {
  // Display a title first.
  System.out.println("Course Schedule for " + getName());

  // Step through the ArrayList of Section objects,
  // processing these one by one.
  for (Section s : attends) {
    // Since the attends ArrayList contains Sections that the
    // Student took in the past as well as those for which
    // the Student is currently enrolled, we only want to
    // report on those for which a grade has not yet been
    // assigned.
    if (s.getGrade(this) == null) {
      System.out.println("\tCourse No.:   " +
        s.getRepresentedCourse().getCourseNo());
      System.out.println("\tSection No.:   " + s.getSectionNo());
      System.out.println("\tCourse Name:   " +
        s.getRepresentedCourse().getCourseName());
      System.out.println("\tMeeting Day and Time Held:   " +
        s.getDayOfWeek() + " - " + s.getTimeOfDay());
      System.out.println("\tRoom Location:   " +
        s.getRoom());
      System.out.println("\tProfessor's Name:   " +
        s.getInstructor().getName());
      System.out.println("\t-----");
    }
  }
}
```

This method is a classic example of ***delegation***:

- We start out asking a Student object to do something for us—namely, to display the Student's course schedule.

- The Student object in turn has to talk to the Section objects representing sections that the student is enrolled in, asking each of them to perform some of their services (methods).

- The Student object also has to ask those Section objects to hand over references to the Professor and Course objects that the Section objects know about, in turn asking ***them*** to perform some of their services.

This multitiered collaboration is depicted conceptually in Figure 14-9.

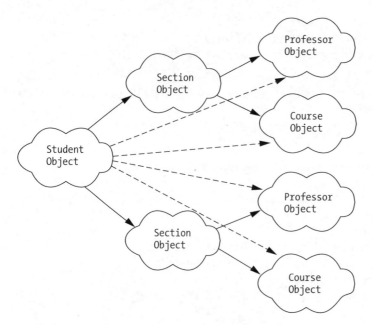

Figure 14-9. *A multitiered collaboration among objects*

The ScheduleOfClasses Class

Figure 14-10 shows the UML representation of the ScheduleOfClasses class. The sections that follow provide more detail about this class.

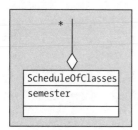

Figure 14-10. *The ScheduleOfClasses class*

ScheduleOfClasses Attributes

The ScheduleOfClasses class is a fairly simple class that serves as an example of how we might wish to encapsulate a collection object within some other class. It consists of only two attributes: a simple String representing the semester for which the schedule is valid (for example "SP2005" for the Spring 2005 semester), and a HashMap used to maintain handles on all of the Sections that are being offered that semester.

```
private String semester;

// This HashMap stores Section object references, using
// a String concatenation of course no. and section no. as the
// key, for example, "MATH101 - 1".
private HashMap<String, Section> sectionsOffered;
```

Aside from a simple constructor, a display method, and accessor methods for the attributes, the ScheduleOfClasses class declares three relatively simple methods, as follows.

addSection()

This method is used to add a Section object to the HashMap, and then to bidirectionally link this ScheduleOfClasses object back to the Section:

```
public void addSection(Section s) {
    // We formulate a key by concatenating the course no.
    // and section no., separated by a hyphen.
    String key = s.getRepresentedCourse().getCourseNo() +
            " - " + s.getSectionNo();
    sectionsOffered.put(key, s);

    // Bidirectionally link the ScheduleOfClasses back to the Section.
    s.setOfferedIn(this);
}
```

findSection()

This is a convenience method that is used to look up a Section in the encapsulated collection using the full section number that is passed in as the lookup key:

```
// The full section number is a concatenation of the
// course no. and section no., separated by a hyphen;
// e.g., "ART101 - 1".

public Section findSection(String fullSectionNo) {
    return sectionsOffered.get(fullSectionNo);
}
```

isEmpty()

This is another convenience method that is used to determine whether the encapsulated collection is empty. Internally, it delegates the work of making such a determination to the sectionsOffered collection.

```
public boolean isEmpty() {
    if (sectionsOffered.size() == 0) return true;
    else return false;
}
```

The TranscriptEntry Association Class (Static Methods)

Figure 14-11 shows the UML representation of the `TranscriptEntry` class. The sections that follow provide more detail about this class.

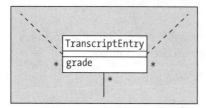

Figure 14-11. *The TranscriptEntry class*

TranscriptEntry Attributes

As you saw earlier in this chapter, the `TranscriptEntry` class has one simple attribute, grade, and maintains associations with three other classes (see Figure 14-12):

- *earns grade*, a one-to-many association with `Student`
- *assigns grade*, a one-to-many association with `Section`
- An unnamed, one-to-many aggregation with the `Transcript` class

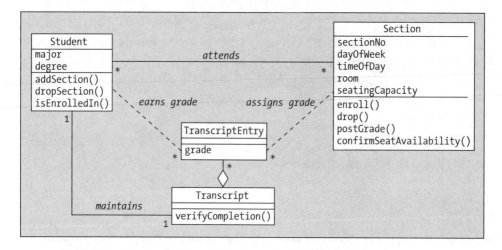

Figure 14-12. *TranscriptEntry maintains numerous relationships with other SRS classes.*

`TranscriptEntry` is at the "many" end of all of these associations, and so it only needs to maintain a single handle on each type of object—no collection attributes are required.

```
private String grade;
private Student student;
private Section section;
private Transcript transcript;
```

TranscriptEntry Constructor

The constructor for this class does most of the work of maintaining all of these relationships.

Via a call to setStudent, it stores the associated Student object's handle in the appropriate attribute.

```
//----------------
// Constructor(s).
//----------------

public TranscriptEntry(Student s, String grade, Section se) {
    this.setStudent(s);
```

Note that we have chosen ***not*** to maintain the *earns grade* association bidirectionally; that is, we have provided no code in either this or the Student class to provide the Student object with a handle on this TranscriptEntry object. This decision was based upon the fact that we don't expect a Student to ever have to manipulate TranscriptEntry objects directly. Every Student object has an indirect means of reaching all of its TranscriptEntry objects, via the handle that a Student object maintains on its Transcript object as a whole, and the handles that the Transcript object in turn maintains on its TranscriptEntry objects. You might think that giving a Student object the ability to directly pull a given TranscriptEntry might be useful when we want to determine the grade that the Student earned for a particular Section, but we have provided an alternative means of doing so, via the Section class's getGrade method.

Even though it may not appear so, we are maintaining the *assigns grade* association with Section bidirectionally. We see only half of the "handshake" in the TranscriptEntry constructor:

```
    this.setSection(se);
```

but recall that when we looked at the postGrade method of the Section class, we discussed the fact that Section was responsible for maintaining the bidirectionality of this association. When the Section's postGrade method invokes the TranscriptEntry constructor, the Section object is returned a handle on this TranscriptEntry object, which it stores in the appropriate attribute. So, we only need worry about the second half of this "handshake" here in TranscriptEntry.

On the other hand, the TranscriptEntry object has full responsibility for maintaining the bidirectionality of the association between itself and the Transcript object:

```
        // Obtain the Student's transcript ...
        Transcript t = s.getTranscript();

        // ... and then link the Transcript and the TranscriptEntry
        // together bidirectionally.
        this.setTranscript(t);
        t.addTranscriptEntry(this);
    }
```

validateGrade(), passingGrade()

The TranscriptEntry class provides our first SRS example of public static methods. It declares two methods, validateGrade and passingGrade, that may be invoked as utility methods on the TranscriptEntry class from anywhere in the SRS application:

- The first is used to validate whether or not a particular string—say, "B+"—is a valid grade. Here we see the business rules disclosed for what constitutes such a grade:

```java
public static boolean validateGrade(String grade) {
    boolean outcome = false;

    if (grade.equals("F") ||
        grade.equals("I")) {
        outcome = true;
    }

    if (grade.startsWith("A") ||
        grade.startsWith("B") ||
        grade.startsWith("C") ||
        grade.startsWith("D")) {
        if (grade.length() == 1) outcome = true;
        else if (grade.length() == 2) {
            if (grade.endsWith("+") ||
                grade.endsWith("-")) {
                outcome = true;
            }
        }
    }

    return outcome;
}
```

- The second is used to determine whether or not a particular string—say "D+"—is a *passing* grade. A slightly different set of business rules is applied in this case:

```java
public static boolean passingGrade(String grade) {
    boolean outcome = false;

    // First, make sure it is a valid grade.
    if (validateGrade(grade)) {
        // Next, make sure that the grade is a D or better.
        if (grade.startsWith("A") ||
            grade.startsWith("B") ||
            grade.startsWith("C") ||
            grade.startsWith("D")) {
            outcome = true;
        }
    }

    return outcome;
}
```

As we discussed in Chapter 7, public static methods can be invoked on the hosting class as a whole—in other words, an object needn't be instantiated in order to use these methods.

The Transcript Class

Figure 14-13 shows the UML representation of the Transcript class. The sections that follow provide more detail about this class.

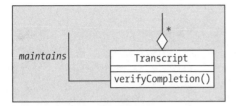

Figure 14-13. *The Transcript class*

Transcript Attributes

The Transcript class participates in two relationships:

- ***maintains***, a one-to-one association with Student

- An unnamed, one-to-many aggregation with TranscriptEntry

The SRS class diagram does not call out any other attributes for the Transcript class, so we only encode these two:

```
private ArrayList<TranscriptEntry> transcriptEntries;
private Student studentOwner;
```

verifyCompletion()

The Transcript class has one particularly interesting method, verifyCompletion, which is used to determine whether or not the Transcript contains evidence that a particular Course requirement has been satisfied. This method steps through the ArrayList of TranscriptEntries maintained by the Transcript object:

```
public boolean verifyCompletion(Course c) {
  boolean outcome = false;

  // Step through all TranscriptEntries, looking for one
  // that reflects a Section of the Course of interest.
  for (TranscriptEntry te : transcriptEntries) {
```

For each entry, it obtains a handle on the Section object represented by this entry, and then invokes the isSectionOf method on that object to determine whether or not that Section represents the Course of interest.

```
    Section s = te.getSection();

    if (s.isSectionOf(c)) {
```

Assuming that the Section is indeed relevant, the method next uses the static passingGrade method of the TranscriptEntry class to determine whether or not the grade earned in this Section was a passing grade. If it was a passing grade, we can terminate the loop immediately, since we need to find only *one* example of a passing grade for the Course of interest in order to return a true outcome from this method.

```java
        // Ensure that the grade was high enough.
        if (TranscriptEntry.passingGrade(te.getGrade())) {
          outcome = true;

          // We've found one, so we can afford to
          // terminate the loop now.
          break;
        }
      }
    }

    return outcome;
  }
}
```

The SRS Driver Program

Now that we've coded all of the classes called for by our model of the SRS, we need a way to test these. We could wait to put our application through its paces until we've built a GUI front-end; however, it would be nice to know sooner rather than later that our core classes are working properly. One very helpful technique for doing so is to write a command line–driven program to instantiate objects of varying types and to invoke their critical methods, displaying the results to the command-line window for us to inspect.

We'll develop just such a program by creating a class called SRS with a main method that will serve as our test "driver."

Public Static Attributes

We are going to instantiate some Professor, Student, Course, and Section objects in this program, so we need a way to organize references to these objects. We'll create collection objects as attributes of the SRS class to hold each of these different object types. While we're at it, we'll declare them to be public static attributes, which means that we're making these main object collections globally available to the entire application; these can then be accessed throughout the SRS application as SRS.*collectionName* (e.g., SRS.faculty).

```java
    // We can effectively create "global" data by declaring
    // collections of objects as public static attributes in
    // the main class;

    public static ArrayList<Professor> faculty;
    public static ArrayList<Student> studentBody;
    public static ArrayList<Course> courseCatalog;
```

```
// The next collection -- of Section object references -- is encapsulated
// within a special-purpose class by virtue of how we modeled the SRS in UML;
// note that we could have encapsulated the preceding three collections in
// similar fashion, and will in fact do so in Chapter 15.

public static ScheduleOfClasses scheduleOfClasses =
            new ScheduleOfClasses("SP2005");
```

The SRS ScheduleOfClasses class serves as a collection point for Section objects; for the other types of objects, we use simple ArrayLists, although we could go ahead and design classes comparable to ScheduleOfClasses to serve as encapsulated collections, perhaps named Faculty, StudentBody, and CourseCatalog, respectively. (We'll actually do so in Chapter 15.)

We don't need a collection for Transcript objects—we'll get to these via the handles that Student objects maintain—or for TranscriptEntry objects—we'll get to these via the Transcript objects themselves.

The main Method

We'll now dive into the main method for the SRS driver class. We'll start by declaring reference variables for each of the four main object types:

```
public static void main(String[] args) {
    Professor p1, p2, p3;
    Student s1, s2, s3;
    Course c1, c2, c3, c4, c5;
    Section sec1, sec2, sec3, sec4, sec5, sec6, sec7;
```

and we'll then use their various constructors to fabricate object instances, storing handles in the appropriate collections (in Chapter 15, we'll explore how we can instantiate objects by reading data from a file instead of hard-coding attributes as we do here):

```
// Create various objects by calling the appropriate
// constructors.  (We'd normally be reading in such data
// from a database or file ...)

// -----------
// Professors.
// -----------

p1 = new Professor("Jacquie Barker", "123-45-6789",
            "Adjunct Professor", "Information Technology");

p2 = new Professor("Claudio Cioffi", "567-81-2345",
            "Full Professor", "Computational Social Sciences");

p3 = new Professor("Snidely Whiplash", "987-65-4321",
            "Full Professor", "Physical Education");

// Add these to the appropriate ArrayList.
faculty = new ArrayList<Professor>();
```

```
            faculty.add(p1);
            faculty.add(p2);
            faculty.add(p3);


            // ---------
            // Students.
            // ---------

            s1 = new Student("Joe Blow", "111-11-1111", "Math", "M.S.");

            s2 = new Student("Fred Schnurd", "222-22-2222",
                    "Information Technology", "Ph. D.");

            s3 = new Student("Mary Smith", "333-33-3333", "Physics", "B.S.");

            // Add these to the appropriate ArrayList.
            studentBody = new ArrayList<Student>();
            studentBody.add(s1);
            studentBody.add(s2);
            studentBody.add(s3);


            // --------
            // Courses.
            // --------

            c1 = new Course("CMP101",
                    "Beginning Computer Technology", 3.0);

            c2 = new Course("OBJ101",
                    "Object Methods for Software Development", 3.0);

            c3 = new Course("CMP283",
                    "Higher Level Languages (Java)", 3.0);

            c4 = new Course("CMP999",
                    "Living Brain Computers", 3.0);

            c5 = new Course("ART101",
                    "Beginning Basketweaving", 3.0);

            // Add these to the appropriate ArrayList.
            courseCatalog = new ArrayList<Course>();
            courseCatalog.add(c1);
            courseCatalog.add(c2);
            courseCatalog.add(c3);
            courseCatalog.add(c4);
            courseCatalog.add(c5);
```

We use the addPrerequisite method of the Course class to interrelate some of the Courses, so that c1 is a prerequisite for c2, c2 for c3, and c3 for c4. The only Courses that do not specify prerequisites in our test case are c1 and c5.

```
// Establish some prerequisites (c1 => c2 => c3 => c4).
c2.addPrerequisite(c1);
c3.addPrerequisite(c2);
c4.addPrerequisite(c3);
```

To create Section objects, we take advantage of the Course class's scheduleSection method which, as you may recall, contains an embedded call to a Section class constructor. Each invocation of scheduleSection returns a handle to a newly created Section object, which we store in the appropriate collection.

```
// ---------
// Sections.
// ---------

// Schedule sections of each Course by calling the
// scheduleSection method of Course (which internally
// invokes the Section constructor).

sec1 = c1.scheduleSection('M', "8:10 - 10:00 PM", "GOVT101", 30);

sec2 = c1.scheduleSection('W', "6:10 - 8:00 PM", "GOVT202", 30);

sec3 = c2.scheduleSection('R', "4:10 - 6:00 PM", "GOVT105", 25);

sec4 = c2.scheduleSection('T', "6:10 - 8:00 PM", "SCI330", 25);

sec5 = c3.scheduleSection('M', "6:10 - 8:00 PM", "GOVT101", 20);

sec6 = c4.scheduleSection('R', "4:10 - 6:00 PM", "SCI241", 15);

sec7 = c5.scheduleSection('M', "4:10 - 6:00 PM", "ARTS25", 40);

// Add these to the Schedule of Classes.
scheduleOfClasses.addSection(sec1);
scheduleOfClasses.addSection(sec2);
scheduleOfClasses.addSection(sec3);
scheduleOfClasses.addSection(sec4);
scheduleOfClasses.addSection(sec5);
scheduleOfClasses.addSection(sec6);
scheduleOfClasses.addSection(sec7);
```

Next, we use the agreeToTeach method declared for the Professor class to assign Professors to Sections:

```
// Recruit a professor to teach each of the sections.

p3.agreeToTeach(sec1);
p2.agreeToTeach(sec2);
p1.agreeToTeach(sec3);
p3.agreeToTeach(sec4);
p1.agreeToTeach(sec5);
p2.agreeToTeach(sec6);
p3.agreeToTeach(sec7);
```

We then simulate student registration by having Students enroll in the various Sections using the enroll method. Recall that this method returns one of a set of predefined status values as defined by our EnrollmentStatus enum(eration), and so in order to display which status is returned in each case, we created a "housekeeping" reportStatus method solely for the purpose of formatting an informational message:

```
System.out.println("================================");
System.out.println("Student registration has begun!");
System.out.println("================================");
System.out.println();

// Simulate students attempting to enroll in sections of
// various courses.

System.out.println("Student " + s1.getName() +
        " is attempting to enroll in " +
        sec1.toString());

EnrollmentStatus status = sec1.enroll(s1);
this.reportStatus(status);
```

Since the preceding three lines of code—the println, enroll, and reportStatus method calls—are going to be repeated multiple times, we have written a "housekeeping" method called attemptToEnroll that does these three things, and will use the more concise attemptToEnroll(...) syntax for the remainder of this program. (The attemptToEnroll method is discussed separately shortly.)

```
// Try concurrently enrolling the same Student in a different Section
// of the SAME Course!  This should fail.
attemptToEnroll(s1, sec2);

// This enrollment request should be fine ...
attemptToEnroll(s2, sec2);

// ... but here, the student in question hasn't satisfied the
// prerequisites, so the enrollment request should be rejected.
attemptToEnroll(s2, sec3);
```

```
// These requests should both be fine.
attemptToEnroll(s2, sec7);
attemptToEnroll(s3, sec1);

// When the dust settles, here's what folks wound up
// being SUCCESSFULLY registered for:
//
// sec1:  s1, s3
// sec2:  s2
// sec7:  s2
```

Next, we simulate the assignment of grades at the end of the semester by invoking the postGrade method for each Student–Section combination:

```
// Semester is finished (boy, that was quick!). Professors
// assign grades for specific students.
sec1.postGrade(s1, "C+");
sec1.postGrade(s3, "A");
sec2.postGrade(s2, "B+");
sec7.postGrade(s2, "A-");
```

Finally, we put our various display methods to good use by displaying the internal state of the various objects that we created—in essence, an "object dump":

```
// Let's see if everything got set up properly
// by calling various display() methods.

System.out.println("====================");
System.out.println("Schedule of Classes:");
System.out.println("====================");
System.out.println();
scheduleOfClasses.display();

System.out.println("======================");
System.out.println("Professor Information:");
System.out.println("======================");
System.out.println();
p1.display();
p2.display();
p3.display();

System.out.println("====================");
System.out.println("Student Information:");
System.out.println("====================");
System.out.println();
s1.display();
s2.display();
s3.display();
}
```

Here is the attemptToEnroll housekeeping method mentioned earlier, along with the reportStatus method that it in turn uses:

```java
private static void reportStatus(EnrollmentStatus s) {
    System.out.println("Status:  " + s.value());
    System.out.println();
}

private static void attemptToEnroll(Student s, Section sec) {
    System.out.println("Student " + s.getName() +
                " is attempting to enroll in " +
                sec.toString());

    // Utilize one housekeeping method from within another!
    reportStatus(sec.enroll(s));
}
}
```

When compiled and run, the SRS program produces the following command prompt output:

```
==============================
Student registration has begun!
==============================

Student Joe Blow is attempting to enroll in CMP101 - 1 - M - 8:10 - 10:00 PM
Status:  enrollment successful!  :o)

Student Joe Blow is attempting to enroll in CMP101 - 2 - W - 6:10 - 8:00 PM
Status:  enrollment failed; previously enrolled.  :op

Student Fred Schnurd is attempting to enroll in CMP101 - 2 - W - 6:10 - 8:00 PM
Status:  enrollment successful!  :o)

Student Fred Schnurd is attempting to enroll in OBJ101 - 1 - R - 4:10 - 6:00 PM
Status:  enrollment failed; prerequisites not satisfied.  :op

Student Fred Schnurd is attempting to enroll in ART101 - 1 - M - 4:10 - 6:00 PM
Status:  enrollment successful!  :o)

Student Mary Smith is attempting to enroll in CMP101 - 1 - M - 8:10 - 10:00 PM
Status:  enrollment successful!  :o)

====================
Schedule of Classes:
====================

Schedule of Classes for SP2005
```

```
Section Information:
    Semester:  SP2005
    Course No.:  ART101
    Section No:  1
    Offered:  M at 4:10 - 6:00 PM
    In Room:  ARTS25
    Professor:  Snidely Whiplash
    Total of 1 students enrolled, as follows:
        Fred Schnurd

Section Information:
    Semester:  SP2005
    Course No.:  CMP283
    Section No:  1
    Offered:  M at 6:10 - 8:00 PM
    In Room:  GOVT101
    Professor:  Jacquie Barker
    Total of 0 students enrolled.

Section Information:
    Semester:  SP2005
    Course No.:  OBJ101
    Section No:  1
    Offered:  R at 4:10 - 6:00 PM
    In Room:  GOVT105
    Professor:  Jacquie Barker
    Total of 0 students enrolled.

Section Information:
    Semester:  SP2005
    Course No.:  CMP101
    Section No:  2
    Offered:  W at 6:10 - 8:00 PM
    In Room:  GOVT202
    Professor:  Claudio Cioffi
    Total of 1 students enrolled, as follows:
        Fred Schnurd

Section Information:
    Semester:  SP2005
    Course No.:  CMP999
    Section No:  1
    Offered:  R at 4:10 - 6:00 PM
    In Room:  SCI241
    Professor:  Claudio Cioffi
    Total of 0 students enrolled.
```

```
Section Information:
    Semester:  SP2005
    Course No.:  CMP101
    Section No:  1
    Offered:  M at 8:10 - 10:00 PM
    In Room:  GOVT101
    Professor:  Snidely Whiplash
    Total of 2 students enrolled, as follows:
        Joe Blow
        Mary Smith

Section Information:
    Semester:  SP2005
    Course No.:  OBJ101
    Section No:  2
    Offered:  T at 6:10 - 8:00 PM
    In Room:  SCI330
    Professor:  Snidely Whiplash
    Total of 0 students enrolled.


=======================
Professor Information:
=======================

Person Information:
    Name:  Jacquie Barker
    Soc. Security No.:  123-45-6789
Professor-Specific Information:
    Title:  Adjunct Professor
    Teaches for Dept.:  Information Technology
Teaching Assignments for Jacquie Barker:
    Course No.:  OBJ101
    Section No.:  1
    Course Name:  Object Methods for Software Development
    Day and Time:  R - 4:10 - 6:00 PM
    -----
    Course No.:  CMP283
    Section No.:  1
    Course Name:  Higher Level Languages (Java)
    Day and Time:  M - 6:10 - 8:00 PM
    -----

Person Information:
    Name:  Claudio Cioffi
    Soc. Security No.:  567-81-2345
Professor-Specific Information:
    Title:  Full Professor
    Teaches for Dept.:  Computational Social Sciences
```

Teaching Assignments for Claudio Cioffi:
    Course No.: CMP101
    Section No.: 2
    Course Name: Beginning Computer Technology
    Day and Time: W - 6:10 - 8:00 PM

    Course No.: CMP999
    Section No.: 1
    Course Name: Living Brain Computers
    Day and Time: R - 4:10 - 6:00 PM

Person Information:
    Name: Snidely Whiplash
    Soc. Security No.: 987-65-4321
Professor-Specific Information:
    Title: Full Professor
    Teaches for Dept.: Physical Education
Teaching Assignments for Snidely Whiplash:
    Course No.: CMP101
    Section No.: 1
    Course Name: Beginning Computer Technology
    Day and Time: M - 8:10 - 10:00 PM

    Course No.: OBJ101
    Section No.: 2
    Course Name: Object Methods for Software Development
    Day and Time: T - 6:10 - 8:00 PM

    Course No.: ART101
    Section No.: 1
    Course Name: Beginning Basketweaving
    Day and Time: M - 4:10 - 6:00 PM

====================
Student Information:
====================

Person Information:
    Name: Joe Blow
    Soc. Security No.: 111-11-1111
Student-Specific Information:
    Major: Math
    Degree: M.S.
Course Schedule for Joe Blow

```
Transcript for:   Joe Blow (111-11-1111) [M.S. - Math]
    Semester:        SP2005
    Course No.:      CMP101
    Credits:         3.0
    Grade Received:  C+
    -----


Person Information:
    Name:  Fred Schnurd
    Soc. Security No.:  222-22-2222
Student-Specific Information:
    Major:  Information Technology
    Degree:  Ph. D.
Course Schedule for Fred Schnurd
Transcript for:   Fred Schnurd (222-22-2222) [Ph.D. - Information Technology]
    Semester:        SP2005
    Course No.:      CMP101
    Credits:         3.0
    Grade Received:  B+
    -----
    Semester:        SP2005
    Course No.:      ART101
    Credits:         3.0
    Grade Received:  A-
    -----


Person Information:
    Name:  Mary Smith
    Soc. Security No.:  333-33-3333
Student-Specific Information:
    Major:  Physics
    Degree:  B.S.
Course Schedule for Mary Smith
Transcript for:   Mary Smith (333-33-3333) [B.S. - Physics]
    Semester:        SP2005
    Course No.:      CMP101
    Credits:         3.0
    Grade Received:  A
    -----
```

We've thus demonstrated a successful test of our model! Of course, the SRS driver program could be extended to test various other scenarios; some of the exercises at the end of this chapter suggest ways that you might wish to try doing so.

The Importance of Model–View and Model–Data Layer Separation

By developing our SRS model classes first, and using a command-line program to put them through their paces, we've virtually guaranteed **loose coupling**—that is, ease of interchangeability—between

- The model classes (aka the *model layer*) of our application and the code that we'll write in Chapter 15 to persist our objects' state from one SRS session to the next, known as the application's *data layer*

- The *model layer* and the code that we'll write to present our model to the users via a GUI, known as the *presentation layer* or *view* of our application

The model layer of an application is typically the layer that changes the least often over an application's lifetime, because the fundamentals of real-world objects (i.e., the business rules for how they operate) are fairly stable, once properly modeled. This is in contrast with both the presentation and data layers of an application, which undergo fairly frequent change due to technology shifts:

- It isn't unusual for the same application to transition from one database back-end to another, or even from one type of persistent storage to another, over its lifetime.

- It isn't unusual for the same application to periodically get a "face-lift" in terms of how information is presented to a user. For example, perhaps an application started out with a client/server desktop sort of GUI, such as the one we'll build for the SRS in Chapter 16 using the Java Swing and AWT APIs, but then later transitioned into a browser-based thin-client user interface, such as the one that can be built with the Java 2 Platform, Enterprise Edition (J2EE) component technologies.

Unfortunately, many developers dive into Java development by acquiring and using a graphics-oriented Java integrated development environment (IDE). As a result, they wind up using the drag-and-drop features of such a tool to build a GUI front-end that directly connects to file system or database back-end, with *no model layer whatsoever* in the middle! Hence, while such applications are, strictly speaking, Java applications, they aren't truly *object-oriented applications*.

If we instead approach OO application development properly, by doing the following:

1. Building the model layer *first*, as a true OO abstraction of the real-world problem that we are trying to automate

2. Architecting the data and presentation layers so as to be easily upgradeable when necessary *without impacting the model*

the resultant applications will be much more resilient to change and will enjoy much longer life cycles, thereby reducing overall software development costs for an organization.

We'll revisit the importance of model–data layer and model–view separation in more detail in Chapters 15 and 16. In particular, we'll see how the *same* model classes that we've used in this chapter to support our command line–driven SRS can be reused with different Java persistence/ presentation technologies.

Summary

You've now seen some ***serious*** Java in action! We've built a command line–driven version of the SRS application. Although this is not typically how most applications are invoked—most "industrial-strength" applications have GUI front-ends—developing such a version is a crucial step in testing our core model classes to ensure that all methods are working properly. And, aside from the various display methods that we encoded for testing purposes, ***all of the code that we've written for the command-line version of the SRS application will carry forward intact*** when we round out the application in the next two chapters.

Exercises

All of the following exercises involve making modifications/extensions to the SRS code presented in this chapter. If you have not already done so, please download the code from the Downloads area of the Apress website (http://www.apress.com) in preparation for these exercises. (See Appendix D for details.)

1. [*Coding*] Expand the SRS class's main method to represent a ***second*** semester's worth of course registrations. (Hint: this will require a second instantiation of the ScheduleOfClasses class.)

    - Change the grades received by some Students in the first semester to failing grades, and then attempt to register the Student for a course in the second semester requiring successful completion of one of these failed courses in a previous semester.

    - Try registering a Student for a course in the second semester that the Student has already successfully completed in the first semester.

2. [*Coding*] Improve the logic of the addPrerequisite method of the Course class to ensure that a Course cannot accidentally be assigned as its own prerequisite.

3. [*Coding*] Improve the logic of the agreeToTeach method of the Professor class so that a Professor cannot accidentally agree to teach two different Sections that meet on the same day/at the same time.

4. [*Coding*] Implement a cancelSection method for the Course class, and then correct the erroneous logic of the scheduleSection method having to do with the manner in which Section numbers are assigned. (Hint: consider introducing a static attribute to the Course class for this purpose.)

5. [*Coding*] The enroll method of the Section class does not take into account the fact that a Student may simultaneously be registered for a course and its prerequisite. Modify this method to allow for this possibility.

6. [*Coding*] The postGrade method of the Section class makes mention of the need for an eraseGrade method, in the event that a Professor wishes to change his or her mind about the grade that has been issued to a Student. Create the eraseGrade method.

7. [*Coding*] Modify the scheduleSection method of the Course class to prevent two Sections from being scheduled for the same classroom on the same day/at the same time.

CHAPTER 15

■ ■ ■

Rounding Out Your Application, Part 1: Adding a Data Access Layer

In Chapter 14, we built our first version of the SRS: a command line–driven version that focused on the model classes called for by our UML class diagram: Person, Professor, Student, Course, Section, ScheduleOfClasses, Transcript, and TranscriptEntry. In essence, we developed what will become the *core* of our SRS application—that is, the SRS application's **model layer**. We then wrote the logic of the SRS class's main method to *test* that model—that is, to instantiate objects of the various types and to put them through their paces as a means of ensuring that we've implemented the logic of their methods correctly.

While the SRS main method proved quite useful as a test driver, the SRS application as written thus far is not useful as a real-world application, however, for the following reasons:

- The application hard-codes all of its objects' data values (e.g., p1 = new Professor("Jacquie Barker", "123-45-6789", "Adjunct Professor", "Information Technology");), rather than obtaining such data interactively from either a user or a data repository.

- The application provides no means of remembering the state of the objects from one invocation of the application to the next. If a student logs on to register, then the next time the student logs back on, all knowledge of what she or he had previously registered for is forgotten.

- Most traditional information systems require significant interaction with a user to drive the applications' behavior, and they rely on a GUI for such interaction. Our SRS as presently written allows for no user interaction whatsoever: once it is launched via the command java SRS, it runs to completion based on the "script" that is laid out by the logic of the main method.

In this chapter, we are going to enhance/extend our SRS application to provide a means for reading/writing data to/from **persistent storage** so that we can remedy the first two of these three shortcomings. Then, in Chapter 17, we'll remedy the third deficiency by adding a GUI front-end to the SRS. The planned evolution of our SRS application is illustrated conceptually in Figure 15-1.

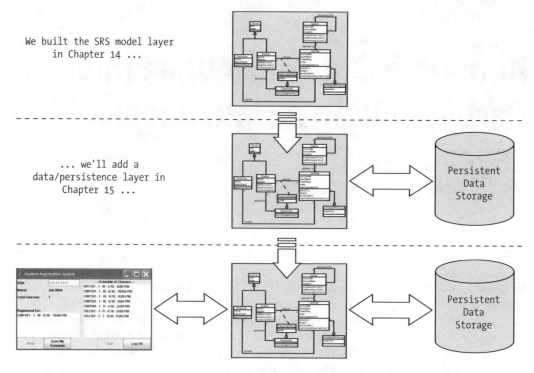

We built the SRS model layer in Chapter 14 ...

... we'll add a data/persistence layer in Chapter 15 ...

Persistent Data Storage

Persistent Data Storage

... and we'll round the SRS out with a GUI view/presentation layer in Chapter 17.

Figure 15-1. *Transforming the SRS into an "industrial-strength" application*

In this chapter, you will learn

- How to perform file input/output (I/O) in Java

- An approach for parsing tab-delimited text records to initialize an object's state, or to initialize a *collection* of objects

- Conversely, a means of persisting an object's state in a record-oriented text file

- The importance of **model–data access layer separation** as a design technique

---

IMPORTANT!

As I've mentioned several times previously, Sun Microsystems introduced some important new features with J2SE 5.0 that significantly increased the power and versatility of Java as an object-oriented programming language. I've thus adopted the J2SE 5.0 approach as of this (second) edition of *Beginning Java Objects*.

Note that the SRS code as presented in Chapters 14, 15, and 17 will **not** *compile with an earlier (pre-5.0) version of the Java compiler*. For readers who are still working with an earlier version of the Java language, a version of the SRS application that will compile with these earlier language versions is also available for download; please see Appendix D for details.

An Overview of Upcoming SRS Enhancements

Here's a high-level road map of what we'll be doing in this chapter to enhance the SRS application as first presented in Chapter 14:

1. We'll modify—and significantly ***streamline***—the SRS driver class, because we'll be able to encapsulate a lot of the "gory details" involved with initializing objects/object collections in six ***new*** classes:

   - SRSDataAccess: A class that provides data access layer functionality to the SRS

   - CourseCatalog: An encapsulated collection of Course objects, patterned after the ScheduleOfClasses class introduced in Chapter 14

   - Faculty: An encapsulated collection of Professor objects, also patterned after the ScheduleOfClasses class

   - Three ***custom exception classes***: SRSInitializationException, InvalidStudentException, and StudentPersistenceException

2. We'll be able to reuse all eight of our model classes—Course, Person, Professor, ScheduleOfClasses, Section, Student, Transcript, and TranscriptEntry—***exactly as designed in Chapter 14*** because of our adherence to the fundamental—and ***critically important***—design principle of **model–data access layer separation**, which we'll spend a great deal of time discussing as this chapter unfolds.

3. We'll also reuse our EnrollmentStatus enum(eration) "as is" from Chapter 14, for a grand total of 16 classes required to support this chapter's version of our SRS application.

We'll revisit this list of extensions/enhancements to the SRS application in detail at the end of the chapter, to reflect on the significance of all that we've done.

As a friendly reminder, all 16 of these classes, plus supporting data files, are downloadable from the Apress web site, as described in Appendix D.

Approaches to Object Persistence

Whenever we run a Java application such as the SRS, all objects that we instantiate reside in memory allocated to the JVM. When such an application terminates, all of the JVM's memory is released back to the operating system, and the internal states of all of the objects created by the application are forgotten—that is, unless they have been **persisted** (saved) in some fashion.

Using various APIs, Java provides a wealth of options with regard to persisting object states.

- Using the **JDBC API**, we can save data to an ODBC-compliant relational database such as Sybase, Oracle, or Microsoft SQL Server in a variety of ways.

  - We may store the attribute values of objects as fields in conventional records, as depicted conceptually in Figure 15-2.

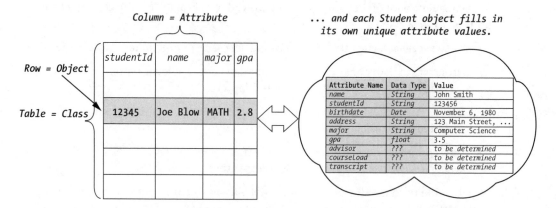

Figure 15-2. *Storing attribute values in fields of conventional records*

  - We may store an entire object in binary form in a ***single*** field within a record, in the form of a **binary (large) object** (**BLOB**), as depicted conceptually in Figure 15-3.

SSN	Name	Advisor
123-45-6789	John	
000-00-0000	Mary	
987-65-4321	Fred	

Figure 15-3. *Objects can also be stored as a whole within a single field as binary objects.*

- We can output an object in a special binary form known as a Java **serialized object**, which is ideal for distributing objects over a network.

- We can save information in a fairly straightforward, human-readable text format, as either of the following:

- With hierarchically organized data using **Extensible Markup Language** (**XML**), we intersperse information—"content"—with "tags" that describe how the information is to be interpreted, such as in the following simple example illustrating a Professor object with two Student advisees:

```
<professor>
    <name>Dr. Irving Smith</name>
    <ssn>123-45-6789</ssn>
    <title>Associate Professor</title>
    <advisees>
        <advisee>
            <type>Student</type>
            <sname>Joe Blow</sname>
            <sssn>987-65-4321</sssn>
        </advisee>
        <advisee>
            <type>Student</type>
            <sname>Mary Jones</sname>
            <sssn>999-88-7777</sssn>
        </advisee>
    </advisees>
</professor>
```

- We can also store the attribute values of objects to a file in the form of simple tab- or comma-delimited record-oriented data.

We'll use the latter form of basic data persistence—***record-oriented file persistence***—in our SRS application. However, ***all of the same design principles*** that we illustrate in doing so are applicable to all of the other forms of persistence, as well. Specifically, we'll demonstrate and emphasize the importance of

- ***Hiding the details of how we persist an object*** by encapsulating them within one or more **data access layer classes**, so that neither our model classes nor client code have to get bogged down with the details.

- ***Adhering to the design principle of model–data access layer separation***, thus ensuring that our model classes serve as pure abstractions of real-world domain objects—without cluttering them with details of persistence (or presentation, as we'll discuss in Chapters 16 and 17)—so that they'll be maximally reusable from one application to the next.

- Ensuring that whatever approach we take to persisting an object today is ***flexible***, so that we can swap out one form of persistence and swap in another—perhaps to take advantage of technological advances in persistence technology—with ***minimal impact*** to our application overall.

- Providing ***graceful error handling*** when something goes awry. Since persistence involves interacting with an external file system, database management system, application server, and/or network, there are many potential points of failure that are outside of an application's immediate control. The best we can do as application developers is to anticipate and programmatically recover from such issues whenever possible.

By the end of this chapter, you'll have a solid appreciation of these matters, regardless of what type of persistence you ultimately choose for a given application.

The Basics of File I/O in Java

In this section, we'll look at the fundamentals of the Java file input/output (I/O), which is based on streams or the reading and writing of data from various sources.

Reading from a File

The basic Java approach that we're going to use for reading records one by one from a text file involves two special types of Java object.

1. First, we'll instantiate a `FileReader`, a type of Java object that knows how to open a file and read data from the file one character at a time.

2. Next, we'll pass a reference to this `FileReader` object as an argument to the constructor for a `BufferedReader`, a more sophisticated type of object that effectively encapsulates the `FileReader`. The `BufferedReader`'s `readLine` method knows how to internally gather up, or **buffer**, individual characters as read by the `FileReader` until an end-of-line character is detected, at which point the `BufferedReader` hands back a complete line/record of data to client code. This process is illustrated conceptually in Figure 15-4.

Both the `FileReader` and `BufferedReader` classes are defined in the `java.io` package.

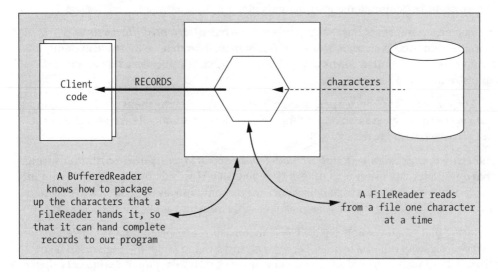

Figure 15-4. *A BufferedReader returns complete records to client code with help from an encapsulated FileReader.*

Here's a bit of pseudocode to illustrate the basics of reading from a file. I've left out some of the fine-point details, but you'll see this process carried out in earnest in the various SRS classes that we'll review later in this chapter.

```
// Instantiate a FileReader, and pass it into a BufferedReader.
FileReader fr = new FileReader(nameOfFileToBeReadFrom);
BufferedReader bIn = new BufferedReader(fr);

// Read the first line from the file.
String line = bIn.readLine();

// As long as the end of the file hasn't been reached ...
while (line != null) {
    // Pseudocode.
    Process the most recently read line however we'd like ...

    // Read another line ("line" will be set to null when
    // the file has been exhausted).
    line = bIn.readLine();
}

// Close the BufferedReader, which automatically closes
// the encapsulated FileReader, as well.
bIn.close();
```

Here are a few points worth noting about the preceding code:

- The two lines of code that instantiate the FileReader and BufferedReader, respectively

  ```
  FileReader fr = new FileReader(nameOfFileToBeReadFrom);
  BufferedReader bIn = new BufferedReader(fr);
  ```

  could also be combined into a single statement as follows:

  ```
  BufferedReader bIn = new BufferedReader(new FileReader(
      nameOfFileToBeReadFrom));
  ```

  because we'll never need to reference (i.e., "talk to") the FileReader object directly.

- A BufferedReader signals that the end of a file has been reached by returning the value null:

  ```
  // As long as the end of the file hasn't been reached ...
  while (line != null) {
      // Processing details omitted ...

      // Remember to read another line, to avoid an infinite loop!
      line = bIn.readLine();
  }
  ```

  An "empty" record, on the other hand (i.e., a record consisting of only a hard return), is instead returned as the String value "".

Here's a trick for skipping blank lines (i.e., lines consisting only of white space), along with "empty" records, when reading from a file:

```
while (line != null) {
    // Use the String class's trim method to eliminate all
    // leading/trailing white space.
    line = line.trim();

    // Skip blank lines.
    if (line.equals("")) continue;

    // Processing details omitted ...

    // Remember to read another line, to avoid an infinite loop!
    line = bIn.readLine();
}
```

- The code involved with reading from a file is liable to throw various types of run-time Exception. We'll discuss this in a moment with regard to both reading from and writing to files.

Writing to a File

The basic Java approach that we'll use for writing records to a text file is similar, but in reverse, to what it takes to read from a file:

1. We instantiate a FileOutputStream, an object that knows how to open a file and write data to the file one character at a time.

2. We pass a reference to that FileOutputStream object as an argument to the constructor for a PrintWriter, a more sophisticated type of object that encapsulates the FileOutputStream. The PrintWriter's println method knows how to transfer an entire record/line's worth of data one character at a time to its encapsulated FileOutputStream object, which then outputs the data one character at a time to the file. This is depicted conceptually in Figure 15-5.

Both the FileOutputStream and PrintWriter classes are defined in the java.io package.

The PrintWriter class also defines a print method, which works exactly like the System.out.print method.

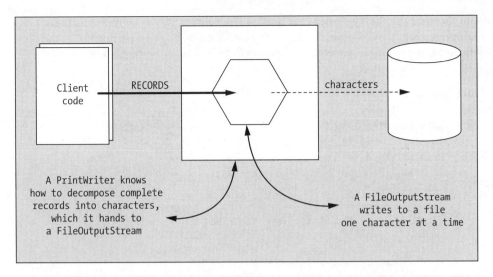

Figure 15-5. *A BufferedWriter uses an encapsulated FileOutputStream to write records, character by character, to a file.*

Here is a bit of pseudocode to illustrate the basics of writing to a file:

```
// Instantiate a FileOutputStream, and pass it into a PrintWriter.
FileOutputStream fos = new FileOutputStream(nameOfFileToBeWrittenTo);
PrintWriter pw = new PrintWriter(fos);

while (we still have more data to output) {
    pw.println(whatever data we wish to output);
}

// Close the PrintWriter, which automatically closes
// the encapsulated FileOutputStream, as well.
pw.close();
```

Here are a few points worth noting about the preceding code:

- Note that the following two lines of code:

    ```
    FileOutputStream fos = new FileOutputStream(nameOfFileToBeWrittenTo);
    PrintWriter pw = new PrintWriter(fos);
    ```

    could also be combined into a single statement as follows:

    ```
    PrintWriter pw = new PrintWriter(
        new FileOutputStream(nameOfFileToBeWrittenTo));
    ```

    because we'll never need to reference (i.e., "talk to") the FileOutputStream object directly.

- It's important to explicitly close a `PrintWriter`/`FileOutputStream` combination when we are through with it, to completely "flush" the data that we've been writing out to the file. In the following example, we've inadvertently forgotten to close the file with a `pw.close();` statement:

```
import java.io.*;

public class ForgotToClose {
    public static void main (String[] args) {
        PrintWriter pw = new PrintWriter(
            new FileOutputStream("test.dat"));
         pw.println("Hi.");

            // Whoops!  We forgot to close the file!
    }
}
```

If we were to run the preceding program, we'd discover that a `test.dat` file would have been *created*, but we'd find it to be *empty*.

- The code involved with writing to a file is liable to throw one of two types of `Exception`. We'll discuss exception handling in a moment with regard to both reading from and writing to files.

Note that if we attempt to open a `FileOutputStream` to a file that doesn't already exist, the `FileOutputStream` object will *create* the file, whereas if we attempt to open a `FileOutputStream` to a file that *does* already exist, we will *overwrite* the file. It's also possible to *append* records to an existing file, rather than overwriting its contents, by using an overloaded version of the `FileOutputStream` constructor, which takes *two* arguments:

```
FileOutputStream(String filename, boolean append)
```

where passing `true` as the second argument will *append* to the designated file, if such a file exists:

```
// If a file by the name of "file1.dat" doesn't already exist, it will
// be created with the following line of code; if a file by this name
// DOES exist, however, it will be APPENDED to, by virtue of the fact
// that we're passing in the value true as a second argument
// to this FileOutputStream constructor.
PrintWriter pw1 = new PrintWriter(
    new FileOutputStream("file1.dat", true));
```

Passing the value `false` as the second argument to this constructor, on the other hand, causes the file to be overwritten instead:

```
// If a file by the name of "file2.dat" doesn't already exist, it will
// be created with the following line of code; if a file by this name
// DOES exist, however, it will be OVERWRITTEN, by virtue of the fact
// that we're passing in the value false as a second argument
```

```
// to this FileOutputStream constructor.
PrintWriter pw1 = new PrintWriter(
    new FileOutputStream("file2.dat", false));
```

The preceding is equivalent to using the single-argument form of constructor:

```
// Overwrite file2.dat if it already exists.
PrintWriter pw1 = new PrintWriter(new FileOutputStream("file2.dat"));
```

Exception Handling with File I/O

As mentioned earlier, reading from and writing to files is liable to generate run-time exceptions. The code involved with reading from a file is liable to throw one of several types of exception:

- `FileNotFoundException`, if the file does not exist; is a directory rather than a regular file; or for some other reason cannot be opened for reading.

- The more general `IOException`, if a problem arises with reading from the file after it has successfully been opened for read access.

- Various application-specific custom exceptions if the data being read in is improperly formatted. We'll talk about the use of custom exceptions when reading from a file later in the chapter.

The code involved with writing to a file is liable to throw these same two types of exception:

- `FileNotFoundException`, if the file exists but is a directory rather than a regular file; if the file does not exist, but cannot be created; or if the file cannot be opened for writing for any other reason

- The more general `IOException`, if a problem arises with reading from the file after it has successfully been opened for write access

Thus, the code shown in our previous examples would need to include proper exception handling measures to satisfy the compiler, as we discussed in Chapter 13.

The following example, which demonstrates an approach to copying the contents of one file to another, reflects all exception handling that would be mandated by the Java compiler when reading from and writing to files (barring any application-specific custom exception handling that we might have introduced):

```
import java.io.*;

public class FileIO {
    public static void main(String[] args) {
        BufferedReader bIn = null;
        PrintWriter pw = null;

        try {
            // Attempt to open a file named input.dat
            // for read access.
```

```
        bIn = new BufferedReader(new FileReader("input.dat"));
    }
    catch (FileNotFoundException e) { ... }

    try {
        // Attempt to open a file named output.dat for
        // write access.
        pw = new PrintWriter(new FileOutputStream("output.dat"));
    }
    catch (FileNotFoundException e) { ... }

    // Count records as we go.
    int recordCount = 0;

    // Transfer one record at a time.
    String record = null;
    try {
        record = bIn.readLine();
    }
    catch (IOException e) { ... }

    while (record != null) {
        recordCount++;

        // Output the current record to output.dat.
        pw.println(record);

        // Read the next record from input.dat.
        try {
            record = bIn.readLine();
        }
        catch (IOException e) { ... }
    }

    // Display record count.
    System.out.println("Total of " + recordCount + " records transferred.");

    // Close both files.
    try {
        bIn.close();
    }
    catch (IOException e) { ... }

    // No compiler-mandated exceptions need be handled
    // when closing a PrintWriter.
    pw.close();
    }
}
```

Populating the Main SRS Collections

In this section, we look at populating the main SRS using collection classes, such as `ScheduleofClasses`, `CourseCatalog`, `Faculty`, and more, in setting up an academic course registration application.

The ScheduleOfClasses Collection

In Chapter 14, the `ScheduleOfClasses` custom collection class was introduced as a means of encapsulating a collection of `Section` objects. We discussed this class's design in depth in Chapter 14, so we won't revisit the code in detail again here. By way of review,

- The class declared two attributes: a `String` representing the `semester` of interest and a `HashMap` called `sectionsOffered` designed to hold references to `Section` objects, using a `String` concatenation of course number and section number as the key (e.g., `"MATH 101 - 1"`).

- The class declared standard accessor methods for these attributes, along with the following other miscellaneous methods:

```
public void display()
public void addSection(Section s)
public Section findSection(String fullSectionNo)
public boolean isEmpty()
```

We won't need to make any changes to the `ScheduleOfClasses` design as presented in Chapter 14 to accommodate persistence, and we shouldn't *want* to. As with all eight of our model layer classes, the `ScheduleOfClasses` class represents a pure abstraction of something in the real-world problem domain that we are attempting to model in software. By allowing this class to remain free of persistence details, it will remain maximally reusable from one application to another. If, on the other hand, we were to embed file I/O logic in the `ScheduleOfClasses` class, we'd thus constrain it to reuse "as is" with only those applications interested in using file persistence (versus some other persistence mechanism).

Two New Encapsulated Collection Classes: CourseCatalog and Faculty

With this version of the SRS, we're going to introduce two new custom collection classes patterned after the `ScheduleOfClasses` class:

- A class named `CourseCatalog` designed to encapsulate a collection of `Course` object references

- A class named `Faculty` designed to encapsulate a collection of `Professor` object references

Introducing these additional classes will facilitate an increased level of abstraction in our application, as we'll demonstrate when we review the revised SRS driver class later in this chapter. (We won't worry about creating a `StudentBody` collection to house `Student` objects, for reasons that will become apparent later.)

These two collections didn't appear in our object model as developed in Part 2 of the book, because they weren't necessary for fulfilling the use cases that we came up with for the SRS back in Chapter 9. These collections represent what we've spoken of before as ***implementation classes*** (aka ***solution-space classes***)—that is, classes that become part of an application's infrastructure, but that needn't appear in the version of the UML class diagram model that we review with users.

Because the code for these two classes is so similar to that of the ScheduleOfClasses class, it's presented here without further narration (please see inline comments for details):

```java
// CourseCatalog.java

import java.util.*;
import java.io.*;

public class CourseCatalog {
    //------------
    // Attributes.
    //------------

    // This HashMap stores Course object references, using
    // the course no. of the Course (a String) as the key.
    private HashMap<String, Course> courses;

    //----------------
    // Constructors.
    //----------------

    public CourseCatalog() {
        // We instantiate empty support collections.
        courses = new HashMap<String, Course>();
    }

    //-----------------------------------------
    // No accessor methods needed for the SRS.
    //-----------------------------------------

    //----------------------------
    // Miscellaneous other methods.
    //----------------------------

    public void display() {
        // Iterate through the HashMap and display all entries.
        for (Course c : courses.values()) {
            c.display();
            System.out.println();
        }
    }
}
```

```java
    public void addCourse(Course c) {
        // We use the course no. as the key.
        String key = c.getCourseNo();
        courses.put(key, c);
    }

    public Course findCourse(String courseNo) {
        return courses.get(courseNo);
    }

    public boolean isEmpty() {
        if (courses.size() == 0) return true;
        else return false;
    }
}

//=========================================

// Faculty.java

import java.util.*;
import java.io.*;

public class Faculty {
    //------------
    // Attributes.
    //------------

    // This HashMap stores Professor object references, using
    // the (String) ssn of the Professor as the key.

    private HashMap<String, Professor> professors;

    //----------------
    // Constructors.
    //----------------

    public Faculty() {
        // We instantiate empty support collections.
        professors = new HashMap<String, Professor>();
    }

    //----------------------------------------
    // No accessor methods needed for the SRS.
    //----------------------------------------
```

```java
//----------------------------
// Miscellaneous other methods.
//----------------------------

public void display() {
    // Iterate through the HashMap and display all entries.

    for (Professor p : professors.values()) {
        p.display();
        System.out.println();
    }
}

public void addProfessor(Professor p) {
    professors.put(p.getSsn(), p);
}

public Professor findProfessor(String ssn) {
    return (Professor) professors.get(ssn);
}

public boolean isEmpty() {
    if (professors.size() == 0) return true;
    else return false;
}
}
```

Initializing the SRS Collections from Record-Oriented Data Files

In the Chapter 14 version of the SRS application, all of the work necessary to populate the ScheduleOfClasses collection was performed in the main method of the SRS class. By way of review,

- We instantiated a ScheduleOfClasses object as a public static attribute of the SRS class to render it globally accessible to the entire SRS application (i.e., so as to be able to refer to it throughout the SRS application's many other classes by the fully qualified name SRS.scheduleOfClasses):

  ```java
  public static ScheduleOfClasses scheduleOfClasses =
      new ScheduleOfClasses("SP2005");
  ```

- We invoked the scheduleSection method on various Course objects named c1 through to c5 to instantiate seven Section objects named sec1 through to sec7, using hard-coded attribute values:

  ```java
  sec1 = c1.scheduleSection('M', "8:10 - 10:00 PM", "GOVT101", 30);
  sec2 = c1.scheduleSection('W', "6:10 - 8:00 PM", "GOVT202", 30);
  sec3 = c2.scheduleSection('R', "4:10 - 6:00 PM", "GOVT105", 25);
  sec4 = c2.scheduleSection('T', "6:10 - 8:00 PM", "SCI330", 25);
  ```

```
sec5 = c3.scheduleSection('M', "6:10 - 8:00 PM", "GOVT101", 20);
sec6 = c4.scheduleSection('R', "4:10 - 6:00 PM", "SCI241", 15);
sec7 = c5.scheduleSection('M', "4:10 - 6:00 PM", "ARTS25", 40);
```

- We then invoked the addSection method on the scheduleOfClasses object numerous times to add these Sections to its encapsulated collection:

```
scheduleOfClasses.addSection(sec1);
scheduleOfClasses.addSection(sec2);
scheduleOfClasses.addSection(sec3);
scheduleOfClasses.addSection(sec4);
scheduleOfClasses.addSection(sec5);
scheduleOfClasses.addSection(sec6);
scheduleOfClasses.addSection(sec7);
```

Rather than hard-coding the information about these Sections in the main method of the SRS class in this fashion, we'd ideally like to acquire this information **dynamically** from persistent storage—specifically, from a record-oriented text file. In fact, while we're at it, we'll acquire the data needed to initialize **all three** of the SRS application's primary object collections—ScheduleOfClasses, CourseCatalog, and Faculty—from text files.

We'll provide five data files to "feed" these three collections, as follows:

- CourseCatalog.dat

- Faculty.dat

- Soc_SP2005.dat

- Prerequisites.dat

- TeachingAssignments.dat

All of these data files are provided with the accompanying SRS code for download from the Apress web site.

Let's discuss the format and contents of each of these files.

CourseCatalog.dat

CourseCatalog.dat contains records consisting of three tab-delimited fields: a course number, a course title, and the number of credits that the course is worth, represented as a floating-point number. The record format is thus as follows (note that <tab> in this and all of the following examples represents the presence of an otherwise invisible tab character):

courseNo <tab> *courseTitle* <tab> *credits*

In other words, each record in this data file represents the attribute values of a **single** Course object.

Here are the actual contents of the CourseCatalog.dat file that we'll use for all of the work that we do in this chapter and in Chapter 17; this data will be used to instantiate Course objects that will in turn be stored within the CourseCatalog collection:

```
CMP101 <tab> Beginning Computer Technology <tab> 3.0
OBJ101 <tab> Object Methods for Software Development <tab> 3.0
CMP283 <tab> Higher Level Languages (Java) <tab> 3.0
CMP999 <tab> Living Brain Computers <tab> 3.0
ART101 <tab> Beginning Basketweaving <tab> 3.0
```

Faculty.dat

Faculty.dat contains records consisting of four tab-delimited fields, representing a professor's name, SSN, title, and the department that the professor works for. The record format is thus as follows:

profName <tab> *ssn* <tab> *title* <tab> *department*

In other words, each record in this data file represents the attribute values of a ***single*** Professor object.

Here are the actual contents of the Faculty.dat file that we'll use for all of the work that we will do in this chapter and in Chapter 17; this data will be used to instantiate Professor objects that will in turn be stored within the Faculty collection:

```
Jacquie Barker <tab> 123-45-6789 <tab> Adjunct Professor <tab> Info. Technology
Claudio Cioffi <tab> 567-81-2345 <tab> Full Professor <tab> Comp. Social Sciences
Snidely Whiplash <tab> 987-65-4321 <tab> Full Professor <tab> Phys. Ed.
```

SoC_SP2005.dat

SoC_SP2005.dat contains the schedule of classes information for the Spring 2005 (SP2005) semester. Each tab-delimited record consists of six fields representing the course number, section number, day of the week, time of day, room, and seating capacity for the section in question. The record format is thus as follows:

courseNo <tab> *secNo* <tab> *day* <tab> *time* <tab> *room* <tab> *capacity*

In other words, each record in this data file represents the attribute values of a ***single*** Section object and, by virtue of the one-to-many association between the Course and Section classes, each record in this file simultaneously represents a ***link*** that the Section object maintains to the particular Course object whose ID is in the first field.

Here are the actual contents of the SoC_SP2005.dat file that we'll use for all of the work that we'll do in this chapter and in Chapter 17. This data will be used to instantiate Section objects that will in turn be stored within the ScheduleOfClasses collection, and will also be used to link these Section objects to their corresponding Course objects:

```
CMP101 <tab> 1 <tab> M <tab> 8:10 - 10:00 PM <tab> GOVT101 <tab> 30
CMP101 <tab> 2 <tab> W <tab> 6:10 - 8:00 PM <tab> GOVT202 <tab> 30
OBJ101 <tab> 1 <tab> R <tab> 4:10 - 6:00 PM <tab> GOVT105 <tab> 25
OBJ101 <tab> 2 <tab> T <tab> 6:10 - 8:00 PM <tab> SCI330 <tab> 25
CMP283 <tab> 1 <tab> M <tab> 6:10 - 8:00 PM <tab> GOVT101 <tab> 20
CMP999 <tab> 1 <tab> R <tab> 4:10 - 6:00 PM <tab> SCI241 <tab> 15
ART101 <tab> 1 <tab> M <tab> 4:10 - 6:00 PM <tab> ARTS25 <tab> 40
```

Prerequisites.dat

`Prerequisites.dat` contains information about which `Course`, listed in the ***first*** column, is a prerequisite for which ***other*** `Course`, listed in the ***second*** column. The record format is thus as follows:

courseId `<tab>` *courseId*

In other words, this file represents the reflexive *prerequisite* association that exists on the `Course` class, and thus each record represents a ***link*** between two specific `Course` objects.

   Here are the actual contents of the `Prerequisites.dat` file that we'll use for all of the work that we'll do in this chapter and in Chapter 17:

```
CMP101 <tab> OBJ101
OBJ101 <tab> CMP283
CMP283 <tab> CMP999
```

TeachingAssignments.dat

`TeachingAssignments.dat` contains information about which professor (whose SSN is reflected in the first column) is teaching which course/section (represented by the **full section number**—that is, the course number, followed by a hyphen, followed by the section number—in the second column). The record format is thus as follows:

ssn `<tab>` *fullSectionNo*

In other words, this file represents the binary *teaches* association that exists between the `Professor` and `Section` classes, and thus each record represents a ***link*** between a `Professor` and a `Section`.

   Here are the actual contents of the `TeachingAssignments.dat` file that we'll use for all of the work that we'll do in this chapter and in Chapter 17:

```
987-65-4321 <tab> CMP101 - 1
567-81-2345 <tab> CMP101 - 2
123-45-6789 <tab> OBJ101 - 1
987-65-4321 <tab> OBJ101 - 2
123-45-6789 <tab> CMP283 - 1
567-81-2345 <tab> CMP999 - 1
987-65-4321 <tab> ART101 - 1
```

Persisting Student Data

One key difference between the way that we plan on handling `Student` data as compared with data for our other model classes—`Professor`, `Course`, and `Section`—is that we are going to store each `Student` object's data in its own ***separate*** file, versus lumping all of the data about all `Students` into a single `StudentBody.dat` file. We plan on retrieving the information for just one `Student` at a time—namely, the data for whichever student user is currently logged on to the SRS. (We'll see how a student logs on and off of the SRS in Chapter 17, when we add a GUI to our application; for now, we'll simulate such logon events in our `SRS main` method.)

The details of an individual student's data file are as follows:

- The naming convention for a student's data file will be to use the student's SSN (ssn) with a suffix of .dat (e.g., 111-11-1111.dat).

- At a minimum, a student's data file will contain a single ***primary*** record, comprised of four tab-delimited fields representing the student's SSN, name, major department, and degree sought:

  ssn <tab> *name* <tab> *major* <tab> *degreeSought*

- If the student in question has already registered for one or more sections during a previous SRS session, then the student's data file will also contain one or more ***secondary*** records, each consisting of a single field representing the full section number of each section that the student is currently enrolled in. In other words, the presence of a secondary record represents the *attends* association in our object model, and any one record implies a ***link*** between a Student and a Section.

We'll simulate three students in this fashion:

- 111-11-1111.dat: This student will be simulated as already having enrolled in one section. The contents of this data file are thus as follows:

  ```
  111-11-1111 <tab> Joe Blow <tab> Math <tab> M.S.
  CMP101 - 1
  ```

- 222-22-2222.dat: This student will be simulated as already having enrolled in one section. The contents of this data file are thus as follows:

  ```
  222-22-2222 <tab> Fred Schnurd <tab> Information Technology <tab> Ph.D.
  ART101 - 1
  ```

- 333-33-3333.dat: This student will be simulated as not yet having enrolled in any sections. The contents of this data file are thus as follows:

  ```
  333-33-3333 <tab> Mary Smith <tab> Physics <tab> B.S.
  ```

As with the previous data files that we discussed, all three of these files are provided with the accompanying SRS code for download from the Apress web site.

Along with these three student data files, we also provide corresponding files named *xxx-xx-xxxx*.dat.orig; these files contain exact copies of the *xxx-xx-xxxx*.dat files as originally downloaded, and can be used to **reset** the contents of the *xxx-xx-xxxx*.dat files back to their original contents, as desired, when you are experimenting with the SRS program for this chapter. The reset.bat script, also downloadable from the Apress web site as part of the Chapter 15 SRS code download, can be executed from a DOS prompt to copy the *.orig file contents to the corresponding *.dat file.

Read vs. Write Access to the Data Files

Note that we'll be both reading from and writing to the *xxx-xx-xxxx*.dat files representing student information, but we'll only be *reading* from the other data files: CourseCatalog.dat, Faculty.dat, Soc_SP2005.dat, Prerequisites.dat, and TeachingAssignments.dat. Why is this?

We're not worried about persisting information about any other type of object besides Student objects because we assume that the rest of the data is *unchanging*. That is, during a particular SRS session, a student user will not be able to alter Professor or Course information; all a student user will be able to do is to add or drop classes (sections) from his or her course load. Such activity changes the status of the *links* between a Student and various Section objects, which are stored as secondary records in the student's data file, hence the need to be able to write to these files.

Note that we aren't giving student users the ability to change their *primary* information—name, ssn, etc.—via the SRS. I'll leave that up to you to tackle as an optional end-of-chapter exercise (see exercise 4).

Configuring Applications with the Java Properties Class

In order to run properly, applications often require information pertaining to their external environment, for example:

- The names of external files to be accessed, such as the various SRS data files that we've been discussing

- The URL of a database server to establish a connection to

- User-specific profile data to control program execution

and so forth. Such information is liable to change over time, as the underlying computer system's infrastructure of an application changes. Thus, rather than hard-coding such information in the source code for a program, it is better to "feed" such information to an application as *data* at run time.

You learned how to pass information into a program in the form of command-line arguments in Chapter 13, which is certainly one way to provide this sort of environmental information to an application. Using command-line arguments, however, is only practical when we have but a few items of information to pass along. The Java Properties class, part of the java.util package, provides us with a convenient alternative way of providing such information to an application in the form of *name/value pairs* known as **properties** that can be read from a simple text file. When used in this fashion, we refer to such a file as a **properties file**.

Specifically, rather than hard-coding the name of a given SRS data file as a String *literal* argument to the FileReader (or FileOutputStream) constructor, as follows:

```
BufferedReader bIn = new BufferedReader(new FileReader("faculty.dat"));
```

we'll initialize the values of String *variables* with the appropriate file names as read from a properties file:

```
// Pseudocode.
String scheduleFileName = read value from the Filenames.properties file;
String facultyFileName = read value from the Filenames.properties file;
String courseFileName = read value from the Filenames.properties file;
// etc.
```

and we'll then pass such variables in as arguments to the FileReader/FileOutputStream constructors instead:

```
BufferedReader bIn = new BufferedReader(new FileReader(scheduleFileName));
```

The FileNames.properties File

The properties file that we'll use for our work in this chapter and again in Chapter 17 is named FileNames.properties (an arbitrary name that I've invented—note that the file name needn't end in ".properties" specifically), and stores name/value pairs, one per record, of the form

symbolicPropertyName <tab> *propertyValue*

Specifically, the file contains the following five records, one per external data file to be used:

```
scheduleFile <tab> SoC_SP2005.dat
facultyFile <tab> Faculty.dat
assignmentsFile <tab> TeachingAssignments.dat
courseFile <tab> CourseCatalog.dat
prereqFile <tab> Prerequisites.dat
```

The FileNames.properties file is another data file that is included with the Chapter 15 SRS code as a download from the Apress web site.

Then, to read this file, we'll employ code such as the following:

```
// Declare String variables to hold the file names as we read them from
// an external properties file - e.g.,
private static String facultyFileName;
// etc.

// Obtain the name of the relevant files from an
// external Properties file.
try {
    // Instantiate an "empty" Properties object.
    Properties fileNames = new Properties();

    // Populate the Properties object with name/value pairs - aka
    // "properties" - read from the FileNames.properties file.
    fileNames.load(new FileInputStream("FileNames.properties"));
```

```
    // Retrieve each file name one by one.
    facultyFileName = fileNames.getProperty("facultyFile");
    // etc.
}
catch (IOException e) { ... }
```

Here are the important points to note:

- Behind the scenes, a Properties object is a form of Hashtable collection (in fact, java.util.Properties is a direct subclass of java.util.Hashtable). We could certainly use a garden-variety Hashtable object instead (or another dictionary type of collection, such as a HashMap or a TreeMap) to store name/value pairs as read in from a tab-delimited file using a BufferedReader/FileReader combination. However, using the load method of the Properties class hides a lot of the details of doing so.

- If the getProperty method is used to attempt to retrieve a nonexistent property, the value returned is null to signal that a property by that name was not found. Returning to our earlier example,

```
    // Populate the Properties object with name/value pairs - aka
    // "properties" - read from the FileNames.properties file.
    fileNames.load(new FileInputStream("FileNames.properties"));

    // If we try to retrieve a property "foo" for which there is no entry
    // in the FileNames.properties file, the value of reference variable x
    // below will be set to null to signal that such a property wasn't defined:
    String x = fileNames.getProperty("foo");
```

The Properties class also plays a valuable role in discovering *system* properties, as discussed in the next section.

Accessing System Properties

Java is a platform-independent language, but certain characteristics of the platforms on which it runs are platform *dependent*—for example, whether we use a forward slash (/) or backslash (\) when describing file paths:

- **Windows**: C:\MyDocs\foo

- **Unix**: /MyDocs/foo

or whether we separate the names of .jar files and/or directories using semicolons (;) or colons (:), as when defining our CLASSPATH for the JVM:

- **Windows**: java -cp *onePath*;*anotherPath* MyApp

- **Unix**: java -cp *onePath*:*anotherPath* MyApp

The predefined System class (of the java.lang package) defines, among other methods, a static getProperties method to enable us to interrogate the platform on which a Java program is running to determine various properties of that platform (detailed in the following section).

Example #1: Platform-Specific Line Separators

Embedding newline characters (\n) in a print statement to force line breaks, as follows:

```
System.out.print("Whee ..." + "\n" + "... Java is FUN!!!" + "\n");
```

is not advised, because line breaks are handled differently on the Unix and Windows platforms. If we were capturing a program's output to a file, for example, use of embedded \n characters in print statements can result in cross-platform inconsistencies.

Here's the output:

```
Whee ...
... Java is FUN!!!
```

We can instead retrieve the ***platform-specific*** line separator, designated by the property name line.separator, as follows:

```
String lineBreak = System.getProperty("line.separator");
```

and can then use it as follows to generate platform-appropriate output:

```
System.out.print("Whee ..." + lineBreak + "... Java is FUN!!!" +
                 lineBreak);
```

Here's the output:

```
Whee ...
... Java is FUN!!!
```

On a Windows platform, the line separator is the combination of a carriage return (Unicode character '\u000a') followed by a line feed (Unicode character '\u000d'), whereas on a Unix platform, the line break sequence is simply a line feed.

Example #2: Determining What Version of Java a Program Is Being Run With

It is possible to programmatically determine what version of the Java Runtime Environment (JRE) is being used to execute a given application, if desired, as the following code illustrates:

```
String ver = System.getProperty("java.version"));
System.out.println("This program is running under JRE version " + ver);

if (ver.startsWith("1.5")) {
    // Pseudocode.
    do something appropriate for newer versions of Java ...
}
else {
    // Pseudocode.
    do something the pre-5.0 way ...
}
```

Here's the output:

```
This program is running under JRE version 1.5.0_01
```

Other Available System Properties

Table 15-1 shows a list of all properties available as of J2SE 5.0.

Table 15-1. *System Properties As of J2SE 5.0*

Key	Description of Associated Value
java.version	Java Runtime Environment version
java.vendor	Java Runtime Environment vendor
java.vendor.url	Java vendor URL
java.home	Java installation directory
java.vm.specification.version	Java Virtual Machine specification version
java.vm.specification.vendor	Java Virtual Machine specification vendor
java.vm.specification.name	Java Virtual Machine specification name
java.vm.version	Java Virtual Machine implementation version
java.vm.vendor	Java Virtual Machine implementation vendor
java.vm.name	Java Virtual Machine implementation name
java.specification.version	Java Runtime Environment specification version
java.specification.vendor	Java Runtime Environment specification vendor
java.specification.name	Java Runtime Environment specification name
java.class.version	Java class format version number
java.class.path	Java class path
java.library.path	List of paths to search when loading libraries
java.io.tmpdir	Default temporary file path
java.compiler	Name of JIT compiler to use
java.ext.dirs	Path of extension directory or directories
os.name	Operating system name
os.arch	Operating system architecture
os.version	Operating system version
file.separator	File separator (/ on Unix)
path.separator	Path separator (: on Unix)
line.separator	Line separator (\n on Unix)
user.name	User's account name
user.home	User's home directory
user.dir	User's current working directory

Defining Custom Exceptions for the SRS

Let's put what you learned in Chapter 13 about designing and using custom exceptions to good use in developing the SRS. As mentioned previously, many things can potentially go wrong when accessing external storage. With file I/O specifically, here's a representative sample of what can go awry:

- A file by a particular name cannot be found.

- The desired file can be found, but cannot be accessed for read (write) purposes, due to inadequate privileges.

- The desired file can be found and accessed, but is of the wrong file type. For example, a user may be trying to read a proprietary Microsoft Excel file as a record-oriented text file.

- The file can be found and accessed, and is a tab-delimited text file, but the record format of the file is found to be incorrect. For example, we are expecting three tab-delimited fields, but encounter a record with two fields.

- The file can be found and accessed, and is a tab-delimited text file with the appropriate record format, but one or more data values within a particular record may be invalid. For example, we're looking for a numeric value for a student's GPA, but encounter a non-numeric value instead.

and so forth. For some of these errors, the Java language automatically throws predefined exception types (e.g., FileNotFoundException); for others that are application specific, we must determine whether or not to ***explicitly*** throw either a predefined or a ***custom*** type of exception.

The first custom exception type that we'll define for our SRS application, SRSInitializationException, is derived directly from the predefined Exception class. We'll use it to report general issues that might arise when initializing any one of our three custom collections. As discussed in Chapter 13, we need do only the bare minimum to declare such a custom exception—namely, we provide an explicit constructor that enables us to pass in a detailed message to reflect the specifics of what has gone wrong in our application to have warranted throwing the exception in the first place.

```
// SRSInitializationException.java

public class SRSInitializationException extends Exception {
    public SRSInitializationException(String message) {
        super(message);
    }
}
```

Then, we'll derive two specialized forms of SRS exception from the previous code: one to use when we're ***reading data in*** about a Student (i.e., when we're instantiating a Student object in memory to represent the human user who is currently logged on to the SRS),

```
// InvalidStudentException.java

// We throw this type of Exception to signal a problem with regard
// to restoring a Student's state from persistent storage.
```

```
public class InvalidStudentException extends SRSInitializationException {
    public InvalidStudentException(String message) {
        super(message);
    }
}
```

and one to use when we're ***writing data out*** about a Student object, based on changes that its human counterpart has made to his or her class schedule while logged on to the SRS:

```
// StudentPersistenceException.java

// We throw this type of Exception to signal a problem with regard
// to storing a Student's state to persistent storage.

public class StudentPersistenceException extends SRSInitializationException {
    public StudentPersistenceException(String message) {
        super(message);
    }
}
```

We'll see these three custom exception types in use in the SRSDataAccess class (to be discussed next), where they'll be thrown as "signal flares" to report issues to our client code, and again in the client code of the SRS driver class's main method, where we'll be catching and responding to such exceptions.

Encapsulating Persistence Details

The data access layer for our SRS will be embodied in a single class called SRSDataAccess. If this were a more extensive application, we might wish to spread the work necessary to access persistent storage across multiple classes, but for an application of this size, a single class will do just fine.

Introducing the SRSDataAccess Class

We'll start with a high-level overview of SRSDataAccess. It consists of the following:

- Five private static String attributes, representing the names of the five different record-oriented text files that we'll be reading our data from:

```
// Schedule of Classes is defined by one file:
private static String scheduleFileName;

// Faculty is defined by two files:
private static String facultyFileName;
private static String assignmentsFileName;

// CourseCatalog is defined by two files:
private static String courseFileName;
private static String prereqFileName;
```

- A static code block, which contains code to be executed when the SRSDataAccess class's bytecode is first loaded into the JVM's memory—in particular, code that will read the FileNames.properties file (discussed earlier in the chapter) to initialize the five String attributes mentioned in the previous bullet.

- Five static methods that provide various data access services to the application:

  - initializeScheduleOfClasses: Populates and returns a ScheduleOfClasses collection instance with Section objects, based on the data that is read in from the scheduleFileName file

  - initializeFaculty: Populates and returns a Faculty collection instance with Professor objects, based on the data that is read in from the facultyFileName and assignmentsFileName files

  - initializeCourseCatalog: Populates and returns a CourseCatalog collection instance with Professor objects, based on the data that is read in from the facultyFileName and assignmentsFileName files

  - initializeStudent: Accepts a String representing a student ID number of the form *nnn-nn-nnnn* as an argument, and returns a Student object whose internal state reflects the data read in from file *nnn-nn-nnnn*.dat

  - persistStudent: Accepts a Student reference as an argument, and stores the (updated) state about this Student's course load in a file named *nnn-nn-nnnn*.dat, where *nnn-nn-nnnn* represents the value of the Student's ID number (ssn attribute)

By hiding all of the details of object persistence in these five methods, we minimize the impact to our application if such details need to change down the road—for example, if we decide to adopt relational database technology as a persistence mechanism because our SRS application has grown in sophistication, such that the "bells and whistles" of a true DBMS (concurrency control, transaction management, etc.) are now warranted. (We'll talk a bit about database persistence at the end of this chapter.)

The following is the overall code structure for the SRSDataAccess class. We'll discuss the specifics of each method in subsequent sections.

```
import java.io.*;
import java.util.*;

public class SRSDataAccess {
    // We declare String variables to hold on to the names of the data
    // files that we need to access, but store the actual file names
    // in an external Properties file rather than hard-coding them here.
    // As discussed earlier, this technique allows us to easily
    // change the paths/names to such files without having to make changes to
    // our code.

    // Schedule of Classes is defined by one file:
    private static String scheduleFileName;
```

```java
// Faculty is defined by two files:
private static String facultyFileName;
private static String assignmentsFileName;

// CourseCatalog is defined by two files:
private static String courseFileName;
private static String prereqFileName;

// We don't need to declare a static String attribute for the
// student file, because this file name is derived on the fly
// when a particular Student logs on, by concatenating his/her
// student ID number with a ".dat" extension.

// Obtain the name of the relevant files from an external Properties file.
// "static" code blocks are executed only once, when the bytecode
// for the class that contains the static code block - class
// SRSDataAccess, in this case -- is first loaded by the JVM
// at run time.

static {
    try {
        Properties fileNames = new Properties();
        fileNames.load(new FileInputStream("FileNames.properties"));

        facultyFileName = fileNames.getProperty("facultyFile");
        assignmentsFileName = fileNames.getProperty("assignmentsFile");
        courseFileName = fileNames.getProperty("courseFile");
        prereqFileName = fileNames.getProperty("prereqFile");
        scheduleFileName = fileNames.getProperty("scheduleFile");
    }
    catch (IOException e) {
        // If the properties file cannot be found, we abort
        // the application.
        System.out.println("ERROR:  unable to read FileNames.properties " +
            "file -- GOODBYE!");
        System.exit(0);
    }
}

// Initialize the Faculty collection.
// Note that we're using a custom Exception type to signal various
// errors that may arise during object "reconstitution"
// from persistent storage.

public static Faculty initializeFaculty()
    throws SRSInitializationException {
    Details explained later in the chapter ...
}
```

```
// Initialize the CourseCatalog collection.
// Note that we're using a custom Exception type (as we did
// for Faculty) to signal various initialization errors.

public static CourseCatalog initializeCourseCatalog()
    throws SRSInitializationException {
    Details explained later in the chapter ...
}


// Initialize ScheduleOfClasses.  Note that we're using a custom Exception
// type (as we did for Faculty) to signal various initialization errors.

public static ScheduleOfClasses initializeScheduleOfClasses(String semester)
    throws SRSInitializationException {
    Details explained later in the chapter ...
}


// Initialize a single Student.  Again, we are using a custom
// Exception -- in this case, InvalidStudentException, which is a subtype of
// SRSInitializationException -- to signal various issues with retrieving
// the Student's state from persistent storage.

public static Student initializeStudent(String sId)
    throws InvalidStudentException {
    Details explained later in the chapter ...
}
// Persist the state of a Student.  This method writes out all of the
// student's information to his/her ssn.dat file when he/she logs off.
// Once again, we use a custom Exception type -- StudentPersistenceException --
// to signal problems.

public static void persistStudent(Student s)
    throws StudentPersistenceException {
    Details explained later in the chapter ...
}
}
```

We'll next look at the initializeScheduleOfClasses method of the SRSDataAccess class in detail.

Initializing the ScheduleOfClasses Collection

The static SRSDataAccess.initializeScheduleOfClasses method will be invoked from the main method of our SRS application to initialize the contents of an instance of a ScheduleOfClasses collection, declared as follows in the main method of the SRS class (which we'll review in its entirety a bit later in this chapter):

```
// Declaration in SRS.java:
public static ScheduleOfClasses scheduleOfClasses;
```

By virtue of its being declared a `public static` attribute of the SRS class, `scheduleOfClasses` can be globally accessed throughout the SRS application as `SRS.scheduleOfClasses`.

The same is true of the other primary collections of the SRS—namely, `SRS.faculty` and `SRS.courseCatalog`.

The `initializeScheduleOfClasses` method starts by instantiating an empty `ScheduleOfClasses` object, soc, along with several other reference variables that will be used in reading records from the `scheduleFileName` file:

```
// Initialize ScheduleOfClasses.  Note that we're using a custom Exception
// type (as we did for Faculty) to signal various initialization errors.
public static ScheduleOfClasses initializeScheduleOfClasses(String semester)
    throws SRSInitializationException {
    ScheduleOfClasses soc = new ScheduleOfClasses(semester);
    String line = null;
    BufferedReader bIn = null;
```

We then attempt to open and read the appropriate file, as referenced by `String` variable `scheduleFileName`:

```
try {
    // Open the file.
    bIn = new BufferedReader(new FileReader(scheduleFileName));

    line = bIn.readLine();
    while (line != null) {
```

We parse tab-delimited records into six `String` values: courseNo, sectionNo, dayOfWeek, timeOfDay, room, and capacity. If we detect that the record we've just read doesn't contain six fields/tokens, we throw one of our custom exceptions, noting the precise error—and the record text in which the error occurred—as the exception's message:

```
StringTokenizer st = new StringTokenizer(line, "\t");

// If there aren't six columns, signal an error.
if (st.countTokens() != 6) {
    throw new SRSInitializationException(
        "File format error on record |" +
        line + "| -- should have 6 tokens -- " +
        "in file " + scheduleFileName);
}
```

If printed, the message might read as follows:

```
File format error on record |foo bar| -- should have 6 tokens --
in file SoC_SP2005.dat
```

If all has gone well up to this point, we parse the record into six String tokens, attempting to convert the second and sixth tokens from a String to an int value. If either of these conversion attempts generates a NumberFormatException, we throw an appropriate custom exception:

```
        else {
            String courseNo = st.nextToken();

            // We have to convert the next value from
            // a String to an int.
            String sectionNumber = st.nextToken();
            int sectionNo = -1;
            try {
                sectionNo = Integer.parseInt(sectionNumber);
            }
            catch (NumberFormatException nfe) {
                throw new SRSInitializationException(
                    "File format error on record |" +
                    line + "| -- invalid section no. -- " +
                    "in file " + scheduleFileName);
            }

            String dayOfWeek = st.nextToken();
            String timeOfDay = st.nextToken();
            String room = st.nextToken();

            // We have to convert the next value from
            // a String to an int.
            String capacityValue = st.nextToken();
            int capacity = -1;
            try {
                capacity = Integer.parseInt(capacityValue);
            }
            catch (NumberFormatException nfe) {
                throw new SRSInitializationException(
                    "File format error on record |" +
                    line + "| -- invalid capacity value -- " +
                    "in file " + scheduleFileName);
            }
```

If all is still well, we use courseNo to look up the appropriate Course object, and then fabricate a new Section object for this Course, adding it to the soc (schedule of classes) collection:

```
                  // Look up the Course object in the Course Catalog.
                  // (Having made courseCatalog a public static
                  // attribute of the SRS class comes in handy!)
                  Course c = SRS.courseCatalog.findCourse(courseNo);

                  // Create a Section object ...
                  Section s = new Section(
                      sectionNo, dayOfWeek.charAt(0),
                      timeOfDay, c, room, capacity);

                  // ... add it to the schedule of classes ...
                  String key = courseNo + " - " + s.getSectionNo();
                  soc.addSection(s);

                  // ... and link it to the Course.
                  c.addSection(s);
              }
```

And, of course, we must remember to read the next line from the file, to avoid an infinite loop:

```
              line = bIn.readLine();
          }
```

Once we reach the end of the file, we wrap up by closing the file, and then throwing custom exceptions if various problems arose. For example, if the schedule of classes data file couldn't be accessed

```
          bIn.close();
      }
      catch (IOException i) {
          throw new SRSInitializationException("Error accessing file " +
              scheduleFileName);
      }
```

or if for some reason the newly created soc collection is found to be empty (this shouldn't happen under normal circumstances).

```
      // If we didn't wind up creating any Section entries, we'll
      // signal a problem in this regard.
      if (soc.isEmpty()) {
          throw new SRSInitializationException("Error initializing " +
              "schedule of classes information");
      }
```

If we make it all the way to the end of the initializeScheduleOfClasses method without throwing any exceptions, we know that we've successfully crafted/populated the ScheduleOfClasses instance required to "drive" the SRS, and can thus return it to the client application (our main method, as it turns out, as we'll see later in the chapter):

```
        return soc;
    }
```

We'll next look at the initializeFaculty method of the SRSDataAccess class, which is used to initialize the contents of the Faculty collection.

Initializing the Faculty Collection

In order to initialize an instance of a Faculty collection, we need to read *two* data files, as discussed earlier in the chapter. The first half of the initializeFaculty method reads the file that defines Professor objects, and is so similar to the code for the initializeScheduleOfClasses method that I'll present it here without narration (please review the inline comments for details).

```java
// Initialize Faculty.  Note that we're using a custom Exception type to
// signal various errors that may arise during object "reconstitution"
// from persistent storage.
public static Faculty initializeFaculty() throws SRSInitializationException {
    Faculty faculty = new Faculty();
    String line = null;
    BufferedReader bIn = null;

    try {
        // Open the first file.
        bIn = new BufferedReader(new FileReader(facultyFileName));

        line = bIn.readLine();
        while (line != null) {
            // We're going to parse tab-delimited records into
            // four attributes -- name, ssn, title, and dept --
            // and then call the Professor constructor to fabricate a new
            // professor.

            StringTokenizer st = new StringTokenizer(line, "\t");

            // If there aren't four columns, signal an error.
            if (st.countTokens() != 4) {
                throw new SRSInitializationException(
                    "File format error on record |" +
                    line + "| in file " +
                    facultyFileName);
            }
            else {
                String name = st.nextToken();
                String ssn = st.nextToken();
                String title = st.nextToken();
                String dept = st.nextToken();

                // Create a Person instance and store it in
                // the collection.
```

```
            Professor p = new Professor(name, ssn, title, dept);
            faculty.addProfessor(p);
          }

          line = bIn.readLine();
      }

      bIn.close();
  }
  catch (IOException i) {
      throw new SRSInitializationException("Error accessing file " +
          facultyFileName);
  }
```

We're not done yet, however—we must now process a second data file, which defines the teaching assignments for each `Professor`. The first part of this processing should by now be very familiar:

```
// Process the second file, which defines teaching assignments.
try {
    // Open the file.
    bIn = new BufferedReader(new FileReader(assignmentsFileName));

    line = bIn.readLine();
    while (line != null) {
        // We're going to parse tab-delimited records
        // into two values, representing the professor's
        // SSN and the section number that he/she is
        // going to teach.
        StringTokenizer st = new StringTokenizer(
            line, "\t");

        // If there aren't two columns, signal an error.

        if (st.countTokens() != 2) {
            throw new SRSInitializationException(
                "File format error on record |" +
                line + "| in file " +
                assignmentsFileName);
        }
        else {
            String ssn = st.nextToken();

            // The full section number is a
            // concatenation of the course no.
            // and section no., separated
            // by a hyphen; e.g., "ART101 - 1".
            String fullSectionNo = st.nextToken();
```

Where we see a bit of unique logic is when it comes time to link the Professor to the Section that he or she is teaching. We look up and retrieve a handle on both the Professor (based on his or her ssn) and the Section (based on its fullSectionNo) from the appropriate collections (one locally created collection, faculty, and one global collection, SRS.scheduleOfClasses):

```
// Look these two objects up in the
// appropriate collections.  Note that
// having made scheduleOfClasses a public
// static attribute of the SRS class
// makes this easy to do!
Professor p = faculty.findProfessor(ssn);
Section s = SRS.scheduleOfClasses.
    findSection(fullSectionNo);
```

and, assuming we've found them both, we link them together via the Professor's agreeToTeach method:

```
// As long as we've found both the Professor
// and Section objects in question, we're
// good to go.
if (p != null && s != null) p.agreeToTeach(s);
}

line = bIn.readLine();
}

bIn.close();
}
```

As with the initializeScheduleOfClasses method, we wrap up with a bit of exception handling, returning a populated Faculty collection instance if all is well:

```
catch (IOException i) {
    throw new SRSInitializationException("Error accessing file " +
        assignmentsFileName);
}

// If we didn't wind up creating any Faculty entries, we'll
// signal a problem in this regard.

if (faculty.isEmpty()) {
    throw new SRSInitializationException("Error initializing faculty " +
        "information");
}

// If we've made it to this point in the code without throwing any
// exceptions, we've successfully crafted/populated the Faculty
// instance required to "drive" the SRS.
return faculty;
}
```

We'll next look at the initializeCourseCatalog method of the SRSDataAccess class, which is used to initialize the contents of the CourseCatalog collection.

Initializing the CourseCatalog Collection

The code for initializing the CourseCatalog collection is virtually identical to that for initializing the Faculty collection just reviewed, hence I'll present the code for the initializeCourseCatalog method without narration (please see the inline comments for details).

```
// Initialize CourseCatalog.  Note that we're using a custom Exception type
// (as we did for Faculty) to signal various initialization errors.
public static CourseCatalog initializeCourseCatalog()
    throws SRSInitializationException {
    CourseCatalog catalog = new CourseCatalog();
    String line = null;
    BufferedReader bIn = null;

    try {
        // Open the file.
        bIn = new BufferedReader(new FileReader(courseFileName));

        line = bIn.readLine();
        while (line != null) {
            // We're going to parse tab-delimited records into
            // three attributes -- courseNo, courseName, and credits --
            // and then call the Course constructor to fabricate a
            // new course.
            StringTokenizer st = new StringTokenizer(line, "\t");

            // If there aren't three columns, signal an error.
            if (st.countTokens() != 3) {
                throw new SRSInitializationException(
                    "File format error on record |" +
                    line + "| in file " +
                    courseFileName);
            }
            else {
                String courseNo = st.nextToken();
                String courseName = st.nextToken();
                String creditValue = st.nextToken();

                // We have to convert the last value into a
                // number, using a static method on the
                // Double class to do so.
                double credits = -1.0;
                try {
                    credits = Double.parseDouble(creditValue);
```

```
                    }
                    catch (NumberFormatException nfe) {
                        throw new SRSInitializationException(
                        "File format error on record |" +
                        line + "| -- invalid credit value -- " +
                        "in file " + courseFileName);
                    }

                    // Finally, we call the Course constructor to create
                    // an appropriate Course object, and store it in our
                    // collection.
                    Course c = new Course(courseNo, courseName, credits);
                    catalog.addCourse(c);
                }

                line = bIn.readLine();
            }

            bIn.close();
        }
        catch (IOException i) {
            throw new SRSInitializationException("Error accessing file " +
                courseFileName);
        }

        // Process the second file, which defines prerequisite relationships
        // between courses.

        try {
            // Open the file.
            bIn = new BufferedReader(
                new FileReader(prereqFileName));

            line = bIn.readLine();
            while (line != null) {
                // We're going to parse tab-delimited records into
                // two values, representing the courseNo "A" of
                // a course that serves as a prerequisite for
                // courseNo "B".
                StringTokenizer st = new StringTokenizer(line, "\t");

                // If there aren't two columns, signal an error.
                if (st.countTokens() != 2) {
                    throw new SRSInitializationException(
                        "File format error on record |" +
                        line + "| in file " +
                        prereqFileName);
                }
```

```
            else {
                String courseNoA = st.nextToken();
                String courseNoB = st.nextToken();

                // Look these two courses up in the CourseCatalog.
                Course a = catalog.findCourse(courseNoA);
                Course b = catalog.findCourse(courseNoB);

                // If both exist, link a to b as a prerequisite.
                if (a != null && b != null) {
                    b.addPrerequisite(a);
                }
            }

            line = bIn.readLine();
        }

        bIn.close();
    }
    catch (IOException i) {
        throw new SRSInitializationException("Error accessing file " +
            prereqFileName);
    }

    // If we didn't wind up creating any course catalog entries, we'll
    // signal a problem in this regard.
    if (catalog.isEmpty()) {
        throw new SRSInitializationException("Error initializing course " +
            "catalog information");
    }

    // If we've made it to this point in the code without throwing any
    // exceptions, we've successfully crafted/populated the CourseCatalog
    // instance required to "drive" the SRS.
    return catalog;
}
```

We'll next look at the initializeStudent method of the SRSDataAccess class, used to instantiate a single Student object representing the student user who is logged in to the SRS application.

Initializing a Student's State

Stepping through the initializeStudent method, we first note that we're using a specialized InvalidStudentException to report any problems that we encounter while attempting to initialize the Student whose unique ID (actually, the student's ssn) is passed in as an argument to this method:

```
public static Student initializeStudent(String sId)
    throws InvalidStudentException {
```

We begin by constructing a "dummy" Student object:

```
Student s = new Student("?");
```

We then attempt to pull this Student's information from the appropriate data file—
nnn-nn-nnnn.dat—by fabricating the file name on the fly based on the student ID number
passed in as argument sId to this method:

```
String line = null;
BufferedReader bIn = null;

// Formulate the file name.
String pathToFile = sId + ".dat";

try {
    // Open the file.
    bIn = new BufferedReader(new FileReader(pathToFile));
```

If we successfully open the file, we'll attempt to read the primary/header record first, parsing it into four fields/tokens, using the data to populate the attributes of Student object s:

```
    // The file consists of a primary/header record, containing
    // the student's basic info. (ssn, name, etc.), and
    // 0 or more subsequent records representing a list of
    // the sections that he/she is currently registered for.

    line = bIn.readLine();

    if (line == null) {
        // Signal the problem via a custom Exception.
        throw new InvalidStudentException("Improperly formatted " +
            "file: " + pathToFile);
    }

    // We're going to parse the primary record into
    // four attributes -- ssn, name, major, and degree.
    StringTokenizer st = new StringTokenizer(line, "\t");

    // If record doesn't have four columns, report an error.
    if (st.countTokens() != 4) {
        // Signal the problem via a custom Exception.
        throw new InvalidStudentException("Improperly formatted " +
            "record |" + line + "| in file " + pathToFile);
    }

    // Populate the newly crafted Student object with the information
    // read from the file.
    s.setSsn(st.nextToken());
```

```
            s.setName(st.nextToken());
            s.setMajor(st.nextToken());
            s.setDegree(st.nextToken());
```

The remaining lines in the file (if any) are secondary records that contain references to sections that the student has ***previously*** registered for during an earlier SRS session. We need to retrieve such Section objects from the SRS.scheduleOfClasses collection:

```
            // If there are no secondary records in the file,
            // the "while" loop won't execute at all.

            line = bIn.readLine();
            while (line != null) {
                // The full section number is a concatenation of the
                // course no. and section no., separated by a hyphen;
                // e.g., "ART101 - 1".

                // Strip off any leading/trailing white space, then use
                // the section number to retrieve the corresponding
                // Section object from the SRS schedule of classes,
                // which was declared as a public static attribute of
                // the SRS class.
                String fullSectionNo = line.trim();
                Section sec = SRS.scheduleOfClasses.findSection(
                    fullSectionNo);
```

We then link the Student and Section objects together via the Section's enroll method:

```
                // Note that we are using the Section class's enroll
                // method to ensure that bidirectionality is established
                // between the Student and the Section.
                if (sec != null) sec.enroll(s);

                line = bIn.readLine();
            }
```

From here onward, the code should be self-explanatory:

```
            bIn.close();
        }
        catch (IOException i) {
            // Use a custom Exception to signal the problem.
            throw new InvalidStudentException("Error accessing file " +
                pathToFile);
        }

        // If we've made it to this point in the code without throwing any
        // exceptions, we've successfully reconsitituted a Student object
        // to represent the student user who has logged on to the SRS.
        return s;
    }
```

We'll now look at the final method of the SRSDataAccessClass, persistStudent, used to persist the state of the Student object representing the student user who is logged in to the SRS—in particular, to record changes to his or her course load.

Persisting the State of a Student

During the course of an SRS session, a student user will presumably be registering for sections and/or dropping sections. So, the *state* of the Student object representing that student user—namely, the attribute values of the Student object and all links maintained by that Student object with Section objects in which the student is enrolled—is likely to change. We must provide a way for the SRS to "remember" these changes from one session to the next; otherwise, the SRS system will be of no practical value. So, we are going to provide a method to persist a Student object's state whenever the student logs off. Specifically, we are going to write information about this Student back out to a file with the *same* name as the file that we originally used to initialize the Student object's state, thereby *overwriting* that file.

Here is the code for the persistStudent method. Because it's fairly straightforward, it's presented in its entirely without narration (please read the inline comments for details).

```java
// Persist the state of a Student.  This method writes out all of the
// student's information to his/her ssn.dat file when he/she logs off.
// Once again, we use a custom Exception type --
// StudentPersistenceException -- to signal problems.
public static void persistStudent(Student s)
        throws StudentPersistenceException {
    FileOutputStream fos = null;
    PrintWriter pw = null;

    // Formulate the name of the file to be written to.
    String pathToFile = s.getSsn() + ".dat";

    try {
        // Attempt to create the ssn.dat file.  Note that
        // it will OVERWRITE one with a similar name if such a
        // file already exists, which is precisely what we
        // want to have happen.
        fos = new FileOutputStream(pathToFile);
        pw = new PrintWriter(fos);

        // First, we output the primary/header record as a
        // tab-delimited record.
        pw.println(s.getSsn() + "\t" + s.getName() + "\t" +
                s.getMajor() + "\t" + s.getDegree());

        // Then, we'll output one secondary record for every
        // Section that the Student is enrolled in.
        Collection<Section> sections = s.getEnrolledSections();
        for (Section sec : sections) {
            pw.println(sec.getFullSectionNo());
        }
```

```
            pw.close();
        }
        catch (IOException e) {
            // Signal that an error has occurred.
            throw new StudentPersistenceException("Error saving student " +
                "information to file " + pathToFile);
        }
    }
}
```

Streamlining the SRS Driver Class

Encapsulating so much functionality into the data access layer of the SRS (i.e., in the SRSDataAccess class) allows us to ***dramatically*** simplify the main method for the SRS driver class. Let's revisit that class to see how it can be changed to accommodate all that we've done in this chapter:

```
// SRS.java

// The main driver for the command line-driven version of the SRS, with
// object persistence added.

import java.util.*;

public class SRS {
```

First, in addition to the public static scheduleOfClasses attribute that we provided in Chapter 14, we're now providing two more such attributes: faculty and courseCatalog.

```
    public static Faculty faculty;
    public static CourseCatalog courseCatalog;
    public static ScheduleOfClasses scheduleOfClasses;
```

That is, we've encapsulated what were previously declared as ArrayLists in the Chapter 14 version of the SRS class—ArrayList<Professor> faculty and ArrayList<Course> courseCatalog—in specialized collection classes named Faculty and CourseCatalog, respectively, to make them a bit more abstract. (Recall that ScheduleOfClasses was implemented this way from the beginning because we recognized the need for such a class when we were first developing the SRS object model in Part 2 of this book.)

As discussed previously, we aren't creating a collection for Student objects because we're only going to handle one Student at a time—namely, whichever Student is currently logged on.

```
    public static void main(String[] args) {
        // Initialize all objects.  The method by which we are accessing
        // data (in this case, from ASCII files) is "transparent" to this
        // application by virtue of our introduction of the SRSDataAccess class
        // as a data layer utility class.
```

The order in which we instantiate and populate the SRS collections is important:

- Creating the ScheduleOfClasses collection relies on the prior existence of the CourseCatalog collection. This is because we must look up the Course that a Section represents in the latter collection so that we can link the Section and Course together when populating the ScheduleOfClasses collection with Section objects.

- Creating the Faculty collection in turn relies on the prior existence of the ScheduleOfClasses collection. This is because we must look up the Section that a Professor is teaching in the latter collection so that we can link the Professor and Section together when populating the Faculty collection with Professor objects.

```
try {
    courseCatalog = SRSDataAccess.initializeCourseCatalog();
    scheduleOfClasses =
        SRSDataAccess.initializeScheduleOfClasses("SP2005");
    faculty = SRSDataAccess.initializeFaculty();
}
```

We're using custom exceptions throughout the SRS to signal various problems that may arise when attempting to reconstitute objects from persistent storage. For example, when creating any of the preceding three main collections, the various initialize*Xxx* methods throw custom SRSInitializationExceptions carrying detailed messages as to precisely what went wrong. Thus, we print the message from any exceptions that get thrown, exiting afterward:

```
catch (SRSInitializationException e) {
    System.out.println("ERROR:  " + e.getMessage() + "-- GOODBYE!");
    System.exit(0);
}
```

If no exceptions have been thrown, we go on to display the contents of the courseCatalog, scheduleOfClasses, and faculty collections to verify that everything has been properly initialized.

```
System.out.println("====================");
System.out.println("Course Catalog:");
System.out.println("====================");
System.out.println();
courseCatalog.display();

System.out.println("====================");
System.out.println("Schedule of Classes:");
System.out.println("====================");
System.out.println();
scheduleOfClasses.display();

System.out.println("====================");
System.out.println("Faculty Information:");
System.out.println("====================");
System.out.println();
faculty.display();
```

Next, since we don't have a user interface yet to allow a ***real*** student user to log on to the SRS, we'll ***simulate*** a student doing so—in particular, we'll simulate a logon by the student whose ssn equals 111-11-1111. The contents of the 111-11-1111.dat data file—reviewed earlier in this chapter and repeated here—reflect that he's previously registered for one course:

```
111-11-1111 <tab> Joe Blow <tab> Math <tab> M.S.
CMP101 - 1
```

Here's our simulated logon:

```
Student student = null;

try {
    student = SRSDataAccess.initializeStudent("111-11-1111");
}
catch (InvalidStudentException e) {
    System.out.println("ERROR:  " + e.getMessage() + "-- GOODBYE!");
    System.exit(0);
}
```

Before we simulate having the student register for another course, we'll view his preexisting class schedule:

```
// Review student's preexisting information.
System.out.println("============================");
System.out.println("Student Information BEFORE:");
System.out.println("============================");
System.out.println();
student.display();
```

Next, we'll simulate having the student enroll in a second course:

```
Section sec = scheduleOfClasses.findSection("ART101 - 1");
sec.enroll(student);
```

We then want to review the student's updated information:

```
System.out.println("===========================");
System.out.println("Student Information AFTER:");
System.out.println("===========================");
System.out.println();
student.display();
```

Finally, we'll simulate having the student log off, so that we may persist his updated course schedule information by overwriting the 111-11-1111.dat file (we'll check the contents of file 111-11-1111.dat to verify that the file has changed after running this program).

```
try {
    SRSDataAccess.persistStudent(student);
}
catch (StudentPersistenceException e) {
    System.out.println("ERROR:  " + e.getMessage() + "-- GOODBYE!");
    System.exit(0);
}
```

Here's an important reminder:

```
        // * * * * * * * * * * * * * * * * * * * * * * * * * * * * * * * * *
        // * Before rerunning this program, use the reset.bat command-line
        // * script to refresh the contents of the 111-11-1111.dat data file.
        // * * * * * * * * * * * * * * * * * * * * * * * * * * * * * * * * *
    }
}
```

Here is the uninterrupted code of the SRS class. Be sure to compare it with the Chapter 14 version of the SRS.java file for an appreciation of how much more concise this version is.

```java
import java.util.*;

public class SRS {
    public static Faculty faculty;
    public static CourseCatalog courseCatalog;
    public static ScheduleOfClasses scheduleOfClasses;

    public static void main(String[] args) {
        // Initialize all objects.
        try {
            // The order in which we create these is important:
            // creating the ScheduleOfClasses relies on the existence of
            // the CourseCatalog, and creating the Faculty relies on the
            // existence of the ScheduleOfClasses.

            courseCatalog = SRSDataAccess.initializeCourseCatalog();
            scheduleOfClasses =
                SRSDataAccess.initializeScheduleOfClasses("SP2005");
            faculty = SRSDataAccess.initializeFaculty();
        }
        catch (SRSInitializationException e) {
            System.out.println("ERROR:  " + e.getMessage() + "-- GOODBYE!");
            System.exit(0);
        }

        // Let's see if everything got initialized properly by calling
        // various display methods.

        System.out.println("================");
        System.out.println("Course Catalog:");
        System.out.println("================");
        System.out.println();
        courseCatalog.display();

        System.out.println("====================");
        System.out.println("Schedule of Classes:");
        System.out.println("====================");
```

```
System.out.println();
scheduleOfClasses.display();

System.out.println("=====================");
System.out.println("Faculty Information:");
System.out.println("=====================");
System.out.println();
faculty.display();

// Simulate one student logging on.

Student student = null;

try {
    student = SRSDataAccess.initializeStudent("111-11-1111");
}
catch (InvalidStudentException e) {
    System.out.println("ERROR:  " + e.getMessage() + "-- GOODBYE!");
    System.exit(0);
}

// Review student's preexisting information.

System.out.println("============================");
System.out.println("Student Information BEFORE:");
System.out.println("============================");
System.out.println();
student.display();

// Simulate the Student enrolling in another course.

Section sec = scheduleOfClasses.findSection("ART101 - 1");
sec.enroll(student);

// Review student's updated information.

System.out.println("===========================");
System.out.println("Student Information AFTER:");
System.out.println("===========================");
System.out.println();
student.display();

// Simulate the Student logging off.

try {
    SRSDataAccess.persistStudent(student);
}
catch (StudentPersistenceException e) {
```

```
            System.out.println("ERROR:  " + e.getMessage() + "-- GOODBYE!");
            System.exit(0);
        }


        // * * * * * * * * * * * * * * * * * * * * * * * * * * * * * * * * * * *
        // * Before rerunning this program, use the reset.bat command-line script  *
        // * to refresh the contents of the 111-11-1111.dat data file.              *
        // * * * * * * * * * * * * * * * * * * * * * * * * * * * * * * * * * * *
    }
}
```

The output produced by running this program is as follows. First, we see proof that all
object collections have been properly established (this output is identical to that illustrated
for the SRS of Chapter 14):

```
====================
Course Catalog:
====================


Course Information:
        Course No.:  ART101
        Course Name:  Beginning Basketweaving
        Credits:  3.0
        Prerequisite Courses:
        Offered As Section(s):  1
```

(etc.—identical to Chapter 14 output)

```
====================
Schedule of Classes:
====================


Schedule of Classes for SP2005

Section Information:
        Semester:  SP2005
        Course No.:  ART101
        Section No:  1
        Offered:  M at 4:10 - 6:00 PM
        In Room:  ARTS25
        Professor:  Snidely Whiplash
        Total of 0 students enrolled.
```

(etc.—identical to Chapter 14 output)

```
====================
Faculty Information:
====================
```

```
Person Information:
        Name:  Snidely Whiplash
        Soc. Security No.:  987-65-4321
Professor-Specific Information:
        Title:  Full Professor
        Teaches for Dept.:  Physical Education
Teaching Assignments for Snidely Whiplash:
        Course No.:  CMP101
        Section No.:  1
        Course Name:  Beginning Computer Technology
        Day and Time:  M - 8:10 - 10:00 PM
        -----
        Course No.:  OBJ101
        Section No.:  2
        Course Name:  Object Methods for Software Development
        Day and Time:  T - 6:10 - 8:00 PM
        -----
        Course No.:  ART101
        Section No.:  1
        Course Name:  Beginning Basketweaving
        Day and Time:  M - 4:10 - 6:00 PM
        -----
```

(etc.—identical to Chapter 14 output)

We next see ***direct evidence*** of our simulated student's SRS session when we compare the "before" version of this student's course schedule, consisting of one course—CMP101, section 1—to the "after" version, which reflects that a ***second*** course—ART101, section 1—has successfully been added:

```
============================
Student Information BEFORE:
============================

Person Information:
        Name:  Joe Blow
        Soc. Security No.:  111-11-1111
Student-Specific Information:
        Major:  Math
        Degree:  M.S.
Course Schedule for Joe Blow
        Course No.:  CMP101
        Section No.:  1
        Course Name:  Beginning Computer Technology
```

```
        Meeting Day and Time Held:  M - 8:10 - 10:00 PM
        Room Location:  GOVT101
        Professor's Name:  Snidely Whiplash
        -----
Transcript for:  Joe Blow (111-11-1111) [M.S. - Math]
        (no entries)


==========================
Student Information AFTER:
==========================


Person Information:
        Name:  Joe Blow
        Soc. Security No.:  111-11-1111
Student-Specific Information:
        Major:  Math
        Degree:  M.S.
Course Schedule for Joe Blow
        Course No.:  CMP101
        Section No.:  1
        Course Name:  Beginning Computer Technology
        Meeting Day and Time Held:  M - 8:10 - 10:00 PM
        Room Location:  GOVT101
        Professor's Name:  Snidely Whiplash
        -----
        Course No.:  ART101
        Section No.:  1
        Course Name:  Beginning Basketweaving
        Meeting Day and Time Held:  M - 4:10 - 6:00 PM
        Room Location:  ARTS25
        Professor's Name:  Snidely Whiplash
        -----
Transcript for:  Joe Blow (111-11-1111) [M.S. - Math]
        (no entries)
```

And, if we take a look at the contents of the file 111-11-1111.dat as a result of running the SRS program, we see that a record of this second course has been persisted in the student's file (**bolded** in the following code):

```
111-11-1111 <tab> Joe Blow <tab> Math <tab> M.S.
CMP101 - 1
ART101 - 1
```

whereas the *original* version of this file—as reflected in the file 111-11-1111.dat.orig—did *not* contain this record:

```
111-11-1111 <tab> Joe Blow <tab> Math <tab> M.S.
CMP101 - 1
```

And so we see that our persistStudent method is indeed working!

Because of the limited amount of error checking built into the SRS, running the SRS program multiple times will cause ART101 - 1 to appear multiple times in this student's data file:

```
111-11-1111 <tab> Joe Blow <tab> Math <tab> M.S.
CMP101 - 1
ART101 - 1
ART101 - 1
ART101 - 1
```

etc. Thus, as mentioned earlier in the chapter, I've provided a DOS script, reset.bat, that will reset the contents of the various student files to their original state, by copying the contents of files *.dat.orig to *.dat.

The Importance of Model–Data Access Layer Separation

Keeping our model classes free of persistence details, as we have in this chapter's version of the SRS, yields two very important advantages:

- First, as we've discussed previously, our model classes are much more reusable across applications if they contain only the essence of the abstraction they were intended to serve as in the first place. For example, if our university later wishes to develop an Alumni Relations System, as an example, they'll be able to reuse our Student class (repeated here) as is because it is ***generic*** code:

```java
import java.util.ArrayList;
import java.util.Collection;

public class Student extends Person {
    // Attributes.
    private String major;
    private String degree;
    private Transcript transcript;
    private ArrayList<Section> attends;

    // Constructor(s).
    public Student(String name, String ssn,
                        String major, String degree) { ... }
    public Student(String ssn) { ... }

    // Accessor (get/set) methods - details omitted.

    // Miscellaneous other methods.
    public void display() { ... }
    public String toString() { ... }
```

```
        public void displayCourseSchedule() { ... }
        public void addSection(Section s) { ... }
        public void dropSection(Section s) { ... }
        public boolean isEnrolledIn(Section s) { ... }
        public boolean isCurrentlyEnrolledInSimilar(Section s1) { ... }
        public void printTranscript() { ... }
        public Collection<Section> getEnrolledSections() { ... }
    }
```

- Just as important, we can totally change the persistence mechanism of *this* (SRS) application, and *the application as a whole will be oblivious to such changes*—only the SRSDataAccess class will need to change—thanks to the power of encapsulation.

To graphically illustrate this latter advantage of model–data access layer separation, let's explore what it would take to retrofit the SRS application with relational database persistence.

My intention is not to cover all of the nitty-gritty details of the Java JDBC API—entire books are devoted to fully exploring JDBC—but rather to give you a jump-start in understanding JDBC conceptually if and when you do decide to delve into it in detail. JDBC is one of the key component technologies of the Java 2 Platform, Enterprise Edition (J2EE), for example, and is a fairly common ingredient in most "industrial-strength" information system applications.

We'll revisit J2EE conceptually at the end of Chapter 17.

Objects and Databases

There is a tendency for folks who are just learning about classes and objects to relate the concept of an *object* to that of a *row* in a database table, where the *table* as a whole represents an entire *class* of similar objects; this is illustrated in Figure 15-6.

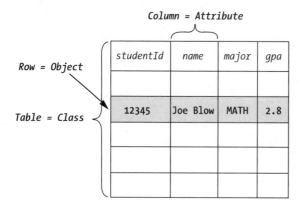

Figure 15-6. *Tables and rows in a relational DBMS correlate directly to classes and objects.*

We often do persist the state of an object within a relational database, as illustrated conceptually in Figure 15-7:

- We query a database to read data in for the purpose of initializing an object's attribute values, temporarily creating an "in-memory" copy of the object as persisted in the database.

- We record changes to the object's state (attribute values) in the database to persist them.

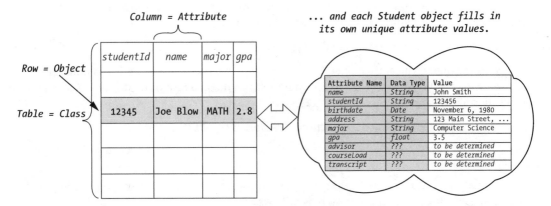

Figure 15-7. *Objects in memory represent "snapshots" of data as persisted in a relational DBMS.*

This works particularly well if an object's attributes are all primitive types, in which case an object's attribute values can be stored as a ***single*** row within a ***single*** table. As we discussed earlier in the book, however, most real-world classes are composite classes, causing the data from a single object to span multiple tables. Nonetheless, this approach to persisting objects is quite prevalent, due to the overwhelming presence of legacy database technology (and legacy data upon which to build an OO front-end).

Using the JDBC API: A Conceptual Overview

The JDBC API provides a number of predefined classes/interfaces via the java.sql, javax.sql, and other packages that enable us to write ***platform- and vendor-independent*** database access code.

At a minimum, we typically make use of the following five key java.sql types (among others) when communicating with a database:

- Driver (interface)

- DriverManager (class)

- Connection (interface)

- Statement (interface)

- ResultSet (interface)

Let's explore the roles that these five predefined Java types play with respect to database persistence.

Driver

Driver is an interface; each DBMS vendor wishing to accommodate Java connectivity must provide a class that implements this interface (e.g., com.sybase.jdbc2.jdbc.SybDriver for Sybase), so as to enable connectivity with that specific vendor's server.

We never command a vendor-specific Driver class or instance directly in our application. Rather, we load the appropriate Driver bytecode into the JVM as a "plug-in" using the Class.forName(...) syntax that we discussed in Chapter 13:

```
Class.forName("com.sybase.jdbc2.jdbc.SybDriver");
```

This bytecode is typically obtained from a particular database vendor within a vendor-specific Java archive (.jar) file (e.g., jconn2.jar for Sybase), which must in turn be made accessible to an application via the application's CLASSPATH:

```
java -cp jconn2.jar;otherApplicationSpecificJarFiles SRS
```

DriverManager

The DriverManager class is used to log on and establish a Connection (another type of interest) to a database. The syntax for doing so is as follows:

```
// Pseudocode.
Connection conn = DriverManager.getConnection(
    vendor-specific URL for locating the database server,
    username, password);
```

as in this representative hypothetical example:

```
String username = null;
String password = null;

// Obtain username and password as Strings via an application's
// user interface; details omitted ...

Connection conn = DriverManager.getConnection("jdbc:Sybase:SRSDB",
    username, password);
```

Connection

A Connection is a conceptual "pipeline" established between an application and the underlying database, through which **Structured Query Language (SQL) statements** are sent (in the form of Statement objects) and results are optionally received (in the form of ResultSet objects). A Connection, once established, is reusable multiple times by the same application as long as the application continues to execute and the Connection is not explicitly closed.

By way of analogy, a `Connection` is like the pneumatic tube at a drive-up bank-teller window: we drive up, "connect" with the teller, and then can conduct as many back-and-forth banking transactions as we wish before driving away ("disconnecting").

There is a great deal of overhead involved in establishing a database `Connection`, so being able to reuse it more than once within an application's execution lifetime is an important performance advantage. On the other hand, an application should not "hoard" an open `Connection` longer than necessary, as most database servers have a limit on the number of connections that can be open simultaneously.

Statement

`Statement` objects are what we actually use to **send** SQL to the database via the `Connection` "pipeline," For example, we might submit the query

```
SELECT * FROM Faculty
```

to retrieve all of the records from the `Faculty` table of the SRS database.

To continue our drive-up banking analogy, a `Statement` is analogous to the little canister that goes **through** the pneumatic tube at a drive-up bank window: we submit a check and a deposit slip into the capsule, and *foop!*—the capsule gets sucked into the bank, as illustrated conceptually in this image:

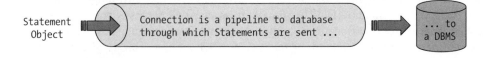

ResultSet

A `ResultSet` is a special sort of collection used to return **rows** satisfying a so-called `SELECT` query to our application—for example, all of the `Professor` rows from the `Faculty` table of our hypothetical SRS database that satisfy the (optional) `WHERE ...` clause of the query:

```
SELECT * FROM Faculty WHERE ssn = "123-45-6789"
```

We can then iterate through the `ResultSet` row by row, perhaps instantiating a `Professor` object in memory based on the data—employee ID, name, etc.—included with every row retrieved.

Doing so is not unlike iterating through the records of a data file one by one, although the syntax for doing so is quite different:

```
// Pseudocode.
Statement stmt = connection.getStatement();
ResultSet rs = statement.executeQuery("SELECT ...);
while (rs.next()) { ... }
```

Now that we've reviewed the five key predefined types necessary for Java database connectivity, let's look at how we can retrofit the SRS for database versus text file persistence.

Retrofitting the SRS with Database Access

Recall a statement that I made earlier in the chapter with respect to SRSDataAccess class:

> *By hiding all of the details of object persistence in these five methods [of the* SRSDataAccess *class], we minimize the impact to our application if such details need to change down the road—for example, if we decide to adopt relational database technology as a persistence mechanism because our SRS application has grown in sophistication, such that the "bells and whistles" of a true DBMS (concurrency control, transaction management, etc.) are now warranted.*

I'll now demonstrate how very true that claim is!

Here is a revised version of the SRSDataAccess class, modified to take advantage of the JDBC API in order to access an underlying hypothetical database. Of necessity, the following example makes heavy use of pseudocode; nonetheless, we've covered enough ground regarding JDBC for you to be able to understand the mechanics of what is going on. The key thing to observe while reviewing this pseudocode is that none of the public features of the class has changed to accommodate database access—all necessary changes have been made to either the private data structure or internal workings of the various methods. Hence, all of the changes are ***transparent to client code***!

```
// SRSDataAccess.java, Take 2 - Modified for database access via JDBC
import java.sql.*;  // new import directive - transparent to client code!
import java.util.*

public class SRSDataAccess {
    // We'll establish and maintain a handle on a Connection to the database
    // as an attribute, so that we may reuse it.  Because this is a private
    // detail of the SRSDataAccess class, it's transparent to client code!
    private static Connection dbConnection;

    // Initialize Faculty.  Note that the method header hasn't changed!
    // We're also still using the same custom Exception type
    // to signal various errors that may arise during
    // object "reconstitution" from persistent storage.
```

```
// Thus, all changes to accommodate database access are internal to
// the method, and hence do not impact client code!
public static Faculty initializeFaculty() throws SRSInitializationException {
    Faculty faculty = new Faculty();

    // Because database operations are prone to numerous issues beyond our
    // control, we'll provide appropriate exception handling.
    try {
        if (dbConnection == null) {
            establish database connection;
        }

        Statement s = formulate query "select * from faculty";
        ResultSet rs = retrieve all faculty data from the Faculty table;
        while (rs.next()) {
            retrieve next record;
            create a Professor object based on this record;
            store the Professor object in the Faculty collection;
        }
    }
    catch (SQLException e) {
        throw a new SRSInitializationException ... details omitted;
    }

    return faculty;
}


// Initialize CourseCatalog.
// Again, no external changes as far as client code is concerned!
public static CourseCatalog initializeCourseCatalog()
    throws SRSInitializationException {
    // Details omitted - similar to the initializeFaculty method.
}


// Initialize ScheduleOfClasses.
// Again, no external changes as far as client code is concerned!
public static ScheduleOfClasses initializeScheduleOfClasses(String semester)
    throws SRSInitializationException {
    // Details omitted - similar to the initializeFaculty method.
}


// Initialize a single Student.
// Again, no external changes as far as client code is concerned!
public static Student initializeStudent(String sId)
    throws InvalidStudentException {
    Student s = null;
```

```
        try {
            submit the query "select * from Student where sid = " + sId;
            if (matching record found) {
                s = create new Student based on record retrieved;
            }
        }
        catch (SQLException e) {
            throw a new InvalidStudentException ... details omitted;
        }

        return s;
    }

    // Persist the state of a Student.
    // Again, no external changes as far as client code is concerned!
    public static void persistStudent(Student s)
        throws StudentPersistenceException {
        try {
            see if a Student with the same ID exists in the Student table;
            if (match found) {
                submit the appropriate "update" SQL statement;
            }
            else {
                submit the appropriate "insert" SQL statement;
            }
        }
        catch (SQLException e) {
            throw a new StudentPersistenceException ... details omitted;
        }
    }
}
```

Now, let's look at the client code—namely, the main method of the SRS class—once again, as it would need to be structured to use our *database* version of the SRSDataAccess class. ***To our delight, the client code remains exactly the same***! From the perspective of the SRS application overall, there's no difference whatsoever in terms of whether we are using file persistence or DBMS persistence. The (unaltered) SRS.java code is repeated here for your convenience (extraneous comments have been removed):

```
// SRS.java

// WE'VE HAD TO MAKE NO CHANGES WHATSOEVER!!!   :o)
// The application is blissfully ignorant that we're now talking to a database
// versus to ASCII files! :o)

import java.util.*;
```

```java
public class SRS {
    // We can effectively create "global" data ...
    public static Faculty faculty;
    public static CourseCatalog courseCatalog;
    public static ScheduleOfClasses scheduleOfClasses;

    public static void main(String[] args) {
        // Initialize all objects.  The method by which we are accessing
        // data (NOW, FROM A DATABASE! :o) is "transparent" to this
        // application by virtue of our introduction of the SRSDataAccess class
        // as a data access layer utility class.
        try {
            courseCatalog = SRSDataAccess.initializeCourseCatalog();
            scheduleOfClasses =
                SRSDataAccess.initializeScheduleOfClasses("SP2005");
            faculty = SRSDataAccess.initializeFaculty();
        }
        catch (SRSInitializationException e) {
            System.out.println("ERROR:  " + e.getMessage() + "-- GOODBYE!");
            System.exit(0);
        }

        // Let's see if everything got initialized properly by calling
        // various display methods.
        // Details omitted ... same as before!

        // Simulate one student logging on.
        Student student = null;

        // EXACT SAME CODE AS BEFORE, when we were using file persistence!
        try {
            student = SRSDataAccess.initializeStudent("111-11-1111");
        }
        catch (InvalidStudentException e) {
            System.out.println("ERROR:  " + e.getMessage() + "-- GOODBYE!");
            System.exit(0);
        }

        // Review student's preexisting information.
        System.out.println("============================");
        System.out.println("Student Information BEFORE:");
        System.out.println("============================");
        System.out.println();
        student.display();

        // Simulate the Student enrolling in another course.
        Section sec = scheduleOfClasses.findSection("ART101 - 1");
        sec.enroll(student);
```

```
        // Review student's updated information.
        System.out.println("===========================");
        System.out.println("Student Information AFTER:");
        System.out.println("===========================");
        System.out.println();
        student.display();

        // Simulate the Student logging off, so that we may persist ...
        // EXACT SAME CODE AS BEFORE, when we were using file persistence!
        try {
            SRSDataAccess.persistStudent(student);
        }
        catch (StudentPersistenceException e) {
            System.out.println("ERROR:  " + e.getMessage() + "-- GOODBYE!");
            System.exit(0);
        }
    }
}
```

And, of course, the various other classes—our eight model classes, our three custom exception classes, our custom collection classes, and our enum(eration)—needn't change, either. Only one class, SRSDataAccess, had to change to accommodate database versus file access.

This example illustrates the ***extraordinary power of model–data access layer separation*** in terms of making an application robust to change when the underlying persistence mechanism changes. We can

- Change the persistence technology that we're using, from files to databases to XML.

- Change the **schema**—record or table design—of an existing persistence mechanism.

- Distribute the data for our application across multiple data sources.

etc., and all such changes will be encapsulated within the data access layer class(es), and hence will be transparent to the user and to the application as a whole.

Our SRS Modifications, Revisited

In summary, here is how our Chapter 14 version of the SRS has evolved to achieve data persistence as of this chapter:

1. We modified—and ***dramatically streamlined***—the SRS driver class, to take advantage of all of the new collections that we created. The new driver class no longer "hard-wires" data about the objects to be instantiated; rather we're reading all such data in from external files.

2. We added ***six new*** classes, as follows:

   - SRSDataAccess: The data access layer of the SRS, encapsulating all of the details of persistence and hence insulating the rest of the application from changes in such details over time

   - CourseCatalog: An encapsulated collection of Course objects, patterned after the ScheduleOfClasses collection of Chapter 14

- Faculty: An encapsulated collection of Professor objects, also patterned after the ScheduleOfClasses collection

- SRSInitializationException: One of several custom Exception types that we invented to signal various issues that can arise when accessing persistent data storage

- InvalidStudentException: A specialized type of SRSInitializationException used specifically when retrieving Student information from persistent storage

- StudentPersistenceException: A specialized type of SRSInitializationException used specifically when saving Student information to persistent storage

We were able to reuse all of our model classes as designed in Chapter 14 as is, *without making any changes whatsoever*, because of our adherence to proper model–data access layer separation principles. ***Wow!***

This concludes the work that we are going to do with respect to persistence in the SRS application. We'll finish rounding out the SRS application by adding a GUI in Chapter 17, after reviewing the basics of Java GUIs in Chapter 16. And, you'll learn that the design technique of **model–view separation**—that is, keeping our model classes free of the details of how objects' states are presented to the user via an application's GUI—is every bit as powerful as model–data access layer separation in terms of building easily extensible, highly flexible applications.

Summary

In this chapter, you learned

- How to approach file I/O in Java, using the FileReader, BufferedReader, FileOutputStream, and PrintWriter classes of the java.io package

- An approach for parsing tab-delimited ASCII records to initialize an object's state, or a collection of objects

- A means of persisting an object's state in an ASCII file

- How to prepare a "test scaffold" main method for testing isolated classes

- A technique for encapsulating collections

- How proper encapsulation streamlines client code (e.g., the SRS main method)

- How Java's JDBC API works conceptually, and how using JDBC can be used to achieve platform independence (and also DBMS *vendor* independence in selected cases)

- How proper model–data access layer separation allows us to easily change our approach to data persistence without affecting the model

You're also getting quite an opportunity to apply the Java language skills that you learned in Chapter 13. I encourage you to work with the SRS code, and to attempt some of the exercises that follow, to reinforce your learning experience.

Exercises

1. Review all of the code associated with the SRS as discussed in this chapter—model classes as well as data access layer classes—and cite all cases where error handling could be improved.

2. The SRS application as presented in this chapter does not do all that it can to "bulletproof" itself against data errors. Test the robustness of the SRS application as currently written against all of the following error situations in either the `CourseCatalog.dat` or `Prerequisites.dat` file—that is, edit these data files to purposely introduce the following problems one by one, and then run the code to see what happens.

    a. The course name is missing from one of the records in `CourseCatalog.dat` (i.e., the record contains only two fields instead of three).

    b. The value for credits (third field in a record) in `CourseCatalog.dat` is a non-numeric value, such as X.

    c. The `Prerequisites.dat` file refers to a course that was not defined in the `CourseCatalog.dat` file.

    d. The `Prerequisites.dat` file is empty.

    e. The `Prerequisites.dat` file contains a record with only one field in it.

    Describe what happens in each case, and discuss what coding changes you'd have to make, if any, to handle each situation gracefully.

3. [*Coding*] Follow up exercise 2 by making whatever changes you deem necessary to the SRS application code to gracefully handle such error conditions. (Suggestion: consider extending the custom exception classes introduced in this chapter.)

4. [*Coding*] ***Advanced***: Design and implement the enhancements necessary to this chapter's version of the SRS so that

    • A student can modify and persist his or her ***primary*** information.

    • A faculty member can modify and persist his or her information.

    • Basic course information (names, credit hour values) can be modified.

    • New courses can be added to the course catalog, and/or courses can be deleted.

    • Sections can be added, deleted, or rescheduled.

    • Teaching assignments can be modified.

    • Course prerequisites can be modified.

5. [*Coding*] ***Advanced***: Retrofit database access to the SRS as downloaded from the Apress web site, using a database vendor of your choosing.

■■■

CHAPTER 16

Rounding Out Your Application, Part 2: Adding a Presentation Layer

In Chapter 15, we greatly improved the usefulness of the SRS application by providing a means for persisting the state of Student objects—in particular, their enrollment status in various classes—from one SRS invocation to the next. However, we still haven't provided a means by which a student user can interact with the SRS. As it is currently implemented, we launch the application from the command line via the command

```
java SRS
```

and from then on, the application runs to completion without any further user input, relying solely on ASCII files and/or hard-coded information as its "fuel"/data.

In Chapter 17, we are going to enhance our latest version of the SRS application once again by retrofitting a graphical user interface (GUI) front-end. With the GUI that we add, we'll provide hypothetical students with the capability to

- Log on to the SRS.

- View the schedule of sections available for registration in the current semester.

- View and modify their individual course load by dropping and adding sections of courses that they are eligible to attend.

- Save these changes to a file before logging off again.

Before we can do so, however, there's a lot to learn about Java GUIs generically, and that's what Chapter 16 is all about. In this chapter, you will learn

- What the two primary Java GUI application programming interfaces (APIs)—the **Abstract Window Toolkit (AWT)** and **Swing**—have to offer

- Details about a number of AWT and Swing **components**—the "building blocks" of GUIs—used to craft the "look" of a user interface

- How we program an application's response to users' interactions with the GUI

- A recommended architecture for GUI applications

- How to prepare a "test scaffold" main method for testing isolated classes

- How to create custom reusable component classes

IMPORTANT!

As we've mentioned several times previously, Sun Microsystems introduced some important new features with Java version 5.0 that significantly increased the power and versatility of Java as an object-oriented programming language. We've thus adopted the J2SE 5.0 approach as of this (second) edition of *Beginning Java Objects*.

Note that the SRS code as presented in Chapters 14, 15, and 17 will *not* compile with an earlier (pre-5.0) version of the Java compiler. *However, the generic GUI examples in Chapter 16 *will* compile with earlier versions of Java, and in fact were tested using Java version 1.3.*

Java GUIs: a Primer

Components

The fundamental approach to graphical user interface programming with virtually any programming language, Java or otherwise, is to assemble graphical building blocks called **components**: buttons, text fields, labels, etc. We assemble components in specific ways to provide the "look," or presentation, that we desire for an application, and then program behind the scenes logic to enable them to do useful things. Users interact with these components to provide information to the system and/or to obtain information from the system in order to achieve some worthwhile goal; in other words, to *fulfill the use cases* that were identified for the application. (Recall that we performed use case analysis for the SRS in Chapter 9.)

Moreover, because it is the model objects that actually carry out the mission of an object-oriented system in terms of their collective business logic, a GUI enables us to *create* and *interact with* model objects. In the case of the SRS, we'll be doing the following:

- *Instantiating objects*: As an example, when a student user logs on to the system, we'll instantiate a Student object as an abstraction of that user.

- *Invoking their methods*: As when we invoke the getEnrolledSections method on a Student object to determine what courses our student user is presently enrolled in.

- *Changing their state*: By modifying attribute values and/or creating new links between them: for example, when a student successfully enrolls in a course, we'll form a link between the appropriate Student and Section objects.

In fact, the GUI *itself* consists of objects! All Java GUI components are created as objects, and hence

- Are declared as classes

- Are instantiated via the new keyword, invoking an appropriate constructor

- Have attributes (that are typically `private`) and methods (that are typically `public`)

- Communicate via messages

- Are requested to provide services by invoking their methods via dot notation

- Participate in inheritance hierarchies

- Are referenced by reference variables whenever we wish to maintain named "handles" on them

- Maintain handles on **other** objects—GUI as well as non-GUI objects

- *Collaborate with other objects—GUI as well as non-GUI objects—to accomplish the mission of the overall system*

Therefore, all of the techniques that you've learned about creating and communicating with objects in general throughout this book will apply to GUI component objects in particular.

Through user interactions with the SRS GUI, the GUI's component objects will be requested to perform services, which in many cases lead them to collaborate behind the scenes with model objects—Students, Professors, Courses, Sections, and so forth—to carry out a particular user-requested service such as registering for a course.

Containers

A **container** is a special type of component that is used to organize, manage, and present other components. We may depict the relationship between components and containers via a UML diagram, as shown in Figure 16-1.

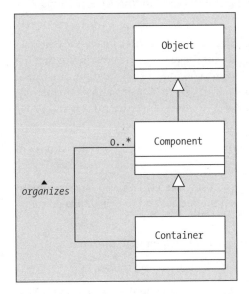

Figure 16-1. *A* Container *is a special type of* Component *that organizes* Components *(including potentially other* Containers*).*

We learn from this diagram that

- A container is a component, but a component is not necessarily a container.

- Since a container can *contain* components, and a container *is* a component, then a container may contain other containers. In fact, this is the way that we build up complex GUIs—by layering components/containers, a technique that we'll explore in depth in this chapter.

By way of analogy, a container is like a directory on a computer system, whereas a component is like an item placed within that directory:

- Just as any one file has only *one* home directory, any one component instance can be directly attached to only *one* container instance.

- Conversely, a container may contain *many* components—including other containers— just as a directory may contain many files and/or other directories.

With Java, when components are added to a container, they are typically positioned through the help of a **layout manager**, a specific type of Java entity that we'll learn more about later in this chapter.

Model–View Separation

A technique known as **separating the model from the view** is an important design approach when developing a graphically oriented application. This concept relates to the **Model–View–Controller (MVC) design pattern**, which was popularized as a formal concept with the Smalltalk language, but is equally applicable to all OO languages, including Java.

MVC is a way of thinking of an application as being subdivided into three cooperating subsystems:

- The **model** embodies the abstract **domain knowledge** of the application: that is, the objects/ classes and their attributes and methods that represent the real-world items/issues that the users are familiar with, often referred to as the *business logic* of the application, as we discussed in Chapter 4. Up until this point in the book, we've been focusing almost exclusively on these so-called *domain classes* (aka *model classes*): Person, Student, Professor, Course, Section, and the like.

- The **view** is the way in which we present this knowledge to the user—typically, although not exclusively, via a graphical user interface.

- The **controller** is the mechanism by which the user interface is displayed, and by which events are communicated back and forth between the model and the view to keep the two in synch:

  - A change in the model must often be simultaneously reflected in the view.

  - A change in the view often impacts the state of the underlying model.

  In the case of Java, this model–view synchronization is handled automatically by the JVM— in conjunction with the underlying windowing mechanism of the computer—based upon application-specific **event handling logic** that we must write to define *how* the model is to change based upon a change in the view (more about this later).

Note that there can be many different views of the same model, in either the same or different applications. For example, with respect to the SRS GUI, we could represent the Students enrolled in a particular Section as a list of their names and student ID numbers:

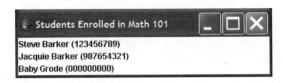

or as photographs:

or as a diagram:

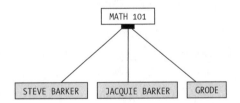

or in any number of other forms.

As OO developers, we must

- Design and program the ***model***, as we did throughout Part 2 of the book and in Chapter 14, respectively.

- Design and program the ***view(s)***. In Java, this is accomplished for ***desktop applications*** through the use of Java's Abstract Window Toolkit (AWT) and Swing APIs, which provide the graphical user interface "building blocks" that we'll focus our attention on for much of this chapter.

And, as we'll discuss conceptually in Chapter 17, we use **Java 2 Enterprise Edition (J2EE) component technologies** to build thin client, browser-based views.

- Understand how the ***controller*** works in order to take advantage of the mechanism for "hooking" the model and view together. This involves learning Java's approach to event handling, which we'll introduce you to in this chapter as well.

When designing and programming an application, if we take care to cleanly separate and insulate the code for the model from the code for the view, then it becomes much easier to

- ***Add or change a view, if need be, without disturbing the underlying model***: That, in essence, is what we'll be doing when we add a desktop GUI to the SRS application in Chapter 17. As you'll see in that chapter, ***the model classes that we've already programmed in Chapter 14 will be reusable precisely as-is when we add a GUI, as will the underlying data access layer that we built in Chapter 15.***

- ***Provide multiple alternative views of the same underlying model***: Sometimes, we provide different views for different categories of user; for example, a professor using the SRS may see different windows and options than a student would see.

We may even give a ***single*** user the ability to switch among multiple views; a familiar example of this can be found within the Microsoft Windows operating system. With Windows, users are able to view the contents of a folder as either large icons:

or as a detailed list:

or even as a DOS window:

```
C:\WINDOWS\system32\cmd.exe                                    _ □ ×

C:\Different Views>dir
 Volume in drive C has no label.
 Volume Serial Number is 786E-44A2

 Directory of C:\Different Views

05/03/2005  09:32 AM    <DIR>          .
05/03/2005  09:32 AM    <DIR>          ..
05/03/2005  09:24 AM                 0 Document 1.txt
05/03/2005  09:25 AM                 0 Document 2.txt
05/03/2005  09:27 AM            26,808 Image.gif
05/03/2005  09:25 AM            12,800 Presentation.ppt
               4 File(s)         39,608 bytes
               2 Dir(s)  19,107,332,096 bytes free

C:\Different Views>
```

Regardless of the view chosen, however, the underlying model in our Windows example is the same: we have a directory entitled "Different Views" on our file system, and it contains four files: two text documents, a GIF image, and a PowerPoint presentation.

- *Modernize the technology with which we present the view*: For example, we may wish to transition from a Java desktop GUI presentation of the type that we'll learn to build in this chapter to a thin client user interface enabled by Java 2 Enterprise Edition (J2EE) technology (again, we'll discuss J2EE conceptually in Chapter 17).

The model should, in essence, be "view free": just as we can change the appearance of a sofa by adding a slipcover without changing its underlying structure or general functionality, so too should we be able to change the appearance of an application without changing its underlying structure. By adhering to the principle of proper model–view separation, the model is indeed insulated from the view: the view can "see" the model, but not vice versa.

One way to help ensure that the model and view are logically separated is to develop the model first, without regard for the view. In theory, if we do a proper job of developing the model, based on the analysis techniques covered in Part 2 of this book, then virtually any view relevant to the original goals (use cases) set forth for the system should be attainable.

The only way that the view should be taken into account when building the model is from the standpoint of considering the application's **concept of operations**: that is, the proposed way in which an external user will view and interact with the application. We'll cover this aspect of OO application development in Chapter 17.

AWT vs. Swing Components

In order for the Java language to truly achieve platform independence, designers of the language had to provide a way for building platform-independent *GUIs*.

With many programming languages that preceded Java, GUI components typically looked different on different platforms. For example, here is a comparison of a pop-up dialog box displayed by Microsoft Word on a Macintosh computer:

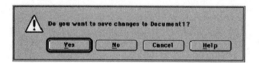

and the same pop-up as it would appear on a Windows PC:

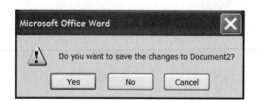

Sun Microsystems designed Java's **Abstract Window Toolkit** API, introduced with version 1.0 of the Java language, to emphasize compatibility with the (platform-*dependent*) graphical-look-and-feel standard for each platform on which a Java application might possibly have run. That is, the express goal of the AWT was to enable the *same* Java application to automatically take on *different* platform-specific "looks," depending on where it was being executed. The rationale was that doing so would increase users' comfort level with a Java application's GUI, thus facilitating Java's acceptance as a mainstream language for application development.

To accomplish this goal, platform-specific versions of all of the Java-supported GUI components were programmed (typically, in the C language) by the developers of the various platform-specific editions of the JVM. (Sun Microsystems traditionally releases JVMs for Solaris [Sun's version of Unix], Linux, and selected versions of Windows; it's up to other vendors to develop JVMs compatible with their operating systems [e.g., SGI's IRIX].) These platform-specific components were then bundled into the JVM.

These so-called **native component peers** did all of the actual work of displaying themselves graphically and interacting with the user. When we, as Java programmers, wrote an application that called for the creation of a Java AWT Button object, for example, then unbeknownst to us, *our* Button object talked to a ButtonPeer object that the JVM automatically created for us; thanks to some magic performed by the JVM, it was the ButtonPeer object that actually appeared on the screen for the user to interact with, as illustrated conceptually in Figure 16-2. Because running Java applications written using the AWT thus involved the invocation of *native (platform-specific) C code*, the AWT components were nicknamed **"heavyweight" components** because of this extra code "baggage."

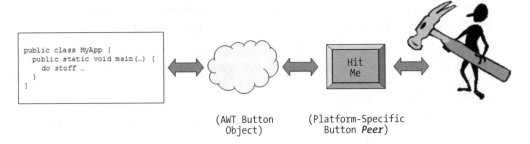

```
public class MyApp {
  public static void main(…) {
    do stuff …
  }
}
```

(AWT Button
Object)

(Platform-Specific
Button *Peer*)

Figure 16-2. *With Java 1.0, our application generated an AWT Button object, which interacted with a platform-specific button peer; the user, in turn, interacted with the button peer.*

Because the same Java AWT application ***intentionally*** looked different when run on different platforms, it therefore became important to test such applications on every platform that they were ever expected to run on to make sure that the various GUI components were properly aligned, that the default fonts used on one platform versus another were suitable such that no labels got truncated, etc.

Sun's official motto of "Write once, run anywhere" informally became "Write once, *test everywhere*, run anywhere."

The Java Swing API became available as an optional add-on API to the Java language with release 1.1, and was officially incorporated into the core Java language as of Java release 1.2 (also known simply as "Java 2"). With the Swing API, a new set of GUI components was introduced to complement the AWT components. Swing components do ***not*** attempt to automatically assume a platform-specific "look"; rather, their default is to assume the *same generic Java-specific look* no matter which computer they are being used on. In fact, Swing components were designed so that most of them no longer need to rely on native peers as did AWT components, and hence Swing components are known as **"lightweight" components** by comparison.

It is possible to control the look of Java GUI components if you wish to have them assume a particular platform-specific look—for example, a Windows look—or some other *custom* look. This is known as assigning a **"pluggable look and feel" (PLAF)**; we won't be discussing how to do this in this chapter, as it isn't relevant to building the SRS GUI.

Most AWT components named "*xxx*" have Swing counterparts named "J*xxx*". For example, the AWT Frame class has a Swing counterpart called JFrame; the AWT Button class has a JButton counterpart; and so forth. It's recommended that, when building a Java GUI

- The Swing version of a component be used in lieu of its AWT version whenever the former is available, as the Swing components generally provide better performance with less overhead; we'll do so in building the SRS GUI.

- The two types of component not be mixed in the same application, as you're likely to run into odd behaviors in a GUI if you mix AWT and Swing components (e.g., screen repainting/"ghosting" issues).

The Swing API also introduced some more advanced GUI components for which there were no AWT equivalents, such as

- JTable, a component for displaying data in a rows-and-columns tabular format, ideal for displaying data that has been returned from a relational database query

- JTree, a way of displaying and navigating hierarchical information similar to the way that Windows Explorer facilitates directory navigation

and others.

Note that the various types of *Swing* Components are in most cases specialized subclasses derived from the java.awt.Component class of the *AWT* API. (And of course, all of the Component classes—like all other Java classes—are ultimately descended from the java.lang.Object class.) Figure 16-3 illustrates the derivation hierarchy of all of the AWT and Swing component classes that we'll need to concern ourselves with in building the GUI for the SRS; asterisks (*) indicate the specific classes that we will be referencing in our code.

Note that there are many more AWT and Swing classes than we've reflected in Figure 16-3; we'll provide a list of some of the other Java component classes that you may wish to explore a bit later in this chapter.

The AWT and Swing classes that we'll be using reside in *four* different packages:

- java.awt: AWT components

- javax.swing: Swing components (note the "x" at the end of the first part of this package name; that's a vestige of the fact that Swing was originally released as an optional Java language extension)

- java.awt.event: Classes related to AWT event handling

- javax.swing.event: Classes related to Swing event handling

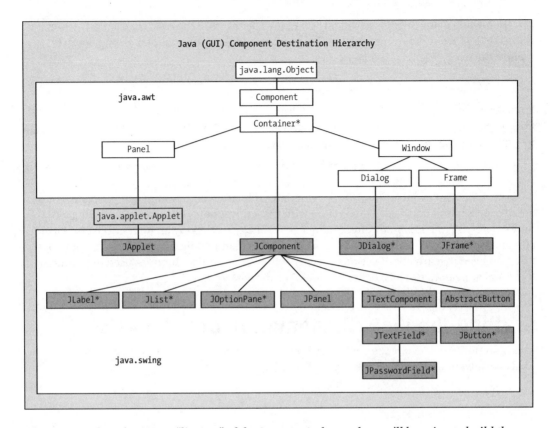

Figure 16-3. *The inheritance "lineage" of the* Component *classes that we'll be using to build the SRS GUI*

Reminder: as we discussed in Chapter 6 when we first introduced the notion of packages and import directives, when we import the entire AWT component set into an application via

```
import java.awt.*;
```

the wildcard character (*) at the end often lulls programmers into thinking that the java.awt.event package will also be imported. This is not the case; if you want java.awt.event classes to be available to your application, you must import that package separately:

```
import java.awt.*;
import java.awt.event.*;
```

The same is true for the two Swing-related packages:

```
import javax.swing.*;
import javax.swing.event.*;
```

Even when using Swing, we still rely on many classes from the AWT, particularly when it comes to GUI event handling, which we'll learn about later in this chapter. Swing doesn't *replace* the AWT API, it *complements* it.

In contrast to Java, C++ has no integrated GUI mechanism. As we discussed in Chapter 2, we typically have to use platform-specific windowing technologies such as Motif or Microsoft Foundation Classes to build a GUI for a C++ application, which compromises an application's portability.

The AWT is an **event-driven** system wherein each visual component can generate a number of events based on a user's interaction with that component. For example, clicking a GUI button, pressing the Enter key after typing in a text field, or clicking an item in a list to select it all generate events. You'll learn more about Java GUI event handling later in this chapter. But first, you need to learn about various specific components and techniques used in producing the visual appearance of a GUI, i.e., its "look," or *presentation*.

Crafting the View/Presentation of a Java GUI

In this section, we'll review the basics of a handful of key Swing/AWT classes/interfaces that we'll take advantage of when building the SRS GUI in Chapter 17:

- JFrame
- JPanel
- JLabel
- Various LayoutManagers
- The generic Component class
- JTextField
- JPasswordField
- JButton
- JList

and we'll demonstrate the use of each of these components by building a simple calculator application, among others.

JFrames

A JFrame is a top-level Swing container/component that serves as a stand-alone window; it cannot be contained by or attached to any other type of component. A JFrame has a title bar and window controls imposed by the native windowing system, and may optionally be equipped with a menu bar, as illustrated in Figure 16-4.

We won't be using menus in our SRS application, but for more information, please explore the Swing JMenuBar, JMenu, and JMenuItem classes.

Title Bar   Native Window Controls

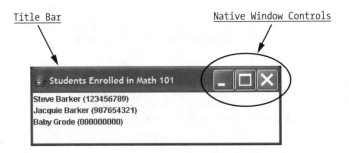

Figure 16-4. *A JFrame with title bar and window controls*

When building a desktop Java application, we typically create a JFrame to host the components necessary to provide the desired GUI appearance and functionality. Nontrivial GUI applications typically consist of *multiple* independent windows—one *main* JFrame and multiple other JFrames and/or transient pop-up windows called **dialog boxes**, which we'll talk about later in this chapter after we've explored event handling a bit.

In contrast with a Java desktop application, a Java **applet**—that is, a Swing-type GUI hosted within an HTML page as viewed by a browser—has no main window of its own. Instead, a browser window serves as the top-level container, and we attach an instance of javax.swing.JApplet as a type of component—a subclass of java.awt.Panel, actually—to the browser "frame." Other than this distinction, however, applets are built using virtually the same AWT/Swing Components with which Java desktop apps are built.

By contrast, thin client J2EE applications typically use neither the AWT nor Swing packages; instead, their user interfaces are delivered as HTML via a browser, as we'll discuss conceptually in Chapter 17.

Let's build our first JFrame. We'll create a program/class called FrameTest, and within the main method of that class we'll perform the bare minimum steps necessary to create and display a JFrame:

```
// FrameTest.java

import javax.swing.*;

public class FrameTest {
  public static void main(String[] args) {
```

We'll instantiate a JFrame object by using one of the JFrame class's constructors, passing in a title for the frame; we'll maintain a handle on the newly created object with a reference variable named theFrame:

```
JFrame theFrame = new JFrame("Whee!!!");
```

Next, we need to set the size of the frame to be something reasonable. We express the width and height of GUI components in **pixels**; a pixel is the smallest addressable graphical unit on a display screen. The default JFrame size is zero pixels wide by zero pixels high, which is effectively invisible.

```
theFrame.setSize(200, 200);    // width, height in pixels
```

Finally, we must explicitly make the frame appear by invoking its setVisible method, passing in a value of true. A JFrame is by default invisible when it is first created, to give us time to assemble all of the components that we wish to attach to the frame before "unveiling" it. (In this example, however, we aren't attaching any components to the frame.)

```
    theFrame.setVisible(true);
  }
}
```

Note that a JFrame can also be made invisible again by calling setVisible with an argument of false.

Here is the code again, in its entirety:

```
// FrameTest.java

import javax.swing.*;

public class FrameTest {
  public static void main(String[] args) {
    // Create the frame by calling the appropriate constructor
    // (we are passing in a title to the frame).
    JFrame theFrame = new JFrame("Whee!!!");

    // Set the size to something reasonable (the default JFrame
    // size is 0 pixels wide by 0 pixels high, which isn't visible).
    theFrame.setSize(200, 200);  // width, height in pixels

    // Make the frame appear on the screen.
    theFrame.setVisible(true);
  }
}
```

The source code for all of the examples in this chapter are available as a download from the Apress web site; see Appendix D for details.

When we subsequently compile, then run, this program by typing these commands:

```
javac FrameTest.java
java FrameTest
```

we see the following window/frame appear in the upper-left corner of the screen:

Of course, Java programs may also be launched through other means, e.g., from a desktop graphical icon. Because the instructions for setting such icons up are operating system dependent and are not Java related, we don't discuss such details in this book. However, in a nutshell, you'd create a shortcut to execute the same command that you'd type to execute your application at the command line—when in doubt, fully qualify all paths, for example:

```
C:\j2sdk1.5.0\bin\java -cp C:\mycode\appdir MyApp
```

There is one slight problem with our program: if we click the close button (⊠) located in the upper-right corner of the frame, the window does indeed close, but our program continues to run! That is, the command line in the Windows command prompt or UNIX window from which we launched the program remains tied up. *Why is this?*

With all of our previous Java program examples throughout the book, as soon as the last line of code in the main method had executed—that is, as soon as the closing brace of the main method body had been reached—the application automatically terminated and the JVM shut down:

```
public class MyApp {
    public static void main(String[] args) {
        System.out.println("Hello ... and goodbye!");
    } // Program terminates and JVM shuts down ...
}
```

What's different here?

This seemingly odd phenomenon has to do with the fact that Java is a **multithreaded language**; that is, the JVM is able to launch multiple *concurrent processes*, or **threads**, as needed. It turns out that whenever we launch a GUI, the JVM spawns *two* threads: in addition to the **main thread**, which is launched for any program, a *second* thread, the event-dispatching thread, is launched that is dedicated to handling GUI events.

The *main* thread of a Java application does indeed automatically terminate when the closing brace of the main method is reached; but, as long as the *GUI* thread is still running, the JVM does not automatically shut itself down. And, the GUI thread will continue to run as long as there is at least one *viable* GUI component still active—e.g., a window-type component such as a JFrame—*whether or not it is still visible to the user*. As it turns out, merely *closing* a window is not sufficient to shut down the GUI event handling thread, because the resources acquired by a window-type component object such as a JFrame are not automatically released—we must do so explicitly and programmatically. We'll learn how to do so via a dispose method when we cover **event handling** later in the chapter.

For now, to regain control of the command line when running one of the demo programs in this chapter, you'll need to do the following:

- Click anywhere in the command-line window from which you typed the java FrameTest command to get the window's "attention"—that is, to cause that window to **gain focus**.

- Press Ctrl+C (the Ctrl and C keys simultaneously) in the command-line window to "kill" (terminate execution of) the program.

Positioning a Frame on the Screen

As you develop a GUI, think of the computer monitor surface as an x-y grid, with the **origin**—a point with (x, y) coordinates of (0, 0)—located in the *upper-left corner* of the screen. As you move to the *right*, the x coordinates of the points *increase*; and as you move *downward*, the y coordinates *increase*.

Points correspond one-to-one with pixels; the lower-right corner of the monitor has coordinates (*maxX, maxY*), depending on the resolution of the monitor in pixels. On a monitor with a pixel resolution of 800 pixels wide by 600 pixels high, the (x, y) coordinate values of the lower-right corner of the screen would be (799, 599), as illustrated in Figure 16-5.

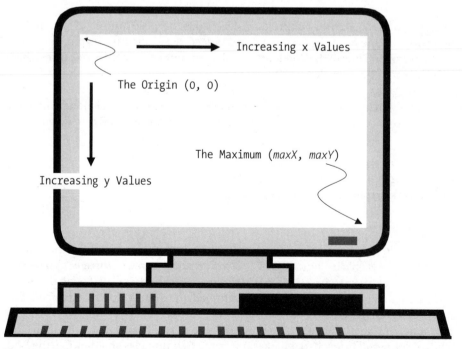

Figure 16-5. *The coordinate system of a computer monitor*

Explicitly Positioning a Frame on the Screen

When we created our first frame with the FrameTest.java program, we didn't explicitly tell the program where we wanted to position the frame, so its upper-left corner was **anchored** at (0, 0) by default, as illustrated in the Figure 16-6.

Our frame was "squished" into the upper-left corner of the display

Figure 16-6. *The default anchor point of a* JFrame *if not otherwise specified is (0, 0).*

If we wish to explicitly anchor a frame somewhere else, we can use its setLocation method to do so. This method takes two int(eger) arguments, representing the x and y coordinates of the upper-left corner of the JFrame relative to the screen surface. Here is a simple example to illustrate this technique:

```
// FrameTest1.java
import javax.swing.*;

public class FrameTest1 {
  public static void main(String[] args) {
    // Create the frame by calling the appropriate constructor
    // (we are passing in a title to the frame).
    JFrame theFrame = new JFrame("Whee!!!");

    // Set the size to something reasonable (the default JFrame
    // size is 0 pixels wide by 0 pixels high, which isn't visible).
    theFrame.setSize(200, 200);
```

```
        // Position the upper-left corner of the frame
        // at the coordinate (300, 400).
        theFrame.setLocation(300, 400);

        // Make the frame appear on the screen.
        theFrame.setVisible(true);
    }
}
```

If you run this program, remember that to regain control of the command prompt you'll need to click in the command-line window to regain that window's focus, and then press Ctrl+C to kill the `FrameTest1` program.

Centering a Frame on the Screen

Often, we would like to center a new frame in the middle of the computer screen when it first appears. Given that screens vary in size from computer to computer, we'll want an approach for computing the center that will be machine independent.

Let's look at a particular example to help us determine the formula that needs to be used in calculating the center of any screen.

- Let's say that we have a frame of size 200 by 200 pixels that we wish to center on a screen of size 800 by 600 pixels. The center of the screen is thus located at $(800/2, 600/2) = (400, 300)$.

- In order to set the location of the frame's upper-left corner so that the frame's *center* coincides with the center of the screen, *half* of the frame's width, or 100 pixels, must fall to the *left* of center, and *half* of the frame's height, or 100 pixels, must fall *above* the center. The upper-left corner of the frame must therefore be positioned at $(400 - 100, 300 - 100) = (300, 200)$, as shown in Figure 16-7.

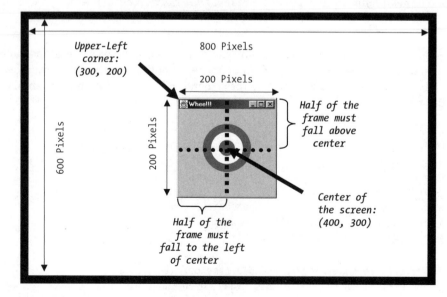

Figure 16-7. *Computing the center of the* JFrame *dynamically, based on monitor size*

Different screens have different physical dimensions and different pixel resolutions, and so we need a way to *dynamically* determine a particular computer's screen size wherever our Java program is run, so that the frame in question will be centered no matter what computer it is physically run on. Fortunately, the AWT provides a Toolkit class that enables us to make such a determination. Let's talk through how this works conceptually first, and then see it in use in code.

- First, we invoke a static method, getDefaultToolkit on the Toolkit class to obtain a handle on the AWT Toolkit object for this computer.

- We then invoke that Toolkit object's getScreenSize method, which returns an object of type Dimension. A Dimension object happens to have two *public* int(eger) attributes— width (in pixels) and height (in pixels).

- We concatenate these two method calls because we don't want to hold onto the Toolkit object for very long: we just want to use it momentarily to retrieve the screen's Dimension object:

  ```
  Dimension screenSize = Toolkit.getDefaultToolkit().getScreenSize();
  ```

  That is, we aren't bothering to assign the handle on the Toolkit object to a reference variable.

- We also invoke the getSize method on the JFrame as a whole to get its size, also as a Dimension object:

  ```
  Dimension frameSize = theFrame.getSize();
  ```

- Armed with all of this size information, we perform the calculation discussed previously.

The preceding approach for centering a JFrame is illustrated by the following sample program; because so much of the code is duplicated from FrameTest1, we've eliminated all extraneous comments:

```
// FrameTest2.java

import javax.swing.*;

// Import a few classes from the AWT API.
import java.awt.Dimension;
import java.awt.Toolkit;

public class FrameTest2 {
  public static void main(String[] args) {
    JFrame theFrame = new JFrame("Whee!!!");
    theFrame.setSize(200, 200);

    // Technique for centering a frame on the screen.

    // First, obtain the size of the frame to be centered. Invoking
    // the getSize method on a Component returns a Dimension
```

```
    // object, which in turn has two public int attributes:
    // width(in pixels) and height (in pixels).
    Dimension frameSize = theFrame.getSize();

    // Now, invoke the static getDefaultToolkit method on the
    // Toolkit class to obtain a handle on the AWT Toolkit object
    // for this platform, and then invoke its getScreenSize()
    // method to obtain a second Dimension object.
    Dimension screenSize = Toolkit.getDefaultToolkit().getScreenSize();

    // Compute the center point of the screen as (centerX, centerY).
    int centerX = screenSize.width/2;
    int centerY = screenSize.height/2;

    // We want half of the frame to be to the left of center,
    // and half to be above center.
    int halfWidth = frameSize.width/2;
    int halfHeight = frameSize.height/2;
    theFrame.setLocation(centerX - halfWidth, centerY - halfHeight);

    theFrame.setVisible(true);
  }
}
```

When we run the program, the frame will indeed appear centered on the screen!
It turns out that there is a shorter calculation that achieves the same result:

```
Dimension frameSize = theFrame.getSize();
Dimension screenSize = Toolkit.getDefaultToolkit().getScreenSize();

// "Split the difference" between the screen size
// and the frame size.
theFrame.setLocation((screenSize.width - frameSize.width)/2,
                     (screenSize.height - frameSize.height)/2);
```

We'll use this more condensed version for centering a frame from now on.

As a bonus, please take a look at the CenteredFrame.java program that we've made available as part of the download from the Apress web site for Chapter 16 code examples—we've created a subclass of JFrame called CenteredFrame that centers itself! This is a **_perfect_** example of how we can use the power of inheritance to extend predefined Java classes.

Adding Components to a JFrame

To add Components to a JFrame, we must first obtain a handle on the JFrame's **content pane**, which is a type of Container:

```
Container contentPane = theFrame.getContentPane();
```

We then use the add method on that Container to add Components one by one.

We've modified our FrameTest2 program to include the lines **highlighted** here:

```
// FrameTest3.java
import javax.swing.*;
import java.awt.*;

public class FrameTest3 {
  public static void main(String[] args) {
    JFrame theFrame = new JFrame("Whee!!!");
    theFrame.setSize(200, 200);

    // Technique for centering a frame on the screen.
    Dimension frameSize = theFrame.getSize();
    Dimension screenSize = Toolkit.getDefaultToolkit().getScreenSize();
    theFrame.setLocation((screenSize.width - frameSize.width)/2,
            (screenSize.height - frameSize.height)/2);

    // Let's create and add a component.
    Container contentPane = theFrame.getContentPane();
    JLabel stuff = new JLabel("I am a label");
    contentPane.add(stuff);

    theFrame.setVisible(true);
  }
}
```

When this program is run, we see that a JLabel appears on the frame with the text "I am a label":

The positioning of the label isn't very interesting—you'll learn how to control this shortly through the intelligent use of layout managers.

Again, remember that, to regain control of the command prompt once any of these demo programs is running, you need to regain the focus of the window from which you launched the program, and then press Ctrl+C to kill it.

Note that we had to use *two* import directives—for `javax.swing.*` and `java.awt.*`—for this example. We'll do this frequently, because we do indeed use a combination of the two APIs for most GUI development:

- Classes `Container`, `Toolkit`, and `Dimension` were introduced with the AWT API, and are still used heavily because the Swing API did not improve upon these.

- On the other hand, classes `JFrame` and `JLabel` were newly added with Swing.

Recall that we can import individual classes, rather than using the wildcard (*) form of import, to better document where each class that we are using originates, as illustrated here:

```
// FrameTest3B.java

// We can import individual classes, to better document where each
// class that we are using originates.
import javax.swing.JFrame;
import javax.swing.JLabel;
import java.awt.Container;
import java.awt.Toolkit;
import java.awt.Dimension;
// etc.
```

JPanels

A `JPanel` is a `Container` (`Component`) that does not have an obvious border. It cannot stand alone, the way a `JFrame` can—it *must* be placed on/in another `Container`, and is used as a convenient way to group multiple other graphic `Components`, such as buttons, lists, text fields, etc. We'll see several creative uses of `JPanel` later in the chapter.

`JPanels` do not make use of a content pane the way `JFrames` do; to add a `Component` to a `JPanel`, we simply invoke the add method on the `JPanel` directly, as this code example illustrates:

```
// Contrast the method for adding a Component to a JFrame ...
Container contentPane = aFrame.getContentPane();
contentPane.add(button1);
// ... or, in a single line ...
aFrame.getContentPane().add(button1);

// ... with that for a JPanel -- no content pane is involved!
aPanel.add(button2);
```

Common Component Properties and Behaviors

Because all of the AWT and Swing components are descended from a common ancestor class, `java.awt.Component`, they all share a number of features inherited from `Component`; we'll review three of these shared features: **color**, **enablement**, and **visibility**.

Color

In Java, colors are implemented as objects belonging to the class `java.awt.Color`. The `Color` class defines a handful of public static attributes, representing the following built-in colors:

black, blue, cyan, darkGray, gray, green, lightGray, magenta, orange, pink, red, white, and yellow. As public static attributes, we refer to them as Color.*xxx*: Color.magenta, Color.cyan, and so forth.

All displayable colors are derived by blending three primary colors—red, green, and blue—in varying intensities from 0 (none) to 255 (maximum), as illustrated for the built-in Java colors in Table 16-1.

Table 16-1. *Built-in Java Colors*

Color	RED Intensity	GREEN Intensity	BLUE Intensity
Color.black	0	0	0
Color.blue	0	0	255
Color.cyan	0	255	255
Color.darkGray	64	64	64
Color.gray	128	128	128
Color.green	0	255	0
Color.lightGray	192	192	192
Color.magenta	255	0	255
Color.orange	255	200	0
Color.pink	255	175	175
Color.red	255	0	0
Color.white	255	255	255
Color.yellow	255	255	0

You can also easily invent your own colors by calling the Color class's constructor, specifying the intensity of the red, green, and blue values that make up the desired color in the range 0 (darkest) to 255 (brightest). For example:

```
Color limeGreen = new Color(50, 205, 50);
```

As a bonus, see the JacquieColor.java and ColorViewer.java classes that we've included with the Apress code download for Chapter 16 for examples of how to define and reuse your own ***named*** custom colors.

All components have both a default **background color** and a default **foreground color**. For example:

- For a JFrame, the default background color is a medium gray color with red/green/blue intensities of (204, 204, 204), and the default foreground color is black.

- For a JTextField, the default background color is white, and the default foreground color, used for displaying the text within the text field, is black.

- For a JLabel, the default background color is the same as for a JFrame, while the default foreground color, used for displaying the text of the label, is a purplish-blue with red/green/blue intensities of (102, 102, 153).

To alter the colors assigned to a component, use the setForeground(Color) and setBackground(Color) methods, respectively, as in the following snippet:

```
// (Assume that 'frame1' and 'frame2' were both declared to be
// JFrames, and that both have been properly instantiated.)

    // Use a standard color ...
    frame1.setBackground(Color.magenta);

    // ... or, invent a color on the fly!
    frame2.setBackground(new Color(20, 30, 40));
```

Enablement

A Component is **enabled** by default when it is created, meaning that it can respond to user input and generate events. Enabled Components provide visual cues to indicate that they have been selected: for example, a JButton has a three-dimensional appearance:

and appears to become pushed in when it is clicked:

 Click!

A Component may be programmatically enabled or disabled by calling its setEnabled(boolean) method, as demonstrated by the following code snippet:

```
    JFrame f = new JFrame("Whee");
    // other details regarding JFrame set up have been omitted ...

    JButton b1 = new JButton("Foo!");
    f.getContentPane().add(b1);
    b1.setEnabled(false);
```

A *disabled* Component *ignores* user interactions: a JButton that has been disabled, for example, will not appear to be pushed in when it is clicked.

To signal to the user that a Component has been disabled, the Component automatically appears to be grayed out in some fashion, as illustrated by the Foo! button here (the Bar button, in contrast, has not been disabled):

It is common practice to disable Components whenever having a user interact with them would be meaningless given the state of an application. For example, if a user is expected to fill in various fields on a GUI "form," but hasn't yet finished doing so, then we might choose to temporarily disable the OK button used to confirm his or her data entry on that form. We'll use this approach with JButtons that we create for the SRS.

Visibility

We've already seen the use of the setVisible method to make a JFrame appear on the screen. Visibility is a characteristic of all Components, as it turns out; some Components are automatically visible when created, and other Components by default take the visibility of the Container to which they are attached. For example, if we create a JButton and add it to a JFrame, then as long as the JFrame is invisible, the JButton will remain invisible, and when we make the JFrame visible, then the JButton will automatically become visible.

We can, however, explicitly make an individual Component invisible while keeping the Container to which it is attached visible by passing the message setVisible(false) to the Component:

```
// Create a frame and add two buttons.
JFrame f = new JFrame("Whee");
JButton b1 = new JButton("Foo!");
JButton b2 = new JButton("Bar ...");

// Details of attaching the buttons to the frame are intentionally
// omitted from this "snippet" ...

// Conditionally hide the first button.
// Pseudocode.
if (some condition) b1.setVisible(false);
```

As a result of the preceding, the Foo! button no longer appears on the frame:

This is an alternative to ***disabling*** individual Components whenever using them would be meaningless given the state of an application.

These aren't **all** of the shared properties of Components, but simply those that we need to know about for building the SRS.

Layout Fundamentals

We can use a special type of object known as a **layout manager** to automatically arrange how Component objects are positioned when they are added to a Container object. We can either use the **default** layout manager that is associated with a particular type of Container such as a JFrame or JPanel, or explicitly assign a **different** layout manager to a container using the container's setLayout method. Then, as we add components to the container, the components will be positioned relative to one another, and to the container as a whole, according to the rules of the governing layout manager.

There are a number of different layout managers defined by the AWT package. We'll be using two of the predefined layout manager types—BorderLayout and GridLayout—to produce the SRS GUI, and so we'll talk about these in some depth. (BorderLayout happens to be the default layout manager for JFrames.)

FlowLayout is another commonly used built-in layout manager. Although we aren't taking advantage of FlowLayout with the SRS application, it happens to be the default layout manager for JPanels, and so it's worth knowing a little bit about how this layout manager behaves, as well.

It is also possible to invent a **custom** layout manager, but this is not a trivial undertaking! The **good** news is that there is generally enough variety among the predefined layout managers to alleviate the need for us to do so.

BorderLayout

A BorderLayout subdivides a Container into five regions, as shown in Figure 16-8 for a JFrame.

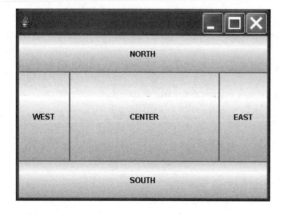

Figure 16-8. *The five regions of a BorderLayout*

- The NORTH region extends across the entire top of the Container. Its height varies, depending on the **preferred height** of whatever sort of Component is inserted into this region.

- The SOUTH region extends across the entire bottom of the Container. Its height also varies, again depending on the preferred height of whatever sort of Component is inserted into this region.

- The WEST region extends from the **bottom** of the NORTH region to the **top** of the SOUTH region, along the **left-hand** side of the Container. Its width varies, depending on the **preferred width** of whatever sort of Component is inserted into this region.

- The EAST region extends from the bottom of the NORTH region to the top of the SOUTH region, along the right-hand side of the Container. Its width also varies, again depending on the preferred width of whatever sort of Component is inserted into this region.

- The CENTER region occupies all remaining space left over in the center of the Container after the NORTH, SOUTH, WEST, and WEST regions all claim their desired amount of space.

If the preceding JFrame is resized by grabbing and dragging an edge of the window with the mouse, the regions change in size and shape but still maintain their relative positions; this is illustrated in Figure 16-9.

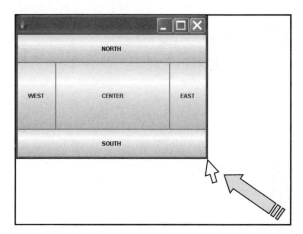

Figure 16-9. *The five regions of a BorderLayout maintain their relative positions when a container is resized.*

When using a BorderLayout to manage a Container, any of the five regions can be left empty; other non-empty regions are then able to expand into the space that has been effectively vacated by the empty region(s). For example, if we were to leave the NORTH region empty in a JFrame, the other regions would expand to consume the available space as shown in Figure 16-10.

Figure 16-10. *A BorderLayout with an empty NORTH region*

If the only region that contains a component is the CENTER region, it expands to consume the entire container, as shown in Figure 16-11.

Figure 16-11. *A BorderLayout with only a CENTER region*

Note that any one of the five regions in a BorderLayout-controlled Container may only contain a single Component. Does this mean that a BorderLayout-controlled Container may therefore only contain a total of *five* Components? The answer is yes—and *no!* If any one of these five Components happens to be a Container itself, such as perhaps a JPanel, then *that* Container can contain as many Components as *its* layout manager allows. In this fashion, we can build up arbitrarily complex GUIs by layering Containers and Components, as shown in Figure 16-12. We'll see several examples of how this is done a bit later in this chapter.

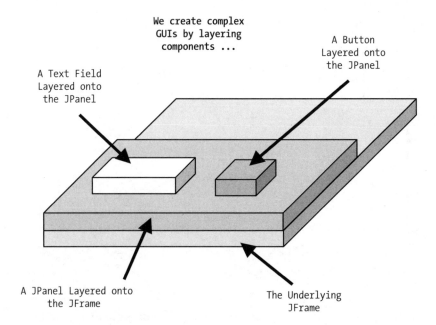

We create complex
GUIs by layering
components ...

A Button
Layered onto
the JPanel

A Text Field
Layered onto
the JPanel

A JPanel Layered onto
the JFrame

The Underlying
JFrame

Figure 16-12. *Layering Containers and Components creates complex GUIs*

Let's modify the FrameTest3 program from a few pages back to explicitly place the label in the NORTH region of the layout simply by changing the add method call to accept a second argument, as follows:

```
contentPane.add(stuff, BorderLayout.NORTH);
```

where BorderLayout.NORTH is one of five public static final attributes (i.e., constants) defined by the BorderLayout class, the other four being BorderLayout.SOUTH, BorderLayout.WEST, BorderLayout.EAST, and BorderLayout.CENTER.

```java
// FrameTest4.java
import javax.swing.*;
import java.awt.*;

public class FrameTest4 {
  public static void main(String[] args) {
    JFrame theFrame = new JFrame("Whee!!!");
    theFrame.setSize(200, 200);

    // Technique for centering a frame on the screen.
    // (Details omitted.)

    // Let's add a component.
    Container contentPane = theFrame.getContentPane();
    JLabel stuff = new JLabel("I am a label");
    contentPane.add(stuff, BorderLayout.NORTH);
```

```
        theFrame.setVisible(true);
    }
}
```

We see the effect of doing so in Figure 16-13.

Figure 16-13. *Adding a component to a specific region*

The label is now at the top of the frame, but it's ***still*** not centered! It turns out that centering a label is a responsibility of the JLabel component itself, not of the layout manager. If we want to ***center*** the label at the top of the JFrame, we must build a label that is ***inherently*** centered by changing one more line of code in our example; namely, by passing a second argument in to the JLabel constructor:

```
    JLabel stuff = new JLabel("I am a label", JLabel.CENTER);
```

where JLabel.CENTER is one of three possible public static attributes defined by the JLabel class, the other two being JLabel.RIGHT and JLabel.LEFT (LEFT is the default justification when none is specified).

```
// FrameTest5.java
import javax.swing.*;
import java.awt.*;

public class FrameTest5 {
  public static void main(String[] args) {
    JFrame theFrame = new JFrame("Whee!!!");
    theFrame.setSize(200, 200);

    // Technique for centering a frame on the screen.
    // (Details omitted.)

    // Let's add a component.
    Container contentPane = theFrame.getContentPane();
    JLabel stuff = new JLabel("I am a label", JLabel.CENTER);
    contentPane.add(stuff, BorderLayout.NORTH);

    theFrame.setVisible(true);
  }
}
```

The result of this code change is shown in Figure 16-14.

Figure 16-14. *Our label is now centered in the NORTH region of the* JFrame.

The AWT and Swing component classes make ample use of public static final attributes to define constant values, such as JLabel.CENTER, BorderLayout.NORTH, Color.PINK, and so on. The generally accepted convention is to use ALL CAPITAL LETTERS to name public static attributes; recall that we did so for attributes FAHRENHEIT_BOILING, FAHRENHEIT_FREEZING, CENTIGRADE_BOILING, and CENTIGRADE_FREEZING in the Temperature utility class that we created in Chapter 7.

Note that we don't have to explicitly tell a JFrame that we wish for it to use a BorderLayout, because BorderLayout is the default layout manager for a JFrame. For other types of Container (like JPanel) that do *not* automatically default to a BorderLayout, we can instruct them to adopt such a layout via their setLayout method, as the following code illustrates:

```
// Create a panel ...
JPanel p = new JPanel();

// ... and set its layout manager to be a Border Layout. (Otherwise, it
// would retain FlowLayout as its default layout manager.)
p.setLayout(new BorderLayout());   // Passing in an "unnamed" BorderLayout
                                   // object.
```

We created a new BorderLayout object without maintaining a named handle on it, since we will never need to address it directly; by passing the layout manager object in as an argument to the setLayout method, the JFrame will maintain a handle on it, such that it won't prematurely get garbage collected.

GridLayout

A GridLayout arranges a Container into a row/column layout, or *grid*. The number of rows and columns is determined when a GridLayout is first created, and cannot be changed; for example:

```
aFrame.getContentPane().setLayout(new GridLayout(3, 2));   // 3 rows, 2 cols.
```

Despite the fact that we cannot change a given GridLayout instance's row/column count once it has been created, we can assign a *different* GridLayout instance, with a *different* row/column configuration, to manage this Container if we wish—even after components have been attached.

Components are then added to the Container in ascending row by column order: the first component added goes into row 1 column 1, the second, into row 1 column 2, and so forth until the first row is filled; then, the next component goes into row 2 column 1, etc., until all components have been added.

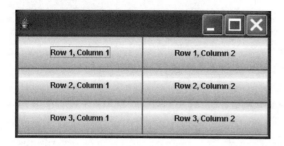

Here is yet another version of our FrameTest program, modified to illustrate the use of a GridLayout:

```
// FrameTest6.java
import javax.swing.*;
import java.awt.*;

public class FrameTest6 {
  public static void main(String[] args) {
    JFrame theFrame = new JFrame("Whee!!!");
    theFrame.setSize(400, 400);

    // Technique for centering a frame on the screen.
    // (Details omitted.)

    // Assign a grid layout to the frame, replacing its
    // default border layout.
    Container contentPane = theFrame.getContentPane();
    contentPane.setLayout(new GridLayout(3, 2));  // 3 rows, 2 cols.

    // Create some components to attach.
    // We'll start with some labels.
    JLabel l = new JLabel("Name:");
    JLabel l2 = new JLabel("Address:");
    JLabel l3 = new JLabel("SSN:");

    // This next component, a text area, is a multiline
    // text component; we're asking for it to be six lines
    // "tall" vs. 20 characters wide.

    JTextArea t = new JTextArea("This is a MULTI-LINE text area, " +
                        "which can contain a lot of text. " +
                        " We've asked it to wrap along " +
```

```
                              "word boundaries.",
                              6, 20);

    // Turn on line wrapping for the JTextArea component ...
    t.setLineWrap(true);

    // ... along word boundaries.
    t.setWrapStyleWord(true);

    // Creating two single-line text fields.
    JTextField t2 = new JTextField("This is a SINGLE LINE text field.");
    JTextField t3 = new JTextField("Another text field.");

    // Add in ascending row by column order.
    contentPane.add(l);       // row 1, col. 1
    contentPane.add(t);       // row 1, col. 2
    contentPane.add(l2);      // row 2, col. 1 (etc.)
    contentPane.add(t2);
    contentPane.add(l3);
    contentPane.add(t3);

    theFrame.setVisible(true);
  }
}
```

The result of running the preceding program is illustrated in Figure 16-15.

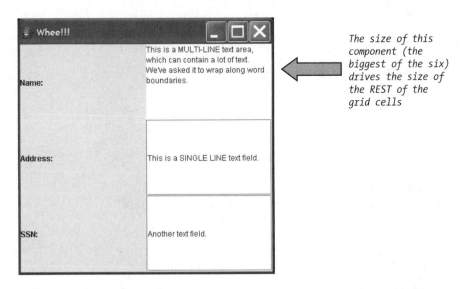

Figure 16-15. *Six cells of equal size appear in the* JFrame—*three rows by two columns overall.*

One problem with using a GridLayout is apparent in the preceding example: the size of all of the cells in a container is driven by the preferred size of the *biggest* component that we've placed on the grid, which can make for an odd looking interface. In this example, we added six components: three JLabels, two single-line JTextFields, and one multiline JTextArea. The text area is the largest component: when we called the JTextArea constructor, we indicated that we wanted it to be capable of showing up to 6 lines of 20 characters each. This drives all other cells to be that *same* size. When we tackle the SRS GUI in Chapter 17, we'll learn a technique for the creative use of GridLayouts in combination with layered JPanels that enables us to work around this shortcoming.

Note that "funny" things happen if we try to add too many Components to a GridLayout-managed Container. For example, if we modify our FrameTest6 program to add *seven* items to the 3×2 grid (please see **highlighted** lines of code in the following snippet):

```java
// FrameTest6B.java
import javax.swing.*;
import java.awt.*;

public class FrameTest6B {
  public static void main(String[] args) {
    JFrame theFrame = new JFrame("Whee!!!");
    theFrame.setSize(400, 400);

    // Technique for centering a frame on the screen.
    // (Details omitted.)

    // Assign a grid layout to the frame.
    Container contentPane = theFrame.getContentPane();
    contentPane.setLayout(new GridLayout(3, 2));  // 3 rows, 2 cols.

    // Create some components to attach.
    JLabel l = new JLabel("Name:");
    JLabel l2 = new JLabel("Address:");
    JLabel l3 = new JLabel("SSN:");
    JTextArea t = new JTextArea("This is a MULTI-LINE text area, " +
                                "which can contain a lot of text. " +
                                "We've asked it to wrap along " +
                                "word boundaries.", 6, 20);
    t.setLineWrap(true);
    t.setWrapStyleWord(true);
    JTextField t2 = new JTextField("This is a SINGLE LINE text field.");
    JTextField t3 = new JTextField("Another text field.");

    // Add in ascending row, then column, order.
    contentPane.add(l);
    contentPane.add(t);
    contentPane.add(l2);
    contentPane.add(t2);
    contentPane.add(l3);
    contentPane.add(t3);
```

```
    // Create ONE TOO MANY component!
    JTextField t4 = new JTextField("ONE TOO MANY! :op");

    // Add it, even though there really is no more room.
    contentPane.add(t4);

    theFrame.setVisible(true);
  }
}
```

then the GridLayout, in an attempt to accommodate seven instead of only six components, adds an extra column (for a total of 3 rows × 3 columns, or nine grid cells), and then adds the seven components to the grid in row by column order as shown in Figure 16-16—this is not at all what we were hoping for!

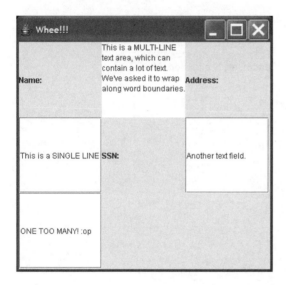

Figure 16-16. *Adding seven components to a grid sized for only six produces cosmetically undesirable results.*

We cannot skip cells in a GridLayout, but may use a blank JLabel to "pad" a cell if need be (see **highlights** in the following code):

```
// FrameTest6C.java
import javax.swing.*;
import java.awt.*;

public class FrameTest6C {
  public static void main(String[] args) {
    JFrame theFrame = new JFrame();
    theFrame.setSize(300, 300);
```

```
// Technique for centering a frame on the screen.
// (Details omitted.)

// Assign a grid layout to the frame.
Container contentPane = theFrame.getContentPane();
contentPane.setLayout(new GridLayout(3, 2));

// Create some components to attach.
JLabel l1 = new JLabel("Name:");
JLabel l2 = new JLabel("Fred");
JLabel l3 = new JLabel("SSN:");
JLabel l4 = new JLabel("123-45-6789");

// Add in ascending row, then column, order.

contentPane.add(l1);
contentPane.add(l2);

// Create two blank unnamed labels as "padding," and add them
// to the 2nd row.
contentPane.add(new JLabel(""));
contentPane.add(new JLabel(""));

contentPane.add(l3);
contentPane.add(l4);

theFrame.setSize(200, 200);
theFrame.setVisible(true);
  }
}
```

The result is shown in Figure 16-17.

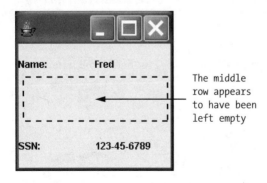

The middle row appears to have been left empty

Figure 16-17. *Padding with blank components*

FlowLayout

Like a GridLayout, a FlowLayout adds Components to the Container that it manages in left-to-right, top-to-bottom order. Whereas a GridLayout divides a Container into rows of equal numbers of evenly sized cells, however, a FlowLayout is much more unstructured: it simply fits as many Components across the Container as it can from left to right to form a row, allowing each Component to retain its preferred size, and then "wraps" to start a new row when a given row is full. (This is similar to the way that words of differing lengths wrap from one line to the next in a word processor.)

Here is a revised version of our FrameTest program, modified to use a FlowLayout (see **highlights** in the following code):

```
// FrameTest7.java

import javax.swing.*;
import java.awt.*;

public class FrameTest7 {
  public static void main(String[] args) {
    JFrame theFrame = new JFrame("Whee!!!");

    // Technique for centering a frame on the screen.
    // (Details omitted.)

    // Override the default layout manager.
    Container contentPane = theFrame.getContentPane();
    contentPane.setLayout(new FlowLayout());

    // Create several labels.
    JLabel l1 = new JLabel("A short label");
    JLabel l2 = new JLabel("A rather long label");
    JLabel l3 = new JLabel("Another fairly long label");

    // Play with the colors.
    l1.setBackground(Color.cyan);
    l1.setForeground(Color.black);
    l2.setBackground(Color.white);
    l2.setForeground(Color.black);
    l3.setBackground(Color.yellow);
    l3.setForeground(Color.black);

    // Make the labels opaque (the default is transparent)
    // so that their background colors show up.
    l1.setOpaque(true);
    l2.setOpaque(true);
    l3.setOpaque(true);
```

```
    // Add them to the GUI.
    contentPane.add(l1);
    contentPane.add(l2);
    contentPane.add(l3);

    theFrame.setSize(200,200);
    theFrame.setVisible(true);
  }
}
```

When this frame is first displayed, it appears as follows:

The first two labels are able to fit side by side in the frame, but the third slips down into a second row by itself.

If we resize the frame by grabbing and dragging an edge of the window with the mouse so that it is wide enough for all three labels to fit side by side, the FlowLayout manager automatically moves them all into the same row:

If we then make the frame sufficiently narrow by grabbing and dragging an edge of the window with the mouse, each label will instead show up on its own separate line:

Note that we had to explicitly set the JFrame's layout manager to be a FlowLayout object in this case, because as we learned earlier, the JFrame's default layout manager is BorderLayout; we did so with this method call:

```
contentPane.setLayout(new FlowLayout());
```

JLabels

As we've already learned, JLabels are a simple type of Component used to display a single line of text, which can be left justified, centered, or right justified. (A JLabel may also be used to display an image, or a combination of text and an image, but we won't be availing ourselves of that capability in building the SRS.)

As is true of so many of the Swing components, the Java language defines many different forms of constructor for JLabels; the only forms of JLabel constructor that we'll be using in building the SRS GUI are

- JLabel(String text, int horizontalAlignment), where horizontalAlignment can assume one of the three different public static final attribute values, JLabel.LEFT, JLabel.CENTER, or JLabel.RIGHT, as we discussed earlier

- JLabel(String text), where left-justified alignment is the default

A JLabel is not meant to be editable by the user directly, but we can *programmatically* affect what a label says in response to what a user does by making use of the setText method; here are a couple of examples:

```
JLabel l = new JLabel("");  // blank for now
// Intervening details omitted ...
// Pseudocode.
if (user chose option X) {
    l.setText("Option X selected ...");
}
// Later ...
// Clear the label.
l.setText("");
```

Or

```
// Pseudocode.
if (error condition X arose) {
    // Make the label red, for emphasis.
    l.setForeground(Color.red);
    l.setText("OH, NO!!! Error X has occurred.");
}
```

We'll use the technique of programmatically changing labels within the SRS application.

JTextFields and JPasswordFields

A JTextField displays a single line of text that is either typed into the field by a user or supplied automatically by the program. We have numerous constructors to choose from for JTextFields; the two that we'll be focusing on are

- `JTextField(int columns)`, where `columns` sizes the text field by describing the number of visible character positions. For proportional fonts—that is, fonts in which not all characters are the same width—the width of the lowercase letter "m" is used as the standard character size/column width.

Note that it is possible to assign specific fonts to a text component, but since we have no need to do so in building the SRS, we will not discuss the details for doing so in this book.

- `JTextField()`, which version creates an empty text field, but doesn't try to mandate its size—in this case, the layout manager of whatever `Container` the field is attached to will decide an appropriate size.

Either way, text fields are **scrollable**, which means that if a user types in more text than can visibly fit into a field, the text will simply scroll off to the left. In the `JTextField` shown in the following illustration, the user has typed `"If I type too much text, the field will scroll."` Note that there is no visual cue given to the user: that is, no scroll bar appears to signal the user that this has happened.

Using the left arrow (cursor) key on the keyboard, we can scroll back to the beginning of the text in this field:

Two of the more frequently used methods defined by the `JTextField` class are

- `String getText()`: Returns a `String` containing the text currently in the `JTextField` (that is, the text that a user has typed into the field). If the field is empty, this method returns an empty `String` (`""`).

- `void setText(String s)`: Allows us to programmatically populate a field with the text specified by s.

Two other useful properties that we often manipulate with `JTextFields` are whether or not a field is **editable** and whether or not it is **enabled**. We talked about the enablement of `Components` in general earlier in this chapter; the editability of `JTextFields` is controlled in much the same way, via the `setEditable(boolean)` method. If a field's editability is set to `false`, a user cannot modify what is displayed in the text field: it **looks** like a text field, but behaves more like a label. To **truly** be modifiable by a user, a `JTextField` must be **both** editable and enabled.

In the sample GUI code that follows, we create four `JTextFields`, and experiment with various settings for the editability and enablement of each field:

```java
// EditableExample.java
import java.awt.*;
import javax.swing.*;

public class EditableExample {
  public static void main(String args[]) {
    JFrame theFrame = new JFrame("");
    Container contentPane = theFrame.getContentPane();
    contentPane.setLayout(new GridLayout(4, 1));

    JTextField l1 = new JTextField("Editable and Enabled");
    l1.setEditable(true);
    l1.setEnabled(true);

    JTextField l2 = new JTextField("Editable and Disabled");
    l2.setEditable(true);
    l2.setEnabled(false);

    JTextField l3 = new JTextField("Not Editable and Enabled");
    l3.setEditable(false);
    l3.setEnabled(true);

    JTextField l4 = new JTextField("Not Editable and Disabled");
    l4.setEditable(false);
    l4.setEnabled(false);

    contentPane.add(l1);
    contentPane.add(l2);
    contentPane.add(l3);
    contentPane.add(l4);

    theFrame.setSize(300, 200);
    theFrame.setVisible(true);
  }
}
```

The resultant GUI is shown in Figure 16-18. Only the *first* of the four of these text fields can actually be modified by the user; yet, note the differing appearances of the other three.

Figure 16-18. *Editable and enabled components vs. not editable and disabled components*

JPasswordField, a subclass of JTextField, is used when we want to provide security with respect to information being typed in. As a user types data into a JPasswordField, each character that is typed is reflected as an **echo character**; in the following figure, the user typed "123" as a password, but it appeared instead as "***":

To set the echo character of a JPasswordField to something other than the default of *, use the setEchoCharacter(char c) method as shown in the following snippet:

```
JPasswordField passwordField = new JPasswordField();
passwordField.setEchoCharacter('#');     // note use of single vs.
                                         // double quotes
```

As mentioned in Chapter 2, we must use *single quotes* to represent a char(acter) literal; this has a very different meaning from "#", which is actually a String literal of length 1.

We have to do a little bit of extra work to retrieve the value that has been typed into a JPasswordField, since the getText method inherited from JTextField is *deprecated* for the JPasswordField class, which means that although the getText method still works as of the *current* version of Java, it is not guaranteed to work in a *future* release of Java. The preferred alternative to using getText is as follows:

- First, we use the getPassword method, which returns an array of char(acters) rather than a String:

  ```
  char[] pw = passwordField.getPassword();
  ```

- Then, we pass this char(acter) array in as an argument to a form of String constructor that knows how to turn the contents of the array into a String:

  ```
  String password = new String(pw);
  ```

  or, as a single line of code:

  ```
  String password = new String(passwordField.getPassword());
  ```

JButtons

JButtons allow a user to initiate an action by clicking what appears to be a three-dimensional button on the GUI. We have to program an **event listener** to define what we actually want the button to *do* when it is clicked (we'll learn about event listeners later in the chapter), but the button is inherently "clickable" just by virtue of creating it—it appears to move in and out of the computer screen.

There are several JButton constructors; the one that we'll use for the SRS is

```
JButton(String text)
```

where text is used as the button's label. (As with JLabels, a button may also carry an image, or a combination of an image and text.)

Note that there is a trick for creating **_multiline labels_** on JButtons.

- Normally, when we create a JButton, we assign its label in one step—for example, JButton b = new JButton(label);—but this doesn't afford us an easy way to split the label onto two or more lines.

- But, because the JButton class is a subclass of JComponent, which in turn is a subclass of the java.awt.Container class, a JButton may itself serve as a container for other components—in particular, of JLabels!

- If we thus set the layout manager for a JButton to be a 2×1 GridLayout, we can then add two different labels to the same button and have them appear one above the other:

```
Button b = new JButton();


// Give the JButton, as a JComponent, a 2 x 1 GridLayout.
b.setLayout(new GridLayout(2, 1));

// Create two labels ...
l1 = new JLabel("Save My", JLabel.CENTER);
l1.setForeground(Color.black);
l2 = new JLabel("Schedule", JLabel.CENTER);
l2.setForeground(Color.black);

// ... and add them both to the JButton.
b.add(l1);
b.add(l2);
```

as illustrated in Figure 16-19.

Figure 16-19. *A multiline JButton label*

This technique can be used with **_any_** component that is descended from the java.awt.Component class.

JLists

A JList is used for presenting a list of choices to a user. These choices can be text, images, or literally any GUI component: for example, a list of JButtons, each of which may be clicked to trigger a different action! We'll be working with simple, text-oriented lists in developing the SRS GUI.

There are various JList constructors; the ones that we'll be focusing on are as follows:

- JList(): Creates an empty JList.

- JList(Object[] listData): This is a very interesting constructor—we hand in an array containing whatever type of Object we wish, and the JList in turn displays a list of *textual* items by invoking the toString method on each of the Objects contained within the array. (Recall our discussion from Chapter 13 of the importance of programming a toString method for all of the classes that we invent.)

Let's look at a simple program that demonstrates the latter form of JList constructor; we're going to display a list of student names based on an array of Student objects. In order for this to work, we must have programmed a toString method for the Student class; we'll use the following simplified version of Student, rather than the more elaborate one we've developed for the SRS, to support this JList example:

```
// Student.java

// * * * * * * * * * * * * * * * * * * * * * * * * * * * * *
// THIS IS AN ABBREVIATED VERSION OF THE Student CLASS,
// FOR USE WITH THE VARIOUS VERSIONS OF JListDemo.
// * * * * * * * * * * * * * * * * * * * * * * * * * * * * *

public class Student {
    private String name;
    private String ssn;

    // Constructor.
    public Student(String ssn, String name) {
        setSsn(ssn);
        setName(name);
    }

    // Typical accessor (get/set) methods for ssn and
    // name also provided -- details omitted.

    public String toString() {
        return this.getName() + " (" + this.getSsn() + ")";
    }
}
```

We start with the basics:

```
// JListDemo.java

import java.util.*;
import javax.swing.*;
import java.awt.*;

public class JListDemo {
    public static void main(String[] args) {
        Frame theFrame = new JFrame("Sample JList");
        Container contentPane = theFrame.getContentPane();
```

Next, we create an array and populate it with a few Student objects:

```
Student[] v = new Student[3];
v[0] = new Student("123456789", "Joe Blow");
v[1] = new Student("987654321", "Fred Schnurd");
v[2] = new Student("000000000", "Englebert Humperdink");
```

We'll now instantiate a new JList object called myList, passing in the array:

```
JList myList = new JList(v);
```

Finally, we round out the program:

```
contentPane.add(myList);
theFrame.setSize(300, 90);
theFrame.setVisible(true);
  }
}
```

Here is the uninterrupted code:

```
import java.util.*;
import javax.swing.*;
import java.awt.*;

public class JListDemo {
  public static void main(String[] args) {
    JFrame theFrame = new JFrame("Sample JList");
    Container contentPane = theFrame.getContentPane();

    // Create a collection of Students.
    Student[] v = new Student[3]; // of Students
    v[0] = new Student("123456789", "Joe Blow");
    v[1] = new Student("987654321", "Fred Schnurd");
    v[2] = new Student("000000000", "Englebert Humperdink");

    // Create a JList based on this collection. The reason that
    // we can do this is because the Student class defines
    // a toString method, which causes each Student object to be
    // rendered in terms of its name and SSN in the list.
    JList myList = new JList(v);
    contentPane.add(myList);

    theFrame.setSize(300, 90);
    theFrame.setVisible(true);
  }
}
```

The preceding program, when run, produces the GUI illustrated in Figure 16-20, as expected.

Figure 16-20. *Student objects are reflected as string values in the* JList.

Had we failed to provide an overridden toString method for the Student class, this example would still work, because as we discussed in Chapter 13, all objects inherit the toString method of the Object class; however, the list wouldn't be nearly as readable, since the default toString method of the Object class returns an internal ID for each object, as illustrated in Figure 16-21.

Figure 16-21. *Relying on the default* toString *method yields a less cosmetically desirable result.*

A Simple Calculator Example

Let's put all that we've learned thus far about GUI components into practice by building a simple little calculator GUI which, when finished, will look as follows:

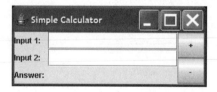

- The calculator provides two input text fields labeled Input 1: and Input 2:.

- To operate the calculator, the user types a numeric value into each field, and then clicks either the plus (+) or minus (–) button, depending on whether he or she wishes to add or subtract the two values.

- The sum or difference of the two values, as appropriate, will (eventually) be displayed as a non-editable value next to the label Answer:

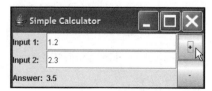

The components that comprise this GUI are visually grouped into three clusters of similarly sized components:

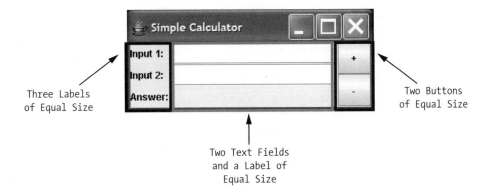

Three Labels
of Equal Size

Two Buttons
of Equal Size

Two Text Fields
and a Label of
Equal Size

Whenever you are able to visually subdivide a GUI into clusters of similarly sized components, think GridLayout-managed JPanels! For our calculator, we'll create three JPanels:

- For each of the leftmost and center panels, we'll create a GridLayout of three rows by one column; and, for the rightmost panel, we'll create a GridLayout with two rows by one column.

- Then, since the default layout manager for a JFrame's content pane is BorderLayout, we can add the leftmost panel to the WEST region of the JFrame, the center panel to the CENTER region, and the rightmost panel to the EAST region to achieve the desired look.

The code used to produce this GUI is as follows. All of the code that we use in this example should by now be familiar to you, so we won't discuss it in detail; please see the in-line comments for details.

```java
// Calculator1.java

import java.awt.*;
import javax.swing.*;

public class Calculator1 {
  public static void main(String[ ] args) {
    JFrame aFrame = new JFrame("Simple Calculator");
    Container contentPane = aFrame.getContentPane();
    aFrame.setSize(250, 100);

    // We don't need to set the layout manager for
    // a JFrame's content pane - it is automatically a
    // BorderLayout by default.

    // Technique for centering a frame on the screen.
    // (Details omitted.)
```

```java
// Let's create the leftmost panel. Note that we use names
// for our components that are somewhat self-documenting.
JPanel leftPanel = new JPanel();

// We'll assign the panel a GridLayout (it would otherwise
// default to FlowLayout).
leftPanel.setLayout(new GridLayout(3, 1));

// We'll create three labels and hand them to the panel;
// there's no need to bother maintaining a named handle
// on any of these labels, since we don't plan on
// programmatically modifying any of them.
leftPanel.add(new JLabel("Input 1: "));
leftPanel.add(new JLabel("Input 2: "));
leftPanel.add(new JLabel("Answer: "));

// Now, we'll attach the panel to the frame.
contentPane.add(leftPanel, BorderLayout.WEST);

// Repeat the process with the center panel.
JPanel centerPanel = new JPanel();
centerPanel.setLayout(new GridLayout(3, 1));
JTextField input1TextField = new JTextField(10);
JTextField input2TextField = new JTextField(10);

// We use a JLabel to display the answer of the
// calculation, although we could have also used
// a non-editable JTextField instead.
JLabel answerLabel = new JLabel();

centerPanel.add(input1TextField);
centerPanel.add(input2TextField);
centerPanel.add(answerLabel);
contentPane.add(centerPanel, BorderLayout.CENTER);

// The third, and final, panel.
JPanel buttonPanel = new JPanel();
buttonPanel.setLayout(new GridLayout(2, 1));
JButton plusButton = new JButton("+");
JButton minusButton = new JButton("-");
buttonPanel.add(plusButton);
buttonPanel.add(minusButton);
contentPane.add(buttonPanel, BorderLayout.EAST);

// (We still need to learn how to add behaviors, so that the
// plus and minus buttons do something useful ... we'll learn
// how to do this shortly.)
```

```
    aFrame.setVisible(true);
  }
}
```

Note that there is no limit to the "depth" of layering that can be achieved with JPanels—in Figure 16-22, we show three levels of JPanel being attached to an underlying JFrame, with varying GridLayout configurations assigned to each. Be creative! We'll see an example of how to do this with the SRS GUI's main window, a class named MainFrame, later in this chapter.

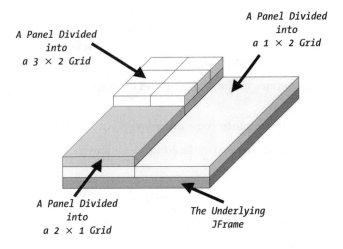

A Panel Divided into a 3 × 2 Grid

A Panel Divided into a 1 × 2 Grid

A Panel Divided into a 2 × 1 Grid

The Underlying JFrame

Figure 16-22. *Layering that can be achieved with* JPanels

Meanwhile, back to our calculator. As currently programmed, it doesn't do anything interesting yet because we haven't programmed any event handling; a user can type values into the Input 1: and Input 2: fields, but clicking either of the two buttons will not cause any computation to occur. Nonetheless, the buttons do reflect movement when clicked.

We'll add functionality to the calculator in just a moment, after we look at ways to restructure our calculator code to conform to a more typical Java software architecture.

An Improved Application Architecture for GUIs

The simple GUI examples that we've seen thus far all involve a single class whose main method instantiates a JFrame, creates and add components to the frame, and finally displays the frame; this basic skeletal structure is summarized here:

```
// Pseudocode.

public class GUIClass {
  public static void main(...) {
    // Create a frame ...
    JFrame f = new JFrame();
```

```
    // ... create and add components ...
    JButton b = new JButton("Foo");
    f.getContentPane().add(b);

    // etc.

    // ... and make the frame appear!
    f.setSize(...);
    f.setVisible(true);
  }
}
```

This is not an appropriate architecture for anything but trivial applications, however. A better architecture for a GUI application is to create a minimum of two classes:

1. A class, ***derived from*** JFrame, which defines the appearance (and behavior) of the main GUI window:

    - All components to be attached to the frame become ***attributes*** of this class.

    - The components are instantiated and attached in the ***constructor*** for this class.

2. An application driver class, which

    - Instantiates an instance of the main window in its main method

    - Handles any other application initialization steps—for example, establishing database connectivity, perhaps with a log-on dialog box

    - Hosts any global data (as public static attributes), constants (as public static final attributes or enums), or convenience methods (as public static methods) for the application as a whole

If more than one window is needed for the GUI (as will be the case for the SRS GUI), additional classes are created, each of which define the appearance and behavior of some other key window (usually either another derivation of JFrame or JDialog). Some simplistic dialog boxes—error message pop-ups, "confirm/cancel" questions, and the like—can be created on the fly, and don't necessarily need their own separate classes; we'll see examples of this with the SRS GUI.

Let's take another look at our calculator example, rearchitected as suggested previously.

- First, we'll create a class called Calculator2, in a file named Calculator2.java, to represent the main window—namely, the calculator itself! We've moved most of the code from the main method of Calculator1.java into the constructor for Calculator2.

- We declare all of the Component "building blocks" of the GUI as attributes of this class, which serves to make them in scope throughout all of the methods of the class. This is not particularly critical for the Calculator2 example, because there are no methods besides the constructor; but, for more complex GUIs, this will prove to be a valuable technique, as we'll see when constructing the SRS GUI in Chapter 17.

By now, most of the code that follows should be familiar to you, so we'll keep our narrative interruptions to a minimum:

```
// Calculator2.java

import java.awt.*;
import javax.swing.*;

public class Calculator2 extends JFrame {
  // Components are treated as attributes, so that they will be
  // in scope throughout all of the methods of the class.
  private Container contentPane;

  // Use descriptive names for components whenever possible.
  private JPanel leftPanel;
  private JPanel centerPanel;
  private JPanel buttonPanel;
  private JTextField input1TextField;
  private JTextField input2TextField;
  private JLabel answerLabel;
  private JButton plusButton;
  private JButton minusButton;

  // Constructor.
  // The constructor is where we create and attach all of the
  // Components to the underlying JFrame.
  public Calculator2() {
    // Invoke the generic JFrame constructor.
    super("Simple Calculator");
```

We are now doing things from *within* the JFrame subclass that we used to do *externally* to the JFrame *instance* from within the main method of the FrameExample class—e.g., getting a handle on the content pane, setting the size of the frame. So, rather than referring to the frame by name—e.g., theFrame.getContentPane()—we use the prefix this. to clarify that the frame in question is *this frame* that we're presently in the process of constructing—e.g., this.getContentPane().

```
    // The content pane container is now declared to be an
    // attribute.
    contentPane = this.getContentPane();
    this.setSize(250, 100);
    // Technique for centering a frame on the screen.
    // (Details omitted.)

    leftPanel = new JPanel();
    leftPanel.setLayout(new GridLayout(3, 1));
    leftPanel.add(new JLabel("Input 1:  "));
    leftPanel.add(new JLabel("Input 2:  "));
    leftPanel.add(new JLabel("Answer:  "));
    contentPane.add(leftPanel, BorderLayout.WEST);
```

```
        centerPanel = new JPanel();
        centerPanel.setLayout(new GridLayout(3, 1));
        input1TextField = new JTextField(10);
        input2TextField = new JTextField(10);
        answerLabel = new JLabel();
        centerPanel.add(input1TextField);
        centerPanel.add(input2TextField);
        centerPanel.add(answerLabel);
        contentPane.add(centerPanel, BorderLayout.CENTER);

        buttonPanel = new JPanel();
        buttonPanel.setLayout(new GridLayout(2, 1));
        plusButton = new JButton("+");
        minusButton = new JButton("-");
        buttonPanel.add(plusButton);
        buttonPanel.add(minusButton);
        contentPane.add(buttonPanel, BorderLayout.EAST);

        this.setVisible(true);

        // We still need to add behaviors!
    }
}
```

Next, we'll create the driver class, CalculatorDriver, in a separate file called CalculatorDriver.
java. For this example, the driver's main method is a trivially simple "one-liner"—it needs merely
to create an instance of the Calculator2 class by invoking the Calculator2 constructor. The
constructor (shown earlier) does all of the work of creating and displaying the GUI!

```
public class CalculatorDriver {
    // If this driver program were to require any "global" data (as public static
    // attributes of the CalculatorDriver class), it would be declared here:
    // ***
    // but this example doesn't require any.

    public static void main(String[] args) {
        // Instantiate the main window -- the Calculator class
        // does the rest of the work!
        new Calculator2();
    }

    // If this program were to require any "convenience" methods (as public
    // static methods of the CalculatorDriver class), these might be
    // declared here:
    // ***
    // but this example doesn't require any.
}
```

Repeating the driver class code again, this time without any in-line comments, we gain an appreciation of how concise it is:

```
public class CalculatorDriver {
  public static void main(String[] args) {
    new Calculator2();
  }
}
```

Note that we didn't have to assign the Calculator2 instance that we created in our main method to a reference variable because, as discussed earlier in the chapter, it's being managed by a separate Swing event handling thread; and, as it turns out, Swing components don't get garbage collected until we explicitly **dispose** of them, as we'll discuss later.

To invoke this new calculator application, we compile both classes, and then pass the name of the driver class to the JVM on the command line:

```
javac CalculatorDriver.java Calculator2.java
java CalculatorDriver
```

This combination of two classes produces the same calculator GUI as before.

We'll use this approach of separating the main window from the application driver when we develop the SRS GUI in Chapter 17.

Adding a "Test Scaffold" main() Method

When we're designing the "look" of a Swing container such as a JFrame, we often want a quick-and-dirty way to display it to see how it is taking shape. For this, we can use a technique that we refer to as creating a **"test scaffold"** main **method**. That is, rather than going to the trouble to program a separate driver class to host a main method if all we want to do is to pop up the frame so as to take a look at it, we'll simply *embed* a main method *within* the JFrame class itself! This main method will be a simple "one-liner" that does nothing more than display an unnamed instance of the JFrame class to which the main method belongs.

Here's a variation on our last calculator example that incorporates a test scaffold main method:

```
// Calculator2B.java
import java.awt.*;
import javax.swing.*;

public class Calculator2B extends JFrame {
    // Components are treated as attributes, so that they will be
    // visible to all of the methods of the class.
    // (Details omitted -- identical to Calculator2 version.)

    // Constructor.
    // The constructor is where we create and attach all of the Components
    // to the underlying JFrame.
    public Calculator2B() {
        // Details omitted -- identical to Calculator2 version.
```

```
        // Note that, because we're making it visible automatically
        // from within the constructor, we needn't make it visible
        // from within the main method.
        this.setVisible(true);
    }

    // A "test scaffold" main method.
    public static void main(String[] args) {
        // Instantiate the calculator!
        new Calculator2B();
    }
}
```

With this version of the calculator, we need only compile one class:

```
javac Calculator2B.java
```

and can execute *its* main method:

```
java Calculator2B
```

rather than bothering with a separate CalculatorDriver class. In fact, note that the main method code body is ***exactly the same code*** that was used in the body of the main method in our CalculatorDriver class from our previous example. Thus, we're going to abandon our use of a separate driver class for all remaining GUI examples in this chapter.

There's no harm in having multiple main methods throughout an application's classes; the only main method that will actually be executed when the application is fully assembled is the one belonging to the class that we name when we invoke the java command—java *MainClass*. We typically leave such test scaffolding main methods in place in our other various classes, reserved for future use, should the look of the component need to be changed and retested.

Other Interesting AWT/Swing Components to Explore

Despite the fact that we've covered a lot of ground so far in this chapter, we've barely scratched the surface with regard to Java GUI components! We've covered the basics of what you'll need to know from the AWT and Swing API perspectives as it pertains to the "look" of the SRS GUI in order to appreciate the SRS solution code later in this chapter. But, you'll almost certainly want to go on to learn about the myriad of other interesting predefined GUI components with Java; in particular, take time to explore some of these other interesting classes/interfaces:

- JMenuBar, JMenu, and JMenuItem

- JDesktopPane and JInternalFrame

- CardLayout

- JFileChooser

- JCheckBox

- JRadioButton and RadioButtonGroup

- JScrollPane

- Image

- JTabbedPane

- JComboBox

- JPopupMenu

- JToolTip

- (Advanced) GridBagLayout

- (Advanced) SpringLayout

- (Advanced) JTree

- (Advanced) JTable

- (Advanced) SwingUtilities

and of course, there are many more!

We'll now turn our attention away from controlling how a GUI looks to controlling how it ***behaves***.

Java Event Handling

Now that you have gotten a sense of how to build a GUI—that is, a "view" of the underlying model layer—you still need to learn how to recognize ***events***—i.e., a user's ***interactions*** with the GUI/view—and how to control the application's ***response*** to such events.

Events: Basic Concepts

GUI events are generated when the user interacts with a component on the GUI: for example, clicks a button, types in a field, selects an item from a list, and so on. As with virtually everything else in Java, ***events are objects!*** There are many different types of event, each represented by its own subclass of the java.awt.event.AWTEvent class; we'll learn about several of these shortly.

When we create a GUI component, it ***automatically*** has the ability to generate events whenever a user interacts with it—we need do nothing to get this phenomenon to occur. What we ***do*** need to explicitly deal with, however, is programming how the GUI should ***react*** to the (subset of) events that we are interested in. This technique is known as **event handling**.

In order to handle events, we need to do two things when programming a GUI:

- *Step 1*: We must design and instantiate a special type of object called a **listener** that is capable of "hearing" and responding to a particular type of event as generated by a particular component. In designing a listener, we must program its methods with whatever behavior that we want it to react with when it *hears* such an event.

  For example, to respond to clicks of a JButton, which generate ActionEvents, we'd create an ActionListener, a type of listener that is capable of listening for and responding to ActionEvents specifically.

- *Step 2*: We must **register** the listener object that we've created with the *specific* Component object(s) that we want that listener to listen to.

A single listener can be registered to listen to *one or more* component objects as illustrated conceptually in Figure 16-23. We thus may choose to have one Listener object assigned to listen to *all* of the JButtons on a given JFrame, as an example; alternatively, we may want a *different* Listener object to react to each individual component.

Figure 16-23. *The same Listener object can listen to multiple components, if desired.*

Whenever a user interacts with a component on a Java GUI, the component generates *numerous* events of various types. For example, if the cursor is moved over a JButton; the JButton is clicked; and the cursor is then moved off the button, the following events are generated:

- A "mouse entered" event is generated when the cursor first enters the boundaries of the JButton.

- Numerous "mouse moved" events are generated as the cursor moves from pixel to pixel within the boundaries of the JButton.

- A "mouse pressed" event is generated when the mouse button is depressed while the cursor is over the JButton.

- *Three* events—a "mouse released" event, a "mouse clicked" event, and an "action" event—are generated when the mouse button is released.

In addition:

- A "focus gained" event is generated for a JButton when the cursor moves inside the boundaries of the JButton.

- A "focus lost" event is generated when the cursor moves outside of the boundaries of the JButton.

This is depicted conceptually in Figure 16-24, where the letters A, B, C, and D represent four different types of events that are generated by interacting with a component—specifically, a JButton labeled Foo!. Note, however, that if no listeners have been created, then these events are not detected (just like a tree falling in the woods when there is nobody around to hear it!).

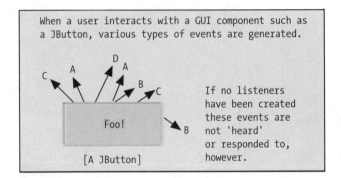

Figure 16-24. *A Component generates a variety of event types in response to a user's interactions.*

In the next figure (Figure 16-25), we conceptually represent creating three different types of listener, capable of "hearing" events of type A, B, and C, respectively. We purposely ***ignore*** event type D, as we are not interested in knowing when such events occur.

As mentioned before, simply creating the listeners is not sufficient; the listeners won't ***react*** to any events unless the listeners are specifically ***registered*** with one or more components that are capable of ***generating*** such events. In our example, the listeners would have to explicitly be registered to listen to the Foo! button in order to hear any of its events.

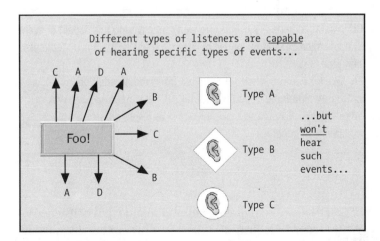

Figure 16-25. *We've created A, B, and C type listeners for the Foo! button.*

In the third and final figure (Figure 16-26), we have registered the A and B type listeners to listen to button Foo! for A and B type events, respectively. However, since we've neither *registered* the C type listener on this component nor *created* a D type listener, then any C and D type events that the Foo! button generates will be ignored.

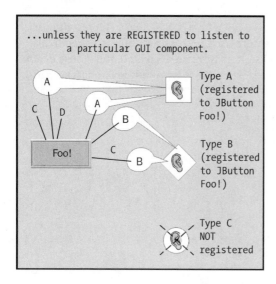

Figure 16-26. *Only A and B type events will be heard for our* JButton.

As a bonus, please compile and run the SimpleGuiDemo program included with the code download for Chapter 16. This program has been designed to print text messages to the command window for *every event* that occurs when interacting with a simple GUI—it's quite eye opening! (We'd recommend that you hold off on looking at the *source code* for this program, however, until you've finished reading Chapter 16.)

Note that it is also possible for *non*-GUI objects to generate events. We won't be covering this aspect of event handling in this book because the SRS application doesn't make use of such a capability, but it is nonetheless a very powerful feature of the Java language.

For further information, research Java's PropertyChangeListener interface. In addition, as a bonus, we've included four files in the downloadable code for Chapter 16—BeanExample.java, ListeningObject.java, ListenedToObject.java, and SomeObject.java—to illustrate how PropertyChangeListeners work for objects in general.

Basic Event Types

There are *many* different types of GUI events, and therefore *many* different types of listeners! Some event types were originally introduced with the AWT API, while others were subsequently added when the Swing API was introduced.

We are only going to be dealing with a few types of events and listeners in building the SRS; these are summarized in Table 16-2.

Table 16-2. *Event Types of Interest for the SRS*

Type of Events That We Care About in the SRS GUI	We'll Be Listening to These As Generated in the SRS GUI by Components of Type	Type of Listener Required for Listening to This Event Type	Defined in Which API/Package?
ActionEvent	JButton, JTextField	ActionListener	java.awt.event
WindowEvent	JFrame, JDialog	WindowListener	java.awt.event
ListSelectionEvent	JList	ListSelectionListener	javax.swing.event

Two important points to note:

- The components listed in the second column of Table 16-2 are capable of generating many more event types than those reflected in the table. For example, *all* of these components generate MouseEvents and FocusEvents, as well, but we aren't going to bother to listen for either of these event types.

- Other components beyond those listed in the second column of the table are capable of generating these *same* event types; for example, JLists also generate ActionEvents, but we aren't going to bother to listen for them when we build the SRS.

Creating and Registering Listeners

In our experience with teaching Java, we've found that one of the most overwhelming aspects of learning Java event handling for most students is understanding all of the *many* ways that Java provides for declaring and instantiating Listener objects.

- There are Listener *interfaces* that we may implement, and/or Adapter *classes* that we may extend;

- There are various ways in which we can structure such classes (as stand-alone classes, as named inner classes, as anonymous inner classes);

- There are various ways to organize listener objects once we instantiate them; and

- There are various ways to associate listeners to the components that they'll listen to.

To keep things manageable, we're going to focus on only one approach for creating Listeners in this book—arguably, the most elegant approach—which involves the use of **anonymous inner classes**.

By way of review, we learned in Chapter 13 that an *inner class* is a class that is wholly defined within the boundaries of another (*outer*) class:

```
public class OuterClass {
    // Declare the outer class's attributes -- details omitted.

    // Declare an inner class within the BODY of the OUTER class.
    class InnerClass {
```

```
        // Declare the inner class's attributes and methods ...
        // details omitted.
    } // end of inner class

    public void someMethodOfOuterClass() {
        // We may instantiate an object of type InnerClass within any of
        // OuterClass's methods. If we were to try to reference the symbol
        // "InnerClass" from anywhere else in our application, however, we'd get
        // a "symbol not found" compilation error.
        InnerClass x = new InnerClass();
        // etc.
    }


    // Declare other methods of the outer class ... details omitted.
}
```

We also learned in Chapter 13 that when a class containing an inner class definition is compiled, we wind up with *two* bytecode files, named *OuterClass*.class and *OuterClass$InnerClass*.class, respectively. Because the inner class in our preceding example has an explicit name—InnerClass—we actually refer to it as a *named* inner class.

What does this have to do with creating and registering listeners? We're going to use a special technique for creating listeners in terms of what are known as **anonymous inner classes**. An *anonymous* inner class is conceptually the same as a *named* inner class—that is, both are nonstatic classes that are wholly defined within the bounds of another class. However, the syntax for declaring an *anonymous* inner class differs from the syntax that we presented in Chapter 13—and again earlier in this discussion—for declaring a *named* inner class. And, when compiled, the bytecode files are given rather "unusual" names, as well. We'll see an example of both of these phenomena shortly.

Since our ultimate short-term goal is to add behavior to our calculator application, let's talk about the specific type of listener that the calculator will be making use of: namely, an ActionListener. To create an ActionListener object, we must implement an interface called ActionListener (recall our discussion of Java interfaces in Chapter 7). This interface specifies only one method, the actionPerformed method, with the following signature:

```
void actionPerformed(ActionEvent e)
```

The intent when implementing this method is to specify the logic of how we want this listener to react when it "hears" an ActionEvent.

We learned back in Chapter 7 that implementing an interface typically involves declaring a class X that states its intention to implement an interface Y via the following syntax:

```
public class X implements Y { ... }
```

Within the body of X, we must repeat all of the method headers called for by interface Y, and then program concrete bodies for all of these methods; otherwise, X must be declared to be an abstract class.

While the *concept* of implementing an interface is the same when it's an anonymous inner class that's doing the implementing, the *syntax* for doing so is a bit unusual. Specifically, we're going to take advantage of a special "shortcut" syntax that lets us create a new "flavor" of ActionListener, implementing the actionPerformed method without going through the full formalities of creating a separate *named* (inner) class. We'll evolve the syntax in stages:

- First, let's start with what appears on the surface to be an ordinary constructor invocation:

```
ActionListener l = new ActionListener();
```

- There's only one "catch": since ActionListener is an interface, and interfaces don't have constructors, we cannot instantiate an object of type ActionListener directly. What we ***really*** want to do is to instantiate an object of some class X that ***implements*** the ActionListener interface:

```
ActionListener l = new X();
```

where class X is in turn declared as follows:

```
class X implements ActionListener {
    // There is one method that we must implement to satisfy
    // the ActionListener interface:
    public void actionPerformed(ActionEvent e) {
        // Program the behind-the-scenes logic that we want to
        // execute when an ActionEvent is detected;
        // details omitted ...
    }
}
```

- Let's now suppose that we can insert the ***entire declaration*** of class X in between the) and the ; of the ActionListener l = ... declaration, as follows:

```
ActionListener l = new ActionListener()
class X implements ActionListener { ... };
```

Note the ending semicolon (;) after the closing brace on this complex statement. We don't normally see semicolons following curly braces; but, this is a special use of curly braces, and the semicolon is needed to terminate the ***single*** statement that begins with "ActionListener l = ...".

- Now, assume that class X has ***no name***—just a body:

```
ActionListener l = new ActionListener() { ... };
```

This, in essence, is how we declare an ***anonymous inner class*** that in turn implements a Listener interface—the ActionListener interface, to be specific.

In the case of an ActionListener, we have to implement the actionPerformed method by enclosing its code within the anonymous inner class body, as follows:

```
ActionListener l = new ActionListener() {
    public void actionPerformed(ActionEvent e) {
        // Program the behind-the-scenes logic that we want to
        // execute when an ActionEvent is detected;
        // details omitted ...
    }
}; // Don't forget the ending semicolon!!!
```

We've just created an inner class! It's known as an ***anonymous*** inner class because we haven't named the class, only the instance variable l that will hold onto the listener object that is returned from instantiating this inner class. We'll utilize this syntax—namely, instantiating a listener object based on an *in-line* declaration of an *anonymous* inner class—repeatedly throughout the remainder of the book.

When we compile an OuterClass that contains one or more *anonymous* inner classes, the compiler assigns names to the resultant inner class bytecode files using "one-up" numeric suffixes. That is, if the bytecode for the enclosing outer class were named OuterClass.class, then the names of any related anonymous inner class bytecode files would be OuterClass$1.class, OuterClass$2.class, and so forth.

Note that the actionPerformed method takes one argument, a reference to an object of type ActionEvent. Just as when Exceptions are thrown, and the JVM automatically passes an Exception object to an appropriate catch block, Events are automatically handed in to event handling methods by the JVM—we never invoke an event handling method explicitly in our own code.

Event objects such as ActionEvent have several methods that can prove extremely useful for discovering information about the *source* of the event; we'll see the use of one such method, getSource, when we program an upcoming version of the calculator program (Calculator4) later in this chapter.

Adding Behavior to Our Calculator

We're now ready to go back and add some event handling to the Calculator2 class/GUI from earlier in this chapter. In this next revision to the class, called Calculator3, we'll instantiate *two* anonymous inner class ActionListeners—one for the plus button and one for the minus button—and will register these listeners with their respective buttons. Here are the highlights of the approach that we are going to take:

- First, we'll use the new technique that we just learned for creating anonymous inner classes to create a listener object to respond to the plus button:

```
ActionListener l = new ActionListener() {
  public void actionPerformed(ActionEvent e) {
    // Get the value the user entered in the JText field and
    // convert it to a double ...
    double d1 = Double.parseDouble(input1TextField.getText());
    double d2 = Double.parseDouble(input2TextField.getText());
    // Add the two values and display them on the GUI.
    answerLabel.setText("" + (d1 + d2));
  }
};
```

  Note the unusual syntax of the following statement:

```
double d1 = Double.parseDouble(input1TextField.getText());
```

  We're using the method call input1TextField.getText() to retrieve the value that the user typed into the input1TextField as a String (because that's the only way that JTextFields know how to report their contents); then, we're passing that value to the static parseDouble utility method of the Double class to convert it to a simple double value.

- We'll then need to register this listener with the plus button:

```
plusButton.addActionListener(l);
```

- We'll then do the same two things for the minus button; note that we are "recycling" reference variable l here, in essence dropping our handle on the *first* listener object so as to grab onto the *second* listener object. This is perfectly acceptable, because as it turns out, the plusButton is still holding onto a reference to the *first* listener that it was passed via addActionListener method. As a result, the first listener won't be garbage collected.

```java
l = new ActionListener() {
    public void actionPerformed(ActionEvent e) {
        double d1 = Double.parseDouble(input1TextField.getText());
        double d2 = Double.parseDouble(input2TextField.getText());

        // Subtract the two values and display them on the GUI.
        answerLabel.setText("" + (d1 - d2));
    }
};

minusButton.addActionListener(l);
```

The code of these two listeners is virtually identical; we'll remedy this redundancy in our *next* iteration of the calculator (Calculator4).

- We must import a new package, java.awt.event, because the ActionListener class is defined therein. (Recall from an earlier discussion that importing java.awt.* doesn't also import java.awt.event classes.) Note that although we are using *Swing* components (JButtons), we are using *AWT* listeners to listen to them, because the Swing API didn't make any improvements to the ActionListener class.

The uninterrupted code of our latest version of the calculator example follows:

```java
// Calculator3.java

import java.awt.*;
import javax.swing.*;
import java.awt.event.*; // added for event handling

public class Calculator3 extends JFrame {
    // Components are treated as attributes, so that they will be
    // visible to all of the methods of the class.
    private Container contentPane;

    // Use descriptive names for components where possible; it makes
    // your job easier later on!
    private JPanel leftPanel;
    private JPanel centerPanel;
    private JPanel buttonPanel;
    private JTextField input1TextField;
```

```java
private JTextField input2TextField;
private JLabel answerLabel;
private JButton plusButton;
private JButton minusButton;

// Constructor.
public Calculator3() {
  // Invoke the generic JFrame constructor.
  super("Simple Calculator");

  // The content pane container is now declared to be an
  // attribute.
  contentPane = this.getContentPane();
  this.setSize(250, 100);

  // Technique for centering a frame on the screen.
  // (Details omitted.)

  leftPanel = new JPanel();
  leftPanel.setLayout(new GridLayout(3, 1));
  leftPanel.add(new JLabel("Input 1:  "));
  leftPanel.add(new JLabel("Input 2:  "));
  leftPanel.add(new JLabel("Answer:  "));
  contentPane.add(leftPanel, BorderLayout.WEST);

  centerPanel = new JPanel();
  centerPanel.setLayout(new GridLayout(3, 1));
  input1TextField = new JTextField(10);
  input2TextField = new JTextField(10);
  answerLabel = new JLabel();
  centerPanel.add(input1TextField);
  centerPanel.add(input2TextField);
  centerPanel.add(answerLabel);
  contentPane.add(centerPanel, BorderLayout.CENTER);

  buttonPanel = new JPanel();
  buttonPanel.setLayout(new GridLayout(2, 1));
  plusButton = new JButton("+");
  minusButton = new JButton("-");
  buttonPanel.add(plusButton);
  buttonPanel.add(minusButton);
  contentPane.add(buttonPanel, BorderLayout.EAST);

  // Add behaviors! Note the use of anonymous inner classes.

  // First, we create a listener object to respond to
  // the "plus" button ...
```

```
ActionListener l = new ActionListener() {
  public void actionPerformed(ActionEvent e) {
    double d1 = Double.parseDouble(input1TextField.getText());
    double d2 = Double.parseDouble(input2TextField.getText());

    // Add the two values and display the answer on the GUI.
    answerLabel.setText("" + (d1 + d2));
  }
};

// ... and then we register this listener with the appropriate
// component.
plusButton.addActionListener(l);

// We do the same for the minus button.
l = new ActionListener() {
  public void actionPerformed(ActionEvent e) {
    double d1 = Double.parseDouble(input1TextField.getText());
    double d2 = Double.parseDouble(input2TextField.getText());
    // Subtract the two values and display the answer on the GUI.
    answerLabel.setText("" + (d1 - d2));
  }
};

// Register this listener with the appropriate
// component.
minusButton.addActionListener(l);

// We set the frame to be visible AFTER registering the listeners.
this.setVisible(true);
}
```

To avoid an intermittent Java "quirk" that plagued early versions of the language, the setVisible(true); method call should ideally come **last** in the constructor, **after** you've attached your various listeners. Under some circumstances, if the setVisible(true); method call is made **before** listeners are created and registered, the listeners don't always work properly.

We also need to make a minor modification to the test scaffold main method within Calculator3.java, to reference Calculator3 rather than Calculator2:

```
public static void main(String[] args) {
  new Calculator3();
}
}
```

When Calculator3.java is compiled, each anonymous inner class produces its own separate bytecode file, and so a total of three .class files are produced:

- Calculator3.class

- Calculator3$1.class (corresponding to the plusButton listener)

- Calculator3$2.class (corresponding to the minusButton listener)

When this version of the program is run:

java Calculator3

we now find that we have the ability to use the calculator as originally intended: if we type in two legitimate numbers in the Input 1: and Input 2: fields and click the plus (+) button, we do indeed see the answer displayed in the Answer: field at the bottom of the JFrame window, as illustrated in Figure 16-27.

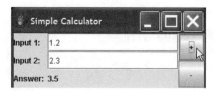

Figure 16-27. *Calculator layout*

We haven't done any exception handling, however, which means that if we type a nonnumeric input value such as "ABC" into either field, or leave either field blank, then the Double.parseDouble method will cause a NumberFormatException to be thrown when either button is clicked. This is not "user friendly" behavior, and so we've included an exercise at the end of this chapter to give you a chance to remedy this shortcoming of the calculator.

Combining Listeners: Utilizing the ActionEvent

The two listeners that we created for Calculator3 were almost identical, and so with a slight modification to our design, we can use a *single* listener to listen to *both* the plus and minus buttons, eliminating this redundancy. We'll do so in this next version of the calculator program, Calculator4.java. Since most of the code for Calculator4 is the same as the previous version, we'll only present and discuss significant changes:

```
// Calculator4.java
import java.awt.*;
import javax.swing.*;
import java.awt.event.*;
```

```
public class Calculator4 extends JFrame {
  // Components are treated as attributes, so that they will be
  // visible to all of the methods of the class.
  // (Details omitted -- identical to Calculator3.)

  // Constructor.
  public Calculator4() {
    // Invoke the generic JFrame constructor.
    super("Simple Calculator");

    // (Details omitted -- identical to Calculator 3.)

    // Add behaviors -- this time we use the SAME
    // listener object to listen to BOTH buttons.
    ActionListener l = new ActionListener() {
      public void actionPerformed(ActionEvent e) {
        double d1 = Double.parseDouble(input1TextField.getText());
        double d2 = Double.parseDouble(input2TextField.getText());
```

Up until now, we've ignored the lone argument to the actionPerformed method—an ActionEvent object reference that we've named e—which we're now going to put to use.

As mentioned earlier, Event objects (such as ActionEvents) are created automatically by the JVM whenever an interaction occurs with a GUI component. The purpose of the Event object is to carry with it some useful information about the circumstances of the event—think of it as a sort of "eyewitness!" Using various methods provided by the Event class, we can gain additional insight into the circumstances of the event.

The getSource method, when invoked on an ActionEvent object, returns a reference to the GUI component that served as the *originator* of the event. By retrieving the source of the event and testing its identity, we can determine where the event originated, and act accordingly: if the source was the plusButton, we *add* the two input values that we've retrieved; otherwise, we *subtract* one from the other.

```
        if (e.getSource() == plusButton) {
            // Add the values.
            answerLabel.setText("" + (d1 + d2));
        }
        else {
            // Subtract the values.
            answerLabel.setText("" + (d1 - d2));
        }
      }
    };
```

We **could** explicitly test for the minus button, as well:

```
    if (e.getSource() == plusButton) {
      // Add the values.
      answerLabel.setText("" + (d1 + d2));
    }
    else if (e.getSource() == minusButton) {
        answerLabel.setText("" + (d1 - d2));
    }
  }
};
```

but, since there are only two buttons on the GUI, and since we are only registering this listener on those two buttons (which we'll do in a moment), then if the origin of the event wasn't the plusButton, it **had** to have been the minusButton.

Finally, we register the **same** listener object l with **both** buttons:

```
plusButton.addActionListener(l);
minusButton.addActionListener(l);

    this.setVisible(true);
}
```

We also need to make a minor modification to the main method within Calculator4.java, to reference Calculator4 rather than Calculator3:

```
public static void main(String[] args) {
    new Calculator4();
  }
}
```

From the user's perspective, this version of the calculator behaves **exactly** as the previous version did.

Closing a Window, Revisited

As shown in Figure 16-28, when we click the close button (⊠) located in the upper-right corner of the Calculator4 frame, the window does indeed **close**, but our program continues to run!

Our program is not doing anything useful, but nonetheless the JVM is waiting for additional user input via the GUI. The problem is that **there is no GUI**, because we've closed it down! As we discussed earlier in the chapter, merely closing a window does not terminate the GUI event processing thread. So, the command line remains tied up, and program resources remain allocated. We learned that we could regain control of the command line if this happens by pressing the Ctrl and C keys simultaneously in the command-line window to kill the program.

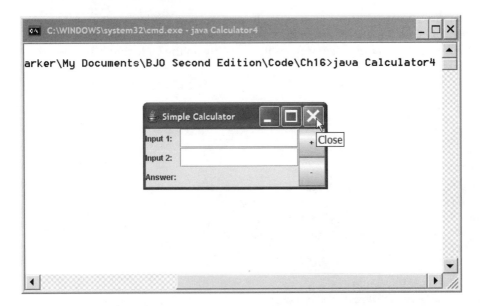

Figure 16-28. *Closing the window doesn't necessarily terminate the application.*

We'd like to be able to respond ***programmatically*** to user-initiated requests to terminate a GUI-oriented application, such as when a user

- Clicks the main application window's close (⊠) button, located in the upper-right corner of the window

- Clicks some other button/menu option that we've provided for this purpose, for example, a JButton explicitly labeled Exit

In order to do this, we'll once again employ event handling techniques: specifically, we'll

- Create a new type of listener called a **window listener**.

- Register the WindowListener as a listener to the JFrame as a whole.

- Program the windowClosing method of the listener so that it shuts down our program via the command

  System.exit(0);

  where exit(int status) is a static method of the System class used to explicitly terminate the currently running JVM. The status argument serves as a status code to the operating system; by convention, a status code of 0 traditionally signals error-free termination.

We haven't previously needed to call System.exit(0); because, up until now, all of our programs were single-threaded, and the **main thread *automatically*** terminates when the main method's terminating brace is reached during normal execution.

We'll illustrate what it takes to programmatically respond to a window closing event with yet another version of our calculator program; again, because so much of this code is identical with the previous version of our calculator, we'll focus only on the code that is relevant to automating the window closing operation.

```java
// Calculator5.java

import java.awt.*;
import javax.swing.*;
import java.awt.event.*;

public class Calculator5 extends JFrame {
  // Components are treated as attributes, so that they will be
  // visible to all of the methods of the class.
  // (Details omitted -- identical to Calculator3.)

  // Constructor.
  public Calculator5() {
    // Invoke the generic JFrame constructor.
    super("Simple Calculator");

    // (Details omitted -- identical to Calculator 3.)

    // Add behaviors.
    // (Details omitted -- identical to Calculator 3.)
    plusButton.addActionListener(l);
    minusButton.addActionListener(l);
```

We want to use a WindowListener to terminate the application when the user closes the window; we'll create the listener as an instance of an anonymous inner class:

```java
WindowListener w = new WindowListener() {
    public void windowClosing(WindowEvent e) {
        // Note the need to preface "this." with
        // the name of the outer class.
        Calculator5.this.dispose();  // See notes after the code
        System.exit(0);
    }
}
```

The WindowListener interface calls for **seven** methods to be programmed; we don't want to do anything in particular when any of the other six situations arise, and yet we must program all seven methods in order for our code to compile, so we "stub out" the other six:

```java
        public void windowOpened(WindowEvent e) { }
        public void windowClosed(WindowEvent e) { }
        public void windowIconified(WindowEvent e) { }
        public void windowDeiconified(WindowEvent e) { }
        public void windowActivated(WindowEvent e) { }
        public void windowDeactivated(WindowEvent e) { }
    };
```

Finally, we register listener w with the frame as a whole, since it will be the JFrame object that generates the window closing event.

```
this.addWindowListener(w);

this.setVisible(true);
}

// etc.
}
```

(Remember that the main method in Calculator5.java must be revised to refer to Calculator5 rather than Calculator4.)

In the windowClosing method of our WindowListener, the dispose method of the java.awt. Window class was used to explicitly request that the Swing event handling thread release its handle on our Component, so that it may be garbage collected.

We followed the call to dispose with a call to System.exit(0), which terminates the application overall; so, strictly speaking, the call to dispose is unnecessary in this particular situation.

Note the syntax *OuterClassName*.this.*methodCall*—for example, Calculator5.this.dispose();— to refer to the instance of the JFrame that we wish to dispose of in the windowClosing method. Had we instead tried to request disposal of the frame as simply this.dispose():

```
public void windowClosing(WindowEvent e) {
  this.dispose();
  System.exit(0);
}
```

then the compiler would have complained with the following rather cryptic error message:

```
Method dispose() not found in local class Calculator5. 2.
```

because the keyword this in this case refers to the instance of the enclosing ***anonymous inner class***—referred to as Calculator5. 2 by the compiler in its error message—rather than to the instance of the ***outer*** class, Calculator5. However, since it's the instance of the Calculator5 (JFrame) object that we wish to dispose of, we must assist the compiler with sorting out what the ***scope*** of this really is.

Adapter Classes vs. Listener Interfaces

With Calculator5, we stubbed out six of the seven methods called for by the WindowListener interface because, while we were uninterested in them, we nonetheless needed to implement them all in order for our Calculator5 class as a whole to compile (recall that implementing an interface is an "all or nothing" proposition, as we discussed in Chapter 7). That code is repeated here for your convenience:

```
WindowListener w = new WindowListener() {
    public void windowClosing(WindowEvent e) {
        Calculator5.this.dispose();
        System.exit(0);
    }

    // We don't care about the other six methods of
    // the WindowListener, and so "stub" them out:
    public void windowOpened(WindowEvent e) { }
    public void windowClosed(WindowEvent e) { }
    public void windowIconified(WindowEvent e) { }
    public void windowDeiconified(WindowEvent e) { }
    public void windowActivated(WindowEvent e) { }
    public void windowDeactivated(WindowEvent e) { }
};
```

Recall from our discussion of anonymous inner class syntax a bit earlier in this chapter that the syntax

```
WindowListener w = new WindowListener() { ... } ;
```

is effectively a shorthand way of expressing the notion

```
WindowListener w =
    new WindowListener() class anonymous implements WindowListener { ... } ;
```

where the expression underlined in the preceding is implied, and hence omitted.

It's often the case that we'll only want to substantively implement one out of x methods that may be called for by a particular listener interface. In addition to the windowClosing example of the WindowListener interface, let's consider another example, this time involving the MouseListener interface.

MouseListener calls for five methods to be implemented: mouseClicked, mouseEntered, mouseExited, mousePressed, and mouseReleased. Often, we'll only care about one such event—perhaps mouseClicked—and will wind up stubbing out the rest:

```
MouseListener w = new MouseListener() {
    public void mouseClicked (MouseEvent e) {
            // We are interested in this circumstance, and so
            // we implement this method body in a meaningful way.
            // (Details omitted ...)
        }
    }

    // Then, we stub out the rest.

    public void mouseEntered(MouseEvent e) { }
    public void mouseExited(MouseEvent e) { }
    public void mousePressed(MouseEvent e) { }
    public void mouseReleased(MouseEvent e) { }
};
```

Java comes to our aid in such cases by introducing the notion of so-called **adapter classes**. That is, for every ***multiple***-method *Xxx*Listener ***interface***, there's a corresponding predefined ***class*** named *Xxx*Adapter. These adapter classes implement the corresponding *Xxx*Listener interface, providing stubbed out versions of ***all*** required methods: e.g., the source code for the predefined WindowAdapter class might look as follows:

```
public class WindowAdapter implements WindowListener {
    // All SEVEN required methods are stubbed out!
    public void windowClosing(WindowEvent e) { }
    public void windowOpened(WindowEvent e) { }
    public void windowClosed(WindowEvent e) { }
    public void windowIconified(WindowEvent e) { }
    public void windowDeiconified(WindowEvent e) { }
    public void windowActivated(WindowEvent e) { }
    public void windowDeactivated(WindowEvent e) { }
}
```

How does this help us out? Rather than having to ***implement*** the WindowListener ***interface*** via our anonymous inner class, we can instead ***extend*** the WindowAdapter ***class***, ***overriding*** the one method we care about and ***inheriting*** the stubbed out versions of all the rest. In terms of our anonymous inner class syntax, we'd therefore replace the rather cumbersome version of code here:

```
WindowListener w = new WindowListener() {
    public void windowClosing(WindowEvent e) {
        Calculator5.this.dispose();
        System.exit(0);
    }

    // We don't care about the other six methods of
    // the WindowListener, and so "stub" them out:
    public void windowOpened(WindowEvent e) { }
    public void windowClosed(WindowEvent e) { }
    public void windowIconified(WindowEvent e) { }
    public void windowDeiconified(WindowEvent e) { }
    public void windowActivated(WindowEvent e) { }
    public void windowDeactivated(WindowEvent e) { }
};
```

with the more streamlined version here:

```
// Note our switch to "WindowAdapter" in this next line.
WindowListener w = new WindowAdapter() {
    public void windowClosing(WindowEvent e) {
        Calculator6.this.dispose();
        System.exit(0);
    }
};
```

See file Calculator6.java, one of the Chapter 16 source code files downloadable from the Apress web site, for a complete example that utilizes this approach.

There's no predefined Action**Adapter** class because there's only one method to be coded for the Action**Listener** interface, namely, actionPerformed; thus, even if there **were** an ActionAdapter class, the code that we'd write to use it:

```
// This won't compile, because there is no ActionAdapter class.
ActionListener l = new ActionAdapter() {
    public void actionPerformed(ActionEvent e) { ... }
};
```

wouldn't be any more streamlined than what we actually **do** have to write:

```
// Implementing the ActionListener interface.
ActionListener l = new ActionListener() {
    public void actionPerformed(ActionEvent e) { ... }
};
```

In retrospect, naming these default listener implementations *Xxx***Adapter** was perhaps not as intuitive a convention as Sun Microsystems could have chosen; we'd have personally preferred that these be named Default*Xxx*Listener instead, to better describe their function. Nonetheless, once you understand the **_purpose_** that these adapter classes are intended to serve, you're good to go!

Selecting an Item from a JList

Similar to the other components that we have seen, we can register a listener—a ListSelectionListener, to be specific—with a JList component, to automatically react whenever a selection is made by clicking an item in the JList.

Let's look at a sample program called JListDemo3 to illustrate the use of a ListSelectionListener. (We're once again going to display a list of student names based on an array of Student objects, and so we'll reuse the simplified version of class Student that we introduced earlier in this chapter.)

The ListSelectionListener and ListSelectionEvent classes were newly added with the Swing API—they didn't exist in the AWT—and so we must import the javax.swing.event package in order for the compiler to recognize these types.

```
// JListDemo3.java

import java.util.*;
import java.awt.*;
import javax.swing.*;
import javax.swing.event.*;  // added for ListSelectionListener/Event
```

For JListDemo3 (and subsequent examples), we've adopted the recommended architecture of having the class in question extend JFrame:

```
public class JListDemo3 extends JFrame {
    super("Sample JList");

    Container contentPane = this.getContentPane();
    Student[] v = new Student[3];
    v[0] = new Student("123456789", "Joe Blow");
    v[1] = new Student("987654321", "Fred Schnurd"));
    v[2] = new Student("000000000", "Englebert Humperdink");
```

Note that since myList is a local variable declared within the constructor, we must declare it to be a final variable; otherwise, the compiler will complain when we try to access myList from the inner class that we create as a ListSelectionListener later on.

```
final JList myList = new JList(v);
contentPane.add(myList);
```

Recall from our discussion in Chapter 7 that a final variable is a variable that may only be assigned a value one time in an application. The need to use the final keyword in this example has to do with the fact that a variable defined **locally** to a method of an **outer** class A is not available to the methods of an **inner** class B unless it is declared to be a final variable. (In a nutshell, this is a scoping problem, the details of which are beyond the scope of this book to address.)

In a subsequent version of JListDemo, we'll declare myList at the **class scope level** (i.e., as an attribute), in which case this complication will go away. However, we've purposely left this issue as-is for JListDemo3 so that if you ever encounter this phenomenon, you'll have been previous exposed to it.

Later on, when we are accessing components as attributes of outer classes from within inner class methods, as we do with the SRS for example, the problem will go away.

Next, we instantiate a ListSelectionListener object to immediately react whenever an item is selected in the JList, and program its valueChanged method:

```
ListSelectionListener lsl = new ListSelectionListener() {
    public void valueChanged(ListSelectionEvent e) {
        // Whenever an item is selected (clicked!) in this list,
        // we'll display it in the command window.
```

We invoke the getSelectedValue method on myList to obtain a handle on the Object that the selected list entry represents. A JList is zero-based, meaning that it indexes the items in the list starting with 0:

- If we click the first entry in the list, we obtain a handle on the first (0th) object in the array that was used to populate the JList.

- If we click the second entry in the list, we obtain a handle on the second object from the original array, and so forth.

Because getSelectedValue returns a generic Object reference, we cast the reference as a Student reference; we then print the value of s, which as we learned in Chapter 13 triggers invocation of the Student's (overridden) toString method:

```
    Student s = (Student) myList.getSelectedValue();
    System.out.println("Selected " + s);
  }
};
```

(Having to cast a reference that is returned from a Swing component is typical; many built-in Java classes deal in generic Objects for versatility.) In this example, we simply print out a message to the command-line window to verify that we have indeed retrieved the desired Student.

As always, we must register the listener with the object being listened to (in this case, the JList):

```
myList.addListSelectionListener(lsl);
```

Here is the program in its entirety:

```
import java.awt.*;
import javax.swing.*;
import javax.swing.event.*;

public class JListDemo3 extends JFrame {
    public JListDemo3() {
        super("Sample JList");
        Container contentPane = this.getContentPane();

        // Create a Collection of students.
        Student[] v = new Student[3];
        v[0] = new Student("123456789", "Joe Blow");
        v[1] = new Student("987654321", "Fred Schnurd");
        v[2] = new Student("000000000", "Englebert Humperdink");

        // Create a list based on this collection.  (We must declare
        // myList to be a final variable; otherwise, the compiler
        // will complain when we try to access it from the inner
        // class that we create as a listener below.)
        final JList myList = new JList(v);
        contentPane.add(myList);

        // Add a listener to note when an item has been selected.
        ListSelectionListener lsl = new ListSelectionListener() {
            public void valueChanged(ListSelectionEvent e) {
                // When an item is selected (clicked!) in this
                // list, display it at the command line.
                Student s = (Student) myList.getSelectedValue();
                System.out.println("Selected " + s);
            }
        };
```

```
        myList.addListSelectionListener(lsl);

        this.setSize(300, 100);
        this.setVisible(true);
    }

    // Test scaffold main method.
    public static void main(String[] args) {
        new JListDemo3();
    }
}
```

An interesting observation: when we click an entry in the list, the itemStateChanged method fires ***twice***—once when the mouse button is depressed, and once again when it is released—causing our printed message to appear twice at the command line:

```
Selected Joe Blow
Selected Joe Blow
```

If we wish to remedy this, we can take advantage of another method of JList—boolean getValueIsAdjusting()—as shown in the following code snippet:

```
// Excerpt from program JListDemo3B.java - available as part of
// the Apress code download.

ListSelectionListener lsl = new ListSelectionListener() {
    public void valueChanged(ListSelectionEvent e) {
        // When an item is selected (clicked!) in this
        // list, display it at the command line.

        // To eliminate the "double display" of this
        // message, perform an initial test.
        if (!myList.getValueIsAdjusting()) {
            Student s = (Student) myList.getSelectedValue();
            System.out.println("Selected " + s);
        }
    }
};
```

Let's now make an adjustment to the demo program so that we no longer have to worry about declaring myList as a final variable. Instead of declaring the JList as a local variable within the constructor, we'll promote it to be an ***attribute*** of the class instead, as mentioned in an earlier note.

```
// Excerpt ...
public class JListDemo3C extends JFrame {
    // By placing the declaration of the JList here, as an attribute
    // of the class as a whole, we avoid problems with accessing it
    // from within the inner ListSelectionListener class below.
    private JList myList;
```

The rest of the example is essentially the same as before, and is presented here in its entirety:

```java
import java.awt.*;
import javax.swing.*;
import javax.swing.event.*;

public class JListDemo3C extends JFrame {
    // By placing the declaration of the JList here, as an attribute
    // of the class as a whole, we avoid problems with accessing it
    // from within the inner ListSelectionListener class below.
    private JList myList;

    public JListDemo3C() {
        super("Sample JList");
        Container contentPane = this.getContentPane();

        // Create a Collection of students.
        Student[] v = new Student[3];
        v[0] = new Student("123456789", "Joe Blow");
        v[1] = new Student("987654321", "Fred Schnurd");
        v[2] = new Student("000000000", "Englebert Humperdink");

        // Create a list based on this collection.  (By having
        // made myList an attribute of the JListDemo3C.
        // class as a whole, we avoid messing around with "final"
        // variable declarations.)
        myList = new JList(v);
        contentPane.add(myList);

        // Add a listener to note when an item has been selected.
        ListSelectionListener lsl = new ListSelectionListener() {
            public void valueChanged(ListSelectionEvent e) {
                // When an item is selected (clicked!) in this
                // list, display it at the command line.

                // To eliminate the "double display"
                // of this message, perform an initial
                // test.
                if (!myList.getValueIsAdjusting()) {
                    Student s = (Student) myList.getSelectedValue();
                    System.out.println("Selected " + s);
                }
            }
        };

        myList.addListSelectionListener(lsl);
```

```
        this.setSize(300, 100);
        this.setVisible(true);
    }

    // Test scaffold.
    public static void main(String[] args) {
        new JListDemo3C();
    }
}
```

We don't necessarily have to connect a listener directly to a JList in order to process a selection from the list. If we don't want to react immediately when an item is clicked, we can forgo the use of a ListSelectionListener, and can instead have a separate JButton that, when clicked, retrieves the selected value from the JList and manipulates it in some fashion. The next example program (a variation of the previous program) demonstrates this alternative approach.

- The program starts out in the same way that the previous program begins: we still create and populate an array of Students to be used as the basis for creating the JList, etc.

- In this example, we want to add two components to the JFrame—a JList and a JButton— and so we attach the JList to the CENTER region of the JFrame's default BorderLayout:

```
myList = new JList(v);
contentPane.add(myList, BorderLayout.CENTER);
```

  and we then create a JButton labeled Select that will pull the selected entry from the JList when the button is clicked, and add it to the SOUTH region of the BorderLayout:

```
JButton selectButton = new JButton("Select");
contentPane.add(selectButton, BorderLayout.SOUTH);
```

- Now, instead of creating and adding a ListSelectionListener to the JList as we did in the previous example program, we instead create and add an ActionListener to the JButton. Note that the internal logic of the actionPerformed method is identical to the internal logic of the valueChanged method in our previous example: we want the exact same behavior to result; we just want it to be **_triggered_** in a different way.

```
// Add a listener to the button.
ActionListener listener = new ActionListener() {
    public void actionPerformed(ActionEvent e) {
        Student s = (Student) myList.getSelectedValue();
        System.out.println("Selected " + s);
    }
};

selectButton.addActionListener(listener);
```

Here is the complete, uninterrupted code:

```
import java.awt.*;
import javax.swing.*;
import java.awt.event.*;
```

```java
public class JListDemo4 extends JFrame {
    private JList myList;

    public JListDemo4() {
        super("Sample JList");
        Container contentPane = this.getContentPane();

        // Create a Collection of students.
        Student[] v = new Student[3];
        v[0] = new Student("123456789", "Joe Blow");
        v[1] = new Student("987654321", "Fred Schnurd");
        v[2] = new Student("000000000", "Englebert Humperdink");

        // Create a list based on this collection.
        myList = new JList(v);
        contentPane.add(myList, BorderLayout.CENTER);

        // Create a button that will pull the selected entry
        // from the list when the button is clicked.
        JButton selectButton = new JButton("Select");
        contentPane.add(selectButton, BorderLayout.SOUTH);

        // Add a listener to the button.
        ActionListener listener = new ActionListener() {
            public void actionPerformed(ActionEvent e) {
                Student s = (Student) myList.getSelectedValue();
                System.out.println("Selected " + s);
            }
        };

        selectButton.addActionListener(listener);

        this.setSize(300, 130);
        this.setVisible(true);
    }

    public static void main(String[] args) {
        new JListDemo4();
    }
}
```

When we compile and run this version of the program, selecting an entry in the list in and of itself doesn't trigger any action on the part of the GUI. A ListSelectionEvent is indeed still being generated at that moment, as it was in our previous example; but, since we haven't programmed a listener to *listen* for it this time around, it is simply ignored. In fact, the user can change his or her mind numerous times, clicking alternative entries in the JList, but no action is taken in response to each individual click. Clicking the Select button, on the other hand, generates an ActionEvent, which we *are* listening for, as shown in Figure 16-29.

   Click!

Figure 16-29. *With* `JListDemo4`, *we've introduced a Select button.*

This triggers the `actionPerformed` method for that button, which "grabs" the user's most recent selection from the `JList` ("Joe Blow", in this case), which in turn results in the following output being displayed in the command-line window:

```
Selected Joe Blow
```

If we happen to click the button without first selecting an entry in the list, we'll get the following output instead:

```
Selected null
```

We'll take advantage of both of these types of `JList` manipulation—direct manipulation via `ListSelectionListeners` and indirect manipulation via `JButtons`—in the SRS application.

More Container Types

There are more types of **containers** or special types of components that are used to organize, manage, and present other components such as dialog boxes and option panes.

JDialog

Dialog boxes are pop-up windows that are typically used to force the user to acknowledge an important message, make a decision, or provide some input. Although we can certainly create windows for this purpose by extending the `JFrame` class, it is often preferable to extend the Swing `JDialog` class instead, because `JDialog` enables us to create pop-up windows that are **modal**. A modal window is one that the user cannot ignore: once a modal dialog box has been displayed, a user cannot interact with any other window belonging to that same Java application until he or she responds to and dismisses the dialog box. This behavior is known as a dialog box **holding the focus of** an application.

There are a number of different `JDialog` constructor signatures; the one that we'll be using with the SRS is

```
JDialog(Frame owner, String title, boolean modal)
```

where

- owner is a reference to the AWT Frame or (preferably) Swing JFrame from which the JDialog was launched.

- title is whatever text we wish to have appear in the title bar of the JDialog.

- modal can be set to true if we want the JDialog to be modal, and false otherwise.

When we create a JDialog, we observe the same general architecture that we used when creating an application's main frame (such as Calculator4). That is, we

- Declare a class that extends JDialog (rather than JFrame, as we did for Calculator4).

- Declare and add whatever components we want the JDialog to display as attributes of the class, optionally changing the JDialog's layout manager from the default BorderLayout if desired.

- Create and register listeners on selected components, just as we would in creating a frame.

Here's a simple example of a class that can be used to produce the following simplistic JDialog:

```
// MyDialog.java

import java.awt.*;
import javax.swing.*;
import java.awt.event.*;
```

We declare all components to be attached to the dialog box (only one button, in this case) as attributes of the class, so that they are in scope throughout all of the methods we write (including methods of inner classes):

```
public class MyDialog extends JDialog {
  // Components as attributes.

  JButton okButton;
```

Note that the constructor for a ***custom*** dialog box should take at least one argument, either of type Frame or (preferably) JFrame, which will be a reference to the (J)Frame from which an instance of this custom dialog box is being launched. We need to provide the dialog box with such a reference because the constructor for the parent JDialog class—which is invoked as the first line of code from within this constructor—expects this reference to be passed in as an argument.

Note that we're also making this dialog box modal.

```
// Constructor.

// We need to pass in a reference to the "parent" frame from
// which this dialog box was launched, because we will need to
// hand it, in turn, to the generic JDialog constructor
// (see the first line of code inside of the constructor).
public MyDialog(JFrame parent) {
    // Let's make this dialog box modal by invoking the generic
    // JDialog constructor with a value of "true" for the
    // final argument. We're also passing through the
    // reference to our parent frame, as the first argument.
    super(parent, "Modal Dialog", true);

    okButton = new JButton("OK");
```

We're using the "padding" technique introduced earlier for GridLayouts to get this single button to appear in the middle of the dialog box:

```
    this.getContentPane().setLayout(new GridLayout(3, 1));
    this.getContentPane().add(new Label(""));
    this.getContentPane().add(okButton);
    this.getContentPane().add(new Label(""));

    this.setSize(200, 100);
```

We're attaching an ActionListener to the okButton, as we've done before for other JButtons. We're using an *even more compact* syntax for declaring and attaching an instance of an anonymous inner class this time, however: rather than using the (now familiar) syntax

```
ActionListener l = new ActionListener() {
    public void actionPerformed(ActionEvent e) { ... }
};

okButton.addActionListener(l);
```

we've collapsed the declaration of listener l and the attachment of l to button okButton into a *single* (complex!) line of code, using the following general syntax:

```
    okButton.addActionListener(DECLARE and INSTANTIATE the listener in here);
```

That is, not only are we using an anonymous inner class, we're also not even bothering to *name* the listener *object*! Here's the full-blown code for adding the ActionListener in this fashion:

```
    okButton.addActionListener(new ActionListener() {
      public void actionPerformed(ActionEvent e) {
        // Close the dialog box.
        System.out.println("OK clicked");
        MyDialog.this.setVisible(false);
        MyDialog.this.dispose();
```

```
      // Note that we won't call System.exit(0),
      // for reasons that we'll discuss in a moment.
    }
  }); // Note UNUSUAL }); syntax!!!
```

The actionPerformed method for our dialog box is doing a few "unusual" things:

- It's closing the dialog box as a whole by sending the message setVisible(false) to the dialog box instance (referred to as MyDialog.this from within the inner class's method).

- When we previously created a WindowListener for use with our Calculator5 program, we used its windowClosing method to dispose of the JFrame, followed by a call to System.exit(0) in order to terminate our application. Typically, we don't want to bring our application to a screeching halt when we close a JDialog, however! So, we simply call the dispose method on the dialog box instance to get the JVM to "recycle" the resources (including memory) that have been allocated to the dialog box.

If we also want to be able to close the dialog box via the close button at the upper-right corner of the dialog box, we have to provide a WindowListener, as well:

```
WindowListener w = new WindowAdapter() {
  public void windowClosing(WindowEvent e) {
    // Note the need to preface "this." with
    // the name of the outer class.
    MyDialog.this.setVisible(false);
    MyDialog.this.dispose();

    // Note that we don't call System.exit(0),
    // because if we did, then the whole application
    // will come to a screeching halt when the
    // dialog box is closed.
    // System.exit(0);
  }
};

this.addWindowListener(w);

// Always make the setVisible call the LAST call in
// the constructor. For some strange reason, if you
// don't, then the listeners don't always work
// properly.

this.setVisible(true);
  }
}
```

Here's the "uninterrupted" code in its entirety:

```java
// MyDialog.java

import java.awt.*;
import javax.swing.*;
import java.awt.event.*;

public class MyDialog extends JDialog {
  // Components as attributes.
  JButton okButton;

  // Constructor.
  public MyDialog(JFrame parent) {
    // Let's make this dialog box modal by invoking the generic
    // JDialog constructor with a value of "true" for the
    // final argument. We're also passing through the
    // reference to our parent frame, as the first argument.
    super(parent, "Modal Dialog", true);

    okButton = new JButton("OK");

    this.getContentPane().setLayout(new GridLayout(3, 1));
    this.getContentPane().add(new Label(""));
    this.getContentPane().add(okButton);
    this.getContentPane().add(new Label(""));
    this.setSize(200, 100);

    // Attach an ActionListener to the button, so that
    // when it is clicked, the dialog box will close.
    okButton.addActionListener(new ActionListener() {
      public void actionPerformed(ActionEvent e) {
        // Close the dialog box.
        MyDialog.this.setVisible(false);
        MyDialog.this.dispose();
      }
    });

    // If we also want to be able to close the dialog box via
    // the "close" button at the upper-right corner
    // of the dialog box, we have to provide a WindowListener,
    // as well.
    WindowListener w = new WindowAdapter() {
      public void windowClosing(WindowEvent e) {
        MyDialog.this.setVisible(false);
        MyDialog.this.dispose();
      }
    };
```

```
    this.addWindowListener(w);

    // Always make the setVisible call the last call in
    // the constructor. For some strange reason, if you
    // don't, then the listeners don't always work
    // properly.
    this.setVisible(true);
  }
}
```

Now, we need some way to display this dialog box; here's a trivially simple driver program that can be used to create and display an instance of MyDialog:

```
// DialogDriver.java

import javax.swing.*;

public class DialogDriver {
  public static void main(String[] args) {
    // Create a frame to serve as the parent for the dialog box.
    JFrame theFrame = new JFrame("Daddy Frame");
    theFrame.setSize(200, 200);
    theFrame.setVisible(true);

    // Now, create and display our custom dialog box!
    // Because the dialog box's constructor contains the
    // logic to make the dialog box visible, we needn't do
    // so in this program.
    MyDialog theDialog = new MyDialog(theFrame);
  }
}
```

This program is not very representative of how such a custom dialog box would really be used; under normal circumstances, we'd only display a dialog box ***conditionally***, when certain circumstances had arisen in our program requiring that we communicate with the user. We'll demonstrate a more conventional use of JDialogs when we introduce the PasswordPopup class as part of our SRS GUI solution in Chapter 17.

One-Step Dialog Boxes with JOptionPane

We often need a very simple, standard form of dialog box to ask the user a quick question or to convey a message. Rather than having to go through the trouble of extending JDialog to invent a custom dialog box class from scratch for this purpose, the Swing API introduced a utility class called JOptionPane which provides a simple way to create various types of standardized dialog boxes with a minimum of effort.

By calling static methods provided by the JOptionPane class, we can instantiate and display various types of dialog box:

- `JOptionPane.showConfirmDialog(...)`: Asks a confirming question, like OK/Cancel?

- `JOptionPane.showInputDialog(...)`: Prompts the user for some "free form" textual input, such as his or her name; automatically provides OK and Cancel buttons for dismissing the dialog box.

- `JOptionPane.showMessageDialog(...)`: Displays a message informing the user of the outcome of some operation or of the state of the application; automatically provides an OK button for dismissing the dialog.

- `JOptionPane.showOptionDialog(...)`: Provides the user with a number of programmer-specified options in the form of multiple buttons, and then returns the user's choice to the client code.

The only type of `JOptionPane` that we are going to be using in the SRS application is a ***message dialog box***. The `JOptionPane.showMessageDialog` method is overloaded, which as we discussed in Chapter 5 means that there is more than one form of `showMessageDialog()`, each having a different argument signature. We are interested in using the following form of the method:

```
public static void showMessageDialog(Component parentComponent,
                                     Object message,
                                     String title,
                                     int messageType);
```

where arguments are defined as follows:

- `parentComponent`: The first argument is a reference to the component that is considered to be responsible for "sponsoring" this dialog box (typically, but not always, a `JFrame`). This `Component` is informally referred to as the dialog box's "parent," but not in the inheritance sense of the word. The message dialog box will be centered relative to its parent component on the screen; if this argument is set to `null`, then the dialog box will instead be centered relative to the screen as a whole.

- `message`: We can pass any arbitrary `Object` as the second argument to this method; the `Object`'s `toString` method will be used to produce an object-appropriate textual message. Of course, since all classes in Java are descended from `Object`, one of the most common types of `Object` to be passed in for this argument is a simple `String` representing the message itself: for example, "Operation completed."

- `title`: A `String` representing the dialog box's desired title.

- `messageType`: This argument determines the default icon to be displayed along with the message text; `JOptionPane` provides a handful of ***final static attributes*** (i.e., constant values) to be used for this argument. For our upcoming example, we'll use `JOptionPane.INFORMATION_MESSAGE`, which displays an exclamation point (!) in a blue circle:

but other choices include JOptionPane.ERROR_MESSAGE:

JOptionPane.WARNING_MESSAGE:

JOptionPane.QUESTION_MESSAGE:

and JOptionPane.PLAIN_MESSAGE (no icon).

Here's a simple class/program that demonstrates the use of the JOptionPane.showMessageDialog method; the main method consists of only one single Java statement, but because it is so long, we've broken it up into multiple physical lines of text and attached comments to help make it easier to understand.

```
// JOptionPaneDemo.java

import javax.swing.*;

public class JOptionPaneDemo {
  public static void main(String[] args) {
    // We'll demo only one of the flavors of JOptionPane:
    // namely, a message dialog box, which simply displays a
    // message, and automatically provides an "OK" button
    // for dismissing the dialog box.

    JOptionPane.showMessageDialog(
      null, // no parent; center dialog box on the screen
      "Click this dialog when you are ready.", // message
      "Whenever", // title
      JOptionPane.INFORMATION_MESSAGE); // type of icon to be used
  }
}
```

These particular argument values cause the dialog box shown in Figure 16-30 to appear when the program is run:

Figure 16-30. *An information message dialog box*

When the OK button is clicked, the dialog box is automatically dismissed.

If we wish to display a multi-line message on a message dialog box, here is a code snippet that illustrates how this is done:

```
// Create a String array of TWO lines of message text plus a blank line.
String[] message = { "Line 1.", "Line 2.", " " };

// Then, we can just hand the String array in to the showMessageDialog()
// call.
JOptionPane.showMessageDialog(null, message, "Multiple Lines",
  JOptionPane.INFORMATION_MESSAGE);
```

We'll see JOptionPane at work in the SRS application in Chapter 17.

Reusable Custom Components

Applying what we've learned about Swing/AWT components and event handling in this chapter plus what we learned about extending classes via inheritance in Part 1 of the book, let's look at how and why we might wish to design custom components of our own.

Let's say, for example, that we wish to provide our users with numerous exit points from an application, by providing exit buttons in a variety of different places across the various windows of our application's GUI.

- No matter where such a button occurs, we'd like them to be easily recognizable, perhaps making them all green with a two-line label as shown in Figure 16-31.

Figure 16-31. *Our custom exit button*

- Furthermore, we'd like to ensure that all of the various exit buttons throughout our application—or perhaps across *numerous* applications—perform in exactly the same manner.

It would be tedious to redundantly program the same look and behavior each time we need an exit button in our application. Rather, it makes much better sense for us to derive a new subclass of the JButton class, perhaps called MyExitButton, giving it the desired look and behavior as shown here:

```
import javax.swing.*;
import java.awt.*;
import java.awt.event.*;

public class MyExitButton extends JButton {
    public MyExitButton() {
        // Craft the two-line label.
        this.setLayout(new GridLayout(2, 1));
        this.add(new JLabel("Press Here", JLabel.CENTER));
        this.add(new JLabel("To Exit", JLabel.CENTER));

        // Color it green.
        this.setBackground(Color.green);

        // Program its behavior.
        ActionListener l = new ActionListener() {
            public void actionPerformed(ActionEvent e) {
                int optionChosen = JOptionPane.showConfirmDialog(
                    null,
                    "Are you sure you want to exit?",
                    "Exit?",
                    JOptionPane.YES_NO_OPTION,
                    JOptionPane.QUESTION_MESSAGE);

                if (optionChosen == 0) { // Yes (first choice).
                    // Do whatever is required to gracefully
                    // shut down the application ... details omitted.

                    System.exit(0);
                }
                // Otherwise, we do nothing.
            }
        };

        this.addActionListener(l);
    }
}
```

Then, wherever we need an exit button in our application, we'd need instantiate and attach a MyExitButton instance, as illustrated in this trivially simple demo program:

```
public class MyExitButtonDemo {
    public static void main(String[] args) {
        JFrame f = new JFrame();
        f.getContentPane().add(new MyExitButton());
        f.setSize(200, 100);
        f.setVisible(true);
    }
}
```

This demo GUI would appear as follows:

And, when our custom exit button is pressed, the following dialog box will appear to confirm whether or not the user truly wishes to exit:

Now, let's return to the scenario of a nontrivial application with perhaps dozens of exit buttons scattered throughout the many windows of its user interface. The **beauty** of this approach is that, should we later wish to change the appearance or behavior of all of our application's many exit buttons, we do so in **one central place**—in the MyExitButton class—and such changes will take effect throughout the entire application!

Summary

In this chapter, we've covered a lot of ground regarding the basics of Java GUI building.

- We discussed the two primary Java APIs—AWT and Swing.

- We've learned specifically about the following building blocks of Java GUIs:

  - Swing top-level **containers**: JFrame, JPanel, JDialog

  - Other key Swing **components**: JLabel, JButton, JList, JTextField, JPasswordField

  - Several AWT **layout managers**: BorderLayout, GridLayout, FlowLayout

  - The JOptionPane utility class (Swing), which provides a convenient way of popping up dialog boxes of various sorts

- We learned about the Java **event handling model**; in particular, about creating and registering **listeners**.

- We discussed several specific AWT/Swing listeners: ActionListener (AWT), WindowListener (AWT), ListSelectionListener (Swing).

- We learned how to create **reusable custom components** (recall our example of a green exit button).

- We discussed the importance of **model–view separation** as a design technique, and will revisit this again in much greater detail in Chapter 17.

Exercises

1. [*Coding*] Improve the `Calculator4` example found in this chapter (and downloadable from the Apress web site—see Appendix D for details) so that it performs proper exception handling. As presented in the chapter, if the user clicks the + or − buttons without typing in two proper numbers, a `NumberFormatException` run-time exception arises. (Hint: you'll need to wrap the code that manipulates the values retrieved from the text fields on the GUI in a `try-catch` block.)

2. [*Coding*] Create a simple class named `SimpleGUI`, derived from `JFrame`, that presents a single component—a `JButton` with the label Push Me, a background color of yellow, and a foreground color of magenta, as shown here:

Use the architecture suggested for the `Calculator2B` example earlier in this chapter to include the use of a test scaffold `main` method.

For this exercise, you needn't worry about event handling—this is covered in exercise 3.

Remember that to terminate a program for which window event handling has not been provided, you must click in the DOS window from which you launched the application to cause that window to gain focus (become the active window), and then press and hold down the Ctrl key while typing C.

You'll need to do this for both exercise 2 and exercise 3.

---

3. [*Coding*] Continuing with the code that you wrote for exercise 2, add event handling to the `SimpleGUI` Push Me button example. Specifically, modify the code to take advantage of an `ActionListener` so that, when the button is pushed the ***first*** time:

   - The color of the button changes from a background color of yellow and a foreground color of magenta to a background color of cyan and a foreground color of black.

   - The button's label changes to Again.

   and, when the button is pushed a ***second*** time, the button's color/label values return to their ***original*** settings. From this point on, successive clicks of the button should toggle the appearance between these two states. (Hint: you'll need to devise some way of keeping track of what the settings are at any given time, to know what to "toggle" to; there are lots of ways to approach this!)

4. [*Coding*] Try adding a `WindowListener` to the `SimpleGUI` example from exercise 3, so that when you click the window's close button (⊠), the application automatically terminates.

5. [*Coding*] ***Advanced:*** Choose three types of Swing/AWT component that you have not previously worked with from the list of components presented in the "Other Interesting AWT/Swing Components to Explore" section of this chapter, and build a simple GUI that demonstrates all three.

■ ■ ■

CHAPTER 17

SRS, Take 3: Adding a GUI

In this chapter, we are going to apply what we learned about Java GUI building in Chapter 16 to retrofit a GUI front-end to the SRS that we built in Chapter 15. With this GUI, we'll provide (hypothetical) students with the capability to

- Log on to the SRS.

- View the schedule of sections available for registration in the current semester.

- View and modify their individual course loads by dropping and adding sections of courses that they are eligible to attend.

- Persist these changes (saving them to a file behind the scenes) before logging off again.

We'll also discuss

- The importance of **model–view separation** as a design principle

- The value of preparing a **concept of operations** for how a GUI is to look and operate before any code is written

- Techniques for sharing information across classes within an application

Finally, we'll close out the chapter by presenting a conceptual overview of **Java 2 Enterprise Edition (J2EE)** technology, used to build **thin client user interfaces**, and will demonstrate the *direct relevance* of what you've learned in this book to building J2EE applications.

Our SRS Code Road Map

Here's a "road map" of the code that we'll need to tackle in building a GUI for the SRS.

We're going to add a GUI *presentation layer* onto our SRS *model layer* in such a way as to *leave the model classes undisturbed* from the way that they were originally designed in Chapter 14. In so doing, the model classes will continue to serve as pure abstractions of real-world objects. This design principle is known as achieving **model-view separation**, aka **model-presentation layer separation**. (We did this same sort of thing when we added a data access/persistence layer to the model in Chapter 15, thus upholding the design principle of model–*data layer* separation.) Thus, *all* of the following model layer source code—as presented in Chapter 14 and as reused unchanged in Chapter 15—is reusable as-is once again with the GUI version of the SRS:

- Course.java

- EnrollmentStatus.java

- Person.java

- Professor.java

- ScheduleOfClasses.java

- Section.java

- Student.java

- Transcript.java

- TranscriptEntry.java

and thus we won't need to revisit any of these classes in this chapter.

By insulating our model classes from the application's user interface, we make it easy to

- ***Modernize the technology with which we present the view***, should we wish to do so at a later date (we'll illustrate this conceptually with J2EE toward the end of the chapter).

- ***Add multiple views to the same model***, to perhaps accommodate multiple different categories of user.

- ***Reuse the same model with different applications entirely!***

Furthermore, all of the classes that comprised the data access layer of our application as introduced in Chapter 15 are also reusable as-is from that chapter:

- CourseCatalog.java

- Faculty.java

- InvalidStudentException.java

- SRSDataAccess.java

- SRSInitializationException.java

- StudentPersistenceException.java

and so we won't need to revisit any of these classes in this chapter, either.

All we're going to need to do to add a GUI to the SRS is to

- Extend two Swing window (Container) classes:

  - MainFrame, a direct subclass of JFrame, to serve as our main application window

  - PasswordPopup, a direct subclass of JDialog, which will be used when logging a student on to the SRS

- Modify our SRS driver class to take advantage of this newly added GUI/presentation layer.

If you haven't already done so, please download and print a copy of the source code for Chapter 17 so that you have it handy to refer to when following along with the discussion that follows. Download instructions are provided in Appendix D.

A NOTE REGARDING MODIFYING MODEL LAYER CLASSES

The fact that we were able to avoid making changes to our SRS model layer classes after they were first established in Chapter 14 is not meant to imply that having to modify the model layer in response to building the data access or presentation layers of an application is necessarily a "bad" thing. In fact, quite the contrary: it is *natural* to coax out additional requirements as an application evolves, particularly if a development approach known as **iterative prototyping** is used. With iterative prototyping, we demonstrate an evolving application to its future users on a frequent and regular basis so that missed/misconstrued requirements can be identified—and midcourse corrections can be made—as early as possible in the development life cycle.

The important point to remember is that *the model layer of an application is not necessarily "cast in stone" when we begin development of the persistence/presentation layers*. When additional insights inevitably arise regarding requirements, regardless of what stage in the life cycle this occurs, we *must* address them if at all possible, *unless* the following two statements are both true:

- It is cost/time prohibitive to do so, *and* (a very *important* "and"!)

- Our client/sponsor/future users *agree* that addressing these requirements is to be deferred.

There is, however, one important caveat: if we find ourselves having to modify the model layer to accommodate user interface requirements, we must nonetheless be certain to *avoid* modifying the model in such a way as to *constrain its reuseability*. That is, we must be certain that any changes we make to the model classes in support of the presentation layer are nonetheless consistent with the "essence" of what the class is serving as an abstraction for. For example, it would be perfectly acceptable to add an attribute such as String abbreviatedCourseName to the Course class if we wanted to be able to display the name of a course in a shortened fashion, but it would *not* be appropriate to add an attribute such as Font courseNameFont to be used in constraining the font with which the course name is to be displayed on a GUI.

We'll revisit this notion when we discuss the PasswordPopup class later in this chapter in the section "The PasswordPopup Class: Sharing Information Across Windows/Classes."

Preparing a Concept of Operations

Before we dive into the code required to automate the GUI, let's quickly talk through how we envision that the GUI will operate.

Sketching out the look and functional flow of a graphical user interface through pictures and accompanying narrative—a technique known as **storyboarding**—is a great way to come to agreement with the future users of a system on how the application should look and behave *before* development begins. Storyboarding can be accomplished informally, perhaps by sketching our ideas with pen or paper or on a whiteboard, or formally, by producing a **concept of operations document** (aka a paper prototype). We'll do the latter in a moment for the SRS.

The story that is told by a concept of operations document is presented from the external viewpoint of a user; it is, in essence, a pictorial representation of how the various use cases for the application will be fulfilled.

As an added bonus, if the application truly evolves as we envisioned that it would, then the concept of operations document can actually be used as the basis for a user's guide and/or on-line tutorial *after* the application is finished.

We've had the good fortune to "morph" a concept of operations document into a user's guide on numerous occasions. Given how the "typical" software developer so seldom finds time to write even minimal documentation and how costly it can be to develop polished documentation, getting this "two-for-the-price-of-one" benefit is significant.

The SRS Concept of Operations

Our concept of operations begins when Joe Blow, a student user, launches the SRS application. The GUI that first appears, shown in the following illustration, presents a list of all sections offered this semester entitled "Schedule of Classes," along with a number of empty fields labeled SSN:, Name:, and Total Courses:. A number of buttons appear at the bottom of the window labeled Drop, Save My Schedule, Add, and Log Off, but these are all grayed out initially to signal that they are disabled; until a user logs on, none of the functions provided by these buttons is relevant.

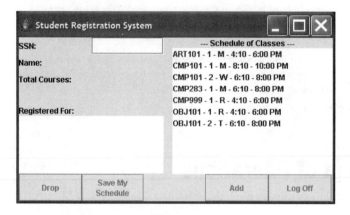

Because the code for the SRS was already developed before this chapter was written, we had the luxury of using actual screen snapshots as illustrations.

Joe logs on to the SRS by typing his social security number, 111-11-1111, in the field labeled SSN:, and then presses the Enter key. The following small dialog window pops up to request that he enter his password to complete the log-on process:

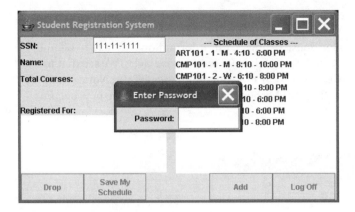

As Joe types in his password (which happens to be 111, the first three digits of his social security number), asterisks (*) appear in place of the characters that he types to ensure his privacy.

After typing in his password, Joe presses the Enter key. Unfortunately, Joe has mistyped his password, and so the following pop-up message appears:

After Joe clicks the OK button on this pop-up to dismiss it, he clicks in the SSN: field to give that field focus, and then presses the Enter key again to redisplay the password pop-up a second time (he needn't retype his SSN, however). Assuming that he types his password correctly this time, he receives this confirmation of a successful logon:

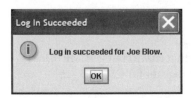

After clicking OK on this confirmation pop-up, Joe sees that the Name:, Total Courses:, and Registered For: components on the main GUI window have been filled in with his current registration information. (Although Joe doesn't know it, this information was read in behind-the-scenes from file `111-11-1111.dat`, courtesy of the SRS data access layer.) We see that Joe had previously used the SRS to register for section 1 of course number `CMP101`. Notice that two of the buttons at the bottom of the GUI—Save My Schedule and Log Off—have now become enabled, as you can see here:

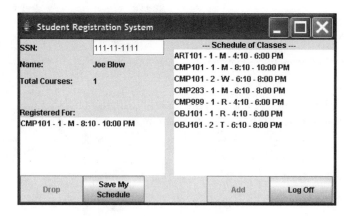

Joe decides to enroll in section CMP101 - 2. He clicks this section in the Schedule of Classes list to highlight/select it, which causes the Add button at the bottom of the screen to automatically become active. Joe clicks the Add button.

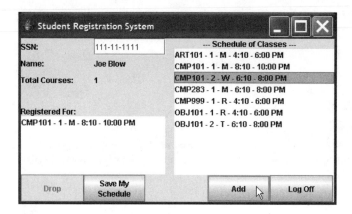

Because Joe is already registered for a ***different*** section of that ***same*** course (CMP101 - ***1***), the system notifies him via a pop-up message that he may not register for CMP101 - ***2***.

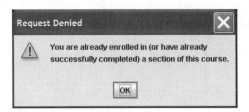

Joe clicks OK to dismiss the dialog box. He next selects CMP999 - 1 from the Schedule of Classes, and again clicks the Add button.

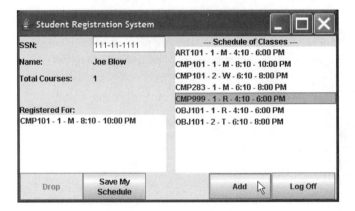

Unfortunately, Joe strikes out again! Course CMP999, "Living Brain Computers," requires students to have successfully completed the prerequisite course CMP283, "Higher Level Languages (Java)." Since Joe's transcript (which is checked behind the scenes) does not show evidence that he has previously completed CMP283, the system once again rejects his registration request with the following pop-up message:

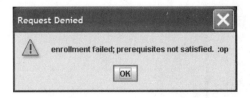

After clicking OK to dismiss this pop-up, Joe selects ART101 - 1 from the Schedule of Classes list, and clicks the Add button yet again.

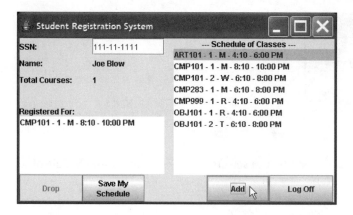

Success at last! ART101—"Introductory Basket Weaving"—has no prerequisites to satisfy, plus Joe is neither currently registered for, nor has ***ever*** successfully completed, a section of this course. Joe receives the following confirmation that he has been registered in ART 101:

After Joe dismisses the confirmation pop-up, he sees the newly added section reflected in the Registered For: list on the main SRS window, with the Total Courses: field reflecting the correct new total of two courses in Joe's course load. (Note that Joe's selection in the Schedule of Classes list has automatically been cleared, and that the Add button is no longer enabled.)

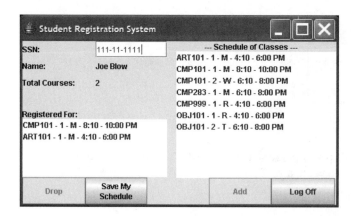

Next, Joe decides that he wishes to drop CMP101. He clicks that entry in his Registered For: list to select it, at which point the GUI's Drop button becomes enabled. He then clicks the Drop button.

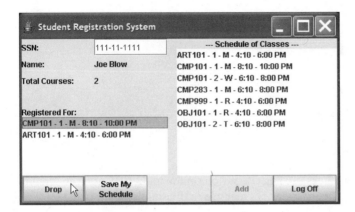

In response, the SRS displays the following confirmation pop-up indicating that the course has been dropped from his course load:

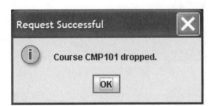

When the pop-up is dismissed, Joe sees that his information has once again been properly updated. (Note that the Drop button has been disabled.)

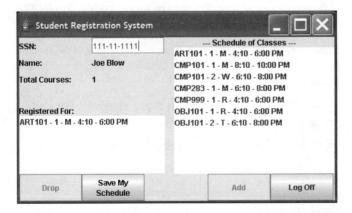

Satisfied with his new schedule, Joe decides to persist this information by clicking the Save My Schedule button, and the system confirms this operation. (Behind the scenes and unbeknownst to Joe, his updated course load information has been persisted to file 111-11-1111.dat, replacing the information that was previously in that file.)

Joe dismisses this pop-up, then clicks the Log Off button on the main GUI, and the screen is cleared of all of Joe's student-specific information, ready for a different student to log on.

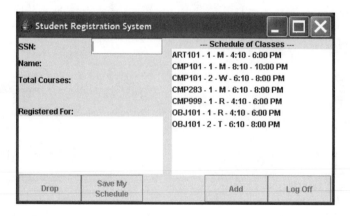

If you haven't yet done so, we recommend that you download, compile, and experiment with the Chapter 17 version of the ***executable*** SRS application before looking at the source code. A few helpful hints:

- Valid SSN values are 111-11-1111, 222-22-2222, and 333-33-3333, based on the contents of the various *xxx-xx-xxxx*.dat files provided with the SRS code. (That being said, be certain to experiment with ***invalid*** values as well, to test the limits of SRS error handling.)

- Valid password values for these SSNs are 111, 222, and 333, respectively. (Again, experiment with invalid values, as well.)

- If at any point you wish to reset the contents of the three data files to their original state, type the (Windows) command

  reset

  to run the reset.bat script provided as part of the download.

The MainFrame Class

Planning the "Look" of MainFrame: Getting Creative with GridLayout

Looking at the desired layout for the SRS GUI, we can visually decompose it into various regions of evenly sized components; as we mentioned in Chapter 16, if we can do this, then the use of layered JPanels with GridLayouts is in order!

- We see a row of evenly sized buttons at the bottom, which we can tackle through the creation of a JPanel—called buttonPanel in our code—with a GridLayout of 1 row × 5 columns, placed in the SOUTH region of the frame's BorderLayout.

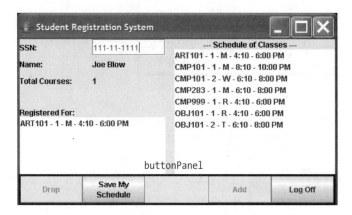

- The remainder of the GUI can be split in half, with the left half being represented by one JPanel and the right by another; we'll refer to them in our code as leftPanel and rightPanel. We can place the left panel in the JFrame's WEST region, and the right panel in the JFrame's EAST region; the CENTER and NORTH regions will remain empty, and hence will "shrink away."

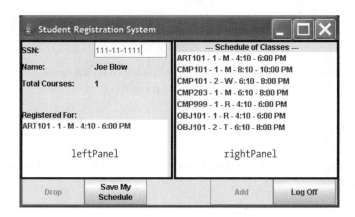

- Focusing on the left panel for a moment, we see that if we manage the left panel with a 2 row × 1 column `GridLayout`, the panel can in turn be subdivided vertically into two equally sized smaller panels, which we'll refer to in our code as `topLeftPanel` and `bottomLeftPanel`.

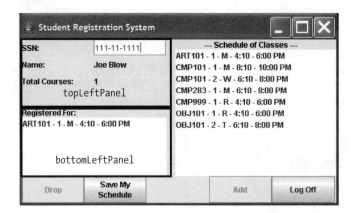

- The `topLeftPanel` can in turn be managed by a 1×2 `GridLayout` to subdivide it into two even smaller panels called `labelPanel` and `fieldPanel`.

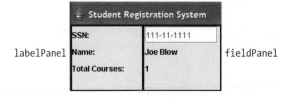

Each of these smallest panels—one to contain unchanging labels, and the other to reflect changeable data (either input by the user or provided programmatically by the SRS application)—can be managed by a 4×1 `GridLayout`. (We could alternatively use a 3×1 `GridLayout` for each of these, but we want to place some white space at the bottom of each, to visually separate it from the list entitled "Registered For:," which falls below this area on the GUI.)

Armed with these decisions, we're now ready to code the first half (i.e., the "look") of class `MainFrame`, which is to be the main application window, based on a `JFrame` container.

Coding the "Look" of MainFrame

We'll now narrate the code of the `MainFrame` class.

We import all of the packages that we'll need both for creating the look of the GUI as well as for implementing its behavior.

```
// MainFrame.java

import java.awt.*;
import java.awt.event.*;
import javax.swing.*;
import javax.swing.event.*;
import java.util.*;

public class MainFrame extends JFrame {
```

We declare all of the components that we're going to be attaching to the MainFrame as attributes of this class; note that we strive to choose descriptive names for most of them so that when we see them referenced in the code further down, we'll remember what purpose each one serves.

```
  private JPanel leftPanel;
  private JPanel topLeftPanel;
  private JPanel labelPanel;
  private JPanel fieldPanel;
  private JPanel bottomLeftPanel;
  private JPanel rightPanel;
  private JPanel buttonPanel;
  private JTextField ssnField;
  private JLabel nameLabel;
  private JLabel totalCoursesLabel;
  private JButton dropButton;
  private JButton addButton;
  private JButton logoffButton;
  private JButton saveScheduleButton;
  private JLabel l1;
  private JLabel l2;
  private JList studentCourseList;
  private JList scheduleOfClassesList;
```

We're going to use reference variable currentUser to maintain a handle on whichever Student object represents the student user who is currently logged in; a value of null for this variable signifies that nobody is officially logged on.

```
  private Student currentUser;
```

Most of the code comprising the constructor for our MainFrame class should by now be familiar, so we'll only explain those items that are particularly noteworthy.

```
  // Constructor.
  public MainFrame() {
    // Initialize attributes.
    currentUser = null;

    this.setTitle("Student Registration System");
    this.setSize(500, 300);
    Container contentPane = this.getContentPane();
```

```
Dimension frameSize = this.getSize();
Dimension screenSize = Toolkit.getDefaultToolkit().getScreenSize();
this.setLocation((screenSize.width - frameSize.width)/2,
  (screenSize.height - frameSize.height)/2);

// Create a few panels.

leftPanel = new JPanel();
leftPanel.setLayout(new GridLayout(2, 1));

topLeftPanel = new JPanel();
topLeftPanel.setLayout(new GridLayout(1, 2));

labelPanel = new JPanel();
labelPanel.setLayout(new GridLayout(4, 1));

fieldPanel = new JPanel();
fieldPanel.setLayout(new GridLayout(4, 1));

bottomLeftPanel = new JPanel();
bottomLeftPanel.setLayout(new BorderLayout());
```

The only panel that we won't assign a GridLayout to is the rightPanel; we'll assign it a BorderLayout instead.

```
rightPanel = new JPanel();
rightPanel.setLayout(new BorderLayout());

buttonPanel = new JPanel();
buttonPanel.setLayout(new GridLayout(1, 4));
```

(We'll allow the main JFrame to retain its default BorderLayout.)

Note that we are adding labels without maintaining permanent handles on them; that's because we won't ever need to programmatically communicate with them as objects again, once they've been attached to the GUI. We do use a ***temporary*** handle l, however, to hold on to each label object just long enough to invoke its setForeground method (the default color for a label's text, or foreground, is a bluish-gray color, but we'd prefer it to be black).

```
JLabel l = new JLabel("SSN:  ");
l.setForeground(Color.black);
labelPanel.add(l);

l = new JLabel("Name:   ");
l.setForeground(Color.black);
labelPanel.add(l);

l = new JLabel("Total Courses:   ");
l.setForeground(Color.black);
labelPanel.add(l);
```

```
// Add an empty label for padding/white space.
l = new JLabel("");
labelPanel.add(l);
```

We do, however, maintain named references as attributes of the MainFrame class to any components that we're going to need to ***manipulate programmatically***; for example, ssnField:

```
ssnField = new JTextField(10);
```

Because these next two items are not going to be editable by the user, we are rendering them both as JLabels. We could have alternatively rendered them as non-editable JTextFields, but we wanted them to ***look*** like labels.

```
nameLabel = new JLabel();
nameLabel.setForeground(Color.black);

totalCoursesLabel = new JLabel();
totalCoursesLabel.setForeground(Color.black);

fieldPanel.add(ssnField);
fieldPanel.add(nameLabel);
fieldPanel.add(totalCoursesLabel);

// Add an empty label for padding/white space.
l = new JLabel("");
fieldPanel.add(l);

// Create the buttons and add them to their panel.
dropButton = new JButton("Drop");
addButton = new JButton("Add");
logoffButton = new JButton("Log Off");
```

We use the technique for creating a multiline button label on the next button, as was discussed earlier in the chapter:

```
saveScheduleButton = new JButton();
saveScheduleButton.setLayout(new GridLayout(2, 1));

l1 = new JLabel("Save My", JLabel.CENTER);
l1.setForeground(Color.black);

l2 = new JLabel("Schedule", JLabel.CENTER);
l2.setForeground(Color.black);

saveScheduleButton.add(l1);
saveScheduleButton.add(l2);

// Assemble the button panel.
buttonPanel.add(dropButton);
buttonPanel.add(saveScheduleButton);
```

```
buttonPanel.add(new JLabel("")); // white space padding
buttonPanel.add(addButton);
buttonPanel.add(logoffButton);
```

In creating the JList used to display all of the Sections that a Student has registered for, it's necessary to use the setFixedCellWidth method to explicitly assign a width to the list entries, because the list will sometimes be empty; without a fixed width assignment, the list would shrink to a width of 0, which would effectively make this component invisible on the GUI.

```
studentCourseList = new JList();
studentCourseList.setFixedCellWidth(200);
bottomLeftPanel.add(studentCourseList, BorderLayout.CENTER);

l = new JLabel("Registered For:");
l.setForeground(Color.black);
bottomLeftPanel.add(l, BorderLayout.NORTH);

l = new JLabel("--- Schedule of Classes ---", JLabel.CENTER);
l.setForeground(Color.black);
rightPanel.add(l, BorderLayout.NORTH);
```

You may recall from Chapter 14 that we declared scheduleOfClasses to be a public static attribute of the SRS driver class so that it would be referenceable/globally accessible from all of the other classes in our application. We now take advantage of this fact to instantiate the scheduleOfClassesList JList.

- As we saw demonstrated in Chapter 16, we may pass in an array of Object references as an argument to a JList constructor, and the JList will automatically use the toString method of the objects contained within the JList to render them as textual entries in the list that is displayed.

- We'll invoke the getSectionsOffered method of the SRS.scheduleOfClasses collection to obtain a HashMap of <String, Section> pairs.

- We'll then feed this HashMap into a housekeeping method called sortSections that will be used to convert the HashMap into an ***array*** of Section references, sorting it in the process. (We'll see the code for the sortSections method later in the chapter.)

All of the preceding takes place within the ***single*** line of code that follows, thanks to the use of nested expressions:

```
// Retrieve a Collection of Sections from the main ScheduleOfClasses,
// then sort it via a private "housekeeping" method,
// sortSections, before displaying it.
scheduleOfClassesList = new JList(sortSections(SRS.scheduleOfClasses.
    getSectionsOffered()));
```

As we did for the studentCourseList, it's necessary to use the setFixedCellWidth method to explicitly assign a width to the scheduleOfClassesList entries, to ensure that this component remains visible even if for some reason the list of available classes were empty.

```
scheduleOfClassesList.setFixedCellWidth(250);
rightPanel.add(scheduleOfClassesList, BorderLayout.EAST);
```

The next line of code is a call to method `resetButtons`, another housekeeping method defined for the `MainFrame` class. This method is responsible for making sure that the various buttons on the GUI are properly enabled or disabled, depending on the student's registration situation, or **state**, at any given point in time. We'll defer a discussion of the `resetButtons` method until a bit later in this chapter, when we discuss the behaviors of the `MainFrame` class.

```
// Initialize the buttons to their proper enabled/disabled state.
resetButtons();

// Finally, attach all of the panels to one another
// and to the frame. Add in ascending row, then column, order.
topLeftPanel.add(labelPanel);
topLeftPanel.add(fieldPanel);
leftPanel.add(topLeftPanel);
leftPanel.add(bottomLeftPanel);
contentPane.add(leftPanel, BorderLayout.WEST);
contentPane.add(rightPanel, BorderLayout.CENTER);
contentPane.add(buttonPanel, BorderLayout.SOUTH);

// -------------------------------------
// Add all behaviors ... coming up next!
// -------------------------------------
```

We'll tackle automating the behaviors of the `MainFrame` class next.

Adding Behaviors to MainFrame

We're going to need to provide listeners for each of GUI components that the user will be interacting with:

- We'll need the GUI to recognize when a user has typed his or her student ID number into the `ssnField` as a signal that he or she wishes to log on.

- We'll need to program the logic for what is to happen behind the scenes when each of the four buttons at the bottom of the GUI—`addButton`, `dropButton`, `saveScheduleButton`, and `logoffButton`—is clicked.

- We'll need to recognize when a user has made a selection in either the `studentCourseList` or `scheduleOfClassesList`.

- We'll also want to close down the application as a whole gracefully if the user clicks the window close button at the upper-right corner of the window.

As mentioned in the comments for this program, different types of components require different types of listeners:

- Text fields respond to an `ActionListener` whenever the Enter key is pressed.

- Buttons respond to an `ActionListener` whenever the button in question is clicked.

- `JList`s respond to a `ListSelectionListener` whenever an item is selected from the list in question.

- We use a `WindowListener` to listen for window closing events.

So, we'll declare a reference variable for *each* of these three listener types:

```
// ------------------
// Add all behaviors.
// ------------------

ActionListener aListener;
ListSelectionListener lListener;
WindowListener wListener;
```

Then, we'll proceed to instantiate the appropriate listeners one by one, using the technique that we learned in Chapter 16 for creating anonymous inner classes.

The ssnField ActionListener

The `ssnField` is the field that the user types his or her student ID into to signal his or her intent to log on. We need to listen for the `ActionEvents` that are generated when a user presses the Enter key after typing in this field.

```
aListener = new ActionListener() {
  public void actionPerformed(ActionEvent e) {
```

We've created a private housekeeping method, `clearFields`, which steps through the three components on the GUI that represent student-specific information—`nameLabel`, `totalCoursesLabel`, and `studentCourseList`—clearing them of any information that is still being displayed for a previously logged on student. You'll see the code for this method, along with several other housekeeping methods, toward the end of this discussion.

```
// First, clear the fields reflecting the
// previous student's information.
clearFields();
```

Next, we use the `getText` method of the `ssnField` to pull whatever `String` value the user has typed into that field.

```
// We'll try to construct a Student based on
// the ssn we read from the GUI.
String id = ssnField.getText();
```

We attempt to instantiate a new `Student` object representing the "real" student user (an example of a ***boundary class***, as we discussed in Chapter 11). Specifically, we utilize the static `SRSDataAccess.initializeStudent` method to attempt to "reconstitute" a `Student` from persistent storage based on the `id` that he or she has typed; if this effort fails, an `InvalidStudentException` is thrown.

```
try {
    theStudent = SRSDataAccess.initializeStudent(id);
}
catch (InvalidStudentException e2) {
```

If the attempt to initialize the Student fails, we reset the currentUser attribute of the MainFrame class to null to signify that no user is logged on; this has the added effect of causing reference variable currentUser to drop any handle that it might still have been holding on a *previously* logged on Student object.

```
    // Drat!  The ID was invalid.
    currentUser = null;
```

We then display a warning message to the user, and exit from the actionPerformed method with a return statement:

```
    // Let the user know that login failed.
    JOptionPane.showMessageDialog(null,
        "Invalid student ID; please try again.",
        "Invalid Student ID",
        JOptionPane.WARNING_MESSAGE);


    return;
}
```

On the other hand, if the Student object *was* successfully created, it's time to ask the user to provide a password before displaying student-proprietary information.

```
    // If we've made it to this point in our code,
    // we found a valid student.  We now need
    // to request and validate the password.
    PasswordPopup pp = new PasswordPopup(
        MainFrame.this);
```

The preceding line of code is responsible for instantiating and displaying a PasswordPopup dialog box, which is a special class that we've defined as a subclass of JDialog. We'll review the code for PasswordPopup in its entirety after we finish stepping through the MainFrame class.

The PasswordPopup dialog box happens to be a *modal* dialog box, which means that as long as the PasswordPopup dialog box is displayed on the screen, the user will be unable to interact with the rest of the SRS GUI. More importantly, though, as long as the dialog box is displayed on the screen, the JVM will be awaiting events from that dialog box, and the code for the MainFrame method that we're in the middle of executing—namely, the actionPerformed method of the ssnField's anonymous inner ActionListener class—is suspended.

By the time we reach the next line of code, we know that the password dialog box has been dismissed by the user (it was modal, after all), so we can use a method that we've written for the PasswordPopup class called getPassword that allows us to "fetch" whatever the user has typed into the dialog box; we'll see the code for that method when we study PasswordPopup a bit later in the chapter.

```
    String pw = pp.getPassword();
```

After we've retrieved whatever password String the user typed in, we can dispose of the dialog box, because we no longer need to "talk" with it to request any of its additional services.

```
pp.dispose();
```

We attempt to validate the password by calling the validatePassword method of the MainFrame class. If the password is found to be valid, we retain a handle on the Student object via attribute currentUser. We then use another housekeeping method, setFields, to populate the various components on the GUI with this student's information so that he or she can see it. (We'll see the setFields method code in a moment.) We also use JOptionPane once again to notify the user that the login succeeded.

```
if (validatePassword(theStudent, pw)) {
        currentUser = theStudent;
        setFields(theStudent);

        // Let the user know that the
        // login succeeded.

        JOptionPane.showMessageDialog(null,
        "Log in succeeded for " +
        theStudent.getName() + ".",
        "Log In Succeeded",
        JOptionPane.INFORMATION_MESSAGE);
}
```

REVISITING AN EARLIER NOTE REGARDING MODIFYING MODEL LAYER CLASSES

Earlier in the chapter, we mentioned that if we find ourselves needing to modify our model classes to accommodate the addition of a user interface, we should avoid modifying the model in such a way as to constrain its reusability. That is, we must be certain that any changes we make to the model classes in support of the presentation layer are nonetheless consistent with the "essence" of what the class is serving as an abstraction for.

With this in mind, note that it could be argued that we should really be asking the Student object to verify its *own* password:

```
if (theStudent.validatePassword(pw)) { ...
```

This would require us to add a validatePassword method to the Student class:

```
public class Student {
    private String name;
    private String ssn;

    // Constructor.
    public Student(String ssn, String name) {
        setSsn(ssn);
        setName(name);
    }
```

```
    // Typical accessor (get/set) methods for ssn and
    // name also provided - details omitted.

    // Validate a Student's password by comparing it
    // to the first three digits of his/her student ID number.
    private boolean validatePassword(String pw) {
        if (pw == null) return false;
        else if (getSsn().startsWith(pw)) return true;
        else return false;
    }

    public String toString() {
        return this.getName() + " (" + this.getSsn() + ")";
    }
}
```

thus *alleviating* the need for a `validatePassword(Student, String)` *utility* method in the `MainFrame` class. *Which approach is better?* This is admittedly a gray area, for the following reasons:

On the one hand, it's arguable as to whether the notion of a password belongs in our generic abstraction of what makes a (human) student a `Student` (object). Human students would continue to designate majors, take courses, be advised by advisors, etc., even if there were no such thing as an SRS; but, would a human student inherently have a *password* if there were no SRS? It's unlikely, but not wholly out the question: for example, a given university may assign each student a student ID number and a password that is to be used throughout the university for a variety of purposes, in which case it would be justifiable to include a `validatePassword` method to the `Student` (model) class for that university. Under such circumstances, it would be advisable to add a (private) `password` attribute to the `Student` class, as well, since using the first three digits of a student's ID as his or her password is not a sound/secure approach.

One way to have our cake and eat it, too, would be to *extend* the `Student` class to create a `SecureStudent` subclass that added a `password` attribute plus perhaps two methods—`setPassword` and `validatePassword`—thus leaving our original `Student` class unaltered. We'd then use the `SecureStudent` class in any application that required password validation, and could use the generic `Student` class for those applications that did not require such security measures, if any.

Returning to our `actionPerformed` method code, if the attempt to validate a Student's password fails, we notify the user of this:

```
            if (validatePassword(theStudent, pw)) {
                // Details omitted ... discussed previously.
            }
            else {
                // Password validation failed;
                // notify the user of this.

                JOptionPane.showMessageDialog(null,
                    "Invalid password; please " +
                    "try again.",
```

```
                    "Invalid Password",
                    JOptionPane.WARNING_MESSAGE);
            }
        }
```

We then force the GUI to refresh itself, to make sure that the new data appears, as appropriate. (It should do so automatically, but this is extra insurance to make *sure* that it does.)

```
        MainFrame.this.repaint();
```

And, since the state of the application has changed—a new user is now logged on—we use a third housekeeping method, resetButtons, to enable/disable the buttons at the bottom of the screen, as appropriate. (We'll see the code for resetButtons toward the end of our discussion of the MainFrame class.)

```
        // Check states of the various buttons.
        resetButtons();
    }
};


ssnField.addActionListener(aListener);
```

The addButton ActionListener

For the Add button, we must first fetch the user-selected line item from the scheduleOfClassesList via the getSelectedValue method. This method returns a generic Object, so we must cast it back into a Section object; we then maintain a handle on that Section object via the selected reference variable.

```
    // addButton

    aListener = new ActionListener() {
      public void actionPerformed(ActionEvent e) {
      // Determine which section is selected
      // (note that we must cast it, as it
      // is returned as an Object reference).
      Section selected = (Section)
          scheduleOfClassesList.getSelectedValue();
```

Next, we invoke the currentUser's isCurrentlyEnrolledInSimilar to determine whether this Student is already enrolled in this section or in a different section of this same course. If the outcome of this method invocation is true, meaning that this would indeed be a duplicate course, we notify the user of this via a JOptionDialog, and our processing of this event is concluded. (Note the technique of displaying multiple lines of message text on the message dialog box by populating a String array.)

```
        // Check to see if this COURSE is already
        // one that the student registered for,
        // even if the SECTION is different.
        // If so, warn them of this.
        if (currentUser.isCurrentlyEnrolledInSimilar(selected)) {
```

```
        // Create a String array of TWO lines
        // of messsage text, so that the pop-up
        // window won't be too wide.
        String[] message = { "You are already enrolled in (or have",
                             "already successfully completed) a section",
                             " of this course.",
                             " " };  // blank line as last line


        // Then, we can just hand the String array in to the
        // showMessageDialog() call.
        JOptionPane.showMessageDialog(null, message, "Request Denied",
            JOptionPane.WARNING_MESSAGE);
    }
```

Otherwise, we attempt to actually enroll the Student in the selected Section:

```
    else {
      // Attempt to enroll the student, noting
      // the status code that is returned.
      EnrollmentStatus outcome = selected.enroll(currentUser);
```

We study the outcome of the enrollment request; if it is other than EnrollmentStatus.success, (one of the values defined by the EnrollmentStatus enum as discussed in Chapter 14), we formulate an appropriate dialog box message with JOptionPane, retrieving the associated String value of our EnrollmentStatus enum(eration) instance via the success.value() method call to serve as the dialog box's "message" to the user.

```
        // Report the status to the user.
        if (outcome != EnrollmentStatus.success) {
            JOptionPane.showMessageDialog(
                null,
                outcome.value(), // retrieve String value of enum
                "Request Denied",
                JOptionPane.WARNING_MESSAGE);
        }
```

If we make it to this point in the code, we've indeed succeeded in getting our student enrolled in the selected class!

```
        else { // success!
          // Display a confirmation message.
          JOptionPane.showMessageDialog(null,
            "Seat confirmed in " +
            selected.getRepresentedCourse().getCourseNo() + ".",
            "Request Successful",
            JOptionPane.INFORMATION_MESSAGE);
```

We must reflect the newly added section to the student's course list on the GUI; it's easy enough to just repopulate the JList with all of the sections for which this student is enrolled presently. Note that a JList likes to be "fed" an array containing the values it is to display, and so we call the toArray method on the Collection returned by the getEnrolledSections method to convert that collection to an array. (Recall our discussion of the toArray method of the Collection interface in Chapter 6: we **must** pass in an array to be "filled" as an argument. However, if the array is too small, as is the case here, it simply gets ignored; we nonetheless must pass one in to satisfy the compiler.)

```
// Update the list of sections that this student is
// registered for.  (We're purposely passing in a too-small
// "dummy" array.)
studentCourseList.setListData(
        currentUser.getEnrolledSections().
        toArray(new Section[1]));
```

We also update the field representing the total enrolled course count:

```
// Update the field representing student's
// course total.
int total = currentUser.getEnrolledSections().size();
totalCoursesLabel.setText("" + total);
```

And, as a housekeeping measure, we clear out the user's selection in the scheduleOfClassesList:

```
        // Clear the selection in the
        // schedule of classes list.
        scheduleOfClassesList.clearSelection();
    }
}
```

and invoke the resetButtons housekeeping method.

```
    // Check states of the various buttons.
    resetButtons();
    }
};
```

```
addButton.addActionListener(aListener);
```

The dropButton ActionListener

The code for responding to a press of the Drop button is quite similar to that for the Add button, albeit a bit less elaborate; here, all we need to do is

- Determine which item the user selected in his or her studentCourseList.

- Drop the course.

- Display a confirmation message.

- Refresh the user-related information displayed on the screen.

We present the code without further discussion; please refer to in-line comments in the code.

```
    // dropButton

    aListener = new ActionListener() {
        public void actionPerformed(ActionEvent e) {
            // Determine which section is selected
            // (note that we must cast it, as it
            // is returned as an Object reference).
            Section selected = (Section)
                studentCourseList.getSelectedValue();

            // Drop the course.
            selected.drop(currentUser);

            // Display a confirmation message.
            JOptionPane.showMessageDialog(null,
                "Course " + selected.
                    getRepresentedCourse().
                    getCourseNo() + " dropped.",
                "Request Successful",
                JOptionPane.INFORMATION_MESSAGE);

            // Update the list of sections that
            // this student is registered for.
            // (Note that a JList likes to be "fed" an Array,
            // so we call the toArray method on the collection
            // returned by the getEnrolledSections method.)
            studentCourseList.setListData(currentUser.
                getEnrolledSections().toArray(new Section[1]));

            // Update the field representing
            // student's course total.
            int total = currentUser.getEnrolledSections().size();
            totalCoursesLabel.setText("" + total);

            // Check states of the various buttons.
            resetButtons();
        }
    };

    dropButton.addActionListener(aListener);
```

The saveScheduleButton ActionListener

The ActionListener for the saveScheduleButton takes advantage of the SRSDataAccess.
persistStudent method to attempt to save the state of the Student (in particular, his or her
potentially modified course load) in persistent storage.

```
            // saveScheduleButton

        aListener = new ActionListener() {
            public void actionPerformed(ActionEvent e) {
                try {
                    SRSDataAccess.persistStudent(currentUser);

                    // If no exceptions are thrown,
                    // let the user know that his/her
                    // schedule was successfully saved.
                    JOptionPane.showMessageDialog(null,
                    "Schedule saved.",
                    "Schedule Saved",
                    JOptionPane.INFORMATION_MESSAGE);
                }
                catch (StudentPersistenceException e2) {
                    // Let the user know that there
                    // was a problem.
                    JOptionPane.showMessageDialog(null,
                    "Problem saving your " +
                    "schedule; please contact " +
                    "the SRS Support Staff for " +
                    "assistance.",
                    "Problem Saving Schedule",
                    JOptionPane.WARNING_MESSAGE);
                }
            }
        };

        saveScheduleButton.addActionListener(aListener);
```

The logoffButton ActionListener

When a user logs off, we clear out various GUI components:

```
    // logoffButton

aListener = new ActionListener() {
  public void actionPerformed(ActionEvent e) {
    clearFields();
    ssnField.setText("");
    currentUser = null;

    // Clear the selection in the
    // schedule of classes list.
    scheduleOfClassesList.clearSelection();
```

```
    // Check states of the various buttons.
    resetButtons();
  }
};


logoffButton.addActionListener(aListener);
```

ListSelectionListeners for studentCourseList and scheduleOfClassesList

Both the studentCourseList and scheduleOfClassesList components are JLists, and so they both generate ListSelectionEvents whenever an item in either list is clicked. For variety, we'll implement a ListSelectionListener for these components, rather than an ActionListener; this requires us to program a valueChanged method rather than an actionPerformed method, but the concept is the same.

Note that we are using these two listeners in such a way as to make sure that there is never an item selected in both lists simultaneously: that is, if a selection is made in one list, we *clear* the selection in the other.

```
// studentCourseList

lListener = new ListSelectionListener() {
  public void valueChanged(ListSelectionEvent e) {
    // When an item is selected in THIS list,
    // we clear the selection in the OTHER list.
    if (!(studentCourseList.isSelectionEmpty()))
      scheduleOfClassesList.clearSelection();

    // Check states of the various buttons.
    resetButtons();
  }
};


studentCourseList.addListSelectionListener(lListener);


// scheduleOfClassesList

lListener = new ListSelectionListener() {
  public void valueChanged(ListSelectionEvent e) {
    // When an item is selected in THIS list,
    // we clear the selection in the OTHER list.
    if (!(scheduleOfClassesList.isSelectionEmpty()))
      studentCourseList.clearSelection();

    // Check states of the various buttons.
    resetButtons();
  }
};


scheduleOfClassesList.addListSelectionListener(lListener);
```

We also add a listener to the frame to enable us to close the window via its close (⊠) button.

```
wListener = new WindowAdapter() {
  public void windowClosing(WindowEvent e) {
    System.exit(0);
  }
};

this.addWindowListener(wListener);

this.setVisible(true);
}
```

Housekeeping Methods

As mentioned throughout this discussion, we've outfitted the MainFrame class with several housekeeping methods; note that these are all declared to be private, meaning that they are only used within MainFrame. Please read the in-line comments in the following code to appreciate what each of these methods does.

```
private void resetButtons() {
  // There are four conditions which collectively govern the
  // state of each button:

  // 1: Whether a user is logged on or not.
  boolean isLoggedOn;
  if (currentUser != null) isLoggedOn = true;
  else isLoggedOn = false;

  // 2: Whether the user is registered for at least one course.
  boolean atLeastOne;
  if (currentUser != null && currentUser.getEnrolledSections().size() > 0)
    atLeastOne = true;
  else atLeastOne = false;

  // 3: Whether a registered course has been selected.
  boolean courseSelected;
  if (studentCourseList.isSelectionEmpty())
    courseSelected = false;
  else courseSelected = true;

  // 4: Whether an item is selected in the Schedule of Classes.
  boolean catalogSelected;
  if (scheduleOfClassesList.isSelectionEmpty())
    catalogSelected = false;
  else catalogSelected = true;
```

```
    // Now, verify the conditions on a button-by-button basis.

    // Drop button:
    if (isLoggedOn && atLeastOne && courseSelected)
        dropButton.setEnabled(true);
    else dropButton.setEnabled(false);

    // Add button:
    if (isLoggedOn && catalogSelected)
        addButton.setEnabled(true);
    else addButton.setEnabled(false);

    // Save My Schedule button:
    if (isLoggedOn) {
        saveScheduleButton.setEnabled(true);

        // Because of the way that we created the latter two
        // buttons, we have to do a bit of extra work to make them
        // appear to be turned on or off.
        l1.setEnabled(true);
        l2.setEnabled(true);
    }
    else {
        saveScheduleButton.setEnabled(false);

        // Because of the way that we created the latter two
        // buttons, we have to do a bit of extra work to make them
        // appear to be turned on or off.
        l1.setEnabled(false);
        l2.setEnabled(false);
    }

    // Log Off button:
    if (isLoggedOn) logoffButton.setEnabled(true);
    else logoffButton.setEnabled(false);
}

//---------------------------

// Called whenever a user is logged off.
private void clearFields() {
    nameLabel.setText("");
    totalCoursesLabel.setText("");

    // Note that a JList likes to be "fed" an array,
    // so we fabricate a "dummy" empty Object array.
    studentCourseList.setListData(new Object[1]);
}
```

```java
// Set the various fields, lists, etc. to reflect the information
// associated with a particular student. (Used when logging in.)
private void setFields(Student theStudent) {
    nameLabel.setText(theStudent.getName());
    int total = theStudent.getEnrolledSections().size();
    totalCoursesLabel.setText("" + total);

    // If the student is registered for any courses, list these, too.
    if (total > 0) {
        // Because we already have a collection containing the
        // sections that the student is registered for,
        // and because these objects have defined a toString()
        // method, we can merely hand the collection to the JList.
        // (Note that a JList likes to be "fed" an array,
        // so we call the toArray method on the collection
        // returned by the getEnrolledSections method.)
        studentCourseList.setListData(theStudent.
            getEnrolledSections().toArray(new Section[1]));
    }
}

//----------------------------

// A utility method used to convert the contents of the HashMap into a
// Section array that is sorted in alphabetic section no. order.
private Section[] sortSections(HashMap<String, Section> sections) {
    // We'll transfer the contents of the HashMap to a TreeMap, which
    // automatically orders its entries in ascending key order.
    TreeMap<String, Section> sortedMap =
        new TreeMap<String, Section>(sections);

    // Then, we convert the contents of the (sorted) TreeMap
    // into a Section array to return it.
    return sortedMap.values().toArray(new Section[1]);
}

//----------------------------

// A utility method used to validate a Student's password by comparing it
// to the first three digits of his/her student ID number.
private boolean validatePassword(Student s, String pw) {
    if (pw == null) return false;
    else if (s.getSsn().startsWith(pw)) return true;
    else return false;
}
}
```

The PasswordPopup Class: Sharing Information Across Windows/Classes

We've already seen one technique for sharing data throughout the various classes of an application, through the use of `public static` attributes of the main class/window (or, for that matter, *any* window), as we do with the various collections declared within the SRS driver program.

Another approach to application-wide data sharing is to allow a class/window A to collect data from the user, and to then have that class A provide accessor methods by which other classes/windows B, C, etc., can request access to the data that A has collected. The `PasswordPopup` class is such a class: the `PasswordPopup` collects the user's password as typed, and then makes it available to client code (the `MainFrame` class, in our application) through the public `getPassword` method.

```
// PasswordPopup.java

import java.awt.*;
import java.awt.event.*;
import java.util.*;
import javax.swing.*;


public class PasswordPopup extends JDialog {
```

We create a `password` attribute, so that this class may remember the information gathered from the user until such time as it is asked to divulge it via a call to the `getPassword` method.

```
    private String password;

    // Attributes representing the GUI components.
    private Container contentPane;
    private JLabel passwordLabel;
    private JPasswordField passwordField;

    // Constructor.
    public PasswordPopup(Frame parent) {
```

Recall that the `parent` of a dialog box is the window (`JFrame`) that launched the dialog box; by making this window the parent, we ensure that the dialog box in question will always appear in front of the parent window, especially important for modal dialog boxes, since if a modal dialog box gets buried, the user will be frustrated as to why he or she cannot interact with any of the other windows of the application.

```
    // Invoke the generic JDialog constructor first.
    super(parent, "Enter Password", true);

    contentPane = this.getContentPane();
    contentPane.setLayout(new GridLayout(1, 2));
```

```
passwordLabel = new JLabel("Password:  ", JLabel.RIGHT);
passwordLabel.setForeground(Color.black);
```

We create an ActionListener to listen to the passwordField component:

```
passwordField = new JPasswordField();
ActionListener aListener = new ActionListener() {
  public void actionPerformed(ActionEvent e) {
```

Recall our discussion of the use of a char[] array to retrieve passwords when we discussed JPasswordField in Chapter 16. When we retrieve the password, we use the trim method of the String class to strip off any leading or trailing white space that may have been erroneously typed by the user.

```
    // Retrieve the password.
    char[] pw = passwordField.getPassword();
    password = new String(pw).trim();
```

Next, we **hide** the window, but do not **dispose** of it; it will wait, invisibly, until client code asks it to divulge the password. Then, as we saw when we reviewed the code of the MainFrame class earlier in this chapter, it is the **client** code's responsibility to call the dispose method on this pop-up.

```
    // Hide, but don't dispose of, this window ...
    // we need to give the client code a chance to
    // retrieve the user's typed response via
    // the getPassword method first.
    PasswordPopup.this.setVisible(false);
  }
};

passwordField.addActionListener(aListener);

contentPane.add(passwordLabel);
contentPane.add(passwordField);

this.setSize(200, 60);

// Center it on the screen.
Dimension screenSize = Toolkit.getDefaultToolkit().getScreenSize();
Dimension popupSize = this.getSize();
int width = popupSize.width;
int height = popupSize.height;
this.setLocation((screenSize.width - width)/2,
  (screenSize.height - height)/2);
this.setVisible(true);
}
```

Here's the method to be used to retrieve whatever the user typed:

```
public String getPassword() {
  return password;
}
```

Finally, we provide our PasswordPopup class with a test scaffold main method:

```
// Test scaffold.
public static void main(String[] args) {
    PasswordPopup pp = new PasswordPopup(new JFrame());
    System.out.println("Password typed:  " + pp.getPassword());
    pp.dispose();
    System.exit(0);
}
```

With the addition of a main method to class PasswordPopup, we can now run it from the command line as

```
java PasswordPopup
```

rather than having to run the main driver program to see it as follows:

```
java SRS
```

This is useful if we want to see how our pop-up looks early on in its development.

Note that, as discussed earlier in the chapter, there is no harm in leaving this main method in the PasswordPopup class even after our testing is finished—it is a handy thing to keep around in case we change the look of this dialog box later, and want to retest it.

The SRS Driver Class, Significantly Streamlined

Now that we have a GUI to use in interacting with the SRS, many of the extra steps that we went through in the Chapter 15 version of the SRS driver class are now unnecessary. Specifically, here are the things we were able to eliminate from our main method:

- We no longer need to hardcode the creation of Student objects to simulate logons, since we now have a GUI for this purpose.

- Neither do we need to simulate a Student enrolling in a Section, since we can drive that behavior via the GUI now, too.

- And, since we can now verify the outcome of our interactions with the SRS in terms of object states simply by viewing the GUI, we no longer need to use our various display methods to inspect the internal state of our objects. (We'll *retain* the display methods in their respective classes, however, to help us with debugging the application at a later date as needed.)

The only new logic that we had to add to the SRS class was the *single* line of code needed to create and display an instance of the main GUI window:

```
// Create and display an instance of the main GUI window.
new MainFrame();
```

(Recall that this can be an *unnamed* object because the event-dispatching thread will maintain a handle on it to keep it from being prematurely garbage collected.)

The resultant streamlined SRS class code is shown here:

```java
import java.util.*;

public class SRS {
    public static Faculty faculty;
    public static CourseCatalog courseCatalog;
    public static ScheduleOfClasses scheduleOfClasses;

    public static void main(String[] args) {
        // Initialize all objects.
        try {
            courseCatalog = SRSDataAccess.initializeCourseCatalog();
            scheduleOfClasses =
                SRSDataAccess.initializeScheduleOfClasses("SP2005");
            faculty = SRSDataAccess.initializeFaculty();
        }
        catch (SRSInitializationException e) {
            System.out.println("ERROR:  " + e.getMessage() + "-- GOODBYE!");
            System.exit(0);
        }

        // Create and display an instance of the main GUI window.
        new MainFrame();
    }
}
```

The simplicity of this client code illustrates the value of encapsulating as much detail as possible within the appropriate model/data access/presentation layer classes; we don't want client code to be concerned with details that we're better off keeping a closely guarded secret!

An Overview of J2EE

We can't do justice to all of J2EE (Java 2 Platform, Enterprise Edition, Sun's standard for component-based, multitier applications) in just a few pages—J2EE is worthy of entire book*s*, plural, and there are plenty of good, in-depth J2EE books already on the market. Nonetheless, we want to provide you with enough of a *conceptual overview* of J2EE to serve as the context for discussing how what you've learned in this book is relevant to building enterprise applications.

We mentioned earlier in the chapter that by observing proper model-view separation in developing an application, we make it relatively easy to modernize the technology with which we present the view should we wish to do so at a later date. As it turns out, the popularity of desktop applications waned a bit when the notion of **thin client computing** surged in popularity in the late 1990s. It's thus quite conceivable that the developers of an application like the SRS might want to replace—or, more likely, *complement*—the Swing desktop GUI that we've just completed with a **Java 2 Enterprise Edition (J2EE)** thin-client version.

As with so many things technology related, there has been a "(technology) pendulum swing" away from the extreme of using J2EE as the "be-all and end-all" solution for building the presentation layer of all apps to a more balanced view that includes Swing GUIs as an acceptable solution for the right problem.

In order to understand why web deployment of apps has garnered such favor, it's helpful to first look at the downside of the *alternatives* to web apps.

There are three primary ways of building a view for a Java application:

- As a *conventional desktop application* using AWT/Swing components, such as the GUI that we've built for the SRS

- As a browser-deployed *applet*, built for the most part using these same AWT/Swing components

- As a *thin client browser-based application*, built utilizing J2EE component technology

Let's compare the pros and cons of each of these approaches, beginning with desktop applications.

The Downside of Desktop Application Deployment

Desktop applications are applications that run wholly on a **client machine**, aka personal computer/workstation. Common examples of desktop apps include Microsoft Word and Excel, Netscape Navigator (and other) browsers, and the Java 2 Standard Edition (J2SE) JVM.

Desktop applications are disseminated in executable form (bytecode in the case of Java, machine code/.exe files in the case of natively compiled applications) to the individual workstations on which they are to run. There are numerous "headaches" with such deployment.

Issue #1: Extra Infrastructure Is Often Required to Run Such Applications

There is potentially a lot of software infrastructure that must exist on a client machine in order for a desktop application to run:

- The appropriate platform-dependent JVM, in the case of a Java application, plus optional supporting jar files

- Various dynamic-link libraries (DLLs), in the case of native Windows apps

and so forth. Because of all of the extra "baggage" that is required to run a desktop application, they are often referred to as **fat clients**. This raises two concerns:

- *A given client machine may not have enough "horsepower"* in terms of memory and processor speed to run the application appropriately; it goes without saying that not all workstations are created equal in this regard.

- Debugging the installation/configuration of all of this infrastructure software can become a *nightmare* when large numbers of users must be supported.

Issue #2: Configuration Management Issues

There also are issues related to whether or not all users will get subsequent **updates** to a given application after it is first deployed.

- We must keep track of everyone who is using a given application—the so-called **installed base**—so that we can alert them to new releases. Despite our best efforts to do so, we may lose track of some users, perhaps for as simple a reason is that a user's e-mail address of record might change.

- Then, for those users whom we do successfully contact, we must rely on **their** initiative to install or download the new version. If someone is too busy, or too disorganized, or is otherwise adverse to doing so, then we'll wind up with different users using different (unsupported) versions of our application. Again, a support **nightmare** can ensue!

The Upside of Web Deployment

"Web" deployment is an alternative to physically distributing executable code to client desktops. When an application is web deployed, it's user interface is delivered to a client machine as a series of HTML pages that are viewable via a browser such as Netscape, Foxfire, or Internet Explorer.

"Web" deployment is more properly phrased **browser-based deployment** because not all so-called web apps are deployed publicly via the World Wide Web over the Internet. Instead, many such apps are deployed **privately** within an organization via the organization's **intranet**. Nonetheless, we'll use the commonly accepted industry slang terminology "web app" and "web deployment" to refer to this broader set of applications for the remainder of our J2EE discussion.

The mechanics of accessing a web app are as follows:

- Whenever a user wishes to use such an application, he or she accesses it by typing the URL of the site hosting the application via his or her web browser.

- The application is in turn delivered just in time to that user's browser for his or her use at that exact moment.

- The user is always **guaranteed** to be accessing the newest release, because a web app isn't stored, or "cached," on the user's machine. When the browser session ends—or even when the user "surfs" to a different site, thus exiting the application—the application ceases to exist as far as that user is concerned until the next time the user types in the application's URL.

The only "remnants" of a web app that typically remain on a client machine are **cookies**—bits of information (silently) deposited as name-value pairs by some web applications on the user's computer, so that these bits of information can be accessed the next time a user returns to the same application, making it appear as though the web server "remembered" the user. One common use of a cookie is to store shopping cart information.

The benefits of a web app over a desktop app are thus as follows:

- In theory, no specialized infrastructure is required to distribute such applications—we rely on the existing Internet/intranet infrastructure and an already present web browser.

This presumes, however, that the view is delivered as ***pure*** HMTL—if other client-side technologies (such as JavaScript or Macromedia Flash) are integrated into these HTML pages, then the user's browser may require specialized plug-ins/configurations, and thus we start running into infrastructure issues once again, as we did with desktop apps.

- Our version control/configuration management problems are ***eliminated***! One ***official*** copy of the executable application is maintained centrally; those who use the application always receive the latest version just in time, in "demand pull" fashion. Conversely, people who ***don't*** receive the latest version by definition didn't ***use*** it, and hence didn't ***need*** it!

- There's a broader potential audience for public Internet-based applications—people can accidentally "discover" an application (via search engines like Google) if it isn't access restricted. This is particularly important with public domain applications—particularly e-commerce web sites—where ease of access is considered a strategic business advantage.

To appreciate the ***dramatic*** difference in the level of effort required to support desktop versus browser-based applications, consider the following analogy. Assume that you are responsible for making sure that everyone in your extended group of family and friends are kept informed of world events on a daily basis. You could

- Make dozens of videotape copies of the nightly news as broadcast on TV to hand deliver to each of your family and friends every day, or

- Simply instruct them as to the time and channel to tune into on their ***own*** televisions to watch the live news broadcast themselves.

This dramatic difference in level of effort is indeed representative of the difference in effort required to support traditional desktop apps ("distributing videotapes") versus to support browser-deployed apps ("live television broadcasts"). It's thus no surprise that large IT organizations have migrated toward web deployment of applications whenever feasible: it's not necessarily cheaper to ***build*** such applications, but it is far cheaper to ***support*** them over an application's lifetime.

As we mentioned in Chapter 7 in a sidebar discussion entitled "One Very Important Caveat," a common misconception, held by many, is that switching to object technology will dramatically reduce the time required to ***develop*** a given application. Unfortunately, due to the learning curve involved in switching to the OO paradigm—particularly for software developers who've been entrenched in non-OO techniques for many years—it will typically take ***longer*** for a team inexperienced with objects to develop their first OO application. Nonetheless, if properly architected, even their first such application will pay big dividends in terms of ease of support, since 80% of an application's cost over its lifetime is typically spent on support, only 20% on development.

What About Applets?

An **applet** is a special type of Java program that is downloadable to a client's machine via an HTML page and hence viewable with/executable by a browser. Applets have GUI interfaces that are built from the same AWT/Swing components that we use to build desktop applications, with one key difference: we use a special type of Container called a JApplet as the applet's main window instead of using a JFrame.

An applet is referenced within an HTML page by a special **HTML tag** that identifies the following:

- The version of the JVM that is required as a browser "plug-in" to run the applet (that is, the JVM that matches the version of the Java compiler used to compile the applet into bytecode)

- A link to a page where the appropriate version of the JVM plug-in can be optionally downloaded from if it isn't already installed in the user's browser

- The name of the class that contains the applet's equivalent of a main method (called an init method)

- The name of the jar file containing *all* of the bytecode comprising the applet: its model classes, the various dialog boxes/windows comprising its GUI, its data access layer classes, and so forth

- The size (width, height) in pixels that has been allocated within the HTML page for display of the applet's GUI

For example:

```
<HTML>
<BODY>
<EMBED type="application/x-java-applet;version=1.4.2" width="300" height="180"
       code="BankingApplet" archive="BankingApplet.jar"
       pluginspage="http://java.sun.com/getjava/download.html">
</EMBED>
</BODY>
</HTML>
```

When we "surf" to such an HTML page, the bytecode of the referenced applet is automatically physically downloaded to our local (client) computer, and is run under the control of our browser's JVM plug-in. The applet's bytecode serves as a form of *temporary* plug-in, in that it becomes part of the browser while it is executing, but is discarded when the browser shuts down. Thus, the bytecode of an applet gets downloaded anew whenever the applet is first accessed in a particular browser session.

An applet's GUI appears to be embedded in the page as viewed by the browser (see Figure 17-1), but *only* if the appropriate plug-in is present. Otherwise, depending on which browser you are using and how it is configured, you may either see a "hole" where the applet should have been (see Figure 17-2) or you may be prompted to optionally download the appropriate JVM plug-in.

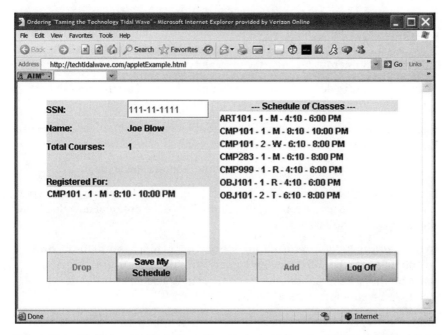

Figure 17-1. *If all goes well, we'll see the applet's GUI embedded in the hosting HTML page.*

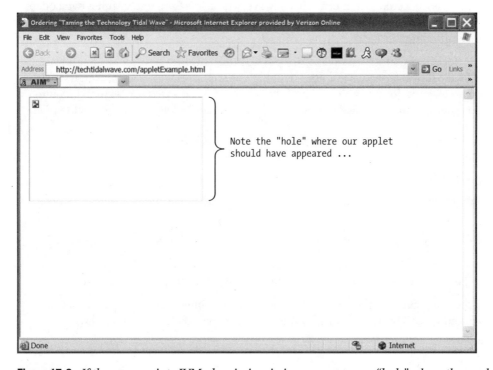

Figure 17-2. *If the appropriate JVM plug-in is missing, we may see a "hole" where the applet's GUI would normally appear.*

Despite the fact that applets are browser-deployed, they are considered to be **thick**, or *heavyweight*, clients, because of the amount of code and supporting data that has to be resident on/downloaded to the client machine (at a minimum, a JVM plug-in and the applet's bytecode jar file). Therein lie numerous problems with applets:

- The bytecode can be slow to download and create an undue load on the underlying network.

- The JVM plug-in can be slow to start up (you'll see the "Loading Java . . ." message in the bottom of your browser window while this is taking place).

- The applet can execute sluggishly if the client machine is underpowered.

- As we discussed a moment ago, the appropriate Java plug-in may be missing from a particular user's browser; that user may not want to bother with the optional download, or may be intimidated about doing so.

Hence, we're liable to get *unpredictable results* from one client machine/user to the next when we rely on applet technology. The bottom line with applets, as with desktop apps, is that we put too much reliance on the "client," in both the machine and user sense of the word.

Are applets "dead" as a technology choice? No . . .

- Sophisticated GUIs may still need the interactive 2D/3D graphics capabilities or other sophistications of Swing, and hence applets may be the only option for web deployment of certain applications.

- Applets are arguably one step ahead of Swing desktop apps, in that the latest version of an applet is delivered just in time virtually every time it is executed. (Applet bytecode is cached only temporarily: as soon as the browser session ends, the downloaded bytecode is abandoned.)

That being said, however, the vast majority of classic information systems type of applications don't *need* heavy-duty interactive graphics. Think of the web sites you've visited lately: most e-commerce web sites, for example, are heavily *forms oriented*—we type textual data into fields, choose items from lists, click buttons—with static graphics (aka eye candy) added for cosmetic appeal.

For these types of applications, *thin client user interfaces are preferred*.

Thin Client Applications

A **thin client application** is one in which the *client* component of a client-server architecture is trivially simple:

- It's involved primarily, if not exclusively, with presenting the view of the application.

- It involves virtually no business logic, and hence no heavy-duty processing occurs on the client machine—the *server* carries the lion's share of the processing load.

The classic thin client approach to presentation layer implementation involves simple HTML forms and a web browser to display them; this is where J2EE comes into play.

For those of us who've been around long enough to remember the days of monolithic mainframe computers and "dumb" terminals, this is another example of the "(technology) pendulum swing" back to a server-centric approach to computing and away from the days of powerful client desktop workstations.

What Is J2EE?

The Java 2 Platform, Enterprise Edition (J2EE) is a collection of over a dozen Java component technologies/APIs that can be used separately or in combination to build **enterprise-level applications**, or simply **enterprise app**(lication)**s**. The J2EE component technologies are used in conjunction with the Java 2 Standard Edition (J2SE) Software Developer's Kit (Java 2 SDK)—that is, the core Java language that we've been discussing, and you've been *mastering*, throughout this book. Thus, being proficient with J2SE is a *critically important* first step to mastering J2EE.

Unfortunately, many folks wanting to gain immediate proficiency with J2EE dive into the deep end of the pool by attempting to learn J2EE without proper grounding in objects and Java first. By reading this book, you are far ahead of the game!

An enterprise application is generally defined as one which is critical to the mission of an organization. Aspects of such an application may include, but needn't necessarily include, the following:

- 24 hours a day × 7 days per week guaranteed availability/"up time"

- Access to a massive amount of persistently stored data (e.g., an employee directory for a large organization)

- Ability to support a high volume of concurrent user sessions

- Implementation/enforcement of business rules that are enterprise wide (e.g., the rules for how an employee's identity should be authenticated)

- Distributed access, such as that which can be easily provided via an intranet/Internet accessible application

- A resultant need for **scalability**: that is, the ability for an application to grow gracefully as the processing demands on the application increase

Different organizations may define "enterprise application" differently, but whatever the definition used by a particular organization, J2EE has become a preferred technology for *implementing* such applications.

The major competitor of J2EE, favored by Microsoft-centric (versus open-standard centric) organizations, is Microsoft's .NET Framework.

The most commonly used J2EE component technologies are

- Servlets
- JavaServer Pages (JSPs)
- The JDBC API

JDBC is actually considered to be part of both the J2SE SDK and J2EE.

We've already conceptually discussed how the JDBC API allows us to access relational databases in a vendor-neutral way in Chapter 15. Let's take a quick look at what two other J2EE component technologies—servlets and JSPs—are all about.

What Is a Servlet?

A **servlet** is a specialized Java program that runs under control of a web server, in essence as a web server "plug-in." In a nutshell, a servlet's mission is to dynamically fabricate and output custom HTML in response to a **request** that's been received by the web server from the client's browser. (We'll discuss the **HTTP request-response cycle** a bit later in this section.)

Common "Java-friendly" web server products include Netscape Enterprise, BEA WebLogic, IBM WebSphere, and Apache Tomcat, among others.

Although the specifics of developing servlets are beyond the scope of this book to address in detail, here is the (pseudo)code for a simple servlet, SimpleServlet.java, that displays a customized "Hello, *name*!" message. (Although servlet technology may be brand new to you, you'll recognize many references to familiar OO/Java techniques in this code: the use of import directives, inheritance, overriding, exceptions, etc.)

```
import javax.servlet.http.HttpServlet;
import javax.servlet.http.HttpServletRequest;
import javax.servlet.http.HttpServletResponse;
import java.io.PrintWriter;
import java.io.IOException;

public class SimpleServlet extends HttpServlet {
    // We must override the doGet method that the
    // predefined HttpServlet class declares.
```

```java
// (Note that objects representing both a
// request and a response are passed into this
// method by the web server.)
public void doGet(HttpServletRequest request,
    HttpServletResponse response) throws IOException {
    // Indicate that the response will be crafted
    // as HTML.
    response.setContentType("text/html");

    // Obtain a PrintWriter from the response object;
    // whatever we output to this PrintWriter will get
    // sent back to the client's browser, wrapped
    // in a response object (as HTML, in this case).
    PrintWriter out = response.getWriter();

    // Formulate our HTML -- this part is "canned."
    out.println("<HTML>");
    out.println("<HEAD>");
    out.println("<TITLE>Simple Servlet</TITLE>");
    out.println("</HEAD>");
    out.println("<BODY>");

    // In order to formulate custom HTML content, we often
    // retrieve values from the request, representing data
    // that was input by the user via an HTML form displayed
    // on their browser.
    String userid = request.getParameter("uid");
    String password = request.getParameter("passwd");

    // Validate this userid/password combination, and
    // create a Person object to represent the user
    // who has just logged on (details omitted).
    // Pseudocode.
    Person user = user who just logged on;

    // Output whatever custom content we wish to display;
    // in this case, we embed the user's name in the
    // "Hello" message.
    out.println("Hello, " + user.getName() + "!");

    // Finish up with more "canned" HTML.
    out.println("</BODY>");
    out.println("</HTML>");
    out.close();
  }
}
```

We see the resultant output from our `SimpleServlet` as viewed via a browser in Figure 17-3.

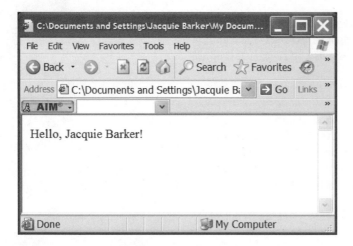

Figure 17-3. *The output that would be displayed in our browser from running the previous "Hello" servlet.*

Again, we'll discuss how this servlet output/response gets transmitted to the user's browser via the HTTP request/response cycle shortly.

What Is a JavaServer Page?

A **JavaServer Page** (**JSP**) is a hybrid of HTML and Java code that gets ***turned into a servlet*** behind the scenes by the web server the first time the JSP is accessed. Thus, writing a JSP is simply a convenient, alternative way of writing a servlet that typically involves writing fewer lines of Java code, as we'll see in a moment.

Although the specifics of developing JSPs is beyond the scope of this book to address in detail, following is a sample JSP that does the equivalent work of the `SimpleServlet` example that we presented earlier—namely, a JSP named `Simple.jsp` that displays a customized "Hello, *name*!" message. A few points of interest:

- We've eliminated the tedium of outputting canned HTML from a servlet (via `out.println(...)` calls) by simply typing it as such.

- Whenever we want to formulate ***custom*** HTML output, we drop into ***Java mode*** by introducing a `<%` tag; from that point on, until we ***leave*** Java mode with a `%>` tag, we are able to write straightforward Java code—as it turns out, the ***same*** code that we used in our servlet a moment ago!

- We're able to combine HTML and Java in the same line using the syntax `<%= Java expression %>`—for example, `Hello, <%=user.getName()%>!`.

Here's the complete JSP:

```
<HTML>
<HEAD>
<TITLE>Simple JSP</TITLE>
</HEAD>
<BODY>

<!-- We drop into Java scriptlet mode here ... -->
<%
// This is the SAME code that we saw in our servlet!
// In order to formulate custom HTML content, we often
// retrieve values from the request, representing data
// that was input by the user via an HTML form displayed
// on their browser.
String userid = request.getParameter("uid");
String password = request.getParameter("passwd");

// Validate this userid/password combination, and
// create a Person object to represent the user
// who has just logged on.
// Details omitted; pseudocode.
Person user = user who just logged on;
%>
<!-- ... and we drop out of Java mode here. -->

<!-- Formulate our custom "Hello" message. -->
Hello, <%=user.getName()%>!

</BODY>
</HTML>
```

When converted into an equivalent servlet and executed by a web server, the preceding JSP would produce the ***exact same output*** as was produced by our earlier servlet, as was shown in Figure 17-3 earlier.

JAVA-LESS JSPS?

The Java content of a JSP is often disguised in the form of **JSP tags** that get translated into Java code when the JSP is translated into a servlet. For example, the lines

```
Person user = user who just logged on;
```

and

```
Hello, <%=user.getName()%>!
```

can alternatively be rendered with JSP tags as follows:

```
<jsp:usebean id="person" scope="request" class="Person" />
Hello, <jsp:getProperty name="person" property="name" />!
```

  The argument in favor of doing so is that folks who are skilled at web page design, but not with Java, can learn the JSP tag language and can design the "look" of a web app while Java experts can develop the model classes that these tags rely upon behind the scenes. Nonetheless, the bottom line is that EVERYTHING in a JSP gets preprocessed into Java code in the form of a servlet before it is actually executed the first time.

If we used our browser's "View => Source" (or equivalent) option to look at the HTML that was *dynamically* generated by either the servlet or the JSP, it would look as shown in Figure 17-4: that is, by the time it reaches our browser, it's indistinguishable from *static* HTML.

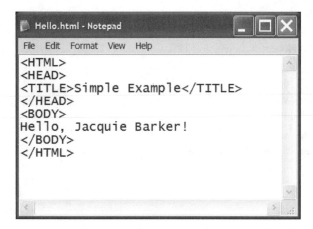

Figure 17-4. *Viewing the source of our servlet- or JSP-generated page*

Let's now talk conceptually about how these three J2EE technologies (JDBC, JSPs, and servlets) can be brought to bear in crafting a browser-based version of the SRS.

Other J2EE component technologies include Enterprise JavaBeans (EJBs), Java Naming and Directory Interface (JNDI), Java IDL, Java Message Service (JMS), Java Transaction API (JTA), and Java Transaction Service (JTS).

J2EE, Model View Controller–Style

The approach for building a J2EE application as endorsed by Sun Microsystems is known as the **Model View Controller** (**MVC**) approach (recall our discussion of MVC in Chapter 16 with respect to desktop applications). In a nutshell, here's how MVC works with regard to J2EE:

1. We design an application's *(thin client) view* as a collection of (a) static HTML forms that are used to *gather information* from the user, (b) servlets/JSPs for generating *custom HTML responses* back to the user. (These take the place of the various Swing JFrames/JDialogs that we use to comprise a desktop application's view.)

2. We then use a servlet as the *controller*/ "traffic cop" for the application, as illustrated conceptually in Figure 17-5.

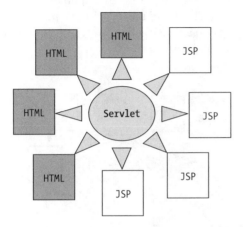

Figure 17-5. *A servlet serves as the "traffic cop" for a J2EE application, whose view is comprised of HTML forms and JSPs.*

3. We kick off the application by having our user "surf" to our application's home page—most likely, a static HTML log-on form.

4. When the user presses the submit button on that form, the information gathered by the form is transferred to the web server as an **HTTP request**, as illustrated in Figure 17-6. The request encapsulates information from the HTML form that the user has just interacted with.

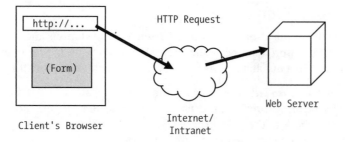

Figure 17-6. *An HTTP request is sent by the browser to the web server via the Internet or an intranet when a user presses a submit button on an HTML form.*

5. Our "traffic cop" servlet receives and processes the request. Based upon the information provided by the user, the servlet decides which page of the "view" to **dispatch** next; it could be yet another static HMTL page or dynamically generated HTML as produced by a servlet/JSP, as illustrated conceptually in Figure 17-7.

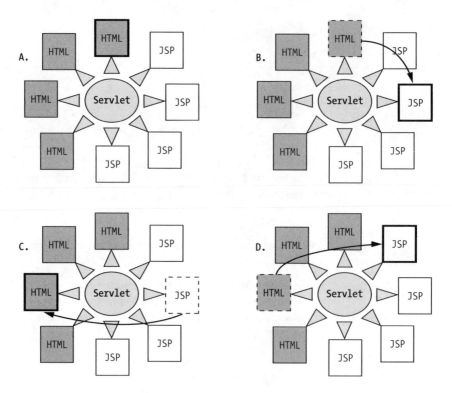

Figure 17-7. *The "traffic cop" servlet decides which page of the view is to be dispatched at any point in time.*

6. Whatever (static/dynamic) page is selected by the servlet is sent back to the browser from which the request came, in the form of an **HTTP response**, as illustrated in Figure 17-8.

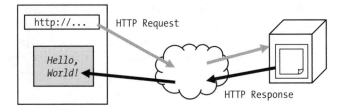

Figure 17-8. *The servlet inspects the request, and formulates an appropriate HTTP response, which is sent back to the browser and displayed.*

7. In formulating custom HTML output, the JSPs in turn rely on model objects—known alternatively as **beans** or **JavaBeans** in the context of J2EE applications—to render behind-the-scenes business logic. ***Note that these bean/model classes are the same model classes that we used in building the SRS desktop application!***

"(Java) beans" in the informal sense are not to be confused with **Enterprise JavaBeans (EJBs)**, another Java component technology that we'll discuss a bit later.

---

8. The beans/model objects typically communicate with the data access layer of our application, using JDBC technology to access an enterprise data repository. ***Note that we use the same data access layer code/classes that we used to support the SRS as built in Chapter 15!***

The architecture of a J2EE application is shown conceptually in Figure 17-9.

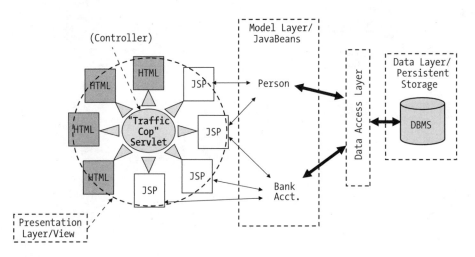

Figure 17-9. *The architecture of a J2EE application consists of a view comprised of HTML forms/JSPs, a servlet "traffic cop"/controller, model/bean objects, and a data access layer to persistent storage.*

Because we are able to ***reuse the model and data access layers*** of the SRS that we've built in Chapters 14 and 15, respectively, ***exactly as-is***, the ***ONLY*** thing we'd need to do to update our SRS application to take advantage of J2EE technology would be to build a new presentation layer (i.e., a thin client view). ***This is a proof-positive demonstration of the incredible power of model-view separation!***

N-Tier Architectures

When we talk about an **n-tier architecture**, "n" typically equals five with respect to J2EE applications, as follows:

- The **client tier**, consisting of a simple browser

- The **presentation tier**, consisting of the HTML/JSP view

- The **application tier**, consisting of our model/bean objects

- The **data access tier**, which encapsulates the details of accessing persistent storage

- The **data tier** (e.g., a relational database or other persistent storage medium)

If we build an MVC web application using servlet, JSP, and JDBC technology as we've just discussed, these tiers break out as shown in Figure 17-10; note that the presentation and application tiers are collocated on, and both are driven by, the web server.

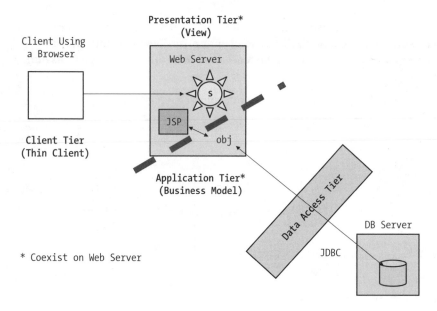

Figure 17-10. *N-tier architecture*

What Are EJBs?

For particularly heavy-duty J2EE applications, we can distribute the presentation and application tiers onto two ***separate*** machines through the use of **Enterprise JavaBeans (EJBs)**—another of the J2EE component technologies.

- With EJBs, we are effectively able to split our model objects into *two* objects—a **stub**, which resides on the web server, and a **remote EJB**, which resides on a separate EJB-capable **application server**.

- Each stub finds a "companion" EJB via a **naming service** (such as JNDI, another J2EE component technology) and connects to the remote EJB via a **remote method invocation (RMI) protocol**.

- From this point forward, the stub and remote EJB work in tandem to serve the application. Whenever a JSP needs data about a model object, it talks to a stub, which talks behind the scenes to its corresponding EJB; the EJB manipulates persistent storage via the data access layer, passing any necessary results back to the stub, which in turn passes them to the JSP. This cooperative relationship between a stub and an EJB is represented conceptually in Figures 17-11 through 17-14.

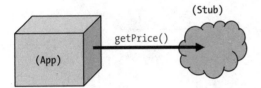

Figure 17-11. *Our web app requests a service of a stub . . .*

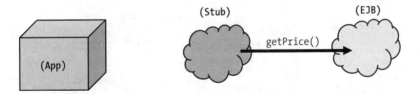

Figure 17-12. *. . . and the stub in turn requests this same service of its companion EJB.*

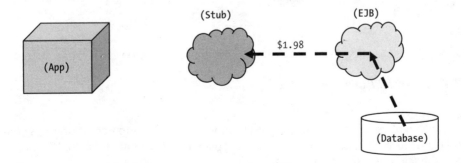

Figure 17-13. *The EJB retrieves the necessary data from the data access layer, returning it to the stub . . .*

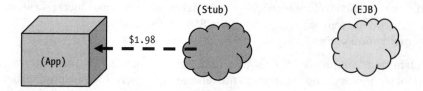

Figure 17-14. *. . . and the stub returns the data to the web app*

- When our application releases its handle on the stub object, the corresponding EJB is freed up to await a connection with a different stub from the same or another J2EE application.

The architecture of an EJB-enabled J2EE web application is illustrated conceptually in Figure 17-15.

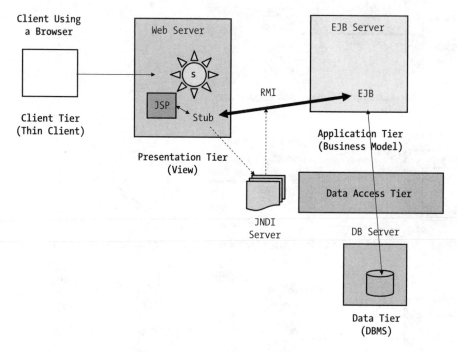

Figure 17-15. *N-Tier J2EE architecture, EJB-style*

Being able to physically separate the presentation and application tiers affords us greater scalability/tunability of a J2EE application. EJBs/application servers are thus used for high volume, 24×7 applications, à la Amazon.com.

Dispelling J2EE Myths

Misconception #1: An application is not considered to be a J2EE application unless EJBs were used to build it.

Reality: Any use of any of the J2EE component technologies—JSPs, servlets, JDBC—is, strictly speaking, considered to be a J2EE application. People commonly misuse the term "J2EE application" to refer only to "an application that uses EJBs, and hence involves an application server." But, it is perfectly acceptable to build an "EJB-less" J2EE application if the usage pattern of the application doesn't warrant the cost/complexity of EJBs. Bottom line: always clarify what someone means by "J2EE app"!

Misconception #2: A "non-EJB" J2EE application is "not worthy" (!).

Reality: A Gartner, Inc. study found that the majority of J2EE applications rely ***exclusively*** on JSPs, servlets, and JDBC, rather than on EJBs. As mentioned previously, using EJBs and an application server is often overkill in terms of expense and complexity.

Misconception #3: J2EE technology is only used for building web apps.

Reality: Any enterprise application can take advantage of J2EE technology, whether it has a thin client user interface or not. Figure 17-16 presents an architecture for an EJB-enabled J2EE application that uses a Swing desktop client to render both the client and presentation tiers of the application.

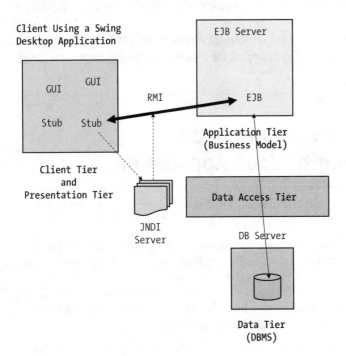

Figure 17-16. *An EJB-enabled desktop application*

The Relevance of What You've Learned in This Book to J2EE

Everything that you've learned about Java and objects in this book is relevant to building J2EE applications! In order to be successful with J2EE, one must be proficient with Java; in order to be proficient with Java, one must be "object savvy." This entire book has been devoted to teach you the essentials of both Java and objects.

Other J2EE-relevant techniques that you've learned:

- The importance of building the model layer/classes as an abstraction of the real world, and the object modeling techniques to support this

- The key design principle of model–data layer separation, and how to carry it out effectively in Java

- The key design principle of model–view separation, and how to carry it out effectively in Java

The only things you haven't been taught in *detail* in this book are

- The nitty-gritty details of using JDBC

- The nitty-gritty details of using the J2EE component technologies

However, armed with the conceptual knowledge that you've gained in this book about these two technology areas, combined with your new-found expertise with Java and objects, you are perfectly poised to master JDBC/J2EE in record time!

Please visit our web site, `http://objectstart.com`, for information about "*Deploying Java Objects On The Web" Self-Study Workbook*, as well as looking into the recommended reading presented in Chapter 18 of this book.

Review of the Architecture of an "Industrial-Strength" Java Application

As we discussed in Chapter 13, the architecture of a nontrivial Java application, such as that which we have built for the SRS, consists of *many* Java source files that, when compiled, yield *many* bytecode files.

- We typically have one `.java`/source code file for each of the *model classes* that we define in our UML class diagram; for the SRS application, we created ten such classes: Course, CourseCatalog, Faculty, Person, Professor, ScheduleOfClasses, Section, Student, Transcript, and TranscriptEntry. These classes jointly comprise the *model layer* of our SRS application—an abstraction of the real-world problem to be automated, encapsulating the *business logic* of the application.

  By keeping this a *pure abstraction*—that is, by not "muddying" it with details of (a) presentation, (b) persistence—we can easily use the same model with different presentation/persistence technologies to support the same or multiple different applications over time, as illustrated in Figure 17-17.

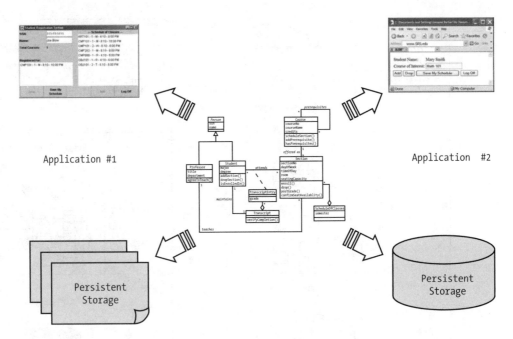

Figure 17-17. *The same model can serve many different views/persistence mechanisms.*

Furthermore, it is quite painless to modernize the view or persistence mechanism of a given application when the three layers are loosely coupled, as represented conceptually in Figure 17-18.

The model layer of an application is the layer least likely to change over time; if the business rules of an organization do change, however, we've learned how to accommodate such changes with a minimum of ripple effects through (a) encapsulation/information hiding and (b) specialization through inheritance.

- We typically need one or more classes to be involved with *establishing connectivity to persistent data storage*. We created one such class for the SRS—SRSDataAccess—which represents the *data access layer* of our SRS application.

We engineered this class to access record-oriented ASCII files, but then demonstrated how easy it would be to retrofit an entirely different persistence mechanism—for example, relational database access—because of our adherence to the key architectural principle of *model–data access layer separation*. That is, in building the data access layer, we focused on keeping the model classes *free of persistence details* to make them maximally reusable.

- We also typically craft a separate .java/source code file to house the class declaration for each of the primary windows comprising the *graphical user interface* of an application, if any. For the SRS application, we declared two such classes—MainFrame and PasswordPopup—which together comprised our application's "view", or *presentation layer*.

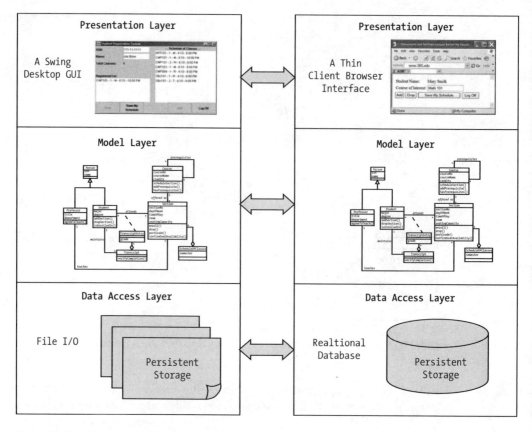

Figure 17-18. *It's easy to adopt a new view or persistence mechanism for the same model when these three layers are loosely coupled.*

We implemented the SRS GUI using the Java AWT and Swing API classes to render a traditional desktop application, but then demonstrated how easy it would be to retrofit an entirely different presentation mechanism—for example, a J2EE thin client user interface—because of our adherence to the key architectural principle of ***model–view separation***. That is, in building the presentation layer, we focused on keeping the model classes ***free of presentation details*** to make them maximally reusable.

- We typically have a separate `.java` source code file to house the class that encapsulates the official `main` method, which as we know serves as the application's starting point; for the SRS application, this class was named `SRS`.

One of the primary responsibilities of an application's `main` method is to instantiate the core objects needed to fulfill a system's mission, accessing persistent storage as needed to "reconstitute" objects in memory. In the final (Chapter 16) version of our SRS `main` method, we instantiated three key collections of objects: `faculty`, `courseCatalog`, and `scheduleOfClasses`.

The main method is also typically responsible for displaying the start-up window of a graphical user interface, if our application has one; in the case of the SRS, the MainFrame window is launched by the main method when our application first starts up.

- Finally, we often have additional "helper" classes to provide behind-the-scenes application support; with the SRS, we had a need for four such classes: an enum(eration) called EnrollmentStatus, and three types of custom exception (SRSInitializationException, InvalidStudentException, and StudentPersistenceException).

All told, we've created a total of 18 source code (*.java) ***files, compiling them into bytecode and integrating them into a single SRS application*** with a graphical user interface and a way to persist the state of our objects from one SRS application session to the next.

Summary

In this chapter, you learned

- How to plan the "look" of a GUI, and creative uses of GridLayout to help you in assembling components into "layers"

- The philosophy and advantages of model-view separation, and the importance of model–data layer separation

- The development of a concept of operations, or "storyboard," as a means for getting sponsor/client/user buy-in before any code has been written, to ensure that the proposed look and flow of a GUI meets the use case requirements for the system

- Data sharing techniques: public static attributes, state retrieval methods

- The basics of J2EE and how all that you've learned in this book provides important foundational skills for building J2EE applications

And, you saw the ***pièce de résistance***: adding a GUI front-end to the SRS application! You've now come through the full life cycle of the SRS application, beginning with an expression of requirements via use cases in Chapter 9, to an object model in Chapters 10 and 11, to a command-line–driven program in Chapter 14; a program with file persistence in Chapter 15; and a GUI-driven application in Chapter 17.

Exercises

1. Write a concept of operations document for the problem area that you selected for exercise 3 of Chapter 1.

2. [*Coding*] Improve the Calculator4 example found in this chapter so that it performs proper exception handling; right now, if the user clicks the + or − button without typing in two proper numbers, a NumberFormatException run-time exception arises. (Hint: you'll need to wrap the code that manipulates the values retrieved from the text fields on the GUI in a try-catch block.)

3. [*Coding*] For all of the catch blocks located in the various SRS classes, use JOptionPane to display an appropriate error message to the user.

4. [*Coding*] ***Advanced***: Modify the SRS application to provide the user with the capability for setting his or her own password. This will involve

   - Adding a Set Password button on the MainFrame that launches a dialog box to solicit a user's new password (consider reuse of the PasswordPopup class for this)

   - Changing the record structure of the Student.dat file to accommodate a password

   - Modifying the model and data access layer classes, if/as appropriate

5. [*Coding*] ***Advanced***: Add a different view for the SRS that a department chairperson would use for purposes of editing the schedule of classes to add/cancel courses and/or to change faculty teaching assignments.

CHAPTER 18

■ ■ ■

Next Steps

Congratulations! You've made it through quite a learning curve, from object concepts, to object modeling, to Java programming. What you do next will depend on what your intentions were for learning this material in the first place:

- **If you're a software developer** primarily interested in building Java applications, you'll want to get some hands-on Java programming experience if you haven't already done so. A good first step is to tackle some of the end-of-chapter exercises in this book; if you've already done so, then you may be ready to try your hand at a full life-cycle object-oriented development project. See the next section in this chapter, "Jacquie's 'Tried and True' Approach to Learning Java Properly," for a game plan on how to proceed, and the "Other Recommended Reading" section later in this chapter for other books that might be appropriate next steps in your continued professional development.

- **If you're a systems analyst** primarily interested in object modeling, be certain to attempt the exercises at the ends of the chapters in Part 2 of the book if you haven't already done so. Then, seek out an opportunity to engage in an object modeling project within your organization, ideally with a senior object modeler to guide and mentor you.

- **If you're a manager** whose goal is to become better versed in these technologies, this may be an appropriate time to conduct a technology review of ongoing projects in your organization to learn how the techniques touched upon in this book are specifically being carried out.

- **If you're an instructor**, please review Appendix A for suggestions on how to use this material as the basis of a beginning object methods/Java curriculum in either an academic or a corporate setting.

Whatever your focus, be sure to visit my web site, `http://objectstart.com`, for additional suggestions as well as links to related web sites that you may find of interest.

Jacquie's "Tried and True" Approach to Learning Java Properly

Here are my recommendations on how to advance through the Java learning curve as smoothly and effectively as possible.

1. Understand OO analysis and design—hopefully, this book has gone a long way toward helping you to accomplish this, and the recommended reading suggestions later in this chapter will help you to deepen this understanding.

2. Obtain a good reference book on Java to complement *Beginning Java Objects*. My book has hopefully given you an excellent jump-start with the language, and the recommended reading suggestions later in this chapter will serve to complement this knowledge.

3. Download and install a free copy of the latest release of the Java Software Developer's Kit (SDK) from the Sun Microsystems web site as described in Appendix C.

4. Compile and run a simple "Hello, World" program from the command line to ensure that all Java SDK components are installed and working properly.

5. Choose a *simple* first problem to automate: one that (a) you're very familiar with the requirements for—perhaps a small-scale application that you've already built in some other language, or an application based upon some hobby—and (b) requires only a handful of domain classes when modeled.

6. Produce a UML class diagram for your application based on the object modeling techniques that you learned in Part 2 of the book.

7. Write the code for your model classes, and get the application to work as a command-line application first, as we did for the Student Registration System (SRS) in Chapter 14. (This is your *model*, *without* a graphical view.)

8. Learn more about Java GUI development beyond what you explored in Chapters 16 and 17, and buy a supplemental reference book on this subject.

9. Add a GUI front-end onto the code that you produced in step 7, as we did for the SRS in Chapter 17. My personal bias is that you should do so by writing GUI code from scratch the first time around, without using a "drag-and-drop" IDE/GUI building tool, as I believe that you'll learn GUI concepts more thoroughly by doing so.

10. Learn more about the JDBC API, and buy a good tutorial book on this subject.

11. Acquire the appropriate Java driver class for your particular DBMS, if necessary, and connect your application to a database back-end so as to persist your objects. Or, visit http://objectstart.com for links regarding free, single-user DBMSs in the public domain that are ideal for educational use.

12. (Optional) If you're inclined to use an IDE, invest in a commercially available Java IDE or obtain a copy of one of the popular free, open source Java IDEs, such as Eclipse (available from `http://www.eclipse.org`), Sun Java Studio (available from `http://java.sun.com`), or a reasonably priced shareware product, TextPad (available from `http://www.textpad.com`).

13. (Optional) Join a Java special interest group, either online or in person. This is an invaluable way to get informal, ad hoc mentorship from colleagues who are more experienced with Java.

From this point forward, your options are open-ended! For example, you may wish to focus on mastering the XML capabilities of Java, or to study the Java 2 Enterprise Edition (J2EE) component technologies that we introduced conceptually in Chapter 17. Whichever direction you choose, you can rest assured that there will be plenty of Java-related technology innovations in the months and years to come.

Taming the Technology Tidal Wave

Virtually all software professionals whom I've met—myself included!—share a common concern: namely, we're **overwhelmed** by how fast technology continues to change. It seems that we barely have time to learn even the **basics** about a new technology X before an even **newer** technology Y comes along to render X **obsolete**! Yet, our career success, if not our very career **survival**, depends on maintaining leading-edge skills in a particular information technology discipline.

What are we to do?

- We certainly can't stop the ever-accelerating pace with which technology is advancing.

- It's not humanly possible to try to learn every new "technology du jour" in our chosen area of specialization, nor should we even try, because many are merely passing fads.

- We can't afford to ignore the problem, either, hoping that it will go away, because it simply won't.

What we **can** do is learn strategies for how to **cope** with this onslaught of new technologies, so that no matter how rapidly technological change occurs, we're able to save ourselves from drowning by

- **Identifying which emerging technologies are worth paying attention to** and, just as important, knowing **when** to dive into each one

- **Utilizing creative, inexpensive ways to master these technologies**

- **Leveraging the skills that we already possess** to help us move into roles where we'll gain on-the-job exposure to these technologies

- Recognizing—and **avoiding**—**pitfalls** that could otherwise lead us off track in our career

- Above all, staying calm—and having **fun**—while we're at it!

Such strategies, once mastered, should last us a professional lifetime, because while technology may be constantly changing, the ways we should approach learning these technologies do not change. And that is precisely what my newest book, ***Taming the Technology Tidal Wave: Practical Career Advice for IT Professionals*** (ISBN: 0-97447-988-8; ObjectStart Press, 2005), is all about: presenting strategies for staying technologically current that have worked for me throughout my 27+ year career as a software engineer, and for countless other technical professionals that I've advised over the years in my roles as manager, colleague, teacher, and friend.

Please visit `http://techtidalwave.com` to learn how you, too, can ***tame the technology tidal wave***!

Other Recommended Reading

Many fine books have been written and published on the subject of OO software development by a variety of publishers, and it would be virtually impossible to do justice to them all here. Consider this list to represent some of my personal recommendations (visit my web site, `http://objectstart.com`, for more recommendations), but please do browse the titles available from your favorite technical bookseller, as new titles are being released literally every day.

- Booch, Grady, James Rumbaugh, and Ivar Jacobson. *The Unified Modeling Language User Guide*. Boston: Addison-Wesley, 1998.

  A definitive reference on the UML, written by its creators. It's definitely worth adding to your library if you're serious about object modeling.

- Rumbaugh, James, Ivar Jacobson, and Grady Booch. *The Unified Modeling Language Reference Manual*. Boston: Addison-Wesley, 1999.

  A second definitive reference by the same gentlemen; see the comments for the preceding title.

- Jacobson, Ivar, Grady Booch, and James Rumbaugh. *Unified Software Development Process*. Boston: Addison-Wesley, 1999.

  And a third!

- Quatrani, Terry. *Visual Modeling with Rational Rose and UML*. Boston: Addison-Wesley, 1998.

  A practical, step-by-step guide for how to use Rational Rose, one of the industry's leading object modeling CASE tools, to prepare UML models.

- Eriksson, Hans-Erik and Magnus Penker. *UML Toolkit*. New York: John Wiley & Sons, Inc., 1998.

  Comes with a CD-ROM containing a demo copy of Rational Rose, numerous UML models, and code.

- Taylor, David A. *Object Technology: A Manager's Guide*. Boston: Addison-Wesley, 1998.

  A classic, high-level review of the direction in which the OO industry as a whole is headed.

- Gamma, Erich, Richard Helm, Ralph Johnson, and John Vlissides. *Design Patterns: Elements of Reusable Object-Oriented Software*. Boston: Addison-Wesley, 1994.

  An in-depth look at identifying and reusing common design patterns.

- Kernighan, Brian W. and Dennis M. Ritchie. *The C Programming Language,* Second Edition. Upper Saddle River, NJ: Prentice Hall, 1988.

  A solid, classic treatment of C, for those of you who are interested in the most basic of Java's "roots"!

And, as mentioned a bit earlier in this chapter:

- Barker, Jacquie. *Taming the Technology Tidal Wave: Practical Career Advice for IT Professionals*. Merrifield, VA: ObjectStart Press, 2005.

  Practical career advice for IT professionals on how to maintain leading-edge technology skills without becoming overwhelmed. Please visit http://techtidalwave.com *for more information.*

Your Comments, Please!

In the interest of making this book as useful as possible to readers, I'd love to hear from you if you have suggestions for how this book could be improved! Please visit my web site at http://objectstart.com to contact me.

PART 4

■■■

Appendixes

■ ■ ■

Suggestions for Using This Book As a Textbook

This appendix presents some ideas for how this book can be used as a textbook for a variety of university level (or advanced high-school level) beginning object-oriented programming (OOP) courses. The suggestions are equally applicable, however, when applied in a corporate training setting.

Recommended Teaching Approaches

As the basis for a single-semester generic OOP course, focus on the subject matter content in Parts 1 and 2 (Chapters 1 through 12). Make sure to give students ample hands-on experience with both Java programming and object modeling through homework assignments as well as in-class group modeling exercises. The latter is particularly important for giving students an appreciation for how subjective object modeling can be. Time permitting at the end of the semester, cover the material in Chapter 13.

This happens to be the way that I'm currently teaching the material at both The George Washington University in Washington, D.C., and George Mason University in Fairfax, Virginia. When I teach this same material for corporate clients, I do so as a series of five full-day lecture/lab sessions, but follow the same basic outline.

For more information about my instructional approach, or to share in my teaching materials, please contact me via my web site, `http://objectstart.com`.

As the basis for a single-semester OO methodology course, adapt the approach described for a single-semester generic OOP course so as to emphasize hands-on object modeling and deemphasize actual programming. However, note that exposing students to the way that an object model translates into the syntax of an OO language such as Java really helps to cement object concepts, even for those students who aren't aspiring to be professional programmers. It's therefore important to examine students on the object aspects of the Java language by giving them simple code examples to analyze on paper.

As the basis for a single-semester comprehensive Java language course, devote the first lecture to reviewing UML notation as covered in Chapter 10, using this lecture as an opportunity to refresh students' memories on the basics of key object concepts. Realize, however, that to do justice to Java as an OO language, students must have previously been exposed to object concepts in depth. Devote the rest of the semester to the Java material in Parts 1 and 3 (Chapters 1 through 7 and 13 through 18).

One significant advantage of using my book as a textbook is that it uses a consistent case study as the basis for object concepts, object modeling, and Java programming. Students can actually see how an object model evolves from a requirements specification, and how that same object model translates into a working Java application—something that few, if any, other books present.

Suitability of Java As a Teaching Language

As a learning/teaching tool, Java is an ideal language for many of the reasons cited in Chapter 1. By way of review,

- *Java is, in my opinion, a simpler language to grasp than C++*, at least as far as the core language is concerned; C++ pointers have historically sent many a student running for a "course drop" slip! The biggest challenge with learning Java is the phenomenal number of APIs and classes therein, but I believe that I've successfully distilled these down to just those that a beginning student needs to know.

- *Java is extremely affordable*. All students need to do programming assignments is Sun's Java Software Development Kit (SDK), downloadable for free as detailed in Appendix C, and a text editor. Or, if you prefer students to use a simple IDE, consider using TextPad (available from `http://www.textpad.com`), an inexpensive yet powerful shareware program.

- *Java is an open standard and, as such, performs consistently across a multitude of platforms*. You will dramatically lessen the "hassle factor" with respect to diagnosing students' problems with both the language and the underlying programming environment as compared with teaching a language like C++ to a group of students who are using a multitude of different vendor-specific programming environments on their home or work computers.

Some Final Recommendations

In addition to the Student Registration System case study that is used as the backbone of the book, I recommend using a consistent second case study as the basis for homework assignments and/or in-class group exercises. Either have students devise their own (see the suggested exercise 3 at the end of Chapter 1), or use the Prescription Tracking System provided in Appendix B.

Each time a new OO concept or modeling technique is introduced in lectures, a classroom exercise or homework assignment should be assigned to the students so that they may experience that concept or apply that technique.

Spend the beginning of each class for which a homework assignment is due discussing students' and instructor's solutions to the assignment.

I often have students submit their homework solutions to me in advance of a class meeting via fax, e-mail, or web posting so that I have time to decide which aspects of their solutions I wish to emphasize. Reviewing a student's (possibly flawed) solution for the first time in front of the class can be confusing to classmates.

For purposes of object modeling, students should be encouraged to work in small teams for both the classroom exercises and the homework assignments. A great deal of the learning that takes place from object modeling comes from "hammering out" differences of opinion among a group, and group projects give students a real taste of the teamwork required in the business world.

It's also enlightening to give the same set of requirements to multiple teams, and to then have the teams review each other's proposed solutions, pointing out what works and what doesn't.

Keep an eye on my web site, `http://objectstart.com`, for additional suggestions on how to use this material effectively in an academic setting. And, if you come up with a particularly effective approach or idea, I'd love to hear about it, so that it may be shared with other instructors.

APPENDIX B

■ ■ ■

Alternative Case Studies

This appendix is meant to be a companion appendix to Appendix A, as well as a supplement to many of the end-of-chapter exercises found throughout the book. This appendix proposes some alternative case studies that can be used as the basis of formal course work or personal study applications.

Case Study #1: Prescription Tracking System

This case study is relatively straightforward, and hence can be tackled by most beginning modelers fairly effortlessly.

Background

Drugs For You pharmacy wishes for us to design and develop an automated Prescription Tracking System (PTS). The requirements are as follows:

- The system is to keep track of the following information for each customer:
  - Customer's name
  - Telephone number
  - Date of birth
  - Insurance provider
  - Insurance policy number
  - A prescription history, detailed next
- Each customer's prescription history will record the following information about each prescription:
  - A unique prescription ID number assigned by the pharmacy
  - The medication being prescribed
  - The prescribing physician's name and telephone number
  - The date of issue
  - Expiration date

- Number of refills authorized

- Number of "units" per prescription refill, where a "unit" might be a pill, a teaspoon, a milliliter (ml), etc. (see the discussion of medications next)

- Whether or not it's OK to provide the customer with a generic substitute, if one exists

- For each medication stocked by the pharmacy, the system will track

  - Its name

  - The "unit" by which the medication is prescribed (pills, teaspoons, ml, etc.)

  - Which medications can serve as "generic" equivalents of which other medication(s)

  - Any common side effects associated with taking the medication

- The system is required to support the following queries (some will be printed as hard-copy reports, whereas others will be viewed online only):

  - A prescription history—that is, a report of all prescriptions ever issued to a given customer—as requested by a given customer

  - A report of all side effects of a given medication, to be enclosed with each prescription dispensed

  - A list of all generic substitutes available for a given medication

  - Whether a given prescription is refillable—that is, whether any refills remain and whether the prescription has yet to expire

All of the preceding will be accessible via a secure web site to individual customers as well as to the in-store pharmacist.

Simplifying Assumptions

A real-life prescription tracking system would be quite complicated. I suggest the following simplifications to make the PTS problem a bit more tractable for beginning-level object modelers:

- The system isn't to be concerned with billing matters in any way; that is, we aren't going to worry about computing the price to be paid for a prescription, and we won't be concerned with trying to get a customer's insurance company to reimburse the pharmacy in any way.

- We'll assume that there is only one Drugs For You pharmacy location; that is, it isn't part of a chain of multiple stores.

- The system isn't responsible for inventory control; that is, we'll assume that "infinite" quantities of all medications are in stock or, conversely, that medications are immediately available on demand from a warehouse.

- Assume that the prescription is always refilled with the same medication as was issued for that prescription the first time around; that is, we'll never initially fill the prescription with a generic medication, and then refill it with a nongeneric equivalent, or vice versa.

Case Study #2: Conference Room Reservation System

This is an advanced case study that involves scheduling complexities and other elaborate requirements, representative of a real-world modeling challenge. It's best suited to an instructor-led group modeling exercise rather than as an individual exercise for a beginning-level modeler.

Background

We've been asked to develop an automated Conference Room Reservation System (CRRS) for our organization.

- A total of a dozen conference rooms are scattered across the four different buildings that comprise our facility. These rooms differ in terms of their seating capacities as well as what audio-visual (A/V) equipment is permanently installed in each room.

- Each of these rooms is overseen by a different administrative staff member, known as a Conference Room Coordinator.

- Reservations are presently being recorded manually by the various Conference Room Coordinators. The name of the person reserving the room, as well as his or her telephone number, is jotted by hand in an appointment book; the start and stop time of the meeting is also noted.

- A separate, central organization called the A/V Equipment Group provides "loaner" A/V equipment to supplement any equipment that may be permanently installed in a given conference room. Equipment that is available for temporary use through this group includes conventional overhead projectors, televisions, VCRs, LCD projectors for use with PCs, electronic whiteboards, laptop computers, tape recorders, and slide projectors. Personnel from this group deliver equipment directly to the locale where it's needed, and pick it up after the meeting is concluded.

The following problems have been noted regarding the present manual system:

- Currently, no supplemental information regarding the number of attendees or planned A/V equipment usage is being noted by the Conference Room Coordinators for a given meeting.

  - If someone planning a meeting involving only 4 people schedules a room with the capacity for 20, the excess capacity in that room will be wasted. Meanwhile, someone truly needing a room for 20 people will be left short.

  - Meeting planners must also be responsible for separately coordinating with the A/V Equipment Group; if they forget to do so, panic often ensues as folks scramble to arrange necessary equipment at the last minute.

- Whenever a given room's Coordinator is away from his or her desk, information about that room's availability is inaccessible, unless the inquirer wishes to walk to the Coordinator's office and inspect the appointment book directly. However, due to the size of the office complex, this isn't practical, so inquirers typically leave a voicemail message or send an e-mail to the Coordinator, who gets back to them at a later point in time.

- People are lax about canceling reservations when a room is no longer needed, so rooms often sit vacant that could otherwise be put to good use. Similarly, they often forget to cancel A/V equipment reservations.

- Pertinent information about the rooms (e.g., their seating capacity, whether or not they have a whiteboard, whether or not they have built-in A/V facilities, whether or not they are "wired" into the company's LAN) isn't presently published anywhere. Someone unfamiliar with the amenities of the various rooms often winds up having to call all 12 of the Conference Room Coordinators in search of an appropriate meeting location.

Goals for the System

We've been asked by management to design a system for providing online, automated conference room and equipment scheduling to remedy the problems of the current manual approach. The goals of this project are to provide the ability for any employee to directly connect to the system to perform the following tasks:

- If the user is interested in scheduling a room for a meeting, he or she will be required to complete an online questionnaire regarding the parameters of the meeting, to include

  - The scheduler's name, title, department, and telephone number

  - The number of attendees anticipated

  - A date range, indicating the earliest and latest acceptable date for the meeting

  - The length of time that the room will be required, in half-hour increments

  - An earliest acceptable start time and latest acceptable stop time

  - A list of all A/V equipment required

- As soon as this questionnaire is completed, the system will present the user with a list of all available suitable room alternatives. The user will be able to select from these options to reserve a room, or change his or her criteria and repeat the search.

Note that the system need not "remember" the conference room criteria after the user logs off.

- When confirming a reservation, the user must designate a subject or purpose for the meeting, such as "Demo of CRRS Prototype."

- After a room has been selected, the system will then determine what "loaner" A/V equipment will be needed to supplement the equipment that is permanently installed in that room, and will automatically arrange for its delivery.

For purposes of this case study, we won't worry about running out of equipment—we'll assume an infinite supply of everything—although in real life this would also have to be a consideration.

- If no rooms meeting the user's requirements are available, the user will be presented with a list of suitable rooms with the number of people waitlisted for each. The user will be able to optionally place his or her name at the end of the waiting list for one of these rooms.
  - When such a request is posted, the system is to send a courtesy e-mail to the person holding that room's reservation, asking that person to rethink his or her need for the room.
  - Should the room on the waiting list become available, it will automatically be temporarily reserved for the first person on the waiting list. An e-mail message is to be sent automatically to the requestor, giving that person 72 hours to confirm his or her selection before the room is either (a) reassigned (again, temporarily) to the next person on the waiting list or (b) becomes generally available if the waiting list has been exhausted.
- A user should be permitted to query the system as to who has a particular room reserved at a given date and time, or to perform a search for a given meeting that the user is to attend based on (a) scheduler or (b) subject.
- The user must be able to cancel a room reservation at any time, whether confirmed or waitlisted.
- The A/V Equipment Group wishes to periodically run a report, sorted by equipment type, indicating how many times a given piece of equipment was used over a 12-month period.

Case Study #3: Blue Skies Airline Reservation System

This is the most complex case study of all. Please see the introductory comments for case study #2.

Background

Blue Skies Airline, a new airline, offers services between any two of the following U.S. cities: Denver; Washington, D.C.; Los Angeles; New York City; Atlanta; and Cleveland.

When a customer calls Blue Skies to make a flight reservation, the reservation agent first asks him or her for

- The desired travel dates
- The departure and destination cities
- The seat grade desired (first class, business class, or economy)

The reservation agent then informs the customer of all available flights that meet his or her criteria. For each flight, the flight number, departure date and time, arrival date and time, and round-trip price are communicated to the customer. If the customer finds any of the available flights acceptable, he or she may either pay for the ticket via credit card or request that the seat be held for 24 hours. (A specific seat assignment—row and seat number—isn't issued until the seat is paid for.)

A limited number of seats on each flight are earmarked as frequent flyer seats. A customer who is a frequent flyer member may reserve and "pay for" one of these seats by giving the agent his or her frequent flyer membership number. The agent then verifies that the appropriate balance is available in the customer's account before the seat can be confirmed, at which point those miles are deducted from the account.

The customer has two ticketing options: he or she may request that a conventional "paper" ticket be issued and mailed to his or her home address, or an electronic ticket (e-ticket) may instead be assigned, in which case the customer is simply informed of the e-ticket serial number by telephone. (With an e-ticket, the customer simply reports to the airport at the time of his or her departure, and presents suitable ID to a ticket agent at the gate. No paperwork is exchanged.) In both cases, the reservation agent records the serial number of the (conventional or electronic) ticket issued to this customer.

The number of seats available for a given flight in each of the seat grade categories is dependent on the type of aircraft assigned to a given flight.

Other Simplifying Assumptions

As with the PTS case study, there are several simplifying assumptions that can be made as compared with a real-life airline reservation system to make this case study more tractable.

- Assume that all flights are round-trip between two cities (no itineraries of three or more legs are permitted).

- Disregard the complication that airlines sometimes have to switch aircraft at the last minute due to mechanical difficulties, thus disrupting the seating assignments.

APPENDIX C

■■■

Setting Up Your Java Development Environment

This appendix presents the basic steps involved in downloading and installing the latest version of Sun Microsystems' Java Development Kit. I also provide troubleshooting tips for how to get Java to "behave" under Windows XP specifically.

If you haven't already read the Introduction to this book, please take time to do so now. In particular, see the section entitled "Sorting Out Java Nomenclature" in the Introduction.

The Java Software Development Kit

The Java 2 Platform, Standard Edition (J2SE) Java Development Kit (JDK) is available as a free download from the Sun Microsystems website. Among other things, the JDK comes with

- A command line–driven compiler (`javac`)

- An executable copy of the Java Virtual Machine (JVM), the engine that runs compiled Java bytecode

and much more. In addition, as a separate (but very worthwhile!) download, Sun Microsystems provides a convenient, online way for you to view Java language documentation from the comfort of your own browser.

Since URLs and links are continuously changing, the instructions for finding the proper location within Sun's domain may change after this book is published.

To download the latest release of the JDK and corresponding documentation from Sun Microsystems, follow these steps:

1. Go to `http://java.sun.com/j2se/`*version*`/download.jsp`, where *version* is the newest "internal" release of Java (e.g., 1.5.0, as opposed to the "external" version, 5.0). Then click the Download JDK link. Be certain to download the platform-appropriate version (as discussed in Chapter 2, while Java is a platform-independent language, the Java compiler and JVM are platform-***dependent*** programs). As of the time of publication of this book, the JDK was available as a download from Sun Microsystems on the following platforms: Windows, Solaris, and Linux/Unix. For JDKs that will run on other platforms (e.g., Apple, SGI Irix, etc.), please consult the appropriate vendor (or do a Google search).

I make an attempt to discuss the implications of installing Java for both Windows XP and Unix in this appendix, where practical; however, when it is impractical to cover both, I defer to a description of the Windows XP approach, and leave it to Unix developers (clever folks that they are!) to execute these in a platform-appropriate fashion.

---

2. On that same web page, click the link for downloading the J2SE *version* Documentation (e.g., the link labeled "J2SE 5.0 Documentation").

3. Then, look for two separate Installation Instructions links on the same `http://java.sun.com/j2se/`*version*`/download.jsp` page for download of the JDK and the documentation, respectively.

Testing Your Installation

Create a working directory in which you plan to store your various Java experiments. In that directory, use a text editor/IDE of your choosing—the Windows Notepad editor or Unix/Linux vi editor will do—to create a file containing the following simple program:

```java
public class Success {
    public static void main(String[] args) {
        System.out.println("Hooray!");
    }
}
```

You must enter the program text ***exactly*** as just shown, including precise use of uppercase and lowercase, into a file named `Success.java`. (Note the precise use of uppercase and lowercase in ***naming*** the file, as well: the "S" is capitalized, and the rest of the name is in lowercase. As discussed in Chapter 2, Java is a case-sensitive language, even when used on a case-insensitive platform such as Windows.)

Open a Command Prompt (Windows) or console (Unix) window, and use the `cd` command to set your **default working directory** to be the directory in which the program resides. Then, type the following command at the operating system prompt to compile the program:

`javac Success.java`

If the program compiles without error, no messages will be generated. The operating system prompt will simply be redisplayed, as follows for Windows:

```
C:\>javac Success.java
C:\>
```

On the other hand, if error messages arise, they might be of the following three forms:

- ***Compilation errors***:

```
Success.java:3: cannot resolve symbol
symbol : Out
System.Out.println("Hooray!");
        ^
```

- ***JVM-generated run-time errors***:

```
Exception in thread "main" java.lang.NoClassDefFoundError: Success
```

- ***Operating system–specific errors***:

```
'javac' is not recognized as an internal or external command,
operable program or batch file.
```

Please see the "Troubleshooting Your Installation," "Common Compilation Errors," and "Common Run-Time Errors" sections later in this appendix for assistance.

Assuming that no error messages arose, use the Windows dir or Unix ls command to verify that an executable Success.class bytecode file has been created in the same directory where the Success.java file resides, then type the following at the operating system prompt to run the program:

```
java Success
```

(As discussed in Chapter 2, we don't type the .class part of the executable file name. Also, note the precise use of uppercase and lowercase in naming the bytecode—***neither of the following variations will work***:

```
java Success.class    <== INCORRECT
java success          <== INCORRECT
```

and each will generate a different run-time error message, as discussed later in this appendix.)

If all goes well, the following should appear as output (shown for Windows):

```
C:\>java Success
Hooray!
C:\>
```

If you get any sort of error message instead, please consult the "Troubleshooting Your Installation" and "Common Run-Time Errors" sections of this appendix.

Troubleshooting Your Installation

The following sections' examples illustrate problems as they might occur under Windows XP. Comparable problems, with potentially different error messages but conceptually similar resolutions, can occur under other versions of Windows and Unix.

PATH and CLASSPATH Settings

Downloading and installing the JDK from the Sun Microsystems website is fairly easy to do; *the biggest stumbling block for most people* is getting Java to "behave" properly, however, which *involves establishing correct settings for the PATH and CLASSPATH environment variables* on their computer system.

What Is the PATH Variable?

The PATH variable is a list of semicolon-separated (for Windows) or colon-separated (for Unix) names of the directories in which the operating system should look for executable programs.

Any operating system comes with a built-in set of commands that it understands (e.g., cd, dir or ls, etc.). However, if we want to be able to run other programs from the command line—for example, java (the Java Virtual Machine [JVM], used to interpret/execute compiled Java bytecode) or javac (the Java compiler, used to compile Java source code into executable bytecode)—then we must inform the operating system of where to look for the executable versions of these programs. *The value of the PATH variable enumerates all of the directories that might contain such executables.*

When a command is typed that the operating system does not inherently understand, such as

```
java -version
```

or

```
javac
```

the operating system searches the locations called out by the PATH setting one by one, from first to last, until it finds the *first* such occurrence of the named program, which it then executes.

Conversely, if the PATH variable is *not* set, or if *none* of the directories that it calls out contains the desired program, the operating system responds with an error message as follows (shown for Windows XP):

```
'java' is not recognized as an internal or external command,
operable program or batch file.
```

To check the value of your PATH setting under Windows, type the command

```
path
```

For the JVM and Java compiler to both run properly, your PATH must contain a reference to the bin subdirectory of your Java "home" directory (e.g., C:\jdk1.5.xxx\bin); otherwise, you'll get error messages such as the following (shown for Windows XP):

```
'javac' is not recognized as an internal or external command,
operable program or batch file.
```

Instructions for setting and modifying the PATH variable's value are provided later in this appendix.

What Is the CLASSPATH?

The CLASSPATH variable is to Java what the PATH variable is to the operating system: namely, a list of semicolon-separated (for Windows) or colon-separated (for Unix) names of the places in which both the JVM and Java compiler should look for **bytecode files** (aka class definitions).

- Java comes with a predefined set of class definitions, delivered in bytecode form; these are stored within a subdirectory of the Java "home" directory—that is, in the directory in which Java was installed (typically, this directory will be [under Windows] C:\Program Files\jdk1.5.*xxx*).

- The JVM automatically knows to look within this "home" directory, at a minimum, for bytecode that you've asked it to execute.

- Similarly, the Java compiler automatically knows to look in this "home" directory for any preexisting class definitions that source code might refer to, in order to compile your code.

- For Java versions 1.4.*x* and later, the JVM and Java compiler additionally know to automatically look in your **default working directory** for bytecode—which can be referred to in commands with the shorthand name of a single period/"dot" (.)—**unless your CLASSPATH setting explicitly instructs the JVM or Java compiler** not **to look there** (more about this later).

- If you want to be able access any other bytecode, then you must inform the Java environment of where to look for such bytecode files. The value of the CLASSPATH variable enumerates all of the directories, .zip **files**, or **Java Archive (JAR) files** that might contain such bytecode (for more information on JAR files, please refer to the appropriate section in Chapter 13).

- When the JVM is launched and instructed to execute bytecode, such as with the command

  java MyApp

  the JVM searches the locations called out by the CLASSPATH setting one by one, from left to right, until it finds the **first** such occurrence of the named bytecode file (MyApp.class), which it then loads and interprets/executes.

- Conversely, if the CLASSPATH variable is set, but **none** of the locations that it calls out contains the desired bytecode file (i.e., if none of the locations refer to your default working directory [.]), the JVM responds with an error message as follows:

```
Exception in thread "main" java.lang.NoClassDefFoundError: MyApp
```

- To check the value of your CLASSPATH under Windows XP, type the command

  echo %classpath%

- If the result displayed is as follows:

```
C:\> echo %classpath%
%classpath%
```

this means that a CLASSPATH variable has not been established on your computer, which is generally just fine if you are using Java 1.4.*x* or later and only want to access bytecode in (a) your default working directory, or (b) the Java "home" directory.

For Java 1.3.*x* or earlier, the CLASSPATH must, at a minimum, contain a single period (.) to reference your default working directory.

- If the result displayed is anything else, for example:

```
C:\> echo %classpath%
.;C:\servlets_2.2b\servlet.jar;C:\Jindent\Jindent.jar
```

then a single period (representing your current working directory) ***must*** be one of the entries in this list (in the preceding example, it is the ***first*** such entry)—otherwise, you'll run into problems of the form shown earlier:

```
Exception in thread "main" java.lang.NoClassDefFoundError: MyApp
```

- Instructions for setting and modifying the CLASSPATH variable's value are provided in the next section.

How Can I Set and Modify the Value of PATH or CLASSPATH?

There are several recommended approaches for setting either the PATH or CLASSPATH value that differ in terms of their permanence. These approaches are outlined in the sections that follow.

Approach #1

The most permanent way to set either of these under Windows XP is by using the Start ➤ Control Panel menu to open the System Properties window. Then go to the Advanced tab and click the Environment Variables button as shown in Figure C-1.

Figure C-1. *The System Properties window*

This brings up the following Environment Variables dialog box, as shown in Figure C-2.

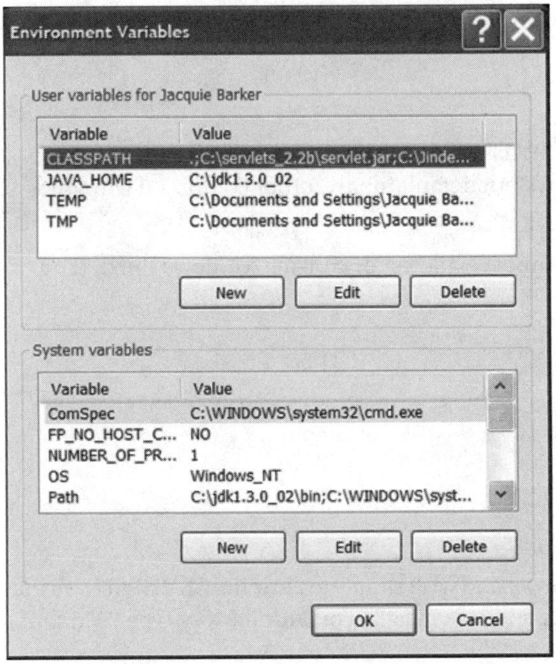

Figure C-2. *The Environment Variables window*

The entry for CLASSPATH, if one exists at all, will typically appear in the User variables list at the top of the window; the entry for PATH will typically appear in the System variables list at the bottom (or, an entry for PATH may appear in **both** lists—if so, you'll ideally want to edit the System versus the User version).

Note that you may not have the necessary administrative privileges to edit the PATH variable on your computer. If you don't, then the Edit button will be grayed-out, and you'll need to seek the assistance of a system administrator to help you.

If you choose to edit either the PATH or CLASSPATH variable, *take care not to disturb their existing settings*. Simply insert whatever new entry you wish to add at the *beginning* of the existing value, *followed by a semicolon (Windows) or a colon (Unix)*.

If you inadvertently disturb what is already there as a value—particularly with respect to the PATH variable—you risk disrupting the way that other programs on your computer operate.

If you alter either variable's setting through the Start ➤ Control Panel menu, you must close any already open Command Prompt windows to use the new variable values; from this point forward, any new Command Prompt windows that you subsequently open will reflect the new value(s) of PATH/CLASSPATH.

These values will be remembered even after the computer has been powered off and back on. They'll persist until such time as you either permanently change them or *override* them via one of the next two approaches.

Approach #2

You can modify the setting of PATH or CLASSPATH so that it only takes effect *within a given command window*, and then reverts to the system default for any other command windows that you subsequently open, as follows:

- Once you've opened a Command Prompt (Windows) or console window (Unix), type the command

  ```
  set path=yourJavaHomeDirectory\bin;%path%
  ```

  to set your PATH (for example):

  ```
  set path=C:\jdk1.5.0_01\bin;%path%
  ```

- Or, to set your CLASSPATH, type (Windows)

  ```
  set classpath=.
  ```

- And, if you are working under 1.4.*x* or newer and wish simply to *clear* the CLASSPATH, so that it refers only to the Java "home" directory and your default working directory, type (Windows)

  ```
  set classpath=
  ```

- Note that the only space in either command comes after the word "set"; do not introduce extraneous spaces! If a directory that you wish to refer to in a PATH/CLASSPATH contains spaces (e.g., C:\My Programs), enclose the entire name within double quotes:

```
set classpath=":\My Programs";C:\Another
```

Approach #3

You can modify the setting of the CLASSPATH so that the setting takes effect for only *one given invocation* of the java or javac commands as follows (where ^ indicates a blank space):

```
java -cp temporaryPathValue bytecodeFilename
     ^   ^                  ^
```

for example:

```
java -cp . MyApp
     ^   ^ ^
```

and for the javac command:

```
javac -classpath temporaryPathValue sourcecodeFilename
      ^           ^                  ^
```

for example:

```
javac -classpath . MyApp.java
      ^           ^ ^
```

Common Compilation Errors

If you get the following error message when attempting to compile:

```
C:\MyDir> javac Success.java
'javac' is not recognized as an internal or external command, operable program,
or batch file.
```

this means that the Java compiler could not be found, which means that you have either (a) improperly installed the JDK download, (b) downloaded the wrong software, or (c) incorrectly set your PATH environment variable.

If you followed the instructions from earlier in this chapter to establish your PATH setting, and you are confident that it is set properly, check to ensure that there is a file named javac.exe located in the Java "home" directory's bin subdirectory. If there is not, then you may have inadvertently clicked the wrong download link—perhaps you downloaded the **Java Runtime Environment (JRE)** by mistake, which doesn't include the Java compiler—in which case you will have to repeat the *JDK* download and installation process.

If you get the following alternative error message when attempting to compile:

```
C:\MyDir> javac Success.java
error: cannot read: Success.java
```

this means that the compiler cannot find your source code. Make sure that (a) you are in the correct (working) directory where the program source code file resides—use the dir command to verify this; (b) you are spelling the name of the file correctly, including proper use of uppercase and lowercase; and (c) your CLASSPATH variable is appropriate, based on our earlier discussion of setting the CLASSPATH.

If you get the following sort of compilation error:

```
C:\MyDir> javac Success.java
Success.java:1: Public class success must be defined in a file called 'success.java'
public class success {
              ^
```

check to make sure that the prefix on the external file name (e.g., Success.java) exactly matches the name of the class in the public class *ClassName* { declaration, including the exact same use of uppercase and lowercase.

If you get a cannot find symbol compilation error:

```
Success.java:3: cannot find symbol
symbol   :  variable Out
location : class java.lang.System
System.Out.println("Hooray!");
       ^
```

it means that in the line in question, you've done one of the following:

- Spelled the name of a method, attribute, class, or other variable differently from how it was declared, including case deviations (in the preceding example, Out should not be capitalized)

- Left parentheses off the end of a method call

- Forgotten to declare the item that you are trying to access

- Forgotten the import directive for a predefined class

or something similar.

For example, let's say that we have declared the following simple Person class:

```
public class Person {
    private String name;

    public String getName() {
        return name;
    }

    public void printIt() {
        System.out.println(name);
    }
}
```

plus a main program as follows:

```
public class PersonExample {
```

```java
    public static void main(String[] args) {
        Person p = new Person();

        // NONEXISTENT METHOD - setName WAS NEVER DECLARED
        IN THE Person CLASS.
        p.setName("Fred");

        // CASE ERROR -- SHOULD BE UPPERCASE "N" in "getname".
        System.out.println(p.getname());

        // FORGOT THE PARENS AT THE END OF THE METHOD CALL.
        System.out.println(p.printIt);

        // TRYING TO USE A PREDEFINED JAVA CLASS FOR WHICH
        // AN import STATEMENT IS REQUIRED.
        ArrayList al;
    }
}
```

Here's what the compiler has to say regarding the preceding code:

```
PersonExample.java:7: cannot find symbol
symbol   : method setName(java.lang.String)
location: class Person
        p.setName("Fred");
         ^
PersonExample.java:10: cannot find symbol
symbol   : method getname()
location: class Person
        System.out.println(p.getname());
                            ^
PersonExample.java:13: cannot find symbol
symbol   : variable printIt
location: class Person
        System.out.println(p.getName);
                            ^
PersonExample.java:17: cannot find symbol
symbol   : class ArrayList
location: class PersonExample
        ArrayList al;
        ^
4 errors
```

If you get a compilation error that doesn't seem to make any sense whatsoever relative to the line it is referring to, check for missing/extra punctuation—parentheses, braces, semicolons, commas—in your code *prior* to that line; it's possible that the compiler has simply gotten "confused." (One such compiler error that often hints at such a problem is an illegal start of type error on a line that otherwise appears to be fine.)

If you get any other compilation errors, for example:

```
C:\MyDir> javac Success.java
Success.java:3: String not terminated at end of line.
        System.out.println("Hooray!);
                          ^
```

these likely represent legitimate programming errors (in this particular example, we're missing the double quote after Hooray!).

Common Run-Time Errors

If you get the following error message when attempting to run a successfully compiled program:

```
C:\MyDir> java Success
Exception in thread 'main' Java.lang.NoClassDefFoundError: Success
```

this could mean one of several different things:

- You are spelling the name of the program incorrectly;

- The program did not compile correctly, thus failing to produce a Success.class bytecode file.

- A bytecode file exists by that name, but the JVM cannot **find** it because your CLASSPATH variable is mis-set.

It's important that you **not** type the .class suffix when attempting to run your program, as you'll get the following error message if you do:

```
C:\MyDir> java Success.class
Exception in thread "main" java.lang.NoClassDefFoundError:  Success/class
```

If you accidentally try to execute a Java **source** file, you'll get a similar error:

```
C:\MyDir> java Success.java
Exception in thread "main" java.lang.NoClassDefFoundError:  Success/java
```

If you misuse uppercase and lowercase in naming a bytecode file when attempting to run a program, as follows (note improper use of lowercase "s" in referring to the Success.class bytecode file), the error message can be rather daunting:

```
java.lang.NoClassDefFoundError: success (wrong name: Success)
        at java.lang.ClassLoader.defineClass1(Native Method)
        at java.lang.ClassLoader.defineClass(ClassLoader.java:605)
        at java.security.SecureClassLoader.defineClass(SecureClassLoader.java:124)
        at java.net.URLClassLoader.defineClass(URLClassLoader.java:260)
        at java.net.URLClassLoader.access$100(URLClassLoader.java:56)
        at java.net.URLClassLoader$1.run(URLClassLoader.java:195)
```

```
        at java.security.AccessController.doPrivileged(Native Method)
        at java.net.URLClassLoader.findClass(URLClassLoader.java:188)
        at java.lang.ClassLoader.loadClass(ClassLoader.java:290)
        at sun.misc.Launcher$AppClassLoader.loadClass(Launcher.java:279)
        at java.lang.ClassLoader.loadClass(ClassLoader.java:236)
        at java.lang.ClassLoader.loadClassInternal(ClassLoader.java:303)
Exception in thread "main"
```

Finally, if you try to execute an otherwise legitimate bytecode file that doesn't declare a proper main method header, the following run-time error message will arise:

```
C:\MyDir> java Student
Exception in thread "main" java.lang.NoSuchMethodError: main
```

Using the Online Java Documentation with Windows

If you downloaded the optional Java documentation from Sun's website, it's most likely located in the docs subdirectory beneath your Java "home" directory (e.g., C:\Program Files\Java\jdk1.5.0.*xxx*\docs). You can access the documentation from your web browser by selecting File ➤ Open (or a comparable menu option), and then opening the file named *javaHomeDirectory*\docs\api\index.html. This brings up the initial Java documentation window as shown in Figure C-3.

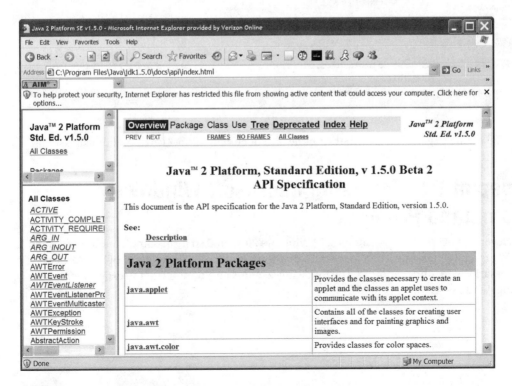

Figure C-3. *Sun Microsystems's online Java documentation*

This page is divided into three frames. The bottom left frame presents a list of links for all of the predefined classes and interfaces that come standard with Java. Clicking any one of these links displays the documentation relevant to that class or interface in the large frame on the right side of the screen, as illustrated for the ArrayList class in Figure C-4.

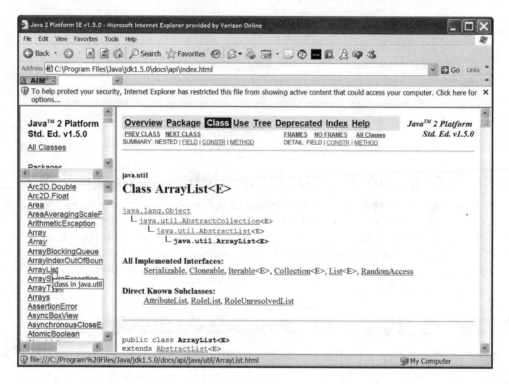

Figure C-4. *Documentation for the* ArrayList *class*

Take time to get familiar with the online Java documentation—it's tremendously useful!

Special Tips for Using Microsoft Windows Command Prompts

Each version of Windows—Windows XP, Windows 2000, and so forth—implements command prompts a bit differently. Therefore, tricks that work under one "generation" of Windows won't necessarily work under another. The following sections outline some of my experiences with using Windows XP.

Capturing Program Output to a File

There are easy ways of capturing program output to a file via the **file redirection symbol**, >; this is known as **redirecting standard output**. For example, the command

```
C:\>java Success > somefile
```

stores what would normally appear as output to the screen (the Hooray! message from the earlier example) in a text file named *somefile* instead.

Alternatively, to capture compilation/run time) *error* messages to a file, the expression 2>, as in the command

```
C:\>javac Success.java 2> somefile
```

should, in theory, do the trick, taking advantage of a technique known as **standard error redirection**.

The use of > for standard **output** redirection seems to work fairly consistently across all versions of Windows, but the use of 2> for standard **error** redirection does not. Both approaches **do** work with Windows XP, however.

Resizing the Command Prompt Window

If you wish to make the Command Prompt window larger so that more lines of text can appear at once, right-click the window header bar and select Properties from the pop-up menu that appears (see Figure C-5). Then explore the settings available for your particular "flavor" of Windows in the window that subsequently appears (shown in Figure C-6 for Windows XP).

Figure C-5. *Accessing the Properties settings of a Windows Command Prompt window*

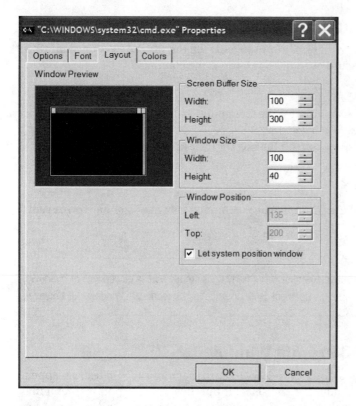

Figure C-6. *Adjusting properties of the Command Prompt window for Windows XP*

In Figure C-6, we'd want—at a minimum—to ensure that

- The Screen Buffer Size is set to Width = 100, Height = 300 or greater
- The Window Size is set to Width = 100, Height = 40 or greater

■ ■ ■

Downloading and Compiling the Book's Source Code

Source code and supporting data files for key examples in Chapters 6, 13, 14, 15, 16, and 17 are available for download from the Downloads area of the Apress web site, http://www.apress.com, as a single file named 1590594576-2.zip.

IMPORTANT NOTE

Sun Microsystems introduced some important new features in J2SE 5.0 that significantly increased the power and versatility of Java as an object-oriented programming language. These improvements were particularly noteworthy with respect to the improved ease with which collections are created and managed. I've thus adopted the J2SE 5.0 approach to collections as of this (second) edition of *Beginning Java Objects*.

Note that the downloadable code examples for this book will *not* compile with an earlier (pre-5.0) version of Java, with one exception: for readers who are working with an earlier version of Java, a pre-5.0-compatible version of the finished (Chapter 17) SRS application source code is included in the .zip file (see notes that follow).

To download the source code .zip file for this book, follow these steps:

1. Access the Apress Downloads page from http://www.apress.com.

2. Left-click your mouse to select the title of this book from scrollable global list of Apress books with source code.

3. Click the Submit button below the scrollable list of books.

4. Now on this book's source code download page, left-click your mouse on the link that reads "Download Source Code File".

5. Left-click the Save button that appears.

6. The Save As window pops up next. Choose where and how you want to save the source code for this book.

Alternatively, you can download the source code .zip file this way:

1. Go to this book's specific Apress.com page: http://java.apress.com/book/bookDisplay. html?bID=406.

2. Left-click the Source Code link.

3. Repeat steps 4 through 6 from the previous instructions.

Downloading the code to an arbitrary directory *xxx* and unzipping it will create the following directory structure. Make sure to use your Zip utility's provision to "use directory names from the Zip file" (or equivalent), so that this directory structure is preserved.

Subdirectory/Folder Name	Contents
xxx/Ch6	Source code from Chapter 6
xxx/Ch13	Source code from Chapter 13
xxx/Ch14/SRS	SRS source code to accompany Chapter 14
xxx/Ch15/SRS	SRS source code to accompany Chapter 15
xxx/Ch16	Source code from Chapter 16
xxx/Ch17/SRS	SRS source code to accompany Chapter 17
xxx/pre5.0_SRS	A version of the finished (Chapter 17) SRS application that will compile under versions of Java that predate 5.0

APPENDIX E

■ ■ ■

Note to Experienced C++ Programmers

This appendix is intended for folks who are C++ "power programmers." I assume a great deal of C++ proficiency in this section, and so as a result I don't explain a lot of the background necessary to understand this material. Therefore, if you are not a C++ expert, please skip this appendix!

Although there are many similarities between the C++ and Java languages—Java was in part patterned after C++—some of the most complex, error-prone features of C++ were eliminated in creating Java to make it a "safer" language. The following section explains one of the most significant changes.

No More Pointers!

Anyone who has programmed in C or C++ knows how easy it is to manipulate memory addresses directly via **pointers**, which can quickly get a programmer into trouble! It is an all-too-common experience to get a **segmentation violation**—that is, an accidental (or intentional!) attempt to access a "forbidden" memory address, such as within the region of memory where the operating system is located. This causes the program to crash.

Instead of using pointers, Java uses **references**. Java references work the same way that C++ pointers do when it comes to instantiating objects dynamically. We declare a reference/pointer variable first, and then use the new keyword to dynamically create the object at run time. Then, we later use the reference to access the object that it references, a process known as **dereferencing**. However, the syntax with regard to references in Java is much simpler than the syntax for pointers in C++, as you'll see in a moment.

Another big difference between pointers and references is that *we can arithmetically manipulate pointers in C++, but not references in Java*. That is, in C++, we can treat a pointer as a "raw" numeric memory address, and can add/subtract arbitrary numeric values to the address before dereferencing it, thus accessing some alternative location in memory. This is not permitted with references in Java.

Dynamic vs. Static Object Creation

With C++, we can create objects in one of two ways:

- At compile time, known as **static instantiation**

- At run time, known as **dynamic instantiation** (see also Appendix F)

Table E-1 shows a comparison of Java versus C++ syntax with respect to *dynamically* instantiated objects (assume the existence of a class named Student in both cases).

Table E-1. *Dynamically Instantiated Object Creation Approaches Using Java and C++*

Approach to Object Creation	Java Syntax for Doing So	C++ Syntax for Doing So

Dynamic Instantiation (i.e., at run time)	`// Declare a reference`
	`// variable (s is not yet`
	`// referring to an object).`
	`Student s;`
		`// Declare a pointer (s is`
		`// not yet pointing at an`
		`// object).`
		`Student* s;`

	`// Instantiate a Student`
	`// object.`
	`s = new Student();`
		`// Instantiate a Student`
		`// object in one of two ways:`
		`// either:`
		`s = new Student();`

		`// or (shorthand form):` `s = new Student;`

	`// Invoke a method on the`
	`// object via dot notation.`
	`s.setName("Fred");`
		`// Invoke a method on the`
		`// object in one of two ways:`
		`// either via dot notation ...`
		`(*s).setName("Fred");`

		`// ... or via "arrow"`
		`// notation.`
		`s->setName("Fred");`

Note that the Java syntax is a lot cleaner, in that we don't use asterisks (*) or arrows (->) when declaring or dereferencing pointers.

In Java, however, there is no concept of static/compile-time object instantiation, as there is with C++. **All** Java objects are created **dynamically** via the new operator. Note that the syntax for creating and manipulating objects **statically** in C++ resembles the syntax for **dynamic** object creation and manipulation in Java, as shown in Table E-2.

Table E-2. *Statically Instantiated Object Creation Approaches Using Java and C++*

Approach to Object Creation	Java Syntax for Doing So	C++ Syntax for Doing So

Static Instantiation (i.e., at compile time)	Not available	```// Declare a reference```
		```// variable.```
		```Student s;```
		
		```// No need to instantiate!```
		
		```// Invoke a method via dot```
		```// notation.```
		```s.setName("Fred");```

Exception Handling

The elimination of true pointers from Java virtually eradicates the potential for getting a segmentation violation, which is one of the main causes of C++ run-time exceptions, or "crashes." Java also has an extensive system of **exception handling**, as discussed in Chapter 13. When something illegal happens, Java throws an exception, which our program can catch and gracefully recover from without crashing.

Exception handling is optional in C++ but ***mandatory*** in Java: if we use a language construct in a Java program that is capable of throwing an exception, but do not explicitly declare it or intercept ("catch") it, a Java compilation error arises. In C++, we aren't advised by the compiler of such potential run-time issues.

"Breaking the OO Rules" with C++

I talk at great length in Part 1 of the book about the advantages of encapsulation, information hiding, inheritance, and polymorphism in OO languages. Although C++ does indeed take advantage of these benefits, it provides a few "back doors" that allow programmers to break the spirit of these features. Here are a few examples:

- **Friend functions**: These functions reside outside the bounds of any class. They are given permission to access `private` attributes of one or more classes, thus breaking the spirit of encapsulation.

- **Virtual functions**: In C++, we have to designate a method as `virtual` in order to get overriding to take place; this means that the developer of a C++ class must anticipate the future need to override a particular method. With Java, the reverse is true: all methods are automatically "overridable" unless they are flagged with the keyword `final`, which ***prohibits*** overriding.

This goes hand in glove with polymorphism. In Java, the ability for objects to perform the correct version of a method is automatic. With C++, if we fail to designate a method in a base class as `virtual`, then we may think we are overriding the method—we may indeed write method code in a subclass to "mask" the superclass's version—but at run time, the subclassed objects will only "see," and hence be able to run, the ***superclass's*** version of the method.

Platform Portability

Another disadvantage of C++ with respect to Java is its relative lack of platform portability, which manifests itself in several ways:

- The executable code that's produced by compiling a C++ program is specific to a certain underlying operating system architecture, and hence is platform dependent, whereas Java executable code is inherently platform independent, as we discuss in Chapter 2.

In defense of C++, a native executable is faster than an interpreted one but, as it turns out, there also happen to be native compilers available for Java. These compromise Java's portability, of course, for the sake of speed.

- Even C++ source code is not necessarily portable. If we stray from the absolute core of ANSI standard C++, we may find ourselves with source code that must be rewritten in order to compile it for a different platform. This is particularly true of C++ applications that avail themselves of platform-specific operating system or windowing calls. As we discuss in Chapter 2, Java provides platform-independent means of doing all of these things, such that source code—as well as executable bytecode—is truly platform independent.

Abstract Methods and Abstract Classes

C++ and Java differ in the specific manner in which methods, and therefore classes, are flagged as being abstract. In Java, we flag the signature of a method with the keyword abstract, and if we have one or more abstract methods in a class, the compiler then forces us to also add the abstract keyword to the class definition as a whole:

```
public abstract class Course {
    // details omitted ...
    public abstract void establishCourseSchedule(Date startDate, Date endDate);
}
```

whereas in C++, we designate a (virtual) method to be abstract with the **pure specifier** (=0):

```
virtual void establishCourseSchedule()=0;
```

which is a bit more obscure. (Such a method, by the way, is called a **pure virtual function** in C++.)

Also, in Java, we are permitted to label a class abstract in order to prevent instantiation of the class even if it contains no abstract methods, whereas we are not permitted to do so in C++.

Other Simplifications

The following are some further simplifications to keep in mind:

- There are no more "memory leaks" with Java—**garbage collection** takes care of this automatically, as we discuss in Chapter 3.

It is possible to get the occasional "out-of-memory" error with the JVM, however, if we consume memory allocated to the JVM faster than the garbage collector can recycle it, or we fail to release memory by letting go of handles on objects that are no longer in service.

- There is no support in Java for multiple inheritance, which as we discuss in Chapter 5 was deemed problematic in C++. Java introduces the notion of interfaces as a workaround, as we discuss in Chapter 7.

For more information on where Java and C++ originally deviated—and why—please see the article "The Java Language Environment" by James Gosling and Henry McGilton (published May 1996) at `http://java.sun.com/docs/white/langenv`.

■■■

How Polymorphism Works Behind the Scenes (Static vs. Dynamic Binding)

Warning: This material is fairly technically deep! The good news, however, is that it is not necessary to understand how polymorphism works behind the scenes in order to make use of it in the applications that you develop, any more than it is necessary to understand how an automobile engine works in order to drive a car. So, if you are curious about the mechanics of polymorphism, read on; otherwise, feel free to skip this material. As long as you feel comfortable with the discussion of polymorphism in Chapter 7, you're good to go!

In Chapter 3, we discussed the fact that with Java, simply declaring a variable to be of type Student doesn't actually make a student object "materialize":

```
Student y;
```

We have to explicitly instantiate an object through the use of the new keyword and a constructor call:

```
y = new Student();
```

The fact that a constructor must be executed to create an object implies that the allocation of sufficient memory to house a Student object takes place when the program runs—that is, at **run time**, **not** at compile time. This is known as **dynamic instantiation**. The concept of dynamic instantiation is closely tied with another concept called **dynamic** or **run-time binding**, which is at the very heart of what makes polymorphism and *overriding* (a concept that we discussed in Chapter 5) "tick."

When the Java code shown previously is compiled, only enough memory is set aside at compile time to hold a reference, which in Java is 64 bits long regardless of the type of object that a reference variable will eventually be referencing.

In contrast to dynamic binding, **static** or **compile-time binding** comes into play with *overloading* (another concept that we discussed in Chapter 5). I'd like to explain these two concepts to round out your understanding of how polymorphism works behind the scenes.

Static Binding

Let's look at static binding first. When a program is compiled, the job of a compiler is to make sure that every line of code you have written makes sense, meaning that, among other things

- All of the variables mentioned in the code—primitive types as well as objects—have been properly declared.

```
int x;
int y;

x = y + z;  // Problem!  z was not declared, and so the compiler
            // will object.
```

- All of the functions (methods) that are called have also been properly declared. That is to say, each method call is compared against all of the method signatures that have been declared to make sure that the call properly agrees with exactly one such signature.

```
int x;
int y;
Student s;

// Details omitted.

s.print(x, y);  // Compiler will look for a method belonging
                // to class Student whose name is "print" and
                // whose argument signature calls for two int(egers).
```

- When the compiler finds such a match, *bingo*! It knows what method body needs to be executed when that method actually gets called at run time, and "locks in" that code at *compile time*, as illustrated conceptually in Figure F-1.

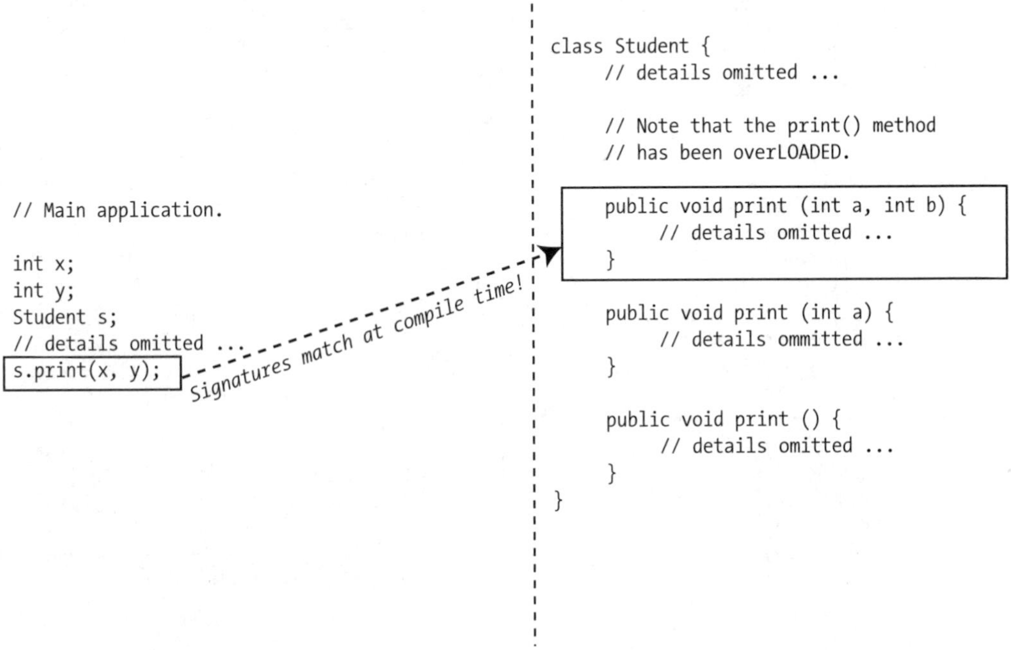

```
                                              class Student {
                                                  // details omitted ...

                                                  // Note that the print() method
                                                  // has been overLOADED.

// Main application.                              public void print (int a, int b) {
                                                      // details omitted ...
int x;                                            }
int y;
Student s;                                        public void print (int a) {
// details omitted ...                                // details ommitted ...
s.print(x, y);                                    }
         Signatures match at compile time!
                                                  public void print () {
                                                      // details omitted ...
                                                  }
                                              }
```

Figure F-1. *Compile-time binding*

Imagine that you are going to take a road trip from Washington, D.C., to Cleveland, Ohio. Compile-time binding is analogous to having a specific driving route planned in advance— route 95N to route 70N to route 83E, etc.—with no flexibility for changing this route when you actually set forth on your trip (i.e., at "run time").

Dynamic Binding

Let's contrast what we've just discussed about static binding with ***dynamic*** or ***run-time binding***, a language feature that defers the decision of which method code body will be exercised for a particular method call until the time at which the program actually runs.

- Figure F-2 shows the main application as declaring a reference p of type Person. The program logic (reflected via an if statement) shows that based upon some condition at run time (e.g., some input provided by the user, perhaps), we will create either a Student object or a Professor object, which p will hold on to.

- At ***compile*** time, since we don't know what the future run-time conditions will be, we can't guess as to whether we'll need to invoke the Student class's version of print() or the Professor class's version, so we have to ***defer*** this decision.

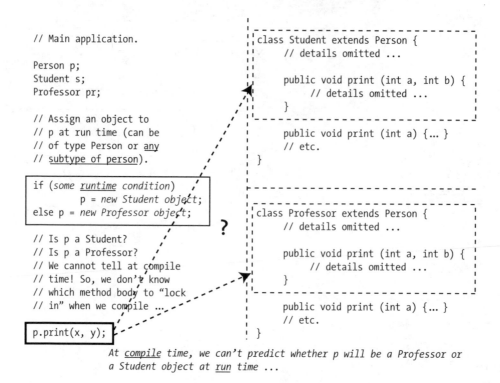

Figure F-2. *Compile-time ambiguity as to which overridden method to invoke*

- At **run** time—that is, at the very moment the print() method is called in our application—p will be referring to a specific object, the run-time environment will be able to determine its type/class, and the proper version of the print() method will automatically be selected, thanks to polymorphism. This is illustrated in Figure F-3.

```
// Main application.                    class Student extends Person {
                                            // details omitted ...
Person p;
Student s;                                  public void print (int a, int b) {
Professor pr;                                   // details omitted ...
                                            }
// Assign an object to                  }
// p at run time (can be
// of type Person or any                    public void print (int a) {... }
// subtype of person).                      // etc.

                                        }
if (some runtime condition)
     p = new Student object;
else p = new Professor object;          class Professor extends Person {
                                            // details omitted ...
// Is p a Student?
// Is p a Professor?         Aha!           public void print (int a, int b) {
// We cannot tell at compile                    // details omitted ...
// time! So, we don't know                  }
// which method body to "lock
// in" when we compile ...                  public void print (int a) {... }
                                            // etc.
p.print(x, y);                          }
```

... but by the time this program is run, we will know what type of object p is referring to, and can choose the right method!

Figure F-3. *Polymorphism at work (aka run-time binding)*

Going back to our road trip analogy, this would be like taking a road trip where you know you plan to travel from Washington, D.C., to Cleveland, Ohio, **and** you know that there is at least one way (if not many!) to get there (because you checked a map), but you nonetheless wish to defer the decision about which route to take until you are actually behind the steering wheel of the car and departing for your trip, to allow for "run-time" road conditions such as ice and snow, road construction, and the like. (That is, you don't wish to lock in your route at the planning stage of your trip.)

Dynamic binding enables polymorphism. If a programming language were not able to hold off on choosing which particular method to execute until the precise moment that such a decision is needed—that is, if a language only supports static, or compile-time, binding—then the compiler's only option in the preceding example would be to play it safe by choosing a version of print() that it knows would work for either a Student or a Professor—namely, the version of print() defined by their common superclass, Person—and polymorphism would not be possible.

■■■

Collections Prior to J2SE 5.0

This appendix first summarizes the collection enhancements made in J2SE 5.0, and then focuses primarily on the Java Collection API available before the advent of J2SE 5.0.

Summary of 5.0 Collection Enhancements

Three new language features were introduced with version 5.0 of the Java language to significantly enhance the manner in which we work with collections. Discussed in detail in Chapter 6, these enhancements are restated briefly as follows:

- **Generics**: These add compile-time type safety to the Java *collections framework* by allowing us to constrain what type of element a particular Java collection is intended to contain when we first *declare* it:

  ```
  // This ArrayList may only contain references to Students
  or subtypes of Student.
  ArrayList<Student> x = new ArrayList<Student>();  // J2SE 5.0 and later
  ```

  so that the compiler can warn us if we accidentally try to put an incorrect type of element into that collection:

  ```
  // This would generate a compiler error as of J2SE 5.0:
  x.add(new Professor());
  ```

  Here's the error message:

  ```
  cannot find symbol
  symbol  : method add(Professor)
  location: class java.util.ArrayList<Student>
  ```

  Chapter 7 introduced the notion of the *Java collections framework* during the discussion of interfaces.

- **Enhanced for loop**: This simplifies the programming effort involved with iterating over collections.

- **Autoboxing/unboxing**: This automatically inserts primitives (such as int) into instances of the appropriate wrapper class (such as Integer) when inserting them into collections, and automatically extracts primitives from such wrapper class instances when retrieving them from collections.

In order to truly appreciate how beneficial these enhancements are, it's helpful to understand what was involved in working with collections prior to J2SE version 5.0. The purpose of this appendix is to illustrate such differences.

Constraining Collection Contents

Prior to J2SE 5.0, we couldn't constrain the type of element that a non-Array collection was to hold when we first declared it; all collection types other than Arrays were designed to hold references to generic Objects.

```
ArrayList x;  // of Object references in Java 1.4.x and earlier
```

We thus were able to mix references of literally any type of object within a particular collection instance, and the compiler didn't object:

```
// This is a PRE-5.0 example.

// Here, we assume that Pineapple, Bicycle, and Cloud are three unrelated
// classes that all have Object as their immediate superclass.

Pineapple p = new Pineapple();
Bicycle b = new Bicycle();
Cloud c = new Cloud();
ArrayList x = new ArrayList();  // of Object references
x.add(p);
x.add(b);
x.add(c);
```

This led to numerous complications when iterating through a collection, which we'll discuss in a moment.

Note that the compiler *did* object if we attempted to insert a primitive type into a non-Array collection prior to J2SE 5.0:

```
int i = 3;
x.add(i); // not allowed prior to J2SE 5.0
```

Here's the error message:

```
cannot resolve symbol
symbol   : method add(int)
location: class java.util.ArrayList
```

Iterating Through Collections

Iterating through non-Array collections prior to J2SE 5.0 required us to *cast* object references as we retrieved them from the collection. For example, to iterate through an ArrayList of Student object references to compute final grades for the semester, we might use a conventional for loop, with the size of the collection serving as our stopping condition. This is illustrated in the following code:

```
// This is a PRE-5.0 example.
ArrayList enrollment = new ArrayList();   // of Object references

// Populate the collection.
Student s = new Student("Fred");
enrollment.add(s);
s = new Student("Bob");
enrollment.add(s);
s = new Student("Chloe");
enrollment.add(s);
// etc.

// Later on ...

// Step through the collection, and process all Students' grades.
for (int i = 0; i < enrollment.size(); i++) {
    // Note cast.
    Student s2 = (Student) enrollment.get(i);
    s2.computeFinalGrade();
}
```

The expression enrollment.get(i) is considered by the compiler to be an expression of type Object because the get(int) method of the ArrayList class is declared to have a return type of Object. Thus, even though *we* know that we've inserted Student objects into the collection, we must convince the *compiler* of this by casting each element as we retrieve it; otherwise, we'd not be able to invoke the computeFinalGrade method on the objects.

If we were to omit the cast, as illustrated by the following alternative version of the for loop code:

```
// Step through the collection, and process all Students' grades.
for (int i = 0; i < enrollment.size(); i++) {
    // Here, we are NOT casting.
    Student s2 = enrollment.get(i);
    s2.computeFinalGrade();
}
```

we'd get the following compilation error:

```
incompatible types
found    : java.lang.Object
required : Student
Student s2 = enrollment.get(i);
                ^
```

Alternatively, if we tried to invoke the computeFinalGrade method on the object reference directly, as follows:

```
// Step through the collection, and process all Students' grades.
for (int i = 0; i < enrollment.size(); i++) {
    // We are once again NOT casting.
    enrollment.get(i).computeFinalGrade();
}
```

we'd get the following compilation error:

```
cannot resolve symbol
symbol   : method computeFinalGrade()
location : class java.lang.Object
Student s2 = enrollment.get(i).computeFinalGrade();
                              ^
```

Thus, the only way to take advantage of the "Studentness" of a Student object when retrieving it from a pre-5.0 collection was to *cast* it as a Student.

Let's return to our example of disparate object references from earlier in this appendix:

```
// This is a PRE-5.0 example.
Pineapple p = new Pineapple();
Bicycle b = new Bicycle();
Cloud c = new Cloud();
ArrayList x = new ArrayList();   // of Object references
x.add(p);
x.add(b);
x.add(c);
```

If we were to erroneously attempt to cast all of the objects in x into Pineapples:

```
for (int i = 0; i < x.size(); i++) {
    // We're attempting to cast all references - Pineapples or otherwise -
    // into Pineapple references.
    Pineapple p = (Pineapple) x.get(i);

    // Pineapples have an eat() method; Bicycles and Clouds don't.
    p.eat();
}
```

the compiler *wouldn't* object, because the whole point of a cast is to effectively say to the compiler "Trust me, I know what I am doing!" Specifically in this example, we're saying "Trust me, at run time, this collection *will* contain only Pineapples." So, the compiler trusts us—after all, the collection does contain Objects, so it is conceivable that they are all Pineapples from the compiler's point of view. However, *at run time*, we'd get a ClassCastException on the line

```
    Pineapple p = (Pineapple) x.get(i);
```

as soon as we encountered the first non-Pineapple reference in x.

With a collection of disparate object types such as x, our only choice when iterating through the collection was to retrieve and command these objects based on their ***common*** identity— that is, we'd have to treat them all as generic Objects, which dramatically limits what we can do with the objects inside of our loop:

```
for (int i = 0; i < x.size(); i++) {
    // We're retrieving all references as their common supertype.
    Object o = x.get(i);

    // We can only invoke Object methods on this object.
    System.out.println(o.toString());
}
```

We could use the instanceof operator, which we learned in Chapter 13 allows us to check the run-time identity of an object:

```
for (int i = 0; i < x.size(); i++) {
    Object o = x.get(i);
    if (o instanceof Pineapple) {
        // Cast - this is safe!
        Pineapple p = (Pineapple) o;

        // Do "Pineapple"-type things to p.
        p.eat();
    }
    else if (o instanceof Bicycle) {
        // Cast - this is safe!
        Bicycle b = (Bicycle) o;
        // Do "Bicycle"-type things to b.
        b.ride();
    }
    else if (o instanceof Cloud) {
        // Cast - this is safe!
        Cloud c = (Cloud) o;

        // Do "Cloud"-type things to c.
        c.photograph();
    }
}
```

This is an inelegant approach, however, because if we add a fourth, or a fifth, or a sixth type of Object to collection x, we'd have to find all cases of if else logic in all of our iterations through x to add additional instanceof tests, which is not practical.

The bottom line is that prior to J2SE 5.0, we had to exercise discipline with regard to putting objects into collections, because the compiler would not restrict us when putting items in, but the compiler and JVM were both liable to complain when pulling items back out.

In contrast, as of J2SE 5.0, the enhanced for loop syntax, combined with our ability to constrain the type of reference that a collection is to hold when we declare it, makes for much simpler iteration logic, as shown in the following code:

```
// This is a 5.0 example.

// Constrain the collection to hold only Student references.
ArrayList<Student> enrollment = new ArrayList<Student>();

// Populate the collection.
Student s = new Student("Fred");
enrollment.add(s);
// etc.

// Later on ...

// Step through the collection, and process all Students' grades.
for (Student s2 : enrollment) {
    // NO CAST REQUIRED!
    s2.computeFinalGrade();
}
```

And, as of J2SE 5.0, if we were to attempt to insert a non-Student object into our enrollment collection

```
// This is a 5.0 example.

// Constrain the collection to hold only Student references.
ArrayList<Student> enrollment = new ArrayList<Student>();

// Attempt to insert a non-student into the collection.
Professor p = new Professor("Claudio");
enrollment.add(p);
```

the compiler would prevent us from doing so with the following error message:

```
cannot find symbol
symbol   : method add(Professor)
location : class java.util.ArrayList<Student>
enrollment.add(p);
         ^
```

As of version 5.0, Java provides **compile-time type checking**, thus greatly lessening the risk of run-time ClassCastExceptions.

Managing Primitive Types with Collections

As mentioned earlier, pre-5.0 collections other than Arrays could not be used to directly organize primitive (nonreference) types such as int, float, etc.; collections were designed to organize object references and **only** object references, and so we had to **"wrap"/"box"** primitive types inside of objects before inserting them into a collection.

For example, if we wanted to create an ArrayList of int values prior to J2SE 5.0, we had to do the following:

```
ArrayList intValues = new ArrayList();

// Let's put the integers from 1 to 10 into this collection.
for (int i = 1; i <= 10; i++) {
    // First, we'll create an Integer object to encapsulate the int value;
    // i.e., we're "wrapping" ("boxing") the int value in an Integer.
    Integer bigI = new Integer(i);

    // Then, we'll add the wrapper object to the collection.
    intValues.add(bigI);
}
```

Let's now turn around and iterate through the collection:

```
for (int i = 1; i <= intValues.size(); i++) {
    // We first retrieve the Integer wrapper object from the
    // collection. (Note the need to explicitly cast.)
    Integer bigI = (Integer) intValues.get(i);

    // Then, we "unwrap" the encapsulated int value from within the
    // wrapper object; i.e., we're "unboxing" the int value.
    int littleI = bigI.intValue();

    // Do whatever we want to do with littleI ... details omitted.
}
```

Thus, prior to 5.0, we had to *manually* box/unbox simple types.

As of J2SE 5.0, this boxing/unboxing happens *automatically/transparently*. We declare our ArrayList to hold Integers:

```
ArrayList<Integer> intValues = new ArrayList<Integer>();
```

but can then directly insert and retrieve int values without boxing or casting them:

```
for (int i = 1; i <= 10; i++) {
    // Insert int values directly.
    intValues.add(i);
}

for (int i = 0; i < intValues.size(); i++) {
    // Retrieve int values directly.
    int val = intValues.get(i);
}
```

The Iterator Class

Iterating through a collection like an ArrayList with a for loop as follows:

```
// This is a PRE 5.0 example.
```

```
// Step through the collection, and process all Students' grades.
for (int i = 0; i < students.size(); i++) {
    Student s = (Student) students.get(i);
    // Do something with s ... details omitted.
}
```

is possible because we have a means for referring to a particular element in an ArrayList by its *index*/position via the ArrayList get method. However, with some of the other Java collection types (e.g., HashSet), objects don't have a relative position, and so we cannot use this type of for loop to iterate through them in indexed fashion.

Prior to J2SE 5.0, the recommended means for iterating through all of the elements in a (nonindexed) collection such as a HashSet was to use an Iterator. An Iterator is a special type of temporary/*exhaustible* collection, used specifically to step through another collection of object references one by one in exhaustive fashion, pulling the references out of the Iterator until it is empty (see Figures G-1 and G-2).

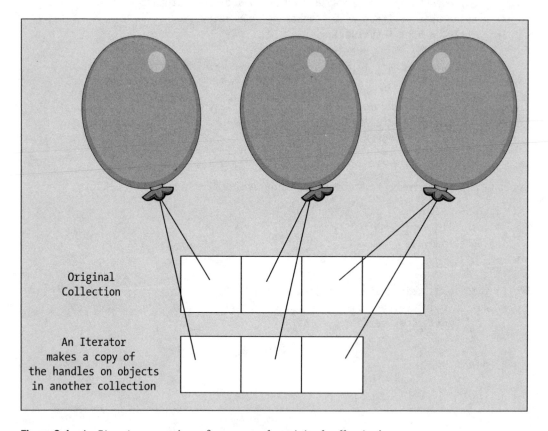

Original
Collection

An Iterator
makes a copy of
the handles on objects
in another collection

Figure G-1. *An Iterator contains references to the original collection's contents.*

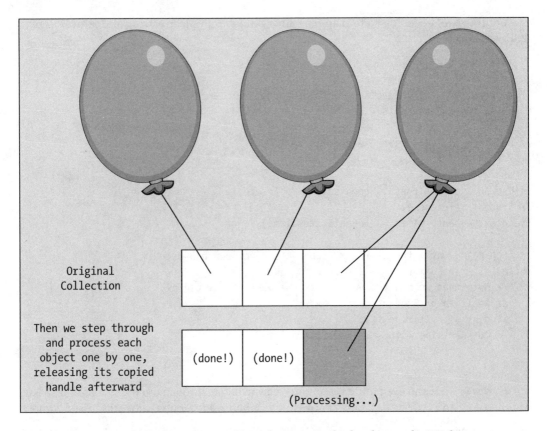

Original
Collection

Then we step through
and process each
object one by one,
releasing its copied
handle afterward

(done!)   (done!)

(Processing...)

Figure G-2. *An* Iterator *is then processed item by item until it has been exhausted.*

We'd obtain an Iterator on the contents of a collection such as a HashSet by invoking its iterator method as follows:

```
// This is a PRE 5.0 example ...

HashSet students = new HashSet(); // of Object references

// Populate the collection -- details omitted.

// Obtain an Iterator on the students collection.
Iterator iter = students.iterator();
```

Then, we'd use the Iterator's hasNext and next methods, respectively, to determine whether or not we'd exhausted the Iterator and, if not, to retrieve the next item:

```
// Keep going until the Iterator's contents have been exhausted.
while (iter.hasNext()) {
    // Pluck the next item out of the Iterator;
    // note the cast.
    Student s = (Student) iter.next();
    // Do something with s ... details omitted.
}
```

Contrast the preceding code example with a similar example involving an `Iterator` as of J2SE version 5.0:

```
// This is a 5.0 example ...

// We constrain our collection to hold Student references.
HashSet<Student> students = new HashSet<Student>();

// Populate the collection -- details omitted.


// Use an Iterator that is constrained to return
// Student references.
Iterator<Student> sIter = students.iterator();

// Keep going until the Iterator's contents have been exhausted.
while (sIter.hasNext()) {
    // Note that we don't have to cast, because of our use of
    // an Iterator<Student>.
    Student s = sIter.next();
    // Do something with s ... details omitted.
}
```

However, there's an even more streamlined way to iterate through our HashSet as of J2SE 5.0, without using an `Iterator` explicitly, thanks to the enhanced for loop that we discussed earlier:

```
// This is another 5.0 example ...

// We constrain our collection to hold Student references.
HashSet<Student> students = new HashSet<Student>();

// Populate the collection -- details omitted.

// Iterate through the collection, no muss, no fuss!
for (Student s : students) {
    // Do something with s ... details omitted.
}
```

Using the -Xlint:unchecked Compiler Option

In migrating from a pre-5.0 version of J2SE to version 5.0 or later, we can locate any "**unsafe**" collection operations—that is, any situations where we've declared a untyped collection and subsequently attempt to manipulate that collection—by using the `Xlint:unchecked` command-line compiler flag.

For example, consider this pre-5.0 code example:

```
// Foo.java
import java.util.*;

public class Foo {
    public static void main(String[] args) {
        // This is an "old style" (pre-5.0) collection declaration;
        // note that we aren't using the syntax ArrayList<...> to specify
        // what type of reference the collection is to contain.
        ArrayList x = new ArrayList(); // of Objects generically
        x.add(new Person());
    }
}
```

If we were to compile the preceding code with a J2SE 5.0 (or newer) compiler

```
javac Foo.java
```

we'd get the following warnings from the compiler:

```
Note:   X.java uses unchecked or unsafe operations
Note: Recompile with -Xlint:unchecked for details
```

If we now recompile the program with the –Xlint:unchecked flag

```
javac -Xlint:unchecked Foo.java
```

we'd get the following *specific* feedback:

```
Foo.java:6: warning: [unchecked] unchecked call to add(E) as a member of
the raw type java.util.ArrayList
    x.add(new Person());
      ^
```

and could thus choose to go back and modify our code, if desired.

■ ■ ■

Programming 101, and the Role of a Compiler

In this appendix, you'll learn how to combine the fundamentals of beginning object-oriented programming with that of a compiler and its role in programming.

A LEGOs Analogy

For starters, a programming language can be thought of like a LEGO set, in that both are kits for building things. In the case of a LEGO set, you get a certain number of different types of pieces—various blocks of different sizes, shapes, colors; various connectors; etc.—and there are rules as to how the pieces can be assembled (e.g., you must set one block on top of another so that the little pegs on the top of the bottom block fit into the holes on the bottom of the top block). But, given this relatively small set of components and rules to start with, the variety of things you can build with the pieces are virtually limitless: castles, rocket ships, skyscrapers, and robots, for example.

The same is true of a programming language. Out of the box, a programming language comes with a relatively small set of predefined "pieces":

- All languages have what is known as a set of ***reserved words***—in essence, a predefined set of symbolic names (aka **symbols**). Each reserved word has a special purpose in that language, which is understood and recognized by the compiler. (There are 50 reserved words [known as ***keywords***] in the Java language: if, boolean, class, static, public, etc.)

- A small subset of these reserved words represent ***primitive (data) types*** for a given language. For Java, we have eight such data types, as discussed in Chapter 2: boolean, char, double, int, etc.

- A compiler understands what ***operations*** we are permitted to perform on elements of these types. For example, we can add two ints together, we can test an int to see if it is equal to another number, and so forth.

- There are a handful of rules about how we can formulate ***expressions*** in a language, as discussed in Chapter 2.

- There are a handful of syntactic rules about special statements, such as the if, for, and while control structures.

- There are rules governing how to write functions (methods, in an OOPL).

- Languages also often come with **libraries** of *predefined* functions—for example, the square root (sqrt) function of the C programming language.

- Finally, there are some "odds-and-ends" syntactic rules, such as the fact that statements in Java end with a semicolon (;), that code blocks are enclosed in braces ({ ... }), etc.

Beyond these predefined language building blocks, it's a programmer's job to **extend** the language. How do we do this? Again, whether we're talking about objected-oriented languages or not, the basics are the same:

- By declaring variables of the various primitive types

- By declaring and programming functions/methods of our own choosing to complement the built-in functions/methods

- In the case of an object-oriented language like Java, by inventing our own **user-defined types** (i.e., **classes**), and by then programming **their** data structure (attributes) and behaviors (methods)

- By assembling all of the above into a working application

The bottom line is that a compiler is rather limited in what it inherently knows; it is by effectively **extending** a language through programming that we dramatically extend the richness of that language.

The Compiler's Job in a Nutshell

A compiler's job is to assess whether we've followed the rules for properly assembling a particular language's building blocks into a complex application, including whether we've **properly declared** anything that we're **adding** to the language. When we compile a program, the compiler studies every line of code, and every symbol in each line, to see if it understands what we are asking of the language. The compiler automatically understands all of the "pieces" of a language that are built in—namely, the items in the first of the two bulleted lists in the previous section—but when it encounters something outside of the core language, it looks to see if you, the programmer, have "invented" (declared) it.

This notion is illustrated by the following sample code. Please pay particular attention to the comments used to narrate this example.

```
// This first line is deemed to be OK by the compiler (i.e., it compiles
// properly), because the symbols "public" and "class" are Java keywords,
// and "MyClass" is a name that we have invented for a class that
// we are about to define for the compiler.
public class MyClass {
    // This next line is also OK, because the symbols "public", "static", and
    // "void" are keywords/recognized symbols; the name "main" is the name
    // of a method that we are in the process of declaring; the symbol
    // "String" represents a predefined Java class/type; and the name "args" is
    // a variable name that we've invented to serve as a parameter to the main
    // method.  Finally, the syntax of this statement conforms to the Java
    // rules for how a method header should be structured.
```

```
public static void main(String[] args) {
      int x;              // OK!  The compiler knows what "int" means - it's a
                          // built-in primitive type, and "x" is
                          // a variable name that we have invented.  This
                          // is known as a DECLARATION:  we are declaring
                          // (to the compiler) our intention to use "x" as
                          // a symbolic name to refer to an int(eger) value
                          // in our program, and thus the compiler records
                          // "x" in the symbol table that it is building.

      float public;       // NOT OK!  The compiler knows what "float" means
                          // (another built-in type), but doesn't like the
                          // fact that we are trying to (mis)use a keyword
                          // -- in this case, "public" -- as a variable name.

      Student s;          // This is OK IF AND ONLY IF we have defined elsewhere
                          // what the "Student" symbol means - namely, if we've
                          // declared a Student class (or borrowed SOMEONE ELSE'S
                          // Student class definition), and are using it as a
                          // user-defined type.  Assuming that the Student class
                          // can be found by the compiler, then the compiler
                          // records that "s" is a variable name that we have
                          // invented to refer to a Student object in its
                          // symbol table.

      foobar y;           // NOT OK!  The compiler has no clue as to what a
                          // "foobar" is.  It is POSSIBLE that we've invented
                          // a CLASS named "foobar", such that y is meant to be
                          // a reference to a foobar object, but the preferred
                          // convention with an object-oriented programming
                          // language is to capitalize the first letter of a
                          // class name - e.g., "Foobar" - as we discussed
                          // in Chapter 3, so "foobar" is probably NOT a properly
                          // defined class/type.

      s = new Student(); // OK!  The compiler recognizes the "new" keyword
                          // and, as mentioned above, also knows what both "s"
                          // and "Student" are all about by consulting its
                          // symbol table.

      t = new Student(); // NOT OK: "t" is not previously declared within the
                          // scope of this class.
```

and so forth.

Whenever the compiler encounters a declaration for a symbol that it wouldn't otherwise have recognized, it records the symbol in a **symbol table**. On the other hand, if a symbol is used that was *not* properly declared, a compilation error such as the following arises (this is the Java-specific compiler message):

```
Cannot resolve symbol
symbol : foobar
```

Programmers must become adept in resolving such compiler errors, as they arise frequently, primarily due to typing mistakes. Recall that Java is a case-sensitive language; thus, even a mistake in the use of uppercase versus lowercase can cause a `cannot resolve symbol` compiler error to arise:

```
int littlex;      // lowercase "x" used in variable name declaration
littleX = 1;      // uppercase "x" typed by mistake
```

Here's the error message:

```
cannot resolve symbol
symbol : littleX
```

Other typing mistakes that will result in a `cannot resolve symbol` compiler error include

- Spelling the name of a method, attribute, class, or other variable differently from how it was declared, including uppercase and lowercase deviations

- Leaving parentheses off the end of a method call

- Forgetting to declare the item (variable, attribute, method, class) that you are trying to access

- Forgetting an `import` directive for predefined classes

or something similar.

For example, let's say that we have declared the following simple `Person` class:

```java
public class Person {
    private String name;

    public String getName() {
        return name;
    }

    public void printIt(int i) {
        System.out.println(name + i);
    }
}
```

The following program illustrates four situations in which a `cannot resolve symbol` error might arise:

```java
public class PersonExample {
    public static void main(String[] args) {
        Person p = new Person();

        // NON-EXISTENT METHOD - setName WAS NEVER DECLARED
        // IN THE Person CLASS.
        p.setName("Fred");
```

```
            // CASE ERROR -- SHOULD BE UPPERCASE "N" in "getname".
            System.out.println(p.getname);

            // FORGOT THE PARENS AT THE END OF THE METHOD CALL.
            System.out.println(p.getName);

            // TRYING TO USE A PREDEFINED JAVA CLASS FOR WHICH
            // AN import DIRECTIVE IS REQUIRED.
            ArrayList al;
    }
}
```

Here's what the compiler has to say regarding the preceding code:

```
PersonExample.java:7: cannot resolve symbol
symbol  : method setName  (java.lang.String)
location: class Person
        p.setName("Fred");
          ^
PersonExample.java:10: cannot resolve symbol
symbol  : variable getname
location: class Person
        System.out.println(p.getname);
                             ^
PersonExample.java:13: cannot resolve symbol
symbol  : variable getName
location: class Person
        System.out.println(p.getName);
                             ^
PersonExample.java:17: cannot resolve symbol
symbol  : class ArrayList
location: class PersonExample
        ArrayList al;
        ^
4 errors
```

Index

From the back cover of Jacquie Barker's lighthearted yet practical career guide for IT professionals:

Maintain leading-edge technology skills
without becoming *overwhelmed*

Jacquie Barker

With this book, you'll learn:

- *Creative, inexpensive ways to come up-to-speed on the latest technology trends.*
- *Ways to recognize which technologies are truly worth mastering and which are just "passing fads."*
- *How to leverage the skills you already have to land an assignment that will give you on-the-job exposure to the new technical skills that you need.*
- *How to recognize – and avoid – common career pitfalls that could otherwise lead you off-track.*
- *Advice for moving back onto a technical career track if you've gotten "derailed."*
- *How to recover from professional burnout and rediscover the joy that led you into an IT career in the first place.*

Most importantly, the tips in this book will help you to develop skills for continually renewing yourself technically that will last a professional lifetime.

Embracing technology change as a life-long habit needn't be overwhelming if you take the career tips presented in this book to heart. Don't wait!

To order, please visit http://techtidalwave.com

Taming the Technology Tidal Wave: Practical Career Advice for IT Professionals,
by Jacquie Barker; ISBN 0-9744798-8-8; ObjectStart Press, 2005.